Praise for Hendrik Hertzberg
and *Politics*

"For Americans interested in the moral and political temper of the republic over the last forty crazy years, Hendrik Hertzberg's *Politics* is a fascinating book—astute, illuminating, and witty."
—Arthur M. Schlesinger, Jr.

"Hertzberg is among the very best: no bellicosity, no moral righteousness, no silly punditry—just the intellectual scrupulosity, the innate skepticism, the uncommon journalistic modesty, the unfailing common sense, the strong sentences, the wit, and the dedication to justice and fair play."   —Philip Roth

"Rick Hertzberg is the most eloquent defender of mainstream American liberalism writing today. Combining passion and common sense, he makes the liberal case on issue after issue seem not just true but obviously true. He makes you wonder: how could any sane person think otherwise?"   —Michael Kinsley

"The *New Yorker* editor and former editor of *The New Republic* has such a good mind, such a strong sense of ethics and honor. There is an almost physical pleasure, like having an itch scratched, in watching him come to grips with some of the thorniest, nastiest, most divisive issues of the past forty years, and slice them cleanly into comprehensible form. Besides, he writes like a dream."
—Molly Ivins

"*Politics* is invaluable for all sorts of reasons—chief among them being decades of elegant writing in the service of surgical intelligence."
—Toni Morrison

"Whenever I read something by Hendrik Hertzberg, like this book for example, my heart goes all aflutter, like a little girl's. Is it because his ideas are so strong and manly? Or is it because his prose is so smooth and suave? I can't tell, I'm too confused. You decide."
—Al Franken

"Hertzberg traffics in the kind of analytical yet, as he says, 'indignant' intellectual discussion that can actually change people's minds, set out in the clear, passionate and clever prose we all wish we could produce ourselves. . . . It is striking how consistent Hertzberg has been over a very long period of time, and how little he has to look back on with regret or embarrassment. . . . Today, in his mature incarnation as a political columnist for *The New Yorker*, Hertzberg's positions have settled into a kind of clearheaded liberalism, minus the heavy-handed wallop or the shrillness characterizing so many on the left. . . . For those who have grown sick of the debased ideological squabbles of the Michael Moores on the one hand and the Sean Hannitys on the other, it's exhilarating to read Hertzberg."
—*Los Angeles Times Book Review*

"Hendrik Hertzberg's *Politics* . . . is the most anomalous of cultural commodities: a book by an author who takes politics very seriously but does not yell, and who can be humorous without resorting to sarcasm. It collects almost forty years' worth of reporting and commentary, beginning in the fog of one war (Vietnam) and ending in that of another (Iraq). But the cumulative effect is not simply that of a chronicle of passing events. They cohere through the force of Hertzberg's style—which is, in turn, the outward form of a certain kind of engaged intelligence."
—*Newsday*

"We have a keen, funny and insightful voice in Hertzberg. . . . Hertzberg's gift is the turn of phrase and the sly dig at his targets, on the right as well as on the left. . . . Taken as a whole, as a walk through both the profound moments of American life and the baser forms of political mudslinging that combine to form our national political life, once can scarcely do better than to read this book. . . . Keeping one's wits during the past several years of wartime partisan rancor have been difficult, but Hertzberg shows, with humor and studied indignation he is up to the task, and is on the scene."
—*San Francisco Chronicle*

"*The New Yorker* is now one of the sharpest, best-informed critics of Mr. Bush and the Republican right. Mr. Hertzberg is part of that success. For a journalist, publishing cuttings is a risk. These ones, which run from 1966 to now, hold up. They are always readable, often funny and almost always have a serious point to make. . . . After the 2000 election, a hardness and an urgency enter Mr. Hertzberg's prose. Angry but lucid, he adopts the tradition of patriotic dissent."
—*The Economist*

"His responses . . . are fresh, relevant and unnerving, and his insights into the two George Bushes are blazingly brilliant. . . . [An] exhilarating volume."
—*Booklist* (starred review)

"Rewarding . . . exhilarating . . . [An] abundant harvest of graceful, amusing, discriminating and public-spirited prose."
—*The Nation*

"Hertzberg . . . is one of the most astute and erudite of American political and cultural commentators."
—*The Globe and Mail* (Toronto)

"In the small world of political essayists, there are stylists: eloquent, elegant, and engaging; and there are thinkers: intelligent and insightful. Rarely do you find a master at both. Hendrik Hertzberg is one . . . read Hertzberg for context, understanding, a profoundly moral perspective, and the pleasure of experiencing the beauty of language perfectly married to thought."
—*The Georgia Straight* (Vancouver)

"What a treat it is . . . to discover that the newly-issued compilation of Hendrik Hertzberg's greatest hits . . . is as swift and sure a read as the last John Grisham thriller. . . . Hendrik Hertzberg now seems securely perched near the very top of a short list of American observers whose words shape opinion and demand careful reading. As a preeminent liberal voice, he has hit mid-career in full stride. This is a fine opportunity to dig in and feast on his observations, regardless of politics."
—*Embassy Magazine* (Ottawa)

PENGUIN BOOKS

POLITICS

Hendrik Hertzberg has been a staff writer and editor at *The New Yorker* since 1992; and was a staff writer there in the early 1970s as well. He has also been a naval officer, a *Newsweek* reporter, President Jimmy Carter's chief speechwriter, and (twice) editor of *The New Republic*, where he (twice) won the National Magazine Award for General Excellence. A 1965 graduate of Harvard, he lives in New York City with his wife and their young son.

POLITICS

Observations
& Arguments

1966-2004

HENDRIK HERTZBERG

PENGUIN BOOKS

PENGUIN BOOKS

Published by the Penguin Group

Penguin Group (USA) Inc., 375 Hudson Street, New York, New York 10014, U.S.A.
Penguin Group (Canada), 10 Alcorn Avenue, Toronto, Ontario, Canada M4V 3B2
(a division of Pearson Penguin Canada Inc.)
Penguin Books Ltd, 80 Strand, London WC2R 0RL, England
Penguin Ireland, 25 St Stephen's Green, Dublin 2, Ireland (a division of Penguin Books Ltd)
Penguin Group (Australia), 250 Camberwell Road, Camberwell,
Victoria 3124, Australia (a division of Pearson Australia Group Pty Ltd)
Penguin Books India Pvt Ltd, 11 Community Centre, Panchsheel Park, New Delhi – 110 017, India
Penguin Group (NZ), cnr Airborne and Rosedale Roads, Albany, Auckland 1310,
New Zealand (a division of Pearson New Zealand Ltd)
Penguin Books (South Africa) (Pty) Ltd, 24 Sturdee Avenue, Rosebank, Johannesburg 2196, South Africa

Penguin Books Ltd, Registered Offices:
80 Strand, London WC2R 0RL, England

First published in the United States of America by The Penguin Press,
a member of Penguin Group (USA) Inc. 2004
Published in Penguin Books 2005

3   5   7   9   10   8   6   4

THE LIBRARY OF CONGRESS HAS CATALOGED THE HARDCOVER EDITION AS FOLLOWS:
Hertzberg, Hendrik.
Politics: observations & arguments, 1966–2004/Hendrik Herzberg.
p.   cm.
Includes index.
ISBN 1-59420-018-1 (hc.)
ISBN 0 14 30.3553 3 (pbk.)
1. United States—Politics and government—1945–1989.   2. United States—Politics and
government—1989–   3. Politics and culture—United States.   4. Politicians—United States.
5. United States—Social conditions—1960–1980.   6. United States—Social conditions—1980–   7. World
politics—1989–   8. Politics and culture.   I. Title.
E839.5.H48 2004
973.92—dc22   2004044332

Printed in the United States of America
Designed by Mary Sarah Quinn

For Virginia Cannon

CONTENTS

6. FOREIGNERS

7. WINGERS

8. THE WAYWARD MEDIA

9. WEDGE ISSUES

10. HIGH CRIMES

11. GHOSTS IN THE MACHINE

12. YUPPIES AND OTHER LEFTOVERS

13. 2000 + 9/11 = 2004

INTRODUCTION

BY DAVID REMNICK

FOR THE PAST dozen years, and with increasing prominence, Hendrik Hertzberg has been the principal political voice of *The New Yorker*. But the voice has always been his own. It is a remarkable voice: at once courteous and ferocious, seductive and caustic, tender and urbane. As an analyst of American public life Hertzberg is logical, humane, and morally acute; as a writer he has tone control the way Billie Holiday had tone control.

I first began reading Hendrik Hertzberg—Rick to his colleagues and his improbably large circle of friends—when he and Michael Kinsley took tag-team turns editing *The New Republic* in the 1980s. *National Review* and *Human Events* may have held sway in the Oval Office, but elsewhere in town (on Capitol Hill, in the office suites of cause lobbyists and consultants, in newsrooms and think tanks, even in odd corners of Reagan's White House) no political publication was more eagerly read or more excitedly discussed than *The New Republic*. The relatively small liberal weekly (its circulation was around eighty thousand) had become an exhilarating cacophony of fractious, even warring, voices of different tones and tempers. In *TNR*'s order of battle, Hertzberg and Kinsley, despite contrasting sensibilities, generally found themselves on the same side. Kinsley was, and remains, a master at lancing an inflated reputation or a fatuous argument. His prose is spare, logical, acerbic. Hertzberg's is a warmer, rounder, more confiding voice, though no less funny and often no less cutting. I had been reading the magazine ever since I arrived in Washington in 1982, but I remember well the first time one of Rick's pieces had on me what I'd later identify as the Hertzberg effect—a twinned zing of provocation and pleasure. The year was 1985, and William Bennett was the Reagan administration's secretary of education and grand inquisitor. (This was long before his Elmer Gantry–Fyodor Dostoevsky moment, when the ever-accusing moralist was forced to reveal he had frittered away millions in family milk money in the gambling dens of Las Vegas and Atlantic City.) In a tone of highest dudgeon, Bennett had complained that the people who *really* ruled the country—the liberals, the judges, the whatever—had consistently displayed what he called "an aversion to religion" and a disdain for the "Judeo-Christian" values that made America great. Hertzberg, a determined secularist born to an unbelieving Jewish father and a Quaker mother, took unforgettable umbrage:

> As a Judeo-Christian who has an aversion to religion, and who is an American as good as or better than any mousse-haired, Bible-touting, apartheid-promoting evangelist on any UHF television station you can name, I must protest.
>
> Where is it written that if you don't like religion you are somehow disqualified from being a legitimate American? What was Mark Twain, a Russian? When did it become un-American to have opinions about the origin and meaning of the universe that come from sources other than the body of dogma of organizations approved by the federal government as certifiably Judeo-Christian? If it is American to believe that God ordered Tribe X to abjure pork, or that he caused Leader Y to be born to a virgin, why is it suddenly un-American to doubt that the prime mover of this unimaginably vast universe of quintillions of solar systems would be likely to be obsessed with questions involving the dietary and biosexual behavior of a few thousand bipeds inhabiting a small part of a speck of dust orbiting a third-rate star in an obscure spiral arm of one of millions of more or less identical galaxies?

Two decades later, I still don't know what to admire most about that passage—its swingy fearlessness, its sly patriotism, or the sheer syntactical gymnastics of its final flourish. The writing is so happy-making, it almost reconciles one to the comic, cosmic smallness of our species and the bleakness of its fate.

Some people are changelings, creating themselves as if in a universe of their own making; others create themselves from what is around. Hertzberg is of the latter kind. There is no doubting the particularity of his voice as a writer, but he comes from a tradition that begins with his parents and their political atmosphere and devotion. His father, Sidney Hertzberg, a son of immigrant garment workers, was a teenage street-corner speaker for the

Bronx Socialist Party who grew up to be an itinerant activist-journalist and a member of New York's small and beleaguered but ultimately influential anti-Stalinist intellectual left. Besides agitating for causes as varied as independence for India, justice for southern sharecroppers, and the political campaigns of Norman Thomas and Hubert Humphrey, Sidney kept the family going with a seemingly endless stream of jobs as a writer and editor at various publications, both mainstream (the *Times, Fortune*) and marginal (*Common Sense*, the early *Commentary*). Rick's mother, Hazel Whitman, was the product of a family far more proper and genteel than one might imagine from the reputation of her famous not-too-distant cousin, Walt. She rebelled, becoming national chairman of the Young People's Socialist League; eventually she became a schoolteacher and then a professor of history at Teachers College, Columbia. When Rick was in first grade, Sidney and Hazel packed up and moved him and his younger sister Katrina out of the city and across the Hudson to Monsey, a sylvan town in Rockland County that is now populated mainly by Orthodox and Hasidic Jews but was then a rural retreat for artistic and intellectual types looking for some quiet and lower real estate prices. By 1952, when Rick was nine, he was handing out Adlai Stevenson buttons door to door. At Suffern High School, he organized a slate of candidates for student council offices. They campaigned against "school spirit," made fun of football, and called themselves the Liberal Party. Not for the last time, the Liberal Party lost.

At Harvard, Hertzberg was managing editor of the student daily, the *Crimson*. Late one morning while he was sleeping off an all-nighter at the paper, he got a telephone call.

"Hello, this is William Shawn."

"Yes," came the answer, "and this is Marie of Romania." Hertzberg hung up, sure that his caller had not been the legendary "Mr." Shawn, editor of *The New Yorker*, but rather a classmate aping the editor's famously whispery tone.

The phone rang again.

"No, this really *is* William Shawn," the small voice insisted.

This time, Hertzberg was more attentive. It would turn out that Lillian Ross had seen him on a television documentary about "concerned youth" called "The Shook-Up Generation," and he had been not only appropriately shook up but eloquent about it. Shawn, therefore, was inviting him to write for his magazine. As it happened, Hertzberg was in the same class, 1965, as

Shawn's son Wallace, and so, too, were Jonathan Schell, Jacob Brackman, George W. S. Trow, and Daniel Chasan, all of whom eventually received similarly welcoming calls from Shawn. "My whole career has been so marked by advantages gained from Harvard's old-boy network," Hertzberg confessed in 2002, in an interview with Craig Lambert for the university's alumni magazine, "that only in the last couple of years have I been getting over the debilitating sense of not deserving anything."

Hertzberg did not take *The New Yorker* job, not right away. First he was briefly the editorial director for the National Student Association, then reported for *Newsweek* out of its San Francisco bureau, and, most consumingly, had to deal with Vietnam. In 1966, he enlisted in the navy, which began a personal drama that he has described with minimal self-dramatics and maximum self-deprecation. The long and short of it, he wrote in 1985, was that he "managed to have it both ways: veteran (sort of), and resister (in a way)." For the details, see, "Why the War Was Immoral," beginning on page 32 of the book you are holding, and "Front Man," beginning on page 222.

Mustered out of the navy in 1969, Hertzberg finally went to *The New Yorker*, where he worked for seven years. It was, despite the times, his least political period as a writer. He did dozens of reporting pieces a year, mostly for the "Talk of the Town" section. He covered antiwar demonstrations and political rallies, but more often he wrote about things like rock concerts, trade shows, countercultural antics, minor-league baseball, local eccentrics, Monty Python's Flying Circus, and movie people—and he grew restless. At the end of 1976, when the call came from James Fallows to join the speech-writing staff of president-elect Jimmy Carter, Hertzberg jumped at the chance.

Hertzberg's four White House years are not represented in this book, unless you count the incisive character assessment of his flawed and saintly boss he wrote fifteen years later. Of course, he was writing like mad during those years, but the results have already been collected—by the U.S. Government Printing Office. Of particular note, for those who care to dig out the nine musty volumes of "Public Papers of the Presidents: Jimmy Carter" from some particularly well-stocked library, are the addresses to the Indian parliament (January 2, 1978), to the Egyptian parliament (March 10, 1979) and the Israeli Knesset (March 12, 1979), at the opening of the John F. Kennedy Library (October 20, 1979), and to the American people on

"Energy and National Goals" (the so-called "malaise speech," July 20, 1979). And, of course, the Farewell Address (January 14, 1981). These speeches, of course, are not exactly "by" Hertzberg. Though his contributions to them were large, presidential speeches involve an authorial cast of thousands. Still, it's not hard to tell which bits are *not* Hertzberg's.

The Reagan tide washed Carter out of the White House, and Hertzberg landed at *The New Republic* at the invitation of another Harvard friend, his old teacher Martin Peretz. The two had been arguing about politics since 1962, when Peretz was Hertzberg's political science tutor; now Marty was paying Rick to tell him he didn't know what he was talking about. While Peretz (and others at the magazine) increasingly listed right, chucking previous convictions overboard as hopelessly dated or naïve, Hertzberg set out the particulars of his persisting liberalism: the squalor of capital punishment, the idiocy of American drug and gun laws, the need for affirmative action as the flawed medicine after generations of institutionalized racism. There was surprise in the argument, surprise, certainly, in the prose, but not in the principles.

Though Hertzberg's title was editor, he sometimes found himself denouncing the editorials he edited. When *TNR* backed military aid to the Nicaraguan contras, he drafted a dissenting letter to—well, to the editor. (It appeared over the names of a majority of the magazine's distinguished roster of contributing editors.) When *TNR* attacked the nuclear freeze movement as a sinister plot manipulated by Soviet intelligence, he defended it as an earnest expression of justifiable popular anxiety. He was quicker than many of his colleagues to credit and welcome the liberal revolutions in Poland and the Soviet Union. The constant internal skirmishing at *TNR* was invigorating, but for the participants it could be wearing, too. The first time Hertzberg quit the editorship, in 1985, he wrote, in a "Washington Diarist" not included in this book,

> My reasons for leaving are complicated. In the current (fiftieth anniversary) issue of *Partisan Review,* Daniel Bell writes that he finally left *The Public Interest,* which he had co-founded with Irving Kristol, because he believes that "friendship is more important than ideology." I believe that too. (In fact, it's a central tenet of my ideology.) I've learned here that I can be friends, good friends, with people who have serious politics of which I deeply disapprove. This is something I wouldn't have thought possible before.

One of the highlights of Hertzberg's time at *The New Republic* was his coverage of the 1988 campaign: Bush-Quayle vs. Dukakis-Bentsen. He got no scoops, influenced not a thing, but bemusedly tagged along with the candidates, all the while writing an ongoing chronicle that combined high comedy with moral disappointment. As a writer and as a man, Rick is almost preternaturally good-natured. Nothing to him is dull or meaningless, even the most meaningless of events. "In the afternoon we fly to South Dakota for a rally at the Sioux Falls stockyards," he wrote of a stint with the Bush (Senior) campaign. "Three hundred people are standing around in a makeshift corral. A sign says WELCOME TO SIOUX FALLS STOCKYARDS. There's livestock nearby. The podium is made of hay bales. The site makes for good visuals. Good olifactuals, too. The smell of bullshit, like the sound, is not wholly unpleasant." It's hard to choose the best of these '88 pieces, but surely the eeriest is the dissection of Dan Quayle. Eerie, because as Hertzberg ruminates about the difference between Bush and Quayle—the generation of noblesse oblige versus the generation of indolence and entitlement—and as he juxtaposes the younger man's limited achievement with his limitless ascent, he might as well be describing Bush (Junior).

HERTZBERG RETURNED to *The New Yorker* as an editor and writer when Tina Brown took over in 1992. For much of that period Rick's office and mine were next door to each other, and I grew accustomed to his undergraduate-style work habits; he was seldom there when I arrived in the morning, unless he had stayed all night. (That began to change somewhat after he married the talented senior editor down the hall, Virginia Cannon, and their son, Wolf, made his appearance.) In 1998, when I moved down the hall myself as Tina's successor, one of my first moves was to make sure that Rick's writing, and his political thinking, would be a regular, not just an occasional, mainstay of *The New Yorker*.

Nearly half of this book is drawn from the "Comment" pieces and longer essays Hertzberg has written for the magazine over the past decade. It has been a time dominated first by the tribulations of the Clinton presidency and then by the darker era of the 2000 election, September 11, and George W. Bush. The Bush era began with impressive rhetoric and cynical action, Hertzberg writes, and it has only gotten worse and more radically conservative. The president has ignored his lack of a mandate and jettisoned the idea of a "compassionate" and conciliatory conservatism for a swaggering reassessment of the American political way of life, foreign and domestic, since the New Deal. One of Hertzberg's more elegiac columns came after Al Gore finally let go the battle for the presidency after the Supreme Court delivered a verdict somewhat different from the electorate's. Hertzberg's choice of a historical analogy was original and apt, with a note of erudite irony worthy, perhaps, of the late Murray Kempton:

That was a tough concession speech Al Gore had to give the other night, but people have had to give tougher ones over the years. In 1633, a prominent, well-connected member of the high-tech community of Florence found himself on the wrong end of a decision by the then equivalent of the Supreme Court. Put on trial by the Inquisition, he was found guilty of advocating a doctrine described in the Holy Office's indictment as "absurd and false philosophically, because it is expressly contrary to Holy Scripture." This was a characterization with which the defendant was known to privately disagree. But he was anxious to avoid being cast as a troublemaker and eager for the healing to begin, so he said the words the occasion required. "I, Galileo, son of the late Vincenzo Galilei, Florentine, aged seventy years," he recited, "abjure, curse, and detest the aforesaid errors and heresies, and I swear that I will never again say or assert that the Sun is the center of the universe and immovable and that the Earth is not the center and moves." Before Galileo was led away to spend the rest of his life under comfortable house arrest, however, he kicked the ground and, according to legend, muttered, "*Eppur si muove*"—"But still, it moves."

It's fair to say that Rick disapproves of George W. Bush. He sees in the president, as he saw in Quayle, a man of incurious mind and crabbed compassion, and it was something that he noted immediately. In Hertzberg's estimation, Bush's inaugural address, as written by Michael Gerson, was a "relative" masterpiece. ("To read all fifty-four addresses, one after another, is to traverse a wasteland where pomposity, banality, and incoherence are more often relieved by mediocrity than by brilliance.") But, as he pointed out, "the dissonance began one day later. The new president's first act was an act of cruelty." He cut off all financial assistance to International Planned Parenthood and other organizations that provide maternal health services in the most wretched corners of the earth and then spent the rest of the week promoting a regressive tax cut calculated to enrich his wealthy friends at the expense of the poor and near poor. "Cruelty" was the word Rick used, and cruelty in politics, I have found, is the quality that he has never been prepared to abide.

AUTHOR'S NOTE

THE NAME OF THIS BOOK is a ripoff, but a ripoff with a pedigree. The catalogue of the New York Public Library lists around thirty books entitled *Politics*, some with subtitles and some without, plus a couple of dozen translations of Aristotle. The "Politics" I was thinking of when I lifted the title (I think of it as a tribute, not a theft), though one of the thirty, is not actually a book per se but a set of bound volumes of a little magazine. *Politics*, founded and edited by Dwight Macdonald, was dreamed up the month I was born—July 1943—and came out forty-two times between the winter of 1944 and the winter of 1949. Its frequency was unreliable (monthly at first, then bimonthly, then quarterly, seldom on time) and its circulation tiny, never getting above five thousand. It published some of the midcentury's most distinguished essayists—Daniel Bell, Bruno Bettelheim, George Orwell, Simone Weil—but was basically a one-man operation. Dwight Macdonald (1906–1982) was the man.

A few yellowing copies of *Politics* could be found tucked away on bookshelves around our house when I was a kid, and once I was old enough to be interested in such things I read them, or read in them. A collection of Macdonald's political pieces, mostly from *Politics*, came out in 1957. A few years later I read it and was electrified by it. It made me see just how good—how vigorous, how funny, how exhilarating—an engaged, indignant political polemic could be; and it confirmed what I had been taught at home: that the most trenchant and passionate critiques of Stalinism (and of liberalism, conservatism, and fascism, too) tended to come from people whose own politics are left-wing, even radical. Macdonald became one of my political-writer heroes—not quite on a level with Orwell, but almost.

Macdonald's collection was reprinted in 1970 under the title *Politics Past*, but the original 1957 edition was entitled *Memoirs of a Revolutionist*. I don't know this for a fact, but I'm pretty sure Macdonald pinched that title from Victor Serge, whose great book *Memoires d'un revolutionnaire* had been published in Paris in 1951. An English translation, *Memoirs of a Revolution-ary*, didn't appear until 1963, but Macdonald was thoroughly familiar with the book and its author, whom he regarded as a hero. Though the two men never met, they were close friends. Victor Serge (1890–1947), a refugee from both Communism and Nazism, was a Belgian-French-Russian poet, novelist, and professional insurrectionist and agitator who lived a life of incredible romance, danger, and courage. He did time in a French maximum security prison for refusing to testify against anarchist comrades, fought for the Reds against the Whites in the Russian civil war, worked as a Comintern official in Moscow, was arrested and persecuted by Stalin's secret police on account of his support for civil liberties and free expression, escaped from the Soviet Union in 1936 one step ahead of the firing squad, fled Paris just as the Nazis were entering the city, and spent his final years in exile in Mexico City. Serge and Macdonald maintained a constant and intimate correspondence from 1940 onward. It was Macdonald and his wife Nancy who made the arrangements for Serge's flight from Paris; they also tried unsuccessfully to get him an American visa, enlisting the lobbying aid of prominent intellectuals like John Dewey, Max Eastman, and Sidney Hook, but the State Department refused to admit Serge on account of his Bolshevik past. From Mexico, Serge contributed regularly to *Politics* until his death in 1947. Macdonald himself translated many of Serge's articles from the French; some of them were excerpts from the manuscript of *Memoirs of a Revolutionary*.

A decade later, Macdonald published his collection. The title was intentionally ironical. As he acknowledged, he called the book *Memoirs of a Revolutionist* (as opposed to, say, *Notes of a Revolutionist*) because he had abandoned the belief that there would or should be a revolution, Marxist or otherwise, in the United States. The allusion to Serge he did not acknowledge, so far as I know; but it was obviously there, both as a token of Macdonald's admiration for Serge and as an almost subliminal fillip to Macdonald's rueful, self-deprecating irony. When it came to revolution, Macdonald had been merely an "ist"—someone who theorized about revolution and vaguely believed in it, but never did much of anything about it beyond speaking and writing. Victor Serge, by contrast, was an "ary," the real thing.

Why am I telling you all this? I'm not sure, exactly, why I feel the need to offer such a tortured explanation for calling a book about politics *Politics*.

Certainly it's not just to argue that because Macdonald borrowed from Serge, it's O.K. for me to borrow from Macdonald.* It's more that there is a whole political and journalistic tradition here (in Serge as well as Macdonald) that has a lot of resonance for me. Macdonald, after a very brief, almost dandyish flirtation with Stalinism, was at different points a Trotskyist, a socialist, a pacifist, and a sort of culturally conservative libertarian anarchist; his politics were exotic, changeable, and all over the place. Mine have all along been boringly moderate and consistent. Even when, as a post-adolescent, I styled myself a radical, I was always what Europeans call a social democrat, which is what we Americans call a liberal Democrat, and I still am. But the cultural roots of my politics are as much in the dissenting, marginalized, Eurocentric, anti-Stalinist intellectual left which Macdonald epitomized as they are in that great amorphous swamp known as the American mainstream. In Macdonald's conception of politics, what counted were the ideas, the ethics, the values—even the aesthetics. He seldom lingered over such trivialities as Democrats, Republicans, and elections. I'm more interested in that sort of thing than he was, but that is at least partly a reflection of our respective political eras.

I admire Macdonald for the fierceness of his opposition not only to communism but to all forms of tyranny. (This was one aspect of his politics that was not changeable.) I admire him almost as much for his refusal to let the horrors of Stalinism and Hitlerism blind him to the injustices and grossnesses of American capitalism, and for his cosmopolitanism, and for his fearlessness, and for his sense of humor. And, while I would never tempt fate by comparing myself to him (I can only wish I had a tenth of his energy, wit, and erudition), I suppose I also identify a bit with his journalistic career, which took him from a big corporate title (*Fortune*) to small left-wing magazines (before starting *Politics* he was a mainstay of *Partisan Review*) and finally to *The New Yorker*. I started at *Newsweek*, and although my small left-wing magazine (*The New Republic*) was neither as small nor as left-wing as either of Macdonald's, we ended up at the same safe, warm harbor. (We were even both unwitting C.I.A. dupes, him at the Congress for Cultural Free-

---

*Nor is it to argue that because both Serge and Macdonald borrowed from Prince Peter Kropotkin, the revered Russian anarchist, it's O.K. for me to borrow from all three of them. (The title of Kropotkin's autobiography, which appeared in 1899, has been rendered in English both as *Memoirs of a Revolutionist* and as *Memoirs of a Revolutionary*. Serge was present at Kropotkin's funeral in Moscow in 1921.)

dom, me a few years later at the National Student Association.) Also, he was a sprinter, not a marathoner; he never quite managed to write a book "in cold blood," as he put it, and had to settle for collections of magazine articles. I can relate to that.

In that connection, a plea to the reader: don't read this book. I mean, don't feel any obligation to read it the way you might read an "in cold blood" sort of book, beginning at the beginning and marching straight through to the end. (Unless you really want to, of course, in which case be my guest.) This is a collection of magazine articles, not a syllogism or a slide show. It is organized thematically, and more or less chronologically within the themes, an arrangement which I hope gives it a modicum of coherence. But the scheme is necessarily somewhat arbitrary. For your purposes, whatever they are, your scheme is as good as mine—probably better. So please feel free to pick, choose, skip, and jump around.

A few selections have been very lightly edited to remove stylistic infelicities that should have been blue-penciled to begin with. Off-the-mark predictions, lapses in political judgment, and moral errors have been left in. The dates given at the end of each piece are magazine cover dates, which can be anywhere from ten days to a couple of months after the piece was written.

New York, January 2005

POLITICS

1. ENOUGH ABOUT THE SIXTIES

Like the 1930s, another decade of rebellion and radicalism, the 1960s were so jam-packed that they spilled over their temporal borders. For Americans, the thirties began with the 1929 crash and ended at Pearl Harbor, three weeks shy of 1942. John F. Kennedy's election kicked off the sixties right on schedule; but not until April 30, 1974, when Saigon fell and the Vietnam War ended, did the decade get a stake driven through its heart.

The day Kennedy was elected I stood on a school desk and delivered a mock victory speech to my mock-cheering classmates at the Lycée Pierre Fermat, in Toulouse, where I was spending the first semester of my high school senior year as an American Field Service exchange student. The Kennedy button I wore on my lapel was a source of wonder to them. In France, they explained, politics was more serious. You'd risk a bloody nose or worse if you were foolish enough to advertise your affiliation in public without a protective crowd around you. That autumn I got my first whiff of tear gas as part of such a crowd, demonstrating against *la guerre en Algérie* and getting chased through the streets of Toulouse by *flics* swinging lead-hemmed capes. The ship that took me home docked on the morning of Kennedy's inauguration. The musty, stuffy, Ike-y fifties were over, and we all felt the brisk joy of "Let us begin." A thousand days later the colors abruptly darkened, and from then on our politics made France's look frivolous.

Kennedy made politics glamorous and exciting. But by mid-decade politics was becoming a matter of life and death, especially for young males. Millions of young men and women began to think of themselves as radical or, at least, as radically at odds with their government and its war in Vietnam. At the same time, for the young, politics was becoming increasingly bound up with a mass counterculture—a tectonic shift in attitudes and mores about sexuality, race, and "consciousness," for which rock and roll provided the soundtrack.

I watched all this, and participated in it, as, successively, a college student, the editor of a skinny magazine published by the National Student Association for distribution to students overseas (and paid for by a "foundation," which, I would learn to my horror, existed to launder funds for the Central Intelligence Agency), a cub reporter in San Francisco at the dawn of hippiedom, a naval officer–part-time antiwar activist, and, by the end of the decade, a *New Yorker* staff writer.

"Enough about the thirties, already," I would sometimes say to my ex-radical mom and dad when they would start to tell me, for the nth time, about the sitdown strikes or the Moscow trials or Gandhi's salt march. But the truth is, I loved those stories. Here are some of mine.

THE SAN FRANCISCO SOUND

THE FILLMORE AUDITORIUM, the gravitational center of the astonishing new San Francisco rock scene, at midnight on a Saturday night:

An enormous red globe of light gurgles liquidly on one thirty-five-foot-high wall, glowing like a hydrogen fireball. On another wall, infinitely complex green light globules flow into each other and pulsate explosively. On a third wall, moiré patterns, giant eyeballs, de Kooning-like abstracts flash past in swift alternation next to an endlessly repeating film of one small boy after another eating jelly bread.

On the floor, two thousand people are watching, listening, and moving. None of them appear to be older than thirty. Many are "straight," like the crew-cut blond boy in chinos and poplin jacket, whose brunette date wears a plaid skirt and knee socks. But most are "hippies," part of the growing society within a society that centers around Berkeley and the Haight-Ashbury section of San Francisco, and, though their tastes obviously tend toward the informal, the bizarre, and the flamboyant, none of them look alike. There are wide mod ties, wispy string ties, and one fellow with a solid aluminum tie. There are boys in silk frock coats, top hats, suede boots, red sweatshirts emblazoned with the zouave who decorates packages of Zig-Zag cigarette paper. There are girls in miniskirts and net stockings, capes and candy-striped pants, paisley socks and bare feet. A few people have adorned their faces with curlicues of phosphorescent paint. The beards range from the trimmed and Schweppesian to the full and piratical to the shaggy and rabbinical. The hair ranges from the merely long to the shoulder-length and beyond. Some people are sitting or standing, but most are dancing. They are not doing the frug, or the monkey, or any other particular dance. They are just dancing—any way they like. And from the platform at the far end of the auditorium, electronically escalated through a two-hundred-watt amplification system, filling every corner and every brain in the room, comes the San Francisco sound, played on this particular Saturday night by one of its principal purveyors, the Grateful Dead.

The Fillmore is the most important part of the San Francisco rock scene, but it is merely the tip of the iceberg. According to one estimate, there are some two hundred and fifty rock and roll bands in the San Francisco Bay area, and of these, in the judgment of at least one record company executive, perhaps forty are of professional quality. Rock and roll is growing all over the country, but here, where the growth is greater than anywhere else, there are differences.

For one thing, as the jazz critic Ralph J. Gleason puts it, "San Francisco bands are oriented toward playing for people. In Los Angeles, the pattern is for a group to practice and practice in a garage until it's good enough to record." There are plenty of places for bands to play for people. Rivaling (though never surpassing) the Fillmore in decibels, imaginative light shows, and general atmosphere is the somewhat smaller Avalon Ballroom, where a group of hippies who call themselves the Family Dog produce weekend dance concerts. Besides the Avalon and the Fillmore, big rock dances are held at California Hall and Longshoremen's Hall in San Francisco, in college gyms, and in big rooms around the Bay Area—places like the San Leandro Rollerena and the San Bruno Armory. Then there are the pure rock clubs—the Matrix in San Francisco, the Jabberwock in Berkeley, the Arc in Sausalito—where people listen to rock and roll as if it were jazz, except that the music is too loud for casual chitchat. Finally, there are the endless go-go and dance clubs, at least one in every little suburban town and all of them hiring live rock music.

The scope of the rock scene in San Francisco sets it apart from other cities. But there are more important differences.

Rock and roll is a field which is subject to an enormous amount of manipulation. A few men—record company executives, radio station programmers, tour promoters, key disc jockeys—exert terrific power. And even when there is no hanky-panky, it is a chancy business. A radio program director who must choose one or two singles out of the two hundred or so sent him every week is bound to make arbitrary or whimsical choices some-times. The record-buying public, like the television-watching public, by de-sign or not, is frequently gulled into liking the worst kind of trash.

But in San Francisco, no one is pulling the strings. There are no shad-owy figures lurking in the background in sharkskin suits and smoked glasses. The discriminating, attentive audiences who attend the big rock-dance con-certs have not been told to like the San Francisco sound, but they like it any-way. As a result, groups like the Jefferson Airplane and the Grateful Dead, neither of which has ever had a hit record, are able to earn upward of two thousand dollars for a weekend's work.

Bill Graham, creator and manager of the Fillmore Auditorium, learned the hard way that San Francisco audiences can't be fooled. In a moment of weakness last August, Graham booked a hokey group called Sam the Sham and the Pharoahs, whose record, "Little Red Riding Hood," was a big na-tional hit at the time. "Only three hundred and eighty-seven people came, and I lost eighteen hundred dollars," recalls Graham. "The people—*my* people—stayed away. It was the best thing that ever happened to me."

THE MUSIC APPEALS to a broad range of people, but it is a definite part of the "hippie scene," San Francisco's new bohemianism. Unlike the sullen Beats of the fifties, who sat around in coffee houses complaining about how rotten and meaningless everything was, the hippies, much more numerous than the Beats ever were, accentuate the positive. They dress wildly, indi-vidualistically, colorfully—"ecstatically," they would say. Like the Beats, they are dropouts from the conventional "status games," but, unlike them, they have created their own happy lifestyles to drop into. "In a way," says Jerry Garcia, twenty-four, lead guitarist of the Grateful Dead and one of the cul-ture heroes of Haight-Ashbury, "we're searching for respectability—not Ford or GM respectability, but the respectability of a community support-ing itself financially and spiritually."

Not many hippies have ever heard of Marshall McLuhan, and fewer have read him, but McLuhan's analysis is useful in understanding them. The old "Gutenberg-era" values of privacy, prestige through money and job, and linear, cause-and-effect logical thinking are out the window. The hippies have embraced the new, "electric," tribal values of total involvement. They are for freedom and "honesty," against categorization, even, in a sense, against language itself. "Maybe the tyranny of the written word is something that is going out," muses Jerry Garcia. "Language is almost designed to be misunderstood."

Psychedelic drugs such as marijuana and LSD are very important to the hippies. Through these drugs the hippie achieves the total involvement, sensory and emotional, that he seeks. On marijuana, he sees, hears, and feels colors and sounds more vividly. On LSD, his ego dissolves and is replaced by an abiding love and appreciation for all people and things. He becomes more existential than the existentialists, because his total immersion in the present is untainted by any sense of the absurdity of the future.

In the light of the hippies' approach to life and sensibility, it is easy to understand why the most creative of them have turned to art forms that offer immediate sensory involvement: experimental films, colorful poster art, abstract light shows, and rock and roll. Unsurprisingly, the hippies have produced little in the way of good writing.

There is no such thing as a hippie who favors the war in Vietnam, but few hippies are political activists. They tend to think in moral and personal, not political, terms. When their lapel buttons are remotely political, they tend to relate political issues to personal ones, as in the slogans "Make Love Not War," and "Keep California Green—Legalize Grass." More often, though, their buttons say things like "Nirvana Now," or simply, "Love."

This is not to say, though, that hippies are uninterested in social change. They take the long view. Their approach is to create their own society of love and light and then wait for everybody else to join up.

Anger is uncommon among hippies. Last month, when California's new law outlawing the possession of LSD went into effect, a group of Haight-Ashbury heads decided to stage a protest. But then they decided that a protest would be "too negative," so they staged a celebration instead. It turned out to be a pleasant afternoon in the Panhandle of Golden Gate Park, with rock bands playing, children finger-painting on the ground, and people wandering among the trees with cans of beer. "Our attitude is strictly laissez-faire," says Jerry Garcia. "Nobody throws rocks at the cops anymore, because we're all human beings in this together." The hippies don't even hate the undercover narcotics agents, whom they call "narcos" or "brain police." A few weeks ago, one such agent, whose picture had appeared in the paper when he received a departmental honor, walked into the Fillmore in his customary hippie disguise. He was applauded.

The benevolent tolerance of the hippie world is obvious to anyone who has ever visited the Fillmore Auditorium on a Friday or Saturday night. Those who go in suits and ties, as many parents, journalists, curious citizens, and record company representatives have done, find absolutely no hostility whatsoever. No one jostles them and hisses, "Get out of our place, you square," or some such. No one is made to feel that he is intruding. "We don't want you to freak out," Bill Graham says. "We want you to melt. A lot of people come in here like blocks of ice against the nasty beatniks. We want to break you down so your pores are open, so you'll look, you'll listen, you'll enjoy."

The breaking down begins as soon as you pay your admission price ($2.50 to $3.50, depending on the talent), walk up the wide, rather dingy staircase, and enter the lobby. The first things you see are a couple of big boxes with a hand-lettered sign on them: HAVE ONE . . . OR TWO. The boxes are filled with apples and lollipops. Graham gives away 2,736 apples and 2,160 lollipops every weekend. "If a guy walks in here worried about what kind of nutty scene he's getting himself into and the first thing that happens to him is somebody gives him an apple," says Graham, "he's bound to loosen up a little." The lobby's walls are covered with signs (ONCE INSIDE, NO OUTSY-INSY), posters, and clippings about Lenny Bruce, Jasper Johns, and Pat Boone.

What the Fillmore does is to have so much going on that the visitor can vary the intensity and quality of his pleasure. It is next to impossible to be bored there. If the visitor gets fidgety listening to the music, he can dance. If he gets tired, he can watch the ever-changing, mesmerizing light show. Or he can look at the fantastic variety of people doing their fantastic free-form dances. Or he can retire to the relative quiet of the lobby for an apple and some browsing among the things posted on the wall. Or he can go up-stairs for a hamburger and survey the scene from the balcony. If he feels like a nap, he can find a quiet patch of floor off in a corner somewhere and go to sleep. No one will mind.

Bill Graham is a thirty-five-year-old Jewish war orphan who fled from Berlin to Chateau Dechaumont, France, to Marseilles to Toulouse to Madrid to Lisbon to Casablanca to Dakar and finally to New York, where he and ten of the sixty-four children with whom he had begun his odyssey disembarked on September 24, 1941. He grew up with a Jewish family in the Bronx and went to Brooklyn College and the City College of New York. He was drafted in 1951 and sent to Korea, where he was busted three times for insubordination and awarded the Bronze Star for valor in combat.

Most summers between 1949 and 1956, Graham worked as a waiter at

Grossinger's, learning the ropes. He was poor, and his "ambition was to make lots of money and become a millionaire and buy everything." He went to work as a statistician, then as a paymaster, and then as an office manager, but it palled. "I got the realization that sitting behind a desk and making good money wasn't all I'd thought it'd be." So in 1959 he started taking lessons at the Actors Studio and tried to make a career out of acting. "I ran the gamut," he says. "Either I didn't have the talent or I didn't get the breaks. But if you're really dedicated to the theatre, you have to be willing to live in a crummy cold-water flat and stand there while hundreds of doors slam in your face. I just couldn't do that. I thought the talent was there to do some character work, but apparently producers didn't."*

Graham got to San Francisco in 1952, flat broke after a trip to Europe. He talked his way into a job at Allis-Chalmers, reduced the staff from forty-seven secretaries in two offices to twenty-one secretaries in one office, and ended up San Francisco sales manager at $14,500 a year.

In February of 1964, Graham quit Allis-Chalmers to go to work as business manager and producer of the San Francisco Mime Troupe, a New Left theatre group which was (and is) raising the ire of the city fathers by performing bawdy commedia dell'arte in the public parks and producing an anti-everybody updated minstrel show called "Civil Rights in a Cracker Barrel." The rock dance scene was three weeks old when Graham got into it. The first dance, sponsored by the Family Dog and entitled "A Tribute to Dr. Strange," had been held on October 16, 1965, at Longshoreman's Hall near Fisherman's Wharf. On November 6, Graham threw a rock benefit at the Mime Troupe's Howard Street headquarters. Some three thousand people showed up to pack the room, whose official capacity was six hundred, and Graham had to soften up a police sergeant by blandly calling him "lieutenant" to keep him from closing the whole thing down.

Clearly a larger place was needed. Graham nosed around and found the Fillmore Auditorium, a run-down old ballroom at Fillmore Street and Geary Boulevard in the city's biggest Negro ghetto. He rented it for sixty dollars, and on December 10 threw another wildly successful rock and roll

---

* Eventually, though, some producers agreed. Besides appearing as himself in numerous rock documentaries, including *Woodstock*, Graham would play character roles in five films, beginning with Francis Ford Coppola's *Apocalypse Now*, in 1971. In 1991, the year he appeared onscreen as Charlie Luciano in Warren Beatty's *Bugsy*, Graham died in a helicopter accident near San Francisco. (2005)

benefit. Shortly thereafter, Graham and the Mime Troupe parted company, and Graham decided to go it alone. He went back to the Fillmore and found that eleven other promoters had already put in bids for it. Graham got forty-one prominent citizens to write letters to the auditorium's owner, a haberdasher named Harry Shifs, and Shifs gave him a three-year lease at five hundred dollars a month. Graham isn't a zillionaire yet, but he's making a comfortable living (he'll probably take home well over fifty thousand dollars this year), and he is beginning to be regarded as a San Francisco institution, like the cable cars, Chinatown, and the topless. "The hippie community," says Jerry Garcia, "has turned out to be something the man from Montgomery Street can point to with pride, in a left-handed way, and say 'these are our boys.' "

It was not always so. Back in April, official San Francisco seemed determined to put Graham and the Fillmore out of business. First the police department turned down Graham's application for a dance permit. The rock impresario took his case to the City Board of Permit Appeals. The police responded by producing a petition of complaint from twenty-eight local merchants.

Graham went through the ceiling. He charged that the police had collected the signatures by accusing Graham of being a "pusher" whose extravagance attracted "the bad element." He went around to the merchants himself and got retractions from twenty-three of the twenty-eight, plus a statement of support from Rabbi Elliot Bernstein of the neighboring Congregation Beth Israel, who had earlier been heard to complain that hippies were urinating on his synagogue.

The appeals board turned Graham down anyway. At this point, when all seemed lost, the *San Francisco Chronicle* came to the rescue on April 21 with an editorial, "The Fillmore Auditorium Case," and a cartoon of a blubbering police officer captioned, "They're dancing with tears in my eyes." "The official hostility is not yet satisfactorily explained," opined the *Chron*. "The police say the dance halls attract disorderly crowds and generate fights—but have reported none at the Fillmore Auditorium since Graham took over."

The police were groggy but still on their feet. An officer showed up in Graham's office, waved the paper at him, and told him the editorial was a "personal affront." The next evening, the police invaded the Fillmore and arrested Graham and fourteen under-eighteen patrons. The charge was violation of a city ordinance prohibiting minors from going unchaperoned to dance halls. The ordinance, passed in 1909 and unenforced for half a century, had been designed for an earlier, wilder San Francisco, when young girls ventured into the Barbary Coast at their peril.

The *Chronicle* struck back with another editorial, "Certain Questions About a Police Raid," which asked, among other things, "Was the Friday night raid vindictive or punitive or the result of police prejudice against the neighborhood? We hope not." Three weeks later, the City Board of Permit Appeals gave Graham his permit.

Since then, police interest in harassing the Fillmore has dropped to zero. Order is kept by seven private policemen, six male and one female, whom Graham calls "swinging cops who know what's happening." One of the joys of the Fillmore is to watch one of these policemen standing quietly in a corner, rocking back and forth to the music, or joking with a long-haired, bead-wearing hippie. But they do their job. "If one of my regulars comes around obviously smashed on pot or booze," says Graham, "the cop'll say, 'Not tonight, man. Come back when you're straighter.' The kid'll say 'Aw, come on,' but he'll go." Very few police are needed, because the hippies will tell them if anyone is smoking pot, picking a fight, or otherwise misbehaving. "It's not 'cause they're stoolies," explains Graham. "It's their scene, too. They know that if we get busted, they lose their scene."

That the *Chronicle* defended the Fillmore so resoundingly was largely the doing of Ralph Gleason. Gleason and entertainment reporter John Wasserman had for months been treating the Fillmore and the Avalon Ballroom as places of serious artistic endeavor. "Some of the *Chronicle*'s editors who had teenage kids had been to the Fillmore to see for themselves," recalls Gleason. "At the editorial meeting, the science editor and a sports columnist came along to urge a strong stand. They knew it wasn't just that nut Gleason, and this made an impression."

Bill Graham himself is a wiry man with light brown eyes, a perpetual five o'clock shadow, and black hair combed into a modified version of old-style Presley rocker. He has a craggy face and a wide mouth that make him look a little like the late Lenny Bruce. He spends most of the day at the Fillmore in his tiny, cluttered office, which looks like the inside of a chimney. He is a gesticulating, nonstop, New York–accented talker. Sometimes his monologues take on the character of a rant. Sometimes he is unnecessarily curt. ("In my conversation," he says, "the 'fuck you' replaces the 'please.' ")

Graham can—and frequently does—talk for hours about the Fillmore and his role in it. His philosophy boils down to the following: "Art in America can only survive within the framework of a sound business structure." He likes making money, but he prefers the challenge of creating a good scene. "If I were to say to you that I don't give a damn about the dollar, I'd be lying," he says. "But the dollar is second to the result. I have my orgasm at one in the morning when I go up to the balcony and see everybody having a good time."

A lot of people dislike Graham for his toughness, but in his management of the Fillmore he has shown taste, imagination, and courage. He combined a dance-concert played by the Jefferson Airplane with a reading by Andrei Voznesensky, the Soviet poet. When he booked the Byrds, the well known Los Angeles folk-rock group, he combined them with a production of LeRoi Jones's play *The Dutchman*. Lenny Bruce made one of his last public appearances at the Fillmore on June 24 and 25.

Graham has run benefits at the Fillmore for such causes as SNCC (the Student Nonviolent Co-ordinating Committee), the Delano grape strikers, the North Beach children's nursery, the San Francisco Artist's Liberation Front, and the Both/And, an experimental jazz nightclub. There was an even, once, a wedding at the Fillmore. Between sets one Saturday night, a young man named Lee "Thunder Machine" Quanstrum married his blonde fiancée, "Space Daisy" (many hippies affect comic-book-type nicknames), in a Unitarian (what else?) ceremony conducted on the bandstand. Graham later got a thank-you note from the couple. Here is its text: "Dear Bill, Thank you for making it possible for us to be married in the style to which we are accustomed."

On the weekend following last month's racial disturbances in San Francisco, when virtually every establishment in the Fillmore District was padlocked after dark, Graham brought off his dance-concerts on schedule. In doing so he went against the advice of his attorneys and many friends (and lost a pile of money), but he succeeded in proving that the Fillmore Auditorium could remain a place of peace and light despite the tribulations of the world outside.

IN ADDITION to their social and artistic role in presenting the new bohemianism and the new music of San Francisco, the Fillmore Auditorium and the Avalon Ballroom have pioneered an essentially new art form, the big light show. Light displays in conjunction with rock music have been used before, and are being used now in other cities (as at the Cheetah in New York). But these efforts have been comparatively primitive. The light shows that go with—and in a sense are part of—the San Francisco sound are unique in scope, brilliance, and technique.

The Fillmore's light man, a twenty-nine-year-old painter named Tony Martin, has led in working out the new methods, both at the Fillmore and at the Tape Music Center of Mills College, Oakland, where his experiments are financed under a two-hundred-thousand-dollar grant from the Rockefeller Foundation. Martin uses a wide variety of equipment to produce his extravaganzas: slide projectors and slides, both conventional (photographs of things like trees and statues of Marc Antony) and handmade (patterns painted directly onto the transparency); movies of every description, including the endlessly repeating type, which are accomplished by running a circular strip of film through a projector bicycle-chain style; colored, flashing footlights, which project elongated, el Greco-like silhouettes of the musicians onto the screen behind them; ordinary theatrical gels and spotlights; and all these in combination.

The most impressive part of the light shows are the bubbling, pulsating, exploding liquid projections, and the technology of these is strikingly simple. The basic piece of equipment is an overhead projector, the kind that college lecturers use to show maps and diagrams to their students. Using a shallow glass dish (actually the crystal of a large clock), the artist mixes vegetable color and water, oil, alcohol, and glycerin. The possibilities are nearly infinite. By tilting the glass, the artist can make the patterns ebb and flow. By raising and lowering the glass, he can shift the focus from soft to sharp. By using two glasses with the liquid between, he can squeeze explosions of light in and out of existence. By putting his hand between the light source and the mirrors which project to the screens, he can vary the intensity of the light or block it off entirely. Even the artist's cigarette smoke adds a subtle touch.

The other main artistic offshoot of the San Francisco sound has been the poster art used to advertise the dance-concerts. The poster style, originated by Wes Wilson, twenty-nine, who does the Fillmore's posters, eschews conventional type faces, no matter how unusual. Lettering, photographs, drawings, and abstract design are woven into a continuous whole, with the words undulating around each other or around photographs or drawings. In their ingenuity and use of distorted lettering, the posters recall their French and German forebears of the 1880s and 1890s. Wilson's posters are coveted by collectors, professional and amateur. The Oakland Art Commission has a complete collection, which it plans to display in its new museum. Graham gives away three thousand posters a week to his patrons at the Fillmore, but even that fails to satisfy the demand. One day last summer Graham put up a hundred and fifty posters along Berkeley's Telegraph Avenue and then stopped at the Forum for a cup of coffee. By the time he got up to go back to his car, only three of them were left.

NONE OF THESE THINGS, however—the lights, the friendliness, the posters, the Avalon and Fillmore "scenes"—could exist without the music.

The San Francisco sound is played by a profusion of groups whose impressionistic, tongue-in-cheek names reflect their determination to make a new kind of music. Generally acknowledged as the best of the San Francisco groups are the Jefferson Airplane and the Grateful Dead. The other prominent bands include the Quicksilver Messenger Service, the 13th Floor Elevator, the Sopwith Camel, Country Joe and the Fish, Big Brother and the Holding Company, Moby Grape, the Loading Zone, the Mystery Trend, the Wildflower, William Penn, the Harbinger Complex, Captain Beefheart and His Magic Band, the Chocolate Watch Band, and the Sir Douglas Quintet. There is even a group called the Five Year Plan, which played its most recent (and perhaps only) gig at the annual picnic of the *People's World*, the West Coast Communist weekly.

The San Francisco sound is a very hard-driving folk-rock with strong blues and electronic influences. A San Francisco band usually consists of three electric guitars (lead, rhythm, bass), drums, and voices. Frequently another instrument (harmonica, electric organ, fiddle) is added. An equally important part of the instrumentation is the electronic amplifying equipment and its accoutrements—microphones, speakers, amplifiers, pickups, tape loops, echo-makers, and reverberators. This equipment can create an energy level that is astonishing. The Fillmore Auditorium's sound system develops enough power to run a small radio station and ten times as much as the biggest home stereo equipment. The sound comes out at roughly a hundred decibels and sometimes ventures as high as a hundred and ten, only ten decibels under the pain level. In this situation the electronic equipment becomes part of the machinery of music, not simply a way of making it audible to people in the back of the room.

Elements of the music have been floating around for years. It's rock dance-music, so the beat is always firmly there: a very basic thump thump thump underpinning the whole thing, a walloping electric bass and drum booming away. The drummers play out of a straight rock and roll bag, except that some of the best of them explode into intricate showers of rhythm that suggest that they have been listening to the music of India. The guitarists chug-chug rock-style, drone folk-style, twang country-style, and wail rhythm-and-blues-style, but they too are increasingly falling into sitar-like improvisations of great color and intensity. Most of them own several Ravi Shankar records. The best guitarists are capable of extended jazzish statements. Instead of wrapping it all up in a three-minute, hit-recordable package, a San Francisco rock group is likely to devote fifteen or twenty minutes to a single number.

The influences which touch the San Francisco sound cover a big slice of the musical spectrum. The Beatles are a stronger influence than ever now that they have ventured into raga-rock and electronic sound processing, and even those San Francisco musicians not directly indebted to the Beatles musically are grateful to them for using their charisma to create a public taste for experimental rock and roll. Another immediate strand of influence is pure folk-rock—the lyrical, harmonic kind popularized by the Byrds, the Lovin' Spoonful, and the We Five (itself a San Francisco group), and the growling, shouting kind popularized by Bob Dylan. Certain kinds of modern classical music have also been influential. Some of the San Francisco groups build their sound to a level of pure white noise, an aspect of the music that John Cage would appreciate. But the most important influence on the San Francisco sound is the blues. At the Fillmore and the Avalon, blues bands more often than not appear on the same bill with San Francisco rock bands. Chicago's Paul Butterfield Blues Band and New York's Blues Project have appeared frequently in San Francisco, and their blend of folk-rock and blues has become part of the San Francisco sound. An older generation of blues singers has exerted considerable influence as well. In the past month alone, three very great blues singers—Muddy Waters, Big Mama Willie Mae Thornton, and Lightnin' Hopkins—have played dance-concerts at the Fillmore Auditorium.

All these strains have been synthesized into a unique sound that is San Francisco's own. Ralph Gleason argues that "it is the first generation of white American musicians who aren't trying to be Negroes. They admire Negro musicians like Otis Redding but aren't interested in imitating them.

They are producing something that cannot be dismissed as merely an imitation of any other kind of music."

THE MOST POPULAR of the San Francisco groups is the Jefferson Airplane.

The Jefferson Airplane is further in a purer folk-rock direction than the other San Francisco groups. Its group vocalizings use folk-style harmony and have a lyricism generally lacking in the San Francisco sound.

The Airplane was organized two years ago by its lead singer, Marty Balin, twenty-three, and the group's main asset is still Balin's strong, clear alto voice. Balin slurs his sibilants, a fortunate speech defect which only adds to the liquid quality of his voice. Broad-shouldered, heavy-browed, and handsome, Balin writes most of the Airplane's material. Like most other San Francisco groups, the Airplane performs largely original material. When it performs other songs (such as "Midnight Hour" and "Tobacco Road," which have become standards among San Francisco rock groups), it uses original arrangements.

The Airplane's five other members include one girl, a slim, lovely brunette named Grace Slick, whose huge, deep blue eyes flash under her bangs. Her throaty contralto and strong vibrato add depth to the group's sound.

When the Jefferson Airplane plays at the Fillmore Auditorium, their set begins with a recording of a jet plane taking off. The sound builds from a low rumble; at the moment it reaches the screaming pinnacle of acceleration, the Airplane launches into its first number. Somehow they manage to maintain the excitement, creating a rolling, building head of steam with each song. They have a joyous sound even though nearly everything they play is in a minor mode. On a song like "My Best Friend," Marty Balin and Grace Slick stare deep into each other's eyes as they sing, and the electricity crackles.

"The Airplane has style," says Ralph Gleason, "and all the people who really make it have got that." And, indeed, it seems more than likely that the Airplane will "really make it." RCA Victor signed them up with a fat twenty-five-thousand-dollar advance. Last week they were in Los Angeles recording their second album. And on January 1 they will appear on television's *Bell Telephone Hour* in a segment taped at the Fillmore.

In preparation for the success its members fully expect, the Jefferson

Airplane is polishing itself up and working hard on new material. But they retain a San Franciscan disdain for crass commercialism. "Sure, we're tightening up," says Skip Spence, twenty-four, the Airplane's drummer. "But we're still not showtime U.S.A. Like we don't all dress the same. One guy'll wear a suit and another guy'll look like he just slept under a train."

They have played in Chicago, Los Angeles, and points in between, but they prefer San Francisco. "It's quiet here," says Jack Casady, twenty-two, the bass guitar player, a dandyish dresser whose nose and pouty mouth are the only parts of his face visible under a Beatles-esque mop of fine hair. "There's no big hassle. The audiences are more demanding here, and you get everybody, from high society to beatniks."

"The thing about San Francisco," adds Marty Balin, "is that everything that happens in the scene is run by the people on the scene. No outside sharpies, no big businessmen."

"The competition here is all friendly," puts in rhythm guitarist and singer Paul Kantner, twenty-four, who looks like a shaggy blond S. J. Perelman without the mustache. "None of that sneaky cutthroat stuff you get in commercial scenes."

"————," concludes Jorma Ludwik Kaukonen, twenty-five, who is tall and angular and has shoulder-length, wavy brown hair. He is quiet but is an exceptionally skillful lead guitarist.

The Jefferson Airplane has invaded territory previously untouched by rock and roll. They played the usually purist Monterey Jazz Festival this summer. More recently (October 19) they performed at the San Francisco Opera Guild's "Fol de Rol," an annual fund-raiser which is also one of the city's most important society events of the season. The Airplane appeared on the same program with members of the San Francisco Opera, who sang pompous versions of "Bess, You Is My Woman Now," "Wouldn't It Be Loverly," and other favorites. Not all the gowned ladies and tuxedoed gentlemen who filled the Civic Auditorium appreciated the intrusion of hard-driving folk-rock—some even hissed—but the Junior Leaguers and their husbands were enthusiastic.

EVERY MEMBER of the Jefferson Airplane wears his or her hair long, but compared to the Grateful Dead, the Airplane looks like the freckle-faced kid next door.

The Dead, nearly as popular as the Plane, play a purer version of the San

Francisco sound. Their music is harder, reedier, eerier, and hoarser. They are five very strange-looking young men. Jerry Garcia—nicknamed "Captain Trips"—is husky and leather-jacketed. He has frizzy hair, like Nancy of Nancy and Sluggo, a homely face, and a gentle smile. Bob Weir, nineteen, the rhythm guitarist, is ethereal and graceful, with light brown locks that wave gently down to his shoulders. Drummer Bill Sommers, twenty-one, and bass guitarist Phil Lesh, twenty-six, have Prince Valiant haircuts, black and blond respectively. Ron McKernan, twenty-one, the organist and lead singer, is commonly known as "Pig-Pen." He has a build like W. C. Fields, a Jerry Collona mustache, and very long, curly hair, which he holds in place Apache-style with a headband. He always wears a black leather vest over a horizontally striped Polo shirt.

Because of the prominent role that LSD plays in their lives and art, the Grateful Dead's music has been called "acid-rock." It's an appropriate tag; during the first months of their existence, the Dead were bankrolled by Owsley Stanley, who is said to have made more than a million dollars manufacturing and selling tiny, eggshell-blue capsules of LSD. Indeed, the name "Grateful Dead" is sometimes interpreted as a reference to the death of the ego under LSD. The Dead do not object to this interpretation, but Jerry Garcia says that in fact he found the name one day when he was leafing through the *Oxford Unabridged Dictionary*. It refers to a family of medieval ballads. Since adopting the name, the Dead claim to have found a reference to it in the Egyptian Book of the Dead: "In the land of darkness, the voices of evil are dispelled by the ship of the sun, which is drawn across the heavens by the grateful dead."

The Grateful Dead may not make it big commercially; they might be too freaky. But Warner Brothers is about to sign them for a record contract.

"I don't think the live sound, the live excitement, can be recorded," says Jerry Garcia. "Rather than trying to turn the living room or the car radio into the Fillmore Auditorium, we'll use the resources of the recording studio—overtracking things, using other instruments."

Garcia acknowledges the importance of LSD to the Dead's development, but he denies that the group is especially drug-oriented. "Consciousness-expanding drugs are a part of the way of life of the community in which we choose to live," he says. "We don't construct our music to be drug music. The way we prefer to play is straight—relaxed and in a good mood. It's always better when something's natural rather than artificial or chemical or whatever."

The Jefferson Airplane, the Grateful Dead, the literally thousands of other groups that are following in their footsteps or branching out on their own, the lights, the art, the dances: all of it adds up to a sound and a scene that is unique.

It is a sound and a scene that supports not one, but two, newspapers: the weekly *Mojo Navigator–R&R News* and the bi-weekly *Deadly Excess*, whose title comes from John Lennon's pun on the London *Daily Express*.

It is a sound and a scene that might sweep the country. Or it might not. San Francisco is a very special kind of city, and things happen here that could never happen anywhere else. If it doesn't, perhaps it will be because, in the words of one Los Angeles record company executive, "these San Francisco groups refuse to co-operate"—meaning they won't make the basic changes in their music that this Angeleno believes are the key to commercial success. But if the San Francisco sound does become the American sound, and the San Francisco scene the American scene, it will be more than just another musical fad. It will mean that the new way of life that is developing in this city is becoming, in some sense, the way of life of the young men and women of the land.

—Unpublished file for *Newsweek*, October 28, 1966*

---

* Newsmagazines used to maintain large domestic and foreign bureaus in interesting cities, allowing cub reporters to have enormous amounts of fun. The bureaus produced "files," which the "writers" in "New York" sometimes glanced at while composing the sentences that actually appeared in the magazine. This "file" was the basis for a 750-word piece in the Music section. It was accompanied by a photograph, taken by me, with the caption, "Jefferson Airplane at Fillmore: 'A big love thing going on.'" Unfortunately, due to a mixup concerning rolls of film, the picture was of Moby Grape. (2005)

WEATHER REPORT:
WHITE TORNADO

WEATHERMAN, as everyone in and out of the movement knows by now, is a faction of Students for a Democratic Society named for a line in a Dylan song ("you don't need a weatherman, etc."), which, in a series of violent street actions, has earned for itself a variety of reputations—militant, courageous, "Custeristic," revolutionary, infantile, bad-ass, "petty-bourgeois subjectivist," and so forth. Weatherman is not the largest of S.D.S.'s three main factions; most observers credit Revolutionary Youth Movement II with having the most followers, though reliable estimates are hard to come by. Nor does Weatherman have the most rigidly ossified ideology; that distinction is usually awarded to the Progressive Labor-Worker Student Alliance faction, now exiled to Boston, where it represents itself as the only true S.D.S. and publishes its own *New Left Notes*. (One is reminded of Liberia, where the governing party is called the True Whig Party and the opposition party is called the Independent True Whig Party.) Yet, far more than either of its rivals, Weatherman has engaged the interest and attention of the public and the press, both within the movement and without it. Its actions, beginning with the artful finessing of the S.D.S. national office out of the hands of P.L.-W.S.A., and continuing with the October "Days of Rage" in Chicago and numerous smaller skirmishes elsewhere, have been nothing if not audacious.

One hardly knows where to begin in discussing the Weathermen. One perhaps ought to begin at the beginning, by asking whether they are in fact a political group at all. A political group, generally speaking, is one which seeks to change (or preserve) social conditions by gaining access to political power, or by causing those who possess power to act in such a way as to bring about the desired change. Using this definition (admittedly an arbitrary one, but again, one has to start somewhere), the Weathermen are *not* noticeably political. It goes without saying that their actions are not designed to persuade the government to change its policies, or even to change public opinion to the point where the government will find it prudent to change its policies. (The principal effect of Weatherman actions on the big public has been to build support for higher police budgets and a freer police hand.) From a radical or "revolutionary" perspective, of course, the notion that problems such as black misery and Vietnam-type wars can be truly solved through "policy changes" is an illusion; what is required is a radical restructuring of the entire society. Yet even from this perspective, it is hard to see in what sense Weatherman is "political." The Days of Rage, for example, did not dramatize any of the injustices ("contradictions") of society; they did not overthrow or even weaken the state; they did not "radicalize" the movement or illustrate the effectiveness of "militant" tactics. You don't even need a dimestore thermometer to see that in terms of its effect on the public (increasing the clamor for a tougher police stance) and on the movement (now badly split and forced to waste energy fighting with itself), the Days of Rage action was a huge, unearned windfall for the forces of repression.

The Weathermen, like the other factions of S.D.S., now present themselves as Marxist-Leninists, and their ideological pronouncements, bristling with oldies like "correct," "objectively," "consciousness," and "running dogs," have the clanging sound of dark Germanic thought. It is a misleading impression. The Weathermen, more "ideological" than ever before, are in full flight from thought. More jawbreakingly "analytical" than ever before, they have abandoned the uncomfortable task of a radical analysis of American society. They have, rhetorically at least, committed themselves to Marxism-Leninism; but they have lost the sense of history which is Marxism's heart.

In place of thought, analysis, and coherent ideology, the Weathermen have evolved a two-point political canon which eliminates the necessity for all three.

The first point is that American revolutionaries must consider themselves as auxiliary to a worldwide battle against U.S. imperialism led by agrarian guerrillas, because it is they who will ultimately bring imperialism (and, by extension, capitalism) to its knees. Bill Ayres, a prominent member of the Weather Bureau, spelled out the implications of this approach when he said, "If it is a worldwide struggle, if Weatherman is correct in that basic thing, that the basic struggle in the world today is the struggle of oppressed peoples against U.S. imperialism, then it is the case that nothing we could do in the mother country could be adventurist."

In other words, since the revolutionary dynamic in American society is coming from outside American society, there is no need to understand American society. No need to worry about what effect a given action might have on the American political climate or on the developing American radical movement. No need to inquire into the possibility that within the 180 million people of white America there might be the potential for an effective radical movement.

To be thus freed from the responsibility of thought is an exhilarating experience. It is pleasant to ride the tide of "history" without having to worry about the political (let alone the moral) consequences. It is thrilling to give oneself over wholly to mindless action without having to face the travail of doubt. It is a relief to rid oneself of troublesome ambivalent feelings about America in a wonderfully simple way—ignore them. Ignore them, "fight against imperialism," and leave the thinking to Fidel, the N.L.F., and Chairman Mao.

One of the strengths of S.D.S., until recently, was its determination to build a native American radicalism, appropriate to American traditions and experience—an American road to socialism. This determination has now been enthusiastically abandoned. "Long live the victory of the people's war!" chanted the Weathermen as they charged through Chicago's Gold Coast. The slogan, meaningless on the face of it (how can a victory live long? what people's war?), becomes almost comic when it issues from the mouths of upper-middle-class kids on a midwestern street. In Chinese, perhaps, "Long live the victory of the people's war" rolls trippingly off the tongue; presumably something is lost in the translation.

Weatherman's view of the movement at home as the servant of a revolutionary dynamic abroad invites comparison with the Stalinists of three and four decades ago. And, indeed, there are similarities: the strange-tasting rhetoric ("running dog," a favorite then as now, is a literal translation from

the Russian); the contempt for internal democracy and the practice of breaking up meetings; the eagerness to bask in the reflected glory of Stalin/
Maochefidel; the atavistic worship of "toughness"; the willingness to ignore domestic conditions. (The differences, though, are at least as great. Unlike the Stalinists, the Weathermen do not take orders from anyone. They
do their own unthinking. On the whole, the Weathermen are the moral su-
periors, and the intellectual inferiors, of the old Stalinists.)

The second point in the Weatherman canon is the notion that "building a fighting force among working-class youth will be the most effective
way to create a revolutionary movement of the whole working class." Having opted for "revolution," Weatherman arrived at this choice of constituency by a process of elimination. As a target for organizing, the
bourgeoisie, big and petty, was out automatically. White workers and college students were too jealous of their privileges to make good revolutionaries. Blacks of any age were the Panthers' turf. Organizing the white poor
had already been tried, without much success. That left white working-
class youth, especially of high school age.

Weatherman's techniques for reaching this constituency have included
picking fights at beaches and drive-ins and running through the halls of
high schools yelling "Jailbreak!" In Cambridge, Weathermen invaded the
Center for International Affairs, beat up a librarian, and later boasted to
neighborhood kids of having "kicked ass" at Harvard as a way of engaging
them in conversation about the Weatherman program. The Days of Rage
were also calculated to prove to working-class youth that Weathermen are
tough street fighters, not dreamy hippies or flabby students.

None of these techniques have been particularly successful, and so the
question of what the Weathermen would do with a youth army once they
had one will probably not have to be answered. The life of a full-time street-
fighting revolutionary may prove satisfying to an upper-middle-class college dropout in a position to reject the meaningless life of the affluent, but
a working-class kid may prefer to find a job that pays something.

The tough-guy techniques suggest that the Weathermen may be trying
to prove something to themselves as well as to those they are trying to recruit. Most Weathermen are bright, and, as noted, upper-middle-class.
When they were in high school, they (generally) got good marks and talked
their way out of trouble. Perhaps they were teacher's pets; perhaps they were
beat up from time to time by the bullies after school. Now, as Weathermen,

they are going back, as if to "do over" their adolescence—only this time they will stand up to the bullies, and, more importantly, earn their respect.

The Weatherman's attitude toward "working-class youth" is ambivalent. On the one hand, these youth are seen as contemptible: the only way to appeal to them is on the lowest, most brutish level. On the other hand (but equally patronizingly), they are seen as a species of Noble Savage, vital and potent. It is the old story, familiar on the Left, of the intellectual's envy of the horny-handed son of toil. There are many resemblances between the Yippies and the Weathermen (the two groups, if the Yippies can be called a group, co-operated at the Justice Department on November 15), but the Yippies are far shrewder politically. There is something inescapably ludicrous about a bunch of kids in football helmets and carrying two-by-fours offering themselves in battle against the armed power of the state, and the Weathermen, in their grim seriousness, leave themselves wide open to ridicule. The Yippies recognize the ludicrousness of the situation and turn it into an important advantage; they understand the magical power of the put-on in an age in which there are no certainties. They understand that the purpose of any announced, public demonstration, no matter how militant, is to get publicity, not to win a victory of arms; by co-opting ridicule, they neutralize it, immunize themselves against it. The Weathermen's humorlessness makes it nearly impossible for them to catch the media off guard.

The reaction of most of the Left to the emergence of Weatherman has been a trifle disingenuous. In its comments on the Weathermen over the past year, the *Guardian* has used words and phrases like the following: "ill conceived . . . without a clear strategy and base of support . . . reckless . . . while we basically agree . . . leaves a lot to be desired . . . glaring deficiencies . . . we deplore . . . confusion . . . inexcusable folly . . ."

If these words and phrases seem familiar, no wonder. They are the same words and phrases used by antiwar liberals who see Vietnam as an exception to (". . . we deplore . . .") a generally benevolent U.S. foreign policy (". . . we basically agree . . ."), rather than as the logical consequence of America's role in international affairs. The Left has been acute in its analysis of the way in which Vietnam arises from a system of imperialism. Unfortunately, the Left seems unable to think about itself equally systematically.

Weatherman is not an accident. Weatherman is a logical consequence of intellectual flabbiness and dishonesty on the Left as a whole. Here are some examples of the kind of thought patterns common in the movement which have now given rise to Weatherman.

1. Movement people who ought to know better have indulged in verbal overkill to the point where language—the basic tool for organizing reality into something that can be understood and acted upon—is no longer descriptive. Terms like "fascism," "racism," "genocide," "police state," and "oppression" have been stripped of meaning. (When and if real fascism comes to this country, it seems we will have no words left to describe it.) The United States is a mess, but it is not, at this moment, a genocidal fascist police state. (Does a government *have* to be a genocidal fascist police state before we can rouse ourselves to oppose it?) When language is corrupted to the point where it becomes impossible to describe the difference between, say, Nazi Germany and Imperial America, no one should be surprised that people begin to make "incorrect decisions." The Weathermen can be forgiven for thrashing about desperately as if the worst were already upon us; in the mad dash to sound ever more militant, the rest of the movement has led them astray.

2. The movement's attack on the American system has degenerated, in too many cases, into an attack on libertarian values generally. The discovery of "corporate liberalism" in the early sixties became, by the late sixties, a widely held conviction that liberals, whatever their positions on the war or any other issue, are "the enemy." (One recalls that the German Communists, when they deluded themselves in a similar fashion about the Social Democrats, ended up voting for Hitler.) "Elections are a farce, the democratic process is warped, justice is a myth, the media is shoddy, etc. I agree," writes David McReynolds in a recent issue of *New Politics*. But he goes on to add: "Yet the hard fact is that our system is open." This is a distinction which the movement increasingly fails to make. Contempt for American democracy has mutated into contempt for democratic— "bourgeois democratic"—procedures generally. Weatherman kept control of national S.D.S. only by flagrantly violating democratic procedures, which the *Guardian*, for example, supported on the grounds that "P.L.'s line and practice on the Vietnam war and the national question is incorrect." (On the other hand, P.L., as a leading exponent of the theory that "freedom is the recognition of necessity," does not inspire much sympathy.)

Freedom of speech and thought should be supported not only because it is good for the movement, but because it is good in itself—before, after, and during the "revolution."

3. Revolution itself is a subject about which there has been a remarkable amount of loose talk. "Revolution," as one of those words everyone to the left of Max Lerner feels he must use relentlessly or be swept into the dustbin of history, no longer means much of anything; it is regularly used to describe everything from opening day care centers to overthrowing the government. It seems fairly obvious that the United States is entering a period of reaction in which the possibility of real revolution is extremely remote, and in which premature activity of an overtly insurrectionary kind is likely to lead to repression. Constant jabber about revolution creates the impression the revolution is imminent, and encourages groups like the Weathermen to "begin class warfare in the streets." When the Weathermen discover that history has not chosen them to bring about the final triumph, they may grow bitter and drop out of the movement entirely, in some cases, perhaps, veering all the way to the extreme right.

4. The movement has been lax about violence, and even a number of prominent pacifists have lately grown wary of speaking out publicly against it (even while doing what they can privately to prevent it). Tom Hayden, writing in the current *Hard Times*, recites a brief summary of official violence in America and then sums up the prevailing movement attitude: "Against this backdrop, the 'violence of the Left' is minor. Our total violence over the last five years has not reached that of a single B-52 raid in Vietnam."

Here Hayden is missing the point in the grand manner. Leaving aside the question of whether keeping our violence down to the level of a B-52 raid is something we ought to be proud of, movement violence is *political* (since there is no question of military victory) and must be judged in terms of its political effect. There is no profit in indulging in political body counts.

5. Finally, there is the question of whether Marxism-Leninism is a worldview to which one wants to lend any support at all. This is a question which it is terribly difficult to discuss within the movement. An atmosphere has enveloped the Left in which anyone who suggests that Marxism-Leninism—orthodox communism—might be a *bad thing*, that it might in fact be diametrically opposed to everything the movement is supposed to stand for, risks being called a "Red-baiter," risks being accused of somehow being in league with J. Edgar Hoover and the Mississippi State Sovereignty Commission. (There is a kind of false civil libertarianism on the Left which equates principled opposition to Communism with support for state repression of those who believe in it.) I feel like a heel for bringing this up,

but all of the countries in the world which are governed by Communist parties have a controlled press, have no freedom of assembly, have pervasive secret police forces, and have no dissident political groups which are allowed to function openly. In the same *Hard Times* article, Tom Hayden offers the following definition: "A police state means: thought control, wage and price control, antistrike regulations, political persecution, endless chaos." I don't mean to be rude, but isn't this an excellent description of China? And, minus the chaos, of the Soviet Union? Is this really the kind of society we want in our country? In its report on the December 27–30 Weatherman conference in Flint, Michigan, Liberation News Service writes: "The Weatherman position boiled down to inevitable race war in America, with very few 'honkies'—except perhaps the four hundred people in the room and the few street kids or gang members who might run with them—surviving the holocaust." LNS reports that Weatherman "digs" Charles Manson, and quotes Bernadine Dohrn as saying, "Dig it, first they killed those pigs, then they ate dinner in the same room with them, then they even shoved a fork into a victim's stomach! Wild!" Is this our movement?

—*Win Magazine*, February 1, 1970*

---

* *Win*—an acronym for "workshop in nonviolence"—was a weekly magazine published in association with the War Resisters League. Its circulation was well under ten thousand, its orientation was radical-left-pacifist-hippie, and its readers were almost all "movement" activists, including plenty of self-styled "Marxist-Leninist" "revolutionaries" who were anything but pacifists. (2005)

EVERYWHERE'S SOMEWHERE

John Lennon Yoko Ono
New York City are your people.
John Lennon Yoko Ono
New York City is your friend.
—*David Peel and the Lower East Side*

SOME GOOD LOCAL NEWS, for a change: John Lennon and his wife and co-worker, Yoko Ono, have become, for most practical purposes, New Yorkers. They have been living here more or less continuously for the past six months: they have rented a studio in the West Village to live in and a loft in SoHo to work in; they have been observed doing New Yorkish things, such as riding their bicycles in the Park, going to the movies in the middle of the night, and picking up the Sunday papers in Sheridan Square. So far, they have not been heard to complain that the city is unlivable. When that happens, we'll know that they're here to stay.

On a recent Saturday, we went down to the West Village to see for ourself how they are getting along in their new home. A long-haired retainer opened the door and steered us toward a curtain in the rear. We ducked through it, into what is surely one of the pleasantest rooms in town. It is a studio in the old, romantic way—high-ceilinged, with serrated skylights, trees outside the windows, and a cast-iron circular stairway, painted muddy green, leading to the roof. The walls are beige, trimmed in the same muddy green. There was a relaxed dishevelment—piles of clothing, electronic equipment, a guitar, magazines in English and Japanese. The only uncluttered horizontal surface was a bed, big and solid, which jutted into the room like the stage in a theatre-in-the-round. A television set, picture on, sound off, perched at the foot—a prompter's box. John Lennon, wearing jeans and a blue tank top, sat cross-legged on the bed. He was a trifle smaller than we had expected, his skin was ruddier, his hair was fairer, but his face was as familiar as an old friend's. Yoko, dressed in green, lounged beside him. We pulled up a chair.

"Why did you choose New York to live in?" we asked.

"We love it, and it's the center of our world," John said.

"It's the first international city, racewise, if you think about it," Yoko said. "It has more Jews than Tel Aviv."

"And more Irish than Dublin," John said.

"And blacks, and Chinese, and Japanese, and they're all living pretty well together," Yoko said. "Right now there's fantastic pessimism, both in the art world and in the general society. Even the most intelligent people in New York are saying, 'Oh, nothing is happening in New York. It's boring. Let's all go to the West Coast.' That was the general tenor when we got here. We're sort of trying to change the wind to a more positive wind."

"I think all of us went through a big depression in the last year and a half, all over the world," John said. "We think there's something in the air that's going to pick us all up again. You know, New York is a fantastic place. Yoko is a New Yorker. She spent fifteen years here before she met me, and she used to go on about New York to me all the time, but I had never really seen it. I was overwhelmed by America in the early days when the Beatles were here, because we were all brought up on Americana. Britain is the fifty-ninth state, or whatever, and America was the mother country of the whole culture. There's an unbelievably creative atmosphere on this little island of Manhattan. Like they say, there just isn't anything you can't get in New York."

"It's a very rich island," Yoko said solemnly.

"It has everything you could possibly want, night and day. That's what I can't stand about England and Europe: it closes down, unless you go to Hamburg or Amsterdam for the nightclub scene, which I don't enjoy. But New York never sleeps."

"If you had all the money in the world and you were in Spain or some-where, what could you do with it?" said Yoko. "Here there's no end to it."

"In a way, it's better to be poor in New York than rich in Spain or Eng-land," John said.

"Exactly, exactly," Yoko said. "I was an artist *cum* waitress *cum* lecturer in New York, and a superintendent also."

"She was the superintendent of the building Jerry Rubin's living in now," John said. "Jerry took us to see it, and it turned out to be a place where Yoko was superintendent ten years ago."

"I was fired," Yoko said, and she laughed. "One night, I was having a con-cert at Carnegie Recital Hall, and I forgot to turn the incinerator on. All the garbage was stuck, and two days later I burned it, and the smoke was everywhere, and the fire department came, and I was fired. I was a waitress and a cook in a macrobiotic restaurant—the Paradox. The critics would come to interview me about my concerts."

"She'd serve 'em macro and then sit down with 'em and talk about her art," John said.

"I thought I was a very rich person then, because this city has that qual-ity, that even a waitress can feel rich about it," Yoko said. "There's no set thing about your fate here. Your fate is what you create in this city."

We said that the talk of riches reminded us of a recent song of John's, "Imagine," which asks the listener, among other things, to "imagine no pos-sessions."

"I wish 'Imagine' would come true," John said. "I've been listening to it myself, because I get an objective view after, and I was imagining. I began to think: I don't *want* that big house we built for ourselves in England. I don't want the bother of owning all these big houses and big cars, even though our company, Apple, pays for it all. All structures and buildings and everything I own will be dissolved and got rid of. I'll cash in my chips, and anything that's left I'll make the best use of. Yoko is a three-tatami woman, and she's been working on me to get rid of this possessions complex, which is someting that happens to people who were poor like myself—not starv-ing but poor."

We asked Yoko about her three tatami, and she said, "One tatami is the length and width of a person lying down. A friend of mine in Tokyo says that in today's society, with its overpopulation, the natural space that a per-son can acquire without fighting or making unnatural efforts is three tatami—one for himself to lie down in, a second for his companion, and a third for them both to breathe in. There is a kind of poverty where you have an excess of things, and all your energy is directed toward getting and keeping them. John was poor, and it was natural for him to strive for wealth, but I come from a background of excessiveness. It was very natural for me to live in New York in a bohemian way, because I was trying to get away from that."

John was still preoccupied with his possessions. "It's *clogging my mind* just to *think* about what amount of gear I have in England. All my books and possessions. Walls full of books I've collected all my life. I have a list this thick of the things I have in Ascot, and I'm going to tick off the things I really want, really need. The rest goes to libraries or prisons—the whole damn lot. I might keep my rock-and-roll collection, but even *that* I'm thinking about."

"Everything you've got in here looks like something you use," we said.

"Yes, it's very casual," Yoko said. "If we lost everything in here, we might be annoyed, but not to the point where it would affect our health. I like the idea of everything being transient, so that all that is with me is somebody I love and myself."

We asked the Lennons how they liked their new neighborhood, and Yoko said, "It's so good! It's like a quaint little town."

"Yes, it's like a little Welsh village, with Jones the Fish and Jones the Milk, and everybody seems to know everybody," John said.

"People don't grab us when we walk in the Village," Yoko said. "They sort of smile from a distance, which is nice."

"We stand out more in Britain than in America as a mixed-marriage couple," John said. "Although there is race hatred in America, you see more different-colored people in America than in Britain."

"Even the white people are different colors here," we said.

"Yes, there are all shades, all different kinds of descent," he said. "In England, everybody south of Calais is a Wog, and that includes the French and the Italians."

"John has a New York temperament in his work," Yoko said. "Liverpool is very much like New York, for an English city."

"Liverpool is the port where the Irish got on the boat to come over here, and the same for the Jews and the blacks," John said. "The slaves were brought to Liverpool and then shipped out to America. On the riverfront in Liverpool you can still see the rings in the side where they were chained up. We got the records—the blues and the rock—right off the boats, and that's why we were advanced musically. In Liverpool, when you stood on the edge of the water you knew the next place was America."

The sun was setting, and the television set glowed more brightly. On the screen, a gigantic lizard was crunching Times Square underfoot. "Do you *like* watching television without the sound?" we asked.

"TV to me is like what the fireplace used to be," John said. "You always get these surreal things happening. I used to watch the fire as a child, but since they took the fire away from us, I've decided that TV is it. It's like the window—only this picture continually changes. You'll see China and the moon, all in ten minutes. You'll see real, surreal, strange, psychedelic—everything."

We got up to go, and said goodbye to Yoko. John walked us to the door, peered out cautiously, and came out on the stoop with us for a moment. "Everywhere's somewhere, and everywhere's the same, really, and wherever you are is where it's at," he said. "But it's more so in New York. It does have sugar on it, and I've got a sweet tooth."

—*The New Yorker*, January 8, 1972

WHY THE WAR WAS IMMORAL

WAS THE WAR in Vietnam wrong? Not just inadvisable, not just a costly mistake, but morally wrong? How one answers that depends partly, I guess, on how one experienced the war and the opposition to it. A few days ago, at the university where I'm spending a semester, I found myself deep in conversation with a tutor in the philosophy department, an intense, articulate man five or six years younger than I am. (I'm forty-one.) We were talking about our experiences in the antiwar movement—ten and fifteen and nearly twenty years ago—and he said that when he looks back on that time he feels mostly a kind of angry regret. He had been a member of Students for a Democratic Society when S.D.S. dropped its homegrown ideology of participatory democracy in favor of mindless Maoism; he had chanted, "Ho! Ho! Ho Chi Minh! N.L.F. is gonna win!"; he had longed for the triumph of the forces of "liberation" not only in Vietnam but everywhere in the Third World and ultimately at home; he had spelled it Amerika and dismissed its political system—"bourgeois democracy"—as a hoax, a cover for racism and imperialism. When the war ended and Indochina vanished into a bloodsoaked totalitarianism (instead of the gentle egalitarianism he had expected), he was wrenchingly disillusioned. Gradually he discovered that the "revolutionary socialism" of the Third World is brutal, that the Soviet Union is armed and dangerous, that for all its flaws American democracy is the moral superior of any form of communism. "I was wrong, just totally wrong," he told me. Last year he voted for Reagan.

I was luckier. I happened to have been brought up in a political and moral atmosphere of left-wing anti-communism. Reared as I was on Or-

well, Gandhi, and Silone, it was no great trick for me to avoid the more blatant naïvetés of New Leftism, and thus also to avoid the subsequent disil-
lusionments. I took my antiwar arguments from Theodore Draper, not
Noam Chomsky; from *Commentary* (yes, *Commentary*) and *The New Republic*, not the *National Guardian* and *Monthly Review*. I was similarly lucky
in my encounter with military service. Opposed to what was then still called
the "Vietnam policy," yet not so fiercely opposed as to be willing to risk
prison, and too straight to dodge the draft, I signed up at the end of 1966
for a three-year hitch in the navy. I asked to be sent to Vietnam, figuring a
desk job in Saigon would be interesting without being unduly risky, but was
sent—catch-22—to a sleepy shore billet in New York instead.

Two years later I *was* ordered to Vietnam (desk job in Da Nang); but
by then my antiwar convictions had grown so strong I preferred jail to further military service, and I announced my intention to refuse the orders. I
hoped for antiwar martyrdom; instead, quite by chance, a medical difficulty
developed, and I was hastily mustered out. I'd managed to have it both
ways: veteran (sort of), and resister (in a way). In the navy and after, I campaigned for Bobby Kennedy and Allard Lowenstein and other antiwar
politicians: went on all the marches; hung around the office of a lively
little pacifist weekly, *Win*, whose editor had two stickers on the bumper of
his Volkswagen; U.S. OUT OF VIETNAM and RUSSIA OUT OF LATVIA. But I
didn't join any of what the inimitable Norman Podhoretz calls (in *Why We
Were in Vietnam*) "the three main currents of the 'antiwar' movement": pro-
communist, anti-anti-communist, and anti-American. I guess that I (along
with more prominent opponents of the war, such as Podhoretz himself)
must have joined one of the non-main currents. Perhaps it was the current
that cheered when Norman Thomas, whom I had been taught to revere
and who never disappointed, advised the movement to wash the flag, not
burn it.

It's no surprise that the differences over Vietnam, rooted as they are in
such different experiences, persist in the form of different histories remembered, different lessons learned. The war turned my tutor friend into
a "communist" and me into a pacifist. A decade later, neither of us is what
we were. We are merely a Republican and a Democrat, passing the time in
earnest conversation. And I still think the war was immoral. So when my
tutor friend told me the story of his days in the movement, I readily agreed
with him that he had been wrong. "It could have been worse, though," I
added. "You could have *supported* the war."

. . .

THERE WERE ALWAYS two main arguments in favor of the war, the geopolitical and the "moral." The war's aftermath has undermined the first argument but has seemingly strengthened the second. For the aftermath proved to be at once worse than the war's opponents had predicted and better than its supporters had feared—worse for the Indochinese, better for everyone else.

The geopolitical argument took many forms, some of which lay in ruins long before the war ended. The notion that the war was needed to stop Sino-Soviet expansionism, for example, had become an embarrassment well before Nixon arrived in Peking. So had the notion that the war was needed to convince the Chinese to abandon revolution and follow the Soviet example of peaceful coexistence.

The most persistent form of the geopolitical argument was the domino theory. Some of the war's retrospective defenders maintain that the fall of Cambodia and Laos proves that the theory was correct. Not so. Cambodia and Laos were Vietnam battlefields long before the Americans arrived, and by the end the three countries became one domino. Anyway, the domino theory always encompassed more than Indochina. Even in its most modest version it envisaged the loss of all Southeast Asia, which is to say Thailand, Burma, and Malaysia. And in its more grandiose form it predicted that Indonesia, India, Australia, and Hawaii would topple too. None of this has happened; on the contrary, the American position in Asia and the Pacific is stronger now than it was before 1975. Such troubles as do exist there, such as instability in the Philippines, cannot remotely be traced to the defeat in Vietnam.

A milder corollary to the domino theory was the argument from will: we needed to go on fighting in Vietnam in order to demonstrate our resolve and reliability. This argument implicitly recognized that the fate of Vietnam was, by itself, peripheral to the national security of the United States; it shifted the ground of discussion from the geopolitics of the map to the geopolitics of the soul. Yes, their will to rid their country of foreigners was stronger than our will to demonstrate our will; but by any reasonable standard, our resolve was strong. We did far, far more than enough to meet our treaty obligations, demonstrate our will, and prove our reliability. We financed a quarter of a century of war in Vietnam. We fought there in strength for ten years—longer than we fought in World War I, World

War II, or Korea, longer than in all of them put together. Fifty-eight thousand American soldiers were killed. We said we would fight, therefore we
must fight: at many a juncture along the way that logic seemed compelling.
But it was not a compelling reason to fight forever. Our guarantees were not
worthless. It was the war that was worthless.

The importance of the collapse of the domino theory to the debate over
the war's morality is that the theory, if correct, could arguably have justified
an enormous degree of suffering and death. What if it had really been true
that the loss of Vietnam would have doomed Australia, India, Hawaii, and
the rest to war followed by communist totalitarianism? A firm moral case
can be made that preventing the certain devastation and enslavement of
many countries can justify the destruction, even the total destruction, of one.
"We had to destroy this village in order to save a hundred villages" is a de-
fensible proposition. But "we had to destroy this village in order to save it"
is a moral absurdity. When the domino theory fell, so, dominolike, did one
of the moral props of the war.

We are left, then, with the "moral case," as Podhoretz calls it—the view
that the war was moral because it was an attempt to save South Vietnam from
communism. My tutor friend, back in his S.D.S. days, did not think this a
moral aim, would not have thought it a moral aim even if it could have been
achieved without cost. In thinking these things he made a moral error, and
he is right to rue it. Even those of us who took the view that it did not make
much difference to the South Vietnamese whether they lived under communism or under the Saigon regime made a moral error. Take away the war,
and the Saigon regime, with all its noisy corruption and repressiveness, was
morally preferable to the totalitarian silence that now rules, with scarcely less
corruption, in Ho Chi Minh City. Except that you can't take away the war.

The overwhelming majority of those who opposed the war did not in any
case reject the aim of saving South Vietnam from communism. And to the
extent that the war was fought for this aim, it was fought for a moral aim.
But this says no more than that the war was fought with good intentions
rather than evil ones, which is saying very little. If good intentions were
enough, there would be no neoconservatives.

In war the moral question is always the same: does the end justify the
means? The calculations are necessarily ugly, but they are unavoidable. Ten
years ago the choice was not between a communist South Vietnam and a
non-communist one. It was between a communist South Vietnam on the
one hand, and the terrible cost of keeping South Vietnam non-communist

on the other. The aftermath of the war—the boat people, the "reeducation" camps, above all the unimaginable horror that engulfed Cambodia—has made the "moral case," the argument that the war was worth fighting solely for the sake of the people of Indochina, seem much more plausible than it did at the time. But for the "moral case" to be clinched, the war must be judged to have been winnable—winnable, moreover, at a lower cost in suffering and death than the cost of the communist victory.

The retrospective defenders of the war must argue that the war could have been won, and their arguments mostly take the form of "if only." If only the bombers had hit "worthwhile targets" on their one thousand sorties a day, says the military analyst Edward Luttwak in a current *Harper's* symposium, it "would have ended the war in a day." If only Lyndon Johnson had allied the country behind the war as a moral imperative, writes Podhoretz in his Vietnam book, then the American people would have remained steadfast. If only the United States had followed a purposeful military strategy, argues Harry G. Summers in *On Strategy: A Critical Analysis of the Vietnam War*, then the conditions for a successful South Vietnamese war against the Vietcong might have been created. If only Congress hadn't voted down supplementary military aid to the Saigon government in 1975, contends Richard Nixon in his new book, *No More Vietnams*, then everything might have turned out fine.

All of these arguments rest on the assumption that there was a point at which North Vietnam, having calculated that the actual costs of war were exceeding the prospective benefits of victory, would have stopped fighting. It seems clearer than ever today that there was no such point. Some people understood this at the time. Ten years ago, this magazine published a special issue devoted to the end of the war. Richard Holbrooke, who had resigned in protest from the foreign service, and who later became an assistant secretary of state, began his essay with these words:

> For at least eight years it seemed reasonable to me to assume that sooner or later, no matter what we did in Vietnam, things would end badly for us. This feeling was not based on any desire to see us humiliated, or any feeling that the other side represented the forces of goodness and light; it just seemed that the only way to stave off an eventual Communist victory was with an open-ended, and therefore endless, application of American firepower in support of the South Vietnamese regime. No matter how much force we were willing to use, this would not end the war, only prevent Saigon's de-

feat. And the human suffering would be bottomless. The war would go on until the North Vietnamese achieved their objectives.

Holbrooke's judgment has stood up well. "The essential reality of the struggle," wrote Stanley Karnow in *Vietnam: A History,* published in 1983, "was that the Communists, imbued with an almost fanatical sense of dedication to a reunified Vietnam under their control, saw the war against the United States and its South Vietnamese ally as the continuation of two thousand years of resistance to Chinese and later French rule. They were prepared to accept limitless casualties to attain their sacred objective. Ho Chi Minh, their leader, had made that calculation plain to the French as they braced for war in the late 1940s. 'You can kill ten of my men for every one I kill of yours,' he warned them, 'but even at those odds, you will lose and I will win.'" William Broyles, Jr., who fought in Vietnam fifteen years ago as a Marine officer, and who recently went back for a visit during which he talked to hundreds of his former enemies, has a similar assessment. Writing in the April *Atlantic,* he concludes, "Whatever the price of winning the war—twenty more years of fighting, another million dead, the destruction of Hanoi—the North Vietnamese were willing to pay it."

If the North Vietnamese were willing to accept limitless casualties, if they were willing to pay any price, then the war could not have been won except by the physical destruction of North Vietnam and the killing of a large proportion of its people. A million? Three million? Six million? The shrill accusation of some in the antiwar movement that the war was "genocidal" was not entirely without justice. Of course no American wanted to kill everybody in North Vietnam. Americans are not monsters. But Americans are not losers, either. Americans are winners. But the logic of winning in Vietnam was inescapably the logic of genocide. We did not lose in Vietnam. We chose not to win. If our entry into the war had something to do with preserving our values, so did our exit from it.

Even Podhoretz, in his book on Vietnam, admits repeatedly that the war could not have been won. In the end, he writes, "The United States demonstrated that saving South Vietnam from Communism was not only beyond its reasonable military, political, and intellectual capabilities but that it was ultimately beyond its moral capabilities as well." Yes, it was beyond our moral capabilities—except that what he understands as a moral failure I understand as a moral success. It wasn't cowardice that finally impelled us to quit. It was conscience.

. . .

THE OLD ARGUMENTS for the war still walk among us, zombielike, in the form of the theory of the Vietnam syndrome, a term calculated to make the American people's desire to avoid another Vietnam sound pathological rather than prudent. Of course, if the war did result in a syndrome, if it did result in a paralysis of American will and so forth, that is hardly an argument that the war was a good idea. Nor do the follies of parts of the antiwar movement somehow vindicate the war. On the contrary, the antiwar movement was created by the war. Is it really so surprising that this unending, unwinnable war became a machine for producing irrationality, hysteria, and rage?

The actual consequences of this so-called syndrome are highly problematic. We "lost" Iran after Vietnam, but we "lost" Cuba before it. A more precise effect of the war upon the American political psyche was diagnosed in 1971 by Nathan Glazer, who wrote in a famous *Commentary* article titled "Vietnam: The Case for Immediate Withdrawal" that "the experience of Vietnam has turned the American people into haters of war." That seems exactly right. By August of 1964, three hundred Americans had been killed and a thousand wounded in Vietnam. Yet there were only a half-dozen American correspondents reporting on the war. (Meanwhile President Johnson was running as the peace candidate, with the support of S.D.S.) Such relative public indifference to a war with American deaths running into the hundreds would be unthinkable today. It took years for any significant movement of protest to develop against the Vietnam War.

The premises of U.S. involvement were scarcely questioned for the first fifteen years. But if the Reagan administration launches an invasion of Nicaragua today, thousands of church people are ready to commit civil disobedience tomorrow. And before giving its support to the new war, the public would insist on a full and prompt discussion of its aims, purposes, and prospects—not out of cynicism or morbid suspicion, but out of a healthy, skeptical, democratic spirit of self-government. War can sometimes be a necessity, but is always to be abhorred. Yes, we were right to oppose the Vietnam War, all of us. Even my friend the Reagan-voting ex-S.D.S.er. Even Norman Podhoretz.

—The New Republic, April 29, 1985

YOU HAD TO BE THERE

GOING TO WOODSTOCK was interesting. Getting the hell out of there was ecstasy.

Four of us set out on the morning of Friday, August 16, 1969—me, fresh out of the navy; my college friend Phil; and our girlfriends, Karen and Mary. We had spent Thursday night at my sister's farm in Rockland County, not too far from where the festival was to be held. She and her husband wanted to come with us, but they had a small child and decided to stay home. They waved goodbye to us from their porch as we pulled out in Phil's beat-up Volkswagen bug. We knew we were in for an adventure of some sort.

Why did we go? Partly for the scene, which promised to be out of the ordinary. Partly for the music: it wasn't every day you could see and hear on the same program the Who, Jimi Hendrix, the Grateful Dead, and the many others whose appearances had been advertised. But mainly, we went because of the persistent rumor that Bob Dylan might show up. Dylan supposedly lived in or near Woodstock, an artsy sylvan village. It was on account of Dylan's glamour that the promoters tried to mount the festival in Woodstock, and then kept the name even after the site had to be changed. The fact that there had been no official announcement proved nothing. The mystery tramp wasn't into official announcements. I'm still convinced that two or three hundred thousand of the half million or so people who eventually showed up were drawn by the mere possibility he might sing. Twenty years later, when every beer-sponsored summerfest seems to have Dylan on its schedule, this may seem incomprehensible. But in 1969 the reclusive young composer of "The Times They Are a Changin'," "Blowin' in the Wind," "Like a Rolling Stone," etc., was for some millions of his fellow citizens the most charismatic creature on earth. His prestige was somewhere between Byron's and Jesus Christ's. So off we went.

The festival began on the New York State Thruway, where every other car was packed with happy, longhaired kids flashing peace signs. On the country roads leading to the site the atmosphere was of a vast medieval gypsy pilgrimage. Besides our tickets, we had low-grade press credentials—not good enough to get us backstage, but O.K. for getting us into some sort of special parking area. I was representing *Win*, a tiny anarcho-pacifist biweekly. My friend Phil was representing *National Review*, for which he would write an article arguing that rock and roll in general and Woodstock in particular exemplified conservative values in action. Somewhere, perhaps, an impressionable Lee Atwater took note.

We kept driving—slowly, because of the traffic and because by now the running boards and bumpers of our VW were piled high with people catching a ride. We came over the crest of a hill, and there, sloping down before us and to our right, was a huge natural amphitheatre covered with the biggest crowd any of us had ever seen. We inched down practically to the stage, abandoned the car, made our way to a spot halfway up the hill, sat down, and waited.

We were well prepared, we thought. We had new sleeping bags and air mattresses, changes of clothes, dozens of sandwiches, jugs of wine and water. The music started—Richie Havens singing "Handsome Johnny," a stirring antiwar anthem, good and loud. The sun shone. The crowd got bigger and bigger. We ate sandwiches and shared some with our neighbors. Everyone was feeling great. Then it rained. Everyone got wet. The music stopped, to forestall the possibility of electrocution. The rain stopped (but everyone stayed wet). It got dark. The music started again—Ravi Shankar. It rained again.

And so on, all night long.

I vividly remember, sometime in the wee hours, Joan Baez's tiny figure spotlighted in the darkness, her pure voice singing a cappella, the crowd calm and still. But most of the time, it wasn't that much fun. Any excursion was a major production. It took an hour to pick one's way through the crowd to the Port-O-Sans and wait in line. It could take another hour to get back, during which, with mounting anxiety, one would become convinced that one's friends were forever lost in the darkness.

Our sleeping bags and clothes got hopelessly soaked and muddied. Our spot was right next to a sort of aisle—a thick, slippery brown river of boots and muck. As we lay there, trying to sleep, a constant, never ending stream of people moved back and forth. All night long, without cease, their feet sloshed and stomped and slammed a few inches from our heads. Some of these passersby were chemically disoriented. Their panic and confusion made them heedless of their steps. The rain, the mud, the unending shifting and tramping, the constant fear of having one's face trodden on—all this made sleep difficult.

We tried going to the car in shifts to get out of the rain, but with the windows closed it was impossibly damp and stifling inside. Saturday afternoon the weather seemed to clear up. We put on our last dry clothes and began to feel tentatively cheerful. Then it rained again, torrentially. Then the key to the trunk broke in the lock, cutting us off from our remaining supplies. But the ignition key still worked. As the engine coughed and rattled, we looked around at each other, nodded, and got in.

We drove slowly through a Mathew Brady phantasmagoria of tents and mud. Tens of thousands of people were fleeing Woodstock. So many of them climbed onto our VW that there was an ominous crack. The car still moved but couldn't take the extra weight. So two of us trotted alongside like Secret Service agents, asking would-be riders not to pile on. Everyone was polite and friendly, just as the legend has it. We spent the rest of the weekend snug and dry at my sister's place, watching reports from the scene on TV. Our one nagging worry was that Dylan would show up after all and we'd have to spend the rest of our lives wishing we hadn't left. When that didn't happen our contentment was complete.

So there you have it. That's what Woodstock was "like."

—*The New Republic*, August 28, 1989

2. BIG MEN

Before I went to work for Jimmy Carter, in 1977, the only time I had ever
met a president was—well, here's what happened. In the summer of 1953,
our family took a car trip from New York to Aspen. We had a light green,
two-door 1949 Ford, a roomy, bulbous car. This was before the interstate
highway system; west of the Pennsylvania Turnpike it was two lanes all the
way. I was nine; my sister was seven. Halfway across the country, we stopped
in Independence, Missouri. My father was the United Nations (and western hemisphere) correspondent for the *Hindustan Times*, of New Delhi, and
my mother was a member of the Rockland County Democratic Committee. Apparently these qualifications sufficed to get us an audience with the
man who, less than six months before, had been president of the United
States. It was dusk, and Mr. Truman's office, on the second or third floor of
a solid old office building, was dark and cozy and the warm colors of worn
wood and worn books. There was a green-shaded lamp on the desk and an
electric fan in the window, which overlooked a street busy with shoppers and
honking cars. To my sister and me, Mr. Truman was kind and clean and
twinkly, like an elderly pediatrician. Just before we left, he handed us each
a mechanical pencil with his picture on it, and said, gravely, "This is so you

can prove to your friends that you met me." Then he patted each of us on the head and shook our hands. (When we got home, our friends didn't believe us. They said we must have got the pencils at a souvenir store.)

My next presidential encounter was in the summer of 1966, when, as a boy reporter for *Newsweek,* I spent a few days following Ronald Reagan, the actor, around northern California as he campaigned to unseat the then governor of the state, Edmund G. "Pat" Brown. Of course, I had no idea that the encounter, such as it was, was presidential. I was pretty sure Mr. Reagan was going to win that election, and it was obvious that he fancied himself a future occupant of 1600 Pennsylvania Avenue. But "President Reagan"? Please. The actor was even more right-wing than Barry Goldwater, and look what had just happened to him. Also, as I pointed out to the *Newsweek* editors in New York at the time, "Reagan may go over big with the smug country-club crowd, but he lacks the common touch." Fourteen and a half years later, as I was packing boxes to move my stuff out of the Old Executive Office Building, I reflected that I might have got that one wrong.

The only time I ever saw Robert F. Kennedy, apart from a few times when I was part of a crowd of thousands cheering him, was at an Upper East Side saloon, P. J. Clarke's, in 1966. Kennedy and a group of friends emerged from the back room, where they had evidently been having dinner. I caught a flash of his extraordinary pale-blue eyes as he and his entourage passed through the bar. It was a fraction of a second, but the memory of it is as vivid as the feel of Mr. Truman's hand on the crown of my head.

A MORAL IDEOLOGUE

THE RELATIONSHIP between a politician and his speechwriter is fraught with awkward emotions. They say that no great man is a hero to his valet; and while there are differences between being a valet and being a speechwriter, from the speechwriter's point of view those differences are not always as striking as the similarities. The relationship is problematical from the politician's point of view as well. The speechwriter's very existence is an affront to the politician, because it intimates that the politician is too lazy or too stupid to decide for himself what it is he is going to say. A retinue of secretaries and bodyguards and advance men and special assistants adds to a politician's glory, because these people are an outward sign of the politician's power and importance. The speechwriter is different from the other members of the court. The politician does not seem bigger or grander because he has a speechwriter. Having a speechwriter is apt to diminish the politician in the eyes of the public, because the one thing a leader cannot delegate is his inner essence, and if what the leader says is not a reflection and product of his inner essence, then what *is*? If someone else is writing the words he speaks, then what *do* those words express? By giving the politician *something* to say, the speechwriter suggests by implication that the politician has *nothing* to say. So a politician is generally a little resentful toward and ashamed of his speechwriter—not ashamed of the particular person who holds the job, simply of the fact that the job exists. By the same token, a speechwriter is always, on some level, just a little bit contemptuous of his politician, even if that contempt is a grain of sand compared to the mountain of respect and even awe in which the squire holds the knight.

There is a peculiar and not always comfortable intimacy about the relationship between politician and speechwriter. This intimacy exists even if the two are not close, even if they seldom or never speak to each other, and it derives from the fact that because the speechwriter, sitting alone in a room by himself, has written certain words and not others, the politician says certain words and not others—says them in a very physical and definite and sensory way, using his tongue and teeth and throat and voice. Speechwriting is what doctors call an invasive procedure. It is not necessarily conducive to a serene, untroubled relationship, free of the emotional complications and hidden agendas historians endeavor to avoid. What a speechwriter says about his president may or may not be insightful, but it should always be viewed with suspicion.

DISCLAIMERS OUT OF THE WAY, then, here is the executive summary of my assessment of Jimmy Carter's character:

Jimmy Carter is a saint.

Now, by saying that I don't mean to assert that Jimmy Carter is perfect, or that he is a total stranger to base motives, or that he is one of the elite of God's elect—though for all I know that third item, at least, may well be true.

Nor am I referring strictly to Mr. Carter's post-presidential career. It is now the conventional wisdom to say that Mr. Carter is a far better ex-president than he was a president. And in this instance the conventional wisdom has got it right. No historian would place Carter among the three or four greatest presidents of our history, and not even his most fervent admirers would place him in the top ten. But as an ex-president he has only a tiny handful of rivals. Most of them, like him, served only a single term in the White House. One thinks of William Howard Taft, who was appointed chief justice of the United States some years after being defeated for reelection, and who performed adequately if without great distinction in that office. One thinks of Herbert Hoover, who after his disastrous term of office did honorable work as founder of the Hoover Institution on War and Peace and as head of the Hoover Commission, the ancestor of today's efforts to tame the federal bureaucracy. One thinks above all of John Quincy Adams, who returned to the capital as a humble member of the House of

Representatives, and who in his final term in Congress stood side by side with a newly elected fellow Whig from Illinois named Abraham Lincoln to denounce the evil of slavery—thus linking together in his person the two greatest upheavals in American history, the Revolution and the Civil War.

Jimmy Carter has taken a different route as ex-president. By inclination as much as necessity, it has not been the route of public office. Carter put his post-presidential ambitions this way in the opening sentence of his farewell address from the Oval Office. "In a few days," he said (and I should note that while I may have typed this line Mr. Carter was its true author), "I will lay down my official responsibilities in this office, to take up once more the only title in our democracy superior to that of president, the title of citizen." In the fourteen years he has held that title, he has brought honor to it. He hasn't just talked about housing the homeless, he has built houses for them with his own hands and has inspired and organized others to do likewise. He hasn't just talked about comforting the afflicted, he has mounted a little-known program through the Carter Center that is well on its way to eradicating Guinea worm disease, a painful, crippling parasite that has inflicted suffering on millions of Africans. He hasn't just talked about extending democracy, he has put his reputation and sometimes his very life on the line in country after country, often with little or no publicity, to promote free elections and expose rigged ones. And, of course, most controversially, he hasn't just talked about peace, he has made peace, or made peace possible, by using his moral prestige, his willingness to take risks, his persistence, his patience, and his stubbornness to bring hostile parties that extra little distance that sometimes makes the difference between war and not-war.

A former president's activities as a former president should not affect our estimation of his performance in office. James Buchanan was a weak and mediocre president, and the fact that he later became a firm supporter of Lincoln and the Union cannot alter that judgment. Millard Fillmore was a bad president and a worse ex-president—he ended up trying to get back into the White House as the candidate of the anti-Catholic, anti-Jewish, anti-immigrant, anti-everything Know-Nothing Party—but his badness as president is not made worse by his worseness as ex-president. As a former president Theodore Roosevelt was on balance a less than constructive force, but that takes nothing away from his glittering accomplishments as president.

Nevertheless, it's useful to look at post-presidential careers, because if they can't change our judgment of a presidency they can certainly deepen our understanding of it. Away from the constrictions and exaggerations of office, undistorted by the powers he wielded and was buffeted by, a president's character and personal qualities may emerge in stronger relief once he is back in private life. We can see which of the qualities he projected as president were authentic and which were fake, which of his strengths and weaknesses were inherent in his character and which were products of chance and circumstance.

In Carter's case, the post-presidential career shows that his inner resources—his inner strengths—are extraordinary, far deeper than they appeared to be when he was president. Many other aspects of the character people saw in him then have turned out to be obviously genuine, and some of them are perfectly suited to the work he has created for himself. His tendency to go it alone sometimes damaged him as president, but in his role as a diplomatic privateer it has served him and the world well. His unshakable sense of his own rectitude did not make him popular on Capitol Hill or in the White House press room, but now it seems to focus him single-mindedly on his good works—and not just when he is within camera range.

His trip to Haiti last September is the best-known example of Carter the ex-president at work. Carter's interference—combined, of course, with President Clinton's determination to use force if necessary—turned what would have been a bloody invasion with casualties and bitterness on all sides into a peaceful and apparently quite successful occupation. Carter was roundly attacked for his efforts, and some of the attacks seemed quite valid on the surface. A lot of people were outraged that Carter treated General Cédras, the Haitian military strongman, with respect and called him a man of honor; that Cédras and his henchmen were permitted to remain in Haiti and keep some of their ill-gotten financial gains; that at one point Carter said he was ashamed of his country for the way it had treated Haiti over the years; and that Carter, in defiance of official State Department policy, allowed Cédras's puppet president to sign the agreement, thus seeming to give legitimacy to an essentially criminal regime. And, of course, a lot of people were outraged, or maybe just baffled, that Carter kept talking about how slender and attractive Mrs. Cédras was. For those of us who still wince at the memory of the "lust in my heart" *Playboy* interview from the 1976 campaign, that detail was what made the episode true vintage Jimmy.

The bottom line was that there was no bloodshed. The elected, legitimate president of Haiti was restored, the killings and human rights violations were stopped, and Cédras and his pals ended up leaving the country, and Haiti now has a better chance than anyone thought possible to become a relatively normal country instead of a nightmare of death and cruelty. Many people, including some of Carter's customary critics, understood this in the immediate aftermath of Carter's trip and were willing to give him credit. And if Carter had just come home and issued a statement saying he was glad to have been of service to President Clinton and the country and had then gone back to Plains and kept quiet for a while, he now would be a universally recognized and celebrated hero. Clearly, this was one of those times when reticence would have been the most effective form of boasting. But Carter didn't do that. He went on television and talked and talked, and ended up saying some rather graceless and foolish things. The result was that he ended up reminding a lot of people of what they had never liked about him—the self-righteousness, the assumption of moral superiority—and quite thoroughly taking the shine off his triumph.

For many of us who love and admire Jimmy Carter, it was an exasperating and all too familiar moment of frustration. But the truth is, a person's character is all of a piece. It would be nice if we could separate out the bits we like from the bits we don't and just have the bits we like. But that's not how life works. A person's character is what it is. It's a little like a marriage—only without the option of divorce. You can work on it and try to make it better, but basically you have to take the bitter with the sweet. The same bullheadedness and perhaps overweening arrogance that misled Jimmy Carter into going on TV after he got back from Haiti and raining all over his own parade were just the flip side of the qualities of perseverance and self-confidence that enabled him to come up with an agreement in the first place. If Carter weren't the kind of guy who can go on the *Larry King* show and offend everybody who wants to give him a break, then he probably wouldn't be the kind of guy who can keep the Pentagon, the State Department, and the White House on hold while he goes ahead and changes their policies for them—all for their own good, of course.

We admire ruthlessness in the makers of war, but we're not quite sure how to respond to it when we encounter it in a maker of peace. We respect George S. Patton because he did what was necessary and didn't give a damn what anyone thought about it. We venerate Ulysses S. Grant because he refused to flinch from taking enormous casualties if he was convinced it would yield victory. Jimmy Carter is a kind of Patton for peace. He is a General Grant of the negotiating table. He may have to flatter a dictator or flirt with a dictator's wife or publicly praise a war criminal in order to avert a bloodbath, but if that's what it takes that's what he does. And if he thereby opens himself to ridicule or scorn, he doesn't give a damn.

One of the most curious charges lodged against Carter after his trip to Haiti—and, even more vociferously, after his trip to the former Yugoslavia, where he tried, with little short-term success and no long-term results, to persuade the Serbs to halt the shelling of Sarajevo—was that he has some sort of compulsion to be nice to dictators. His critics recalled that as president, he toasted the Shah of Iran and the authoritarian rulers of the Philippines and South Korea, described Marshal Tito of Yugoslavia, preposterously, as one of his "best friends," and, at the SALT II signing ceremony in Vienna, embraced Leonid Brezhnev and kissed the startled apparatchik on both cheeks. But these gestures spoke not to any admiration for tyrants but to a Christian eagerness to redeem sinners—and, as in the later case of Cédras and the Serbs, to a not-so-Christian willingness to manipulate the emotions of his negotiating partners. In practice, Carter has always showed himself as ready to anger authoritarians as to flatter them, in pursuit of peace and human rights. He kissed Brezhnev, yes; but he also defied him by receiving Alexander Solzhenitsyn, corresponding with Andrei Sakharov, boycotting the Moscow Olympics, and sending arms to the Afghan resistance. And in his post-presidential travels, with the power of the U.S. government no longer at his command, he has sometimes filled the gap with a display of physical courage. When he denounced the rigging of a Panamanian election by the Manuel Noriega regime, he did so not from the safety of Washington or Atlanta, but from a sidewalk in Panama City, under the eyes—and the guns—of Noriega's armed secret police.

THE HAITI EPISODE illustrates some of the qualities in Jimmy Carter I've chosen to call, only half-unseriously, saintly. Being a saint isn't all kindness and sweetness and compassion. Being a saint, especially a saint in politics, is a very mixed proposition and not always a completely attractive one. Saints can be intensely annoying. They can be hard on the people around them. They can be blind to ordinary human feelings and ordinary human failings, including their own.

George Orwell began his famous essay on Mahatma Gandhi with these words: "Saints should always be judged guilty until proved innocent." Later in the essay, referring to Gandhi's self-denying way of life and uncompromising moral standards, he wrote, "The essence of being human is that one does not seek perfection, that one is sometimes willing to commit sins for the sake of loyalty, that one does not push asceticism to the point where it makes friendly intercourse impossible, and that one is prepared in the end to be defeated and broken up by life, which is the inevitable price of fastening one's love upon other human individuals." And Orwell continues, making a point that today would be judged medically if not politically incorrect, "No doubt alcohol, tobacco, and so forth are things that a saint must avoid, but sainthood is a thing that human beings should avoid."

I should add, before anybody gets the wrong idea, that Orwell's overall assessment of Gandhi is a very positive one. Carter is no Gandhi (and I'm no Orwell). But the fact that it is not completely unnatural to mention the two of them, Gandhi and Carter, in the same breath is suggestive of something worth exploring. This is not something one would be tempted to say about many presidents or many politicians.

Carter's style of leadership was and is more religious than political in nature. He was and is a moral leader more than a political leader. I think this helps explain not only some of his successes as president but also some of his failures.

Look at how he was elected in the first place. In the early and decisive days of his campaign, he spoke the language of religion and morality far more, and far more effectively, than he spoke the language of politics. He spoke openly and convincingly about his Christian faith—and he managed to do this in a way that was inclusive, tolerant, and undogmatic. Nowadays every politician seems to feel obligated to talk about being born again, as in decades past politicians seemed to feel obligated to have themselves photographed wearing an Indian chief's war bonnet. But Carter was Christian before Christian was cool. Carter was the first and is still the only candidate for president who ever used the word "love"—in its specifically religious and Christian sense—in virtually every campaign speech he delivered.

Carter was nominated because of a number of circumstances. The liberal wing of the Democratic Party formed its usual circular firing squad, splitting its vote among several candidates and leaving Carter with a narrow plurality within the party. Carter alone understood the peculiar timing and dynamics of the nominating season. He used the previously ignored Iowa caucuses to leverage himself a victory in New Hampshire and some other early primaries; by the time he started losing one primary after another, as he did toward the end, it didn't matter because he was able to pick up enough delegates here and there to put himself over the top. Carter won the general election partly because the incumbent, Gerald Ford, had been damaged by the Nixon pardon and then by a bruising primary campaign against Ronald Reagan. But in a deeper sense, Carter was nominated and elected on account of a pair of profound and painful moral dramas in American life—the centuries-long drama of race and the decade-long drama of disillusion over Vietnam and Watergate.

Carter's nomination and election marked the end of the Civil War as a determining factor in American party politics. Carter's political career was a product of the civil rights movement as surely as were those of his fellow Georgians Andrew Young and John Lewis. In his inaugural address as Governor of Georgia Carter said, "The time for racial discrimination is over." Because he was so clear about that, because he made that simple and electrifying declaration, he was able to become the first president of the United States from the heart of the Old Confederacy. Carter's historic role in the Democratic Party was that he was the agent of the final destruction of the Southern racist wing of the party. Carter was not the only "centrist" or "moderate" Democrat who sought his party's nomination in 1976; the professionals regarded Senator Henry Jackson of Washington State as a far more formidable figure. But Jackson had been a diehard supporter of the Vietnam War, and Jackson lacked the moral prestige Carter gained by humbling George C. Wallace and ridding the party of what Wallace represented.

Carter was certainly not the first New South politician. Atlanta had long prided itself on the slogan "The city too busy to hate." But that very slogan implied that if the good people of Atlanta weren't so darn busy, well, maybe they *would* find time to hate. Carter's rejection of racist and racial politics was not based on the idea that racism was bad for business. It wasn't based on technocratic or pragmatic considerations. It wasn't based on notions of legal equity. It was based on Christian love. Carter appealed to blacks—and also to a stratum of Southern whites—not on the basis of interest group politics, but on the basis of a fervent shared vision of Christian love, forgiveness, and reconciliation.

There was a remarkable scene at Madison Square Garden after Carter's acceptance speech. On the stage, Carter and his running mate, Senator Walter Mondale, stood arm in arm and side by side with an extraordinary array of friends and former adversaries: Coretta King, the widow of Martin Luther King, Jr., and King's civil rights comrades Ralph W. Abernathy, Jesse Jackson, and Andrew Young; the wheelchair-ridden George Wallace, the one-time racist firebrand; Mayor Richard J. Daley with former Senator Eugene McCarthy, whose youthful followers had been clubbed by Daley's police in the streets of Chicago eight years before; Senators Hubert Humphrey, George McGovern, and Henry M. Jackson, who had struggled with each other over policy and power for a decade; and many more. It was a political Peaceable Kingdom. The anthem of the evening was "We Shall Overcome." I had not yet joined the Carter team; I was there as a reporter. But I wept. Everyone in the room wept. Everyone—even in the press section—linked arms and swayed and sang. The moment carried tremendous emotional power. It was as if the agonies of slavery and war and racial hatred and the fratricidal bitterness of Vietnam and the lies of Watergate—it was as if all this were being washed away, washed in the blood of the lamb; and at the center of it was this small, slight, soft-spoken man from a tiny hamlet in the depths of the Deep South.

The rest of the campaign was something of an anticlimax. The simple verities that had propelled Carter to the nomination—the promise not to lie, the assurance that we could govern ourselves through goodness and love—were not quite enough to power a general election campaign. Carter left his convention with a huge lead in the polls. His lead melted steadily in the brutal furnace of the national arena. If the election had taken place a few days later, he might well have lost. But he won, if only by a hair.

IN THE WHITE HOUSE, Carter established a style of leadership that was pointedly humble. The candidate who had carried his own suit bag became the president who walked down Pennsylvania Avenue in his inaugural parade. President Carter got rid of door-to-door limousine service for top White House staff. He dispensed with fancy tablecloths and seating by rank in the White House Mess. He put a stop to the constant serenades of "Hail to the Chief."

It was completely typical of him that one of the first things he did was to sell off the presidential yacht, the *Sequoia*. The truth is that this was a mistake. It was a mistake because the *Sequoia* was one of the most cost-effective items in the federal budget. A president could take some important senator out on that yacht and give him a few drinks and flatter him and they could sit together on the deck and watch the sun go down in the cool of the evening, and when they got back to the dock the president would have that senator's vote on some important bill. Without the yacht, the president might have to offer something more concrete and expensive to get that senator's vote—like agreeing not to close a big military base in the senator's state. That yacht had paid for itself many times over every year.

Carter didn't look at it that way. He should have, but he didn't. He simply thought it was wrong for the people's servant to put on airs by sailing around on a yacht. He thought it was unseemly for a man in his position to live like a millionaire at the taxpayers' expense.

In a way there was a religious aspect even to this little detail, in my opinion. Unlike President Carter, I don't come from a long line of Baptists. But my mother was a Congregationalist, and she taught me the difference between low church and high church. Jimmy Carter was and is emphatically low church. His discomfort with pomp and circumstance isn't just a matter of personal taste. It goes straight back to the Protestant Reformation.

Fortunately for Carter, his distaste for show worked very well for him as a candidate—almost as if it had been a calculated ploy dreamed up by image consultants. The public was sick and tired of artifice, insincerity, and slick packaging—sick of lies and anything that smacked of lies. Carter's simplicity, his lack of bombast, even his Sunday-school-teacher awkwardness—all this the public found very appealing. These things were part of his outsiderness. His communications director, Gerald Rafshoon, took advantage of these qualities by making ads that were calculatedly amateurish and unslick looking.

This religious style of leadership continued in the Carter White House. In our speechwriting office, which was populated mostly by diehard secular humanists, we used to joke that it was no accident that the man's initials were J.C. It seemed like one of those odd coincidences that make you think maybe there is a God after all and that He has a pretty good sense of humor—like the fact that the anti-welfare leader of the Senate Republicans is named Dole, or that the reptilian Speaker of the House is named Newt, or that the tax-cuts-for-the-wealthy former Republican national chairman was named Rich Bond, or that Ross Perot had a campaign manager named Swindle.

Carter's disdain for artifice served him well as long as things were going his way, but when things weren't going his way it created problems for him, because it essentially deprived him of the full use of one of the basic tools of statecraft. He didn't like to perform—in the sense of giving a performance. He hated to pretend to be feeling emotions he wasn't actually feeling at that moment. And of course that kind of pretending is essential to making an effective political speech, which is a theatrical turn. You have to act like you're feeling pride or sorrow or the swell of patriotic feeling, even if at that particular moment, the moment the speech is scheduled for, what you really want is to be home in bed—or, in Carter's case, back in the little study next to the Oval Office, reading memos and making decisions.

Carter considered making decisions to be by far the most important aspect of his job. Communicating those decisions—communication in general—took a distant second place. Naturally this was frustrating for those of us who were writing his speeches. He didn't much like to prepare or rehearse. He often removed emotive or inspirational language from his speech drafts.

Sometimes his dislike of artifice reached comic lengths. One day he was scheduled to announce the elimination of several thousand pages of federal regulations. We got a big stack of paper for him, and the idea was that he would sweep it off the table or dump it in the wastepaper basket to illustrate how many regulations he was getting rid of. We thought that this would be very dramatic—excellent footage for the evening news. The only problem was, the president didn't follow the script. Instead he pointed to the stack and said something like, "This is a prop prepared by my staff. It's supposed to represent the thousands of pages of regulations. Actually, it's just a pile of blank sheets of paper." He then ignored it for the remainder of his statement. The evening news found something else to lead with that night.

On this point, of course, the contrast between Jimmy Carter and the man who beat him in 1980 could hardly be stronger. We Carter speechwriters, after we left office, sometimes felt a twinge of envy for our successors in the Reagan administration. Ronald Reagan *did* know how to follow a script—and I say that meaning no disrespect. (Well, maybe a little.) If Reagan understood nothing else, he understood the importance of speechmaking and communications.

But Reagan and his speechwriters had an advantage over us that was a good deal more important than his superior talents as a thespian: Reagan always knew far ahead of time what he wanted to say—and we didn't.

This was not because Reagan had stronger convictions. It was because Reagan had a fixed political ideology, and Carter did not—at least, he had much less of one.

A political ideology is a very handy thing to have. It's a real time-saver, because it tells you what you think about things you know nothing about. Reagan never had to agonize over the merits of this tax versus that tax—if it was a tax, he was against it. He never lost sleep over the proper design of some environmental regulation—if it was an environmental regulation, he was against it. He never worried about whether to build up the navy at the expense of the army, or the army at the expense of the navy. His view was, if it was military, build it all—and damn the expense.

Another way to put this same point is that Reagan did all of his thinking and made most of his decisions long before he became president. He had a complete ideological framework that answered virtually every policy question in advance. So as president he was able to devote all his time and energy to selling and implementing the ideas he had adopted during his years in the wilderness as leader of the conservative wing of his party.

This observation applies as much to ideologues of the left as to ideologues of the right. If, say, a Hubert Humphrey or an Edward Kennedy had ever become president, then he, like Reagan, would not have had to spend a lot of time developing a program. A fully developed, fully worked-out political ideology provides a model of how the whole organism works. It may not provide you with the details, but it does provide you with a clear general direction.

Jimmy Carter did not have the advantage of a dogma. In this respect he was like all other presidents of recent times—all except Reagan, who was the only leader of the militant wing of one of the two parties to come to power since World War II. All the other postwar presidents—Eisenhower, Kennedy, Johnson, Nixon, Ford, Carter, Bush, and Clinton—have been drawn from the pragmatic center. (No leader of the left or liberal wing of the Democratic Party has ever become president—which is one reason that the conventional assumption that liberalism has been tried and found wanting is a little unfair. Unlike unalloyed conservatism, unalloyed liberalism has not been tried.) And Carter, even more than Kennedy, Johnson, and Clinton, was a centrist. His only strong tie to the party's liberal wing was through the Southern civil rights movement, which was limited both regionally and ideologically.

In Carter's case, the matter was complicated by three other factors. First, he came from a one-party state, Georgia, where politics was traditionally a matter of maneuvering within a single party, usually without much ideological content. Second, Carter—unlike Johnson, the veteran Senate leader, and Clinton, the cosmopolitan Rhodes scholar, former antiwar protester, and one-time Senate staffer—had had no exposure to national issues and national politics before he started running for president. And, third, Carter was brand-new. He had played no role in national political life and was almost entirely unknown outside his region. When I first heard about Carter, in 1975, my first thought was that it would be interesting to have a country singer in the White House. It wasn't until several months later that I realized that Jimmy Carter was not the same person as Jimmie Davis, the singing governor of Louisiana.

Because he was so new, Carter had no ties or commitments to the traditional constituency groups of the Democratic Party, such as labor and the cities. This was a strength for him, because he could argue, correctly, that he would not be a prisoner of pressure groups. But it was also a weakness once he became president, because he did not have the loyalty of those groups. Again, the contrast with Reagan is instructive. Reagan could say to a Republican constituency group like the Christian right, "I'll get to your concerns about abortion and school prayer eventually, but right now I have to concentrate on my economic program. Be patient." Because of his long years in the wilderness with these people, he had the authority to ask them to wait. Carter didn't have the standing to make that kind of request. He couldn't tell the unions or the cities or the women's rights advocates to be patient. As a result, he was too weak politically to resist pressures from the various Democratic constituency groups to propose legislation on behalf of each and every one of them, and to assure each in turn that its particular concern—youth employment, the Equal Rights Amendment, labor law reform, consumer protection, health care, whatever—was his "top priority." Is it any wonder he quickly earned a reputation for scattering his energies, for failing to set clear priorities, and for getting swamped in details?

The truth is, he was damned either way. If he had set firm priorities, choosing to emphasize one or two issues to the exclusion of others, the disappointed interest groups would have turned on him immediately, making it impossible for him to accomplish even limited goals. So he chose to try to appease the interest groups for a while, and hope for the best. As it was, once they realized he would be unable to deliver on most of his promises, they turned on him anyway.

The interest groups had very high expectations, which were based on their experience with President Johnson. But Johnson, who had won a huge mandate at the polls after President Kennedy's assassination, had governed at a time when liberal reform was sweeping all before it. (The tide of reform was so strong that it continued well into the Nixon administration, bringing about the creation of such agencies as the Environmental Protection Administration and the Occupational Health and Safety Administration.) Carter, elected in a squeaker, had no such mandate. And he came to office at an essentially conservative moment: his election had more to do with moral revulsion at Watergate than with political enthusiasm for large-scale programmatic innovation. (The interest groups never quite admitted this, but they seem to have learned enough from the experience that they have been willing to give the current Democratic president a little—though only a little—more leeway.)

Carter approached domestic issues one by one, as a problem-solver. He studied each issue separately and tackled each on its own terms. He didn't have the kind of big-picture framework that might have enabled him to explain how the issues all fit together. And he didn't have the kind of political strength that might have enabled him to bring the unruly constituencies into line. So it was difficult both conceptually and politically for him to set priorities. He had little choice but to spread himself too thin.

Though Carter didn't have a political ideology, he did have what I would call a *moral* ideology—and on this he was faultless. He knew the difference between right and wrong. This may sound like faint praise—after all, doesn't everybody know the difference between right and wrong?—but it isn't. It is very high praise.

Let me explain. I came to the Carter White House from the liberal wing of the Democratic Party. I voted for Carter in the 1976 election, of course, but in the primaries I had first been for Harold Hughes and then for Fred Harris and then for Mo Udall. My liberal friends would sometimes say to me, "How can you work for that guy?" Their questions became more insistent as 1980 approached and Ted Kennedy began making moves to get into the race.

Well, I never had any problems of conscience about working for Jimmy Carter—for two reasons. The less important reason was that I was absolutely certain that Ted Kennedy could never be elected president of the United States—not because he was too liberal, but because of Chappaquiddick. Even if the public had been willing to forgive Kennedy for the drowning of Mary Jo Kopechne, they would not have been willing to forgive him for the more politically damaging but less widely known aspect of the scandal: his abortive attempt in the hours after the accident to establish an alibi and shift the blame to a family retainer. By the time the Republicans were through, I feared, every American would be familiar with the details. For the Democrats to nominate Ted Kennedy, I believed, would be tantamount to turning the country over to the Republicans without a fight.

The second and more important reason had to do with this matter of Carter's moral ideology. I used to say to my liberal friends, "Jimmy Carter is the first president of my adult life who is not criminally insane." I had in mind the legal definition of criminal insanity: the inability to tell right from wrong. It is wrong to kill people for no reason other than political gain or political fear. Lyndon Johnson and Richard Nixon did that. They escalated and continued the Vietnam War, thus causing the deaths of tens of thousands of Americans and hundreds of thousands of Vietnamese, long after it became clear that the war could not be won—and they did this not because they seriously believed that their actions would help America to be secure or Vietnam to be free, but because they were afraid of looking weak. Gerald Ford was not in the same category by any means. Indeed, his simplicity and forthrightness contrasted markedly with the tortured Machiavellianism of his two predecessors. But in what became known as the Mayaguez incident, even the gentle Ford sent some fifty men to their deaths needlessly. Jimmy Carter never did anything like that.

Carter's moral ideology—his ability to tell right from wrong—would have made him a great president for a time of moral crisis. If the overriding problem facing America in the late seventies had been racial segregation, for instance, or the Vietnam War, Carter would have known how to rise to the occasion because he knew how to do what was right—even when the political cost was high.

Carter was elected in the backwash of a moral crisis, but the biggest problems he faced as president, especially in the domestic arena, were not primarily moral problems. They were primarily managerial, technical problems, involving tremendous vested interests and offering few political rewards. There was no right or wrong way to solve these problems—just effective ways and ineffective ways.

Energy is a good example. Carter devoted enormous amounts of time and political capital to the energy problem. One might argue that he achieved a certain success—you don't hear much about the energy crisis these days, I notice. But he suffered many legislative defeats along the way and alienated many groups of people.

On one occasion, Carter, seeking to go beyond technocratic approaches, tried to cast the energy problem in sweeping moral terms. This was the so-called "malaise" episode, widely recognized as one of the most memorable moments of the Carter administration and almost as widely scorned as one of the most contemptible. The received version of what happened is simple. It goes like this: in the summer of 1979, President Carter was overwhelmed by energy and economic crises. In desperation, he made a disastrous speech blaming the American people and a national "malaise" for his own manifest failures of policy and leadership. The American people, horrified, turned him out of office at the first opportunity.

Variations on this version were used effectively by both Edward Kennedy and Ronald Reagan in the 1980 election campaign. The "malaise" has proved to have a long shelf life. At the 1988 Republican convention and again in 1992, speaker after speaker trooped to the podium to denounce "Jimmy Carter and the days of malaise." Attacks on Carter and "malaise" have served the Republicans in the eighties and nineties almost as sturdily as attacks on Hoover and "prosperity is just around the corner" served the Democrats in the forties and fifties.

It goes almost without saying that the historical reality and the political caricature do not comport with one another. For example, here are four details of the episode that are at variance with how most people seem to remember it: 1. Carter himself never mentioned the word "malaise." 2. The speech itself was an enormous popular success. It generated a record amount of positive mail to the White House, and Carter's approval rating in the polls zoomed up by eleven points literally overnight. 3. The sudden political damage came not from the speech but from the cabinet firings a few days later. 4. Although Carter has been flayed for blaming others, the first third of the speech is devoted to the most excoriating self-criticism ever heard from any American president. As these details suggest, the "malaise" episode has become encrusted in myth.

The episode came at a moment of great political and human vulnerability for Carter. He and his staff had been preoccupied with two difficult overseas trips—one to Vienna to complete and sign the SALT II Treaty with the Soviet Union, the other to Japan and Korea. He and his staff were completely exhausted. Meanwhile, back at home, the country was in an uproar because of gasoline lines triggered by the fall of the Shah in Iran. Carter had hoped to stop over in Honolulu for a couple of days and get some rest, but that was politically impossible given the gas lines at home. Almost as soon as we got back to Washington, it was announced that Carter would address the nation on July 5th. Actually, Carter had not agreed to deliver a speech, only to look at a draft and then decide. But the premature announcement put him in a corner.

Even so, when Carter got his speech draft he decided that he didn't want to do it. He said he had made the same points about energy policy over and over again, and the people weren't responding, and, as he pungently put it in the conference call in which he told his staff he was cancelling the speech, he didn't want to "bullshit the American people." He remained at Camp David and began an extraordinary series of meetings with leaders from all walks of American life. For a long time, Patrick Caddell, Carter's brilliant young pollster, had been saying with increasing urgency that Americans were losing faith in their institutions. The things Carter heard from his visitors at Camp David seemed to confirm Caddell's analysis.

I was the designated writer for the speech that emerged from this curious process. In truth I was more stenographer-typist than author, smoothing and coordinating bits of draft from various people, including Caddell, Stuart Eizenstat, and Carter himself. The speech had three parts. In the first part of it, wholly conceived and written by Carter, the president criticized himself through the words of those he had spoken to over the previous ten days: "Mr. President, you're not leading this nation—you're just managing the government," and so on. The second part described the erosion of public faith in institutions, in the future, and in the economy—an erosion begun by the shocks of Vietnam, the Kennedy and King assassinations, and Watergate, worsened by inflation and energy shortages, and manifested in declining rates of savings and voter participation. The third and final part outlined a series of proposals for tackling the energy problem and, in the process, beginning to pull ourselves out of the crisis of confidence.

The speech engendered a mixed reaction among the elites, although it did get mostly favorable editorial comment in its immediate aftermath. But three days later, Carter asked for the resignations of the whole of his cabinet and senior staff, telling them he would decide which ones to accept. He hoped that this would be the beginning of a regeneration of his administration—an infusion of new blood and new ideas, and a signal that even those whom he would decide to keep on would be starting anew. Instead, the mass resignations created an unanticipated and unwelcome global sensation; many foreign newspapers and governments, whose grasp of the intricacies of the American political system was imperfect, actually believed that the United States government had "fallen." It was at this point, I think, that the elites decided that Carter was finished. Within a few weeks this view had trickled down to the public, and Carter's popularity ratings dropped back to the abysmal level where they had been at the outset.

The episode was consistent with the religious cast of Carter's leadership. It had elements of sin, confession, and redemption, via a process of "witnessing," prayer, and rededication. It was part of a pattern of symbolic death and resurrection that had marked Carter's personal and political life. He had been politically reborn before—after his first, unsuccessful runs for state senator and then governor, and then, as an obscure Southern ex-governor, to the presidency itself. And of course he had been "born again" as a Christian. The "malaise" episode was his most spectacular effort to be "born again"—and, this time, to bring the country with him.

The episode was an exercise in national pastorship—in national psychotherapy, to use secular terms. Acknowledging the trauma (the "crisis of confidence" brought on by Vietnam, Watergate, and the sense of national vulnerability triggered by energy shortages) was to be the key to healing it. The therapy's failure, of course, opened the way to a period of hedonism and boastfulness.

The episode may also be seen as mythmaking, in the sense popularized by Joseph Campbell. It was an attempt to create one myth (the notion of a crisis of confidence that could be overcome by tackling the energy problem) that inadvertently created another (the notion of Carter as the personification and cause of national weakness and vulnerability). A side effect was the discrediting of candor about unpleasant truths and the enshrinement of "optimism." Carter's diagnosis of the country's spiritual ills was accurate and was recognized as such by millions of people, but when he proved unequal to the task of curing those ills (or even palliating them, as Reagan did), he was reviled with special bitterness.

In the cabinet and staff shakeup that followed the speech, Carter got rid of a number of officials who, it is fair to say, were disloyal but competent. If he had first gotten rid of a few who were loyal but incompetent, the episode might have turned out quite differently. That, apparently, he could not bring himself to do. The rebirth was stillborn. The speech was a truthful and prescient diagnosis of what was wrong with the country and what in many ways continues to be wrong with the country. But a president who sets out to diagnose a problem had better be able to offer a plausible solution to it. The Carter of the "malaise" episode was a prophet. But he was not a savior.

IN FOREIGN POLICY, where Carter could pursue his vision relatively unhampered by the built-in frustrations and roadblocks that hamper our political system in the domestic arena, his moral ideology was a clearer guide to action. He was very much in charge of his own foreign policy. His two top foreign policy advisers, the hawkish Zbigniew Brzezinski and the dovish Cyrus Vance, were often in disagreement with each other. I don't know whether he intended it to work this way, but the result was that he himself made all the important decisions.

Carter believed in peace—in preventing war—and in human rights. These two values were the lodestars by which he guided his conduct of foreign affairs. And, again, these values were expressions of his sense of religious and moral duty.

Four areas of Carter's foreign policy show his character and style of leadership quite clearly: his human rights policy, his fight for the Panama Canal treaties, his Middle East diplomacy, and his handling of the Iran hostage crisis.

Carter's advocacy of human rights as a central goal of American foreign policy was an innovation, but it was one that connected directly with the values of the American civic religion. He said several times that while America had not invented human rights, human rights had invented America. The United States was unique among nations in that its very sense of nationhood was based not on ties of blood or faith or ethnicity or language but on the shared political and moral values of the American political compact—especially the value of universal human rights.

Carter insisted on applying the human rights test not only to our adversaries—to the Soviet Union—but also to countries allied with us. This angered a number of dictatorial governments that had traditionally done our bidding in the Cold War and now found themselves upbraided by their patron. It also angered a good many foreign policy experts in this country. They saw it as naïve and moralistic and even dangerous. Some of them saw in it a squeamish failure to understand that the global struggle against Soviet Communist totalitarianism carried an overriding moral imperative of its own, one that sometimes required the use of dirty methods and unsavory allies.

Carter's human rights policy invited charges of hypocrisy and inconsistency. It was inevitable that there would be times when specific strategic concerns had to take precedence over human rights concerns. And there were times when the policy did indeed weaken leaders of governments that had been American clients—Somoza of Nicaragua, for example, and the Shah. But on balance the policy was a success. It saved thousands of lives and won freedom for thousands of prisoners of conscience. It was crucial in launching the process that has seen country after country in Latin America replace military dictatorships or oligarchies with constitutional democratic governments.

The implication of the human rights policy was that America's enemy was not Communism per se but tyranny in general, regardless of ideology. Many assumed that the policy would succeed only in weakening America's friends while having no effect on the countries of the Soviet bloc, which understood only force and strength and could not be swayed by lectures about human rights. This view prided itself on being hard-headed and tough-minded, but it turned out to be less hard-headed and tough-minded than it claimed to be. We have it on no less an authority than Vaclav Havel that Carter's human rights policy undermined the legitimacy and self-confidence of the Communist bosses and gave hope and encouragement to the dissidents. Communism collapsed from within, non-violently. America's embrace of human rights played a role in that magnificent triumph.

The human rights policy is one reason that Jimmy Carter remains a hero today in much of Latin America. Another reason is his fight for the Panama Canal treaties. This was an epic struggle, though it is now almost completely forgotten in this country. But the truth is that if Carter had ducked that fight, or if he had lost it, Central America would have been plunged into instability and probably into war.

The Panama struggle was fairly typical of the kind of fights Carter took on. Though failure would have been disastrous, success offered no political rewards—Carter could hardly run for reelection on the boast that he had successfully given away the Panama Canal. The opposition to the treaties was led by Ronald Reagan, who used the issue to galvanize his political movement and build up its mailing lists and fundraising apparatus. Perhaps Reagan was sincere in saying that the loss of the Canal would be a blow to America's vital national security interests. Yet the fact is that once Reagan became president, he did absolutely nothing to abrogate—or even to modify—the treaties he had so passionately denounced.

President Carter's most important single foreign policy achievement was making peace between Israel and Egypt—an extraordinary breakthrough, one that permanently changed the dynamics of events in the Middle East and laid the groundwork for all the progress that has been made since. Carter's role at the Camp David summit with Anwar Sadat and Menachem Begin is well known. His perseverance, his determination, his ability to listen, his refusal to quit when others lost hope—these qualities of his came into focus like a laser beam at Camp David. But six months later, negotiations on the peace treaty itself had stalled, and it looked as if the entire agreement might collapse.

So in March 1979 Carter decided to go to the Middle East. I went along on that trip. It was very different from any other presidential trip that I had ever read about, let alone experienced. Presidential trips abroad are carefully scripted. Advance teams go to the site weeks or months beforehand to make preparations down to the tiniest detail. If there are agreements to be signed, they are worked out well ahead of time. Nothing is left to chance.

This trip wasn't like that. The decision to go was made only five days before Air Force One took off. There was very little time for preparation. As we flew across the Atlantic, everybody tried to get some sleep—everybody except me. I was up working on the address Carter would make to the Egyptian parliament after we landed. I remember tiptoeing down the plane's darkened hallway and seeing Cyrus Vance, the secretary of state, and Zbigniew Brzezinski, the national security adviser, sleeping head to toe next to each other on a banquette. When these men were awake there was a sometimes intense rivalry between them. But now, as the plane sped east through the night, they had their little Air Force One pillows under their heads and their socks peeking out from under their little Air Force One blankets over them, and they looked as peaceful as a couple of kids at a slumber party.

Not just for me but for many of us, that journey was the high point of our White House service. What it showed about Carter is that he was willing to risk everything for peace. There was absolutely no guarantee of success. In fact, right up to the last day of the mission we were convinced that it was going to fail. It would have been a very public, very costly, very humiliating failure, which would have cemented the notion that Carter was a well-meaning incompetent.

But the mission didn't fail. The reason, I think, was that Begin and, especially, Sadat were deeply impressed by Carter's courage. He had put his presidency on the line. He had made it personal. He had taken the leap into the abyss and dared them to follow. They could not refuse.

Coming home from that trip, being greeted at Andrews Air Force Base by our friends and co-workers and loved ones, we all got a taste of what it must be like to return in triumph from a victory in war. The fact that it was a victory in peace made it all the sweeter.

Again, though, the political rewards were minimal. We had an easier time of it on Capitol Hill for a few weeks, and then the bump in the polls faded and we were back to the normal backbiting and bickering. But the satisfaction remains to this day; and every time ex-President Carter goes on one of his quixotic journeys, those of us who went with him to Cairo and Jerusalem remember and smile.

If the Middle East journey was the high point of those four years, the night of Desert One was the low point.

Five months into the Iran hostage crisis, on the night of Thursday, April 25, 1980, in conditions of absolute secrecy, eight helicopters and a number of C-130 transport planes took off for a site in the Iranian desert. The plan was to set up a staging area there, and then use the helicopters to fly into Tehran—first to the outskirts of town and then to the American Embassy itself in the heart of the city, where most of the fifty-two American hostages were being held by armed student militants. The militants, with tacit but increasingly open Iranian government support, had seized the building and the people in it the previous November, supposedly to protest the admission of the deposed Shah into the United States for medical treatment. Diplomatic efforts, though tirelessly pursued, had proved unavailing, and Carter had reluctantly given his approval for a rescue mission. The Desert One base was the point of a big spear. Men and materiel had also been infiltrated into Tehran itself over the preceding several months. It was an enormous, elaborate effort.

But three of the helicopters broke down or never made it to Desert One, because of sandstorms. There was still a chance to carry out the mission with the remaining five, but the margin of error was gone. The commander on the ground recommended that the mission be postponed. The choppers and C-130s would be flown out again, along with a busload of very surprised Iranians who had stumbled upon the scene and suddenly found themselves in the middle of a bewildering bustle of men and machines.

Then, horror descended upon the desert. In the darkness, a C-130 crashed into a helicopter as it was taking off. Eight commandos were killed. The mission ended in failure and chaos. There would be no second chance.

Like everyone in the White House who didn't have a "need to know," I had been kept in the dark about the mission. In fact, I took it for granted that a rescue mission was impossible. Many of us suspected that some kind of military action was imminent, but we thought it would involve the bombing or mining of Iranian ports and cities. I was against that kind of military action; I thought it would worsen the situation, perhaps start a war, and have no effect on the hostages except perhaps to get them killed. The week before, I had spoken up against such an attack at the regular morning senior staff meeting. Word of my closed-door antiwar heroics was instantly leaked to the press. At the next day's meeting, Hamilton Jordan rebuked the staff for publicly airing internal differences about something so sensitive. (Naturally, I fretted that he and Carter thought I was the leaker, which I wasn't.) Jordan went on to say that military action had not been ruled out, and he added, as if parenthetically, that the idea of a rescue mission had been explored and deemed unfeasible. This too was promptly leaked. Later, I realized that the whole sequence of events was probably part of an improvised deception to mislead the Iranians.

When the mission failed, I was at home, asleep. I was awakened by a frantic phone call from Pat Caddell, Carter's pollster, who was in California and had heard the news on television. I immediately went to the White House to see if I could help out, and was put to work writing a statement for Carter to deliver in the morning. It was a night of shock and grief. Staff members moved about like zombies, or stood with faces stained by tears, or sat with their faces in their hands, or tried to distract themselves with work. Jody Powell, the president's press secretary, was a calm center, comforting the rest of us and bucking us up.

The Iran rescue mission became the ultimate symbol of what people considered Carter's incompetence and haplessness. The magazine I would later edit, *The New Republic*, cleverly but cruelly called it "The Jimmy Carter Desert Classic." Everyone complained that it was typical of Carter that he tried to scrimp on helicopters and didn't send enough. But in truth the number of helicopters had to be balanced between the requirements of sufficiency and the requirements of secrecy.

When the mission failed, we realized that we would probably lose the election. But I've thought a lot about it over the years, and to me the disaster in the desert was one of Jimmy Carter's finest hours. This was not a careless or excessive or immoral use of force. In amount and kind, the force was calibrated to the goal—freeing the hostages, and freeing them directly, as opposed to raining down destruction on Iran in order to put pressure on an Iranian government that was probably too unstable and divided to respond. And the potential payoff was very high. As I wrote in my diary a few days later:

> What made us saddest was thinking of the historical moment we missed. If the mission had succeeded, the explosion of joy in this country would have been unlike anything anyone in our generation has ever seen. It would have been a catharsis that would have wiped away ten years of spiritual, yes, malaise. So it was worth trying.
>
> Paradoxically—despite the fact that this is on one level a metaphor for three years of Carter administration screwups—it has made me feel better about the administration. This was a rational, intelligent thing to have tried. It would have been a solution to the problem. There is all the difference in the world between this and a blockade or mining. I just wish it had worked. I just wish it had worked.

Carter said afterward that the mission had been "an incomplete success"—a line I don't mind mentioning I didn't write. Naturally, he was roundly ridiculed for saying that. But the funny thing is, he was right. The incomplete part I don't have to explain. But the mission *was* a success of sorts. It convinced the Iranians that we were ready to use force—and that they had better make sure the hostages did not come to any harm. Along with Carter's patient diplomacy—and, yes, along with the Iranians' fear that President Reagan would not be so patient—the rescue mission, for all its horror and disappointment, ultimately achieved its goal.

Jimmy Carter was an interesting experiment for the American presidency. Electing him to the job was as close as the American people have ever come to picking someone out of the phone book to be president. He was a man of faith and morality—a kind of Christian pacifist—a man whose quest was as much spiritual as political.

Here is how Orwell ends his essay on Gandhi:

> One may feel, as I do, a sort of aesthetic distaste for Gandhi, one may reject the claims for sainthood made on his behalf (he never made any such claims himself, by the way), one may also reject sainthood as an ideal and therefore feel that Gandhi's basic aims were anti-human and reactionary: but regarded simply as a politician, and compared with the other leading political figures of our time, how clean a smell he has managed to leave behind!

Is Carter a saint? On second thought, I'll leave God to be the judge of that. Were his aims anti-human and reactionary? Of course not. But I do think we can say of Jimmy Carter, as Orwell said of Gandhi, "how clean a smell he has managed to leave behind!"

—Prepared for *Character Above All*,
a PBS series on modern presidents, May 31, 1995

THE CHILD MONARCH

I.

HARD TO BELIEVE: Only a couple of years have passed since the Reagans went away. It was a touching moment, we now learn. "Look, honey," Ronnie whispered tenderly to Nancy as the helicopter banked back for one more sweep across the South Lawn, "there's our little shack." That's according to *An American Life,* by Ronald Reagan. According to Lou Cannon's *President Reagan: The Role of a Lifetime,* he whispered tenderly, "There's our little bungalow down there." Whatever.

It's taken a while for the full weirdness of the Reagan years to sink in. Not that the unnerving facts weren't available; but nobody—not even Reagan's political opponents—really wanted to face them. We've known for some time, for example, that Reagan's schedule was drawn up in consultation with an astrologer. Reagan's sacked chief of staff, Donald T. Regan, told us so in a book published a full eight months before the administration left office. Thanks to Nancy Reagan, Kitty Kelley, and now Lou Cannon, we've since learned about the weekly astrology classes Nancy took during the 1950s and 1960s, the "zodiac parties" the Reagans attended in Hollywood, Nancy's annoyance when the White House astrologer insisted on being paid for her horoscopes, and the humiliation felt by aides such as James Baker, Richard Darman, and Michael Deaver at having to explain away absurd and arbitrary changes in the schedule that they knew were being made on the basis of supersecret astrological prognostications.

Cannon finds no evidence that astrology had any direct effects on substantive policy. But he finds plenty of evidence that this was a government of, by, and for the stars. And astrology, as it happens, is a pretty good metaphor for the peculiar qualities of that government.

REAGAN, as portrayed in Cannon's book and in his own, is a childlike and sometimes childish man. His head is full of stories. He is unable to think analytically. He is ignorant. He has notions about the way things work, but he doesn't notice when these notions contradict each other. He has difficulty distinguishing between fantasy and reality. He believes fervently in happy endings. He is passive and fatalistic. He cannot admit error.

Within the White House, Reagan himself was consulted precisely as one consults a horoscope. To his frazzled assistants he had mystical power, but was not quite real. Like a soothsayer's chart, he required deciphering. "Reaganology," Cannon writes, "was largely based on whatever gleanings could be obtained from body language." The president's pronouncements in meetings, which usually took the form of anecdotes that might or might not be relevant to the matter at hand, were open to various interpretations. When the conversation ranged beyond the handful of *Animal Farm*–type certainties that made up what Cannon calls Reagan's "core beliefs" (taxes bad, markets good; government bad, defense good), Reagan was lost. Though the people who served with him respected him for his occult powers—his rapport with the television audience, his ability to read a text convincingly, the powerful simplicity of the core beliefs—they viewed his intellect with contempt. They thought he was a big baby, and they were right.

This is a point that Cannon makes over and over, in one way and an-other. His book is devastating and superb. He has covered Reagan for a quarter-century and is looked upon by Reagan's friends and enemies alike as a fair witness and an impartial judge. Having read not only Cannon's new blockbuster but also several thousand of his stories and columns in the *Washington Post*, I still have no idea if he is pro-Reagan or anti-Reagan. His only discernible ideological predisposition is that he has no ideological pre-disposition (though this ideologically predisposes him to underestimate ide-ology's importance, as well as to be more sympathetic to the administration's "pragmatists" than to its movement conservatives).

Cannon's book braids a biography of Reagan together with a detailed and lively account of Reagan's presidency. Much of it is necessarily about Reagan's advisers and cabinet secretaries, for it was on them that the day-to-day burdens of the presidency actually fell. A good deal of what Cannon shows us about Reagan is seen through their eyes. It's quite a spectacle:

> The sad, shared secret of the Reagan White House was that no one in the presidential entourage had confidence in the judgment or capacities of the president.

> Pragmatists and conservatives alike treated Reagan as if he were a child monarch in need of constant protection.

> Reagan's reliance on metaphor and analogy for understanding made him vulnerable to arguments that were short on facts and long on theatrical gimmicks.

> He made sense of foreign policy through his long-developed habit of devising dramatic, all-purpose stories with moralistic messages, forceful plots, and well-developed heroes and villains.

> The more Reagan repeated a story, the more he believed it and the more he resisted information that undermined its premises.

> His biggest problem was that he didn't know enough about public policy to participate fully in his presidency—and often didn't realize how much he didn't know.

> [I]t was commonplace for Reagan's principal policy advisers to find the president inattentive, unfocused and incurious and to depart from meetings not knowing what, if anything, had been decided.

> Ronald Reagan's subordinates often despaired of him because he seemed to inhabit a fantasy world where cinematic events competed for attention with reality.

Cannon stresses the movie angle as a way of understanding Reagan, which is interesting in light of how little public discussion of this angle

there was during Reagan's twenty-five years as an active politician. Governor Pat Brown of California, whom Reagan unseated in his first bid for public office in 1966, humorously likened him to John Wilkes Booth. The joke
backfired, but the "actor issue" was a perfectly legitimate one. If it is fair to
examine how a candidate's background as a soldier or a corporate lawyer or
a civil rights agitator might affect his cast of mind, then surely it was fair to
ask if the mental habits instilled by spending most of one's time until the
age of fifty-three dressing up in costumes and playing out elaborately
mounted wish-fulfillment fantasies was good preparation for high office.
But partly because it hadn't worked for Brown and partly because mentioning Reagan's profession somehow got classified as bigotry ("jobism," it
might be called nowadays), the actor issue was never aired in any of Reagan's subsequent campaigns.

As president, Reagan spent a lot of time at the movies. According to
Cannon, he saw some three hundred and fifty feature films at Camp David
alone. He also saw several more a month at the White House family theater, plus an unknown number in the private screening rooms of rich friends.
And those were just the ones requiring the services of a projectionist. In addition, the Reagans watched TV every night they were free. Reagan loved
war pictures. He had starred in several during World War II (*International
Squadron, Rear Gunner,* and *For God and Country*, among others) and had
absorbed hundreds more. Some of his best anecdotes—the B-17 pilot who
cradles his wounded gunner's head in his arms as they ride their crippled
plane down together; the black sailor who saves his white shipmates by
grabbing a machine gun and swiveling to shoot a Japanese fighter out of the
sky; the American army officer (Reagan himself) who helps liberate the
death camps—were twisted, hoked-up, or falsified versions of experiences
that Reagan had encountered in movie theaters, not in real life.

We knew about Reagan and war movies. What Cannon adds is that
Reagan loved peace movies, too. He couldn't stop talking about *War Games,*
a Matthew Broderick vehicle about a teenage hacker who breaks into the
NORAD computer and saves the world from being destroyed by trigger-
happy Pentagon generals. He watched *The Day After,* the 1983 made-for-TV
nuclear holocaust weepie that his own people spent weeks trying to dis-
credit, and found it powerful and affecting. His strategic defense proposal
was strikingly reminiscent of one of his own pictures, *Murder in the Air*
(1940), in which the future president, playing Secret Service agent Brass

Bancroft, foils a foreign plot to steal the "Inertia Projector," an American ray gun that can shoot down distant enemy aircraft. And according to Colin Powell, Reagan's last national security adviser, Reagan's proposal to share strategic defense technology with the Soviets was inspired by *The Day the Earth Stood Still*, a gripping 1951 science fiction movie in which a flying saucer descends on Washington. The saucer disgorges Michael Rennie, the urbane representative of an advanced civilization, who warns earthlings to put aside their petty quarrels among themselves or face the consequences.

If the war-movie side of Reagan had been all there was to him, as many of us feared in the early 1980s, we might all now be radioactive ash. But because he also had his peace-movie side, he turned out to be a somewhat less predictable and altogether less frightening character. He was, in fact, a precursor, a kind of spiritual grandfather, of what has become a standard Hollywood type: the autodidactic, self-righteous, "issue-oriented" star who is full of opinions about politics and who also dabbles in "New Age" phenomena. These last, in Reagan's case, included (besides astrology) extrasensory perception, precognition, sci-fi, people from other planets, and prophecies about Armageddon. It was only natural for him to be interested in such things, given that the Reagans had spent most of their lives (as Nancy puts it with screwball reasonableness in *My Turn*) "in the company of show-business people, where superstitions and other non-scientific beliefs are widespread and commonly accepted."

REAGAN'S STAFF kept most of the wigginess from spilling over into the public arena. "Here come the little green men again," Powell used to tell his staff whenever the subject arose of Reagan's preoccupation with how an alien invasion would unify the earth. Powell, Cannon writes dryly, "struggled diligently to keep interplanetary references out of Reagan's speeches." They couldn't be kept out of informal conversations, though—much to the bafflement of Mikhail Gorbachev, who, when Reagan started in about invasions from outer space at the 1985 summit in Geneva, politely changed the subject.

The wildest aspect of Reagan's premature New Agery was his obsession with the Battle of Armageddon. The closest anyone ever came to flushing out this particular bit of Reaganuttiness came during the second televised campaign debate in 1984, when Marvin Kalb asked Reagan if the matter of

Armageddon had had any effect on American nuclear planning. Reagan just made it through his answer safely, saying that while he had engaged in "philosophical discussions" on the subject, "no one knows" whether "Armageddon is a thousand years away or the day after tomorrow," and therefore he had never "said we must plan according to Armageddon."

Had Walter Mondale picked up on this opening and used the rest of the debate, and maybe the rest of the campaign, to harass Reagan on what could have become the "Armageddon issue," the election might have been less one-sided. A little more drilling in Armageddon territory could have yielded a political gusher. Cannon has conducted his own archaeological dig into the matter and unearthed enough shards to warrant his own conclusion that "Reagan is hooked on Armageddon." In 1968 Billy Graham visits Reagan and they talk about portents of the end of days. In 1970 Pat Boone brings a couple of radio evangelists to see Reagan in Sacramento, and one of them, seized by a supposed visitation of the Holy Spirit, prophesies rapturously that Reagan will be president and tells him about the approaching mother of all battles, and then listens as Reagan ticks off modern events, such as the founding of the State of Israel, that seem to fulfill the biblical preconditions for the big one. In 1971 Reagan tells his dinner partner, the president pro tem of the California Senate, that the end is nigh and that one of the portents is that Libya has gone Communist. In 1980 Reagan announces on Jim Bakker's TV show that "we may be the generation that sees Armageddon."

The obsession continues after Reagan is president. His national security aides grow used to hearing him talk about it. Robert McFarlane becomes convinced, in Cannon's words, "that Reagan's interest in anti-missile defense was the product of his interest in Armageddon." When Frank Carlucci tries to persuade Reagan that nuclear deterrence is a good thing, Reagan astonishes Carlucci by telling him about Armageddon. When Caspar Weinberger tries to make the same case, Reagan gives him the same Armageddon lecture. On March 28, 1987, at the Gridiron Club dinner, Reagan tells James McCartney of Knight-Ridder that because Chernobyl is the Ukrainian word for "wormwood" and Wormwood is the name of a flaming star in the Book of Revelation, the accident at the Soviet nuclear plant was a harbinger of Armageddon. (In a hilarious footnote, Cannon adds that Reagan, in telling the story to McCartney, misremembered the name of the star and called it "Wedgewood." Shades of Nancy's china!) On May 5, 1989, Reagan tells Cannon that Israel's possession of the Temple Mount is a sign that Armageddon looms. There are other omens, too, he tells Cannon. What, for example? "Strange weather things."

II.

THE BOOK TITLED *An American Life* omits any mention of strange weather things. It is as much a star autobiography as a presidential memoir, but a star autobiography of the pre-Geraldo type. There are no shocking confessions, no harrowing addictions, no twelve-step recoveries. This is *Photoplay* circa 1940, not *National Enquirer* circa 1990.

Has Reagan read this book? Besides the printed tome, there is also an audio version—two cassettes with a total running time of three hours, on which Reagan, in his seductive announcer's voice, recites excerpts aloud. According to my calculation, the tapes represent about thirty-two thousand of the roughly two hundred and sixty thousand words in the printed text. The evidence, then, is that Reagan has read at least 12 percent of his book. Trust, but verify.

The actual author of *An American Life,* as the opening acknowledgments more or less proclaim, is a "thoroughly professional team" of about two dozen people headed by Robert Lindsey, who has written several readable best-sellers. "Even though I am glad to have this book finished, I will miss my conversations with Bob," writes Reagan, or writes Bob, or writes somebody. There's no way, really, to be sure. Anyway, the conversations with Bob didn't yield much. Almost everything in the book could have been gleaned, perhaps was gleaned, from the public record—from newspapers, old speech and interview transcripts, other books, and White House news releases.

But if there are no revelations, there is a portrait—no, there are two portraits. On the surface is the golden personification of the American dream: the small-town lifeguard who saved seventy-seven people from drowning, the movie star who saved the girl and the day in many a B picture, the citizen-politician who saved the conservative movement from sullen irrelevance, the triumphal president who saved his country from drift and decline. Below the surface—but only a little below, since these depths are not very deep—is the child monarch, a person of stunning narcissism and unreflectiveness.

Reagan, as all the world knows, is a big-picture man. His famous "hands-off management style" seems to have evolved early and to have extended to the smallest details of his own life. His most politically potent qualities—the placidity of his temperament, the smooth-surfaced simplicity of his politics, the magical ease with which he waves away inconsistency and irresponsibility—are all related, first, to his ability to ignore contradictions (more precisely, his inability to notice them), and, second, to the effortlessness that has attended all his achievements.

"I was raised to believe that God has a plan for everyone and that seemingly random twists of fate are all a part of His plan," he writes. "My mother—a small woman with auburn hair and a sense of optimism that ran as deep as the cosmos—told me everything in life happened for a purpose. She said all things were part of God's plan, even the most disheartening setbacks, and in the end, everything worked out for the best." But then, a few sentences later, he tells us what his father taught him: "that individuals determine their own destiny; that is, it's largely their own ambition and hard work that determine their fate in life."

Reagan is untroubled by the stark incompatibility of these two conceptions of will and destiny. He just forges blithely ahead, and before long it becomes clear which of the two views he finds more congenial:

> Then one of those series of small events began that make you wonder about God's plan.

> Once again fate intervened—as if God was carrying out His plan with my name on it.

> Then one of those things happened that makes one wonder about God's having a plan for all of us.

> If ever God gave me evidence that He had a plan for me, it was the night He brought Nancy into my life.

And finally, as he and his wife emerge from the elevator on the second floor of the White House on the evening of the inaugural:

> I think it was only then, as Nancy and I walked hand in hand down the great Central Hall, that it hit home that I was president . . . it was only at this moment that I appreciated the enormity of what had happened to me.

Even the presidency was something that happened to Reagan. This is more than just the affectation of a becoming modesty. The political philosophy that Reagan adopted in his forties may have stressed ambition and hard work, but Reagan himself has never had to do much more than go with the plan. Even in his own telling, it is striking how easy he has had it (which makes his denunciations of "giveaway welfare programs" especially unattractive).

After graduating from Eureka College in 1932, he tells us, he was bitterly disappointed when someone else beat him out for a job running the sporting goods department at the local Montgomery Ward in Dixon, Illinois, for $12.50 a week. That's about it as far as reversals go. A few months later he was making $25 a week as a radio announcer, and then $75, and then, after a quick screen test taken during a trip to California to cover the Chicago Cubs in spring training for his radio station in 1937, $200 a week as a contract player at Warner's—the equivalent today, after taxes, of well over $100,000 a year.

Reagan was twenty-six when he arrived in Hollywood in the depths of the Depression, and after that it was just a matter of adding zeroes to his income. Even World War II was easy for him. Lieutenant Reagan spent it narrating training films for the Army Air Force at a movie studio in Culver City. His first picture after his discharge involved riding horses, which made it, he writes, "like a welcome-home gift." Of course, he was already home. He had been home all along—though he genuinely believed, at the time and after, that he had been to war.

In 1954, after Reagan's movie career had begun to falter, the Plan intervened in the form of an offer to serve as the host of a television series, *General Electric Theater*, and to give speeches at G.E. plants as a company spokesman. Taking this job, perhaps more than any other decision Reagan ever made, was what made him president. Reagan had turned down other TV offers because, as he notes shrewdly in *An American Life*, "most television series expired after two or three years, and from then on, audiences—and producers—tended to think of you only as the character you'd played in the TV series." Being the host, however, was different. It put him before the public every week for eight years (plus another two years as the host of *Death Valley Days*), not as a cowpoke or a private eye or a bumbling husband but as a congenial, dignified man in a business suit, a man called Ronald Reagan.

Cannon's book stresses Reagan's pride in his acting and his movie career, but Reagan's book confirms Christopher Matthews's insight that Reagan's real calling in life was not as an actor but as an announcer—and, by extension, as a giver of speeches. Reagan offers no reflections on the craft of acting, but plenty on the craft of announcing and speechmaking. (Can you picture the young Reagan waiting on tables for a chance to play Hamlet? Neither can I.) The speeches for G.E. became The Speech, a compendium of free enterprise bromides and fabulous anecdotes about government waste that he polished to a high gloss in hundreds of repetitions, and which, when he delivered it on national television in 1964 on behalf of Barry Goldwater, led to the governorship of California and eventually the presidency of the United States.

III.

CHARACTERISTICALLY, Reagan sees no contradiction between the cozy cartel system of the Hollywood studios in which he prospered and the cut-throat laissez-faire doctrine he would later espouse. On the contrary, he deplores the antitrust suit that forced producers "to make movies purely on the speculation theatres would want to show them." This kind of ideological incoherence contributes to Reagan's opacity about just when and how he became a conservative. His wife is more straightforward on this point. Referring to Reagan's years shilling for G.E. in the middle and late 1950s, she writes in *My Turn:* "It was during this period that Ronnie gradually changed his political views."

From Nancy's account, and from Cannon's, it seems clear that during his G.E. spokesman days Reagan became persuaded by the sound of his own voice, which was also his master's. More flatteringly to himself, Reagan depicts the change as starting much earlier. He pretends to recall, anachronistically, that as a small-town boy he learned "to know people as individuals, not as blocs or members of special interest groups." He claims, improbably, that his support for Franklin D. Roosevelt was a function of F.D.R.'s call in 1932 for a cut in federal spending. While making a picture in England in 1949 he observes, omnisciently, "how the welfare state sapped incentive to work from many people in a wonderful and dynamic country." He makes much of having called on the Democrats to nominate Dwight D. Eisenhower for president, but this was a popular position within Americans for Democratic Action, the leading liberal pressure group of the day. (A.D.A.'s 1948 ticket was Ike and William O. Douglas.)

Reagan also portrays his battles with Hollywood Communists in the Screen Actors Guild, the United World Federalists, the American Veterans Committee, and other organizations as a factor in his conversion to conservative Republicanism. This makes a nice, heroic-sounding story, but it's demonstrably untrue. He writes that "after the war, I'd shared the orthodox liberal view that Communists—if there really *were* any—were liberals who were temporarily off track, and whatever they were, they didn't pose much of a threat to me or anyone." But this was not the "orthodox," i.e., mainstream, liberal view. By 1946, and unmistakably by 1950, the great majority of American liberals, leftists, and Democrats were firmly anti-Communist. This was the case even in Hollywood, where a fair amount of poolside Stalinism (like today's hot-tub Sandinismo) persisted right through the mid-1950s.

Reagan after the war was a dupe, an enthusiastic joiner of Communist front groups. He expresses no remorse about this. On the contrary, in his memoir you can almost hear the fond, indulgent chuckle in his voice as he describes himself during this period. He "was speaking out against the rise of neofascism in America." He "joined just about any organization I could find that guaranteed to save the world." But heck, he just "hadn't given much thought to the threat of communism." Darn that headstrong, idealistic Reagan kid anyway—somebody forgot to tell him about the Moscow trials. In any case, he doesn't mention such things in explaining his awakening to the problem of communism. Instead he recounts a visit from a couple of F.B.I. agents and his agreement to become an informer for them. ("They asked if they could meet with me periodically to discuss some of the things that were going on in Hollywood. I said of course they could.")

Whatever his reasons for turning against communism, he remained left of center long after he did so. As late as 1952, by which date he had been publicly denouncing Communists for six years, the Los Angeles County Democratic Central Committee declined to endorse him for an open House seat because they thought he was too liberal. It's tantalizing to speculate on what might have been had the Democrats of Los Angeles not made this bonehead decision. Would Representative Reagan have become Senator Reagan? Might he have ended up as J.F.K.'s running mate? Would he have drifted to the right and become a marginal crank like Sam Yorty? Or would he have stayed left and won the White House four or eight years earlier than he did? And—most delicious thought of all—would the ultimate sneer-word of today's conservatives be not McGovernism or Carterism but Reaganism?

THE FACT THAT Reagan converted to anti-communism long before he converted to conservatism may have had an important consequence. Evil though he thought the empire was, his conservatism did not depend on an emotional attachment to a permanent, Manichaean East-West struggle. This may be one reason why he was so much readier than were the ideologues among his aides when Gorbachev came along and announced that the struggle was over.

Reagan is not, nor has he ever been, ideologically sophisticated. He was a sentimental liberal who became a sentimental conservative. His liberalism was a product of inertia combined with a vague sympathy for the little guy; his conservatism was a product of convenience combined with sympathy for guys who weren't so little—the G.E. managers and executives who had his ear for eight years. ("By 1960, I realized the real enemy wasn't big business, it was big government.") This lack of intellectual sophistication—an inability to think, really—is one of the themes of Cannon's book that manifests itself over and over again in Reagan's. For example, when he becomes governor of California, two years after the Watts riots, Reagan decides to "find out what was going on" by paying secret visits to black families around the state:

> One of the first things I heard was a complaint that blacks weren't being given a fair shot at jobs in state government. I looked into it and confirmed that virtually the only blacks employed by the state were janitors or those working in other menial positions, largely because state civil service tests were slanted against them.

His response was to change the testing and job evaluation procedures to make up for the fact that "blacks just hadn't had the opportunity to get the same kind of schooling as other Californians"—in other words, to rewrite the tests and the qualifications so as to guarantee equality of outcome. A good-hearted act, no doubt about it; but Reagan shows absolutely no awareness that this aggressive instance of affirmative action was precisely the sort of thing that his Justice Department would soon enough denounce as an affront to American values.

Another example. A lodestar of the Reagan administration's foreign policy was the distinction between authoritarian regimes, which are by nature reformable because they permit competing centers of social power to exist, and totalitarian regimes, which are by nature unreformable because all power has been seized, or is in the process of being seized, by a party-state professing a messianic ideology that claims a total monopoly on truth. This analysis was the heart of a famous article by Jeane Kirkpatrick in *Commentary* in 1980. Reagan was so impressed by this piece that he made Kirkpatrick his ambassador to the United Nations.

The doctrine of the immutability of totalitarian regimes has turned out to have no predictive power, and it was therefore a poor basis for long-term policy; but the analytic distinction between the two types of dictatorship was sound enough. The idea that there's a difference between plain old undemocratic governments, however brutal, and those with totalitarian pretensions is not hard to grasp. Furthermore, this idea underlay some of the Reagan administration's most important foreign policy innovations. Even so, it comes as no real surprise that the authoritarian-totalitarian distinction was utterly lost on Reagan. Discussing policy options for the hemisphere in *An American Life*, he writes:

> Sure, we could send in the troops, but the threat of communism wouldn't diminish until the people's standard of living was improved and the totalitarian countries of Latin America gave them more freedom.

Discussing the Falklands War, he writes:

> Margaret Thatcher, I think, had no choice but to stand up to the generals who cynically squandered the lives of young Argentineans solely to prolong the life of a corrupt and iron-fisted totalitarian government.

The Argentine military junta, remember, was Kirkpatrick's beau ideal of an authoritarian government. And the totalitarian prototype in the Kirkpatrick scheme was pre-Gorbachevian Soviet communism, which Reagan describes as a system of—what else?—"authoritarian rule."

Or perhaps it isn't Reagan but his "thoroughly professional team" that is confused. I must acknowledge that the sentences quoted above are not recited on the cassettes, so there is no hard proof that Reagan was ever familiar with them. But *An American Life* does have passages that Reagan can be credited not only with having read but with having written. These are excerpts from a diary that he seems to have kept as president, of which a total of about forty pages are scattered through the ghosted text. To appreciate fully the flavor of these diary entries, one needs to sample more than one or two. The three entries below are given in their entirety. They are typical. I categorically deny that I am being unfair.

Feb. 22

Lunch on issues. I'm convinced of the need to address the people on our budget and the economy. The press has done a job on us and the polls show its effect. The people are confused about economic program. They've been told it has failed and it has just started.

June 30

Word came that the hostages were going to leave in a Red Cross motorcade for Damascus. It was a long ride. We then were told that celebrations in small villages along their route were delaying them. About a quarter to three our time, they arrived at the Sheraton hotel in Damascus.

Out to George Shultz's home for dinner with George and O'Bie. A very nice and finally relaxed dinner. Before that, however, I spoke to the nation on TV from the Oval Office, then George took questions in the press room. When I spoke our people were just leaving Syrian air space in a military aircraft.

Sept. 26

High spot was swearing in of Chief Justice Rehnquist and Justice Scalia in the East Room. After lunch meeting with George S., Cap. W., and Bill Casey plus our White House people, Don R., John P., etc. It was a sum up of where we stand in the negotiations between George and Shevardnadze. The difference between us is their desire to make it look like a trade for Daniloff and their spy Zakharov. We'll trade Zakharov but for Soviet dissidents. We settled on our bottom line points beyond which we won't budge. Then we picked up Nancy and helicoptered to Ft. Meade for the opening of the new National Security Agency complex. I spoke to the NSA employees. Then we helicoptered to Camp David and topped the day with a swim.

The entries from the diary that were chosen for publication in *An American Life* are presumably the best of the lot, and this is as good as they get. One can imagine the sick disappointment of Lindsey and the rest of the team when they got their first look at them. There are no portraits of friends and enemies, no thumbnail sketches, no gossip, no peeves, no wisecracks, no outbursts of principle, no anecdotes—no nothing, really, except simple-minded digests of news bulletins and appointment logs. For authenticity's sake, the team has left in a few grammatical howlers and preserved a Reagan habit, which some will find endearing, of taking the hyphens out of compound phrases like "tight rope," "plane side," and "heart breaking" and saving them up for use in low-octane swear words, such as "h--l" and "d--m" (hang on, shouldn't that be "d-m-"?).

Many entries combine childish diction with childish thinking, as in this reflection on the flap over the visit to the Waffen SS cemetery at Bitburg, Germany:

> I still think we were right. Yes. The German soldiers were the enemy and part of the whole Nazi hate era. But we won and we killed those soldiers. What is wrong with saying, "Let's never be enemies again"? Would Helmut be wrong if he visited Arlington Cemetery on one of his U.S. visits?

And then this follow-up, after Kohl suggested that they balance the Bitburg ceremony with a tour of Dachau:

> Helmut may very well have solved our problem re the Holocaust.

And then there is this innocuous reference to a negotiation on the budget:

> The big thing today was a meeting with Tip, Howard Bohling, Jim Wright, Jim Baker, Ed Meese, Don Regan, and Dave Stockman.

Howard Bohling wasn't at the meeting, or on the planet. Our diarist is conflating two of the actual attendees, Howard Baker and Richard Bolling. Are the identities of these men a mere detail? You could say that about Bolling, a mere House member (though a prominent one) and a Democrat to boot. But Senator (and Majority Leader) Baker was the second-most-powerful figure in the Republican Party. He would later become Reagan's chief of staff. It is deeply weird that the president was so vague about who he was.

THE EMPTINESS of Reagan's diary is one of many indications that the president's narcissism was of the babyish, not the Byronic, variety. And a happy baby he was. His perfect obliviousness to the feelings and the thoughts of others protected him from emotional turmoil. And his emotional tranquillity in turn helped to cushion him from what otherwise might have been the political impact of the contrast between his beliefs and his life. He listed "family" first among his public values, yet his emotional remoteness so wounded his own children that during the White House years three of them published books attacking him. And he treated his closest aides, Cannon tells us, "as indifferently as he did his children." Once they left his employ, they would never hear from him again.

There were times when Reagan's lack of self-awareness was merely goofy. At other times, however, his inability to see himself clearly takes on a somewhat more unpleasant edge. Consider this anecdote:

> I've never liked hunting, simply killing an animal for the pleasure of it, but I have always enjoyed and collected unusual guns; I love target shooting, and have always kept a gun for protection at home. As I had done when I was governor, I sometimes did some target shooting with the Secret Service agents who accompanied us to the ranch, and occasionally managed to amaze them with my marksmanship. We have a small pond on the ranch that sometimes attracts small black snakes, and every now and then, one would stick its head up out of the water for a second or two. After I'd see one, I'd go into the house and come back with a .38 revolver, go into a little crouch, and wait for the next snake to rise up. Then I'd shoot.
>
> Well, since I was thirty feet or more from the lake, the Secret Service agents were shocked that I was able to hit the snake every time. They'd shake their heads and say to each other, "How the hell does he do it?"
>
> What they didn't know was that my pistol was loaded with shells containing bird shot—like a shotgun—instead of a conventional slug. I kept my secret for a while, but finally decided to fess up and tell them about the bird shot.

This little story has a chilling, brightly lit creepiness, like something out of David Lynch. Its trajectory, from Reagan's pious and no doubt sincere disavowal of killing animals for pleasure to his almost sensuous description of the fun of blowing the heads off inoffending water snakes (and doing it in an unsporting manner, too), suggests an obliviousness that is potentially sinister. One begins to suspect that, for all his generic charm, Reagan may not be such a nice guy after all. We are dealing here with the same insensibility that enables Reagan to believe that he never traded arms for hostages, that the deficit was all the Democrats' fault, that his economic policies helped the poor at the expense of the rich.

IV.

BUT WAIT. If he was dumb, superstitious, childish, inattentive, passive, narcissistic, and oblivious, how come he won the Cold War and brought peace and liberty to all mankind?

Good question. The answer, in two words, is Mikhail Gorbachev. Reagan, always lucky, was never luckier than to find himself president of the United States at just the moment when a Soviet leader decided to lift the pall of fear and lies from his empire, thus permitting the system's accumulated absurdities and contradictions to come into plain view and shake it to pieces.

Everyone agrees that the West, led by the United States, deserves credit for creating the conditions under which this could happen. But in order to assign to Ronald Reagan the largest share—to assign to this particular president more than the equal slice of credit that is due each of the eight postwar presidents who carried out the Western policies of containment, nuclear deterrence, conventional military readiness, support for NATO, support for non-Communist economic development, and political and diplomatic opposition to Soviet expansionism—you have to believe that the *marginal* differences between Reagan's policies and his predecessors' were the ones that brought about the Gorbachev breakthrough.

These marginal differences included bigger increases in military spending; intransigence in, if not outright hostility to, arms control negotiations; an emphasis on ideological attacks on Leninism in American public diplomacy; suspension of the anti-Soviet grain embargo; assistance to the guer-

rillas fighting the Soviet-supported Sandinista regime in Nicaragua; a somewhat more aggressive program of military aid to the Afghani *mujaheddin*
than might otherwise have been pursued (though this program was begun
under the Democrats and was popular with both parties); the anti-missile
defense proposal; and the military interventions in Lebanon and Grenada.

The effect, such as it was, of these policies on changes within the Soviet
Union was probably mixed. Reagan's admirers argue that the American
military buildup encouraged Soviet reform by persuading Gorbachev that
the arms race was a pointless rathole. It could also be argued that the buildup
retarded reform by strengthening the worst-case paranoids within the Soviet military. More plausible than either argument is the view that Gorbachev's determination to disengage from the Cold War was the product of
forces far deeper and stronger than whether American military spending increased a lot or a little during the early 1980s, that the forces that made and
unmade Gorbachev were indigenous, historical, Russian.

Nor were the other Reagan policy innovations—whether "hawkish" like
the contra obsession or "dovish" like the grain-embargo cancellation,
whether wise like the president's vigorous attacks on Leninist ideology or
foolish like the Lebanon fiasco—truly central to the epochal decisions being
made in the Kremlin. And the argument that these innovations were decisive requires us to believe that without them Gorbachev would not have
come to power; or that he would have come to power but would not have
embarked on the path of glasnost and perestroika; or that he would have embarked on this path but would have been deflected or replaced long before
he could follow it as far as he did. None of these propositions seems persuasive to me.

The issue of nuclear weapons increasingly occupied Reagan's attention,
and it presents a special case. How much he knew about the topic was the
subject of much speculation while he was in office. Cannon shows that
Reagan's ignorance was actually more comprehensive than many of us suspected. The president did not know that submarines carried nuclear missiles, or that bombers carried them. He did not know that land-based
ballistic missiles made up a much larger proportion of the Soviet nuclear
force than the American one, and therefore he did not realize that his proposal for halving the numbers of such missiles on both sides was far from
being the even-handed basis for serious negotiation he believed it to be.
Though he had campaigned against the "window of vulnerability"—the

alleged ease with which a Soviet first strike could destroy America's land-based missiles—he did not know that his own plan to put such missiles in stationary silos would open the "window" wider.

Throughout Reagan's first term his strings were being pulled by officials who privately opposed the whole idea of arms control agreements with the Soviet Union because they thought such agreements weakened the West's will to resist. These officials concocted bargaining positions that the Soviets could be relied upon to reject, which is exactly what the Soviets did under Brezhnev, Andropov, and Chernenko. Then along came Gorbachev. He wanted a deal so badly that he systematically probed until he found a question Washington was unable to answer no to. And so the "zero option" for European-based intermediate-range missiles—a proposal that the Defense Department had crafted to be unacceptable—became, presto chango, the great and crowning achievement of Ronald Reagan's foreign policy.

Whatever happens in the aftermath of the coup in Moscow, the central achievements of the Gorbachev years—the dissolution of the Soviet Union's Eastern European empire, the demolition of Leninist ideology, and the defusing of East-West confrontation—will almost certainly remain. Could Gorbachev have done all this without Reagan? Probably, yes—but he probably couldn't have done it without accepting Reagan's (that is, the West's) view of the Cold War. Gorbachev recognized that the cause of the Cold War was not superpower tensions or capitalist encirclement or the arms race, let alone the international class struggle. The cause of the Cold War was simply the Soviet Union's refusal to become a "normal" country. As a corollary, Gorbachev recognized that the Soviet Union faced no military threat from the West, however bulging Western arsenals might be. So he knew he could accept what his predecessors would have seen as preposterously disadvantageous arms control deals without putting his country's physical security at risk.

There was another point of agreement between Gorbachev and Reagan. They both thought Gorbachev's country was redeemable. Reagan had a recurring daydream that someday he would take a Soviet leader up in his helicopter and together they would fly low over an American suburb. The Soviet leader would see the tidy little houses of American workers, with their plastic pools out back and a car or two out front, and he would decide that maybe it was time to scrap communism and try a little democracy and free enterprise instead. Is this sentimental fantasy really so different from what actually happened?

When Reagan called the Soviet Union an "evil empire" and "the focus of evil in the modern world," conservative op-ed writers expressed their satisfaction that at last we had a president who had a moral vocabulary and a tragic sense of history, a president who recognized that some political systems are irredeemably tyrannical and aggressive, a president who rejected the contemptible claptrap that attributes every international conflict to "lack of understanding." These commentators, and many of their friends inside the Reagan administration, saw Gorbachev as simply cleverer than his predecessors, and therefore more dangerous. Reagan did not agree. When he said "evil," he just meant bad. He didn't really believe in immutable malevolence. The villains of Reagan's world were like the ones in Frank Capra's movies— capable of change once they saw the light. And Reagan thought that Gorbachev was a pretty good guy.

AS PRESIDENT, of course, Reagan was the ex officio high priest of the nuclear cult. He was followed everywhere he went by a military aide handcuffed to the "football," the sacred object containing the codes that would enable him to launch the final conflagration. And the propinquity of the thermonuclear Excalibur gave him, in this one area of policy, a consciousness of personal power unparalleled in history and shared only with his Soviet counterpart. By the same token, the rituals of nuclear summitry required his personal participation, and he found the drama irresistible.

Resplendent in the vestments of the nuclear episcopate, Reagan announced his astonishing heresies. In 1983, just when the whole of the conservative foreign policy establishment, and many centrist and liberal nuclear worthies besides, had geared up to defend the morality of nuclear deterrence against freezeniks, Catholic moralists, Euro-accommodationists, and other unsound elements, the president proclaimed that nuclear deterrence was . . . immoral. To replace it, he proposed an exotic space shield that would protect America (and Russia, too—why not?) against nuclear attack.

Whatever progress is ultimately made in anti-missile defense technology, the idea of an impenetrable space shield was then, and remains today, a lunatic notion. The notion's provenance was lunatic, too. "The dream," writes Cannon, "was the product of Reagan's imagination, perhaps of Brass Bancroft and the Inertia Projector and *The Day the Earth Stood Still,* and certainly of the vivid prophecy of Armageddon that Reagan accepted as a valid forecast of the nuclear age." The Strategic Defense Initiative was pure Reagan.

Useless as S.D.I. would be as a shield against a determined missile attack, it would not be at all useless as a supplement to a first strike launched by the side that possessed it. This—plus a superstitious awe of American technology—was why S.D.I. alarmed the Russians, even Russians as well-disposed toward the United States as Gorbachev. Reagan did not understand this. He thought they were lying when they said they were worried about Americans attacking them with nuclear weapons, because they had to know Americans would never do such a thing. McFarlane, who didn't think they were lying, saw how the dross of Reagan's "dream" could be turned into gold. In a negotiating ploy so one-sided that he privately called it "The Sting," the United States would abandon S.D.I.—a research program of dubious practicability—in exchange for the destruction of thousands of actually existing Soviet nuclear weapons. McFarlane didn't mind that Reagan kept saying S.D.I. was not a bargaining chip, because every such avowal drove up its value as a bargaining chip.

McFarlane didn't realize that the old boy meant what he said. And Reagan had another dream, which prompted him to utter another heresy, the most dangerous one that the priesthood could imagine. He said he wanted to rid the world of nuclear weapons altogether. Total nuclear disarmament was a silly old chestnut of Cold War propaganda, especially Soviet propaganda. But Reagan believed in it. He had said so in a number of speeches before he became president, but no one paid any attention because everyone assumed that it was just drivel that he'd thrown in to soften his right-wing image. As president, Reagan continued to believe in the desirability of complete nuclear disarmament, even after it was explained to him that nuclear weapons were good because they had kept the peace for forty years. His advisers, he writes in *An American Life*, included "people at the Pentagon who claimed a nuclear war was 'winnable.' I thought they were crazy."

Reagan knew that his own secretary of defense, for example, was "strongly against" nuclear disarmament. Still, he told Gorbachev that he wanted exactly that. In October 1986, at the Reykjavik summit, the principals agreed on principles: the Soviet Union and the United States would scrap all their ballistic missiles within five years and all the rest of their nukes within ten. The only thing that stood in the way of the deal was S.D.I. Gorbachev wanted it confined to the laboratory, and he simply refused to take seriously Reagan's offer to share it. Reagan, all accounts agree, became angry—so angry he stalked out of the room while Gorbachev was still talking to him. The session, and the summit, ended. Reagan's "dreams" had fratricided, like incoming missiles bunched too closely together. He and Gorbachev had to settle for the Euromissile treaty, which would be signed a year later.

Cannon blames Reagan for the failure at Reykjavik. "Reagan," Cannon writes, "clung to his competing dreams of a world without nuclear weapons and a world in which people would be protected from nuclear war by an anti-missile defense." But were these "dreams" really so inherently contradictory? If both sides still had nuclear arsenals, then S.D.I. would indeed be "destabilizing," because it would create an obvious, if conjectural, temptation to strike first: smash the other side's forces, and even a leaky defense might be enough to repel what was left. But if "a world without nuclear weapons" were actually to be achieved, then might not shared anti-missile defenses (of a suitably modest kind) be just what Reagan was saying they'd be—insurance against cheaters or crazies?

In retrospect, it's clear (at least to me) that both Reagan and Gorbachev blundered at Reykjavik. If one of them had given in, both superpowers might be dismantling the last of their ballistic missiles right now. But Gorbachev's stubbornness was less excusable than Reagan's. Gorbachev should have realized that it didn't much matter what he conceded about S.D.I.: once nuclear disarmament was a reality, there would be little political support in the United States for spending hundreds of billions of dollars on exotic space lasers designed to shoot down weapons that were being eliminated anyhow. Gorbachev should have tried to understand why Reagan was so angry. S.D.I. was Reagan's baby, Reagan's pride was at stake, and therefore Reagan was the one who was overvaluing it. Gorbachev should also have realized that Reagan meant what he said about sharing the technology— that on this point, as on the space shield itself, Reagan was willing to brave ridicule and the weight of expert opinion.

All this is, admittedly, a little moot. Once Gorbachev decided to forgo rule by terror, the arms race was going to melt away no matter what anyone else did. The peace that reigns between the United States and the Soviet Union is obviously more of Gorbachev's making than of Reagan's, whereas Reagan alone is responsible for a domestic legacy that includes, besides a wonderful revival of the American Spirit, a soul-crushing national debt, an ignoble Supreme Court, stark economic stratification, the impoverishment of public institutions, and a make-my-day brand of social discourse that revels in ugly contempt for losers. Yet none of that (except the debt) is a surprise. We—those of us who voted against him— knew he was going to be that way from the start.

Reagan was the plaything of whichever of his aides most deftly pushed his hot buttons, but on the nuclear question he lurched into leadership— and that *was* a surprise. The same ignorance that made him a pawn in the struggles among his advisers also made him a savant—an idiot savant, but a savant all the same—in the surreal universe of nuclear strategy. He may not have known which end of the missile has the warhead on it, but he was an expert on the end of the world.

It was Reagan's genius to paste a smiley-face on Armageddon's grinning skull. It turned out he didn't view the biblical account of Armageddon as a prophecy of something inevitable, let alone desirable. He viewed it as a sci-fi story, a cautionary tale about a big awful disaster that could and should be prevented. This is a misreading of the text of the Book of Revelation, but Hollywood always rewrites the classics. Too many downbeat endings.

And how was Armageddon to be prevented—or, rather, who was to prevent it? Something McFarlane observed about Reagan is instructive on this point. "He sees himself as a romantic, heroic figure who believes in the power of a hero to overcome even Armageddon," McFarlane told Cannon. "I think it may come from Hollywood. Wherever it came from, he believes that the power of a person and an idea could change the outcome of something even as terrible as Armageddon. . . . He didn't see himself as God, but he saw himself as a heroic figure on earth." Not as God, but maybe, *pace* Jack Warner, as God's best friend.

Perhaps, in true Hollywood style, there will be a sequel. The happy ending was not the only unusual feature of our hero's interpretation of the tale of Armageddon. "As Reagan understood the story," Cannon notes, deadpan, "Russia would be defeated by an acclaimed leader of the West who would be revealed as the Antichrist." Residents of Pacific Palisades, beware of strange weather things. What rough and chuckling beast, its hour come round at last, slouches toward Beverly Hills to be born?

—*The New Republic*, September 9, 1991

SCALING MT. KENNEDY

IN AN EARLY CHAPTER of *Robert Kennedy: His Life*, Evan Thomas notes that in 1952, when Bobby Kennedy, then twenty-six, was in charge of John F. Kennedy's campaign for the Massachusetts Senate seat held by Henry Cabot Lodge, Jr., no detail was too small for the personal attention of the candidate's kid brother and campaign manager. Bobby, Thomas writes, "would personally go door to door handing out a campaign tabloid newspaper extolling J.F.K.'s virtues, which he had ordered printed up at great expense."

Reading this, I felt a jolt. In the spring of 1968, I was only a little younger than Bobby Kennedy was in 1952. By day, I was a lieutenant, junior grade, in the navy, stationed, thanks to some slipup in the Pentagon, in a sleepy office in lower Manhattan; by night and on weekends, I atoned for my complicity in the Vietnam War effort, ludicrously marginal though it was, by doing grunt work for antiwar causes. As part of that, I was spending some furtive time as a low-level volunteer in the New York storefront headquarters of the Robert Kennedy for President campaign. My task was to do layout and write headlines for—a campaign tabloid newspaper extolling R.F.K.'s virtues. I assumed then, and had assumed since, that our tabloid, which we called the *Kennedy Current*, was the brainchild of one of the harried strategists whom we occasionally glimpsed dashing upstairs to a bank of offices on a mezzanine overlooking the main space. Now I wonder if the person who ordered our little paper printed up at great expense wasn't Bobby himself. Glory!

If you were more or less young, more or less on the left, and more or less active in the peace movement in 1968, then you had strong feelings about Bobby Kennedy. If you hated him (a majority sentiment, if the peaceniks I knew were a fair sample), you saw him as a preeningly "tough," calculating, bloody-minded young man (the shorthand was "ruthless") who had amply proved that he would stop at nothing to serve his family's will to power and who, unlike his Senate colleague Eugene McCarthy, had refused to challenge Lyndon Johnson when it really counted. If you loved Bobby, you didn't necessarily disagree with any of that. But you also thought that he knew these things about himself. And you thought that he had changed, especially after his brother's assassination, and was changing still—that the unimaginable wave of grief and loss that engulfed him after November 22, 1963, had washed him as if in the blood of the lamb, after which he had climbed out of despair to find his true voice in solidarity with those who were suffering from and struggling against war, racism, and poverty. In the present climate of complacency and protective irony, it sounds corny. It didn't seem that way then. It was thrilling.

Bobby Kennedy was a wildly romantic figure in 1968, and the mean, hard chrysalis from which he had emerged only made him seem more so. He was at once slight and strong, with pale-blue eyes full, alternately, of hurt, anger, and curiosity, and a shock of dark hair that he'd push back from his forehead as he shyly ducked his head. It was a year of fearful portents and strange exhilarations. Everything—on every scale, from the global to the personal—seemed to be coming unmoored. The sweep of events was like a hurricane. War in Vietnam and antiwar uprisings on American streets and campuses, insurrections in France, Mexico, and Czechoslovakia, the transfiguring martyrdom of Martin Luther King, Jr., and the burning cities afterward—these public turmoils and many more had their private analogues in millions of individual psyches. To many of us, Bobby Kennedy's appeal was that he seemed open to all of it, that he seemed both defenseless and defiant, that he seemed to be rushing toward his feelings, that he had lifted his feet from the ground and was ready to ride the hurricane to an unknown and unknowable destination. We were projecting, of course. But so what? (According to Evan Thomas, Bobby couldn't stand his campaign poster—the same poster, by the way, that has hung on my living-room wall these thirty-two years. He thought it made him look like a guitar player. We thought so, too.)

The R.F.K. phenomenon has prompted the writing of a lot of prose. It inspired David Halberstam, Jack Newfield, and Peter Maas to do some of their strongest work; Halberstam's *The Unfinished Odyssey of Robert Kennedy* (1968) is especially fine. The best of the Bobby books remains, and probably will always remain, *Robert Kennedy and His Times,* by Arthur M. Schlesinger, Jr., published in 1978. Its nine hundred-plus beautifully written pages combine the virtues of memoir, biography, and history, giving it the crystalline depth of field of an Ansel Adams photograph. Thomas's book is less than half the length of Schlesinger's; it necessarily leaves out a lot, especially the richly textured context of events through which Schlesinger's Kennedy moves. But it has something to add, too—not only the cool perspective of time but also quantities of new information, some of it the fruit of Thomas's own research. Thomas is an experienced biographer and, as *Newsweek*'s main man in Washington for ten years, an accomplished political journalist. His style is clear, a little homely, and anything but overwrought, and this allows the almost operatic nature of the tale he tells to speak for itself. Much of his story was invisible to the public eye as it was happening, and has emerged only in recent years. He is respectful of evidence and measured in his judgments. He is neither an apologist nor a debunker. But his portrait of what it was like to grow up in the Kennedy clan is fraught with more unhappiness and anxiety than that of earlier biographers. And he shows that the secret side of the Kennedy administration—the obsession with Cuba, especially Bobby's, and the immense dangers posed by J.F.K.'s sexual recklessness, which it was part of Bobby's job to conceal—sometimes distorted its priorities and stunted its possibilities. Thomas's spareness makes the story sad—sadder, maybe, than it really deserves to be.

MOST PEOPLE'S LIVES, if plotted as a graph with time and intensity as axes, would look like a bell curve, climbing toward a smooth hillock of accomplishment and then trailing down gently into old age. Robert Kennedy's would look like one of those scary diagrams of the population explosion, rising gradually at first and then zooming exponentially off the chart. The unbelievably eventful period from his brother's election as president to his night of victory and death after the California primary covered a span of years shorter than the Clinton administration. He barely reached middle, let alone old, age. He was forty-two when he was murdered.

Robert Francis Kennedy, born on November 20, 1925, was the third of Joseph P. Kennedy's four sons and the seventh of his nine children. He was a sweet child, so much so that his father initially wrote him off as a mama's boy. As an adolescent, he was pious, moody, touchy, and a little lonely. Struggling to compete, he was given to reckless gestures: once, before he knew how to swim, he jumped off a sailboat into the sea and had to be rescued by his brother Joe, prompting Jack to remark, "It showed either a lot of guts or no sense at all, depending on how you looked at it." At a succession of boarding schools, he was an outsider with a chip on his shoulder. At Milton, where he landed after withdrawing from Portsmouth Priory under suspicion of cheating on an exam, he found comfort in a close friendship with David Hackett, a football hero and "schoolboy god" who would become the model for the main character of John Knowles's novel *A Separate Peace*. But Bobby was never part of the in-crowd, either at school or at home, where he was outshone by the glowing trio of Joe Jr., Jack, and Kathleen, the second-oldest sister.

To anyone from a normal or, at least, relatively typical home, the pressures of growing up in the Kennedy clan—that was the word they themselves used, often with a touch of irony—can only be guessed at. This was a family in which wealth and fame were taken for granted, yet every advantage had to be earned, through constant displays of courage and determination. Failure was unthinkable. The father's ethic of competitiveness pitted the children against each other and the clan against the world. That there were secrets to be kept—the shadowy sources of the family's wealth, the father's string of mistresses (including Gloria Swanson), the botched lobotomy that destroyed the brain of Rosemary, the second daughter—only increased the clan's sense of wary exceptionalism. By the time of Pearl Harbor, when Bobby was sixteen, Joe Sr., who had supported Neville Chamberlain's policy of appeasing the Nazis, had been forced out as President Roosevelt's ambassador to Britain and had transferred his ambitions to his sons. The eldest, the gregarious Joe Jr., was the one designated for politics, although Jack had already made a down payment on the family's political rehabilitation: at twenty-three, he was famous as the author of an implicitly pro-intervention tract, *Why England Slept*, a Harvard senior thesis turned (with the help of Arthur Krock, of the *Times*) best-selling book. By 1946, Jack was more famous still; his PT-109 exploits had been chronicled by John Hersey in *The New Yorker*, and he was running for Congress. Joe

Jr., was dead. He had volunteered to fly a bomber full of high explosives on a one-way trip to a German rocket base on the French coast; he was supposed to bail out before impact, but his plane exploded shortly after take-off. He had died in the service not only of his country but also of his father's harsh ethic: he was trying at once to vindicate the family and to outdo Jack within it. Bobby, for his part, had joined the navy in 1943, just after his eighteenth birthday, and combined officer training with studies at Harvard. But he washed out of flight school as the war was ending, and it was over by the time he went on active duty—as an enlisted man aboard a destroyer named for his dead brother.

Jack and Bobby could hardly have been more different. Jack dealt with the pressures of being a son of Joseph Kennedy by keeping the patriarch at arm's length; Bobby did so by trying to please him. Jack's strategy was ironic detachment; Bobby's was humorless loyalty. Jack's Catholicism was nominal, Bobby's fervent. Jack was the clan's prince, Bobby its foot soldier. The differences showed in, among other ways, their relations with women—a topic on which, unsurprisingly, Thomas is franker than Schlesinger. Thomas writes that, according to Lem Billings, Jack's roommate from Choate, the two brothers lost their virginity, years apart, at the same Harlem whorehouse; Billings accompanied Bobby to the establishment, paid the bill, and was reimbursed by Joe Sr. But there were few other parallels. Jack was elusive, glamorous, relaxed; he had many liaisons, often simultaneous. Bobby was bashful, at once tense and intense, a little priggish. Bobby's "first true love," a Lauren Bacall look-alike named K. K. Hannon, told Thomas many years later that Bobby had been "wry and very dear. He was interested in everything, curious. He didn't have good manners, but he tried. He was like a ten-year-old in a grown-up's suit." Bobby asked her to marry him; she gently put him off. Some time later, as the two walked down a Boston street on the way to the movies, they ran into Jack, who took one look at K.K. and invited himself along. "The next morning," K.K. told Thomas, "Jack called up. I thought he was terrific. That was the end of Bobby. It was very awkward." Bobby showed no anger at this exercise of *droit du seigneur*. He simply deferred.

Thomas tells of another failed romance, one that occurred in the spring of 1948, while Bobby was touring Europe alone before starting law school at the University of Virginia. Kathleen—the most beautiful, spirited, and independent of the Kennedy girls, who went by the marvellous nickname of Kick, and whose husband, an English aristocrat, had died in the war—had just been killed in a plane crash. Thomas writes:

> In deep mourning, Kennedy wandered on to London, where he gloomily attended a popular play called "The Chiltern Hundreds." The play was based partly on the much-publicized drama of Kathleen's marriage, outside the faith and against her mother's wishes, to the son of the Duke of Devonshire. In the starring role—as the American millionairess who marries the son of an earl—was a blond twenty-seven-year-old actress named Joan Winmill. Smitten, Kennedy asked Winmill out to dinner the next night. She later recalled his boyishness—his freckles and toothy smile—and the intensity of his stare. The two began a secretive and slightly lugubrious romance, visiting Kathleen's grave and her late husband's ancestral home, Chatsworth. Inevitably, Joe, Sr., found out and disapproved. He would not have his son marry a showgirl. Promising he would return, Bobby said goodbye to Winmill in August. According to Winmill's memoirs, Bobby wrote her often, sending her chocolates and perfume and hand-me-down dresses with expensive labels from his sisters. She considered herself "in love," she later wrote, until she received a letter from him in the summer of 1949. The letter said, "I am getting married to Ethel Skakel."

It's an astonishingly suggestive episode, like a dream in the way it smashes and rearranges elements of the family's (especially the father's) experience, and in its intimations of repressed or forbidden fantasies—of escape, of resurrection, even of incest. Thomas simply records it, leaving the interpretation to the reader. In any case, Bobby, with his marriage to a woman whose devotion to him was total and uncomplicated, founded a clan of his own, one that eventually surpassed the patriarch's in size. (In the brothers' division of the father's labor, it was Jack who specialized in showgirls.)

In law school, Bobby earned a reputation for rudeness and pugnacity. He invited his father's friend Joseph McCarthy to speak there. But he also invited Ralph Bunche, the black American diplomat who had won a Nobel Peace Prize as a United Nations negotiator. The university was all white, and its seat, Charlottesville, was a Jim Crow town. Bunche stipulated that he would not speak to a segregated audience, and Kennedy insisted that the meeting be integrated and open to the public. When other student leaders hesitated, he told them they were "gutless"—a favorite word of his. Addressing the university's governing board, he grew angry to the point of incoherence. He got his way.

Jack's 1952 Senate race brought the two brothers together in a sustained fashion for the first time and prefigured the genuine closeness that would begin to develop eight years later. "J.F.K. liked to remain above the fray, coolly elegant and sardonic," Thomas writes. "He let Bobby deal with the hacks and favor-seekers, as well as run interference with their father." The governor of Massachusetts, Paul Dever, who was running for reëlection on the same ticket, observed that Jack was the first Irish Brahmin and Bobby the last Irish puritan. It was a Republican year—Dever lost, and General Eisenhower swept the state—but the Kennedys had built their own organization, separate from the Democratic machine, and Jack won by a hair.

For most of Jack's eight years in the Senate, Bobby was down the hall, as a lawyer on the staff of the Permanent Subcommittee on Investigations. His father got him the job, and his initial stint with the committee, when he worked for its Republican chairman, Joseph McCarthy, earned him the lasting mistrust of many liberals. But the work he did, Thomas says, was conscientious and, except by association, unsullied by McCarthy's demagoguery and falsehoods. Bobby's attachment to McCarthy was more personal than ideological. McCarthy had been a visitor to the family compound in Hyannis Port, even an occasional escort of Bobby's sisters Jean and Pat. (Jean recalled his M.O. as a half-hour of chitchat about Commies followed by abrupt, "very hard" kissing. Ugh.) McCarthy's rough-hewn Irishness, his unsophisticated Catholicism, and his resentment of the establishment elite appealed to the truculent adolescent in Bobby. (They did nothing for Jack, who advised his brother against taking the job.) After five months, Bobby quit, frustrated by having to work under McCarthy's chief counsel, the reptilian Roy Cohn. He returned after a brief hiatus, but it was as counsel to the Democratic minority, and his principal antagonist was not some real or imagined Communist but Cohn. The two nearly came to blows during one well-publicized altercation, and Kennedy, by helping Democratic senators like Henry Jackson to bait Cohn during the climactic Army-McCarthy hearings of 1954, actually contributed to McCarthy's downfall. But he continued to defend McCarthy to his appalled friends; one of them, Kenneth O'Donnell, blew up at him at the 1954 Harvard-Yale game, shouting, "What the hell is wrong with you?" Bobby's obtuseness about McCarthy reflected not only his temperament but his upbringing; the clan's insularity and the father's prejudices weighed more heavily on Bobby than on Jack. It took him more than a decade to admit that he had simply been wrong.

When the Democrats recaptured the Senate in the 1954 elections, the committee—urged on by its new chief counsel, Robert Kennedy—shifted its attention to organized crime and labor racketeering, and Kennedy began his long pursuit of Jimmy Hoffa, the thuggish leader of the Teamsters Union. Joe Sr. objected bitterly to this tack, and Thomas credits Doris Kearns Goodwin's view that there was an Oedipal element in it. It was Bobby's declaration of independence, and it was so successful that his fame—aided by his own best-selling book about it, *The Enemy Within*— soon eclipsed that of all but a handful of senators and rivalled his brother's. Nevertheless, when J.F.K. announced for president, Bobby dropped everything to manage the campaign.

IT WAS ANOTHER of Joe Sr.'s ideas that Bobby should be attorney general. The president-elect took a lot of political heat over it, but the fact that Bobby's confirmation was never in doubt shows how profound have been the changes over the past four decades. It would be simply inconceivable for a new president in this new century to announce that he was appointing to his cabinet as the nation's chief law-enforcement officer a person who was (a) his little brother, (b) his campaign manager, (c) barely thirty-five years of age, and (d) wholly without experience in the practice of law. Yet Robert Kennedy turned out to be one of the most energetic and effective attorneys general ever, with a first-rate staff that included Byron White, Nicholas Katzenbach, Burke Marshall, Archibald Cox, John Doar, John Seigenthaler, and Edwin Guthman. He drove them as hard as he drove himself, and he earned their devotion and respect.

The role Bobby played was unique in the history of the presidency, unprecedented and unrepeatable. After the Bay of Pigs fiasco, which took place three months after the inauguration and shook J.F.K.'s confidence in his advisers, Bobby's writ expanded, especially in foreign policy. Because the principal crises in the Kennedy administration concerned either foreign policy or civil rights, and because the personal and political trust between the brothers was very nearly total, Bobby became a kind of informal deputy president.

In Thomas's account of the White House years, three often interweaving themes stand out: Bobby Kennedy's almost pathological obsession with Cuba, his growing understanding of and, finally, identification with the civil-rights movement, and his uneasy relationship with his nominal subordinate J. Edgar Hoover, the director of the Federal Bureau of Investigation.

R.F.K.'s fixation on punishing Fidel Castro produced a plethora of covert (and unsuccessful) sabotage plots and off-the-books task forces with schoolboy names like the Special Group (Augmented) and Operation Mongoose. The C.I.A.'s notorious attempts to use American gangsters to assassinate Castro predated the Kennedys but did not end with their arrival. Thomas painstakingly sifts through the evidence, concluding that if the Kennedys did not know of the assassination intrigues, as seems probable, it was because they chose not to know, and that Bobby's personal pursuit of the secret war against Castro created the atmosphere in which those intrigues flourished. Meanwhile, Kennedy's commendable pressures on Hoover to shift resources away from monitoring the Communist Party (which "couldn't be more feeble and less of a threat, and besides its membership consists largely of F.B.I. agents," the attorney general said at the time, though not to Hoover) were mostly unavailing, and, to the extent that they succeeded, produced horribly ironic results. The bureau's wiretaps on Sam Giancana, the Chicago Mob boss, yielded evidence of murder and extortion, but all of it was unusable in court because the wiretaps were illegal. Nor was that all. The Mafia wiretaps gave Hoover an unlooked-for windfall: through them, he learned of the Mob's and Giancana's involvement in the Castro assassination plots, the tangled relations among Giancana, Frank Sinatra, and President Kennedy, and, best of all from Hoover's point of view, the fact that Giancana and the president were sharing a mistress, a member of Sinatra's circle named Judith Campbell.

Less well known is the case of Ellen Rometsch, who came to Hoover's attention in the middle of 1963, in connection with a Capitol Hill scandal of the time involving Bobby Baker, the secretary of the Senate. Rometsch was twenty-seven, beautiful (like Campbell, she was dark-haired and curvy), an immigrant from East Germany, and a call girl. When, in mid-1963, Hoover unctuously advised R.F.K. of suspicions that she was a Communist spy and was sexually involved with the president, the attorney general arranged to have her deported. She was spirited out of the country on an Air Force transport, accompanied by LaVern Duffy, a colleague of Bobby's from his Senate staff days, who, Thomas notes, "was so close to R.F.K. that he baby-sat for the Kennedy children." (Duffy was also a natural choice for the assignment because he too had been sleeping with Rometsch.) The deportation did not end the danger, however. In October, just weeks before J.F.K.'s final trip to Dallas, the investigative reporter Clark Mollenhoff, of the Des Moines *Register*, picked up the Rometsch trail. His story, headlined U.S. EXPELS GIRL LINKED TO OFFICIALS, came out on October 26th. It named no names but was not especially cryptic. It reported that "an exotic 27-year-old German girl"—a "part-time model and party girl," a "beautiful brunette"—had been deported in August, and that her playmates had included "high executive branch officials" and "prominent New Frontiersmen." Nowadays, as Thomas notes, a story like this would provoke a cable-news feeding frenzy. Then the frenzy was confined to the White House. Thomas's examination of the phone logs shows that the switchboard lit up; the ringing phones included those of, among others, the president, the attorney general, trusted aides like Kenneth O'Donnell and Ed Guthman, J. Edgar Hoover himself, Mollenhoff's publisher John Cowles, and LaVern Duffy. R.F.K., who was worried less about the press than about the Senate's ongoing hearings on the Bobby Baker mess, went to Hoover as a supplicant. Hoover saw to it that the Senate stayed away from Rometsch, a task simplified by the fact that her acquaintances included members of that august body. "In the end," Thomas notes, "the F.B.I. never turned up any solid evidence that she"—Ellen Rometsch—"was either spying for the communists or having sex with President Kennedy."

Nevertheless, it's easy to imagine circumstances under which unsolid evidence would have sufficed. Thomas, in his understated way, shows how close the administration came to self-destructing in a public scandal that would have made the Lewinsky episode look like the social notes in a church newsletter. But the real scandal was, if anything, worse. Thomas's chronology demonstrates that the Rometsch revelations track exactly with R.F.K.'s decisions to approve extensive F.B.I. wiretaps on the telephones of Martin Luther King, Jr.—wiretaps that would later provide Hoover with the raw materials of his vile campaign to destroy King. The dismaying truth is that the Kennedys not only allowed but invited themselves to be blackmailed, and the nation damaged, by the criminal chief of America's secret police.

ROBERT KENNEDY was relaxing on the patio of Hickory Hill, his home in the Virginia suburbs, when a telephone call brought him the news from

Dallas. The caller was J. Edgar Hoover. Malcolm X would say a few days later (and was universally denounced for it) that the chickens had come home to roost. Robert Kennedy evidently thought so, too. That afternoon, he summoned the director of the C.I.A. and demanded to know if his people were responsible; called his closest friend among the Cuban exiles and asked—by way of accusation ("One of your guys did it")—the same question; brooded that Southern racists might be behind the murder; called his staff specialist in the activities of Jimmy Hoffa; called a Chicago labor lawyer who was his best source on the Mafia. But his efforts to find the killer or killers ended there; he was through with playing the prosecutor, and he was evidently afraid of what a thorough inquiry might discover. His Catholic faith offered him little solace; the notion of a beneficent, loving God seemed, for the moment, a mockery. Instead, he sought consolation in the pagan fatalisms of the Greek tragedians and the bleak courage of Camus. He lost himself for months in a dark sea of suffering, deepened, no doubt, by obscure guilts. Thomas:

> Robert Kennedy seemed devoured by grief. He literally shrank, until he appeared wasted and gaunt. His clothes no longer fit, especially his brother's old clothes—an old blue topcoat, a tuxedo, a leather bomber jacket with the presidential seal—which he insisted on wearing and which hung on his narrowing frame. To John Seigenthaler, he appeared to be in physical pain, like a man with a toothache or on the rack. Even walking seemed difficult to him, though he walked for hours, brooding and alone. He admitted to Seigenthaler that he could no longer sleep, and then seemed to regret his confession. He tried to anoint his wounds with daubs of black sarcasm. "Been to any good funerals lately?" he asked one friend. "I don't like to let too many days go by without a funeral," he told another.

The brother and the successor of the slain president disliked one another. Bobby had tried to keep Lyndon Johnson off the ticket in 1960 and had humiliated him in meetings more than once. But the mutual loathing stayed, for the most part, hidden, expressing itself openly only in the sadistic games they played over the vice-presidential nomination for 1964. Bobby could hardly object to the fact that L.B.J. was fulfilling Jack's nascent plans for civil rights and anti-poverty legislation—fulfilling them with a vengeance, so to speak. Vietnam was still a cloud, not yet a storm. Johnson, running against

Barry Goldwater, was the peace candidate in 1964. The Democratic party, including the rank and file of its Kennedy wing, was still in love with L.B.J.; during that brief honeymoon, the new president's crudeness was still seen as more endearing than repellent—an expression of Bunyanesque, larger-than-life Americanness.

At the 1964 Democratic Convention, in Atlantic City, Johnson—who, baselessly, feared a revolt—made sure that Bobby's appearance, to introduce a film about his late brother, was delayed until after the president and his running mate, Hubert Humphrey, were safely nominated. In the darkened convention hall, Bobby stood alone and unsmiling in a cone of light as, for twenty long minutes, the vast throng roared and wept. (I was in the hall that afternoon, and it was then that I became a Bobbyphile.) His words were modest and moving. Thomas writes (as does Schlesinger, by the way) that he "concluded" the speech with a verse from *Romeo and Juliet*—

> *When he shall die,*
> *Take him and cut him out in little stars,*
> *And he will make the face of heaven so fine*
> *That all the world will be in love with night,*
> *And pay no worship to the garish sun.*

—in which "the allusion to the 'garish sun' was obvious and galling to the followers of Lyndon Johnson." That interpretation exaggerates Bobby's hostile intentions, if in fact he had any. The Shakespeare passage, which had been suggested to Bobby by Jacqueline Kennedy, comes not at the end but seven paragraphs before it; the speech actually concludes with some lines from Frost ("And miles to go before I sleep"). Midway between the two quotations, Kennedy says, "The same effort and the same energy and the same dedication that was given to President John F. Kennedy must be given to President Lyndon Johnson and Hubert Humphrey." Whatever their personal feelings toward each other, Johnson and Kennedy were political and substantive allies in 1964. Ten weeks after the convention, Kennedy rode to victory in the New York Senate race on Johnson's coattails; his slogan was not "Kennedy for Senator" but "Johnson-Humphrey-Kennedy." Bobby won by seven hundred thousand votes, but he ran a full two million behind L.B.J. in the state. "I guess I pulled you through up here," the senator-elect deadpanned to the president on Election Night.

During the three and a half years left to him between his Senate swearing-in and the pistol shots in Los Angeles, Kennedy lived his life at a pitch of almost unbearable intensity. He seemed forever lashing his courage in a desperate race with his fears. He performed a series of feats of physical daring, some premeditated (he rafted dangerous rapids; though afraid of heights, he grimly scaled the highest unclimbed peak in North America, which Canada had renamed Mt. Kennedy), some spontaneous (he leaped from a yacht into icy Maine waters to retrieve his brother's bomber jacket; he swam through heavy seas to a Coast Guard cutter because he had received word that a daughter of his had been injured). The hero worship that he had once lavished on generals like Maxwell Taylor and Edward Lansdale now bonded him to nonviolent warriors like Cesar Chavez, the saintly leader of the farm workers' union. The former enthusiast of "counterinsurgency" (Kennedy coined the term, Michael Forrestal, a national-security staffer, told Thomas) and goad of the C.I.A. now met secretly with the leader of South Africa's anti-apartheid students, showing him how to disrupt electronic listening devices by jumping up and down on the floor.

As the war in Vietnam escalated and Kennedy's opposition to it deepened, his private race between fear and courage played out as indecision over whether to challenge Johnson for the 1968 nomination. Kennedy feared not only defeat but the destruction of his party, not only the loss of his political career and maybe his life but also the possibility that the antiwar message would be drowned out by the noise of clashing ambitions. In the months before the primaries, Ethel Kennedy, Walter Lippmann, and the antiwar organizer Allard Lowenstein begged him to run; among those who begged him not to were Kenneth O'Donnell, Arthur Schlesinger, and "the Two Teds," Kennedy and Sorensen. Bobby had everything to lose; Eugene McCarthy, who answered Lowenstein's call after Bobby agonized and declined, had everything to gain. Not until the beginning of March did Kennedy determine to take the leap. Almost offhandedly, he decided to wait until after the New Hampshire primary, on March 12th, to make his announcement. He did not wish to upstage—anyway, to be seen as upstaging—McCarthy's children's crusade.

Big mistake. The hatred and contempt that rained down on Kennedy from McCarthy's (almost all white and middle-class) supporters would be hard to credit unless one felt it oneself—as I did, from many of my friends— though it was more than matched by the love of his (mostly minority or working-class) followers. The campaign, which for Bobby lasted only twelve weeks, was a howling, deafening wind tunnel. Johnson dropped out two weeks after Kennedy jumped in. The tested tactics of Jack's old advance man Jerry Bruno—book a hall too small for the expected crowd, the better to whip up sweat and excitement—were counterproductive when deployed for Bobby: the near-hysteria of his supporters, and the candidate's own emotionalism, reminded voters of the disorder in the streets, which exploded after Martin Luther King was murdered, on April 4th. Bobby won in Indiana but was defeated in Oregon—the first time, Thomas notes, that a son of Joseph Kennedy had ever lost an election. Bobby's victory in California, on June 9th, was less than overwhelming; he won a plurality but not a majority.

"The inevitability of Kennedy's triumph—at the Democratic Convention in August and in the presidential election in November—has long since hardened into myth," Thomas writes. That view is indeed myth, though it is also myth that historians agree with it. No one can say with certainty what would have happened—the year and the country were too volatile for that—but the likelihood is that, while Kennedy would have eventually seized the antiwar banner from McCarthy, the nomination would still have gone to Humphrey, who entered no primaries at all. If a Kennedy victory had begun to look probable, things might have got very ugly indeed. The recipient of J. Edgar Hoover's useful, poisonous memos was now Lyndon Johnson.

After Bobby was killed, many of his supporters immediately began campaigning for McCarthy, though he never deigned to ask us to. My McCarthy friends had railed against Bobby—his ruthlessness, his presumption, his opportunism. All the same, they mourned him. As some of them told me, they had assumed, somewhere in the back of their minds, that the day would come—maybe not that year, but eventually—when they, too, would be supporters of Robert Kennedy for president. His death put them in the unhappy position of someone whose estranged parent or brother has died before there could be a settling of accounts and a reconciliation.

Rose Kennedy, Thomas tells us, heard the news of her third son's death on television the next morning as she was dressing for Mass in Hyannis Port. A little later, she was seen in the driveway of her house, bouncing a ball like a small child. Inside, old Joseph Kennedy—who, since suffering a massive stroke in late 1961, had uttered not a word except "no," which he said

often, angrily and repeatedly: "No, no, no, no!"—sobbed inconsolably. A funeral train brought the coffin from New York to Washington, moving slowly
past huge, silent crowds all along the route.

"IN THE YEARS since his brother's death, Kennedy had shown a capacity for growth," Thomas writes, "but the myth of his transformation, like
most Kennedy legends, has been exaggerated." I'm not so sure. It is the biographer's business to find the connecting threads in apparent discontinuities—to see in the child the father of the man. But the change in Kennedy
was not merely a matter of growth. After Dallas, no more was heard of his
get-Castro and get-Hoffa obsessions. He was finished with getting people.
His commitment to the cause of racial equality, tinged with resentment
and defensiveness during the White House years, was something akin to
total. His identification with the dispossessed had melded with, in some
ways even superseded, his identification with the clan; the choked tender-
ness and cold anger were the same, but their objects had changed. Winning
was still better than losing, but it was no longer the only thing.

Robert Kennedy, on his own, left no great legislative legacy, founded no
great institution, led no great movement. His most extraordinary accomplishment—and it was extraordinary—was to embody in himself, and create in others, a kind of transcendent yearning for the possibility of
redemptive change. Thomas has persuaded me that the Bobby I imagined—
the beautiful existential hero—was a less complicated figure, less shadowed
and tormented by darknesses of his own and his family's making, than the
Bobby who lived and died. As much because of that as in spite of it, the
poster stays on the wall.

—The New Yorker, November 20, 2000

3. SPEECHIFYIN'

I have a professional interest in this topic, acquired the hard way: four years of unremitting toil as a drafter of addresses, proclamations, jokes, and casual remarks for President Jimmy Carter, in whose service I eventually acquired the Gilbert and Sullivanish title, at once grandiose and humiliating, of "Chief Speechwriter to the President." President Carter was not an easy man to be a speechwriter "to," mostly for reasons that reflected well on him, such as a dislike of artifice, a feeling that there was something wrong with the whole idea of hiring someone to tell you what to say, and an aversion to bullshit—other people's, at any rate. No doubt vanity and stubbornness (his, not mine) also played a role. Mr. Carter was not a particularly good deliverer of prepared speeches, except when he cared to be, but this was less of a problem for me than my non-speechwriting friends often assumed. People pay attention to what a president says, whether or not he pauses for emphasis in the right places. Sometimes they even read the text.

I became a speechwriter haphazardly. In 1976, through my friend Jeff Greenfield, now of CNN, whom I had known since the early sixties, I heard about a temporary job writing speeches for Hugh Carey, then the governor of New York. A few months later, having satisfied my curiosity about

Albany, I drifted back to *The New Yorker*. A few months after that, James Fallows was putting together a "speechwriting shop" for President-elect Carter. Jim called an old *Washington Monthly* friend of his, Suzannah Lessard. Suzannah, like me, was a *New Yorker* staff writer. (We barely knew each other, which was typical of the magazine.) Jim asked Suzannah if she knew someone, anyone, who knew how to write a speech. Suzannah said no, but offered to go down the hall and put the question to Andy Logan, our city hall correspondent, who was a kind of office den mother. Andy said, "How about Rick Hertzberg?" So it was off to Washington, where I spent most of the next fifteen years.

The White House job was extraordinarily satisfying, notwithstanding horrible luck (oil crises, stagflation, hostages) and political defeat. The satisfaction had less to do with speechwriting per se than with the experience of being part of a serious political enterprise which, despite frustrations and disagreements, corresponded with the general arc of my beliefs and values. Of course, the element of boyish fun should not be underestimated: to travel everywhere by motorcade and Air Force One within a bubble that feels as if it's at the center of the whole world's attention is to partake of pure narcissistic pleasure. But there was more. The combination of high stakes and a ticking clock made for an intensity that cranked up the senses like a powerful drug. And there was the pleasure of total commitment, the exhilaration and comradeship of combat without the chaos and terror of violence. As awful as I felt after Carter's defeat in the 1980 election, I think I would have felt worse if I had not worked my heart out to trying to prevent it.

All the essays in this section are informed by that experience in one way or another, though none of them are directly about it. Most are about the speeches of presidents or would-be presidents. Some are about the uses of rhetoric in a broader sense. Only the first is an actual speech, and that one is basically a joke. It is an "address," delivered by me, to the founding dinner of an association of former White House speechwriters, an association which exists solely to have self-congratulatory dinners. Speaking of self-congratulation, I'd like to take this opportunity to record that the idea of forming such an association was mine, as was the notion of naming it the Judson Welliver Society. The person who did something about it—who did everything about it—was William Safire. That is why he is honored, and properly so, as the founder. I take a certain pride, however, in being the Paine to Safire's Washington, the Greece to his Rome, the Hegel to his Marx, the Briton Hadden to his Henry R. Luce, the John the Baptist to his—but this is beginning to sound distressingly like a speech.

IN PRAISE OF JUDSON WELLIVER

MY FELLOW SPEECHWRITERS:

We come tonight to honor many things and many people. We honor our host and founder, Brother William Safire. We honor the profession of speechwriting. We honor the statesmen and politicians, great and small, for whom we have toiled in that trade. But most of all, we come to honor—to praise, even to revere—ourselves. Because if we don't do it, nobody else will.

As part of honoring ourselves, we honor the man whose quiet, selfless, pioneering work made it all possible for us who followed him.

Now, I know that there are those who say that Alexander Hamilton, not Judson Welliver, was the first White House speechwriter. And it must be admitted that on occasion Hamilton did work up some language for his boss, President Washington. (By the way, if you think I had problems, imagine trying to write a speech for a guy who had *wooden* teeth.)

But we know better than to accord Hamilton the honor. First of all, there was no White House back then, so by definition there could be no White House speechwriter. And, second, Hamilton was not a speechwriter at all but was in fact the natural enemy of the presidential speechwriter—one of the many natural enemies of the presidential speechwriter—a cabinet officer.

No, it was Judson Churchill Welliver—may his name henceforth be as famous as it has heretofore been obscure—who was the first person in the history of the republic ever to be employed in the capacity already mentioned. Our source for this is no less than Irwin Hood "Ike" Hoover, whose service as Head Usher stretched from the presidency of Benjamin Harrison to that of Franklin D. Roosevelt. Permit me to read, in very nearly its entirety, a short chapter from Ike Hoover's memoir, *42 Years in the White House*. The chapter is entitled "A New White House Office: The Professional Speech-Writer:

> Until the time of Harding, all the presidents, so far as I know, wrote their own speeches. With his coming a man was appointed to prepare whatever set and formal speeches he was called upon to make. The first man to hold this office was Judson Welliver, a widely known newspaper man. He had been with the president through the campaign, being close to the throne, so to speak, and naturally came along to the White House. No doubt he had made himself useful along this very line during the campaign and it was most natural that he should be kept on.
>
> When Coolidge came, he found Welliver on the job and continued to employ him, no doubt finding him a very handy man. . . .
>
> As the whole scheme was a new one, there were many embarrassments for the individual holding down this job. For example, there was no legal appropriation for his salary. It was skimmed from here, there, and everywhere. At one time it was taken from the fund for the payment of chauffeurs and the upkeep of the garage.
>
> Much jealousy was also aroused by this office. The regular secretaries seemed to resent the fact that, owing to the confidential nature of the work, the man holding this job had an entrée to the president which they themselves did not enjoy. He seemed always to be a separate part of the Executive Offices, under orders of no one but the president.

The life of Welliver, like the life of any saint, is well worth studying. We know as yet relatively little about this great man, for the field of Welliver studies is still in its infancy. We do know that he was born on August 13, 1870, in Aledo, Illinois. We know that he worked for newspapers as varied as the Sioux City *Journal,* the Des Moines *Leader,* and the Sioux City *Tribune*. We know that in the first decade of this century he served as an editorial writer for the *Washington Times*—a position that even today would be regarded as ideal preparation for White House service. And finally, we know that the most inspiring and exemplary moment of his career came immediately after the White House years, in 1925, when he resigned from the service of President Coolidge to accept the position of public relations director for the American Petroleum Institute. Here truly was a man ahead of his time—a man of genuinely modern sensibilities—a man, indeed, who would be comfortable here in this room tonight.

So much, then, for the man. What of the work?

Most of Welliver's finest work as a speechwriter was done in the service of candidate and then President Warren Gamaliel Harding. And so, while Welliver is properly revered by all speechwriters, he is especially sacred to those scribes who have written for that select group of presidents who—whether deservedly or not—are seldom if ever quoted by their successors. Judson Welliver is indeed the patron saint of the unquotables. It is now more than sixty years since the Harding administration was so tragically cut short. Despite the unkind things said about the prose of that administration by H. L. Mencken and others, the work of Harding and Welliver is coming to be recognized and appreciated by specialists. For example, as noted in the authoritative reference *Safire's Political Dictionary,* Harding and thus Welliver coined the term "Founding Fathers." Yet even the passage of six decades has not made it any easier for a tired speechwriter, groping for a peroration at three o'clock in the morning, to end a draft by inserting some appropriate quote introduced by the phrase, "In the immortal words of Warren G. Harding . . ."

Tonight, let us right this great wrong. Let us quote Warren G. Harding— or, rather, let us quote our own Founding Father, Judson Welliver, as he spoke through the strangely marionette-like figure of the great Gamaliel.

On world trade:

"The United States should adopt a protective tariff of such a character as will help the struggling industries of Europe get on their feet."

On the legacy of the 1914–1918 war:

"Here is the chief difficulty of the world today. In the turbulence and upheaval of World War, when all humanity was distracted and distressed, the vandals who operate amid calamity have sought to hoot suffering civilization."

"Have sought to hoot suffering civilization"—what a marvelous phrase.

On the duties of the press:

"There's good in everybody. Boost—don't knock."

On Japan:

"We know little about Japan."

On thinking:

"Normal thinking will help more. And normal living will have the effect of a magician's wand, paradoxical as the statement seems. The world does deeply need to get normal, and liberal doses of mental science will help mightily."

On normalcy—from perhaps Welliver's finest speech, the address to the Home Market Club of Boston on May 14, 1920:

"America's present need is not heroics but healing; not nostrums, but normalcy; not revolution, but restoration; not agitation, but adjustment; not surgery, but serenity; not the dramatic, but the dispassionate; not experiment, but equipoise; not submergence in internationality, but sustainment in triumphant nationality."

Finally, let me conclude with a passage from a lesser-known but perhaps more typical work of Welliver, the address at the General Grant Dinner—edited very slightly to remove gratuitous partisan references. Savor, if you will, its sublime, incomparable emptiness. Truly, this is a speech for all seasons:

Mr. Toastmaster, in that retrospection which makes for inspiration, there grows the conviction that progress, written in half a century of accomplishment, seems more like the miracle of a national destiny than the story of a political party and its tasks in statecraft. But the truth abides, incomparable and incontrovertible. We have not only made a nation, rough-hewn and popularly governed, the marvel of development among great nations; we have contributed to the uplift and elevated the standard of living; we have not only become leaders in finance and industry; we have not only become equals in education and rivals in art, but we are the inspiration and example of other republics, and ought to be, could be, influencing the idealization of the government of the earth. It justifies our pride in the past, explains the nation-wide turning to the party for the country's restoration, and gives every assurance of glorious triumphs in the future.

Now that's what I call *speechwriting*.

—Address at the founding dinner of the Judson Welliver Society, an association of former White House speechwriters, *The Washington Post*, October 20, 1985

WASCALLY WOSS

COME NOVEMBER, it looks like, the elephant and the donkey are lookin' to get their sorry gray butts kicked by a rampagin' . . . a rampagin' what? Which of our furry or feathered friends ought to have the honor of becoming the official mascot of the Ross for Boss presidential campaign? The personal choice of the candidate himself would undoubtedly be the eagle, as in "Eagles don't flock" (ruggedly individualistic slogan of candidate) and *On Wings of Eagles* (drugstore paperback about candidate's hostage-freeing heroics). But that would be a little too contrived, don't you think? A bit of a cliché? No, the better way is to look for a creature that springs unbidden from the candidate's unconscious.

As it happens, Perot is haunted by a beast along these very lines. In the payoff sound bite from his March 17 appearance at the National Press Club, the Texas Billionaire reminded the electorate of his up-front conditions for condescending to become our president. "If ordinary people in fifty states went out on the streets," the T.B. instructed, "on their own initiative, not programmed, not orchestrated like **rabbits** the way we try to do everything now, did it on their own and put me on the ballot in all fifty states—not forty-eight, not forty-nine, but fifty—then I would run." Good, good—but what color rabbits? Presciently, Perot had already given the answer, in the famous Larry King interview of February 20. "We're the owners of this country," he said. "We don't act like the owners. We act like **white rabbits** that get programmed by messages coming out of Washington."

Encouraged by rising poll numbers, Perot has been developing the leporine theme, especially with respect to the abortion issue: In another CNN interview, this one with Robert Novak, the T.B. argued that "there's far more to it than just the woman's choice. We are not **rabbits**. We are thinking, reasoning human beings." A few seconds later he added: "It's more complex than just saying 'the woman's right.' We are not **rabbits**." On the line to Diane Rehm's call-in program on Washington's public radio station WAMU-FM, he put it this way: "Can we agree that each human life is precious? And surely we can. And can we agree that we are not **rabbits**?" A few days later, talking to Dan Balz of the *Washington Post:* "You will always hear me say never forget, we aren't **rabbits**, we are thinking, reasoning human beings. . . . Now, it is absolutely irresponsible for two thinking, reasoning human beings to get drunk, get high, get pregnant, and get an abortion just because they act like **rabbits**." And on a second appearance on Larry King's TV show, April 16: "We are not **rabbits**. We are thinking, reasoning human beings. . . . We aren't **rabbits**. Let's just—See, I can generally get a consensus on that, Larry."

O.K., Ross, have it your way: we aren't rabbits. Even—no, especially—those of us who are presidential candidates with unusually large ears.

As everyone knows, Perot has been getting a bit testy lately. ("You're off on an absolute **rabbit** chase," he snapped the other day when a CNN investigative reporter inquired about one of his quasi-military adventures.) But he was affable—expansive, even—when a caller on that April 16 Larry King show asked him if he belongs to any clubs that exclude Jews or blacks. "Yes, I do," he replied forthrightly.

KING: And?

PEROT: And I go there about once a year. And all my Jewish friends in Dallas, they've had a great deal of fun with me over this. If it bothers the people—

KING: Why don't you quit?

PEROT:—I will quit immediately. But I have to tell you this story. So my Jewish pals one day gave me a mezuzah as a gift, and they said, "Now you can put this on your door, Perot." And I said, "Well, which door?" They says, "Any door you want to." And this was all in great spirit, as you can imagine. So a few days go by and they come back to me. They all know that maybe once a year I'll go down there for a lunch or something like that. I don't play golf, don't have a golf locker. They all know that. And the reason we belong is, it's a good safe place for the children to swim—that sort of thing. They come back in a few days and say, "Perot, have you put your mezuzah up?" And I say, "It's up." They says, "Where did you put it?" I says, "I've got it on my locker door at the country club." And they all says, "My gosh, Perot, they'll throw you out!" I says, "No, nobody knows what it is. It's absolutely safe."

KING: Why—Why—

PEROT: So around Dallas it's not a problem. If it's a problem—

KING: But why belong to a club that excludes anything, anyone?

PEROT: The only reason is it's a safe—I have an interesting problem in terms of security—it's a safe place for my family to swim and do things like that. We don't use it that much. In terms of is it—I would sort of—You know, from my point of view, I'll save the dues.

Or was that "I'll save the Jews"? Either way, it must be acknowledged that Perot's jocular though unironic use of the some-of-my-best-friends defense is anachronistic at best. No doubt this reflects insularity rather than actual prejudice. (Perot is a deeply provincial figure.) It is harder to find a charitable explanation for his fantastic claim that his membership in restricted country clubs (not one but two of them, by the way) is dictated by the quest for a safe place to swim. If that is truly the grail he seeks, he needn't search so far. There is a perfectly adequate swimming pool on the grounds of his own house. It is not far from the tennis courts, hard by the riding stables, and is only a short walk from the two-story family athletic complex containing basketball court, Nautilus machines, bowling alley, racquetball court, and weight room. And indoor swimming pool, in case the outdoor one has been seized by terrorists.

The mascot question remains. Some will object to the designation of the rabbit on the ground that Perot's feelings about the creature are in some sense negative. I admit that some of his statements might be open to such an interpretation. For example, his remark to a *Life* magazine interviewer in 1988 that "people don't change from lions into **rabbits** in midflight." (If they did: *On Feet of Rabbits*.) Or this comment six months ago, when he was telling the *Los Angeles Times* that the research laboratories of American car and computer companies harbor too much irrelevant work: "You go back in research centers, electronic companies, car companies, you may find a guy with **white rabbits**. What does that have to do with making a better computer or a better car?" But a case can be made that the T.B. actually loves bunnies. How else to explain the news, reported by *Computerworld* for May 21, 1990, that a computer firm called Atlantix Corp. has "named **Rabbit Software Corp.** founder and former executive Charles Robins as president"? The man from Rabbit was brought on board, the story continues, "in the wake of a major equity investment received in March from The Perot Group, an investment group headed by industry entrepreneur H. Ross Perot." Maybe the "H" stands for "Harvey."

—Washington Diarist, *The New Republic,* June 29, 1992

SPEEDING TICKET

ON THURSDAY, JULY 9, 1992, the presidential campaign of Bill Clinton ascended to the mystic plane of political satori, where, with ever-mounting bliss, it remains. That was the day Clinton chose Al Gore to be his running mate, a metaphor the two have since made literal with their daily tandem jog. Even those of us who thought the choice of Gore would be a good one had no idea it would turn out to be a magical one. The whole ticket seems to be vastly greater than the sum of its two parts. The unlooked-for synergy of the Gore choice ignited the campaign for its breathtaking acceleration through a nearly perfect convention and on into its sequel, the triumphal bus tour (if that's not an oxymoron) across the Rust Belt. In picking Gore, Clinton rejected balance, that false god of politics (and journalism), in favor of amplification and consistency—harmonic convergence, you might say. Balance, at least of the conventional kind (regional, ideological, generational), is an act of cautious calculation. Amplification is an act of self-confidence, of clarity. The one aims for equilibrium, the other for dynamism. Of course, it helps when what is being amplified is youth, energy, intelligence, and open-mindedness.

Nothing actually happened at the convention in the way of concrete events except parties and speeches. The best of the former must have been one I missed, though Monday night's boozy reunion of old McGovernites, where Arnold Schwarzenegger, son-in-law of McGovern's No. 2 No. 2 Sargent Shriver, stood bicep by jowl with a succession of diminutive lefties, was pretty good. The best of the latter was Mario Cuomo's nominating address for Clinton. The libretto had some brilliant lines; the music, however, was the thing, and it was grand opera. As in his national debut during the 1984 season, Maestro Cuomo used his Italian baritone to devastating effect. The most striking aspect of his performance, also as in '84, was his effortless control of the audience. With outstretched palms and sinuous body movements he played the crowd like a resonating instrument, damping and releasing its roars as if touching the pedals and pistons of some great cathedral organ. All admired the Cuomo speech; but unlike eight years (or eight months) ago, few indulged fantasies of "if only." By now we know this Pavarotti will never be Rudolf Bing. The difference is that in 1984 Cuomo showed the Democrats something they otherwise lacked; his masterfulness contrasted with the party's lassitude. In 1992 his speech was an act of feudal fealty, an expression of Clinton's power rather than his own.

EVERY DEMOCRATIC CONVENTION has its emotional high point. Two stand out in my memory: the twenty-two-minute ovation for Robert F. Kennedy in 1964, and the closing tableau of racial and regional healing in 1976, when the first ever nominee from the Old Confederacy stood surrounded by blacks and whites singing "We Shall Overcome." This year's festivities had nothing to match either of those in political meaning or depth of feeling. The 1992 high point was light and joyful: it came when Gore, buoyed by music and applause after his acceptance speech, swept the divine Tipper into his arms for a dance. And why not? The speech had been good by any standard, awesome by Gore-in-'88 standards. Unlike Clinton's shapeless, endless mess, which stopped just short of being bad enough to spoil the convention's by then firmly established story line of unmitigated success, Gore's address was crisply written. And well delivered: the Gore who called down thunderbolts upon the Republicans in Madison Square Garden was not so much wooden as Woden.

I wept buckets during Gore's recounting of his son's near-fatal accident. It didn't occur to me at the time that there might be something exploitative about it, or about the avalanche of intimate details set forth in the two acceptance speeches and the films preceding them: not just Gore's son's ordeal and Gore's sister's death from lung cancer but also Clinton's father's death in a car crash before he was born, his stepfather's drunken violence against his mother, his separation from mom at age three, her breast cancer, how he met his wife and proposed to her, what his daughter looked like ("all sqwunched up") as she emerged from his wife's womb while he watched, how he took care of his wayward brother, and, of course, how his daughter reacted to his and his wife's televised discussion of their marital difficulties. You can't really blame Clinton and Gore for foisting all this on the public. The "character issue" is there, the "family values issue" is there, and they must be dealt with. The fact that we have to hear about young Bill Clinton threatening to coldcock his stepdad is an unintended consequence of the press defenestration of Gary Hart four years ago. The problem is that once all the "positive" personal stuff that supposedly attests to good "character" gets trotted out, it becomes harder to argue that the "negative" personal stuff is none of anybody's business.

One thing's for sure: if F.D.R. were running today, his aides would wear little gold wheelchairs on their lapels. And John F. Kennedy's 1960 acceptance speech written under 1992 conditions would have sounded less like Cicero and more like Geraldo. No doubt it would've started out with a vivid description of precisely how his brother Joe was killed in World War II, tying that in with the theme of sacrifice as well as the need to find peaceful solutions. Then a couple of grafs on his mentally retarded sister, Rosemary, and how her plight brought all the members of the family closer together while sensitizing them to the issue of community-based health care. Something about the candidate's chronic back pain as a metaphor for economic suffering, and a line or two about how his experiences as a recovering cortisone addict deepened his commitment to making drug treatment available to all who seek it. Nor would a reference to how much he had learned about compassion and understanding from living in a dysfunctional family with an intermittently pro-Nazi dad be out of place, along with a candid acknowledgment of the now-overcome troubles in his own marriage. The strumpet summons us again. . . .

—New York Diarist, *The New Republic*, August 10, 1992

TWO SPEECHES

PRESIDENT CLINTON had barely stepped back from the rostrum after delivering his Inaugural Address before people began comparing it—unfavorably, on the whole—with John F. Kennedy's. Clinton was faulted for being too much like Kennedy, and for being too little like him—for aping him, and for not aping him. Clinton's speech, one gathered, borrowed shamelessly from Kennedy's, with which, one gathered, it had nothing in common. Some observers pointed disapprovingly to the similarities, from the opening sentence of each address (Kennedy said that the day was "a celebration of freedom" which signified "renewal as well as change"; Clinton said, "Today we celebrate the mystery of American renewal," and a couple of lines later he noted the need for "change"), through matching calls for public responsibility (Kennedy said, "In your hands, my fellow citizens, more than mine, will rest the final success or failure of our course"; Clinton said, "My fellow Americans, you, too, must play your part in our renewal"), to the parallel evocations of generational transition (Kennedy called his contemporaries "a new generation of Americans, born in this century, tempered by war, disciplined by a hard and bitter peace, proud of our ancient heritage"; Clinton said, "Today, a generation raised in the shadows of the Cold War assumes new responsibilities in a world warmed by the sunshine of freedom but threatened still by ancient hatreds and new plagues"; Kennedy said, "Now the trumpet summons us again"; Clinton said, "We have heard the trumpets, we have changed the guard"). Other observers pointed, also disapprovingly, to the differences, grumbling that Clinton's language, unlike Kennedy's, did not sing, his rhetoric did not soar, his calls for service were insufficiently stately and cadenced.

Of course, the Kennedy comparison is not one that President Clinton can complain about. He has gone to some trouble to encourage it. He mentioned Kennedy often on the stump (but not, interestingly, in his inaugural text, which mentioned only Jefferson and Roosevelt among Democratic presidents); he affects certain Kennedyish mannerisms (the thumb-topped fist jab, the stiff slouch with hand in jacket pocket); and a black-and-white clip of a glowing sixteen-year-old Clinton meeting President Kennedy in a Rose Garden reception line was the climax of Clinton's convention film. But it would have been natural to compare the two presidents—both of them conspicuously vigorous men in their forties, both of them reform-minded centrist Democrats succeeding Republicans old enough to be their fathers—even if Clinton had not invited it. And it is natural, and instructive, to compare the words they spoke and the thoughts they chose to express at the beginning of their presidencies.

It's true that Clinton's address was far less polished than Kennedy's. (Clinton's opening metaphor about the changing seasons—"in the depth of winter . . . we force the spring"—owed more to Chauncey Gardiner than to Cicero.) Kennedy was a writer by trade (insofar as he had a trade beyond politics), while Clinton's vocation—not just his profession—has been that of government executive. But part of what gave Kennedy's speech its elegance was how firmly anchored it was in the simple (in retrospect) dualities of the Cold War. From the distance of thirty-two years, this is its most striking aspect. Kennedy's speech didn't just emphasize foreign affairs in general and the Soviet-American competition in particular, it was about absolutely nothing else. The context of its most famous line—"Ask not," etc.—is unmistakably that of global struggle. Kennedy's only reference to the domestic problems that Americans were facing in 1961 came at the end of the "new generation" passage, where he spoke of "those human rights to which this nation has always been committed, and to which we are committed today at home and around the world." Two words—"at home"—out of a text of nearly fourteen hundred: that was the total treatment of domestic policy in John F. Kennedy's Inaugural Address.

In more ways than one, Clinton's address was made of homelier stuff than Kennedy's. All the same, it was a good speech, even a very good speech, and remarkable for having been written mostly by its deliverer. It was frank in its recital of American ills, consistent in its appeals for renewal and change, surprisingly brief (Clinton, as many noted, not only called for discipline but exercised it), and, in its fashion, eloquent. Clinton took the generational theme a step further than Kennedy had, using it as a bridge to the idea of investment in and sacrifice for the future well-being of American society. Some observers deplored the strain of conservatism in Clinton's emphasis on discipline, on responsibilities as well as rights, but in fact his entire speech was an implicit refutation of the laissez-faire that has dominated American government for the past twelve years and an explicit endorsement of the need for, and the nobility of, public action to attack a whole range of public ills: economic stagnation, poverty, crime, health-care costs, environmental degradation, AIDS, political corruption, and more.

According to Kennedy's co-worker, Theodore C. Sorensen, it was the president-elect himself who banished any such matters from his Inaugural Address. "Let's drop out the domestic stuff altogether," Kennedy told Sorensen. "It's too long anyway." Kennedy, Sorensen writes in his memoir, thought that each attempt to outline domestic goals sounded partisan, divisive, "too much like the campaign." It is to Bill Clinton's credit that his Inaugural Address sounded very much like the campaign.

In 1961, the combination of Cold War and Kennedy cool made for a speech that yielded more fire than warmth. Clinton, in contrast, said, "This is our time. Let us embrace it," and he was eager, last week, to embrace every living thing that came within his reach. Clinton is an unusual character. If he is, in his way, Kennedy's political son, he is also, in his earthiness, his populism, and his hunger for power, Lyndon Johnson's, and, in his earnestness and empathy, Hubert Humphrey's. But Clinton's graceful farewell to George Bush, the last president of Kennedy's generation, was also a farewell to his own Democratic forebears.

Between Kennedy's time and Clinton's, a series of moral and practical failures at the highest level gave rise to widespread public alienation from politics. In recent months, that alienation has shown a few small signs of lessening, but if public trust in the institutions of self-government is truly to be restored, so must the link between what candidates say and what presidents do. No one expects President Clinton to keep every promise he made in his long march to the White House. But by reiterating main themes and goals of his campaign in his Inaugural Address he has taken an essential first step.

—*The New Yorker*, February 1, 1993

BIG TALK

SO MANY WORDS! At the national political conventions just completed, a couple of hundred thousand of them issued from the podiums—and that was on top of millions more poured forth at caucus meetings, delegation meetings, press conferences, and panel discussions, and into the microphones of an immense journalistic horde. Cascades of words, cataracts of words, great rolling tsunamis of words—all spoken for the purpose not of enlightening or entertaining, or even tricking, the public but of inducing it, by any verbal means necessary (including enlightenment, entertainment, and trickery, if that's what it takes), to vote the right way come November.

So little meaning! For when the object of the game is to sway the emotions of the largest possible masses of people vagueness is a precision tool. Politicians are not essayists; their purpose is not to make themselves clear but to make themselves, and their ideas, acceptable to a fleeting majority. The more precise a formulation is, the more it invites disagreement. If the essayist is a sculptor, chipping away at each thought until its significance is exact and unmistakable, the politician is a truck driver, hauling as much raw granite as his vehicle will hold. Both follow honorable trades, but each of them bears watching by the other.

In the verbal war for political domination, the big guns are the focus-group-tested "themes"—the Republicans' "Restoring the American Dream," the Democrats' "Putting Families First," the endlessly repeated references to values, strength, community, opportunity, diversity, work, responsibility, and the like. The parties invest enormous quantities of energy, ingenuity, and money in trying to create associations in the public mind between themselves and feel-good bromides of this kind. But there's some small-calibre ordnance lying around, too.

For example, the minute Bob Dole selected Jack Kemp as his running mate, a drumbeat went up from operatives of the Clinton campaign. Senator Christopher Dodd, the Democratic Party's general chairman, immediately went around describing Kemp's views as "totally out of the mainstream." George Stephanopoulos, a senior adviser to the president, added, "His economic ideas, while interesting, are certainly outside the mainstream, and in some cases even flaky." And deputy campaign manager Ann Lewis, speaking of Kemp's hard line on abortion, chimed in, "Let us be clear that is an extreme position. That is not in the mainstream." The chorus continued right through the Democratic Convention, and it shows no signs of letting up.

It's not true, of course. Kemp's views may indeed be flaky (as is, arguably, his attachment to the gold standard). They may even be extreme (as is, certainly, his support for a constitutional amendment that would criminalize abortion in all instances). But, by definition, the long-held, well-known views of a major-party candidate for national office cannot be outside the mainstream. Beyond that, though, this sanctification of the mainstream as a political Ganges, a sacred river whose waters cleanse all impurities, is a thoroughly bad business. Mainstream-mongering suggests that the test of an idea is not logic, reason, or merit but conventionality. It implies that an unpopular, or even an unfamiliar, idea is per se a bad idea. Yet the list of ideas that were good many years before they were mainstream is a long and distinguished one; it includes abolitionism, woman suffrage, social security, child-labor laws, and the income tax. Without tributaries, the mainstream dries up.

The season's most noticeable vogue word, however, is an innocent-sounding preposition. Having been thoroughly tested by the advertising and fashion industries, "about" has now become the new universal solvent of political language. Everything is about something, and, by contrast, is not about something else. The Republican Party is about inclusion. The Democratic Party is about working families. The Reform Party is about—or not about—Ross Perot. The beauty of "about" is that it suggests some sort of causal or programmatic relationship without having to specify one. "About" represents a technological leap over its predecessor, the verb "to address." Addressing problems long ago became the rhetorical substitute for solving them. But "addressing" calls a little too much attention to its own cluelessness. If "addressing" is a vacuum tube, the far speedier and more versatile "about" is a silicon chip.

The country's leading aboutnik, of course, is Bob ("That's what Bob Dole's all about") Dole. Yet the Republican nominee's acceptance speech in San Diego contained not a single instance of that invidious usage. More remarkably, it contained scarcely a single cliché, even in the pedestrian—and occasionally (such as an attack on United Nations Secretary-General Boutros Boutros-Ghali for having a foreign-sounding name) vulgar—passages that had obviously been shoehorned into the original draft, which, as was widely reported, was the work of the novelist Mark Helprin. Dole offered little of the usual vacant blather about "dreams," especially "the American dream," which the Republicans are "about" restoring. On the contrary, Dole won the hearts of at least a few skeptical listeners by declaring that "facts are better than dreams," thus trashing the whole carefully devised theme of the convention. The speech was a beautifully written exercise in old-fashioned rhetoric—so old-fashioned that it owed more to Pericles than to, say, Daniel Webster. In simple, elevated, rather archaic language, Dole embraced "God, family, honor, duty, country," and expressed a dignified contempt for money: "The triumph of this nation lies not in its material wealth but in courage, sacrifice, and honor."

Fine words, but the virtues they praise are martial, civic, public virtues. The great flaw in the speech was the absence of any connection between those virtues and the program they supposedly require: a huge, unfinanced tax cut skewed to the already well-off. Yes, Dole's was a wonderful speech, but its formal style was so remote from the candidate's usual way of talking, and its charm so much a result of its literary qualities, that one is hard put to imagine how it can endure and be replicated on the stump. What's more likely to endure in the public mind is the program: that great big tax cut, which Dole argued would simultaneously spur people to work harder and allow them more time to spend at home with their families—a neat trick, but perfectly manageable, no doubt, in the supply-side fantasy world Dole has chosen to enter, where cutting taxes raises revenues.

President Clinton, in accepting renomination two weeks later in Chicago, used up his opponent's allotment of clichés as well as his own. The president's speech was interminable and uninspiring. Its try for the vision thing, "a bridge to the future," was lifted directly from Dole's far more eloquent paean to the past: "Let me be the bridge to an America that only the unknowing call myth." But Clinton's lengthy list of modest, practical, specific proposals—here a community-development bank and a bit of gun control, there a flextime law and an extra day in the hospital—is truer to his tinkerer's heart, and is probably more in tune with a public made wary of big promises and big plans. In any case, all was back to normal the next day. "It's about America," Dole told his first post-convention rally. "It's about America's children. It's about the future."

—*The New Yorker*, September 9, 1996

STAR-SPANGLED BANTER

TED TURNER set off a firecracker of his own this Fourth of July. Speaking in front of Independence Hall, in Philadelphia, he argued that it's time to dump "The Star-Spangled Banner." Over the years, Mr. Turner has had many capital ideas—CNN, Turner Classic Movies, and interrupting Jane Fonda's career as a serial monogamist, to name three. Now he has come up with another, and one cannot but agree with him. By all means, let us ease the old chestnut into well-deserved retirement. But not for the reason he offers, and not to make way for the alternative he recommends.

Mr. T notes that the national anthem is warlike, whereas the age we live in is (relatively) peaceful. He is right on both counts, but his second point makes his first less compelling. Just as gun control is more urgent in Detroit than in Lausanne, bellicose songs are more worrying in bellicose times than in times of tranquillity. "The Star-Spangled Banner" is warlike, yes. But so are a lot of first-rate national anthems. ("The Marseillaise," with its ghoulish call to "drench our fields" in "impure blood," makes its American counterpart sound like something by Joni Mitchell.) In any case, there are plenty of better reasons for getting rid of "The Star-Spangled Banner." Its tonal range corresponds to that of the electric guitar, as Jimi Hendrix proved, but not to that of the human voice. The lyrics include some fine phrases— "the twilight's last gleaming," "the ramparts we watched"—that are a reliable source of titles for the type of potboiler novel that goes in for raised lettering on the jacket, but on the whole the words don't convey what politicians call core American values. Francis Scott Key's poem was written to immortalize the siege of Fort McHenry, Maryland, during the War of 1812—a silly war, a minor war, a war that ended in what was at best a tie. (The British torched the White House and smashed our hopes of gobbling up Canada. We got to keep our independence.) The poem lends itself to mishearing, from the traditional "José can you see" opening, through "O, sadists that stars spank," to the closing "Orlando D. Free and Homer D. Brave." Congress designated "The Star-Spangled Banner" our national anthem during the Hoover administration, when the country's judgment was impaired by clinical depression. The relevant bill—whose sponsor hoped to promote the tourist trade in his district, which included Fort McHenry—was rejected three times by the House before it finally passed, on a slow day. It was supported by the "Americanism" busybodies of the Daughters of the American Revolution and the American Legion but opposed by music teachers—an important group at a time when pianos were more common than phonographs. The complaints then were identical to the complaints now: too martial, too irritating, too hard to sing.

What's the alternative? Mr. T suggests "America the Beautiful"—the music teachers' choice back in 1930, by the way. It's nice, but, like so many nice things, it's also wimpy. The best that can be said for it is that it's more singable than the incumbent. A third contender—"America (My Country, 'Tis of Thee)"—has O.K words, but the tune is the same as that of "God Save the Queen." This would make for an unusually severe "Is there an echo in here?" problem during joint appearances by Bill Clinton and Tony Blair. How about "This Land Is Your Land"? Plenty of progressive-school pupils already think Woody Guthrie's populist jingle is the national anthem, but the tune is a little too Barney the Dinosaurish, and the lyrics have a musty, Popular Front feeling about them.

Our country has at hand what is perhaps the greatest patriotic hymn ever written: "The Battle Hymn of the Republic." But secularists would object that it is too God-filled, and Southerners—white Southerners, at least—would complain that the vineyards it advocates trampling were their vineyards. ("The Star-Spangled Banner" was also popular with the Union Army, but never mind.) Perhaps "The Battle Hymn of the Republic" could be twinned with "Dixie," as in the Elvis Presley version, but "Dixie" has its own problems. Anyhow, serious countries do not have national medleys.

This space would like to offer a recommendation of its own: "Lift Ev'ry Voice and Sing." James Weldon Johnson, a poet of the Harlem Renaissance, wrote it, in 1900, for a Lincoln's Birthday celebration. It is already a national anthem of sorts; its alternative title, in fact, is "The Negro National Anthem." Its tune (by J. Rosamond Johnson, the poet's brother) is stirring, and so are its words. The opening verse, the one that would be sung at ballgames, goes, in part:

> *Lift ev'ry voice and sing,*
> *Till earth and heaven ring.*
> *Ring with the harmonies of liberty . . .*
> *Sing a song full of the faith that the dark past has taught us,*
> *Sing a song full of the hope that the present has brought us;*
> *Facing the rising sun of our new day, begun,*
> *Let us march on till victory is won.*

No bombast, no boasting, no wimpishness—just good, solid values that are both American and universal. How about it, Ted?

—The New Yorker, July 21, 1997

TALKING POINTS

THE END OF JANUARY is a busy season for superannuated speechwriters. The news industry gears up for the president's State of the Union address, and veteran political wordsmiths, like retired ballplayers at World Series time, are suddenly in demand. All-news cable interviewers and newspaper reporters assigned to sidebar duty want to know: How does "the process" work? Does somebody tell you what to write, or do you just dream it up? Do you kick around ideas with the president ahead of time? Does he do a lot of editing or just take what you've written as is?

When the topic is speechwriting, the first name on every booker's list is Peggy Noonan's. Only if she is unavailable does the call go out to someone else—me, for example. (I was President Carter's speechwriter, a job that my predecessor, James Fallows, once likened to being F.D.R.'s tap-dancing teacher.) Unlike many of the rest of us, Ms. Noonan is not at all superannuated. She is beautiful, blond, and glamorous—which doesn't hurt, but isn't why, or mainly why, she gets the call. She gets it because she is a very good speechwriter, perhaps the most accomplished in the country. During the 1980s, she was responsible for the lioness's share of whatever memorable rhetoric issued from the mouths of Presidents Reagan and Bush. She didn't do "evil empire"; her colleague Anthony Dolan came up with that. But she did do Mr. Reagan's celebrated remarks at Normandy Beach for the fortieth anniversary of D-Day. ("These are the boys of Pointe du Hoc. These are the men who took the cliffs.") She wrote Mr. Reagan's simple, sombre statement of grief after the *Challenger* disaster. And she wrote Mr. Bush's startlingly effective 1988 acceptance speech. That was the one with "kinder, gentler" and "a thousand points of light" and "read my lips: no new taxes"; the one that wiped out Michael Dukakis's lead in the polls; the one that arguably swept Mr. Bush into the White House (and, via "read my lips" blowback following the 1990 budget agreement, arguably swept him right back out again).

Like sexual excess and substance abuse, speechwriting has been around awhile. What's new is the fact that we talk about it openly, without shame. It was known, in a general sort of way, that Alexander Hamilton helped draft President Washington's farewell address, that William Seward contributed notes that, rewritten and much improved, ended up in Lincoln's First Inaugural, and that people like Samuel Rosenman and Robert E. Sherwood were sometimes seen in the vicinity of the West Wing before one of Franklin Roosevelt's fireside chats. But such services were performed discreetly. And the speechwriters of old had day jobs: Hamilton was the secretary of the treasury, Seward the secretary of state, Rosenman a New York State judge, Sherwood a Pulitzer Prize–winning playwright. Theodore Sorensen and Harry McPherson, who wrote speeches for John F. Kennedy and Lyndon Johnson, respectively, did so as a sideline to their main work, as policy advisers and operatives. By the time the Carter crowd moved in, the White House had established what was brazenly called the Office of Speechwriting and put it in the care of someone styled Chief Speechwriter to the President. These attest to the gravity and importance of his official responsibilities. But a Chief Speechwriter? He might as well have a Chief Toothpaste Squeezer, or an Office of Coffee Stirring. Aren't there some things that even a president should at least appear to do for himself?

As with sex and drugs, though, the new candor about speechwriting has the merit of demystifying an activity that was once shrouded in darkness. Everyone knows that presidents—and governors and senators and C.E.O.s—have neither the time nor, in most cases, the inclination to write their own speeches from scratch. Why not be frank about it? In 1990, Ms. Noonan gave us her political memoir, *What I Saw at the Revolution*. A how-to book was a logical next step. *Simply Speaking: How to Communicate Your Ideas with Style, Substance, and Clarity* is self-help of the aspirational variety. Unlike a cookbook, but like one of those mass-market paperbacks that tell you how to run a Fortune 500 company, *Simply Speaking* is more apt to guide the typical reader in fantasizing about doing something than in actually doing it. "We are all asked sooner or later to say a few words at the annual meeting, the parent-teacher gathering, the awards dinner, the memorial service, the wedding." Perhaps so. And for these rare occasions Ms. Noonan has some harmless, if obvious, advice: keep it short, use humor, don't be stentorian, have something to say and know what it is, be yourself, rehearse. But giving a public speech, let alone writing one for someone else to give, is something normal people seldom do. Anyhow, Ms. Noonan is a little perfunctory about the how-to stuff. She tries gamely, peppering her text with zippy chapter headings ("Be You") and admonitions that may ("Put your points and stories in order") or may not ("Always ask, if you can, for a car service") be useful in helping you prepare for that talk at the P.T.A. But her heart isn't in it. What she really wants to do is go over some of the speeches she has written and analyze some she has heard or read, and when she does that she becomes engaged.

MS. NOONAN didn't know Reagan terribly well. She writes with uncharacteristic annoyance that after he was wounded in the March 1981 assassination attempt his aides were told "to limit nonessential demands on the president's time, and they were more than happy to define meetings with speechwriters as nonessential because they viewed the speechwriters as idiots, i.e., serious conservatives." But this didn't much matter, because these particular idiots knew "what he thought, why he thought it, and how he'd say it." She notes—with, I must disclose, a graceful compliment to me—that this was an advantage denied to Carter's speechwriters. (I'd put it differently, though: because Mr. Carter was an undogmatic empiricist, not an ideologue, he had no fixed opinions on matters he knew nothing about.) Ms. Noonan made up for the lack of personal feedback with a mental exercise. "I used to imagine [Reagan] in my mind as an old sailor, a wise ol' salt ambling down a rolling deck as the ship rolled in the sea," she writes. "He never fell or had to grab the rails, he just rolled with the swells as they rose and fell. George Bush, on the other hand, was like a man briskly walking down a city sidewalk, stopping all of a sudden to greet a friend and then plowing on, slowing briefly for a light, going forward with the crowd, turning to say hello to the man at the hot dog stand, moving on."

Poor Bush: pedestrian even in a young woman's fantasy, while Reagan was Popeye. But this only makes Olive Oyl's triumph with the 1988 Bush acceptance speech all the more impressive, and she lingers over it lovingly in an extended *explication de texte*. She shows how the speech cast Bush's lack of a distinct public identity in the noble light of service to Reagan, while suggesting almost subliminally that he might not have agreed with every last thing the old boy did: "Ronald Reagan asked for, and received, my candor. He never asked for, but did receive, my loyalty." She reminds us of how the speech dealt with Bush's silver-spoon problem:

> Yes, my parents were prosperous, and their children were lucky. But there were lessons we had to learn about life. John Kennedy discovered poverty when he campaigned in West Virginia; there were children there who had no milk. And young Teddy Roosevelt met the new America when he roamed the immigrant streets of New York.

In other words, Ms. Noonan paraphrases, "I know the press is playing me as a rich preppy, but look what the rich preppies Jack and Teddy became—great men." And the Bush equivalent of rural hollers and urban streets?

> I learned a few things about life in a place called Texas. . . . Lived the dream—high school football on Friday nights, little league, neighborhood barbecue.

I was up in the cheap seats while these words were being delivered, trading sarcastic wisecracks with some fellow members of the liberal media. But even our biased little anti-claque couldn't help noticing that this stuff was going over big. The speech (as Ms. Noonan does not mention) ended with the candidate leading the throng in the Pledge of Allegiance, thus highlighting an "issue" that Dukakis would absent-mindedly allow to distort the campaign. I didn't see Ms. Noonan in the hall that night, but I imagine she must have looked the way Tim Russert had looked during Mario Cuomo's keynote address at the Democratic Convention four years earlier: Russert, who was then a close Cuomo aide, stood mouthing the words his boss was speaking, his broad mug suffused with an expression of total ecstasy.

For the person in the analogous position four years earlier still—me—the experience was not so blissful. As the nominal author of President

Carter's 1980 acceptance speech (in reality there were many authors, and my main role was to do the suturing, like an emergency-room trauma surgeon after a gas-main explosion), I had an excellent seat right up on the platform of Madison Square Garden. Mr. Carter had barely begun speaking, though, when, taking advantage of a pause after one of our carefully crafted applause lines, he urgently signalled that something was wrong with the teleprompter. I rushed below decks to alert the technicians to the problem. When I got back, Mr. Carter was in the middle of the "We're the party of" litany, and I guess he was feeling expansive, because when he got to the part where the text said "Hubert H. Humphrey" he improvised: "the party of a great man who should have been president, who would have been one of the greatest presidents in history—Hubert Horatio Hornblower! Er, Humphrey." Horatio was, in fact, Senator Humphrey's middle name. Horatio Hornblower was the hero of C. S. Forester's popular series of seafaring adventure yarns. The conflation that rocketed out of the president's mouth at this inopportune moment, I later learned, had been the 1976 Carter campaign staff's derisive nickname for their most feared rival. Ever since that night in the Garden, I have had to endure a taunt that I suppose must be familiar to William ("I am not a crook") Safire and, for all I know, to Peggy ("We begin bombing in five minutes") Noonan as well: "Was that yours?"

Charles Peters, the editor-in-chief of the *Washington Monthly*, once wrote that this speech of Carter's was what put Reagan in the White House. I've always thought that this was giving it (and me) too much credit. The speech wasn't all *that* terrible. While Carter was delivering it, his pollster, Patrick Caddell, had a roomful of citizens somewhere watching television and wired up to some sort of gadget that allowed them to register approval or disapproval by turning a dial. Caddell assured me later that the needles stayed over to the right almost throughout. And we did get a bump in the polls after the convention.

But then presidential candidates always get a bump in the polls after their conventions. That speech was not one of our team's better efforts. On my wall is a framed copy of a speech that *was* one of our better efforts—the farewell address that Carter delivered just before leaving office. The inscription reads, "Rick—not bad for a 10th draft. Maybe we should have been more careful on earlier speeches, & saved this one 4 more years. Jimmy Carter." Right again, Mr. President.

Too many cooks—that was the trouble with Carter's 1980 convention speech. Peggy Noonan would understand. In her exegesis of her convention speech, she contemplates what might have been its best line, if only the suits hadn't tampered with it:

> This is America: the Knights of Columbus, the Grange, Hadassah, the Disabled American Veterans, the Order of Ahepa, the Business and Professional Women of America, the union hall, the Bible study group, LULAC, Holy Name—a brilliant diversity spread like stars, like a thousand points of light in a broad and peaceful sky.

"People around Bush," Ms. Noonan complains mildly, "eager as people around candidates always are to include every single group in every single litany, kept shoehorning in groups that were, well, interest groups: the Disabled American Veterans and so on."

She's right, of course. The line would have been better without LULAC (whatever that is) and the rest. But perhaps it wouldn't have been as true to who Bush actually was. Ours (it is frequently lamented) is an age of inauthenticity. The fact that the speeches of politicians are ghostwritten by committees is often adduced as proof. The existence of celebrity speechwriters like Peggy Noonan presumably clinches the case. But perhaps the ghosted committee product is the authentic voice of the modern presidency. Ms. Noonan's complaint simply shows that the speech, in the end, was Bush's, not hers. Ms. Noonan may have been the author, but Mr. Bush was the auteur.

—*The New Yorker*, February 2, 1998

THE WORD FROM W.

GEORGE W. BUSH'S first week as president of the United States began with a speech that, taken as a whole and judged purely as a piece of writing, was shockingly good. It was by far the best Inaugural Address in forty years; indeed, it was better than all but a tiny handful of all the inaugurals of all the presidents since the republic was founded. That praise is not, or not necessarily, quite as high as it may sound: except for Lincoln's imperishable Second Inaugural, scattered passages from his first and from the speeches of certain of the greats (Washington, Jefferson, Franklin Roosevelt, one or two others), and, arguably, Kennedy's 1961 address, the presidential Inaugural is not a distinguished branch of American literature or even of American rhetoric. To read all fifty-four addresses, one after another, is to traverse a wasteland where pomposity, banality, and incoherence are more often relieved by mediocrity than by brilliance.

The speech Bush read was different. It was tightly constructed. Its rhythms flowed pleasingly. Its sentences were sculpted. Its sentiments, however familiar, were expressed in language that was consistently fresh, at once elevated and unpretentious, and almost entirely free of bombast, cliché, or sloganeering. By the "We're No. 1" standards of patriotic speechmaking, the version of the American civic religion it set forth was without arrogance, and its admissions of imperfection abjured scapegoating. Its description of America as "a slave-holding society that became a servant of freedom" was a cleansing acknowledgment of America's original sin. In affirming that what binds America is not "blood or birth or soil" but "ideals that move us beyond our backgrounds," and that "every immigrant, by embracing these ideals, makes our country more, not less, American," it rejected nativism and deftly sketched both the relevance and the limits of multiculturalism. And consider this passage, outstanding but by no means atypical:

> In the quiet of American conscience, we know that deep, persistent poverty is unworthy of our nation's promise. And whatever our views of its cause, we can agree that children at risk are not at fault. Abandonment and abuse are not acts of God, they are failures of love.

Here the cant phrase "at risk" is freshened by juxtaposition with "at fault," making the point that the origins (and, by extension, the pathologies) of poverty are rooted more in social than in personal responsibility. In substance if not in expression, it was a speech that, with five minutes of blue-pencilling, could as easily have been delivered by the rightful winner of the election. Bravo, then, to its author, the former journalist Michael Gerson, and to Bush himself for recognizing its merits and protecting it from the "improvements" that were no doubt suggested by other members of his staff. ("It's gotta mention missile defense! It's gotta say the words 'compassionate conservatism'! That was the theme of the whole campaign!")

The dissonance began one day later. The new president's first act was an act of cruelty. He ordered an end to federal assistance to overseas organizations, such as the International Planned Parenthood Federation, that, in his words, use taxpayer funds "to pay for abortions or advocate or actively promote abortion." These organizations do no such thing, of course; nor, by law, can they. The federal money they receive is used for family planning—that is, to prevent unwanted pregnancies (and therefore to reduce the occasions for ending them). Nor do these groups promote or advocate abortion, though the clinics they operate sometimes use private funds to provide abortion counselling and services. Bush's order is calculated to placate his pro-life supporters, while avoiding the political storm that would ensue if similar restrictions were imposed at home. (The underlying logic—that public money "frees up" funds that might otherwise be devoted to purposes of which some taxpayers disapprove—is not likely to deter the administration's plans for aid to "faith-based" organizations.) "Where there is suffering, there is duty" were among Bush's inaugural words. His inaugural act will increase suffering by shirking duty.

The president spent the rest of the week promoting his proposals for improving education and for a hugely regressive tax cut. The former was the subject of some of his speech's finest passages, the latter of its one descent into grossness: a pledge, high-fived by the crowd on the Mall, to "reduce taxes, to recover the momentum of our economy and reward the effort and enterprise of working Americans." Bush's "education package" is expected to amount to some ten billion dollars a year. Meanwhile, his income-tax cut would confer more than thirty billion dollars a year on the richest one percent. His abolition of the estate tax would funnel another thirty billion a year to the well-off. Nearly half of that would go to an average of twenty-four hundred families a year. The economics columnist Matt Miller has calculated that each of these sets of heirs would get an average windfall of $6.2 million—a reward not for effort, enterprise, or work but simply for having been, like Bush himself, born rich.

This, so far, is the context of the Inaugural Address, and where speeches of this kind are concerned context is all. "The only thing we have to fear is fear itself," F.D.R. said, on March 4, 1933. But, if his programmatic response to the Great Depression had been limited to making psychotherapy tax-deductible for anxious stockbrokers, that great line would be little remembered. What President Bush does, not what he says, will determine whether his speech ultimately redounds to his credit, or only to Michael Gerson's.

—The New Yorker, February 5, 2001

GRINDING AXIS

A POLITICAL BY-PRODUCT of the modern cult of personal authenticity is a tendency to treat a president's off-the-cuff remarks as more revelatory than the prepared kind. And so they can be. But the prepared kind are a better guide to policy, especially when an administration is as disciplined as Bush II. No presidential speech is worked over more obsessively than the annual message on the State of the Union, which every administration treats as the year's most important guide to policy. And in George W. Bush's first State of the Union address, delivered last Tuesday evening, the most carefully worked-over line was probably this one, which followed hard upon a condemnation of North Korea, Iran, and Iraq: "States like these, and their terrorist allies, constitute an axis of evil, arming to threaten the peace of the world."

"Axis of evil" is a phrase worth lingering on. By combining allusions to the two great global struggles of living memory, it raises—rhetorically, at least—the stakes of the campaign against terrorism. But Bush's evil axis, unlike the Axis powers of the Second World War (the coinage was Mussolini's), is not an alliance. Apart from being three in number and nasty in disposition, North Korea, Iran, and Iraq have little in common with the Germany, Italy, and Japan of 1940; and, apart from an appetite for weapons of mass destruction and a history of dabbling in terrorism, they have little in common with each other. Indeed, the biggest war either Iran or Iraq has ever fought was fought between them.

North Korea is a hermit kingdom ruled by a hereditary Communist monarch. It has no powerful friends and partakes of no worldwide move-ment. The threat that it presents is almost certainly manageable via a com-bination of diplomacy and economic inducements, a path that South Korea seems determined to pursue, despite discouragement from Washington. Until now, the administration has viewed North Korea more as a trope than as a country, seeing it chiefly as an argument for missile defense. Its inclu-sion in Bush's list seems designed both to buttress that argument, which has little to do with the events of September 11th, and to keep the list from con-sisting entirely of Islamic countries.

Iran is a special case. It has feisty internal politics and, nominally, an elected government, but the real power lies with a shadowy council of mul-lahs. (Bush was referring to them when he noted that "an unelected few re-press the Iranian people's hope for freedom.") Iran's support for terrorism begins with Hezbollah but does not end there. And yet, for any number of reasons, there is essentially no possibility that the United States would choose to go to war against Iran.

That leaves Iraq, the most hostile and dangerous of the three. The Bush speech, on its face, appeared to be laying the groundwork for a war aimed at toppling the regime of Saddam Hussein and thereby completing a job that the president's father had left unfinished. It is not at all clear, however, how the administration intends to proceed. A war, unless it were to be con-cluded as briskly as was the much easier task of subduing Afghanistan, would carry the risk of alienating Europe and Russia, rattling the tacit global consensus behind the anti-terrorist fight, and provoking an attack on Israel. Other options—such as offering supplies and training to insurgents inside Iraq—are evidently under consideration. By rhetorically combining Iraq with Iran and North Korea under the rubric of an axis, Bush evoked the memory, and raised the spectre, of war on a terrifying scale. But by the same token he left himself the option of dealing with all three in a consis-tent and necessarily less bellicose manner.

The other half of Bush's formula recalled, no doubt intentionally, Ronald Reagan's most famous phrase. "Evil empire" is now chiselled on history's wall next to "iron curtain" as an example of prescient moral clarity. But it is worth recalling that in 1983, when President Reagan pinned that tail on the Soviet donkey, he touched off a good deal of justifiable anxiety. It was easy to infer that he was ruling out the possibility of a peaceful future: one does not compromise with evil. At the time, though, the Soviet Union's days of evil were mostly behind it. As Reagan understood, the Soviet Union was a ramshackle, dysfunctional mess whose inheritors were flailing about for ways to fix it. War, it turned out, was the last thing on Reagan's mind; his eagerness to compromise alarmed many of his admirers, some of whom now serve the present administration. But the phrase touched off a kind of rhetorical inflation, and Bush now freely spends the currency that Reagan printed.

So "evil" doesn't have the buying power it once did. At the same time, it applies far more aptly to the terrorists of Al Qaeda and their ilk than it did to the Soviet Union in its dotage. The latter was an unhappy assemblage of three hundred million, most of whom yearned for peace with the United States; the former consists, as Bush accurately put it, of "thousands of dangerous killers, schooled in the methods of murder, often supported by outlaw regimes." Bush was right to stress that the struggle against them does not end in Afghanistan, and that it will be long and difficult. But there is danger in the conflation of terrorists and states. A government, even one as tyrannical and aggressive as Iraq's, always has something to lose and something to gain. Saddam Hussein is a murderer, but there is no evidence that he is a suicide, or that he is incapable of rational calculation. The war against terrorism was and is unsought, unavoidable, and existential. It is a war of necessity. That, in the end, is why it commands the public's nearly unanimous support. Certainly, the fall of Saddam Hussein is devoutly to be wished for. But an American war aimed at achieving that goal—a war of choice, a war that, in all likelihood, would be long, bloody, and fraught with unanticipated and unpleasant consequences—is not.

—*The New Yorker*, February 11, 2002

4. JUDEO-CHRISTIANS

As I note a little more than half-seriously in the piece that opens this section, I am a Judeo-Christian. This has nothing to do with religious belief, especially the sort that involves directives and other messages from supernatural beings. It's more of a sensibility, combined with a demographic-ethnic-cultural category. My father was indisputably a Jew, even though he was a militant enough atheist by the age of thirteen to refuse to be bar mitzvahed. His Jewishness manifested itself through the ethics of socialism and through an easy familiarity with *Yiddishkeit.* (I didn't understand this until I read Irving Howe's *World of Our Fathers,* which, for me, became something like a sacred text.) My mother was a Protestant—a follower of the Social Gospel, a Congregationalist and sometime Quaker, an agnostic on the subject of God. My wife is a Catholic who, although completely nonobservant, regards my sometimes obstreperous impiety as jejune. So what am I, really? I don't know, which suits me fine. The Nuremberg laws would say I'm Jewish, the Law of Return would say I'm not. Like George W. Bush, I admire Jesus as a philosopher, but unlike him (Bush, that is) I do not consider him (Jesus, that is), or anybody else for that matter, my personal savior. I consider myself to be a product equally of Judaism (or, more precisely, Jewishness) and Christianity (or, more precisely, Christendom)—as traditions if not as religions. From a strictly aesthetic point of view, I prefer Christian liturgy to the Jewish kind, though I am admittedly more familiar with the former than the latter, thanks partly to the compulsory chapel policy of the Episcopal boarding school where I spent my ninth grade year (and got an A in Bible class). I'm pretty sure there's no such thing as God. I'm even surer that revealed religion is an unsound basis for morality, because the idea that we should behave in a certain way because a big, powerful, possibly vengeful being tells us to doesn't sound to me like moral reasoning. It sounds like authoritarianism, pure and simple. Might doesn't make right, even if the might is almighty. On the other hand, I'd rather not call myself a secular humanist, because it sounds vaguely cultish, and because I'm not entirely sure just what a secular humanist is. But I'm perfectly happy to be called one by the sort of people who consider secular humanists the devil's spawn.

If a person doesn't feel like sharing, then his or her religious beliefs shouldn't really be anybody's business but his or her own. Political candidates, in particular, oughtn't to feel the slightest obligation to discuss their theological beliefs, beyond assuring the public that they will scrupulously avoid trying to use the power of the state to promulgate them. It ought to be that way, but it isn't. Unfortunately, that particular barn door has been open for quite some time, and the horse has taken up residence in the public square, where the rest of us must either clean up after it or tiptoe around the results. (I'm doing a full disclosure here in a spirit of fairness, or maybe preemption, because if politicians have to bare their souls then no doubt those of us who presume to judge politicians deserve to be next.)

Americans are bigger believers than the peoples of other advanced countries, but then they always have been. Tocqueville noticed this back when the republic was still being run by politicians born as British subjects. If we had polling data from the eighteenth, nineteenth, and early twentieth centuries, I suspect it would show that the percentage of Americans who believe in God, Satan, Armageddon, Heaven, Hell, and the like has not materially changed for the past three hundred years. Yet the framers of the Constitution made sure the text would contain no mention of God, while the Declaration of Independence refers merely to a "Creator" and to "Nature's God"—deist code words, crafted to avoid any suggestion of the sort of deity who interests himself in the outcome of wars, elections, or athletic contests. Four score and eight years later, Lincoln, who had admired Paine's *Age of Reason* in his youth and who (as his widow put it) had never been a "technical Christian," used the beautiful, Bible-echoing rhetoric of his greatest speech, the Second Inaugural, not to claim God's favor but to point to the unknowability of divine intentions.

A cruder kind of public piety began elbowing its way in during the 1950s. Yet compared to what has followed, the prayer-breakfast, god-of-your-choice, BOMFOG (brotherhood of man, fatherhood of God) brand of Eisenhower-era sanctimony now seems blessedly anodyne. Now every presidential speech ends with the commander in chief ordering God to bless America, and every presidential hopeful feels obligated—or at least pressured—to announce how many times he or she has been born. Some hold Jimmy Carter partially responsible for this state of affairs, and perhaps there is a drop of justice in the charge. But Carter's religiosity stressed love and tolerance, including (luckily for me) tolerance for unbelief. (In Carter's White House no one was chastised for missing Bible study, nor would Bible study have been regarded as a fit use for federal property.) The new fundamentalist dispensation that has reached its apotheosis under George W. Bush has, after a brief flirtation with "compassion," stressed confrontation between absolute evil and presumably absolute good and is obsessed with controlling the reproductive and sexual freedom of women and the young.

The atmosphere of piety in American public life has become stifling. At the same time, religion appears to have become curiously brittle, as if subjecting its tenets to public questioning or criticism would shatter it. Believers and nonbelievers alike used to be made of hardier stuff. During the 1870s and beyond, one of the most prominent Republicans in the country was a wildly popular barnstorming lecturer who denounced Democrats as little better than traitors and who, at the 1876 Republican Convention, delivered the nominating speech for James G. Blaine, indelibly dubbing him the "Plumed Knight." But the speeches Robert Ingersoll was most famous for, the ones that really packed 'em in at lecture halls from coast to coast, were the ones that ridiculed the Bible and lampooned Christianity. "We have heard talk enough," Ingersoll thundered, four years before he nominated Blaine. "We have listened to all the drowsy, idealess, vapid sermons that we wish to hear. We have read your Bible and the works of your best minds. We have heard your prayers, your solemn groans and your reverential amens. All these amount to less than nothing. We want one fact. We beg at the doors of your churches for just one little fact. We pass our hats along your pews and under your pulpits and implore you for just one fact. We know all about your mouldy wonders and your stale miracles. We want this year's fact. We ask only one. Give us one fact for charity. Your miracles are too ancient. The witnesses have been dead for nearly two thousand years."

One and one-third centuries later, it seems unlikely, somehow, that a person who so frankly avowed views like these would rate a place of honor on the podium of a major-party convention. Nowadays, his bloodcurdling Republicanism notwithstanding, Bob Ingersoll wouldn't even get past the bookers at Fox News.

ANTIDISESTABLISHMENTARIANISM

RETURNING AFTER an absence of some months, I find Reagantown in the grip of one of its periodic religious frenzies. Possibly it's the weather, which as usual in August is unwholesomely swampy and feverish. More likely it's just the zeitgeist, which is that way all year round. The current mania was touched off by the secretary of education, William J. Bennett. He gave a speech saying that the bad guys who still supposedly run everything (liberals, the Supreme Court, etc.) have an "aversion to religion." The situation is so grave that the administration is prepared to put aside its usual reliance on the private sector in favor of more government programs. These government programs will promote what? They will promote the "Judeo-Christian tradition." That's the big thing right now, apparently—the "Judeo-Christian tradition."

This gets to an area that, to me, is close to home. As it happens, my ancestors are exactly half Jewish and half Christian as far back as can be traced. In other words, unlike Bennett and 99.99 percent of his fellow followers of the currently fashionable antidisestablishmentarian line, I actually *am* a Judeo-Christian. And I must say that we Judeo-Christians are beginning to get a little testy about the uses to which our name is being put. The past decade or so has brought about an alarming deterioration. Back in the old days, most of the people who talked about the "Judeo-Christian tradition" were nice, high-minded clerics from the mainstream Protestant denominations who wanted to include Jews in on things like Brotherhood Week. The sentiments may have been a bit treacly, but the underlying purpose—

to make people less inclined to hate each other on the basis of religious af-filiation—was praiseworthy. The underlying purpose of the new crowd seems altogether different. Being inclusive is not what they have in mind. On the contrary. It looks to me like what they want to do is to slice off those of their fellow citizens who don't meet their standards for admission to the "Judeo-Christian tradition"—e.g., those who have an "aversion to religion," by which they presumably mean an aversion to organized religion and/or religious dogma—and then to read these citizens out of American society. As a Judeo-Christian who has an aversion to religion, and who is an Amer-ican as good as or better than any mousse-haired, Bible-touting, apartheid-promoting evangelist on any UHF television station you can name, I must protest.

Where is it written that if you don't like religion you are somehow dis-qualified from being a legitimate American? What was Mark Twain, a Russian? When did it become un-American to have opinions about the ori-gin and meaning of the universe that come from sources other than the body of dogma of organizations approved by the federal government as certifi-ably Judeo-Christian? If it is American to believe that God ordered Tribe X to abjure pork, or that he caused Leader Y to be born to a virgin, why is it suddenly un-American to doubt that the prime mover of this unimagin-ably vast universe of quintillions of solar systems would be likely to be ob-sessed with questions involving the dietary and biosexual behavior of a few thousand bipeds inhabiting a small part of a speck of dust orbiting a third-rate star in an obscure spiral arm of one of millions of more or less identi-cal galaxies? What is so terrible about being averse to religion?!? (Diarist suddenly pitches violently backward in chair and disappears from view, à la John Belushi.)

I think I know who these people—not Bennett, necessarily, but certainly some of his religious-right allies—are talking about when they talk about the Judeo-Christian tradition. By Judeo-Christian, I suspect, they mean Christian. By Christian, they mean Protestant. By Protestant, they mean evangelical. (And by evangelical, I'll bet, they mean anti-abortion, pro–school prayer, anti–gay rights, pro–Star Wars, extreme right-wing Rea-ganite Republican.) A specimen of this type of Judeo-Christian, as opposed to the type represented by your Diarist, is John Lofton, correspondent and columnist for the *Washington Times*, a newspaper owned by Sun Myung Moon, the Korean messiah and tax-fraud artist. About a month ago, Lofton did a Q&A interview that ran under the priceless headline JEANE KIRK-PATRICK: THOUGHTS ON RELIGION, ABORTION AND TAXATION. (The holy trinity?) Lofton harassed Mrs. Kirkpatrick with questions like

> Q: You mean, then, that you don't believe the Bible when it says it is the sole source of truth?

and

> Q: Goodness. We've just plunged headlong into heresy here. You mean God doesn't govern civil government?

and, best of all,

> Q: Reading your writings, you seem to be taken by some of these Greek philosophers. But can they really be relied on? . . . [Plato and Aristotle] were horrible people when you judged them by Christian standards.

Mrs. Kirkpatrick handles her interlocutor tactfully and skillfully, but you can almost see her eyes checking to make sure she has a clear path to the door. She obviously believes that her new political role obliges her to curry favor with these people; still, it's hard to believe this was the fire she had in mind when she jumped out of the "blame America first" frying pan.

—Washington Diarist, *The New Republic*, September 16, 1985

VATICAN'T

PROVIDING THE COMMENTATING community with a bit of relief from Iran-contra, along comes what might be called Vatican't. The new prohibitions from Rome are outlined in a document entitled "Instruction on Respect for Human Life in Its Origin and on the Dignity of Procreation: Replies to Certain Questions of the Day." (The document is not, repeat not, entitled "Sex Tips for Modern Girls from Sixty-Year-Old Bachelors Who Have Taken Vows of Chastity.") Surrogate motherhood is out, artificial insemination by donor is out, in vitro fertilization of wives by husbands is out. And of course contraception, still, is out. Having been told they have to get pregnant, women are now being told they can't. More precisely, fertility is mandatory for those who are able to conceive but don't want to, forbidden for those who want to conceive but aren't able to. Catch-XXII.

The Sunday morning talk shows, secular humanism's answer to hymns and sermons, zero in on the Vatican document. A personable young Irish monsignor answers respectful questions via satellite from Rome. Back in the studio, bishops and senators react. The American clerics interviewed seem glumly aware that Catholics who badly want children will be apt to choose parenthood over obedience. A questioner points out to a bishop that the prohibition against in vitro fertilization appears to fly in the face of both charity and experience, and says she can't understand the argument against it. "The argument is an argument from faith," the bishop replies irritably. His curtness surprises me. There must be more to it than that.

Curious, I dig out the previous Wednesday's *New York Times* and read the full text of the Vatican's instruction. Sure enough, there is an argument of sorts buried in the dense prose of the Congregation for the Doctrine of the Faith. It is the same as the argument against contraception. There is an "inseparable connection, willed by God and unable to be broken by man on his own initiative, between the two meanings of the conjugal act: the unitive meaning and the procreative meaning." Contraception is forbidden because it sacrifices the procreative meaning to the unitive, in vitro fertilization because it sacrifices the unitive to the procreative. Q.E.D. The argument is coldly and relentlessly deductive, depending as it does upon a bald assertion of what is "willed by God." A Catholic couple unable to conceive without medical help might protest that the husband's low sperm count is also "willed by God"; more to the point, so is the human ingenuity that enables them to overcome it. But the argument is over. The bishop was right after all: it's an argument from faith, which in this case means an argument from authority. Take it or leave it. And the anguish of the couple? "Spouses who find themselves in this sad situation," replies the document, "are called to find in it an opportunity for sharing in a particular way in the Lord's Cross, the source of spiritual fruitfulness."

This is not to say that there is nothing for a secular humanist like me to admire in the Vatican document. It is refreshing, even uplifting, to read a committee-produced 1987 text that has so little awe of modern science and modernity in general, that asserts that no human being can "be reduced in worth to a pure and simple instrument for the advantage of others," that is so manifestly unguided by public opinion polls, and that nowhere contains the word "incentives." Yet there are unwelcome reminders of the old authoritarian ways. Artificial insemination by donor, for example, is not only proscribed for Catholics; it is also, if the Church has its way (admittedly a highly unlikely prospect), to be criminalized in civil law. And of course non-Catholics thus forced into barrenness by state power would be denied even the dubious comfort of metaphorical crucifixion. William Jennings Bryan, where are you?

I HEAR a startling report from Alabama, where a federal district judge named W. Brevard Hand—known to courthouse regulars as Unlearned Hand—has rendered a decision banning forty-five textbooks from the public schools. According to Judge Hand's reasoning, since the textbooks in question do not promote Christianity, it follows that they promote "the religion of secular humanism." Therefore the textbooks constitute an establishment of religion by the state of Alabama. This is unconstitutional, as Judge Hand learned when an earlier decision of his got blown away on appeal. That was the one where he declared that it was perfectly O.K. for Alabama to have an established state religion, adding that (a) the Bill of Rights only applies to the feds and (b) "a member of a religious minority will have to develop a thicker skin if state establishment offends him." The new Hand decision won't last long either, but for now it seems that secular humanism is indeed an officially recognized religion. This is welcome news for the unchurched among us, who didn't even know we had a religion until the fundamentalists gave us one. I suggest to my fellow secular humanists in the Cotton State that they hasten to claim the privileges to which their new station entitles them: clergy parking spaces; favorable consideration in the awarding of UHF television licenses; and (since both the federal and state governments are secular humanist institutions) the total deductibility of all tax payments from taxable income. If my calculations are correct, this should reduce secular humanist tax liability to zero. But better act fast. Judge Hand may like us, but the Supreme Court isn't as hospitable to our religion as it used to be.

—Cambridge Diarist, *The New Republic*, April 6, 1987

SECULAR SERMON

A COUPLE OF DAYS after the Salman Rushdie story started to break, I happened to be at one of those innumerable conferences that right-wing think tanks put on in Washington. During the coffee break, one of the people I was standing around with, a young aide to a hard-right senator, said, "This Rushdie business is really something." "Unbelievable," I said, pleased to have something to agree with this fellow about. "Yeah," he went on. "You know, these so-called writers and intellectuals have been laughing at religion for hundreds of years. It's about time somebody blew the whistle on it."

I peered closely at my interlocutor, hoping to discern some sign—a smile, a wink, a crinkling around the eyes—that this was a joke. None was forthcoming. If it was irony I wanted, I'd come to the wrong conversation.

A few days later I read a syndicated column that began with apparent relish, "If the ayatollah has his way, the last sound the trendy leftist Salman Rushdie will hear is the swish of a scimitar." The rest of the column was devoted to denouncing Rushdie as "an artistic delinquent" and a "scoundrel," his work as "vandalism" that depicts Islam as "a gutter religion" and is "the moral equivalent of an anti-Semitic book," and "the Western literary herd" as hiding behind "the First Amendment, artistic freedom and all that." The author was not some obscure crank, but rather a famous crank: former White House confidant of Presidents Nixon and Reagan and current television star Patrick Buchanan.

Such views, happily, remain marginal in this country. For most Americans, including most American conservatives, the Rushdie case is a pretty obvious call. On one side, a fanatical terrorist-theocrat, the unchallenged ruler of a large and powerful state and an even larger and more powerful movement, a despot who has ordered the execution of tens of thousands of his countrymen for their opinions and has sent hundreds of thousands more to their deaths in war against their co-religionists. He offers a million dollars to anyone who will kill the author of a book deemed blasphemous. On the other side, a novelist in his quiet London study. He taps out fictions, trying obliquely to understand the real world by creating imaginary ones. On one side, howling mobs, the burning of books, serious hatefulness. On the other side, calm discussion, the reading of books, serious playfulness. On one side, murder. On the other, art. Which side are you on?

That's an easy one, or should be, for Westerners who think of themselves as defenders of liberty. Even so, it took a week for President Bush to get around to acknowledging that something was amiss, and when he did he addressed himself only to the grossest aspect of the affair. "However offensive that book may be," he said, "inciting murder and offering rewards for its perpetration are deeply offensive to the norms of civilized behavior. And our position on terrorism is well known."

This did not go very far, and it was not even all right as far as it went. "However offensive that book may be," for the president to choose this moment of terrible vulnerability to dismiss it as such was considerably more so. The Ayatollah Khomeini is out to murder more than a man, more even than a book. He is out to murder freedom, and he is out to murder one of the political arrangements that make freedom possible: secularism.

The ayatollah cannot succeed in murdering freedom, but he has nicked it, and the wound is visible and not yet stanched. Rushdie has had to cancel his tour of the United States; his American wife, Marianne Wiggins, who also has just published a new (and acclaimed) novel, has had to cancel hers. Indeed the Rushdies have had to cancel what had been their lives, in order to save them. They are in hiding, possibly for good. *The Satanic Verses*—"that book"—was withdrawn from sale at thousands of chain-owned bookstores; that will not prevent it from reaching more American readers than it would have done without Khomeini's threats, but the firebombing of stores that still carry the book has begun. The more lasting result will be insidious and unmeasurable: the books and articles that will never be proposed, commissioned, written, or published because of Iran's intimidation.

Other despots—too many—have murdered writers within their borders, or have sent assassins to murder writers without them. Other despots have banned books and outlawed thoughts. What is unique and unprecedented about Khomeini is the global ambition, and the threatened global reach, of his censorship-by-threat. He has created the first planetary civil liberties case. This is his distinctive contribution to the history of tyranny.

The case imposes a special responsibility on two groups in the West: Rushdie's fellow writers and Khomeini's fellow clerics. The writers, for the most part, have understood the stakes and have reacted accordingly, even if one or two among them, fearing to be added to the ayatollah's little list, were sluggish about doing their duty. The clerics, for the most part, have been slower and sorrier. Some have condemned the (prospective) murder, few have condemned the (proscriptive) motive. Cardinal John O'Connor of New York, for example, let it be known through a spokesman that while the Catholic Church does not condone acts of terrorism, His Eminence "encourages everyone not to dignify the publication of this work, which has been viewed by Muslims as highly sacrilegious and offensive." This is "moral equivalence" with a vengeance.

We are accustomed in the West to defending freedom of speech and freedom of the press. We are much less accustomed to defending secularism. Secularism is not the same as anticlericalism or irreligion. It is simply the recognition that the civic and religious spheres should be kept separate—not only to protect religion from the corruptions and temptations of state power, but also, and more important, to protect civil society from the potential absolutism of religious belief.

In the United States, secularism has come in for some rough treatment in recent years. A large part of the religious right has declared war on "secular humanists," who are sometimes pictured as tools of Satan. More thoughtful conservatives (and a few liberals), troubled by what they see as a decline in the public's sense of right and wrong, look to religion as a means of social control and call upon the state to abandon its religious neutrality.

Our secularism is hard-won, the product of centuries of political, intellectual, and sometimes physical courage. Secularism is the institutionalization of doubt, or more precisely of respect for doubt, and it is harder to love doubt than to love freedom. So we are grudging about our secularism, and some of us are a little ashamed of it. Maybe it takes Rushdie's nightmare and Khomeini's rage to remind us how precious it is, and how fiercely it must be guarded.

—TRB from Washington, *The New Republic*, March 20, 1989

TWO LITTLE WORDS

THE PLEDGE OF ALLEGIANCE—much in the news just now, on account of a soon-to-be-overturned court decision declaring its "under God" clause unconstitutional—has a curious history, one that encapsulates many of the oddball contradictions of American life. The original author of the Pledge, one Francis Bellamy, called himself a Christian socialist. Some people might detect a contradiction right there. But in 1892, when Bellamy came up with his epic one-liner, socialism—in its main American variant, at least—was a genteel movement of reformist uplift, like temperance. Bellamy himself was a Baptist minister, and a holder of one of the most famous names in America: his first cousin was Edward Bellamy, whose utopian novel of 1888, *Looking Backward,* was one of the three biggest best-sellers of the second half of the nineteenth century. (The other two were *Uncle Tom's Cabin* and *Ben-Hur.*) *Looking Backward,* whose mock preface is dated "December 26, 2000," envisions a future America that has peacefully evolved into a paradise of fairness, prosperity, and fraternity.

In 1891, Francis Bellamy left a Boston pulpit to work with an admirer of his, the publisher of *The Youth's Companion,* a mass-circulation family magazine devoted to instilling virtue in young people. The magazine was spearheading a campaign for patriotic observances in the schools, keyed to the quadricentennial of Columbus's voyage. Bellamy joined in with gusto. "I pledge allegiance to my flag and the republic for which it stands; one nation indivisible, with liberty and justice for all," published in the September 8, 1892, issue, was one of his contributions. He was thirty-seven.

The Pledge was a monster hit, thanks largely to what its principal historian, John W. Baer, has called "one of the first nationwide advertising and public relations campaigns in the United States." (Bellamy himself went on to a long and successful career as an advertising executive.) The Pledge really took off in the 1920s, when "my flag" became "the flag of the United States of America" and a coalition of citizens' groups, prominently including the Ku Klux Klan, got behind it. Millions of schoolchildren learned to recite it, accompanying the recitation with a stiff-armed, flat-palmed salute. (By 1942, for obvious reasons, the salute had been replaced with the hand-over-heart gesture that is used today.)

As a lot of people have been learning for the first time, the words "under God" weren't added until 1954, as part of a general outbreak of Cold War public piety. The campaign to stick them in was led by the Knights of Columbus, and got a big boost from President Eisenhower's Presbyterian pastor, the Reverend Dr. George M. Docherty, who sermonized that there was "something missing" in the Pledge. Without "under God," he said, "I could hear little Muscovites repeat a similar pledge to their hammer-and-sickle flag in Moscow." The change was gavelled through both Houses of Congress by voice vote without audible dissent. "Wedge issues" had not yet been invented, but politicians already knew that they had nothing to gain from quibbling about whether there's a God up there.

Thus it was that on a bright June morning in 1954 schoolchildren across the country were told that the Pledge of Allegiance would be different from then on. "One nation indivisible" was suddenly divisible—by the Supreme Being, no less. "Liberty and justice for all" was still intact, though it was unclear whether "all" now encompassed towheaded little Master Atheist and pigtailed little Miss Agnostic. For some, the experience left a small residue of disillusionment with the machinations of the grownup world—not as bad as when the Dodgers moved to Los Angeles, perhaps, but a palpable addition to the stultification that, come the 1960s, would generate an opposite and more than equal reaction.

All was quiet on the Pledge front for the next third of a century. Then, in 1988, when George Bush the elder and Michael Dukakis the hapless were running against each other for president, the Pledge got weaponized. As governor of Massachusetts, Dukakis had vetoed a bill that would have forced teachers to force their pupils to recite it. By the time Bush got through with him ("What is it about the Pledge that upsets him so much?"), the Duke was well on his way to a professorship at Northeastern.

Small wonder, then, that the other day, when a three-judge panel of the federal Court of Appeals for the Ninth Circuit, which covers eleven Western states and territories, ruled that "under God" falls afoul of the establishment-of-religion clause of the First Amendment, politicians rose as one in ostentatious wrath. The president led the way, squeezing off Bushisms. ("America is a nation that values our relationship with an Almighty." "You know, it's interesting, there is a universal God, in my opinion.") This time, the Democrats weren't about to let themselves be outpledged. "Just nuts," said Tom Daschle. Hillary Clinton pronounced herself "offended." Most egregious, the famously thoughtful Joseph Lieberman announced his eagerness to "amend the Constitution" so as to "make clear" that "we are one nation because of our faith in God."

Technically, the court's ruling was probably O.K. But the harm caused by those two words has not been serious—and it's nothing compared with the potential harm of poking this particular beehive with a stick. The only service performed by the court was the wholly redundant one of exposing the politician class in full pander mode. Anyway, all that Congress was doing this time was trying to keep something that has acquired the sheen of tradition from being taken out. It wasn't trying to shoehorn something in to suit the political panic of the moment. (After "under God," insert "and we don't mean Allah.")

Finally, W.W.F.B.D.? What would Francis Bellamy do? He wouldn't have liked the politics behind "under God," but the phrase itself probably wouldn't have bothered him. In his own speech at the ceremony where the Pledge was introduced, Bellamy praised the public schools as "the masterforce which, under God, has been informing each of our generations with the peculiar truths of Americanism." As an editor and rhetorician, though, Bellamy would notice that the phrase has been inserted in the wrong place. It should be "one nation indivisible, under God." As is, it sounds as if it's God that's indivisible (which would be news to the trinitarians among us). Also, the flow would be better. For a white guy from Boston, Bellamy had a pretty good sense of rhythm.

DIVIDENDS

THE CURRENT ADMINISTRATION likes its initiatives faith-based, and there has never been much secret about which faith constitutes the base. "Christ," Governor George W. Bush replied during a 1999 primary debate, when asked to name his favorite political philosopher. In the ambit of Bush the president, piety is next to godliness. According to a former Bush staffer, Evangelical Christianity is the "predominant creed" at the White House, and a tardy arrival is apt to be greeted with the reproach "Missed you at Bible study."

After the unveiling last Tuesday of Bush's "economic stimulus package," though, one has to wonder, and not for the first time, just which Bible these good people have been studying. It must be some sort of Heavily Revised Nonstandard Version, whose verses are familiar yet subtly different:

> He that hath pity upon the rich lendeth unto the Lord; and that which he hath given will pay him again. (Proverbs 19:17)

> Jesus said unto him, If thou wilt be perfect, go and sell what thou hast, and give to the rich, and thou shalt have treasure in heaven. (Matthew 19:21)

> For the love of money is the root of all good. (I Timothy 6:10)

The stimulus plan, which the president outlined in a speech to an audience of friendlies at the Economic Club of Chicago, exercises what the pope might call, if the pope were a Bush-style evangelical instead of a Catholic, a preferential option for the rich. It is fully consistent with the economic and fiscal policies that the administration has pursued from the beginning, which have combined small, cheap, and increasingly feeble gestures toward the bottom four-fifths of the income scale with enormous reductions in the taxes paid by the top tenth, and, especially, by the couple of hundred thousand families with annual incomes greater than a million dollars. Most of the claimed ten-year cost of the new plan—$364 billion out of $674 billion (the real cost is closer to $900 billion, because of interest payments on a higher public debt)—is accounted for by a proposal to make stock dividends tax-free. According to Citizens for Tax Justice, whose computations are generally regarded as reliable, half the cash will flow to the richest 1 percent of taxpayers. Another quarter of the benefits will go to the rest of the top 5 percent. Wealthy rentiers will thus be freed from the indignity of having to pay ordinary income tax on their dividend income, as if it were the vulgar sort of money that is earned by the sweat of one's brow—as if it were a coal miner's wages or a schoolteacher's salary. Much of the rest of Bush's plan consists of speeding up rate reductions from his 2001 tax cut, which are also overwhelmingly skewed in favor of the affluent.

"These tax reductions will bring real and immediate benefits to middle-income Americans," Bush said in Chicago. "Ninety-two million Americans will keep an average of $1,083 more of their own money." The first of these claims, as the *Financial Times* editorialized the day after the speech, is "obviously bogus." The second is true, but only in the sense that it is also true that if Bill Gates happened to drop by a homeless shelter where a couple of nuns were serving soup to sixty down-and-outers dressed in rags, the average person in the room would have a net worth of a billion dollars. Average, yes; typical, no. A typical taxpayer—one right smack in the middle of the income range—will get a couple of hundred dollars. And a worker in the bottom 20 percent will get next to nothing—at most, a dime or a quarter a week.

The Bloomberg financial news service performed the useful exercise of calculating what this latest Bush package would deliver to Bush himself. If his income this year is unchanged, he could get a windfall of as much as $44,500. Not bad—more, in fact, than the total income, before taxes, of a substantial majority of American families. Dick Cheney does even better. His tax break comes to $327,000—more than the before-tax income of 98 percent of his fellow citizens. At the presidential and vice-presidential level, it seems, there is no conflict of interest between public policy and private gain. The two are in perfect harmony.

The question naturally arises: have these people no shame? Well, yes, they have a little. They don't say outright that they regard giving money to the rich as a worthy end in itself. They say that their goal is to create jobs. That's what Bush said in his speech, not once but two dozen times. There are better ways to do this. The various Democratic proposals for smaller, faster, temporary tax cuts aimed at people who actually need money would be one such way. A payroll-tax holiday would be better still, because the payroll tax is a direct tax on jobs and therefore on job creation. Even better would be for the government to buy things that people need—social goods that markets cannot provide unassisted, things such as schools, cops, and hospitals. To provide economic stimulus, after all, the money has to be spent; and the surest way to guarantee that it will be spent is to spend it.

The notion that the elimination of income tax on dividends has something to do with stimulus is, to quote the *Financial Times* again, "dishonest and seems to be designed to prevent a proper discussion of the long-term fiscal costs and benefits." The proposal makes sense only as part of the administration's apparently iron determination to shift the tax burden downward. In that connection, here's a suggested text for the next meeting of the White House Bible-study group. The real thing this time, from the King James version, not the Prince George one:

And Jesus sat over against the treasury, and beheld how the people cast money into the treasury: and many that were rich cast in much.

And there came a certain poor widow, and she threw in two mites, which make a farthing.

And he called unto him his disciples, and saith unto them, Verily I say unto you, That this poor widow hath cast more in, than all they which have cast into the treasury:

For all they did cast in of their abundance; but she of her want did cast in all that she had, even all her living. (Mark 12:41–44)

Thus endeth the lesson, and thus might beginneth an enlightening discussion of the virtues of progressive taxation.

—*The New Yorker*, January 20, 2003

5. A CAMPAIGN

It would be convenient if I could maintain that the presidential campaign of 1988 was the most gripping and important of the twentieth century—or of the 1980s—with a straight face. But even if I could, no one would believe me. The nominees of both major parties were, after all, figures of striking mediocrity. One, the winner, was the overprivileged, syntax-mangling scion of a second-rate political dynasty. He glossed over his Andover and Yale background to present himself as a Texan, though he was all beanie and no cattle. He now seems destined to be remembered mainly as his son's father, like Efrem Zimbalist, Sr. The other, the loser, was the son of Mediterranean immigrants and the governor of a northeastern state, though he was not, alas, Mario Cuomo. He gave 'em neither hell nor heaven, was politically mugged but declined to press charges, and campaigned as if he had been nominated at the Technocratic National Convention. There was no third-party mischief to liven things up. Passions remained disengaged.

On the other hand, the fact that the White House was up for grabs in 1988, with no incumbent running for reelection and no prohibitive favorite, attracted a large supporting cast of odd and interesting characters, including Gary Hart, Pat Robertson, Bob Dole, Al Gore, and Bruce Babbitt.

With the Cold War sputtering to an end, no visible existential threats on the horizon, and a pair of nominees who, while dull, did not appear to be dangerous or insane, it was possible to enjoy the political spectacle without worrying overmuch about what it all might portend for the future.

The big advantage of the 1988 campaign, for my purposes here, is that it's the only one I ever covered from start to finish. When I wasn't on the road, I was living in Boston in a roomy Beacon Hill sublet and riding my bike every day along the Charles River to Cambridge, where I had an office at the Shorenstein Center on the Press, Politics, and Public Policy, which is part of the John F. Kennedy School of Government, which is part of Harvard. I was a "fellow"—no salary, no expenses, but a desk, a phone, and the run of the university's libraries and athletic facilities. Michael Dukakis's campaign headquarters was a subway ride away, New Hampshire an hour's drive. All the candidates and most of their handlers dropped by the Kennedy School. The company of eager undergraduates and tweedy professors seemed to soothe them, making them relatively relaxed and candid. My colleagues at the K-School knew plenty about politics, but they were more interested in the bigger social patterns, the wider historical sweep. This helped me keep the shenanigans of the campaign in perspective. And while Cambridge, Massachusetts, is not exactly Main Street America, it's just remote enough from Washington and Washington's obsessions to offer a bit of protection from the constantly stampeding conventional wisdom. I had as much fun as I've ever had in my life. Campaign '88 was a little like my only LSD trip, which, as it happens, occurred that same year. It was fascinating and intense; it produced unusual but temporary perceptual effects and one or two lasting insights (just don't ask me what they were); and, while I greatly enjoyed it, I have had no desire to repeat it. The occasional toke is more than enough.

SLUICEGATE '88

GARY HART has now become the first American victim of Islamic justice. He has been politically stoned to death for adultery. The difference is that in Iran, the mullahs do not insult the condemned prisoner by telling him that he is being executed not for adultery but because of "concerns about his character," "questions about his judgment," or "doubts about his candor."

As far as I can determine, Gary Hart is the first presidential candidate, president, prime minister, cabinet member, congressional committee chairman, party leader, or television evangelist, American or foreign, ever to be destroyed solely because of what David S. Broder, the dean of American political reporters, calls "screwing." In the past, for a public person's private sexual life to be considered a fit subject for exposure in respectable newspapers, some additional factor had to be adduced in order to establish a connection, however tenuous, between the screwing and the screwer's performance of his public duties. At Chappaquiddick a young woman was drowned and the accident was not reported promptly. In the Profumo affair Miss Keeler's other clients included Soviet diplomats. In the Jeremy Thorpe scandal an innocent dog was cold-bloodedly murdered.

But Gary Hart is held to be different, because in Gary Hart's case "concerns" had been raised about his "character." The business with Donna Rice was said to be part of a pattern. What else was part of this pattern? Well, the name change thing. The age thing. The signature thing. Anything else? No. The list ends there. What all these things have in common is that they are trivial. Character, however, is not trivial. It is the collection of qualities that make one person distinct from another; it is the overall moral pattern of a life and work. Character, by definition, is woven through the total pattern of a person's life; a man does not leave his character at home when he goes to the office. If Gary Hart is a man of bad character, surely the voluminous public record of his actions, decisions, statements, writings, and political maneuvers over the last fifteen years must be replete with examples. Those who have condemned his character on the basis of the Donna Rice affair have been unable to point to such examples. If character is something that manifests itself solely in a person's private sexual behavior, yet leaves no trace in the rest of his life, including his work life, then "character" is not very important after all—and the sexual details tell us nothing. If character is something that manifests itself in the totality of a life, then we don't need the sexual details to discern it.

The fact of Gary Hart's adultery—we must stipulate it for the sake of the argument—is being seen as the philosophers' stone that converts the rest of his life to dross. It certainly did that to his chances of being president. But to regard sexual facts as having a special, magical power of revelation that makes them superior to all other facts as clues to character is a vulgar distortion of psychoanalytic thinking. It's voodoo Freudianism.

The entire political and journalistic community "knew" about Gary Hart's marital infidelities long before the *Miami Herald* staked out his house, as did any intelligent newspaper reader capable of picking up hints and reading between the lines. For this large group of people the *Herald*'s tawdry scoop provided absolutely no new information by which to judge Hart's character. The only new information was provided by the manner in which Hart behaved when the catastrophe struck. In the face of what *Time*'s Walter Shapiro accurately described as "the most harrowing public ordeal ever endured by a modern presidential contender," Gary Hart showed an iron gut. His fortitude was remarkable, his coolness under fire exemplary, his courage admirable. Before all this happened I too had questions about Hart's character, as I have questions about the characters of all the candidates. But I think rather more highly of his character now than I did before.

Gary Hart is held to be different, because in Gary Hart's case "questions" were raised about his "judgment." And it was certainly an error in judgment for him to imagine that he could enter his own house, on a dark street, in the middle of the night, without being observed by reporters hiding in parked cars. Perhaps, given the way the press behaved, it was also an error in judgment for him not to have anticipated what have turned out to be the public consequences of his private life—though that comes perilously close to saying that the fact that he has been destroyed is proof that he deserved to be destroyed. If judgment, not sex, were truly "the issue," as we have been told over and over, then Hart's campaign would still be alive. And the headline in the *New York Post* would have been HART'S JUDGMENT REVEALED AS FAULTY, not GARY'S LOVE BOAT FOLLIES.

Gary Hart is held to be different, because in Gary Hart's case "doubts" were raised about his "candor." The issue is truthfulness, we are told, not adultery: the fact that he lied about his adultery shows he's a liar. The difficulty with this is that lying comes close to being an intrinsic part of adultery. The fact that a person will lie in the context of adultery proves nothing about his general propensity to lie. Whatever one thinks about adultery itself, lying about adultery has less in common with Watergate-style lying than with such social fictions as the practice of saying "Glad to see you" to people whom one is not in fact glad to see. The point is that if Hart is a liar there must be one or two more lies among the millions of words he has spoken as a public man. Let them be produced.

"THIS IS NOT about screwing," David Broder told a Harvard forum last week. "This is about the ability or inability of a candidate to sustain a human relationship over time." If that is what this is about, then it is not immediately apparent why Hart, who for all his personal troubles has been married to the same woman for twenty-eight years, is to be condemned more than the several other candidates who have divorced and remarried. Still, Broder is edging toward the only even remotely persuasive argument that Hart's sexual behavior is relevant to his ability to govern. This is what might be called the feminist argument. Writing in *Newsweek,* Suzannah Lessard defended the relevancy of a candidate's adultery as a measure of his "awareness of the dignity and equality of women." Yet even Lessard added that "a candidate's behavior in this respect is significant but not the kind of issue that by itself ought to decide one for or against a candidate." It's worth mentioning, by the way, that no major presidential candidate in American history ever put women in such influential and important posts in his campaigns as did Gary Hart. If Hart is a misogynist of some kind, no hint of it ever carried over into any aspect of his work.

The famous dare Hart put to E. J. Dionne, Jr., of the *New York Times*—

"If anybody wants to put a tail on me, go ahead"—was both the candidate's biggest mistake and the press's luckiest break. The *Miami Herald's* stakeout was widely rationalized as a response to this challenge—though how a challenge can be taken up before it is issued remains a mystery. (The Miami vice squad was outside Hart's house the night before Dionne's piece was published.) But it is infantile to think that Hart's foolish dare somehow freed the *Herald* from any obligation to decide for itself how it ought to behave. That level of moral reasoning is better suited to a grammar school blacktop than to a newsroom.

The bottom line is that no matter what Gary Hart says, Gary Hart's private life is none of my business, none of your business, and none of the respectable press's business. The *Miami Herald* editor who got the tip should have said, "I'm sorry, ma'am, you have the wrong number. You want the *National Enquirer."* The reporter who got the order to do the stakeout should have said, "I'm sorry, sir, but it's more than this job's worth to be a Peeping Tom." And when Gary Hart noticed the carful of men parked in the gloom outside his house, he should have called the police and told them he had reason to believe a Libyan hit squad was shadowing him. A couple of reporters spread-eagle against a fender, surrounded by cruisers with red lights flashing and radios barking, might have done wonders for journalistic ethics.

THE GROSS VIOLATION of the privacy of Gary Hart, Lee Hart, and their children is part of a general degradation of the public sphere and a general weakening of the distinction between the public and the private realms of life in the United States. This is a social phenomenon with many sources—the Reagan administration's delegitimation of public action, the human potential movement's hostility toward "hypocrisy" and exaltation of "authenticity," and the feminists' dictum that the personal is the political, to name three. But none of this justifies the *Miami Herald* and the *Washington Post* any more than the correlation between poverty and crime justifies mugging.

I don't mean this to be a defense of Hart, whose public behavior was in many ways foolish. I do mean it to be an attack on the *Herald* and the *Post,* which deliberately opened a sluice gate that will not be easy to close. The papers are full of assurances that there will be no peeping into other candidate's bedrooms without "probable cause." There was probable cause in

Hart's case because (a) many people knew of the rumors of Hart's infidelities; (b) the currency of these rumors constituted presumptive evidence that Hart was recklessly indiscreet; and (c) his presumed indiscretion legitimately "raised questions about his judgment." One might call this the Gossip Standard of Probable Cause. The problem is that Hart is not the only candidate whose "judgment" is called into question by the Gossip Standard. In the current field, for example, I have heard that Candidate A is as notorious a womanizer as Gary Hart, that Candidate B is having an affair with his secretary, and the Candidates G and H are adulterers. If I have heard these rumors, thousands, perhaps millions, of others must have heard them too. The Gossip Standard of Probable Cause. I'm confident that the *Herald* and the *Post* will not stoop to going after any of this, but there are many newspapers in this country, and not all of them are so scrupulous. If some fourth-rate paper somewhere does a story, and it moves on the wires, and people start calling radio phone-in shows, and the story gets picked up by a couple of third-rate papers, and "concerns" start getting "raised" . . .

Allah preserve us!

—*The New Republic*, June 1, 1987

SPORTING NEWS

WITH THE PUBLICATION of the Gary 'n' Donna vacation snapshots in the *National Enquirer*, the 1988 presidential "character" story has at last found its natural level. But before the story takes its place on that big front page in the sky, there to join such other all-time greats as the *Boston American*'s Toodles and Honey Fitz Fitzgerald story (1913) and the New York *Evening Graphic*'s Peaches and Daddy Browning story (1926), a couple of final examples of press pathology deserve to be recorded. The first concerns the *Washington Post* and its lead political reporter, Paul Taylor. It was Taylor of the *Post* (not some hireling of Rupert Murdoch or Lyndon LaRouche) who achieved a Fawn Hall–like fifteen minutes of fame by asking Hart the two key questions, "Do you consider adultery immoral?" and "Have you ever committed adultery?" Taylor has now offered his apologia, in the form of a letter to the editor of the *New York Times*. The letter is written in the slangy, regular-guy style much prized at the *Post* ("Let's review the bidding here," "What in heaven's name are these guys talking about?" etc.). Taylor's argument is essentially that Hart asked for it, both by fooling around after telling his staff he wouldn't, and by saying, after the *Miami Herald* scoop, that he'd done nothing "immoral." But there's another explanation for Taylor's line of questioning. Six hours after Taylor popped his questions, the *Post*, as he boasted in his story the next day, "presented a top campaign aide with documented evidence of a recent liaison between Hart and a Washington woman with whom he has had a long-term relationship." Given that, it looks very much as if Taylor's real reason for asking Hart if he had ever committed adultery was to elicit a denial and thus to establish a "cover-up" rationale for going with the "recent liaison" story the *Post* was sitting on. This proved unnecessary, in the event, because Hart decided to drop out of the race, in exchange for which the *Post* agreed not to print the name of the "Washington woman." I'm sure there is a moral distinction between this transaction and simple blackmail, though it escapes me for the moment.

By the way, according to rumor (or "persistent reports," as the *Post* would say), the "documented evidence" of the "recent liaison" was in fact collected by a private eye hired by a jealous husband, himself a prominent politician. So here we have a new "role" for the press: adjudicating the love triangles of the rich and famous.

Taylor wrote to the *Times* because the *Times*'s Anthony Lewis had named him as the questioner, and because Lewis, William Safire, Tom Wicker, Russell Baker, and former executive editor A. M. Rosenthal, in a rare display of op-ed unanimity, had all deplored the *Post*'s and the Miami *Herald*'s handling of the story. (The *Times*'s sixth columnist, Flora Lewis, whose specialty is foreign affairs, merely reported Europe's bafflement that such things were considered serious news.) But in its own coverage, the *Times* went haywire, too. On Monday, May 5, the day after the *Herald*'s big score, the *Times* confined itself to a story on page A16 under the discreet headline PAPER AND HART IN DISPUTE OVER ARTICLE. On Monday, May 6, though, the newspaper of record kicked out the jams. At the top of page one was a glamorous publicity still captioned, "Portrait of Donna Rice purchased from a Miami photographer who asked not to be identified." The story, headlined AN ACTRESS IN TURMOIL," was not yet six paragraphs old when it hit pay dirt: "Three years ago she posed partially nude for a photograph used to publicize a Miami-area country-western saloon, standing at a bar in jeans and"—here the story jumped, forcing the reader to turn with trembling fingers to page B6, column 5—"a cowboy hat, with a Confederate flag draped across her front." Hubba hubba! At the end of the story was a box headed HOW PICTURES WERE OBTAINED that bragged breathlessly, "The New York Times yesterday purchased two pictures, about three years old, of Donna Rice, an actress and model identified as the woman in the controversy embroiling former Senator Gary Hart. . . . The photos were exclusively provided to The Times by a photographer who insisted on anonymity." For some reason the *Times* printed only one of the pictures, the head shot. The Confederate flag one was omitted. Space considerations, probably. I describe all this because it appeared only in early editions, such as the one we get in Boston. By the time of the late edition, the one most New Yorkers (and most *Times* staffers) see, the publicity still had been replaced by a news photo and the box had been pulled. Future researchers looking for those exclusive pix will scan the microfilm in vain; only the late edition lives in history. A close shave. I mean, I'm all for glasnost, but could it be that de-Rosenthalization has gone too far?

—Boston Diarist, *The New Republic*, June 15, 1987

G.O.P. FOLLIES

GEORGE BUSH "won" the Republicans' first debate for a lot of reasons, but the biggest was his association with somebody higher ranking than he is, a popular politician and skilled communicator who believes in the economic magic of the market and who, despite some sniping from the right wing of his own party, is about to enjoy a foreign policy triumph made possible by massive concessions to a hostile power he has spent most of his career describing as a dangerous and malevolent empire.

Yes, Bush has reason to be grateful to Mikhail Gorbachev. By meeting Ronald Reagan nine-tenths of the way (ten-tenths when necessary), he has set the stage for a splashy stateside summit next month, at which the president and the general secretary will sign a treaty banning intermediate-range ballistic missiles from Europe. The I.N.F. treaty has been dismissed by many a Washington Strangelove as unimportant at best and dangerous at worst, but it is neither. And it is the easiest arms control sell since the Kennedy-Khrushchev test ban, because unlike SALTs I and II it is nice and simple. Here's how George Bush sold it during the debate: "I like an agreement that takes out sixteen hundred Soviet warheads for four hundred of ours. . . . This is the first time in the nuclear age that we're getting rid of an entire generation of nuclear weapons, and that's good for my grandchildren and the rest of the world."

Bush and Gorbachev had plenty of help. During the debate, a two-hour edition of William F. Buckley, Jr.'s *Firing Line* broadcast from Houston, all five of Bush's opponents managed to position themselves on what is almost sure to be the politically wrong side of the issue, even within the Republican Party. Reading from right to far right, Robert "Bob" Dole prescribed a "dose of healthy skepticism." Alexander M. "Al" Haig, Jr., said that "Europe is unnerved about this agreement." Pierre S. "Pete" du Pont IV said, "I cannot support a treaty we may not be able to verify made with a nation we cannot trust." Marion G. "Pat" Robertson called the treaty "badly flawed." And Jack "Jack" Kemp said, "I wouldn't sign a new agreement with the Soviet Union until they're required to keep the previous agreements they signed with the United States of America." Kemp added, using a bit of think-tank shorthand certain to baffle viewers unaware that it is good to be nuclearized, "I can't understand why we're rushing into an agreement that threatens to denuclearize Europe."

Bush's rivals thus lashed themselves to the rails on the very track down which the Moscow-Washington Express is scheduled to roar on December 7, with Bush in the cab of the locomotive sitting next to the engineer. Of the five, only Dole tied himself loosely enough to permit himself to escape without severe rope burns and in time to hop aboard the caboose.

Thanks to the expectations game, the fix was in for Bush before the debate even started. Bush had a bad reputation as a debater, the hangover from his goofy performances in the 1980 Iowa debate against Reagan and the 1984 debate against Geraldine Ferraro. Delivering a widely held press verdict, Evans and Novak wrote that Bush won "mainly by not losing." Robertson benefited from a similar dynamic: he gained simply by appearing affable and by not having his head rotate 360 degrees with the sign of the beast tattooed on his forehead. Dole, meanwhile, was destined to be counted a flop no matter what he did. Forced to pick between being too nasty or too nice, he chose (probably wisely) too nice.

But Bush was more than just lucky. With surprising grace and subtlety, he also established a certain distance from Reagan—starting with his answer to the first substantive question of the debate, posed by Robert Strauss, the Washington operative who served as Buckley's Ed McMahon: Could you please name some areas where the administration should have done things differently? "The answer is, I could but I won't," Bush replied, neatly establishing both fealty and independence. He went on to list his own priorities, beginning with education and arms control, neither of which has been a passion of the Reagan regime.

Bush's best moment, however, came in an exchange with du Pont. The panel was sunk in a numbing discussion of how grateful they all were to Robertson for bringing his evangelical followers into the Republican Party—a discussion that for hypocrisy and condescension was more than a match for the Democratic candidates' similar go-rounds with Jesse Jackson. Du Pont, with little to lose, decided to change the subject and strike. Bush had "heroically followed America into war" and followed Nixon into China and followed Reagan into tax cuts. "But the question is, in a Bush presidency, where would he lead America?" Illogically, he tied this complaint back to the I.N.F. question: "We're waiting for details and we're hearing generalities." Bush's reply:

> Pierre, let me help you on some of this. One, I think it's a nutty idea to fool around with the Social Security system and run the risk of [hurting] the people who've been saving all their lives. . . . It may be a new idea, but it's a dumb one. On the question of the I.N.F. treaty, I told you all these European leaders were for it. I'm for it. The president's for it. The Joint Chiefs are for it. . . . It's fine when you're outside, carping, criticizing a president and it's different, I've found, it is very different when you're in there having to make the tough calls.

For Bush, a more advantageous foil than du Pont cannot be imagined. Patronizing, humorless, and ice-cold, du Pont is the perfect picture of a banker about to foreclose on the mortgage. The bumper stickers may say Pete, but the glasses, clothes, haircut, and narrow, thin-lipped face all scream Pierre the Fourth. Bush doesn't need to worry about seeming too preppy when du Pont is in the room. He makes Bush look like the Godfather of Soul. Bush and du Pont are on different sides of the ideological fault line that divides the traditional Republicans (Bush, Dole, Haig) from the movement conservatives (du Pont, Kemp, Robertson). But they are on the same side of another fault line, the one between the upper-crust, to-the-manor-born types (Bush, du Pont, Robertson) and the non-U's (Kemp, Dole, Haig). Bush could therefore slap du Pont around at will without the risk of awakening class resentments in the audience.

Du Pont's thrust was a crafty blending of poll data that show voters perceiving Bush as a vague, visionless, wimpy follower. By telling du Pont where to get off, Bush showed he could play the tough guy. His sarcastic "Pierre, let me help you" was the evening's knockout punch, the equivalent of Reagan's "there you go again" in the 1980 debate with Jimmy Carter. As it happens, Reagan's 1980 "there you go again" crack had come in response to Carter's (correct) accusation that Reagan had advocated making Social Security voluntary—precisely the idea, suitably updated, that du Pont has made the centerpiece of his 1988 campaign. By attacking du Pont on this issue, Bush implicitly attacked Reagan—not Reagan himself, but the side of Reaganism that voters find least appealing in the light of the stock market crash and the intimations of hard times to come. Thus Bush may have helped to free himself from his president's increasingly palsied grasp.

Bush made his share of foolish statements too, mostly about taxes, but in that company he was not likely to be called on them. "As president," he pledged, "I will not raise taxes." Seconds later he added (referring to the efforts of Dole and other congressional leaders to reach a budget compromise), "I think it's right to do what Bob's engaged in. I think it's time to lay partisan politics aside, get it solved, and then as president not raise taxes." That is, it's O.K. to raise taxes between now and January 20, 1989, but not O.K. between January 20, 1989, and January 20, 1993. And the list of Bush priorities that began with education and arms control ended with this voodoo prayer: "reducing the capital gains [tax] rate to add five billion dollars' worth of income for the federal government." Say what?

PAT ROBERTSON did better than expected, mostly by chuckling a lot and going easy on the Bible-thumping. He invoked his friend God only in his closing statement, which was calculated to reassure. "The first thing we've got to do in America is get back to basics," he said. "And many of the things are not governmental solutions. We can't make through government husbands love their wives, or wives love their husbands, or families bring up their children as law-abiding, God-fearing citizens. That's got to be done in the private sector." "The private sector" is a curious way to evoke the sanctity of the hearth. It sounds a bit like the plan is to contract out bedroom-snooping to the business community. (Moralco, Inc.?) Nevertheless, the point was made.

Yet for all his attempts to seem normal, the Howdy Doody-faced evangelist did contribute the debate's one moment of transcendent lunacy. It came when Robertson advanced the theory that banning abortion is the solution to the problem of financing Social Security:

We've got a true genetic problem in these United States of a magnitude beyond what we could conceive of. By the year 2020 we're going to be running out of workers. There won't be enough to support the retirees. As a matter of fact by the year 2000 we will have aborted forty million children in this country. Their work product by the year 2020 will amount to $1.4 trillion, the taxes from them would amount to $330 billion, and they could ensure the fiscal stability of the Social Security system, which is going to be near bankrupt by the year 2015.

Robertson promised to address the Social Security crisis by vetoing all federal funding for Planned Parenthood.

The press gave Bob Dole lousy marks; "lackluster" and "tranquilized" were among the unkinder cuts. But then, as noted, Dole was trapped in an "expectations" double bind. That's something he'll just have to wait out. Meanwhile, even as he referred to his rivals as "all these fine candidates," he managed to convey a (to me) attractive impatience with the low company he was being forced to keep. He showed a similar subtle scorn for some of the positions he apparently believes himself obliged to take. "I'm a strong supporter of S.D.I., and I think we're making progress," one Dole observation began. "We know that the Russians are spending millions or maybe billions of dollars on the same thing. In fact we get recent reports that they may be catching up, or whatever." That "or whatever" was a nice contemptuous touch. But Dole used most of his time to construct a persona—laconic, plain-spoken, occasionally witty—that seems built for the long haul. His savage side, made famous by his 1976 vice-presidential debate with Walter Mondale, came through only once. Haig had just started talking when Dole interrupted with a cutting "Tell that joke, Al, about Haig & Haig." Poor Haig could think only to reply, gamely but lamely, "I'm going to do that." Sure enough, the general then told his joke: "Beware of Dole & Dole, it's only watered-down pineapple juice. Haig & Haig is the real McCoy." Not that bad, actually, even if the punchline lacked surprise.

—The New Republic, November 23, 1987

TUESDAY NIGHT PATBALL

A COUPLE OF THOUSAND YEARS from now, perhaps, when faint electronic signals from this corner of the galaxy are picked up on some distant world, the alien exobiologist assigned to decipher them may well conclude that there once was a planet called Earth and that it was ruled by a biped named Brokaw. It's hard to imagine a more powerful symbol of television's political primacy than the NBC anchorman's back-to-back nights of glory. On December 1st he imperiously asked a gaggle of politicians why they thought they were qualified for the honor of sitting across the table from Mikhail Gorbachev. Someone had actually sat across that table just the night before, and that someone was Tom Brokaw. Maybe the politicians are seeking the wrong job.

Brokaw was the most obvious "winner" of Tuesday evening's two-hour, one-party-after-another extravaganza, but he wasn't the only one. As in Houston on October 28th, George Bush won by default on the Republican side, and again for the same reason: he is the only candidate of his party who unequivocally supports the wildly popular Euromissile arms control treaty. On other subjects, however, the vice president was not so impressive. His gee-whiz side seems to be acting up again. "Can I say something on this Ollie North thing?" was how he began one comment, which ended with the observation that sure, North and Poindexter "did some things wrong," but "I don't want to let these guys [the Democrats, not the Iranamok gang] off by just criticizing all the time two patriotic people."

Bob Dole, for his part, made it clearer than before that his suspension of judgment on the treaty is simply a matter of senatorial ritual, and that he'll be for it in the end: "I've never let the president down yet, but I have a right to read and study and have my experts take a look at this thing." Al Haig—whose overall performance was surprisingly good—was murkier. On the one hand, "It's too late to scuttle what has already happened," on the other, "It seems to me we need some absolute preconditions," including solving the problems of strategic nuclear weapons and conventional force imbalances in Europe. Since there is no chance these "preconditions" can be met, it will require some powerful Haigspeak for the general to talk himself around to supporting the treaty.

Part of the format called for the candidates to ask each other questions. Most of these were what Haig called "patballs," but his own, directed at Bush, was not: "George, you've claimed to be the co-pilot of this administration, and we've known that on occasion you were the pilot. The president put you in charge of the task force to deal with terrorism. One of the recommendations of that task force was that we will never engage in paying blackmail to terrorists. Now, where were you when the administration made a decision to do precisely that? Were you in the cockpit or were you in an economy ride in the back of the plane?" Bush's rather lame answer included this weird boast: "I wrote the antiterror report. It was the best antiterror report that any country has ever had." The best *darn* antiterror report, you could almost hear him say.

Pierre S. du Pont IV got to be Pete all night long, as he, Jack Kemp, and Pat Robertson fought over the crumbs at the far right end of the table. Kemp forthrightly called for pardoning North and Poindexter. Robertson announced in shocked tones his discovery that "the Soviets, in my estimation, have been trying to undermine NATO for years." He added later that he "would believe in the Great Pumpkin and the tooth fairy" before he'd trust the Communists—not so unthinkable an eventuality, given that he already believes that TV evangelists can divert hurricanes.

On the Democratic side, Michael Dukakis was able to float above the battle, saying little of note but projecting calmness and stability. Al Gore was the most impressive of the bunch. He was cogent (as he showed in a well-constructed verbal essay on how to achieve savings at the Pentagon), passionate (as in a denunciation of official inaction on AIDS), and even mildly witty. When Jesse Jackson began a question to Gore, "Since I'm the Southern candidate," Gore shot back, "South Chicago"—earning a laugh and a handshake from Jackson. Under pressure from Gore (and from the Republicans in the wings), the other Democrats sounded a bit more hawkish than usual. Even Jackson, who now swims in the mainstream like Mao in the Yangtze, said he wouldn't deflag the Kuwaiti tankers.

Paul Simon had perhaps the most to lose, and by and large he lost it. He was unable to give a plausible answer to the question of where he would get the money to pay for the many New Deal-style programs he has proposed. Richard Gephardt, who designated himself to lead the attack on Simon ("Simonomics is really Reaganomics with a bow tie"), damaged both himself and his target in the process. Bruce Babbitt, with nothing to lose, tried a bit of stage business: he climaxed his call for the candidates to "stand up" to the budget deficit issue by literally standing up. It was hokey and it cost him a bit in the dignity sweepstakes, but at six foot three, he couldn't be ignored.

Jackson, in his remarks on AIDS, made this point: "The last night on earth of Jesus the Christ, he stayed with Simon the leper, who was quarantined with the so-called sin sickness of his day." At the word "Simon," the incredibly alert NBC director instantly switched to a shot of the senator from Illinois. Poor guy. He was better off when they confused him with the singer.

—*The New Republic*, December 21, 1987

MONSTER FROM THE ID

THE BEST BUMPER STICKER of this campaign is still the one a friend of mine claims to have spotted about a year ago: HE'S TAN. HE'S RESTED. HE'S READY. NIXON IN '88.

Gary Hart's December 15th redeclaration of candidacy brought that bumper sticker to mind again, and not just because of the memory of the nice little note Hart received last May, shortly after dropping out, from the man who proved for all time that one's last press conference need not be one's last press conference. In the days following Hart's sudden lurch from the political grave the Nixon comparison was all over the place. It's an unfair comparison, mostly. Both Hart and Nixon have a grievance against the press, but Hart's is justified: his privacy *was* invaded, and he was essentially blackmailed out of the race by the threat of more such invasions. Both men are proven liars, but from the standpoint of statecraft Hart's lies have been uniformly trivial (why he changed his name, where he spent the night), while Nixon's were about rather more important things, such as what countries he was bombing and whether or not he was committing high crimes and misdemeanors. Morally, Hart is no Nixon. Yet there are points of similarity, and one of them is this: Hart, like Nixon, knows how to keep things interesting.

Things got awfully interesting awfully fast when Hart jumped back in. It was politics as theatre, politics as guerrilla tactics, politics as psychotherapy. And it was superb as all three. Only from the point of view of politics as politics—that is, politics as how a free people govern themselves and choose their leaders—did it leave something to be desired.

As theatre, Hart's reentry made for great television. News is only television's hobby; comedy and drama are its business. David Letterman's gibes ("In, out, in, out—isn't that what got him in trouble in the first place?") were shown not only on the Letterman show but on news programs such as *Nightline* and *The MacNeil/Lehrer News Hour* as well. Other jokes (such as: "It's safe to vote for Gary Hart, but only if you're wearing a condom" or "This proves that you really *can* fuck your brains out") were too strong for TV, but traveled at the speed of light all the same. The comedy was a bit tired, most of it, but the drama was downright compelling, drawing as it did elements from almost every known genre of popular entertainment: soap opera, romance, suspense, horror, domestic melodrama, Westerns. In his reannouncement speech a cowboy-booted Hart provided the trailer (rated G) for his own movie (rated R). "This will not be like any campaign you have ever seen," he promised thrillingly. "Because I am going directly to the people . . . . I don't have pollsters or consultants or media advisers or political endorsements. But I have something even better. I have the power of ideas." It was *High Noon* crossed with *Rambo*, directed by Frank Capra (second unit director Russ Meyer).

As political guerrilla tactics, Hart's reentry was just what Patrick Caddell, his occasional colleague, adviser, and enemy, called it: brilliant. When the storm broke last May, Hart really had no choice but to withdraw. Had he stayed in he would have been slowly, excruciatingly crushed between two kinds of stories: the unearthing, liaison by liaison, of all his romantic interludes; and the collapse, departing staffer by outraged contributor, of his campaign organization. Better to quit, and so let the liaison stories sputter out and the antipress reaction take hold unmolested. Better to quit, and so cut the losses in his organization. That horse had a broken leg anyway. Better to quit, and so let the press and the party pros spend seven months deriding the remaining candidates as bores and midgets. Hart meant it when he left the race, but he wouldn't have behaved all that differently had he been plotting his return from Elba all along.

His timing was perfect. He waited until the last possible moment: the day of the New Hampshire filing deadline, in time for the evening news. Gorbachev had taken his bows and swept into the wings, the crowd was standing to leave the theatre—and Gary Hart leaps, arms outstretched, from the balcony to the apron of the stage. Ta-da! His supernova of publicity engulfed the week before the holiday break: thirty-nine-and-a-half minutes on the three network news programs (out of fifty minutes devoted to politics that week), an hour of *Nightline,* the cover of *Time,* huge punning tabloid headlines: HAVE A HART (New York *Daily News),* CHANGE OF HART *(Newsday),* HART TO BELIEVE! *(New York Post),* and at the end of the week a relaxed-yet-emotional chat with Ed Bradley on *60 Minutes.* The Bradley interview was seen by forty million people, the largest political audience of the year. After the holidays and their sluggish aftermath, a two-hour televised debate from Des Moines, on January 15th, will mark the reborn candidate's return to the fold. Three weeks later, the Iowa caucuses. A nice, crisp, three-week campaign, like England's: just what the reformers always wanted.

But it is as psychotherapy that Hart's decision makes most sense. He has often said, still says, that office-seeking is something he can take or leave. After the collapse he could have started anew—could have moved to Los Angeles, say, where new beginnings and complicated personal lives are routine—but he didn't. He became the wraith of Denver, stewing in his law office and tormenting himself by giving speeches few paid attention to. When Bradley asked him how he had liked it, thus was his reply: "Worst period of my life. Worst period of my life. Worst period of my life." In this interview, in all the interviews, you could see the relief washing over him. He says he's running because he thinks his ideas are better—he can hardly be expected to say he thinks they're worse—but at the same time he implicitly admits, and with far more feeling, that his real reasons for running are existential and psychological. Consider this exchange from the *60 Minutes* interview:

BRADLEY: How long are you in this race?

HART: For the duration.

BRADLEY: And if the voters say no, Gary, we don't want you?

HART: I'm gone. I'm out. This is not a dog-in-the-manger operation. I know when I'm not wanted.

BRADLEY: What would you do with the rest of your life?

HART: Oh, there are a lot of things I could do.

BRADLEY: But I mean, if there are a lot of things you could do with your life, you could have done them without getting back in the race.

HART: Yeah, but now I will know. Now I will know. Otherwise I would never have known. It's that simple. How would you like to go through the rest of your life having a major unanswered question? This way, I'll have it answered.

BRADLEY: And those who say that you got back in because you need the voters more than the voters need Gary Hart?

HART: Let the voters decide that. I mean, I'm taking certain risks. The voters can say no. But even if they say no, I'll feel better about myself than if I'd just sat up there on that mountain, wondering.

There it is: the man is running so he can feel better about himself. It's not the highest motive in the world, but it's not the basest either, and it's both more believable and less alarming than the motives of contempt, recklessness, revenge, and cynicism so widely ascribed to him. One would have to be awfully callous not to hope he finds the tranquillity he seeks (and more callous still not to wish Lee Hart and Donna Rice some of the same). But what has all this got to do with who ought to be president of the United States? Not a thing.

There has been much overwrought commentary about the threat that Hart's candidacy poses to the party and the nation. Clearly Hart himself will not be nominated (and if he is rational, his goal is rehabilitation, not nomination). Clearly Hart's entry ups the ante for Michael Dukakis in New Hampshire. And clearly Hart burns up some of the air the less well known but more electable candidates, such as Albert Gore and Bruce Babbitt, need to breathe to stay alive. Beyond that, though, things are not so clear. If the press is not too quick about pronouncing candidacies dead after New Hampshire and Super Tuesday, then maybe states like California and New York might actually be allowed something to say about who gets the nomination. That would be a nice change. Perhaps the convention might even be forced to act like a deliberative body and choose the nominee itself. That wouldn't necessarily be so terrible either.

BY REVIVING HIS CAMPAIGN, Hart has also revived the argument about the private lives of public people. In the toughest of his post-announcement interviews, the one with Jim Lehrer of PBS, the candidate stuck to his new insistence that his private life is no one else's business:

LEHRER: Now why isn't it anyone else's business?

HART: Because it isn't. It hasn't been the business of the American public for two hundred years and it isn't today.

LEHRER: You don't think it speaks to the question of judgment as to what a person would do as a candidate for president of the United States?

HART: Jim, if I may call you Jim, let's reverse the logic. Does it suggest that because Ronald Reagan used poor judgment on Irangate that therefore he's unfaithful to his wife?

LEHRER: I don't understand what you mean.

Well, *I* understand what he means, and he has a point. The two realms, public and private, are distinct and ought to be kept that way. Misbehavior in the one does not necessarily entail misbehavior in the other. But Hart goes further, implicitly arguing that the individual soul—the character, if you will, of a particular human being—is itself correspondingly divisible. Praising his wife to Ed Bradley, Hart said: "She has had a remarkable ability to detach her relationship to me as my wife from my role as candidate for the Senate or the presidency." Obviously Hart himself has that "remarkable ability" too. But many others balk at accepting, let alone admiring, such a radical internal dissociation. This is the hard nub of truth beneath all the vague and pompous moralizing about "the character issue."

Hart asks us to accept, and admire, an analogous split between "politics as usual"—that is, politics—and "ideas." His ideas are fine (though they are not as unique as he makes them out to be), and he expresses them more cogently and convincingly than ever. But he is wrong to insist that he be judged on them alone, in isolation from any assessment of his ability to carry them out in the messy rough-and-tumble of our messy political system. In boasting of a campaign free of such encumbrances as alliances to be built and a staff to be administered, Hart is partly just making a virtue of necessity. But he is plainly glad to be rid of all that. The campaign a candidate runs is a miniature mock-up of the government he would give us. Do we really want a government free of "politics"? It's hard to argue with a slogan like "Let the people decide," but do we really want a quasi-plebiscitary government in which the president, seen as a disembodied generator of ideas, communes directly with "the people" without the intervening institutional cushions of Congress, the press, and the political process? Whether he wants to or not, Hart is also calling into question the legitimacy of politics itself. He takes the "anti-government" themes of the last three elections a fateful step further. He stokes the fires of alienation, and others may get burned.

I happen to think that Hart got a raw deal last May. He was engulfed in a story of private passion and family intrigue, and now, however unfairly, he can't get loose from it. That's why his campaign cannot now finally be about "ideas." His revived candidacy is a long, bony arm that reaches down shoulder deep into the collective id and dredges up muck. The muck clouds the waters; it diverts our attention from public questions; it makes us respond inappropriately and disproportionately. Hart wants to provoke our thinking about public policy, but all he does is roil our feelings about love and sex and the drama of family life—subjects, as Hart is the first to insist, that don't belong in the political arena. Hart stirs the wrong kind of passions, and that is why he won't, and probably shouldn't, be president. It's hard to imagine a more ironic denouement for Gary Hart, the hyperrational candidate of ideas.

—*The New Republic*, January 18, 1988

FIRST RETURNS

THE 1988 CAMPAIGN woke up with a start last Monday night. The sitzkrieg ended; the blitzkrieg began. The Iowa caucuses put a shocking stop to a long, dreamy year in which every event or pseudoevent that came drifting into view could be analyzed and reanalyzed, and then the analyses could be languorously analyzed in their turn. There was no hurry, even when, as happened from time to time, the events themselves lurched quickly. Whatever the distraction of the moment, it could be savored at leisure like a glass of port. The candidates and their staffs, of course, were all frenetic activity; but they were seen, if they were seen at all, as if through the wrong end of a telescope, tiny figures gesticulating in the distance, their voices faint and tinny. Inconclusiveness had become a settled way of life. It had begun to seem as if things might just go on that way forever, that we might all grow old together, lulled into somnolence by the gentle rhythms of endless poll results and murmured complaints about the length of the campaign, the absurdity of the process, and the inadequacies of the candidates. Then, *blam!* Iowa. Suddenly we're at Mach 2, and the landscape is a giddy blur below. To quote *All About* (Election) *Eve:* Fasten your seat belts. It's going to be a bumpy ride.

On the Democratic side, there were two unambiguous winners (Richard Gephardt and Jesse Jackson), two ambiguous winners (Paul Simon and Michael Dukakis), one ambiguous loser (Al Gore), and two unambiguous losers (Gary Hart and Bruce Babbitt). Among the losers, none showed his pain more chillingly than Hart. From May to December, Hart was consumed by a single question: to run (again) or not to run. He never thought beyond that question. Eight weeks ago, when he made his existential leap into the void, he was beatific with relief. But in Iowa the pavement came up to meet him, and on caucus night his face was drawn into a mask of bitterness. In a tight, angry voice he told interviewers that his invisible showing didn't mean that much, that he'd do better in New Hampshire, that he'd only had a couple of weeks to campaign while everybody else had been at it for a year. The reality is that he has been campaigning for six years. New Hampshire will be the end for him.

Babbitt deserved better than the 9 percent of the vote Iowa gave him. His calls for fiscal honesty had won him, briefly, the attention of the voters; but once they were listening he simply repeated himself, instead of telling them what (other than a tidy balance sheet) the taxes he advocated might buy them. He too will be out after New Hampshire, but if the next administration is a Democratic one there surely ought to be a place for him in it. As for Gore, his Southern strategy had looked for a clean Simon victory. Gore is ill served by Gephardt's emergence (and by Robertson's—more conservative Southern Democrats will now cross over on Super Tuesday). Gore survives, but his immediate future is as cloudy as his long-term prospects are bright. (He won't be Hart's age, for example, until the year 2000.)

The big Democratic winner, of course, was Richard Gephardt, a man who puts me in mind, unreasonably to be sure, of an earthling whose body has been taken over by space aliens. I keep expecting him to reach under his chin and peel back that immobile, monochromatic, oddly smooth face to reveal the lizard beneath. Perhaps the aliens are from the planet Bryan. How else to explain the fact that Gephardt, who until a few months ago was a sort of neoconservative neoliberal, has suddenly begun talking, in his slow, robotic voice, like a devotee of the cult of Populism? Whatever its provenance, though, Gephardt's message, as expressed in his extraordinarily skillful TV commercial and his own quick sound bites, is manifestly effective. The message is that our standard of living is going down, that foreigners and establishmentarians are to blame, and that we need new economic and trade policies to get better jobs at better wages. Not very uplifting, not very noble, but very, very clear.

The clarity of Gephardt's message, not the margin of his victory, is what makes him so formidable coming out of Iowa. Paul Simon's second-place finish was good but not quite good enough, and his backward-looking, Humphreyite campaign has stasis written all over it. Michael Dukakis acted triumphant on caucus night. His showing so far from home was strong, but not so strong as to tempt New Hampshire voters to take him down a peg. His record over the years is far more consistent than Gephardt's, but his campaign is intellectually and "thematically" adrift, wandering aimlessly from the Massachusetts Miracle to the Nicaraguan Nightmare by way of the New American Frontier. The danger, for Dukakis, is that he will imagine he can get by with more of the same. And Jackson? Well, he got five times as many white votes as black ones. He has made no blunders of the "Hymie-town" variety, or any other variety. He will do better, maybe much better, than he did four years ago.

Among the Republicans, meanwhile, George Bush was giving new meaning to the term "Skull and Bones." That's why Al Haig, who amassed a vote total that would embarrass Lyndon LaRouche, looked so happy. Maybe Bush will recover, but, as he showed in 1984, he does not find adversity invigorating. He has become a voodoo doll for everything Republican voters dislike about Reagan and almost nothing that they admire. Like Mondale in '84, he has a safety net of money and organization, but unlike Mondale he commands little loyalty among his party's constituencies. New Hampshire suddenly yawns before Bush like a great black pit. Pat Robertson was a surprise, but he has peaked. Fortunately he comes with a built-in ceiling. On caucus night he accused Tom Brokaw of religious bigotry for referring to him as a television evangelist, a charge that is sure to baffle the infidel majority. His function in Iowa was to humiliate Bush. His function now will be to destroy the chances of his fellow right-wingers, Jack Kemp and Pete du Pont. Right now it looks a lot like Bob Dole.

Dole versus Gephardt? Dole versus Simon? Dole versus Dukakis? Gee, thanks, Iowa. Mario, Mario. Where art thou, Mario?

—Campaign Diarist, *The New Republic*, February 29, 1988

DOLE'S CHARM

Nashua, New Hampshire

IN THE THEATRE of American politics in 1988 Bob Dole is the mask of comedy and tragedy. A doubleness runs through him and all his works, and it begins with his body. From the back of a big hall Dole's injury is unobtrusive. One's attention is captured instead by his tall silhouette, pivoting from side to side, and by his flat, cutting voice. In television interviews one most often sees only a sharp-featured face atop broad shoulders. But up close and in person, without a mediating camera to choose what shall be seen and not seen, one can contemplate at leisure the wound, still raw after forty-three years, that has marked him in body and spirit. Dole's left side is buoyant and energetic. His left arm is in constant motion, arcing and slicing with hand flat, pumping and punching with fist clenched. His right side, as if in silent reproach to all that hopeful animation, is still and crabbed. The right arm is crooked at waist level and noticeably shorter than the left, the right hand smaller, darker, wrinkled, and always twisted around the ever-present pen he clutches to warn off any unwelcome touch.

With Dole, metaphors of duality are inescapable. His physical doubleness is more than matched by doubleness of heart and mind. But Dole's is not the serene dualism of a harmonic yin and yang; it is more like the positive and negative poles of some infernal electric machine, and part of what makes him so obsessively interesting to watch is that one never knows when the spark will snap and crackle, leaving behind a strong whiff of ozone. The spark may take the form of acrimony or of humor; the shock may be painful or it may be pleasant, but it always comes. The tension in Dole is not between anything so banal as unhappiness and happiness. Rather it is between an almost unfathomable bitterness, on (literally) the one hand, and a kind of rough wisdom touched by compassion, on the other.

On the night of the New Hampshire primary Dole showed the grimacing half of his mask. In Iowa he had come from behind to beat George Bush (with some help from Pat Robertson). Here in New Hampshire the polls had shown him going from a one-to-two deficit against Bush two weeks before the voting to dead even two days before. But in "the only poll that counts" he got 42,878 votes, or 29 percent, against Bush's 56,393, or 38 percent. Appearing before his supporters at the Merrimack Hilton, Dole introduced a kid who had stood for him in a fourth-grade mock election, and then added bleakly: "The only difference is, he won." But the real shocker came later, when Tom Brokaw brought the two front-runners together electronically, Bush in NBC's Manchester studio and Dole on a monitor, and asked Dole if he had any message for the vice president. Dole's answer was a five-word snarl: "Stop lying about my record."

The Republican result here was a disappointment to the traveling press corps, which had collectively settled upon a story line for New Hampshire to which only a Dole triumph over Bush could have provided a satisfying climax. The story line was the humiliation of Bush-the-wimp, and the press pursued it with gusto. The vice president provided plenty of help. He engaged in wan regular-guy gestures, such as steering an eighteen-wheeler slowly around a truck-stop parking lot (with Secret Service men perched on the running board). He made a pathetic plea for votes, at the end of Saturday evening's televised debate, on grounds of his inability to express himself ("I don't talk much, but I do believe. I may not articulate much, but I feel"). And he repeatedly made a faintly off-color defense of the environmental benefits of the Alaska pipeline ("There are more darn caribou rubbing up against that pipeline and having babies").

By contrast, Dole got a mostly free ride. But if the story line of the moment had been something less favorable to him, then the press's obvious liking for Dole would have given him less protection. Consider his behavior at a Friday appearance at the University of New Hampshire. During the question period, a neatly dressed young man stepped to the microphone and began, "I'd like to ask a question about South Africa, which hasn't been a forefront issue in this campaign but will definitely be a problem for the next president—" "Aren't there any conservative students here?" Dole interrupted. "Gotta be one or two. Good to see you," he added as a few students waved. The audience laughed. "Senator Dole—" the questioner continued, but Dole interrupted again: "I'd like to see some future taxpayers." That cut the laughter short, and it fumed to boos. If the press's story line that week had been different—if it had been, say, the comeuppance of Dole-the-meanie—that little tiff might have made the news as the day's sound bite, perhaps accompanied by a pointed reminder of Richard Nixon's attacks on campus "bums."

Like a puff adder, Dole emits jets of venom when poked. Yet he is enormously seductive, not only to reporters but also to a great many Democrats. I have heard more Democrats than I can count say that Dole is the only Republican who might tempt them to stray, especially if their own party nominates someone they dislike or are indifferent to. Some say they like Dole because he is funny, others because he is cynical, others because he is a practical man impatient with ideology. Yet this uncanny appeal of Dole's surely goes deeper than these pat formulae suggest, and it is somehow rooted in the complicated layerings of doubleness in the man.

Start with his humor. Nothing quite like it, so far as I know, has ever been seen before in American politics. It is not of the folksy, reassuring, yarn-spinning, countrified variety, nor is it the urbane wit of the cosmopolitan sophisticate; and it has nothing whatever to do with the packaged, professionally supplied jokes on which other candidates rely. Dole's humor is bleak, savage, often deeply subversive. It has less in common with Lincoln's or Will Rogers's or Adlai Stevenson's than with Lenny Bruce's.

Dole knows essentially nothing about popular culture. He cannot remember the last movie he saw. He reads newsmagazines for relaxation. It happens that the most energetic part of American popular culture right now is comedy. Bob Dole has probably never heard of Andy Kaufman or David Letterman, yet his humor shows every sign of coming out of a similarly modernist, minimalist, almost dadaist sensibility. God only knows how this happened, but there it is.

An example. In Iowa Dole said that when President Reagan needed something done he called Dole, not Bush. Bush shot back that when Reagan wanted someone to take his place should something happen he called Bush, not Dole. Apprised of this sally, Dole asked, "Did he call collect?"

Another example. In the Iowa debate sponsored by the Des Moines *Register*, Jack Kemp asked Dole why he's for an oil import fee. Dole answered seriously, explaining that he hadn't been an advocate of such a fee but would support it under certain conditions, as a means to price stability and energy independence, and that a five-dollar-per-barrel fee, for example, would raise about five billion dollars. Then he added, totally deadpan: "You'd have to rebate probably most of that to those who use heating oil in New England, particularly in those early states like New Hampshire."

One more. Last week, at the Peterborough Town Hall in New Hampshire, he told how as a young man he had challenged the local Republican chairman to "give me one good reason" Dole should join his party. " 'I'll give you the best reason I know of,' " came the reply. " 'There are twice as many Republicans in this county as Democrats.' So I made a great philosophical judgment right there on the spot."

All this is pure Dole: laconic, acerbic, dry as a bleached skull on a Kansas plain. The "call collect" line skewers Reagan as doddering and out of it, ridicules Bush as choking on a silver spoon, and throws in a bit of dada blindsiding for good measure. The "early states" line sounds cynical, but since the effect is to sandblast away the cant in an otherwise conscientious answer, the result is actually less cynicism, not more. On the surface the line is "self-deprecating" (that holy grail of political joke writers), but it is at least equally aimed at his opponents, who, Dole subtly suggests, offer the cant without the antidote. (Dole's humor is never without political purpose.) Moreover, the line is subversive to the whole enterprise in which they all are engaged; Dole aims his shafts at the grotesqueries of politics, just as Letterman aims his at television's. The "philosophical judgment" line is similarly subversive. Dole's jokes and comic asides are part of his doubleness, a continuous running commentary on himself, his rivals, his trade, and whatever the ostensible subject of his remarks happens to be.

The "philosophical judgment" line begins to get at one of the reasons so many Democrats like Dole: they suspect he doesn't believe a lot of what he says. (Unfortunately for Dole in New Hampshire, there are apparently conservative Republicans who share that suspicion.) This does not come across only in his humor. He often sends double messages. Certainly he did so in a foreign policy speech to the New Hampshire legislature a week before the primary. It was studded with right-wing crowd-pleasers such as calling Russia a godless Communist state and quoting Jeane Kirkpatrick on those who always blame America first. And on the red-meat issue of aid to the contras Dole made all the right noises, blasting "liberal Democrats" for "throwing in the towel on freedom" and showing "naive faith in a Marxist dictator like Daniel Ortega." But he was careful to define the threat not as "Daniel Ortega's army" but rather as "Soviet bases and intelligence facilities and advisers." I heard him go further over the next few days. At the University of New Hampshire he excoriated the Sandinistas and then said, "I would question that form of government. Does that give me the right to say we're gonna topple it? No. But if there's some legitimate group that's fighting for their freedom I might want to get Congress to go along with offering assistance." At the Derryfield School he said, "We're not afraid of Ortega. We're not afraid of the Sandinista army. They're no threat to us. But now they're talking about increasing the army and bringing in sophisticated Soviet weapons. If we ask the American people, 'Do you want another Soviet base in this hemisphere?,' they'd say no. We haven't articulated our policy very well."

One can discern in all this the outlines of support for a deal whereby the Soviets would forgo bases and withdraw advisers in exchange for an end to U.S. support for the contras—exactly the deal Gorbachev has reportedly been offering, and the administration rejecting, for months. I like to think that Dole is simply too intelligent and too realistic to think much of the current policy of keeping a nasty, inconclusive war going and hoping for the best. He offers rhetorical red meat to the faithful, but for a true Doleologist like me his real intentions are there to see, cryptic but decipherable. To me this looks like ruthless shrewdness in the service of ultimately reasonable policy. To someone else, of course, it might look like duplicity.

Dole misses no chance to refer to himself as a conservative, and his conservative credentials date back a long way. Like Reagan, he was a charter supporter of Barry Goldwater in 1964. He was always a slashing partisan, and he is one of the few prominent Republicans who still uses "Democrat" as an adjective. But ideology is foreign to him, and to the extent that partisan loyalties have given way to ideological ones, Dole is a far less divisive figure than he used to be. When he touts his leadership abilities, he mentions two examples: working with Daniel Patrick Moynihan and Tip O'Neill to rescue Social Security in 1981, and defying the Reagan Justice Department to get the Voting Rights Act renewed in 1982. His record, on the whole, remains that of a hidebound Reaganite. But judging from what he says, and the feeling with which he says it, that is not the side of himself he values.

Dole is never more laconic than when he talks about the wound that felled him in the Po Valley in 1945, paralyzed him from the neck down for a year, put him in the hospital for thirty-nine months, and left him reluctant to this day to look in the mirror. He does not speak of himself as a hero and (unlike Bush) he was not in fact a hero, merely a kid who "got shot." The experience made him, he says, "a bitter young man." Of course, he always adds, it also made him more sensitive to the handicapped and to unfortunates in general. Still, it is remarkable in this age of empty optimism that he dares to use a word like "bitter" about himself, even in the past tense. At some level he remains bitter, and his defeat here will do nothing to gentle him.

—*The New Republic*, March 7, 1988

THE FATHER, THE SON, AND THE
HOLY POLITICIAN

MARION G. "PAT" ROBERTSON does not wish to be known as a former television evangelist, although he is one, because poll data show that the overwhelming majority of American voters regard television evangelism as an unsuitable preparation for the presidency. He wishes to be known as a lawyer, economist, and educator. Most of all, he wishes to be known as a businessman. His argument is that he founded and for twenty-six years ran a business, the Christian Broadcasting Network, or CBN, which grew from nothing to become the country's fifth-largest cable-TV network, and which, with its various subsidiaries and offshoots, employs four thousand people and grosses two hundred million dollars a year. Therefore Pat Robertson is a businessman. What's wrong with that?

What's wrong with it is that if CBN is a business, then a gigantic fraud has been perpetrated upon tens of thousands of simple Christian folk. Three-quarters or more of the income of CBN is in the form of contributions, mostly small contributions. The lonely, desperate, and pious people who made those contributions did not do so in the belief that they were fattening a business. They thought they were giving to a ministry. They thought (as did the Internal Revenue Service) that it all had something to do with God, Jesus Christ, and the Bible. Now they are being told that the bottom line was—well, the bottom line. This is why Robertson's portrayal of himself as a businessman is not just a matter of exaggeration, like Jimmy Carter's calling himself a nuclear physicist, or of emphasis, like Ronald Reagan's preference for being known as an ex-governor rather than an ex-actor. It's nastier than either of those, not least because it reveals the shepherd's implicit contempt for his flock. The only question is when the lie took place. If Robertson was a businessman at CBN, he was a liar then; if he was an evangelist at CBN, he is a liar now.

The fantasy that Pat Robertson might somehow actually win the Republican nomination for president evaporated in South Carolina on March 5th. On Super Tuesday, March 8th, the remaining wisps got blown away in a hurricane of votes even prayer could not divert. But the fantasy was still moist and healthy the morning I caught up with the Robertson entourage, at the First Baptist Church, in Dallas. The First Baptist Church is reputed to be the largest Protestant congregation in the world, with twenty-six thousand members; it is certainly one of the richest (H. L. Hunt was a prominent member) and meanest (less than 0.4 percent of its income goes to help the poor). First Baptist has long been a bastion of political and theological reaction. At its private school, founded a generation ago to promote racial segregation, young minds are unsullied by Darwinism, unless it is social.

The pupils of that school got that morning off from classes for a special chapel meeting. Times have changed: a few black faces were among them as they filed into the church, a roomy white interior with red carpets, movie theatre–style red plush seats in the balcony, a terrific sound system, and acoustics that magnify applause. The girls wore white shirts, red sweaters, and tartan skirts; the boys, ties of the same tartan. On the stage a pretty senior sang pop-flavored hymns to a rich recorded accompaniment, holding the microphone in her hand as she walked confidently back and forth behind a flower-bedecked pulpit. Then somebody snapped in a cassette of "Strike Up the Band," and everybody rose excitedly, heads craning and hands clapping, as Robertson entered dramatically from the rear and worked his way up the aisle.

Russell Kammerling, chairman of the school's Bible department, introduced the guest speaker. "When God decides to do something really big, he selects out an individual," Kammerling said. "He selected Moses to lead his children out of Israel and David to be king over Israel. He called Jeremiah to call Israel back to repentance and faith in God, Peter to preach Pentecost, and Martin Luther to nail the ninety-five theses to the wall of Wittenberg Castle. . . . And I believe that in these 1980s God separated out a man to keep us steered toward those issues which are of light and truth and good and of eternal significance. I sat in his office two years ago and talked with him then about the potential of his running for president. I'll never forget when he said, 'Russell, the only thing that will get me in the presidential race is a clear word from the Lord that says that's where I am to be.' I believe his announcement is a result of that, and it's a real privilege for me to introduce to you—Pat Robertson!"

The smug smile never left Robertson's face as he listened to this amazing recital. He is a chunky man with a large, eerily cubical head, pointy ears, and childlike features. As he speaks, self-satisfaction seems to bubble up in his body, and when it bubbles up to mouth level, his voice gets gurgly with suppressed chuckles and the corners of his mouth stretch out as if his smile was shooting its cuffs. This time, he began by asking the kids to raise their hands if they knew anybody in their age group who uses drugs. Up went a forest of hands.

God, Robertson told the kids, gave man dominion over the animals and the plants. "We have people today who have become slaves to a plant," he went on, warming. "Cannabis is a plant. So called Mary Jane, marry-wanna, is a plant. People are slaves to a plant! Cocoa, cocaine, the coca plant—people are hooked on a vegetable!"

Up in the balcony, reporters exchanged glances of guilty pleasure. This was the sort of stuff we had come to hear, and it gave promise of more and better to come. Robertson, at this point, had been on almost a gaffe-a-day schedule: the claim that there are still Soviet nuclear missiles in Cuba, the accusation that the George Bush campaign had engineered the Jimmy Swaggart scandal, the assertion that CBN had known the whereabouts of hostages in Beirut. He was due for another.

But he got through his speech and his answers to prescreened questions from students without incident—or almost. The last question was about the Middle East, and he seemed to have finished his answer with a statesman-like conclusion. "The long-range interests of the United States of America should really coincide and track with Israel." Then, however, he got expansive, and added an afterthought: "But I would say this, and I said it to a good friend of mine who is with the AIPAC, which is the Israeli group that pushes for their legislative initiatives: I said, 'I'm for free enterprise. I'm a capitalist. And although I'm with you on these issues, I have no intention of sending American taxpayer money to go to Israel to support a socialist form of government. I want you to move toward free enterprise over there and not the Eastern European liberalism which came with some of your early settlers.'"

This sounded very much like a threat to cut off aid to Israel in the event of a Labor Party victory, the Israeli Labor Party being a member of the Socialist International. It wasn't a full-fledged Robertson gaffe, perhaps, but enough of one, I thought, to set off a minor flap. Alas, it was not to be. The story went nowhere; this was one lump of lead, it turned out, that not even the overwrought alchemy of campaign-trail coverage could turn to gold.

ABOARD ROBERTSON'S campaign plane later in the day, I was called to the front for a brief interview with the candidate. The Robertson plane, a British BAC-III, is on the large side for a corporate jet. As befits a plane that supposedly once belonged to Kenny Rogers, it is luxurious, with a large color television set and VCR, stained-wood appointments, mock-gold bathroom fixtures, and oversized seats of dark-green crushed velvet.

Robertson had been sounding a conspiratorial, persecutory note of late, with dark references to the Eastern Wall Street foreign policy establishment, and I decided to forgo confrontation and try instead to draw him out on this theme. I asked about the Trilateral Commission and the Foreign Policy Association. "The people at the grass roots don't like illogic, and it seems illogical to spend vast amounts of money on arms while at the same time we're aiding our enemies," Robertson said. "The people can't understand this. The only explanation is that somebody has a financial interest, possibly, that would transcend it, or else a philosophy of one-world government."

There was more in this vein. But the plane had landed, and an aide fidgeted nearby. I shuffled politely as if to go, but Robertson suddenly wanted to talk about the supposed Cuban missiles, even though I hadn't asked about them. "This Cuban loophole is an incredible gaffe in the drafting of this I.N.F. treaty—an incredible gaffe!" he said. "I have committee records from the Internal Security Subcommittee of the Senate Judiciary Committee in 1967 where a State Department employee went over detailed evidence of people who had seen missiles in Cuba in 1967. It's all on the record, and yet somehow we have acted as if none of that material was around when this treaty was drafted. And I have had reports from within the cabinet of the United States that George Shultz literally bulldozed everybody there. He was so insistent on pushing this treaty through that he did it over the vigorous objections of almost everybody that was there!" He added that maybe the Russians didn't take out all the missiles after the 1963 missile crisis, and that in a recent phone-in poll 82 percent of the people who called in said there are missiles in Cuba. "Well, my heavens! Whether they're there or not is not the issue. The issue is, shouldn't a conservative president be saying, 'Wait a minute—let's go down to Cuba and verify'?"

"We've gotta go, guys," said the aide, and we went—Robertson to give another speech, me to reel from the revelation that Robertson's Cuban missile charge is apparently based on a twenty-year-old scrap of secondhand testimony before a long since discredited and abolished anti-"subversion" Senate subcommittee, and that anyway, he doesn't think it really matters whether the missiles exist or not.

THERE WAS NEVER the slightest chance that Pat Robertson would win the Republican nomination for president, and all Super Tuesday did was allow everybody to say so out loud. But if he did less well than his supporters had hoped in the afterglow of Iowa, he has done far better than anyone imagined he could at the outset. There is still an outside chance he will end up brokering the nomination between Bush and Bob Dole. And simply as a character in the picaresque saga of 1988 Robertson remains a fascinating figure—one who, however, is better apprehended by the categories of psychoanalysis than by those of politics or religion.

The story of Pat Robertson's life forms the unmistakable pattern of an Oedipal drama. He is a son who rebelled against his father, fulfilled his mother's dreams, and finally returned by a circuitous route to outdo the father on his own ground.

Robertson is the son of A. Willis Robertson, who was elected a congressman from Virginia in 1932, when Pat was two years old, and a senator in 1946, when Pat was sixteen. The father's plans for the son were firm: young Pat would go into politics. He guided the boy to the right schools (Washington and Lee, Yale Law), looked after him while he was in the Marines (arranging for him to be in the Korean combat zone without actually being in combat, according to evidence adduced in Robertson's abandoned lawsuit against former Representative Pete McCloskey), got a job for him on the staff of the Senate Appropriations Committee, lined up a Virginia law firm for him, even introduced him to nice, suitably well-connected Baptist girls from the right Tidewater families. On the surface Pat seemed a dutiful enough son, but underneath he was in fitful, rebellious agony. One by one, he thwarted his father's plans for him. He got a girl pregnant—a Catholic girl, no less—and married her in her seventh month. He flunked the bar exam. He moved to New York and went into business in a firm making audio components. He drank, swore, played poker, and, as he once told a *Washington Post* interviewer, spent his evenings in "upholstered sewers called nightclubs." He was drifting and depressed.

The keynote of Robertson's father's life was right-wing politics; of his mother's, fundamentalist religion. As she grew older, Gladys Churchill Robertson gradually withdrew from the society of her husband and his political friends, becoming, in the words of one family chronicler, "a religious recluse." It was she who, in 1958, introduced her son to the man who converted him to born-again, speaking-in-tongues, charismatic Christianity, a Dutch evangelist named Cornelius Vanderbreggen. And it was she, a year later, who told him about a bankrupt UHF television station in Portsmouth, Virginia, that could be had for thirty-seven thousand dollars. Two years later he was on the air and on his way.

Robertson had found a heavenly Father powerful enough to sanction rebellion against his earthly one, and awesome enough to win him the place of honor in his mother's heart. "No longer did I remember I was the son of a senator," Robertson wrote in his autobiography, *Shout It from the Housetops*, published in 1972, the year after his father's death. "I was the son of the King." Furthermore: "I knew this was mother's dream, to evangelize the world for Jesus. And suddenly it became my vision, too."

The Oedipal drama reached a climax in 1966. Senator Robertson faced a hard fight for renomination. He turned for help to Pat, who by this time was a locally prominent TV evangelist with a following big enough to count. Pat refused—on orders from God, who said to him, according to a passage excised from the latest edition of the autobiography, "I have called you to my ministry. You cannot tie my eternal purposes to any political candidate." Senator Robertson lost by a narrow margin. Now his son is a candidate for president, assured of a place in the political history of the United States far beyond his father's.

In our interview on the plane, Robertson offered a thought about his father: "I've found, interestingly enough, that although I had never heard or read what he had said on certain issues, I've made speeches in which my words are almost the same as some of the things he was saying twenty and thirty years ago."

Pat Robertson hears a voice. Sometimes the voice is in his heart, sometimes it is plainly audible to him—"level and conversational," he once wrote. This voice, he has said many times, is the voice of God.

When God speaks to Robertson, his words make up in specificity for what they lack in majesty:

"Congress is going to pass a bill requiring all television sets to be equipped with UHF." This in 1959, when Robertson was contemplating buying his first station.

"Don't fire Jim Bakker." This in 1965, when the boyish star of a CBN puppet show had gone AWOL from work.

"Don't go over two and a half million dollars." This in 1969, when Robertson was negotiating the purchase of some electronic gear.

"I have something else for you to do. I want you to run for president." This in 1987, when Robertson was exploring his political options.

These dicta may seem rather mundane to have been uttered by the Creator of the Universe even if, as the saying goes, God is in the details. But God also speaks to Robertson about more consequential matters, such as the end of the world. One intelligent examination of Robertson's views on the apocalypse came on a recent edition of the CBS program *West 57th*, on which Meredith Vieira interviewed a former CBN producer named Gerard Thomas Straub. In 1969, Straub told Vieira, Robertson "received a prophesy that said that he was chosen to usher in the Second Coming of Jesus. We actually had plans made on how to televise the Second Coming, as incredible as that may seem. That is why we had a television station in Jerusalem. They were convinced the Second Coming would happen there. His whole ministry was pointing toward a message that Armageddon was going to happen, and when it failed to materialize as he predicted, in 1982, I think he began to suddenly realize, or refocus his energies to realizing, that the way this was going to happen was through the political process."

Vieira asked the Reverend Warner Dunlap, the pastor of the church where Robertson was ordained, whether the thought of Robertson with his finger on the nuclear button worried him. "Absolutely," Dunlap replied. "A person who was functioning totally with an apocalyptic view of history would have less restraint on the button than someone who was not apocalyptic in his view of history."

"Why?"

"That could be perceived as a way of assisting God in bringing about what God had intended."

Robertson dismisses Straub as a disgruntled former employee. But the public record of Robertson's predictions of apocalypse is ample, and the relevance of that record to any consideration of how Robertson might behave as president seems too obvious to argue. As an evangelist, he said repeatedly that Armageddon would come during his lifetime, and that it would begin with a war in the Middle East. If he believed this then and believes it now, he is plainly too dangerous to be allowed anywhere near the nuclear button. If he believed it then but does not believe it now, he is guilty of a flip-flop on a cosmic scale. And if he believed it neither then nor now, he truly is Elmer Gantry.

IN 1958, enraptured by his conversion, Robertson suddenly announced to his wife, Dede, that the voice of God had told him to go off to the Canadian woods to meditate. She was almost destitute, she had a toddler at home, she was eight months pregnant with their second child, and she was frightened. "I'm a nurse," she pleaded, according to Robertson's own account. "I recognize schizoid tendencies when I see them, and I think you're sick."

Thirty years later, Dede Robertson too has become a born-again, Spirit-filled Christian, campaigning at her husband's side. But the voice in Pat Robertson's ear has not stilled. What are we to make of it? On the general subject of voices, a psychoanalyst friend, Dr. Peter Mezan, tells me, "Auditory hallucinations—particularly of a command variety, which is to say voices telling one to do things—are certainly a primary symptom of schizophrenia. They're not specific for schizophrenia, they are also typical of many forms of psychosis. But they are certainly one of the things that you would see in an acute schizophrenic episode."

That is secular humanism talking. There are other explanations of such phenomena, as Dr. Mezan points out. "Of course," he says, "auditory hallucinations may be divinely inspired and given. They may be symptoms of sainthood as well. But how is anybody supposed to know?" There is always the possibility that Pat Robertson really is divinely inspired. But if God is Robertson's campaign manager, then he is, as Super Tuesday showed, far from Almighty.

—*The New Republic,* March 28, 1988

THE TORTOISE

PITY GEORGE BUSH. His people have been saying for a long time that they would like nothing better than to run against Michael Dukakis (except maybe to run against Jesse Jackson). Well, it looks like they're going to get their wish, and they may yet regret it.

It's understandable that the Republicans have tended to look upon Dukakis as easy pickings, almost as their dream opponent. How much trouble can they really expect from a short, uninspiring Northeastern liberal with a funny name, no previous experience in national politics and none at all in foreign policy, and a political career that has been played out entirely within the confines of a state that was the only one carried by George McGovern in 1972 and has since been known principally as the home of those favorite bogeymen of Republican fund-raising letters, Tip O'Neill and Edward Kennedy?

Dukakis will be a more formidable opponent than the Bush people could have imagined as recently as a month ago. They had to have been impressed, as were Dukakis's detractors in his own party, by the assurance with which the governor of Massachusetts walked cool and unscorched through the hellfire of the New York primary campaign. Dukakis went into that primary as a rather shaky front-runner, still haunted by his Michigan loss and dogged by doubts about how well he could compete in a state where passions are large and volatile, voters cynical and unpredictable, and politicians shark-like and imperious. He emerged the nominee in all but name, having obliterated Albert Gore, tamed (for the moment) Jesse Jackson, and increased his own stature at least as much as the two non-candidate Democratic players in the New York game, Mayor Edward Koch and Governor Mario Cuomo, diminished theirs. As many have noted, Koch helped Dukakis by drawing off the state's racial poisons to himself, thus damaging both the candidate he endorsed (Gore, who was embarrassed and humiliated by Koch's attentions even as he welcomed them) and the candidate he attacked (Jackson, whose populist message was drowned out by the Koch-abetted cacophony about blacks versus Jews). Cuomo could have helped Dukakis by endorsing him. But he helped him almost as much by not endorsing him, thus allowing him to win his majority on his own, out of Cuomo's (now smaller) shadow.

It will soon be George Bush's turn to discover what the Democratic pack has learned over the past two months: it is very, very hard to get a handle on Michael Dukakis. There are no rough edges, no jagged outcroppings to grab hold of. Dukakis is a candidate whose weaknesses are his strengths. If his character has hidden depths, if his soul has dark corners, no one has ever been able to find them—not even his wife, Kitty, who has called him "the most uncomplicated man in the world." The simplicity, banality, consistency, stolidity, matter-of-factness, and emotional equanimity that make him an unsuitable vehicle for political fervor also make him an elusive target for political attack. He is not exactly a cardboard cutout; his sense of himself is too firm and palpable for that. But the aspect he presents is sufficiently two-dimensional that to his opponents, who see him from the side, he is practically invisible. (Fortunately for him, television is a two-dimensional medium.)

Dukakis was the eye of the long hurricane of multicandidate primaries. At the outset he established the well-financed, well-disciplined organization that, along with his own unflappable temperament, would enable him to absorb setbacks along the way. In speeches and debates he stuck to a series of propositions that made up in durability and unexceptionability what they utterly lacked in transcendence: I have a record of accomplishment, I have integrity, I have competence, I have brought "good jobs at good wages" to Massachusetts and I can do the same for the country. He then proceeded to put one foot in front of another. While he plodded, his opponents, who had no choice but to take larger risks, played with fire; and, one by one, they flared up and flamed out. They aimed their darts at each other, not least because Dukakis presented such a faint and elusive target. In the last desperate days in New York, Gore could find nothing better to attack Dukakis for than for not attacking Jackson.

Like Dukakis, Bush has trod a cautious, steady, money-cushioned path to his own de facto nomination. Bush does not play with fire (though he has been known to sit unprotestingly through meetings with pyromaniacs), and Dukakis cannot count on the vice president to immolate himself. But Bush and the Republicans will have a hard time forcing Dukakis into the categories against which they have spent a generation perfecting their attacks. It will not be easy, for example, to depict Dukakis as a tax-raising paleoliberal who thinks the answer to every problem is a government spending program, because the emphasis of both his rhetoric and his record, at least since his second term as governor, has been on economic growth and on the use of state power to promote it equitably through the private sector. It will not be easy to depict him as a cultural radical, because his own style of life is such an eloquently homely affirmation of such middle-class values as work, family, neighborhood, and self-discipline. It will not be easy to depict him as a captive of "interest groups," because he has resisted the more egregious forms of pandering (for example, in his appearance before the Conference of Presidents of Major Jewish Organizations in New York, he declined three opportunities to rule out the possibility of a Palestinian state), and because he has avoided the Mondale error of rhetorically slicing up the electorate into segments, making special appeals to each, and mistaking letterheads for constituencies.

The Republicans have already begun to target two areas of potentially serious Dukakis vulnerability, foreign policy and crime. But circumstances may help him to limit the damage. The recent spate of negotiated settlements or quasi-settlements—on European missiles, in Nicaragua, and in Afghanistan—tends to make the "strength" issue less useful for Bush even as it makes the "peace" issue less useful for Dukakis.

On crime, Bush is sure to make much of the Massachusetts prison furlough program, under which at least two first-degree murderers escaped to repeat their crimes. That will hurt, and there's not much Dukakis can do about it. Bush is already calling for applying the death penalty to big drug traffickers, and Dukakis has always been an opponent of capital punishment. But Dukakis will be able to reply that some of the biggest drug lords, from Panama's Noriega on down, reaped their harvests of cocaine cash under what has amounted to a grant of immunity provided by the administration's eagerness to keep arms flowing to the contras.

Dukakis's greatest weakness—his famous inability to inspire—happens to be identical with Bush's. This is a lucky break for Dukakis (and for Bush, too). In terms of what Bush perplexedly calls "the vision thing," the fall campaign will be a wash. Neither man is capable of saying—to all evidence, even of thinking about—how his presidency would advance the great romantic drama of American history. In place of a vision, Bush has the lift of a driving résumé. What Dukakis has is a set of proven personal qualities (competence, confidence, integrity), a set of comprehensible and relevant accomplishments for which the conventions of politics allow him to take credit (most notably the Massachusetts economic recovery), and, of course, the story of his own family's rise from poverty in Greece to prominence in America in a single generation.

For someone like Cuomo, the immigrant heritage is a fact that becomes a metaphor that becomes a vision. For Dukakis it remains a fact, albeit a moving one. As Dukakis has been telling audiences lately, "It says something about America that the two leading candidates for president are the son of Greek immigrants and a black man who grew up poor." (It also says something about America that the second fact, even at this late date, is more moving than the first.)

At Cuomo's urging, Dukakis made his immigrant ancestry part of his stump repertoire when he began running for president. Before that, he had seldom spoken of it. One reason, perhaps, was that Dukakis's experience growing up as a doctor's son amid the middle-class Jews and Irish of Brookline, the Boston suburb where he still lives, was more like that of a third-generation than a second-generation American. His father, Panos Dukakis, on his own made the jump that takes most immigrant families at least two generations, graduating from Harvard Medical School just twelve years after arriving in 1912, nearly penniless and unable to speak English at age fifteen. Dukakis's mother, Euterpe Boukis Dukakis, came to the United States and Massachusetts in 1913, when she was nine, and twelve years later graduated Phi Beta Kappa from Bates College in Maine. By the time Michael was born in 1933, the Dukakis family's struggle for survival had been won.

Dukakis's ethnicity has been an unobtrusive but distinct asset to him in the presidential campaign. Compared with the full-bodied Cuomo *vino*, Dukakis is Ethnic Lite. There has never been as much nativist prejudice against Greeks in this country as there has been against such larger immigrant groups as Italians, Irish, or Jews. As an assimilated Greek-American

Dukakis has succeeded in being a mirror for other ethnics without displeasing non-ethnics. In Brookline he was often taken for Jewish, an electoral advantage there. Through his first cousin Olympia Dukakis, who last month won an Academy Award for playing Cher's Italian mother in *Moonstruck,* he is a kind of honorary Italian. His fellow Greek-Americans welcome him across party lines not merely as one of their own but also as a way to wipe away the dishonor of Spiro Agnew. Though his religion is Greek Orthodox and his wife's is Jewish, he and his wife brought their children up in both traditions, and their ethic is quite thoroughly Protestant. Dukakis is a generic ethnic, anything but unmeltable.

One group that is sure to greet Dukakis's advent with enthusiasm is cartoonists. Dukakis is a caricature waiting to be drawn. He has oversized features on an oversized head, a trait he exaggerates by wearing suits so tight they look like they were spray-painted on. His needlelike trousers end at enormous, suspiciously thick-soled black shoes that resemble bumper cars. If he wins, his bushy eyebrows will join F.D.R.'s cigarette holder, Nixon's nose, Carter's teeth, and Reagan's pompadour in the cartoonists' pantheon.

Impressionists will like Dukakis too. It's easy to "do" him. First, pretend that your elbows are stapled to your sides. Then splay your hands as if you were holding a beach ball, or make a post-coin-flip fist. Then shake your head slowly, shrug slightly, and say in a rapid, faintly nasal, risingly inflected voice, "I happen to be a guy who believes deeply that if we're serious about creating good jobs at good wages, and I mean good jobs at good wages, then we've gotta do nationally what we did in Massachusetts."

DUKAKIS GENUINELY LOVES public policy—a quality that is easy to mock but is no more to be deplored in a politician than a love of auto mechanics is in a racing driver. He is a legitimate expert in it, at least in its domestic aspect, and in the processes by which it is forged. On this ground he is sure of himself, perhaps too sure. After the most devastating experience of Dukakis's public life, his 1978 defeat for renomination as governor after his first term, he easily could have set himself up in a big law firm and made a pile of cash. But for him the pleasures of money are public, not private. (The private Dukakis would rather scrimp than spend.) Instead, he joined the faculty of Harvard's John F. Kennedy School of Government.

At Harvard he had every incentive to settle in as just another politician-in-residence. He could have spent his time working the phones and taking long lunches with his political friends as he plotted his comeback, and that was exactly what some of his new colleagues expected him to do. He surprised everybody: he became a real teacher. He won over his suspicious colleagues with his seriousness, his diligence, and his modesty. "What made a real impression was his complete lack of egomania," says one ex-colleague, Steven Kelman. "He was perfectly indifferent to the lack of grandeur of his surroundings. His office was a cubbyhole. He shared a secretary. I'm sure it never entered his mind to complain about such things. He simply decided that as long as he was going to teach, he would do it right. He was accessible to students and junior faculty. He was a regular participant at faculty research seminars. He stood in line for lunch with everybody else. He didn't put on airs. It was almost touching."

He taught a full schedule, even splitting one class into two sections when it was oversubscribed, doubling his workload. His reviews in the course evaluation guide published by the Kennedy School Student Association make interesting reading today for the glimpses they give of his character. One had this telling comment: "Several mentioned that Dukakis cut student comments short. In presenting 'one man's view of the world' I occasionally felt that no other contradictory views would be strongly considered." But Dukakis's notices improved with time:

M-662, INSTITUTIONAL LEADERSHIP AND THE AGENCY MANAGER. Instructor: Dukakis.

Students were highly impressed by Dukakis's personality and teaching effectiveness. They found him to be an "excellent," "outstanding," "first-rate," "super" instructor. *He also was described as a charismatic personality* who effectively conveyed to the class his interest and enthusiasm for the subject he was teaching. However, a few students mentioned that they found him opinionated. . . . Similarly, while the structure and content of the course were generally judged to be quite good, there were complaints about a bias in favor of the East Coast. (1981–82)

Italics mine. Of course, it may be that only someone who would voluntarily take a course with a title like "Institutional Leadership and the Agency Manager" could actually believe what Al Gore gracefully said in his withdrawal speech, that "competence is charisma."

The cliché about the Kennedy School is that it views politics with disdain, as an annoying impediment to the rational shaping of rational public policy. Be that as it may, Dukakis returned to the governorship in 1983 with a greater, not a lesser, aptitude for the rough-and-tumble. The arrogance his students had noted did not disappear entirely. But Dukakis did manage to transform himself from a stiff-backed confrontationist into a careful coalition-builder who looks for common ground with any potential allies, from a disdainer of schmoozing into a massager of legislators, from the Torquemada of patronage to its Toscanini. Despite the frequently drawn comparisons to Jimmy Carter, Dukakis as president would be extremely unlikely to blanket Capitol Hill with a blizzard of proposals unaccompanied by other consultation or follow-up. He would set priorities, budget his time and attention, cement his alliances beforehand, and limit his legislative goals to those that had a reasonable chance of achievement. Now that Dukakis is all but sure to be the nominee, Democrats, however relieved they may be, are also feeling a vague disappointment. But if Dukakis wins, they may learn that it is better to be disappointed at the beginning than at the end.

—*The New Republic*, May 16, 1988

IVY SCOREBOARD

SCHMOOZING WITH REPORTERS not long ago, Senator Al Gore remarked solemnly that he was pleased that the overarching issue of the 1988 presidential campaign had at last been joined. "All right, senator," said one of the reporters, "Which do you think is more élitist, Harvard or Yale?"

"Isn't it obvious?" replied Gore (Harvard '69). "One of them is the exclusive preserve of the rich and privileged. While the other"—and here he gnarled his hands into fists and deepened his voice to a guttural peasant growl—"is *of the soil.*"

BUT WHICH IS WHICH? It was George H. W. Bush (Yale '48) who put the issue on the nation's agenda, by assailing Michael Dukakis for "making some sort of macho statement out of Harvard." He followed up on this seemingly oxymoronic attack by accusing Dukakis of having "foreign policy views born in Harvard Yard's boutique." Thus did the bulldog go bow wow wow.

The Duke didn't bark back, contenting himself with the observation that, strictly speaking, he isn't a Harvard guy at all. "I'm a Swarthmore guy," he said.

"How come?" I asked him. "Doesn't the top student at Brookline High School always go to Harvard?"

"Not always, no," Dukakis said. "I wanted, first, to go to a coed school, and, second, to stay active athletically, [so] for me the Ivies just weren't a factor. . . . My brother . . . was the one who got me interested in Swarth-more. He said, 'You like cities, and there's a school that's supposed to be very good outside Philadelphia.' I'd never heard of it. I'm not sure I knew what a Quaker was, to tell you the truth. But it was a great experience."

To a truly effete Harvard snob, the fact that Dukakis went to Harvard Law School and later taught at the John F. Kennedy School of Government no more makes him a Harvard man than the fact that he might secure his bicycle with a Yale lock would make him a Yale man. Referring to these places as "the Ivies" is a dead giveaway that he is a product of none of them.

On the other hand, no Yale snob, however effete, could possibly see George Bush as being any color but the deepest blue. He went to Yale. His father, Senator Prescott Bush of Connecticut, went to Yale, took a gradu-ate degree at Yale, got an honorary doctorate from Yale, and served as a fel-low of the Yale Corporation. His brothers went to Yale. His uncles went to Yale. His sons went to Yale. His brothers' and sister's sons went to Yale. Moreover, George Bush had the kind of Yale panache that might have turned the head of Daisy Buchanan. He wore the sacred Y as captain of the varsity baseball team. And he was "tapped" for membership in Skull and Bones, the most prestigious of Yale's secret societies—probably the most élite experience that an American college student can have.

But this does not resolve the question of the relative élitism of the two institutions themselves. Let us consider it from a variety of perspectives.

Longevity. Harvard was founded in 1636. Yale was founded in 1701, both in imitation of and in opposition to Harvard, which was seen as having grown theologically lax. Yale's anxiety about its status as against Harvard dates from Year One. "[A]ll persons admitted to any Degrees," wrote Samuel Sewall in a letter to Yale's founders, "shall have the same Honor & Respect shown them that Students have or ought to have had who recd. Degrees at Harvard College at Cambridge." From Sewall to Bush, the eyes of Yale have been on Harvard rather more than the reverse. In this category, Har-vard must be judged more élitist.

Class. Neither university is noticeably proletarian. Only 6.7 per cent of the fathers of the Harvard class of 1982 worked in blue-collar occupations, compared with 47 percent of the country's total male work force. Four-fifths of the Harvard dads were managers or professionals. I couldn't lay my hands on the figures for Yale, but I did find some comparative statistics on students admitted from private schools, a good indicator of élitist tendencies. Between the world wars around 75 percent of Yalies had "prepped," as against roughly 55 percent of Harvardians. During the 1940s, Bush's era, Yale was 65.8 percent prepster, Harvard 50.4. By the 1950s both schools were admitting mostly public school boys, but to this day Yale's ambience remains preppier than Harvard's. Award this category to Yale.

Snobbery. Harvard's tends to be coy—"I go to school in Boston." Yale's is more robust—"Boola boola!" Within the two institutions, the principal snobbery involves social clubs. (Fraternities to you.) Yale's are called "secret societies," with names like Skull and Bones, Scroll and Key, and Wolf's Head. Harvard's are called "final clubs"—the Porcellian being the most prestigious. The societies and the clubs both have elaborate physical plants and large alumni endowments. Blacks and Jews are no longer excluded from any of these organizations; all but two of the secret societies, but none of the final clubs, admit women.

In the final clubs, activities include drinking, wearing tuxedoes, and loafing. In the secret societies, the principal activity is a twice-weekly mandatory dinner. What goes on at these dinners is supposed to be secret, but it is universally believed by non-members at Yale that the rituals of Skull and Bones include nude mud wrestling, masturbating into a coffin, and detailed recountings of personal sexual histories. (As Bush was already married when he was tapped, he was presumably able to enlighten his fellow Bonesmen on what it was like to "go all the way.")

Membership in the secret societies is said to be marginally more meritocratic and less dependent upon family connections than membership in the final clubs. On the other hand, these institutions matter much more at Yale, and yet are smaller. Therefore more people's feelings get hurt by being excluded at Yale—an important plus, élitismwise. This category must be counted a draw.

SO WE HAVE A TIE. But Bush's literal point wasn't that Harvard is élitist. It was that Harvard is the center of, as he put it, "a philosophical cult normally identified with extremely liberal causes." In this he may be on slightly firmer ground. In the 1948 *Harvard Crimson* student poll, Thomas E. Dewey ran behind President Truman, Henry A. Wallace, and Norman Thomas. In the *Yale Daily News* poll, Dewey got 88 percent. Even today, Republicans are fairly common at Yale. Harvard gave us John Reed and

W.E.B. DuBois. Yale gave us William F. Buckley, Jr., even though Buckley made his reputation denouncing the atheism and collectivism of the Yale faculty. The Kennedy School, presumably the boutique to which Bush had reference, does indeed count a couple of Dukakis foreign policy advisers on its faculty. But they are cautious centrists, not "extremely liberal" philosophical cultists. And the K-School faculty also includes many Republicans, including Richard Thornburgh, Reagan's new attorney general–designate, whom Bush has promised to retain.

As for the non–Ivy League Middle American voters to whose presumed prejudices Bush was trying to appeal, they are likely to regard the controversy, if they regard it at all, in the same light as George Bernard Shaw. Offered an honorary degree as an inducement to participate in Harvard's tricentenary celebration in 1936, Shaw replied, "If Harvard would celebrate its three-hundredth anniversary by burning itself to the ground and sowing its site with salt, the ceremony would give me the liveliest satisfaction as an example to all the other famous old corrupters of youth"—sound good, Mr. Vice President? hang on—"including Yale, Oxford, Cambridge, the Sorbonne etc. etc. etc." Shaw didn't mention Swarthmore, possibly because, like Dukakis before his brother clued him in, he had never heard of it.

—The New Republic, August 8 & 15, 1988

DYNASTIES, OLD AND NEW

LIKE A LOT OF THINGS about Michael Dukakis, his choice of Lloyd Bentsen appeals more to the head than to the heart. I understand the rationale. I've even become persuaded that it makes political sense. Bring back the Reagan strays, get Texas, motivate the quadrennially torpid conservative Democrats, reassure business, raise big money, display ruthless determination to win, scare the hell out of Bush—all very sensible. But don't ask me to like it. When I heard the news I could feel energy leach from every cell of my body. Bentsen's record is that of a big-business Tory Democrat, and within the Texas tradition he's more unguently reminiscent of John Connally than of Lyndon Johnson. Politicians like Bentsen always have made life miserable for Texas liberals, a brave and noble breed once epitomized by Ralph Yarborough, the incumbent Democratic senator whom Bentsen defeated for renomination in 1970 before disposing of Representative George Bush in the general election. Bentsen is more of a partisan Democrat than Sam Nunn, but he is fully as conservative. Of course, the fact that people like me can't stand the Bentsen choice but will still support the ticket in November is probably the clinching argument that the choice was a political masterstroke.

One nice thing about the Bentsen nomination: assuming the ticket wins, he's almost guaranteed to be a one-term vice president. Once Bentsen has served his one-shot electoral purpose Dukakis will have every incentive, four years hence, to give him a comfy ambassadorship somewhere and replace him with someone younger (Bentsen will be seventy-one in 1992) and more compatible—someone Dukakis might actually want to succeed him. There will be plenty of possibilities: Bill Clinton, Bill Bradley, Bob Kerrey, Bill Gray, Al Gore. . . . Another consoling thought is that Bentsen's elevation to the depths of the vice presidency would open up his Senate seat for Jim Hightower, the populist Texas agriculture commissioner whose little speech to the convention Tuesday night was a tiny taste of the punishment he would be capable of dishing out to whatever hapless interim Republican would be appointed pending a special election.

THIS CONVENTION, by the way, is absurd. It is an allegedly deliberative body whose success is measured precisely by the degree to which it does no deliberating, since any sign of dissent or controversy is seen as lèse-majesté. The delegates wear funnier hats than they do in the Supreme Soviet, but their scope for discretionary decision-making is more limited. The nominating role of conventions having been displaced by the primary system, their only remaining function is to be the pretext for a gigantic press Woodstock. The most impressive sight here is not the convention hall itself—which is too small to hold all the delegates, let alone the armies of V.I.P.s, contributors, and hangers-on—but the enormous indoor press encampment across the street, where hundreds of news organizations have divided a room as big as a half-dozen airplane hangars into an endless Casbah of work spaces marked off by blue curtains. To walk through this impromptu mediapolis is to be overwhelmed by the elephantine extravagance and pointlessness of it all. The work spaces are full of tables piled high with expensive computers, fax machines, laser photo developers, television sets, and of course free food. Ten thousand journalists stand around telling each other how much better off they'd have been if they'd stayed home and watched the whole thing on C-Span.

The same might be said of the delegates, many of whom, come to think of it, actually are watching the whole thing on C-Span, in a spillover auditorium set aside for the purpose. But the delegates don't even have the minimal dignity of being able to busy themselves telling people about what they are passively observing. "Everybody is a spectator here," Bruce Babbitt told me, "and the spectators with status are the reporters." Babbitt was sporting press credentials himself, as a representative of two newspapers and four television stations. "You know, it's absurd," Babbitt added. "They spent a year and a half panning me for my television technique, and now they're paying me for it."

Tuesday night was set aside for the party's premier orators, Ted Kennedy and Jesse Jackson. They did fine, especially Jackson, whose closing litany of solidarity with the poor and discouraged, with its tender refrain of "I understand," left many black and white faces wet with tears. But the unexpected star speakers were the ones who immediately preceded the two veteran spellbinders. Introducing his uncle from the podium, John F. Kennedy, Jr., was poised, calm, and so handsome that Walter Isaacson of *Time*, who was standing next to me, remarked that the roof almost buckled from the sudden drop in air pressure caused by the simultaneous sharp intake of so many thousands of breaths. John Kennedy has none of the slightly edgy boisterousness of his cousin Joe, who backslapped and kissed his way across the convention floor on opening night. John's charm is simpler, quieter, and more modest than his congressman cousin's. But I would guess that his political career, should he choose to pursue one (he is a law student), will ultimately take him further. The other young star was Jesse Jackson, Jr. All five of the Jackson children spoke briefly in introducing their father, but Jesse Jr., who spoke last, gave a mini-speech that was well above the convention average in the forcefulness and clarity of its delivery. He said that just as the Kennedy children are proud to be Kennedys, he and his brothers and sisters are proud to be Jacksons. Young Jesse, twenty-three years old and a graduate of both Washington's snooty St. Alban's prep school and his father's alma mater, North Carolina Agricultural and Technical State University, is said to be interested in running for office. The Adamses, the Harrisons, the Roosevelts, the Tafts, the Stevensons, the Kennedys, and now the Jacksons: we may have been witness to the debut of America's first black political dynasty.*

—Atlanta Diarist, *The New Republic*, August 8, 1988

---

* In 1995, Jesse Jackson, Jr., was elected to Congress from the Second District of Illinois. (2005)

FRONT MAN

THE BUSH-QUAYLE TICKET is a powerful symbol of the moral decline of the American ruling class. Consider the response of each half of this generationally balanced ticket to its generation's war.

In 1941 George Herbert Walker Bush, scion of a rich and politically influential family, was a seventeen-year-old senior at a prestigious New England prep school. A secure and idyllic childhood, spent in the bosky suburban towns of Milton, Massachusetts, and Greenwich, Connecticut, and in summerhouses and sailboats on the Maine coast, was behind him. An equally secure future beckoned, first at Yale and afterward in some appropriate branch of business. Then his country called—but let Bush (and Vic Gold) take up the story, as told in Bush's autobiography, *Looking Forward:*

> When the Japanese bombed Pearl Harbor, December 7, 1941, there wasn't any doubt about which branch of the service I'd join. My thoughts immediately turned to naval aviation. College was coming up the following fall, but that would have to wait. The sooner I could enlist, the better.
>
> Six months later I got my diploma from Phillips Academy Andover. Secretary of War Henry Stimson came from Washington to deliver the commencement address. He told members of our graduating class the war would be a long one, and even though America needed fighting men, we'd serve our country better by getting more education before getting into uniform.

After the ceremony, in a crowded hallway outside the auditorium, my father had one last question about my future plans. . . . "George," he said, "did the secretary say anything to change your mind?"

"No, sir," I replied. "I'm going in."

Dad nodded and shook my hand.

In that exchange, so long ago, between Prescott and George Bush, there is real nobility; it is a perfect expression of the upper-class ethos at its tight-lipped, firm-jawed best. These were not people brought up to talk endlessly, or at all, about their "feelings." A nod and a handshake were more than sufficient to convey the father's pride in the son. With that handshake the boy became a man; and the man went on, as the world knows, to become the youngest aviator in the Navy, flying fifty-eight combat missions off the pitching decks of aircraft carriers, getting shot down in his TBM Avenger and rescued at sea by an American submarine, and coming home with the Distinguished Flying Cross on his chest. He need not have left home at all. A word from Prescott Bush to Secretary Stimson or some other highly placed acquaintance, and George might have had a comfortable billet in the Pentagon or as an adjutant on some general's staff behind the lines. But that was not his way, or the way of his class. "War," writes Nelson W. Aldrich, Jr., in *Old Money: The Mythology of America's Upper Class,* "is the ultimate in the series of ordeals, beginning at boarding school, going on through the trial by nature, through which the Old Rich discover their personal powers and enter at last into the line of descent and succession that marks their place in time." George Bush took his place in that line, and it would carry him to the threshold of the White House.

NOW FLASH FORWARD to 1969. J. Danforth Quayle III, scion of a rich and politically influential family, has a problem. Like millions of others, he has held off the draft for four years with a Selective Service rating of 2-S— a student deferment. But now he has graduated, from DePauw University, and because his grades weren't so good it's going to take some doing to get him into law school. Meanwhile, he has had his physical examination, the last step before the machinery of Selective Service will grind out his induction notice. He applies for a spot in the National Guard, as the state militia is called, but the demand for places is so great that he will have long since been drafted if he waits his turn. Fortunately, a senior employee at one of the family's newspapers is a retired major general in the Guard. Telephone calls are made. A spot is found. Quayle is inconvenienced: he has to spend six months in training, and for five and a half years after that he has to spend one weekend each month and two weeks each summer at meetings. But he is out of danger. The 120th Public Information Detachment of the Indiana National Guard is not a hell-for-leather outfit, and anyway the chances that it or any other unit of the militia will be activated for duty in Vietnam are close to zero. On paper Quayle "served his country," as we have been told so often in recent days; in reality he served himself.

So did a lot of other people, of course. On the exquisitely calibrated moral scale of that period, Quayle fell somewhere in the middle. The aristocrats were the fighters and the resisters—those who volunteered for combat duty and sometimes lost their lives in the war, and those who chose to go to prison to demonstrate their opposition to it. In the second rank were the draftees and the C.O.s—those who accepted induction and obeyed orders, even if that meant going into combat (which in the majority of cases it did not), and those who, in obedience to religious conscience, did alternative service in hospitals or nursing homes. In the third rank were the joiners and the exiles—those who, like Quayle, signed up with some branch of the service in a way that guaranteed they could discharge their military obligation without incurring physical risk, and those who moved to Canada or Sweden, placing themselves beyond the reach of army or jail but sacrificing home, and sometimes career and relations with friends and family, in the process. The fourth rank were the evaders—those who arranged their lives to correspond with one of the categories exempt from the draft. (Graduate school, marriage with children, and civilian defense work were the most common ploys.) Bringing up the rear were those who faked or exaggerated physical or mental infirmities with enough success to obtain 1-Y status (a temporary medical deferment) or, best of all, the coveted 4-F. Only those in this final category truly deserved the name of draft dodger. Outside this scheme of moral ranking were the genuine 4-Fs with true medical disabilities.

I'm not running for vice president, but since I'm judging people who are, full disclosure is in order. By the end of 1966 I had held off Uncle Sam for five years, first by going to college and then by working for the National Student Association, which was mysteriously able to shelter its staff from the draft. (The mystery was cleared up in 1967, when it was disclosed that the

C.I.A., which was secretly funding the N.S.A., would simply request one's file from one's local draft board and sit on it.) I'd quit N.S.A. to work for *Newsweek*, my draft status was 1-A, and certain induction was only weeks away. I was too straight to malinger and too glad to be out of school to want to go back; and I doubted that my opposition to the Vietnam War was single-minded enough to sustain me through a jail term. So I joined the Navy for a three-year hitch. After Officer Candidate School I requested assignment to Vietnam (where I would have been in no great danger—my specialty, like Quayle's, was "public information"), but with typical military logic they gave me a desk job in Manhattan.

After a year and a half in the passionately antiwar atmosphere of Greenwich Village, I decided I was a conscientious objector after all and applied for discharge as such. My application was long (twenty-five thousand words) and earnest, containing what I considered an ingenious and convincing plan for the non-violent national defense of the United States. My commanding officer, Vice Admiral Andrew Jackson, was sympathetic, but the Navy Department wasn't buying. Instead of a discharge they sent me my long-deferred orders to Vietnam. I politely announced my intention to disobey, and looked forward to a court-martial and fame as an antiwar hero. It was not to be. A friend from the office who was a former guard at Portsmouth Naval Prison, where I was expecting to finish out my military career, strongly advised me to have any pending dental work done before rather than during my stay at Portsmouth. (He cautioned that the prison dentists' sole remedy, no matter what the complaint, was extraction.) I followed this advice, bled more spectacularly from the procedure than I should have, was found to have a mild clotting-factor deficiency, and was returned, with breathtaking speed, to civilian life. In sum, I was an evader turned joiner turned C.O. whose ambition to be a resister was frustrated by the fact that he'd been 4-F from day one.

How one served or didn't was not the only variable in the moral calculus of the time. There was also where one stood on the war, and how one's actions comported with one's words. Many a draft evader or dodger partially redeemed himself by participating in the movement to end the war, sometimes running real risks (though of course of a much lower order than the risks to which combat troops exposed themselves) in the process. Such men also "served their country." The Quayle, however, was one of the most irritating species in the aviary, the "chicken hawk" who cawed loudly in support of the war while fluttering far from the theatre of combat. The antiwar equivalent was the saber-toothed dove, the draft dodger who jeered at soldiers and sailors. (Strolling in uniform around Sheridan or Harvard Square, I was often the object of unsolicited abuse from birds of this type. My policy was to inquire about the Selective Service status of my tormentor. If the answer was 1-A, or the person was out on bail for draft resistance, I'd nod or try to engage him in conversation. If the answer was 2-S or 1-Y, I'd tell the son of a bitch to fuck off.)

In the hours following his selection as Bush's running mate, Quayle all but acknowledged the moral ambiguity of his position, saying he chose as he did because he wanted to go to law school and get on with his career, and adding, with coarse candor, that "I did not know in 1969 that I would be in this room today, I'll confess." By the time he gave his acceptance speech (in which he identified the Republican themes as "Freedom, Family, and Future"—a fourth F and he wouldn't have had to join the Guard), the line had changed. Now he was "proud" of what he did. Quayle's problem is that he has no really good answer to the questions that are being raised. But both he and the country would be better off if he would say something like, "The choice I made twenty years ago was not a dishonorable one, but I'm not especially proud of it either. It takes nothing away from the respect and gratitude we owe to those who fought and died to say that it was a wrenching time for all Americans, and particularly for young men of my generation. I've learned a lot since then, and our country has come a long way toward healing the wounds of that terrible time. I want that healing to continue. I hope that in the end this controversy will help that process along, not retard it."

Of course, that's a bit long for a ten-second sound bite, and in any case the Republicans have chosen another route: demagogic, defensive anger. Speaking before the Veterans of Foreign Wars, George Bush said of Quayle, "He did not go to Canada, he did not burn his draft card, and he damn sure didn't burn the American flag." More's the pity; those who did do such things—twisted, bitter, and self-defeating though their actions sometimes (not always) were—at least acted from motives higher than individual convenience. Quayle made a separate peace; now Bush proposes to refight the war. *Aux armes, citoyens.*

—*The New Republic*, September 12 & 19, 1988

ROBOFLOP

DESPITE HIS PEE-PANTS performance in the Omaha debate against
Lloyd Bentsen, it looks as if Dan Quayle, forty-one, will be president one
of these days. Consider the politico-actuarial probabilities. Assuming the
Republican lead endures, the junior senator from Indiana will be elected vice
president. This alone will give him an even chance of becoming president.
Three out of the last five presidents were vice president first. Seven out of
the last ten vice presidents have ended up heading a national ticket, and four
(five if you presumptively count George Bush) got all the way to the Oval
Office. Of this century's vice presidents Quayle's age, all became president.
Admittedly, the sample is small: T. Roosevelt, vice president at forty-two in
1901, and R. Nixon, vice president at forty in 1953. Still, makes you think,
doesn't it?

Vice President Quayle is sure to make his move sooner or later. Maybe
later—skinny Yankees like Bush are notoriously long-lived. But maybe
sooner. Life is a fragile thing. We live in a hazardous world. A lot of things
can happen. Let's say it's next April, and President Bush is out having a brisk
springtime sail off Kennebunkport. Maybe he gets his tie caught in the jam
cleat. Or maybe, just maybe, he doesn't hear the cry of "Hard to lee!" when
the boom sweeps over the deck. Suddenly—*bonk! splash!*—a vacancy occurs,
and J. Danforth Quayle III, maybe still dressed in his lime-green golf pants,
putter in hand, standing at the club bar, takes the oath of office as the forty-
second president of the United States.

At this point, the question becomes the one Quayle so conspicuously
failed to answer in Omaha: once we've all had a good pray, what next? The

answer, probably, is that the United States would enter a brief Regency period. The regent, in those first panicky months, would be Secretary of State James Baker. For a while, Quayle would perform as he performed in the debate, fearful of disobeying the instructions of his programmers. But as President Quayle gained confidence, the struggle between the Republican moderates and the ideological hard right, formerly assumed to have been settled in the moderates' favor by the nomination and election of Bush, would flare up again. Quayle would grow bored with taking orders from Baker (who, after all, had let it be known during the convention that he had wanted Bush to pick a different running mate) and his Ivy League buddies in the cabinet junta. The instincts of the vain and unreflective young president would begin to reassert themselves. We can imagine what those instincts might be, given a political character shaped by a grandfather who was one of the most prominent reactionaries of his time, by a father who takes pride to this day in his membership in the John Birch Society, which declared that Dwight Eisenhower was a conscious agent of the Communist conspiracy, and by a wife who has spent dozens of hours in her parents' home listening to the tape-recorded rantings of a fundamentalist sect leader named Colonel Robert Thieme, who often wears his uniform in the pulpit and who believes that the United States government is in the grip of a "Satanic conspiracy."

On the foreign policy side, out-of-favor right-wingers who had been careful to praise Quayle during the post-convention days when everybody else was damning him—Richard Perle, Jeane Kirkpatrick, Kenneth Adelman— would ascend to glory. On the domestic side, on-the-shelf "cultural conservatives" such as William Bennett and Gary Bauer would stage a similar comeback. With Central America in flames, Soviet-American relations in ruins, NATO turning toward Gorbachev as a source of stability, and police hosing down crowds demonstrating against the appointment of Orrin Hatch to the Supreme Court, conflict between the White House and the Democratic majorities in the House and Senate would escalate to red alert. In 1992 President Quayle would run for a full term as the feisty Midwestern underdog giving "the do-nothing, blame-America-first 102nd Congress" hell. After Reagan's clay-animation cartoon of F.D.R., Quayle's Truman impression. From the daddy to the caddy.

OR MAYBE the Age of Quayle will never dawn. The Omaha debate seemed to hold out that possibility. Never in the twenty-eight-year history of televised joint appearances by national party nominees has any candidate "lost" so decisively without committing an obvious suicidal gaffe.

The debate was preceded by an unusually Byzantine "expectations" game. Complex signals were coming from the journalists, consultants, and spin doctors who collectively make up what might be called the expectorate. (Or, for purposes of vice presidential commentary, the warm expectorate.) The expectorate's thinking went something like this. Quayle was expected to do poorly. Therefore, Quayle was expected to do well because expectations for him were so low that he could hardly fail to do better than expected. On the other hand, most observers expected Bentsen to do well, but because most observers expected him to do well most observers couldn't see how he could meet the expectations most observers expected of him. That's why most observers expected him to do poorly. In other words—oh, never mind.

By these low standards, I thought Quayle would surely "win." He didn't. He did all right for about the first fifteen minutes, handling the tough, often harsh questions of the panel of reporters in a functional if robotlike manner. Then Tom Brokaw sadistically asked him to describe the last time he had visited a poor family and to tell how he had explained to that family his votes against the school breakfast program, the school lunch program, and the expansion of the child immunization program. In a quavering voice Quayle said he had too met with "those people" and that "they didn't ask me those questions on those votes, because they were glad that I took time out of my schedule to go down and talk about how we're going to get a food bank going. . . ."

With this unpleasant display of condescension the debate began to go sour for Quayle. Some of his barbs were still effective, such as his attack on Bentsen's now abandoned ten-thousand-dollar-a-time "breakfast club" for lobbyists ("I'm sure they weren't paying to have corn flakes"). Others were not, such as his demagogic promise never to have another grain embargo—or, as he jumpily called it, "another Jimmy Carter grain embargo, Jimmy, Jimmy Carter, Jimmy Carter grain embargo, Jimmy Carter grain embargo." As the minutes ticked away, the admixture of gibberish grew richer, the candidate's manner more and more tense and rigid.

Bentsen's now famous saber thrust to the belly—"Senator, you're no Jack Kennedy"—won both ears, the tail, and the debate. But by then Quayle's affect had been thoroughly flattened by the repeated questions about his qualifications. Actually, they were questions about what he would do if he suddenly succeeded to the presidency. But the only *answer* Quayle could find in his mental card file was about his qualifications, so he repeated it—twice, three times, four times—with what appeared to be mounting anxiety. Quayle was like a teenager in a horror movie who thinks the monster has finally been killed, only to have it leap out again from behind a tree. The ritual words they'd given him—I have twelve years of experience in Congress, here are the three big issues, I'll know the Cabinet personally—had no effect. The thing kept coming. When in desperation he used the ultimate incantation, the sacred name of J.F.K., all it did was bring forth an even worse horror—and this time not from the cackling coven of the press, but from the tall white-haired wizard who until then had seemed courtly if not kindly.

Quayle could have simply said that he would continue the policies of the president he would be succeeding, and then dared Bentsen to say the same. Instead Quayle kept talking about how ready and qualified he was to take over the ultimate power, a prospect he seemed to find as frightening as many voters do. In short, he turned himself into one of those "President Quayle" bugaboo buttons the Democrats were handing out beforehand.

THE FLOPSWEAT was all over Quayle in the second half of the debate. While his slide was less a matter of particular statements than of general demeanor, three moments of supreme silliness do stand out.

Asked to name a "work of literature or art" that had impressed him lately, Quayle cited a book by . . . Richard Nixon. Also a book by the other senator from Indiana, Richard Lugar, and *Nicholas and Alexandra* by Robert Massie. One CBS guest commentator said that this answer "came across as non-prepared." I didn't think so, as I had heard it before—in an interview with Quayle a few days earlier.

Asked to describe some key experience that had shaped his political philosophy, Quayle said there had been a lot of them, but there was one in particular that he kept coming back to, that he talked about in commencement addresses, that he talked about in high schools, that he talked about in job training centers, that he talked about to his own children, that he talked about to other people's children—on and on went the buildup, and to what? To an incredibly banal piece of advice from his grandmother, namely, "You can do anything you want if you put your mind to it." When the Democratic claque laughed at this, Quayle added petulantly, "Now the Dukakis supporters sneer at that because it's common sense. They sneer at commonsense advice, midwestern advice, midwestern advice from a grandmother to a grandson, important advice, something that we ought to talk about." His problem was immaturity; yet he chose to present himself as a child at his grandma's knee.

Finally there was his closing statement, which he began by saying, somewhat rashly, "You have been able to see Dan Quayle as I really am," and ended by saying, in a flourish that sounded like a literal translation from some language other than English, "George Bush has the experience, and with me the future—a future committed to our family, a future committed to the freedom." What?

THE DAN QUAYLE I followed on his last big predebate swing was a happier man than the fearful, angry zombie of the television debate. The three-day trip through the South was probably the least stressful interlude Quayle has had or will have in this campaign. The National Guard business had quieted. Quayle hadn't had a press conference in nearly two weeks (not since the one in which, memorably, he had called the Holocaust "an obscene period in American history" and then, trying to explain that he meant this century's history, blurted out, "I didn't live in this century") and had no plans to have another. He was traveling in magnificent style. His ticket was looking like a winner. All this made for a contented candidate.

To travel with Quayle is to be made more than usually aware of the absurdity of "covering" a fully entouraged American political candidate. It's fun, of course. Traveling with a candidate is always fun, because it's always fun to pal around with one's fellow reporters, ride in chartered airplanes, stay in hotels, and pass through barricades into press sections from which regular people are barred—all at company expense. One enters a movable cocoon of privilege and adventure, a zone of magic. But in the case of Quayle, the zone was touched by twilight. The ratio of miles traveled, pizzas eaten, and expense receipts collected to insights gleaned was unusually high.

Take day two. Quayle "did" a total of seven "events," but only three were open to the press; the other four were closed fund-raisers. At the open events, the press was kept at a distance. We watched Quayle's speech to the students of McNeese State University in Lake Charles, Louisiana, from the balcony of the auditorium. We watched his remarks to Asian Americans in Houston, Texas, from the far end of a hotel ballroom. We watched him address a tarmac rally in El Paso, Texas, from a roped-off section thirty yards away. I had brought a pair of binoculars powerful enough to see the moons of Jupiter. These were much in demand. The plane had two entrances, so there was no danger of encountering the candidate when embarking or disembarking. Total time spent airborne: three and a half hours. Total time spent riding in motorcades: two hours. Total time spent waiting around: three hours. Total time spent watching the candidate read speeches: fifty-five minutes.

Quayle's role was mostly limited to reading aloud. In speeches, he was permitted to interpolate an occasional interjection—for example, he might say, "And you know what? That's the big difference between us and our opponents," instead of just "That's the big difference between us and our opponents"—but apart from that he stuck closely to the texts handed to him by his minders. I call them "minders" rather than "handlers," the usual term, because the part of the candidate's person they substitute for is the mind, not the hands. Perhaps someday we could have a political campaign in which this pattern is reversed and the staff does the handshaking while the candidate does the thinking.

The tone was set at the very first event, a joint appearance with Bush at a big rally near Nashville. Quayle sailed immediately into his assault on Michael Dukakis. "He is for abortion on demand," Quayle read. "He is against the death penalty for cop killers and drug kingpins. He is for cutting the muscle out of our strategic defense. He is opposed to cutting taxes. He is opposed to asking teachers in his state to lead students in the Pledge of Allegiance. He supports the American Civil Liberties Union and its extreme positions." And so on. Then the peroration. "Here's my summary. When you review all his positions, you could call him Mr. Tax Increase. You could call him Mr. Polluter. You can call him Mr. Weak on National Defense. You can call him Mr. Weekend Furlough. But lemme tell you, my friends, come November 8th there is one thing the American people will never call the man from Massachusetts and that is Mr. President!"

There was a good deal of this sort of thing. The indictment of Dukakis was wrong, or at least distorted, in every particular. Dukakis is against capital punishment on principle, but shows no special solicitude for cop killers or drug kingpins. Our strategic defense has no muscle to cut out. Dukakis has no generic opposition to tax cuts; he does oppose the capital gains tax cut for the rich that Bush and Quayle are campaigning for. Dukakis is not opposed to "asking" teachers to lead the Pledge, he's opposed to forcing them to do so. Dukakis supports the A.C.L.U., but, like many other members, he does not support its more extreme positions.

The minders chose to have Quayle expand on the A.C.L.U. point at the Houston meeting of Asian Americans for Bush. It was faintly nauseating to watch this audience of Asian American faces cheering Quayle's attack on one of the few groups that provided leadership in the fight against the internment of Japanese Americans during World War II. Nor did they know what they were cheering about. Of the dozen or so I talked to afterward, all said they approved of Quayle's attack, and all said they knew nothing about the A.C.L.U. other than what they have heard from Bush and Quayle.

There were two unscripted talks: in New Orleans to the National Alliance of Business and at a Job Corps center in El Paso. Quayle could be trusted to go off the cuff because the subject was the Job Training Partnership Act of 1983, his single legislative achievement. It replaced the old Comprehensive Education and Training Act with a more decentralized, more business-dominated program. Quayle co-sponsored the bill with Edward Kennedy, and when he talks about it he sounds almost like a liberal—a neoliberal, anyway.

"For the first time in our nation's history we've said that a dislocated worker, someone that has no real chance of going back to their place of employment, has the opportunity and the right to receive help through the Job Training Partnership Act. Before, under the program, they were excluded. But we recognize the dynamics that were changing in our society, the dynamics that you have six hundred thousand businesses that start up in a year, but you also have businesses that don't make it. And we changed the culture and attitude of the work force around to say, 'You shouldn't feel that it's your fault that you lost your job. It's not because you didn't work hard. It's not because you didn't come to work on time. It's not because you weren't willing to invest. The reason you lost the job was because the company made a decision not to continue, through no fault of your own. . . .' "

This side of Quayle is a puzzlement. To be sure, he faithfully represented business interests in his work on the job training program. Still, it's essentially a liberal program, because it sanctions public intervention in the job market. His work on it is vastly outweighed by an otherwise almost spotless record of opposition to civil rights bills, environmental controls, prolabor legislation, and measures aimed at helping the poor. Yet his pride in the job training program must mean something. The question is whether it means he is potentially open-minded, intermittently softhearted, or just too intellectually inert to care about being consistent.

IF QUAYLE'S TRAINING PROGRAM is aimed at workers who do nothing wrong but whose careers suffer anyway, his own experience is exactly the opposite. Most of us pay some sort of price for screwing up. Quayle never has. His high school guidance counselor told him his grades were too low for admission to DePauw University, where his grandfather was a trustee and major donor, but he got in anyway. In college he flunked the departmental exam that was supposed to be a prerequisite to graduation, but he graduated anyway. Although it was 1969, the height of the Vietnam War, a year when more than a quarter million young men were drafted and other Indianans were being told it would take years to get into the National Guard, Quayle landed a spot in a week flat, after a retired Guard general who worked for his family made a call on his behalf. Quayle was rejected by Indiana University Law School, but he got in anyway—under an affirmative action program, after he visited the dean of admissions, a Republican judge in a city (Indianapolis) where Quayle's grandfather owned the newspaper. (Soon thereafter, the grandfather made a large contribution to the law school.) Quayle was an indifferent law student, but he got a job in the state attorney general's office anyway. (His father had made a few calls.) He was a twenty-nine-year-old employee of his father's paper, but he got elected to Congress anyway, with the help of the paper and his own good looks. He was a poor congressman, but he got elected to the Senate anyway, in the 1980 Reagan landslide. Two years later the DePauw faculty voted against giving him an honorary degree, but he got it anyway. He was a mediocre senator, but Bush put him on the national ticket anyway. He blew the debate, but he'll probably be elected vice president anyway. At this rate he'll be president by cherry blossom time.

TO MY SURPRISE, I was given an interview with Quayle during the flight back to Washington. It had been a successful trip. The minders were feeling expansive. From a distance of two feet Quayle looks younger than he is, his face smooth and creamy, as if unmarked by life. He's good-looking, no denying that. If he were a woman he would be described as beautiful. His facial bones are delicate, and his mouth is what pulp fiction writers call sensual. This gives the lower half of his face a look that is either weak or sensitive, depending on your political predilections. Like his looks, his character seemed soft (in the sense of being unformed). My subjective impression was of a man who has no intellectual depth and not much imagination or empathy, but who is shrewd about the emotional texture of whatever situation he finds himself in. To me, he talked about "our" generation.

I started by asking him how, if at all, experience had caused him to modify the extremely conservative opinions he had been inculcated with since childhood.

"I would say that I've changed on many of the social issues—like civil rights, and things like the Job Training Partnership Act," said Quayle. "Getting government involved in a limited but effective way is a new type of conservative approach. Another difference is an understanding toward the environment and its importance. That gets more into this generational thing. I mean, we grew up with Martin Luther King. I didn't agree with everything he said, but certainly the goals of Martin Luther King are something we all subscribe to, whether you're conservative, liberal, Republican, Democrat—the only exceptions in our generation are those that are on the fringe. The same way with the environment. We are the ones that first experienced this global effect of looking at the problems of the environment.

"Those aren't things that we discussed a lot at the dinner table. The dinner table discussion was more along the lines of very strong anti-Communist feelings. And then there were a lot of good discussions about what you would do on campus, or whether girls would be allowed to visit one's room—things of that sort. So it was a normal type of chitchat that sometimes got confrontational about what was socially acceptable and what wasn't. . . .

"In our generation things were changing so fast and going on so quickly that I think all people of my generation had that little bit of rebellion and independence with your parents. But in my case never anything that was too extreme. There wasn't any social rebellion where I said, 'Parents, you really don't know what it's all about.' Because I was too close to my parents for that."

"Any intellectual rebellion?" I asked.

"I think my intellectual rebellion, my interests in what I wanted to do from an intellectual basis, was formed much later than most. It wasn't formed in college, but later."

"What were the influences of that later development in terms of people or books?"

"Well, it wouldn't be an intellectual rebellion. I guess I read Charles Reich's *The Greening of America* in '68 or '69 and at the time I thought it was an interesting book. I haven't reread it, but I've read enough about it that I was really somewhat confused at the time. The sort of thing with the three layers. . . . That was sort of *the* book at the time. We all read it and we all talked about it. But as I look back now it was sort of an exercise in frivolous intellectual curiosity. As far as now, since I've come to the Senate I've been much more interested in trying to focus on what my intellectual approach is. Over spring vacation I read three books that I think were important."

At this point I got the full book report of which Quayle's "work of literature or art" debate answer was merely the executive summary. Hold on to your hat, here it comes:

"I read Nixon's book, *1999*. I read Richard Lugar's book on the *Letters to the Next President*. And I read Bob Massie's book on *Nicholas and Alexandra*. Nixon's book was about the Soviet Union and how we ought to handle them in the future, in 1999. Lugar's was much more of a foreign policy review—the Philippines, South Africa, what we ought to be doing in Nicaragua. . . . And then Massie's book on Nicholas and Alexandra, which is a really interesting book on the downfall of the Russian czar and the empire and the coming of Lenin and how that whole thing just crumbled when his father passed on unexpectedly and Alexandra had to take it and they had that child that had hemophilia. And it came through Queen Victoria and everybody sort of thought that the hemophilia was from the high living and they didn't realize it was hereditary. It comes through the mother. And Alexandra was from Germany. And it was a very good book of Rasputin's involvement in that, which shows how people that are really very weird can get into sensitive positions and have a tremendous impact on history."

I lifted an eyebrow; Quayle took a breath.

"Let's see. And then I read other things. Like I read Rick Smith's book on Washington power [*Power Game: How Washington Works*]. It's a good book, and, I thought, very accurate and to the point. So what I've been doing in the last eight years, I've been forming much more of my intellectual basis and pushing on how I really view the world and what the world means to me and how we're going to go forward. I've reread over the last four years both Plato's *Republic* and Machiavelli's *Prince*. I've enjoyed that. I was going to go back this summer and make myself read *The Republic* again but I never got around to it. I don't know if I would have gotten it done on the August break or not. But I was tempted to, because you always learn something by reading the classics. Particularly *The Prince*. I go through and look at this from this intellectual point of view, which I think is your question. Machiavelli had these three classes of mind, and it fits in so much with Plato's state. The first class was the person that was creative enough to be leader and be able to lead a great nation without much help. The second class of mind was one that wasn't creative but could take ideas, put people around him, and be able to lead nations forward. And the third class of people didn't really know much of anything. And they were the worst kind of leaders, because not only were they not creative, but they didn't know what was right or wrong and they just sort of went by whatever they felt like. I've tried to figure out where I am. I know I'm not the first one because I don't think I have that creativeness that Machiavelli talks about. If I go back and reread it I might figure it out exactly where I put myself. I'm somewhere in between two and one."

I'M NOT SURE what I can add to this. Quayle seemed like a pretty nice guy, and he can be charming. His political views, which is to say the political views of his grandparents and parents and minders, are of course awful. But they are awful in a way that unfortunately has become routine in recent years. The question raised by the prospect of President Quayle is the same as the question raised by the likelihood of President Bush and for that matter by the reality of President Reagan: How long can a great nation afford to have silly leaders?

—*The New Republic*, October 31, 1988

AND WHAT IF . . . ?

FROM THE VERY OUTSET of the second and final presidential "debate" of the 1988 general election campaign, there were intimations that this one was going to be different. Miraculously, Michael Dukakis had at last decided to *say* something. That was clear from the way he handled Bernard Shaw's brutal opening question.

"Governor," the Cable News Network anchor asked, "if Kitty Dukakis were raped and murdered, would you favor an irrevocable death penalty for the killer?"

"God forbid," said Dukakis, frowning. "God forbid any harm should come to the person who is dearer to me than anyone or anything on earth. But I'd react the same as anyone. I'd want to kill the scum that did it. I'd want to rip him limb from limb."

The applause was sharp and sudden. But Dukakis was already shaking his head to silence the crowd.

"Now wait, wait. Yes, I would want revenge in that situation. Of course I would. But you don't run a government on that basis. I believe that the premeditated killing of a human being is wrong. Period. I don't care how much the person may deserve it. It's wrong. And it's doubly wrong when the government does it. That's how I feel. So I'm against capital punishment.

"I know that position doesn't get me a lot of political points. I saw a poll the other day where something like 70 percent of the voters disagree with me on this one. It'd be a lot easier for me if I could just stand up here and yell death, death, death, as if that was the answer to the problems of crime and drugs in our society. But I don't think it is the answer. I don't think it works. And more important, as I say, I think it's wrong. And I say this without any disrespect to those who have a different opinion. I know a lot of good people who don't feel the way I do on this. But I have to go with what my conscience tells me.

"One more thing. Violent crime is not some abstract issue to me. It's not something I learned about in a Clint Eastwood movie. My father, a doctor, seventy-seven years old, was gagged, beaten, and robbed by a thief looking for drugs in his office. My brother was killed by a hit-and-run driver. Violent crime is something I take personally. So as governor of my state I've gone out and done something about it. We've put violent criminals in jail. We've built more jails. We've shaken up the criminal justice system so that punishment is swifter and surer. And now my state has the lowest murder rate of any industrial state."

After Dukakis's passionate appeal to conscience, George Bush's talk of "values" as a reason for executing what he termed "narcotics drugs kingpins" sounded a trifle tinny. Even so, the vice president nearly held his own for the first half of the debate. The decisive exchange came when *Newsweek*'s Margaret Warner asked Bush about abortion: "Why should a woman who discovers through amniocentesis that her baby will be born with Tay-Sachs disease, for instance, that the baby will live at most two years and those two years in incredible pain, be forced to carry the fetus to term, and yet a woman who becomes pregnant through incest would be allowed to abort her fetus?"

Bush told Warner she had "left out one other exception"—"the health of the mother." He then spoke haltingly and rather touchingly of his late daughter Robin, who died a few months after being diagnosed with leukemia. Bush added that medical science often makes such rapid advances that there is hope even for the most seemingly intractable cases. "And so I just feel this is where I'm coming from," concluded Bush, employing a bit of bell-bottom slang.

Dukakis's memorable reply began in all mildness. "Margaret, Kitty and I had very much the same kind of experience that the Bushes had. We lost a baby, not even an hour old. So we have nothing but sympathy and respect for what they went through. But we're not talking here about what advice we might give to a woman who has to make that agonizing choice. We're talking about taking the choice away from her.

"Let's be clear about the vice president's answer. What is Mr. Bush saying to that young woman who learns that the fetus she is carrying is damaged or deformed? He's saying: No. You can't end that pregnancy. He's saying, too bad you weren't raped, because then maybe we could do something for you. He's saying, if you terminate that pregnancy you're guilty of a criminal act and if you don't go to jail your doctor will.

"George Bush seems like too nice a guy to say this. But it's the clear logic of his position. George, maybe this is another case where you haven't sorted things out. Because what you're saying now is thoughtlessly cruel. That terrible decision about ending a pregnancy under these nightmarish circumstances—that's not George Bush's decision to make, or Michael Dukakis's, or the federal government's. It's up to the woman to make that decision. We can offer her advice. And when she's made her decision we can offer her support and help and love. But let's not add to her suffering by telling her she's a criminal."

Dukakis's answer on abortion wasn't the only time he scored points by expressing a bit more feeling than usual. Bush, responding to a suggestion from Andrea Mitchell of NBC that the voters are fed up with negative campaigning, said that the Democrats were the ones who started it, at their convention—"Do you remember the senator from Boston chanting out there, and the ridicule factor from that lady from Texas that was on there?" Dukakis replied: "Yes, George, you're right—some of our folks did make fun of you a little bit. That's in the great American tradition of political irreverence. But there is no excuse for what you and your campaign have done. You've questioned my patriotism. You've pictured me as a friend of criminals. You've used ugly code words like 'card-carrying' to imply that I am a subversive of some kind. Clean it up, George. You and I are both old enough to remember a guy named Joe McCarthy. In 1954 I was a college kid visiting Washington. I was in the gallery of the Senate chamber when your father, Senator Prescott Bush of Connecticut, courageously voted to censure McCarthy. It's not my place to say what he would have thought of the campaign you've been running. But I can say this: what you've done is little better than McCarthyism."

When Bush attacked Dukakis for being "a liberal" who takes positions that are "very liberal," Dukakis shot back, "If it's liberal to feed the hungry and house the homeless, George, you can call me a liberal. If it's liberal to make sure a young mother can see a doctor when her baby's sick, call me a liberal"—that whole litany. And when Dukakis was asked to name some heroes of today, he hesitated briefly but then, warming to the subject, came up with a surprisingly interesting list: Henry Steele Commager, Lech Walesa, Andrei Sakharov, Robert Coles, Marian Wright Edelman, Everett Koop, Oscar Arias, Leonard Bernstein, Cory Aquino, "and two young men named for a county in Ireland, who fought valiantly in Vietnam and who today fight for peace and justice at home—John Kerry, who was my lieutenant governor in Massachusetts and who now serves our state in the United States Senate, and former Governor Bob Kerrey of Nebraska, who will be joining John in the U.S. Senate next year."

MOMENTS AFTER Dukakis's eloquent closing statement, with its talk of "mastering the future," the spin doctors poured into the press center in UCLA's student union building. You could tell who had "won" by watching the flow of reportorial flesh. There was a near-stampede to get to Susan Estrich, Paul Brountas, and the other Dukakis operatives; around James Baker, Lee Atwater, and the other Bushies the crowd was sparse.

Since then, the campaign has taken a dramatic turn. Dukakis's five-point "bounce" in the polls has him almost even with Bush and gaining fast. Local Democratic office-seekers are fighting to get into the picture at Dukakis rallies. Reporters have even spotted a few "jumpers" along Dukakis motorcade routes. The race is still far from over; just a couple of weeks ago, after all, Bush was being touted as a sure winner. He could still make a comeback. He's done it before. But right now the election looks like Dukakis's to lose, or my name's not Joe Isuzu.

—*The New Republic*, November 7, 1988

AROMA OF BULL

MIDWAY THROUGH THE WEEK before the week before the election, the George Bush campaign caravan is making its way west. I catch up with it in Detroit, at the end of the day.

It's 11:29 P.M. Most of the members of the bloated, redundant Bush press corps (some one hundred and twenty persons all told) are in their rooms in the tower of the Westin Renaissance Center Hotel. Sixty stories below, urban ruin twinkles prettily. At 11:30 eyes shift from windows to TV screens. On comes ABC's *Nightline*. Ted Koppel asks Michael Dukakis his first question. Unlike Bernard Shaw of CNN, who during the second Bush-Dukakis debate took the subtle, indirect approach of asking Dukakis how he would like it if someone raped and murdered his wife, Koppel goes straight to the root of the problem: How does the candidate respond to the fact that the Bush campaign has been, as Koppel puts it to Dukakis, "kicking you in the groin?"

Dukakis's answer banishes hope he might have learned something from the debate debacle. He ignores the violence of the question. No expression crosses his face. His tone is flat. He speaks of his determination to go on "expressing concerns" about issues. He explains that his plan is to "address the concerns of average Americans." He adds that he and his campaign "will do everything we can to address those concerns."

"What a hopeless wanker," remarks one of the two British correspondents with whom I am watching the show.

To be sure, Dukakis says many sensible things over the next ninety minutes. But he says them in an overpoweringly boring way. The familiarity of the stock answers intensifies their inherent dullness. The drone is all. The word "concerns" continues to get a heavy workout.

As the minutes tick slowly by, our attention turns to the uncanny resemblance between the two men on the screen. They appear to be exactly the same size. They both have enormous round heads topped by low-slung swirls of thick hair. They wear identical looks of thoughtful concern. Their stilted body movements are indistinguishable. Their nasal, resonant voices are interchangeable; if you close your eyes and ignore the content, it's hard to tell which of them is talking. The only difference is that one is blond and the other dark, like Betty and Veronica.

"If only they were wearing dresses," one of the Brits says glumly.

"Yes," says the other. "That would add interest."

IN THE MORNING I notice that the Bush campaign has assumed the gargantuan proportions of a presidential entourage. Secret Service men are everywhere. A huge motorcade is forming up out front. Everyone is consulting thick, pocket-sized schedules full of numbing detail ("3:32 P.M. The VICE PRESIDENT arrives Off-Stage Area and Holds Briefly," etc.). There hasn't been a press conference in ten days. A press aide laughs at my request for an interview. Obviously I'm not going to get within a mile of the guy. It's as if he's already won.

At 10:08 A.M. I am stumbling along one of the walkways that honeycomb the Renaissance Center, trailing Walter Mears of the Associated Press in an attempt to find the temporary press center. I encounter a group of men in suits plus one in a U.S. Olympic Team warm-up jacket and sweatpants. The one in the sweatpants is George Bush. He greets Mears with great friendliness. "You missed my big press availability over there," he says, gesturing vaguely in the direction of the hotel's health spa. "Missed a great opportunity to see me naked." Mears smiles. "Guy from *Newsday* was next to me in the sauna," Bush continues. "*Newsday* guy says, 'I don't want to take advantage, but I have to report to my colleagues. When are you going to have a press conference?' I gave him my two hundred and seven press conferences thing. 'We've had two hundred and seven press conferences since the campaign began. Once every ten days.' He said, 'You haven't had one in ten days.' I said, 'Hey, look at those numbers.' "

Bush then asks after Mears's wife and, after lingering a few moments longer, lopes off on his way.

An hour later Bush is dressed and reading a speech to the Economic Club of Detroit. The text plugs his proposal for a capital gains tax cut and contains this sublime two-sentence non sequitur, this haiku of self-refutation: "Let's cut through the demagoguery. America is No. 1."

After the speech Bush takes some softball questions that members of the audience have passed to the dais on bits of paper. His answers contain a few of the syntactical nuggets for which I have grown used to panning the stream of his spontaneous talk like an old-time prospector. On the homeless, he admonishes: "Don't drum the private sector out of the homeless business." On drugs, he observes: "Governor Dukakis and I both have position papers on this—mine, many pages."

The goofiness gets more substantive when he tackles a question about whom he would appoint to be secretary of state.

"All through this campaign there have been questions asked about who you might appoint, who you might have in the cabinet," he says. "I've stayed out of that for two reasons: One, I *think* it may be against the law. I'm not sure about that. That would be somewhat persuasive, I think. 'Cause you cannot—there's a rule about promising appointments and all this. Second, to respond to questions of that nature conveys a sense of overconfidence that I do not feel." This is absurd, of course. Though selling offices is against the law, no law forbids a presidential candidate from saying whom he intends to appoint to any post. Odd that Bush, who has sought both presidential appointments and the power to make them as vigorously as anyone alive, does not know this. Besides, a few minutes earlier he was saying he is intent on "having a drug czar" and on "placing the vice president of the United States in charge of drugs"—which would seem to add up to something along the lines of "promising appointments and all this."

IN THE AFTERNOON we fly to South Dakota for a rally at the Sioux Falls stockyards. Three hundred people are standing around in a makeshift corral. A sign says WELCOME TO SIOUX FALLS STOCKYARDS. There's livestock nearby. The podium is made of hay bales. The site makes for good visuals. Good olifactuals, too. The smell of bullshit, like the sound, is not wholly unpleasant.

Bush gives his stump speech. "The liberals have been all over my case all across this country because of my differences with him on what I think of as family values," he says. "I don't think there's anything wrong with having a voluntary prayer in a public school," he says. "I think it's right that the teachers lead the kids in the Pledge of Allegiance," he says. "There's a wide array of these social issues and values that the liberals don't like to hear about," he says.

Then the whole entourage—a couple of hundred people, a like number of tons of equipment and baggage—goes to Billings, Montana, so that Bush can give essentially the same speech to another rally, this time in a college gym. Eleven Sioux chiefs stand behind him in full feathers. The speech yields only a single nugget to the syntax prospector, but it's a glittering one: warming to the issue of gun control, Bush calls himself "a violent opponent" of it. It's dark by the time we get back to the airport, and a vicious wind is howling across the tarmac. Air Force Two gets airborne en route to Tacoma, Washington, after a brief delay occasioned by some fuel vapor that got blown back into the cabin. But after two hours and three tries, the press plane still has not left the ground. Each time it lumbers down the runway, a couple of alarming thwacks can be heard in the left engine and the plane slows and stops. "That's a pressure stall 'cause of the strong crosswinds," the pilot announces laconically and not very reassuringly. The press starts taking votes. We vote to try taking off for Tacoma. Then we vote to forget Tacoma and go directly to California. Then we vote to stay in Billings. All day we've been herded from place to place, given carefully prepared things to read, and fed more frequently than newborns. The pilot ignores us and our ridiculous votes. On the fourth try the plane takes off. Our infantilization is complete.

Early the next morning, in Tacoma, Bush accepts the endorsement of the Marine Engineers Beneficial Association, a pro-Reagan union. The proletariat is giving its noisy blessing to the Bushoisie. The press corps is not in a particularly good mood. Nothing resembling news has come its way on this trip. But now, as Bush blathers on about the need to subsidize the shipping industry, a scuffle breaks out. The reporters brighten up. A respectable-looking young man, his hands cuffed behind him, is being hustled out of the hall by a couple of uniformed cops and a heavy-set plainclothesman in a mud-brown jacket. The young man is bleeding from the nose.

I follow the young man and his escorts outside. "A Bush supporter assaulted a man and I complained about it and I'm gettin' my head bashed against the floor!" the young man is yelling. As reporters pepper the young man with questions, he gives his age (twenty-one), occupation (college student), and political affiliation (Democrat). "What's this guy under arrest for, officer?" I ask one of the uniformed cops who is frog-marching the young man toward a paddy wagon. "I have no idea," says the cop. "What's he under arrest for, officer?" I ask the plainclothesman in the brown jacket. He says nothing. "That man, in the brown sports coat!" the young man is yelling. "He was bashing my head against the floor, against the cement floor!" "What's he under arrest for?" I again ask the brown jacket. Brown jacket gives me a long look. Finally he says, "Failing to disperse when told to."

On the plane to San Jose, we are told that the young man was arrested for resisting arrest, a favorite ontological puzzler of local law enforcement agencies. A Bush press aide tells us that the young man was a Bush supporter who got his bloody nose from a Dukakis supporter's fist. The sound of clicking keyboards fills the plane as reporters rewrite their leads to include the "violence" that "marred" the rally. "It isn't much of a story, but it'll have to do," a reporter remarks to no one in particular. "At least it's better than these speeches."

Near San Jose Bush tours a Silicon Valley high-tech plant. He wears a white coat. It suits him. He looks like a doctor recommending a pain reliever in a television commercial. He gives his speech under a white tent with a green carpet. The audience sits on white folding chairs. It looks like a Connecticut wedding, except that everyone has on a laminated badge. There are no scuffles.

The trip ends in Los Angeles, with a party at the home of Bob Hope, the great eighty-five-year-old comedian. In the dark, Hope's house blends into his enormous lawn. A podium has been set up. Hope, old and small but in nose and voice still recognizably Hope, mentions the Secret Service. "This afternoon they brought in the dogs to sniff out the bombs. They stopped twice by my joke files." Everybody laughs.

When it's Bush's turn he tries a joke about Hope being old enough to have known Martin Van Buren, but it's not that boffo. So he turns sincere. "I'm not gonna bore you with all the issues," he says. "But Barbara and I do feel good about it. . . . We're not going to be talking on the negative side anymore. I'm sorry Clint Eastwood isn't here. Remember how he'd say 'Make my day'? Now my opponent says 'Have a nice vacation' as the prisoners come out of the jails. But now it's gonna be a kinder and gentler finish to this campaign. I do feel good about it."

Everybody's feeling good about it, apparently. Not just George and Barbara, but also Hope and the fabulous galaxy of stars he has assembled for the evening. This is not exactly the brat pack. There they are: Jane Russell, Telly Savalas, Danny Thomas, Esther Williams, Efrem Zimbalist, Morey Amsterdam, Glenn Ford, Pat Boone, Gene Autry, Phyllis Diller, Barbara Eden, Jack Jones, Tony Martin, Cyd Charisse, Robert Mitchum, Donald O'Connor, Don Rickles, Abby Lane, Ruta Lee, and many, many more. And you know what? They look marvellous.

For eight years we've been watching *Death Valley Days,* with your host, Ronald Reagan. For a while there some people thought the replacement would probably be something more educational, say a remake of the old PBS series *The Advocates.* No way. That got cancelled before it ever aired. With George and Barbara heading a kinder, gentler cast, the next four years will be one long episode of *The Love Boat.*

—*The New Republic,* November 21, 1988

RECRIMINATIONS '88:
HELL, I DUNNO

THE DAY AFTER the election, Mario Cuomo was asked for his analysis of George Bush's victory. As usual, Cuomo was eloquent.

"How do I know why the guy won?"

The governor of New York was then asked for his analysis of Michael Dukakis's defeat. Again his reply was incisive.

"He got fewer votes."

I'll buy that, both halves. For the rest, though, I don't really know. There are a lot of theories kicking around. I'm of a minimum of two minds about most of them.

First, there's the peace and prosperity theory. We've got p & p, or a reasonable facsimile thereof, goes the theory. The outs can't beat the ins when these conditions obtain. Maybe. But how does this theory account for the fact that Dukakis was seventeen points ahead in the summer and seventeen points behind in the fall? The amount of peace and prosperity was the same in July as in October. When fully a third of the electorate is swinging back and forth like a busted gate in a hurricane, it becomes hard to put much stock in economic determinism or indeed in any notion that people are deciding whom to vote for on the basis of some sort of considered judgment about objective conditions. I'm more inclined to think that these crazy swings confirm what Ralph Whitehead has discovered in his focus-group research and Jonathan Schell has described in his reporting (in the unjustly neglected small classic *History in Sherman Park*)—to wit, that a lot of voters no longer see much connection, if any, between political choice and the conditions of their lives. For such voters, of whom there are surely enough to swing a national election, picking a presidential candidate is like switching the channels on a television set.

To the extent that prosperity explains the outcome, the most politically salient form of prosperity is evidently low inflation. That's pure gold. The stuff the Democrats had to work with—the budget and trade deficits, the slow rate of job creation, the loss of economic sovereignty, the low savings rate, the fact that there has been no federal tax cut for most Americans, the huge increases in economic inequality—is low-grade ore: not exactly worthless, but requiring skillful processing before it can be spent as the coin of the realm.

Second, there's the negative campaign theory. The Pledge of Allegiance, the furlough program starring Willie Horton, the carrying of the A.C.L.U. card, Boston Harbor—all that high-yield political ordnance with which the Bush campaign carpet-bombed the Dukakis campaign from before Labor Day onward. This theory comports more convincingly with the polling data, as well as with the observed reality of the campaign. Bush, this certifiably sweet guy, this amiable goof who spends hundreds of hours each year writing great stacks of nice little personal notes, ran the most vicious campaign of the second half of the twentieth century. It was a campaign that quite openly exploited primitive racial-sexual fears. More subtly, as Philip Roth has argued, the Bush negative campaign exploited nativist prejudice as well. Dukakis is not a real American, Dukakis is different: this was the unwholesome subtheme that tied together the Pledgehammer assault on Dukakis's patriotism with the unrelenting rhetorical effort to place Dukakis outside the "mainstream." Maybe Bush would have used the same or similar attacks against an Al Gore or a Joe Biden. But it's hard to resist the supposition that some among the Bush people calculated that these particular attacks would be particularly effective against a swarthy, big-nosed, beetle-browed Mediterranean type with a Jewish wife and a funny name.

THIRD, and closely related, there's the slow-response theory. What did Dukakis in wasn't so much the negative campaign as his failure to respond to it swiftly and effectively. In other words, Dukakis made a tactical error that cost him the presidency. This theory happens to be the conventional wisdom, but that doesn't make it wrong. In fact there's a lot of evidence for it. In an Election Day piece in the *Wall Street Journal*, David Shribman and

James M. Perry reported that Dukakis was being inundated with pleas to respond all throughout the crucial August and September period when the other side was "defining" him as a weak, unpatriotic, rapist-loving crypto-Communist. For example, John Glenn, who is the flag made flesh, was all set to film an ad that would have eviscerated Bush for questioning Dukakis's patriotism. If the spot had been made, and if it had turned out to be half as effective as a similar one Glenn did for his Ohio senatorial colleague Howard Metzenbaum, that would've been the end of the Pledge travesty. But the Duke said no. And this is far from the only example of his refusal to save himself. What was the guy's problem?

Well, stubbornness, a.k.a. arrogance, for one thing; and what Ellen Goodman called "the candidate's irrational belief in reason," for another. It's laudable, in a way, to want to stick to reasoned, positive argument. From a moral point of view, that is infinitely preferable to a Bush-like willingness to debase reason and truth in order to gull the voters. But emotional resonances must be taken account of. To ignore the irrational, to pretend it doesn't exist, is to disarm oneself in the struggle against it. That's what Dukakis did by failing to respond.

His own inclinations might not have mattered if he'd had someone on his staff who could've stood up to him and told him what to do. But John Sasso, his first campaign manager, was gone by then, and Susan Estrich, his second, wasn't close enough to him to enforce her will. This leads to a fourth theory, the Burgoyne's Nail theory, which holds that Michael Dukakis lost the presidency because Neil Kinnock gave a good speech over in England (and Joe Biden stole it and John Sasso leaked this and Dukakis fired him); and a fifth theory, which holds that Dukakis lost because the campaign brought out his character flaws such as stubbornness and emotional deafness, and that if it hadn't been one thing it'd have been another. I agree with both theories even though they're mutually exclusive.

(By the way, you would think from the retrospective commentaries that back in August it was obvious to absolutely everyone that Dukakis had to strike back and strike back hard. Not so. The conventional wisdom at the time was that Dukakis's problem was not that he wasn't responding to the attacks, but rather that Bush was "controlling the agenda," and that what Dukakis therefore needed to do was avoid the trap of being drawn into "Bush's" issues, such as the Pledge, and talk instead about "his" issues, such as jobs and education.)

Theory No. 6, a familiar one by now, I suspect, to readers of this jour-

nal, is that Dukakis lost because he was too liberal. The scourge of Mc-
Governism claims another victim, and so forth. It is certainly true that liberalism is in disrepute among a plurality of Americans, and that Dukakis
allowed Bush to define him as a liberal and to define a liberal as someone
whose disdain for God, the flag, and national defense is exceeded only by
his eagerness to release murderers from prison. But Dukakis too liberal? This
centrist reformer? This skinflint with a clipboard? Dukakis is scarcely more
liberal than, say, Gore, and less so than Cuomo. Does anyone doubt that either of them would have run a stronger race? If Dukakis was too liberal, then
any Democrat is probably too liberal. And there is the awkward fact that
Dukakis's last-ditch ascent in the polls corresponded quite precisely to his
belated embrace of the L-thing.

SO WHO KNOWS? Meanwhile I'm left not so much with conclusions as with
a feeling. The feeling is one of triviality. I'm sure that the election was very gratifying for those who have accepted George Bush as their personal savior. Some
of the rest of us found the triumph of the Bushoisie less enjoyable. It's not that
one is unused to being on the losing side. On the contrary, over the past twenty
years these quadrennial electoral disasters have become a fixed part of the
leap-year calendar. The television maps covered with spreading blue;* the relieved, slightly guilty faces of Democratic senators spared the ax; the more or
less graceful concession speech by the Democratic nominee—it's all become
quite familiar. Yet each defeat has its own special quality.

What was different about this one was the triviality of its apparent
causes. In 1968 and 1972, in 1980 and 1984, the events that did in the Democrats had a certain grandeur. In '68, foreign war and civil disorder; in '72,
more war and disorder, plus revolution within the party and impeachable
crime against it; in '80, Islamic revolution and runaway inflation; in '84, a
Republican incumbent of F.D.R.-level popularity and political skill. It is
never easy to lose, but there is dignity in being undone by large historical
forces. In '88, Dukakis and those of us who voted for him have been denied
even that dubious solace.

—*The New Republic,* December 5, 1988

---

* The color scheme has since reversed itself. Now the hue that spreads across the map is red, even when,
as in 2000 and 2004, the election is close, because the states Republicans do well in are numerous, large
in acreage, and thinly populated. (2005)

6. FOREIGNERS

A surprising number of knowledgeable people look back upon the Cold War with something like nostalgia. They remember the "long twilight struggle" between the Soviet Union and the democracies as a period of stability and order. Alliances were firm. The world was unchangingly bipolar, like a child's globe. Ultimate power had known, visible addresses—the Kremlin and the White House—and was wielded by men who had something to lose, understood the basic principles of rationality, and were capable of communicating with one another. There were frequent disturbances at the periphery, but the territory of the superpowers—North America and Western Europe on one side, Great Russia and Eastern Europe on the other—remained inviolable. World peace was the misty goal to which, with varying degrees of cynicism, all subscribed; but world peace—in the sense of the absence of world war—was also a reality, underwritten by the balance of terror.

The balance worked—it must have, or we'd all be dead. But it helps to remember the terror. As a child in the 1950s I felt it nearly every day. We lived in "the country"—a bucolic presuburb thirty miles north of New York—but we trained for the front lines. In school we were taught that if the sirens sounded for nuclear attack we would file into the hallway, squat along the walls, and wrap our arms around our heads. If there was no siren, just a blinding flash of light, we were to get under our desks right away. Certain buildings, or parts of buildings, were marked with orange-and-black signs designating them as air raid shelters, but how these places differed from non-shelters remained a mystery. The signs were scary.

I'm pretty sure I took this to heart more than most kids. I had carefully studied an issue of some popular magazine—*Collier's* or *Look*—which had page after page of artists' renditions of what a nuclear attack would do to New York. For several years I tried not to look at doorknobs, because they were shaped like mushroom clouds. I was terrified of flashes of light. My bedroom was situated in such a way that the headlights of cars coming over the crest of the nearby hill would sweep across the ceiling, and I felt a little spike of fear every time. I thought that the Russians would probably attack during a thunderstorm, because they figured we would mistake the bomb's flash for lightning and fail to "duck and cover." The best birthday present I ever got was a little Zenith table radio when I was ten, because if I was alarmed by a flash or a noise in the middle of the night I could turn it on and assure myself that New York was still there. One night, unable to sleep, I crept downstairs and tearfully asked my father if there was going to be a nuclear war. In a calm, serious voice, he said that he had thought a great deal about the matter and had concluded that it would not happen. I felt better for months afterward. Decades later, he told me that at the time he was in fact convinced that nuclear war was extremely likely. Perhaps that was why we had moved out of the city. Perhaps, now that I think of it, fear of the bomb was a factor in the postwar stampede to the suburbs.

My childish fears were quite reasonable, it would turn out. Rational men with something to lose nearly destroyed civilization in the Cuban missile crisis, which, we now know, was an even closer call than it seemed at the time. Much later, I got a very small taste of what Kennedy's men must have gone through. For a brief period in early 1980, mostly unbeknownst to the public and even to most of the White House staff, nuclear fear touched the circle around President Carter. A confluence of events—the Soviet invasion of Afghanistan, followed by the revolution in Iran and the hostage crisis— created a situation in which it seemed possible that the Soviets might make a military move on the Persian Gulf. On January 23, in his State of the Union Address, Carter had put forth his "doctrine": "An attempt by an out- side force to gain control of the Persian Gulf region will be regarded as an assault on the vital interests of the United States of America, and such an assault will be repelled by any means necessary, including military force." The difficulty was that we had no "means," other than nuclear weapons, ca- pable of making this warning stick. For a few days, serious people thought we might be two or three perfectly imaginable Soviet miscalculations away from the ultimate catastrophe; and serious people were frightened. I was frightened, too—almost as badly as when I was a child.

Ever since the morning of September 11, 2001, it has been chillingly clear that the probability that a nuclear explosive will at some point be used somewhere in the world is extremely high—higher, perhaps (though I know of no way to measure such things) than at the height of the Cold War. The specific danger to certain cities—New York and Moscow, for example—is greater still. But the possibility of general, worldwide annihilation has been reduced nearly to zero. For that reason alone—quite apart from the fact that it liberated millions from a stifling tyranny—the end of the Cold War de- serves to be celebrated unreservedly.

Most of the pieces in this section involve events surrounding the final decade of the Cold War. Some of them were written from exotic locales. For others, I let my fingers do the traveling.

POLAND'S REVOLUTION

IF KARL MARX were alive today, he would not be surprised at what is happening in Poland. Exactly as he predicted, a conscious movement of the entire working class, consisting of the great majority of the population, has risen in spontaneous revolt against the exploiters of labor, the owners and administrators of the means of production. The character of that revolt, as he knew it would be, is democratic and, at the same time, disciplined by an awareness of its own interests. Only one thing would astonish Marx about this first genuine proletarian revolution in history: it has occurred against and within a regime that for thirty-five years has claimed to rule in his name.

The emergency congress of the Communist party of Poland has come and gone; and if it leaves behind a faint aura of anticlimax, that is because it was less an instrument of a revolution than an imperfect reflection of one that has already taken place. The revolution was made by the ten million members of Solidarity, and it has worked one miracle after another in the past year. It has made the Polish press interesting, reliable, and, to a very large extent, free; it has won recognition for a truly independent trade union federation of industrial, intellectual, and agricultural workers—including the right to strike; it has turned the rubber-stamp parliament into a contentious body which, in televised sessions, rejects as many government bills as it passes; it has won important new rights for Catholicism, including the right to build new churches; it has harnessed the traditionally reactionary force of Polish nationalism and directed it to democratic ends. It has done all this, and more, without the slightest hint of violence, and without the loss of a single life. Now the Polish revolution has done something else that would have seemed impossible a couple of years ago, something that is rather small in the context of its own accomplishments but immense in the context of the history of the Soviet empire: it has turned a Communist party into a political party, and a Communist congress into a political meeting.

The powers that will ultimately decide the fate of Poland are Solidarity and the Soviet Union, so it was not surprising that the Polish people seemed to regard the deliberations in the Palace of Culture as in some sense irrelevant. In any case, the Poles are too preoccupied with the gravity of their economic problems, and too aware of the continuing menace on their eastern border, to feel much like celebrating. Nevertheless, the congress was something wholly new, and wholly salutary, in the history of ruling Communist parties. Democratic centralism was stood on its head—or, rather, put on its feet, however unsteadily. There was no "prolonged and stormy applause" on cue for boilerplate speeches, no unanimous show of hands for prearranged results. Instead of "one post, one candidate" it was "one man, one vote." Two thousand delegates, themselves chosen by secret ballot in contested elections, elected their central committee—by secret ballot, in a contested election, after a session in which the candidates were subjected to questioning by the full congress. These new procedures cost most of the old Politburo members their jobs. All but four of the fifteen members of the new Politburo, like most of the delegates themselves, are newcomers; one of them, Zofia Grzyb, is the first member of Solidarity (and the first woman) to be chosen. If she and First Secretary Stanislaw Kania and the rest of them run for reelection at the next congress, it will be their last hurrah; for the new party rules specify, in addition to the secret ballot, a limit of two five-year terms for positions of leadership.

No one knows how lasting or significant these reforms will prove to be, assuming the Polish revolution is allowed to take its course. The Communist party is better equipped to play its "leading role" than it was before its congress; but it is still a deeply discredited organization, held in contempt by most Poles, and its rule would melt away in an hour without the threat of Soviet armed force. The greatest trials, for the party and the country, are still to come. The prime minister, Wojciech Jaruzelski, said in his closing address to the congress that the price of food, fuel, and shelter will soon double, and that wage increases must end. Such sacrifices cannot possibly be exacted without Solidarity's full cooperation, and the price of that will be more political freedom, more economic reform, more democracy—in short, more revolution.

Nor does anyone know what the Soviet Union will do. Many Western analysts thought the party congress would never come off, but the troops did not march in; and every day, every reform, and every democratic change that is incorporated into the national life of Poland makes it more certain that they would be met with armed resistance. The Russians are afraid of that, afraid of the enormous cost of assuming (or repudiating) Poland's foreign debt, and afraid of the damage an invasion would do to their relations with the West, especially Europe. They are even afraid, in a small way, of world opinion. This time, if the Russians go in, it will be different. In 1956 and 1968, the West was distracted and morally disarmed. Soviet troops invaded Hungary under the cover of Suez and Czechoslovakia under the cover of Vietnam. There is no such camouflage for them today.

The Soviet army has performed ironic services for the Polish revolution. It is the guarantor of the discipline that enables Solidarity to end a one-hour strike precisely at the sixtieth minute; the source of the Polish Communists' recognition that they have more in common with "anti-Socialist elements" at home than with "fraternal parties" to the east; and the cause of the realization by the state and the police that they had better not bite off more in the way of repression than they can chew alone. Just as capitalism generates the class that undoes it in Marx's theory, Soviet communism has generated Solidarity. Soviet armed force may yet crush what it has helped to create. Or the Poles, wearying of bread lines and cacophony, may flee from freedom. But the possibility that Poland will become a real democracy on the Finnish model, or, barring that, a genuinely pluralist one-party state on something like the Mexican model, is no longer just a romantic fantasy. If that were to happen, it would crack open a window for evolutionary change in the rest of Eastern Europe and even in the Soviet Union itself. Whether or not the Polish revolution survives, the fact will remain that it happened, and no matter how it is rewritten in the *Great Soviet Encyclopedia* or its Polish counterpart, it can never be extirpated. It has already more than earned its place in Polish history alongside the uprisings of 1768, 1830, 1863, and 1944; and we can dare hope it will take its place in world history with the revolutions of Jefferson, Mazzini, and Gandhi.

—Editorial, *The New Republic,* August 1 & 8, 1981

LE CHANGEMENT

FOR EARNEST AMERICAN LIBERALS of a social-democratic bent (myself, for example), there has traditionally been an ideological motherland somewhere—a land across the seas that provides political inspiration. For a long time it was Sweden. The only bad thing anybody knew about the place was that it has a high suicide rate. In order to win an argument about Sweden, therefore, all you needed to know was that the Swedish suicide rate is, was, and always has been identical to that of white Protestant Americans. Checkmate. Except that a few years ago the Swedes unaccountably went and elected themselves a conservative government, thus rendering themselves useless for inspirational purposes. So now it's François Mitterrand's France.

After a two-week stay in the new Valhalla of the democratic left, though, I am unable to report that France has become a workers' paradise. An eater's paradise, yes—but that was true before. I'm dividing my time between Paris and a little village in Provence. In neither place is there much evidence of a great Socialist Experiment. In Paris the only sign of the new order is a weakening of social stratification on the Metro. Holders of second-class tickets are now free to ride in the first-class subway cars—but only before 9 A.M. and after 5 P.M. This is reform, not revolution. In Provence there's no sign of the *changement* at all, unless you count the tattered Mitterrand poster that the sun is slowly bleaching pale blue on the wall in the village square.

Of course, these things take time—and with six more years of his term left to go, time is the one thing Mitterrand has plenty of. Still, most of my French friends who voted enthusiastically for the Socialists seem puzzled that they haven't moved faster or more boldly. It's true that the biggest remaining private banks and some very big corporations have been nationalized, but it's hard to say exactly how this change of *patrons* will add measurably to the national store of liberty, equality, or fraternity. When I pressed one friend to name something, anything, that the government had done that really makes a difference, all she could come up with was the abolition of capital punishment. There is a nice symmetry in the fact that the guillotine has gone out as it came in, under a government of the left. But stopping executions hardly adds up to a reform of society. The Socialists are determined to confound the right's predictions that their inexperience and ideological rigidity will lead the country briskly to disaster. Hence their caution, and the rather wistful disappointment of many of their supporters.

One aspect of the Mitterrand program that is proceeding on schedule is his systematic demolition of the Communist Party as a consequential political force. It's a little ahead of schedule, actually: in the recent regional elections, the Socialists did better than ever, but the Communists (with an assist from General Jaruzelski) lost so many votes that the conservative coalition ended up with a narrow majority. The right incessantly refers to the government as the "Socialo-Communist regime," but the Communist leaders know perfectly well that Mitterrand maneuvered them into his embrace so that he could smother their organization and co-opt their followers. That's exactly what he's doing, and at this stage the Communists have no choice but to smile and pretend they're enjoying it. The president clearly is willing to go to great lengths to avoid giving the Communists a usable issue to take into opposition with them. To this end he even sacrificed an important and imaginative reform, the thirty-five-hour work week. The original proposal envisioned a thirty-five-hour work week at thirty-five hours' pay. This would have been an exemplary exercise in social solidarity, since it would have required workers to sacrifice part of their income (in exchange for more leisure time) so as to create jobs for the unemployed. The CFDT labor federation, which is generally aligned with the Socialists, was willing to go along with the idea. But the Communist-led CGT said no, insisting demagogically on thirty-five hours' work for forty hours' pay, and threatening a strike. A good many Socialists think Mitterrand should have taken them on; the CGT's position was unpopular, and a CGT strike might have done for Mitterrand what the air controllers did for Reagan. But Mitterrand decided otherwise, and the final proposal calls for a thirty-nine-hour week at forty hour's pay. It's inflationary and it doesn't do much for the jobless, but it does keep the Communists right where the president wants them: under his thumb.

IN FRANCE, people are still making noise about the repression in Poland. In the basement of the Pompidou Center, the big culture radiator in the Marais, there is currently a fascinating exhibit called "Lessons of Solidarity." It's a show you have to read as well as look at. There are Solidarity manifestos, Solidarity programs, Solidarity newspapers, even Solidarity lampoons of officialdom. Visitors are invited to write their own thoughts in a fat blank book; it contains hundreds of pages of comments in a dozen languages—mostly expressions of grief, anger, hope, or gratitude. "Lessons of Solidarity" is not an official propaganda exercise, by the way. It was mounted by the Pompidou Center's own workers, through their union locals—the CFDT local, and, in defiance of their federation's national leadership, the CGT local as well.

TO BE AN anti-Communist is a less reflexive, more thoughtful, more politically relevant act in France than in the United States, because every tenth person you see in the street is a real, live, flesh-and-blood Communist. Every Sunday, at the corner of the Rue Rambuteau and the Rue Beaubourg, down the street from where I'm staying in Paris, a couple of nice old party duffers sit on folding chairs and try to hawk a few copies of *L'Humanité Dimanche*—in much the same spirit, I suppose, as some of their neighbors go to mass. The friend I'm staying with, a Socialist writer, has his Sunday routine too: he buys bread at the bakery and milk at the grocery, and when he gets to the corner on his way home he always raises a clenched fist and hollers, *"Vive la classe ouvrière polonaise!"* The corner Communists don't seem to mind being yelled at. They've had to take much worse from their own party for the sake of their faith.

—France Diarist, *The New Republic*, May 5, 1982

DEATH OF A PATRIOT

"SOME OF YOU were here when John F. Kennedy was assassinated," Count Wilhelm Wachtmeister, Sweden's ambassador to Washington, told a doleful press conference the day after Olof Palme was murdered. "If you were, then you know something of how we feel." The comparison was apt, and not only because of the shocking manner of both men's deaths. Like Kennedy, Palme came to power in his early forties and personified youth, vitality, and sophistication. Palme's politics, like Kennedy's, evolved in spite of a family background of wealth and reaction. (Palme's father was an industrialist, his mother a Russian Czarist turned Swedish conservative.) And Palme, like Kennedy, was an inspirational figure to many in the Third World. There were differences between the two men, of course. One difference is this: from the beginning, Palme was considerably more at home with the American liberal left—the stretch of political ground bounded roughly by the views of Norman Thomas at one end and Hubert Humphrey at the other—than Kennedy ever was.

At his press conference the Swedish ambassador found it necessary to deny, for what must have been the thousandth time, that Palme had been "anti-American." Yet that is essentially how he was being pictured in the days after his death. "He often seemed to favor the Soviet Union in East-West disputes," the obituarist of the *New York Times* complained. And in a follow-up story a couple of days later, Barnaby Feder accused him of backing "Communist-led revolutions from Indochina to Nicaragua" and of being "too quick to criticize the United States and too quiet about such matters as human rights in the Soviet Union," a view of Palme unconvincingly attributed to "many Swedes." The overall impression is of Palme as a routine *New Statesman*-type Euro-leftist, blaming the world's troubles on U.S. imperialism and finding little to choose between American democracy and Soviet totalitarianism. That impression could hardly be more wrong.

Olof Palme was more than "pro-American," he was "American"—as American as apple pie with lingonberry sauce. He spent what he always described as the most formative year of his life, the year he turned twenty-one, in the United States. He got his bachelor's degree in politics and economics from Kenyon College, a small Episcopal college in the incorrigibly American environs of Columbus, Ohio, in 1948. He wrote his senior honors thesis on the United Automobile Workers union. He then hit the road, hitchhiking all over the country for three months, meeting hundreds of citizens along the way and learning something about their wealth and their poverty. He ended up in Detroit, where he spent hours talking with one of his heroes, Walter Reuther.

Why did the president of the U.A.W. take time out of a busy schedule to shoot the breeze with an itinerant foreign student? I suspect it was simply because the student was Swedish. It would be hard to overestimate the prestige Sweden had in those days among Americans of Reuther's views. For C.I.O. unionists, ADAers, moderate socialists, Democrats of the Minnesota farmer-labor stripe, and the like, Sweden was a magic land, a place of pilgrimage, a concrete demonstration that a society could be both just and free. Such Americans were accustomed to learning from Swedes. Young Palme reversed the usual pattern. This time it was the Swede who was doing the learning, the Swede who was making the pilgrimage. Palme was in the habit of remarking, during his many subsequent visits to this country, that the United States had made him a socialist. And it wasn't because he was repelled by what he found here, but because he was inspired by it.

When Palme began to speak against the war in Vietnam, beginning in 1965, he did so with the special passion, the outraged indignation, of an American. Unlike certain other European leftists, he did not greet the war with the smug satisfaction of one who has at last been proved right about those nasty Americans. He thought more highly of us than that (and in this sense he did indeed have a "double standard"). Unlike certain other European Socialist statesmen—Harold Wilson comes to mind—he did not regard silence on Vietnam as an act of friendship to the United States. And unlike many other "moderate" protesters on both sides of the Atlantic, he did not consider that he had anything to prove where anticommunism was concerned.

Palme learned anticommunism as much from his friends on the American democratic left as from his comrades in the European social democracy. He understood, of course, that anticommunism alone, like antifascism alone, is a poor guide to action unless it is a by-product of a positive democratic vision. Unlike many conservatives, he understood that the basic trouble with communism is a shortage of political freedom, not an excess of economic egalitarianism. And his was an anticommunism of action.

In 1948 he went from Detroit to Prague, where, representing Sweden at a meeting of the Soviet-controlled International Union of Students, he made a speech attacking Stalin; after that speech, a group from the Russian delegation came to his hotel room and beat him up. (His American counterpart at that I.U.S. meeting, by the way, was Allard Lowenstein, whom he resembled in many ways and with whom he later worked to set up the rival International Student Conference.) While he was at it, Palme married a young Czechoslovak woman he had met at the Prague meeting. The reason was simply to help her get out; once she was safe in Sweden, they divorced as planned.

His services to democracy tended to be similarly concrete. He was instrumental in mobilizing the cash and muscle that built a strong democratic left for post-Franco Spain and post-Salazar Portugal—a crucial precondition for the consolidation of liberty in those countries and the consequent decline of their Communist parties. Every obituary of Palme mentioned the famous photograph of him marching alongside a North Vietnamese diplomat in an anti–Vietnam War demonstration in 1968. But the biggest demonstration in which Palme marched in 1968—it also happened to be the biggest demonstration in the history of Sweden—was a massive protest against the Soviet occupation of Czechoslovakia.

As Palme's assassin knew very well, he was accessible. I don't run into prime ministers that often, but I did see Palme a half-dozen times in one setting or another. The first time was in 1975, at a party thrown by Michael Harrington's Democratic Socialist Organizing Committee at the Workmen's Circle in New York. The last time was in 1984, at Harvard's Kennedy School of Government, where Palme had just delivered the first Jerry Wurf

Memorial Lecture. Both times Palme stayed late and ended up in the middle of a knot of American labor-union people, students, and intellectuals, disputing and laughing and asking as many questions as he was answering. He seemed right at home. And why not? He *was* right at home.

—*The New Republic*, February 28, 1986

CASUALTIES OF WAR

ON WEDNESDAY, February 15, 1989, something happened that was not supposed to happen. The Red Army got out of Afghanistan.

What's left behind is a ruined charnel house. Hundreds of thousands of Afghans and tens of thousands of Russians are dead. Countless villages have been destroyed, their rubble salted with land mines that will continue to maim for years. Half the fifteen million surviving Afghans are refugees.

There are ideological casualties, too—and for these we need feel no grief. One of them is the Brezhnev Doctrine, which is the idea that Communist advances are irreversible (and which has as fervent a following among American as among Soviet conservatives). Another is the Brezhnev Doctrine's American cousin: the notion that the Western democracies are too irresolute and guilt-ridden to resist Soviet expansion.

Some on the right are unable to accept the idea that even the Russians can't win 'em all. "Are the Soviets really leaving Afghanistan?" asks Elie Krakowski of Boston University, former director of the Pentagon's Office of Regional Defense, in the current issue of *The National Interest*, the conservative foreign policy journal. "Or is the recently announced 'pause' in their departure one of a growing list of indications that the much-touted Soviet 'disengagement' is more a product of American wishful thinking than it is of serious analysis of Soviet actions and intentions?"

Unless we are the victims of an unusually elaborate Kremlin hoax, the Soviet disengagement, despite being much-touted, is real. This calls for an explanation. And the people who have some explaining to do are those who have spent the past nine years dismissing this very outcome as inconceivable.

For example, George Will. Shortly after the invasion, Will noted that Senator Joseph Biden had said that U.S. economic sanctions against the Soviet Union should remain in place as long as Soviet troops remain in Afghanistan. Will then made this prediction: "Biden, thirty-seven, will not live to see the troops withdrawn, and I'll bet he changes his mind."

Senator Biden, now forty-six, has had some serious health problems during the past year, but lately he's been feeling fine. He never did change his mind. And the Soviet troops are out.

Similar predictions were issued by many of Will's fellow conservative and neoconservative commentators. Over and over again, from December 1979 right down to the last few months, we were told that the essential nature of the Soviet regime, regardless of who might be in charge, made it unthinkable that Moscow would accept anything short of victory—and that Soviet totalitarianism was a juggernaut that democracies, by their very nature, are unfit to resist.

Perhaps the most influential exponent of this point of view has been Jean-François Revel, whose book *How Democracies Perish* caused a great stir four and a half years ago. One of many things American neoconservatives have in common with the old American New Left is an apparent need for a pet French intellectual to validate their views. Mr. Revel is the right's Régis Debray.

The salient points in Revel's book appeared in an excerpt in the June 1984 issue of *Commentary*. The excerpt begins with this dramatic sentence: "Democracy may, after all, turn out to have been a historical accident, a brief parenthesis that is closing before our eyes."

The heart of Revel's argument is that "democracy faces an internal enemy whose right to exist is written into the law itself." That's us liberals. By contrast, "Totalitarianism liquidates its internal enemies or smashes opposition as soon as it arises; it uses methods that are simple and infallible because they are undemocratic. But democracy can defend itself from within only very feebly; its internal enemy has an easy time of it because he exploits the right to disagree that is inherent in democracy."

Revel writes about Soviet might and democratic weakness in a tone of voluptuous masochism. When he contemplates the Soviet system, his language is that of a trembling virgin admiring the ruthless strength of the brute who is about to ravish her.

He writes: "Communism and the Soviet empire are unprecedented in history. None of the classic concepts that make the past intelligible explains Communist imperialism. The Soviet empire does not follow the bell-shaped expansionist curve of previous empires. Yet the democracies persist in believing that it will decline of itself and inevitably grow more moderate."

And further: "Other totalitarian systems were defeated or simply crumbled with age. . . . Only Communist totalitarianism is both durable and immutable."

In the light of what has happened in Afghanistan, and in the light of what is happening inside the Soviet Union itself, this theory of Communist exceptionalism—this insistence that communism is unchanging and unchangeable—now seems shockingly ahistorical. It has been shown to have no predictive value, an important test for any theory.

Revel's ideas achieved enormous currency on the American right. They trickled down from his book through journals like *Policy Review* and the *American Spectator* before finding their final resting place in the opinion section of Sun Myung Moon's *Washington Times,* the swampy repository of the conservative conventional wisdom. When this process was about half complete, toward the end of 1984, the editors of *National Review* were struck by the following Revelation:

"Five years ago, liberal opinion predicted that Afghanistan would be the 'Soviets' Vietnam.' How could that be, without a free press and the freedom of opposition that liberalism also prescribes? . . . A society that has only *Pravda* may be less blessed than a society that has the [*New York*] *Times,* but it enjoys a strategic advantage."

It happens that the analogy between Afghanistan and Vietnam is quite a good one as historical analogies go—much better, for example, than the analogy between Munich and Vietnam. The more important error here is the doctrine that a free and critical press is a strategic disadvantage. That doctrine is now being questioned even in the Soviet Union itself. It's time for it to be questioned by American conservatives as well. A free and critical press may sometimes be a *tactical* disadvantage for a society. But surely it is a huge advantage strategically, because it enables a society to apprehend and correct its own defects.

The Russians' Afghanistan fiasco just might help American conservatives rid themselves of what somebody once wisely called an inordinate fear of (as distinct from a principled opposition to) communism—and maybe even an inordinate fear of democracy, too.

—*The New Republic*, March 3, 1989

DEMOCRACIA

WHERE WERE YOU when you learned about the fall of the Wall? Me, I was in a grubby, dimly lit roadside police station in rural Costa Rica. Having just emerged from two days of shooting rapids on a rubber raft through jungle mountains, followed by a morning at a remote, coconut-covered beach on the Atlantic coast where the sand and the inhabitants alike are mostly black and mostly untroubled, I was out of touch with everything except the elements. In the ramshackle port town of Limón I'd stood with two gringo traveling companions on a litter-strewn sidewalk teeming with dogs and drunks and watched haplessly as the last bus of the night, packed solid with campesinos, pulled out for San José. Somehow we'd managed to find a transplanted Panamanian taxi driver willing to make the trip. We'd been speeding for an hour down a dusty highway flanked by moonlit banana fields when a roadblock loomed. Green-uniformed men, pistols holstered at their rib cages, waved us to the side of the road behind trucks that had passed us long before. While the Civil Guardsmen picked through our luggage, looking for cocaine, I wandered into their grubby headquarters. On the floor was a wrinkled, day-old copy of *La República*, a San José newspaper. The page one headline: ¡CAYÓ EL MURO DE BERLIN! I rushed out and demanded of the taxi driver, "Is it true? Is it true they tore down the Berlin Wall?" "Oh, sure," he said. It was already old news. For two days I'd lifted mine eyes unto the hills, and when I looked down again they'd abolished communism.

. . .

OBVIOUSLY I had some catching up to do. At the newsstand around the corner from my hotel in San José the *Miami Herald* was on sale (along with the *National Enquirer* and, weirdly, *The New Republic*). I paged eagerly through the paper, looking for Washington's reaction to the great events. I found it in the stirring words of the Secretary of Defense, Richard Cheney: "We must not be euphoric." Of course not. Very sage advice. Quite right. Why be euphoric just because a non-violent, leaderless, joyful, unvengeful civic revolution has erased the Berlin Wall overnight, eviscerating the strongest Stalinist regime in Europe and leaving its temporary custodians desperately promising free elections and a total transformation of society? Why get all happy just because Poland already has an elected non-Communist government and because a year or two from now Hungary and East Germany will almost certainly be parliamentary democracies with a vigorous free press and harmless little Portugal-sized Communist parties (if the Communists luck out) and because Czechoslovakia and Bulgaria (Bulgaria!) may not be far behind? Why give way to elation just because this vast, peaceful, unprecedented liberation is taking place with the explicit blessing of the leader of the Soviet Union? No. We must not be euphoric. We might lose sight of the important things, like the need for "nuclear modernization."

AS MY UNSCHEDULED rest stop showed, Costa Rica may be a trifle weak in the unreasonable search and seizure department, but it's the only country in Central America in which one can be flagged down by armed representatives of the state without fearing for one's life or liberty. The place is incorrigibly democratic. In fact, democracy is as important to Costa Rica's sense of nationhood as it is to the United States'. I happened to be in San José for a big nighttime celebration of the day—November 7, 1889—when Costa Ricans took to the streets to force the bloodless departure of a president who had lost an election but had refused to leave office. Now, a hundred years later, the main square of the city—called Democracy Plaza, naturally—was filled with perhaps ten thousand happy people. At one end of the square, on the steps of the floodlit National Museum (which was the main military fortress until 1949, when Costa Rica wisely abolished its army), President Oscar Arias, his cabinet, and members of the one-house

National Assembly sat on folding chairs. Security for these dignitaries was provided by Boy Scouts and Girl Scouts holding hands. The big attraction was a sort of pageant in which fifteen hundred kids wearing white shirts and hats and carrying torches pretended to storm the fortress. Then speeches praising democracy and boasting about having no army. Then the wistful-sounding Costa Rican national anthem, which all sang feelingly. Finally a fireworks display, consisting of two rickety wooden signs lit up by sputtering sparklers—VIVA COSTA RICA and 100 AÑOS DE DEMOCRACIA—and a few skyrockets that would have been rejected as insufficiently spectacular by the volunteer fire department in my home town. Some of the skyrockets blew up on the roof of the museum before they could be launched. Costa Ricans are not good with explosives. It was all touchingly sweet—something one does not normally associate with politics in Central America.

At a reception following the festivities, one of President Arias's aides told me that the National Endowment for Democracy (N.E.D.), a U.S. government agency, has been pumping cash into right-wing Costa Rican think tanks that oppose Arias and consistently try to undermine his efforts for peace in Nicaragua and El Salvador. I later learned that the money in question actually comes through the National Republican Institute, which gets it from N.E.D.—a distinction of greater moment in Washington than in San José. Even so, I'm not sure which was more irritating: the idea that U.S. taxpayers' money is being used to promote opposition to a democratic leader who has done far more to promote the true national interests of the United States than any number of contras or colonels, or the fact that such funds are being spent in Costa Rica at all. Costa Rica requires no lessons in democracy. Instead of sending N.E.D. money to Costa Rica, maybe we should send it to East Berlin. And maybe we should get the Costa Ricans to tell us how to spend it.

—Costa Rica Diarist, *The New Republic,* December 4, 1989

CIVICS, NICARAGUA-STYLE

I'D BEEN PRIMED to expect a lot of things in Managua—revolutionary fervor, totalitarian sullenness, grotesque poverty, churchy North American "sandalistas"—and, sure enough, a bit of each was on view during the days I spent there. But no one had told me about the weird beauty of the place.

Managua was flattened by an earthquake in 1972 and never rebuilt. Somoza stole the relief money that poured in after the quake, and the Sandinistas had other priorities. So nature took its course. As a consequence, downtown Managua is more rural than urban. A few shells of old buildings remain, now weathered into mossy ruins in a haunting tableau softened by lush vegetation. The main square now commands a panoramic view of Lake Managua. A herd of oxen wanders in a nearby meadow. The walls of the old cathedral still soar, but the roof is long gone. Inside, you look up and stone angels blow their horns against the bright blue sky; you look down and the weeds that carpet the floor are waist-high. In this neighborhood there is very little motorized traffic. The smell of exhaust, which in many Third World cities is so strong you can taste it on your tongue, is entirely absent. Instead the air has a faint aroma of charcoal. At the Eastern Market, a mile away, crowds trudge through a muddy warren of ramshackle stalls offering faded plastic trinkets, loose cigarettes, and expired pharmaceuticals. In an alley of food stands, dull-eyed children wave clouds of flies from chunks of fatty organ meat. Here the poverty is palpable. But the quiet, green center of town is a romantic ruin, more like ninth-century Rome than the modern focus of the waning Cold War.

Along with my North American traveling companions—journalists from the *Los Angeles Times, The Nation, The Atlantic,* and *Vanity Fair*—I spent most of my time in Nicaragua's magic-realist capital talking with Sandinista spokesmen, their political opponents, and representatives of the United Nations and the Organization of American States, who are responsible for observing the February 25 general election. Voters are to choose not only a president and vice president but also a new National Assembly and hundreds of local officials. Despite everything—which is to say despite the sputtering contra war, despite the government's suspension of the cease-fire, despite the horrors in neighboring El Salvador, and despite the fabled hostility of anti-Yankee revolutionaries to bourgeois democratic institutions—the election will probably come off as scheduled. If it does, it will be the freest, fairest election ever held in Central America outside Costa Rica.

The reason is all those international observers. They are uniformly independent, well informed, and well organized, and to all appearances they are competent. The U.N. will have a hundred and fifty observers running around the country during election week, the O.A.S. will have three hundred, and free-lance non-governmental groups like the one organized by former President Carter—who was invited by both the Sandinistas and the opposition—will have a couple of hundred more. A sizable advance guard of this horde has been in place for three months, monitoring the registration process (which was unanimously pronounced fair) and the campaign itself.

Nicaragua has 4,394 polling places, and the observers obviously won't be able to watch the voting and counting at them all. Their plan, as Iqbal Riza, a suave Pakistani diplomat who heads the U.N. contingent, explained it to us, is to visit all or nearly all the rest after the polls close. At each polling place, the votes will be counted by the president of the local election *junta* in the presence of a poll-watcher from the Sandinista party and one from the United National Opposition (UNO), the fourteen-party alliance whose presidential candidate is Violeta Chamorro. The U.N. or O.A.S. observer will make sure all three agree on the totals, and if they tally the assumption will be that the count was fair.

This system should be foolproof—assuming, of course, that UNO manages to get itself sufficiently organized to have poll-watchers at every polling place. "That's one of the points we've been stressing to the opposition," Riza said. "They have a major responsibility. They have to be there." After some early doubts, it now appears certain that UNO will be able to recruit (or hire) enough volunteers to ensure a fair count.

The international kibitzing is unprecedented in both scope and duration. "We have observed many elections, but we have never before observed a process," Mario Gonzalez, the Colombian chief of the O.A.S. team, told us. "In Chile and elsewhere, our observers were in the country for a week at most. This time we will be around for more than six months. We've had eighteen O.A.S. observers here since August 4, living in all nine regions of the country. We'll be able to render judgments not only on the registration and the voting but also on things like access to the media."

If the margin on election night is wider than a few percentage points, the election will be very hard to steal. But if it's very close, the Sandinistas will in theory be presented with a powerful temptation to jiggle the figures a bit and preemptively announce a victory. The antidote to this danger would be a "rapid count," an effort to sample the returns independently of the official national counting center and with comparable speed. A "rapid count" dissuaded the Chilean authorities from falsifying the results of last September's referendum on keeping Pinochet in power, and another exposed the crude fraud in Panama last May. Such an effort will likely be undertaken in Nicaragua. The Carter group is consulting with the O.A.S. and the U.N. about mounting one.

And the election could well be close. The three high Sandinista officials we met with—Vice President Sergio Ramirez, Deputy Foreign Minister Victor Hugo Tinoco, and Foreign Ministry Secretary General Alejandro Bendaña—all predicted that President Daniel Ortega and Ramirez would win with at least 60 percent of the vote. The Sandinistas are well organized and well disciplined, and in a country where the police, the army, and the education system are run as branches of the ruling party, incumbency offers more than the usual advantages. Opinion surveys, however, show a dead heat. The most reliable one, taken a month ago by the Washington political consultant Sergio Bendixen for Univision, the U.S.-based Hispanic TV network, shows 40 percent for Ortega, 39 for Chamorro, 5 percent for one of the seven other parties on the ballot, and 16 percent "undecided." (North American political obsessives will remember Bendixen as a strategist for Alan Cranston in 1984 and Bruce Babbitt in 1988.)

No one thinks all the "undecideds" are really undecided. Bendaña insists that "people don't like to be asked. They've been told that their vote is secret, and they're not going to tell any pollster." But if he's wrong, and if some voters declining to reveal their preferences are motivated less by rugged Nicaraguan individualism than by fear that the authorities might somehow find out and be displeased, then the poll numbers are bad news for his side.

The campaign, which formally begins this week, will not be anything like as fair as the voting itself. The print press will not be a problem for UNO— Chamorro, after all, is the publisher of *La Prensa,* the largest of Nicaragua's three daily newspapers—but television will be. The parties get free time on the box, and the Supreme Electoral Council, Sandinista-controlled but re-markably well behaved, recently ordered that these broadcasts be moved from Channel 2, which yields a snowy picture in Managua and none at all in outlying areas, to Channel 6, which comes in clearly throughout most of the country. But UNO has to rotate its slots with minor parties that stand no chance of winning, and the Sandinistas control the news broadcasts.

For UNO, however, this problem may not be a problem. As the recent experience of countries as various as India, Panama, and Poland demon-strates, oppositionists can win elections handily even if the government shuts them out of television entirely. In Nicaragua, everybody knows who's running. Everybody knows the race is between the Sandinistas and UNO. If the election becomes a referendum on the status quo, UNO will win eas-ily, and the less people know about UNO—beyond the already well known fact that it represents change—the better. The Sandinistas' own campaign slogan, *"Todo será mejor"* ("Everything will be better"), reflects in its choice of tense a nervous recognition that the country is a mess. But if the elec-tion gets cast as a choice between two prospective governments, the San-dinistas could do better. UNO is a taped-together coalition of groupings ranging from the Communist Party to former Somocistas, with democrats of varying stripes in between. This does not make for a "clear message." Chamorro launched her campaign by announcing that her martyred hus-band, Pedro Joaquín, who has been dead for ten years, had told her he en-dorses her candidacy, as had God—which in most countries would have been a fatal gaffe. This sort of thing goes down better in Nicaragua, where there's a good deal of primitive religiosity, but not much better. If there's a televised debate—still an outside possibility—Daniel is likely to come across as competent if humorless, Violeta as a nice lady way out of her depth.

The Sandinistas have national pride on their side. They stood up to the colossus of the north. They whipped the contras. They carried out land reform, which even the opposition admits will be an enduring achievement of their rule. UNO, for its part, appeals simultaneously to high motives and low. The high motive is democracy. The low motive is money. The millions of dollars the U.S. government is giving UNO is a campaign issue, but it doesn't cut against UNO alone—and not just because the Sandinistas have received large amounts of Soviet logistical aid. Asked why his side had decided to accept the money, Alfredo Cesar, an important UNO spokesman, told us, "If we don't take it, the Sandinistas will say we took it anyway"— which, when you think about it, is a pretty lame argument. The money from Washington is important not so much for what it will buy in the way of buttons and bumper stickers as for the message it sends about future largesse from up north. If UNO can pry loose nine million dollars when it's still in opposition, many voters are bound to reason, think how the Yankee cash will flow if UNO wins!

The most interesting question will arise after voting and the counting are done. If UNO wins, will the Sandinistas accept it?

The Sandinista officials I spoke with all said they would go peacefully if they lost. "If we lose we'll become an opposition party—but we're going to be a hell of a strong opposition party," Tinoco told me toward the end of a long evening of conversation. "To be perfectly honest, I wouldn't want to be the party in power and have to deal with an opposition party like the Sandinista Front. I wouldn't wish that on anybody."

The next morning, over breakfast at the incongruously Swedish Modern convention complex called the Olof Palme Center, I asked Vice President Ramirez how he could square the possibility of electoral defeat with such tenets of Marxism-Leninism as "democratic centralism" and the leading role of the party.

"The truth is we've never described ourselves as a Marxist-Leninist party," he replied. "Yes, some of our perspectives reflect Marxist insights. But the great difference between us and traditional orthodoxy is that we've never talked about a single party without opposition or a command economy without private property. We are not carrying out measures to let people enter or leave the country freely, because they already can. We are not deleting 'Socialist Republic of Nicaragua' from our constitution because we never put it in. We are not changing from a single-party system because we never had one. If somebody has something to learn here, it's not us. It's those countries in Eastern Europe."

All very stirring. Yet there is reason for doubt. In Eastern Europe, Communist regimes now abdicate power on an almost daily basis, but the Communists of Eastern Europe are quislings in a state of moral collapse. The Sandinistas are genuine revolutionaries who won power on their own, and who brought with them a vision of the revolutionary state as an instrument of utopian transformation. That vision ill comports with the humdrum notion of parties alternating in power through regular elections until the end of time, especially when the other party represents the class enemy. And when the Sandinistas boast about the cleanliness of the current electoral process, they tend to do so in a way that suggests they regard the election as a concession they have made to the United States and to the internal opposition. In a real democracy, of course, elections are not concessions. They are the basis of legitimacy.

In the wake of the carnage in El Salvador, Nicaragua's political atmosphere has darkened. The Central American "peace process" is in deep trouble. As the crash of the plane carrying surface-to-air missiles establishes, the Sandinistas have been supplying arms to the Salvadoran rebels in violation of Ortega's explicit promises to the other Central American presidents not to do so. The Sandinistas, it would seem, are perfectly capable of playing for keeps. If they become convinced they are going to lose the election, it is far from unimaginable that they could find a pretext to cancel it. Washington has helpfully provided one such pretext by keeping the contras, who by regional agreement were supposed to have been demobilized by now, in business.

And then there is the awkward matter of the military. Even if the election takes place and the Sandinistas lose, they will retain, at the very least, significant influence in the army. UNO recognizes this and is prepared to live with it. One possibility, especially if the UNO victory is narrow, is a "national unity" government in which the Sandinistas hold on to the Defense Ministry. Another possibility, familiar in this part of the world, is a civilian government headed by one party in which the army is under the de facto control of a different political tendency, one with a less than perfect record of respect for democracy. Nicaragua could become a sort of El Salvador in reverse—minus (and this is a big minus) "death squad activity."

And what if the Sandinistas win? Will the United States accept it? So far there is no sign Washington has made up its mind. Governments, like individuals, prefer to avoid thinking about an outcome they dread.

When the economist Richard Parker, who organized our trip to Nicaragua, asked UNO's Alfredo Cesar if UNO favors lifting the U.S. trade embargo if the Sandinistas win a fair election, he replied emphatically, "Yes. Yes. Without any doubt." The Bush administration has not yet given a clear answer to that question. One thing, though, is clear: the U.S. policy of thwarting contra demobilization makes it considerably likelier that the question will have to be faced.

President Bush ought to ponder some figures from the Bendixen-Univision poll. Nicaraguans, the poll shows, view the contras unfavorably by an overwhelming 65 percent to 20 percent margin. Only 29 percent think they're "freedom fighters," while 44 percent see them as "tools of imperialism." Asked whose pressure made the election possible, 53 percent say it was the Central American presidents, while only 14 percent say it was the contras. Fifty-nine percent say the United States is Nicaragua's enemy, considerably more than any other country. On the other hand, 55 percent blame the Sandinistas fully or partly for Nicaragua's economic crisis, and a full 61 percent say life was better under Somoza than it is now. Only 24 percent think times are better under the Sandinistas. Obviously, if Bush is serious about helping UNO the best thing he could do would be to eliminate the contras as an issue and allow Nicaraguans to focus their full attention on the dismal state of the economy.

I left Managua with rather more respect for the intelligence and suppleness of the Sandinistas than I had brought with me. Even so, as a North American I hope for a UNO victory. Nicaragua was never a threat to our security, but for ten years it has been a threat to our sanity. If UNO squeaks by, perhaps the United States' Nicaragua neurosis will at last be cured.

It will take a lot more than a new government, however, to cure what ails Nicaragua. Decades of dictatorship and another of war and revolutionary rapture have left the country with a devastated economy and a wounded political culture. No matter who wins, the weeds will grow waist-high for a long time to come.*

—*The New Republic*, December 25, 1989

---

* On February 25, 1990, to the surprise of nearly everyone, UNO won by a crushing margin of 55 percent to 45 percent. After a tense couple of days, Daniel Ortega agreed to step down, partly as a result of Jimmy Carter's persuasion. Daniel's brother Humberto, who was also his minister of defense, gave up that job but became chief of the army, a post he held until 1995. (2005)

NON-PARTY LINES

TWO THINGS are everywhere in Moscow this spring—lines, and the sounds of debate. At the Lenin Mausoleum in Red Square the line is not so long as it is reputed to be; but not far away in Pushkin Square, in front of the largest and abruptly the most famous McDonald's on earth, a thick, still river of patient humanity folds back and forth against itself and then undulates out along the edge of the square, around a corner and past the block-long Rossiya movie theatre, around another corner and past the Bauhausy *Izvestia* building, and around still another corner past the statue of the poet, until it disappears behind the trees. It takes four hours to get to the hamburgers. This McDonald's—a *real* Lenin's tomb—is built in the familiar roadside architectural style. But nestled against the gray Moscow buildings it looks as exotic and powerful as a gleaming spacecraft from some distant alien civilization—which, of course, is pretty much what it is.

A few steps away, in front of the dingy headquarters of the *Moscow News*, the lines are of a different sort. Though the circulation of this weekly paper, one of the most daring of "official" Soviet publications, is up around eight million, the demand is far greater than that; so each week's issue is posted in glass cases along the building's outside wall. People are standing four deep to read the current issue, which includes an interview with Boris Yeltsin, a report on the disintegration of the Warsaw Pact ("with its critical internal conflicts, its economy in a 'free fall,' and its nationalities raging, the Soviet Union is perhaps the main potential destabilizing factor in Europe . . ."), and an article by Elena Bonner, Sakharov's widow, attacking the blockade against Lithuania. The wall next to the glass cases is plastered with samizdat, ranging from crude mimeos to the well-printed papers of the new Christian Democratic Party, the new-old Constitutional Democratic Party, and Sajudis, the Ukrainian nationalist party. An English-speaking kibitzer helpfully reads out a few of the headlines for me: LIFE AFTER GORBACHEV; LENIN WAS GUILTY, TOO; COMMUNIST DICTATORSHIP OR PEOPLE'S POWER? In this corner of Pushkin Square, the crowds are so thick one can barely move, and the din of argument drowns out the noise of traffic.

In Pushkin Square the lines are more for spiritual than for physical sustenance, even at McDonald's. Matters are grimmer in the state-run neighborhood food store I visit. The Tagansky Gastronom is as large as a Safeway and is similarly organized: you push a shopping cart around, serve yourself, and then stand in line to make your purchases. To get into the place you show your Moscow internal passport (though the word "foreigner" works just as well). Scattered here and there among the gray, mostly empty shelves, some forty-odd items are for sale. A pile of cabbages (40 kopecks a kilogram) is the only nominally fresh produce, apart from some rotted garlic. Gory pigs' heads and skinny Russian ducks are the only nominally fresh meat, though there are also frozen Hungarian geese (2 rubles per kilo) and turkeys (3.2 rubles). Lard, margarine, salt, cooking oil (50 kopecks per liter), mineral water (60 kopecks). Latvian sardines. Dark bread at 20 kopecks a kilo, white at 60. Yogurt and milk (40 kopecks a liter). Eggs, but you can only buy ten at a time. Sugar, but you can only buy two kilos a month. Not much else. Are the prices high or low? Judge for yourself: a ruble is 100 kopecks; the official exchange rate is 6 rubles to the dollar, the street rate upward of 12; and a good monthly salary is 200 rubles. The wait at the checkout counter is around twenty minutes; but in a subqueue within the store for Bulgarian deodorant, it's more like half an hour.

THE DEBATE COMES at you wherever you go. It comes from TV sets overheard through open windows, from taxicab radios, from boom boxes on park benches. If it's not Gorbachev's all-union Supreme Soviet then it's Yeltsin's Russian Supreme Soviet or Popov's MosSoviet, the insurgent-dominated city council. At least one of them seems to be on the air all the time, and people listen. It reminds me of the spring of 1965 in Cambridge, when the Beatles' *Rubber Soul* album was released and all you had to do to hear it was walk down the street, because everybody was playing it turned up loud. For a Westerner steeped in the democratic mythos this is very moving. But it's hard to find a Russian who isn't a little cynical about it, a little disgusted with all the talk-talk-talk. Still: they listen.

ALONE IN A FRIEND'S APARTMENT after dinner one evening, I watch the tube for an hour, zapper in hand. *Click* A costume movie, powdered hair and knee britches. *Click* A guitar-playing folksinger, blue and soulful. *Click* A documentary about Old Russia: onion domes, long beards, sepia tones. *Click* A talk show featuring a psychic who is apparently reading someone's auras; he draws one on a big sheet of paper after sculpting it in the air around his subject's head. *Click* Yeltsin speaking in the Russian Supreme Soviet. He is strong-voiced, emphatic, unhurried, and when he gets off a good line he accompanies it with a wry little conspiratorial smile. Unlike C-Span's congressional coverage back home, here there are plenty of reaction shots. Delegates yawn, read newspapers, whisper among themselves—though mostly they listen attentively. Yeltsin calls for a vote to fill some office, and the tally is shown on an electronic tote board that records not just the number of votes but also the percentages. There are six candidates; the winner of this round gets 38 percent, the runner-up, 36. *Click* A town-meeting-like discussion program, apparently about the upcoming Communist Party congress. The talk is animated, with people interrupting each other to make their points. Even if you don't speak Russian, there are so many cognates that you can catch the drift. The words rush by: capitalist Stalin perestroika totalitarianism democratic ideology multiparty Lenin transition . . . *Click* The World Cup soccer championship, live from Florence. Yeltsin or no Yeltsin, this has to be what most people are watching. The Soviet team is getting trounced by Argentina. During a break, a commercial for Adidas running shoes. Consumerist porn.

ON MY LAST NIGHT in town, I take a walk with a Russian friend in the Arbat, a famous old street that Yeltsin, back when he was mayor, turned into a pedestrian mall. Though it's late—after eleven—dusk has only just begun to fall. The light is soft, the spring breeze caressing. The crowds have started to thin. We stop for a snack at a state-owned food stand. Everyone gets the same fare: two reddish sausages twisted like cheroots, some bits of boiled potato (slightly rotted but still edible), some flavorless red sauce, and a cup of watery red liquid that tastes of cranberries. We carry our paper plates to one of the chest-high round tables nearby. On it is a glass filled with battered metal forks. We each take one and dig in. At a neighboring table stands a gaggle of very young Soviet marines. A stout old woman, the babushka in charge of busing the tables, shuffles over. One of the marines produces a half liter of vodka in a paper bag. "Grandma," one of the marines says, "is it all right if we drink here?" The babushka's impassive face breaks into a smile, showing gaps between stumpy brown teeth. "Why not?" she says. "That's perestroika!"

—Moscow Diarist, *The New Republic*, July 9 & 16, 1990

TEAM PLAYER

EVERYBODY, it seems, is having elections, including a lot of unlikely countries that haven't had much luck with them in the past: Nicaragua, Chile, Panama, Czechoslovakia, Romania, Bulgaria, Russia . . . Dispatches from such places often make mention of "teams" of "international observers," who put out statements saying that the elections were "free and fair" (as in Nicaragua), or that they were neither (as in Panama), or that they fell somewhere in between (as in Romania). Last week it was Pakistan's turn, and mine.

I went to Pakistan as one of forty members of a "team" organized by the National Democratic Institute for International Affairs, known as N.D.I., which is loosely affiliated with the Democratic Party. Half of us were Americans (including a fair number of Republicans); the other half were from sixteen countries in the first, second, and third worlds, including Britain, Sweden, Japan, Turkey, Poland, Egypt, South Africa, and Sri Lanka. I'd often wondered what international election observers actually do. Now I know. I know what our group did, anyway. We read—great sheafs of clippings, election laws, and speech texts. We listened—to officials, party representatives, and independent journalists. And we "observed."

I observed a rally. This was two nights before the election, in Rawalpindi, a small city near Islamabad, Pakistan's hideous, sterile capital. It was put on by the Islamic Democratic Alliance, known as the IJI from its Urdu initials, a coalition of rightist and religious parties united by antagonism toward Benazir Bhutto and her Pakistan People's Party. The IJI has been in power since August 9th, when Benazir (as she is called by friend and foe alike) was peremptorily dismissed from the prime ministership. Packed into two cars, accompanied by an armed policeman and by Husain Haqqani, a suave young IJI spokesman, we rushed through warrens of streets, horns blaring, and were deposited at a scene of overwhelming exoticism. In a vast oblong space hemmed in by leafless trees spangled with strings of red and green lights, under a lurid, purplish pall of smoke and dust, was a human carpet—tens of thousands of people, all male, squatting on the ground, faces turned upward to a high, floodlit platform. The blare of overamplified oratory swept over everything, punctuated by the pop of fireworks and firearms—a man in the crowd, signaling his approval of the speaker, was firing a pistol into the air. Heavy banners of dark green, the IJI's color, waved slowly back and forth. So did bicycles, the IJI's symbol, mounted on poles. Here and there, sheaves of fluorescent bulbs cast a faint, eerie light against the darkness. We were taken up a ladder to the platform, which was covered with layer upon layer of red-patterned rugs, and where perhaps fifty men sat on folding chairs. Then we were taken down again, to one side—where we finally saw some women, in a roped-off section; all were fully veiled, their eyes floating in a sea of black. "Fellini crossed with David Lynch," one of my companions whispered. And a bit of Riefenstahl.

The cadenced shouting continued over the loudspeakers. Smiling languidly, Haqqani translated snatches for us. *The PPP of old once had great leaders—now it is led by an incompetent woman, who takes instructions from Washington and Moscow!* (The crowd chanted in response: "Traitors! Traitors!") *We are accused of supporting the armed forces of Pakistan—at least we do not support the armed forces of our enemies!* Startlingly, the speaker pronounced names that needed no translation: Salman Rushdie, Mark Siegel, Stephen Solarz. *They are friends of Israel, they are friends of India, but are they friends of Pakistan? American senators, you can keep your aid! You can keep Benazir Bhutto! You are conspiring against Islam! An Islamic resurgence is sweeping through Central Asia—it may not be good for British shopkeepers or American businessmen hungry for the Russian market, but it is good for Muslims!* It was past midnight; the rally had been going on since 4 P.M., and the main speaker, Nawaz Sharif, the probable next prime minister, had not yet arrived. We made our way back along the roiling edge of the crowd to our cars.

I observed a "news" broadcast on government-controlled Pakistani TV—in English, but identical to the Urdu version, I was told. Six minutes of speeches by the IJI's caretaker prime minister; one minute of our delegation, filmed on a visit to the Electoral Commission; four minutes of Nawaz Sharif at a rally ("We must get rid of leaders of the past who looted the public treasury," "The IJI will help the downtrodden," etc.); forty seconds of Benazir at a rally, unflatteringly filmed ("Only the PPP has roots in all four provinces"); four more minutes of government officials making political points ("The minister pointed out that the PPP has helped U.S. senators put pressure on Pakistan," etc.). In our delegation's statement a few days hence, we will say delicately that the TV coverage was "not balanced."

I observed voting. At dawn election morning, October 24th, three of us set out from Lahore, a city of melancholy beauty, and in an hour's time we were in the fourteenth century. Every mile or two we encountered a village of one-story mud-brick buildings, teeming with people, cattle, and goats. At each randomly picked polling station, usually in the village school, always separate for men and women, we found idyllic scenes of civic peace. The voters lined up, clutching their identity cards. Election officials, seated behind a table, punched a corner of the cards, checked their names off a list, marked their thumbs with (supposedly) indelible ink, affixed their thumbprints to a receipt for the ballot paper. The voter would go behind a makeshift curtain, mark the paper with a rubber stamp, fold it, and drop it into a green ballot box sealed with cord and wax. Outside the polling stations, the two big parties had their "camps," tents made of colorful blankets. "No problems," was the universal reply to our questions.

The election returns showed an unexpectedly overwhelming IJI victory. In Karachi two days later, after many meetings and drafting sessions, our group issued its preliminary statement and had its press conference. The statement carefully avoids the standard formula a similar N.D.I. group had used to praise the previous Pakistani election—"free and fair"—but this subtlety was missed by the press. We say that the elections, "as we observed them at the local level," were "generally open, orderly, and well administered." We mention irregularities, violence, the caretaker government's political use of its incumbency powers, and statistical anomalies in the voting patterns; and we stress that our report is "preliminary." I am left with a nagging feeling of unease. Perhaps our report should have mentioned that most of us had never been to Pakistan before, that we had little or no familiarity with Pakistani politics or culture, that we did not speak the language, that Pakistan is vast and our team's resources small, and that we had no way of independently verifying the vote count. If rigging was done, it was not done under our noses. I'm impressed with what we saw, and our honest initial judgment, for what it is worth, was that the results as announced more or less reflected how the people voted. But I'm even more impressed with what we did not see, what we do not know.

—Pakistan Diarist, *The New Republic*, November 19, 1990

GREMLINS AND GOBLINS

AS WE ALL KNOW, the Union of Soviet Socialist Republics is no more. It has ceased to be. It has rung down the curtain and joined the choir invisible. It is a late Union. Bereft of life, it is pushing up the daisies. It is an ex-Union. (It's not just "resting," either.) The landmass it formerly occupied is now taken up by new countries with old names, such as Russia, Ukraine (out, damned "the"!), Kazakhstan, and Byelorussia, which I half expect, once capitalism takes hold, to rename itself Sellhighrussia. Yet even though the corporeal and temporal actuality of the Soviet Union has ended, the Soviet Union is not nowhere. It has simply moved to a different plane of existence. It has fled to the realm of myth and mystery, of fright and fable, where it abides with other empires that must be imagined to be believed (whether or not they were ever real)—empires good and empires evil—empires like Atlantis, Ancient Rome, the Middle Kingdom, Oz, and the Third Reich.

Of course, even when it was alive the Soviet Union was a fabulous kingdom, a place of the blackest black magic. How could it have been otherwise? After all, here was a country founded upon a vast and elaborate fantasy, the fantasy of the Workers' State, a fantasy sustained not only by the cruel and blood-soaked apparatus of fear but also, and above all during its wickedest decades, by the blind goodwill of millions of believers within and without its borders. The literature of and about the Soviet Union was steeped in weird phantasmagoria. Almost every word of Soviet journalism was fiction disguised as fact; by the same token, any Soviet writer wishing to publish a bit of honest social analysis had to disguise his facts as fiction. Many of the books written in praise of the Soviet Union described an imaginary place. Some of the most eloquent attacks on it did likewise, albeit in a more conscious way—Zamyatin's *We*, Orwell's *Animal Farm* and *1984*. The most spookily on-target visual portrait of the pre-collapse U.S.S.R. is Terry Gilliam's great cult film *Brazil*. The movie has nothing directly to do with the Soviet Union (or with Brazil either), and I doubt that Gilliam had the Soviet Union in mind when he made it. He captured its essence all the same. If you want to know what the texture of this very odd country was like before the fall, see *Brazil*.

I've been here three times now. The first time, Moscow seemed to me less like a foreign city than an alien planet—a planet that had developed along amazingly similar lines to Earth. This faraway planet, like our own, is populated by bilaterally symmetrical bipeds who, like us, garb themselves in clothing differentiated by gender, use four-wheel motorized vehicles for transport, live in boxlike structures, and consume grain-based products for both nourishment and recreation. They have equivalents of almost everything we have—shoes, newspapers, traffic lights—yet there is always something about these everyday items that makes them seem utterly strange. It is hard to say which is more eerie, the resemblances or the differences. They have shops, for example, but the signs on the outside say harsh generic things—PRODUCTS, REPAIRS, MILK, PHOTO—and inside there are only drab, empty display cases and coiled lines of shuffling people. That was three years ago.

It's still basically the same, only now this exotically gray planet has begun to be colonized by earthlings. Three years ago there were still a few big signs of the COMRADES! WE ARE BUILDING COMMUNISM! variety to be seen. On my second visit, a year and a half ago, I saw only one sign of this type—red background, block letters—but when I asked someone to translate it for me it turned out to say YOUNG PEOPLE! INVEST IN HIGH-YIELD SECURITIES! This time, the signs are advertising Mars candy bars, Hyundai cars, Panasonic electronics. The consistent thread is that all the signs, whether Communist, perestroika-ist, or post-communist, advertise things that are either non-existent or unavailable.

Some other changes. The lines at the state stores are longer than they were eighteen months ago, but elsewhere there is much more evidence of non-state commerce. The Metro corridors and the passageways under the broad Moscow avenues are lined with card tables where people sell books, magazines, scarves, flowers, chewing gum, cans of German beer. There are musicians on the subway, too—another absolutely new development. Homeless people, too—ditto. Three years ago the hot newspaper was *Moscow News,* which had emerged from decades as a weekly for tourists published by the Novosti Press Agency to become the voice of glasnost. A year and a half ago it was *Commersant,* a business weekly. Now it's Moscow's *Nezavisimaya Gazeta (The Independent),* a sober thrice-weekly broadsheet, and St. Petersburg's *Chas Pik (Rush Hour),* a spunky afternoon daily. Three years ago, an American in Moscow felt utterly invulnerable. Now every foreigner knows someone who's been mugged or burgled.

But Moscow still feels a lot safer than New York. And if you have dollars and a few Russian-speaking friends to guide you, the Commonwealth of Independent States is, for the moment, a vacationer's and shopper's paradise. I traveled here on frequent flyer miles courtesy of Pan Am (another institution that has gone the way of the U.S.S.R.) and stayed in the apartment of a friend of a friend. A couchette on the night train to St. Petersburg set me back about 26 cents' worth of rubles; on the return trip I bought a whole four-passenger compartment. Lunch for three at a "cooperative" restaurant (pickled veggies, not-bad pizza, cognac), about 38 cents. Reverse-chic Soviet neckties at TSUM (Central Universal Stores), the Gimbel's to Moscow's Macy's, the more famous GUM (Government Universal Stores), a nickel each. Subway rides, about two-tenths of a cent each. The whole nine-day trip has cost me about two hundred dollars, mostly for gifts and meals for Russian friends and souvenirs to take home.

I've been asking people if communism left anything worthwhile behind. Everyone gives the same answer: the Metro, the legendary Moscow subway that served as an argument clincher for a generation of American Communists. True enough: the Moscow subway is the only Soviet institution that is indisputably the best of its kind in the world. Like the pyramids of Egypt, the temples of the Incas, and the Roman coliseum, it has a brutal splendor that transcends the moral squalor of its origins. A Russian friend adds something else to the list: the "Seven Stalinist Sisters," the mock-gothic, wedding-cake skyscrapers that dot the cityscape. "I hate them, myself," the friend says, "but my eight-year-old daughter loves them. She says they're magic castles. She says gremlins and goblins must live there." A wise little girl.

—Moscow Diarist, *The New Republic,* January 20, 1992

THE KOSOVO PRECINCT

IN 1950, after the United States sent troops into battle for the first time since the end of the Second World War, President Truman took to calling America's military defense of South Korea a "police action." This was a euphemism that made a lot of people angry. It was widely derided as mealy-mouthed, ignoble, or simply false. Some on the left saw Truman's phrase as an effort to criminalize one side of a civil conflict. Some on the right saw it as part of a sinister campaign to subsume the United States into a global superstate. And many—left, right, and center—recoiled from the term as a prettying-up of the slaughter of what was, by any commonsense understanding, a war, and a bloody one.

In truth, Truman's phrase was less any of these than it was the product of an uneasy mixture of idealism, prudence, and wishful thinking. Calling the Korean War a police action was aspirational, not descriptive. Yes, the American G.I.s who fought in Korea served under the United Nations flag, side by side with soldiers and medics from twenty other countries, including not only Britain and France but also Thailand and India. At bottom, though, the Korean War was an old-fashioned conflict among states, a proxy war fought against the background of big-power politics and the global struggle between liberalism and totalitarianism.

Now, a half century on, the United States has fought a war that actually was what the Korean War only pretended to be. No one has called the air war to drive Slobodan Milosevic's marauders out of Kosovo a police action. Perhaps there are still too many people around who remember the heat that Truman took for his choice of words. But a police action is exactly what it was.

Police power is something that is normally wielded within a state. Its effectiveness depends on monopolizing violence, but its legitimacy depends on nonviolence—on subordination to a liberal democratic political structure with enforceable rights. (Without that subordination, the police function gobbles up the state, and the state becomes a police state.) The checks on the police function are political, not military—checks and balances, not balances of power. The legitimacy of the police power also depends on the ability to use force precisely. In 1985, in Philadelphia, a police helicopter bombed a house occupied by an outlaw cult, and the resulting fire engulfed an entire neighborhood. Everyone recognized this as a catastrophe, deeply alien to the purposes and practices of policing. But the bombing of Belgrade was so accurate that it went seriously wrong only when the targeters made a mistake about an address, like a drug squad breaking down the wrong door.

Sovereignty in Europe is fluid right now. The various Continental structures—NATO, the European Union and its parliament, and so on—are still a few post offices short of constituting a true government, but Europe has come very far from being a congeries of independent states with clashing territorial and ideological ambitions. Europeanness is an increasingly viable identity, and Europe is an increasingly solid confederation, reminiscent in some ways of the early United States. It even has its own version of manifest destiny. Ultimately, as everyone agrees without quite saying so, the Balkans will be part of that confederation. They are certainly part of Europe, and now they are part of what confederated Europe, with American prodding, sees as its area of responsibility.

The Kosovo conflict had at least analogues of all the elements that distinguish a police action from a traditional war. Though NATO obviously did not possess a monopoly of force, its precision weapons, plus the enormous power it held in reserve, gave it something that came close. After a decade of vacillation, NATO at last committed itself to the proposition that mass slaughter is intolerable on Europe's home ground, even when that ground is technically beyond the jurisdiction of Europe's institutions. (The strength of those institutions, more than racism or cultural Eurocentrism, explains the difference in the international response to similar humanitarian outrages in Africa.) And the indictment of Milosevic by the Hague tribunal made the police model explicit.

It is clear, in retrospect, that President Clinton and Secretary of State Albright have conducted this episode wisely. Even the most widely criticized aspect of their strategy—their initial refusal to consider the use of ground forces—now appears prescient. Maintaining the solidarity of the nineteen NATO governments was indispensable—more important by far than the notionally greater pressure that the threat of ground troops might have put on Milosevic. Early talk of a ground war would have strained that solidarity to the breaking point, and might even have brought down Germany's coalition of Social Democrats and Greens. At the beginning, a ground war was unthinkable (and not for the Germans alone); by the end, failure was what had become unthinkable. If ground troops had been needed, it now seems clear, ground troops would have been used.

In terms of achieving its goals at an acceptable cost, the Kosovo war was at least as successful as the Gulf War. Yet its conclusion has engendered none of the euphoria that accompanied the liberation of Kuwait. It may seem strange that the authors of such a success should receive so little political credit for it. It may seem even stranger that the fact that NATO suffered not a single combat casualty should be an occasion for disapproval—as if this omission were somehow unsporting, or as if there were any evidence that military deaths on NATO's side would have meant fewer civilian deaths among the Albanians and the Serbs. Yet the absence of triumphalism is in many ways entirely appropriate. It is a sign of realism and of maturity. Police work is routine, and cops learn not to expect laurels for doing their jobs. Something has changed. With America's help, Europe has taken a long, quiet step toward normality.

—*The New Yorker*, July 12, 1999

A TALE OF TWO CUBAS

IF THERE'S ANY NOSTALGIA still lingering for the era of the Cold War—that supposed time of moral clarity, when good was good, evil was evil, and transcendent ends overrode qualms about sometimes squalid means—it ought to be laid to rest by the sad struggle over Elián González, the little castaway who has now become the most famous citizen of Cuba apart from Fidel Castro himself. Many of the vices of that era have returned to center stage: self-righteousness; polarization; ideological rigidity; the use of innocents as pawns in games that are anything but innocent; the deployment of false accusations carrying suggestions of treason (soft on Communism! imperialist stooges!); the exaltation of materialisms, dialectical and consumer, over simpler, worthier values. The sufferings of the González family—the mother drowned, the son traumatized and bewildered, the father bereft—are all too real, and, because their scale is comprehensibly small, they are vivid in a way that the sufferings of faceless millions can seldom be. But, if the real Cold War was grand opera, this tiny remnant, this Cold Spat, is operetta, and comic operetta at that. The combatants are not superpowers but a couple of palmy, balmy banana republics: on the one side Cuba, with its absurd world-historical pretensions; on the other the semi-autonomous province of South Florida, a kind of upside-down Taiwan. The nuclear shadow that once darkened every Cuban crisis has lifted, taking existential terror with it. The Soviet Union is gone, and the United States, for its part, is not so much a direct party to the dispute as it is a mediator, trying to keep the shrill squabble between Cuba (Havana) and Cuba (Miami) from breaking the crockery.

The two Cubas have been behaving like mirror images of each other, but they are not, to use a catchphrase of Cold War polemics, morally equivalent. The ultimate cause of the real Cold War was not the arms race, or mutual misunderstanding, or (least of all) Western imperialism; it was the refusal of one side, the Soviet Union, to become what Mikhail Gorbachev used to call, plaintively and rather touchingly, a "normal country." The ultimate (if not the proximate) cause of Cuba's civil cold war is the same. No Castro regime, no crisis—no Helms-Burton Act, no apparitions of the Virgin in Miami bedrooms, no watery *muerte* in the straits between *patria* and Florida.

The Soviet Union was abnormal because it had a messianic ideology that combined what might be called exceptionalist universalism—the idea that it represented the next stage in human history, a quantum leap into an inevitable future—with a political economy made (barely) workable by fear alone. By the late 1980s, the ideology had become an inherited relic, as moribund as the cult of Jupiter in fifth-century Rome; and once Gorbachev made it clear that he would never use mass violence to defend the system, the fear dissolved and the party-state withered away. In Cuba, the official ideology still has at least one influential adherent. "I accept with pride that we are a Communist country," Castro told NBC not long ago, adding that Cuba's system "has much more internal support than any system anywhere, because it is more sharing, more fraternal, it is not self-centered, and all the people genuinely participate in its construction and development." The simplest explanation for why Fidel utters such fatuities is that he believes them. As for mass violence, his regime's willingness to use it has never been tested, thanks largely to the Miami safety valve: Cuba's biggest export, its monocrop, is active discontent.

If Castro is the cause of the trouble, though, it doesn't necessarily follow that endless confrontation with Castro is the solution. To the extent that Western policy brought down the Soviet state, military containment was only half the story; the other half was engagement—political, diplomatic, and economic. The Soviet glacier melted a dozen years ago, but the Caribbean iceberg is still afloat. The policy of embargo has had thirty years to prove itself. No one believes any longer that it is going to end, or even alter, the regime; even those who support it do so for other reasons, mainly because it enables them to strike a pose of romantic heroism. It's not that we can no longer afford such posturing. We can, all too easily. But why not try something different? Can anyone imagine an alternative policy that could fail more abjectly than the present one? To visit Cuba these days is to come away convinced that the embargo has become the main prop of Castro's political legitimacy, to the extent he still has any. That is not why American business interests are increasingly against it, of course; but that is most certainly why the dissidents living in Cuba (as distinct from the Miami diaspora) oppose it—and with something close to unanimity.

The Clinton administration, in its determination to return Elián to his father, is following a policy that, besides being legally correct, is morally sound. Not all the moral arguments, however, are on one side. Far from it. And no such arguments could be determinative—to use one of Al Gore's Latinate lawyerisms—if sending Elián back would have the effect of keeping the regime in power unchanged for a day longer. But it won't have that effect. Wherever Elián grows up, Cuban communism will be history by the time he reaches manhood. If the embargo were to be lifted, however, he might not have to wait that long. Conservatives have been suggesting darkly that President Clinton wants to "make a deal with Castro"—that he secretly wants to move toward normalizing relations with Cuba as a feather in the cap of his legacy. Let's hope they're right.

—*The New Yorker*, April 17, 2000

7. WINGERS

When I was fourteen and spending my one and only private-school year as a "third former," i.e., ninth-grader, at the Millbrook School, a sort of vest-pocket Andover, I had a mail subscription to the *New York Post*. It came rolled up tight in a brown wrapper. One day a sixth former, seeing me try to flatten my *Post* enough to read it, asked me in a southern drawl what I was doing with such trash. I said loftily that I read the *Post* for its editorials and its liberal columnists—Murray Kempton, Max Lerner, James Wechsler, Tristram Coffin, William V. Shannon. (This was true, though I also liked the way the *Post* reminded me that there was a jazzy urban world out there where every building wasn't made of white clapboard and situated on a leafy quad.) The sixth former, Clark Woodroe, was the school conservative, and the only other person around who wanted to talk about politics as much as I did. We became fast friends. Clark was a member of the quaintly named Intercollegiate Society of Individualists, the leading (perhaps the only) conservative youth group in the country at that time. He worshipped Edmund Burke and John C. Calhoun. He subscribed to *Modern Age*, the seminal right-wing intellectual quarterly edited by Russell Kirk, and to *National Review*, which was two years old at the time. Its founder and editor,

William F. Buckley, Jr., who was all of thirty-two, had gone to Millbrook and was already its most famous alumnus. During spring break, Clark took me on a pilgrimage to *National Review*'s offices in Manhattan. We had an audience with Mr. Buckley, who was courtly and genial. When my friend warned him that I was a liberal, possibly a socialist, he said "Mmmm," and, flatteringly, opened his eyes wide in mock alarm. I have followed the activities of conservative intellectuals with interest ever since.

National Review was the beginning of what might be called cargo cult conservatism—the American right's attempt to take over the world by imitating what it imagined to be the methods and structures of the left. Liberals had *The New Republic* and *The Nation*; therefore conservatives, too, must have a weekly journal of opinion printed on non-glossy stock and aimed at an educated élite, with unsigned editorials up front and book reviews in the back, presented in a classically restrained format featuring gray columns of type and no photographs. Other institutions followed in due course: think tanks full of tweedy, pipe-smoking "senior fellows"; tax-exempt foundations eager to fund "studies" confirming tenets of the faith; "alternative" campus newspapers devoted to provoking campus authorities; endowed university chairs in subjects like "traditional values"; and, at less rarified levels, television and radio propaganda outlets. In contrast to the South Seas variety, cargo cult conservatism has been a spectacular success.

At midcentury American conservatism was nearly synonymous with anti-intellectualism. Conservatism was represented by philistine organizations like the Daughters of the American Revolution and the American Legion, special interests like the American Medical Association and the National Association of Manufacturers, and potato-faced wielders of arbitrary authority like J. Edgar Hoover, Francis Cardinal Spellman, and Joseph R. McCarthy. The border between these quasi-respectables and outriders like the White Citizens Councils, the John Birch Society, and the Christ-ian Anti-Communist Crusade was porous.

Today's conservative "movement" is of course vastly more powerful than its fifties ancestor, and its face is at once prettier and uglier. Thanks to Buckley, and to the neoconservatives, who migrated from the left during the late sixties and early seventies, conservatism has acquired a respectable in-tellectual component, which does not welcome anti-Semites, overt racists, and the cruder sort of nativists. (Making fun of intellectuals qua intellectu-als is no longer deemed conservatively correct.) At the same time, an enor-mous infrastructure of right-wing populist demagogy heaps hatred and contempt upon Democrats and liberals, mainly via round-the-clock syndi-cated talk radio programs that blanket the country on powerful stations. The obnoxiousness of these radio "hosts" has to be heard to be believed. In cyn-icism, vulgarity, and incivility, they much surpass their cable-TV comrades, such as Bill O'Reilly and Joe Scarborough. Rush Limbaugh is far from the worst of them. (The worst of them, probably, is a truly wicked and de-praved creature who uses the *nom de diffusion* "Michael Savage" and is based in San Francisco, of all places.)

Neoconservatives get a lot of space in this section, partly because when I was editor of *The New Republic* I kept stumbling across them. (A few, I'm sorry to say, had offices there, like hermit crabs occupying the shells of de-ceased crustaceans.) Buckley's *National Review* featured the work of ex-Communists who had become embittered reactionaries, such as Frank S. Meyer.* The neocons were and are a friskier breed. They brought with them the old left's taste for sectarian combat and intense argumentation and its

---

*"I knew Frank Meyer," my late mother, who was a veteran of the Communist versus Socialist battles in the student politics of the late thirties, once told me. "He was the hatchet man for the Y.C.L."—the Young Communist League—"at the University of Chicago. A real bastard. Not like Murray Kempton and Jimmy Wechsler—they were Y.C.L.ers, too, back then, but what a couple of sweethearts."

contempt for liberal softies, but their intellectual style was ex-Trotskyist as opposed to ex-Stalinist. Their ascendance under the Bush administration, post-9/11, has given Republican security policy its sheen of missionary militarism. But they have not moved the center of gravity of the Republican creed in domestic affairs, which is to weaken social controls on private economic power, "incentivize" the rich by bestowing rewards and the poor by inflicting punishments, and use the tax code to effect an upward redistribution of wealth and income.

McGOVERNIST CONSPIRACIES

THE NEW YEAR has arrived, but it's not too late for a few last-minute re-criminations about the old year, judging by the January 1985 issue of *Commentary*. The lead article is "Why the Democrats Lost," by my old comrade Joshua Apparatchik, I mean Joshua Muravchik. Back in the late 1960s, Josh and I, both of us sons of old Socialists, were members of the tiny Socialist Party, U.S.A. We were both strong anti-Communists, of course, as was everybody in the S.P.; but he was in the pro-Vietnam War faction (yes, there was such a thing), while I was in the antiwar, pro-Michael Harrington faction. My politics haven't changed that much over the years, though I've come to agree with Tom Hayden that in the American context "social-ism" is just a word that confuses the voters. (If I must have a label, I'll take "Democrat," or "liberal," or even "neoliberal.") Josh, meanwhile, has evolved into a stalwart neoconservative, to the point where, as noted, he can be trusted with so important a task as codifying the official neocon line on what's wrong with the Democratic Party. And what is wrong with the Democratic Party, according to Joshua Muravchik and *Commentary?* Can you guess? Yes, that's right—"McGovernism." (This is the only correct answer, though if you said "New Politics" or "the adversary culture," you get partial credit.) The article is quite long, well over ten thousand words, because when your foreordained conclusion is that "the McGovernization of the Democratic Party is complete" you need a lot of space to explain away the fact that the party (a) rejected McGovern himself and (b) nominated Hubert Humphrey's protégé, Walter Mondale, who proceeded to run as a centrist with the enthusiastic support of the A.F.L.-C.I.O. "McGovernism" is a deeply wicked and deceptive thing, like fluoridation—even when it's invisible, it saps our precious ideological fluids.

Muravchik, by the way, seems to have discovered something even more terrifying than McGovernism: Cuomoism. Possibly you thought the New York governor's speech at the Democratic Convention was an inspiring statement of bedrock Democratic themes and values. That had certainly been my impression. It seems we were wrong. According to Muravchik, Cuomo's speech was "radical" and "extreme"—indeed, it was "among the most radical given at the convention," which in Josh's book is saying a lot. What made it so radical? Well, first of all, Cuomo didn't couple each of his criticisms of Reagan with a corresponding criticism of the Soviet Union. That was bad enough. But far worse—the "most radical" thing about the speech, in fact—was Cuomo's metaphor of the country as a family. ("We believe we must be the family of America, recognizing that at the heart of the matter we are bound one to another, that the problems of a retired school-teacher in Duluth are our problems," etc. Remember?) According to Muravchik and *Commentary,* this homely, innocent-sounding figure of speech is actually a sinister "confusion of polity and family" that leads directly to—here it comes—"the totalitarian state." Quack! Quack! Down comes Groucho's duck. Now really, what is it with these guys at *Commentary?* It's not enough for something they disagree with to be illogical, or wrong, or even dangerous. It has to be "totalitarian." C'mon, Josh. Give us a break. Lighten up a little.

—Washington Diarist, *The New Republic,* January 21, 1985

NEOCONFAB

HAVING MISSED what probably should have been but possibly wasn't the farewell tour of the Rolling Stones, I was not about to make the same mistake with the neoconservatives. So I hastened to the Omni Shoreham Hotel, to attend what probably should have been but possibly wasn't the farewell conference of the Committee for the Free World. Atmosphere: surprisingly mellow, faintly melancholic, mildly chummy. Attendees: a couple of hundred "New Class" types—editors, polemicists, academics, and think tankers, most of them ex-radicals, ex-socialists, ex-liberals, ex-bohemians and/or ex-Democrats, some of them ex-Reagan administration officials lately eased out by the pragmatic Bushies. Explicit topic: "Does the 'West' Still Exist?"— a characteristically gloomy way of putting a question most people would phrase as "Does the 'East' Still Exist?" Implicit topic: What are neoconservatives supposed to do now?

These are, as always, contentious times for neocons. Some of them revel in the collapse of Soviet power while others denounce glasnost et al. as a ruse designed to make Uncle Sam drop his guard. Midge Decter, executive director of the Committee for the Free World, is of the former persuasion (though she still thinks Gorbachev is nothin' but a damn Communist). But in a pre-conference fund-raising letter, she argued that even though Bolshevism is kaput the Committee will always have a role—"as long as the media demoralize us with their smug, lazy, ignorant misreporting; as long as the schools miseducate our children on the racist assumption that real standards of achievement are inherently unfair to expect of minority children; as long as the universities are permitted to defraud their hard-pressed consumers by purveying anti-intellectual formulas packaged as learning; as long as the arts and publishing industries continue to demand the kind of conformity of which theocracies only dream . . ." Hang on—aren't Americans who endorse this sweeping anathema thereby joining what the letter elsewhere calls a "chorus of disaffection toward their own country and its political and social institutions"? But as true aficionados of neocon rhetoric are aware, condemning American business or American military interventions is "anti-American," whereas wholesale vilification of American newspapers, American schools, American universities, American movies, American museums, and American book publishers is the least that can be expected of defenders of American values. (By the way, I do not use the term "neocon" in an unfriendly spirit, at least not very. Like Quakers, cops, suffragists, contras, and freaks, the neocons have taken an appellation tailored to discomfort them, slipped it on, and worn it till it's as snug as an old leather jacket.)

Nobody covered this meeting. To put it another way, the *Washington Times* covered this meeting. No newspaper not owned by a tax-evading Korean messiah covered it. Yet surely it was news that the neocons, who after all have been an important intellectual force for well over a decade, were, as the *Washtimes* reported on page one, riven by "internal strife," that they "showed deep divisions," that they were "at odds." Who, for instance? Well, Norman Podhoretz and Jeane Kirkpatrick. He said the West's response to the Lithuanian crisis is "something of which we all should be ashamed." She said, "I am not ashamed of the West because of the decision on Lithuania." He said the Russians will never let the Lithuanians go unless the United States makes them. She said that even if the United States does nothing, "the Baltic states will have their independence within three years." He said, "Gorbachev's smile is the most powerful weapon the Soviets have," because this smile is beguiling the United States into taking its troops and missiles out of Europe. She said, "It's not Gorbachev's smile but his restraint in the use of force in Eastern Europe." Who else? Frank Gaffney and Irving Kristol. Gaffney, who used to be Richard Perle's Richard Perle and now runs an ultra-hawkish think tank, said that owing to "the Machiavellian schemes of Gorbachev," the Soviets "are closer to achieving their strategic goals than at any time since World War II"—goals like loosening NATO, getting credits from the West, and "maintaining buffer zones." Kristol, editor of *The*

Public Interest (the leading neocon domestic policy magazine) and publisher of *The National Interest* (the leading neocon foreign policy magazine), said, "Listening to Frank Gaffney, I thought I was listening to someone in a time warp." Gaffney said Kristol had a "passive and appeasing point of view." Kristol said, "That's not the world as I see it." Biff! Pow! Blam!

I HAD LONG BEEN curious to lay eyes upon Jean-François Revel, who was the third panelist on the Podhoretz-Kirkpatrick panel. Having pictured him as the vulpine type, I was surprised to see that he looks like Erich von Stroheim, only more so. Revel said that the Soviet Union's economic collapse is what keeps it from using force, though I'm pretty sure I read an article by him not long ago that said economic trouble would make the Russians more aggressive. Revel is the author of *How Democracies Perish*, which, according to Peggy Noonan in her memoir of the Reagan White House, "everyone" read. That book argued that democracies are at a possibly fatal disadvantage in the great global struggle because they allow peace movements and radicals to do their worst, while totalitarian countries enjoy corresponding advantages. I was eager to ask Revel if recent events had not thrown doubt on this thesis. At the question period I waited in line behind the floor microphone. Unfortunately, the moment I got to the front of the queue was the exact moment the session was declared to be "out of time."

The discussion on Western culture took up the troubling question of why Vaclav Havel has a picture of John Lennon on the wall of his apartment. Hilton Kramer, editor of *The New Criterion*, bemoaned the fact that the East European dissidents liked Allen Ginsberg and the Beatles. John O'Sullivan, editor of *National Review*, said this was only because the authorities had censored them, though he didn't trouble to say *why* they had censored them. "Is rock and roll always bad?" asked a questioner from the floor. Richard John Neuhaus, the Lutheran-turned-Catholic theologian, said he didn't know because he wasn't masochistic enough to listen to the stuff. O'Sullivan said he disliked all popular music after Cole Porter. Kramer suggested that Lennon and his friends "used to sing the praises of Ho Chi Minh." (Untrue, by the way.) Oh, well. Western civ may be as decadent as Kramer says, but at least he doesn't blame it on the Stones. He blames it on the Beatles.

—Washington Diarist, *The New Republic*, May 21, 1990

SWEET AND SOUR

DUE TO AN awkward deadline, the Republican convention is only half over as I write. So there are necessarily a few things you know that I don't. For example, you know that George Bush and Dan Quayle delivered acceptance speeches of such felicity of phrase, such cogency of analysis, such sweep of vision, that by the time the stunned and happy delegates had dispersed from Houston to go back to their home states, the overnight opinion polls were already showing the massive swing that has wiped out Clinton's lead and produced the historic political turnaround that is now the talk of Washington, the nation, and the world. Or perhaps things haven't worked out quite that way. As I say, I have no way of knowing. All I am in a position to know at the moment is that as of Day Two of the big conclave, the electoral prospects of the Grand Old Party were looking distinctly iffy.

The problem, or one of them, is that into the howling vacuum where the Bush record and the Bush philosophy ought to be has rushed the crazed political theology of the far right. The 1992 Republican platform reads like a collection of articles from *Human Events*, which means that while it is somewhat more clearly written than most such documents, its content is fully intelligible only to the faithful. "This," goes a typical passage, referring to the Democrats' deliberate plot to destroy the American family, "is the ultimate agenda of contemporary socialism under all its masks: to liberate youth from traditional family values by replacing family functions with bureaucratic social services." One sees what they're getting at, but the murky, paranoid, know-it-all ideology is as thick as in any Trotskyite tract.

Undiluted right-wingery of a simpler sort was on tap at Monday's

"Christian Coalition God and Country Rally" at the Sheraton Astrodome Hotel, where I went for a look at one of the G.O.P.'s 1996 (or sooner) presidential possibilities, Dan Quayle. The Christian Coalition is Pat Robertson's political arm. While Quayle was speaking, Robertson aides were handing out copies of the Coalition's newspaper, which featured an article attacking the Rio environmental summit as a "giant step" in "the Establishment's strategy for a New World Order." This seemed impolite, in view of the fact that this same New World Order is the explicit goal of Quayle's boss. "The cultural élites laughed at my reference to Murphy Brown," Quayle told the cheering Christians. "It wasn't just me they were laughing at. It was you." Resentment and martyrdom ("I don't care what the élites say, I don't care what the critics say, I will never back down") were the vice president's themes. But Quayle was overshadowed at the rally, I thought, by a far more enduring figure: Pat Boone, the singer, who looked as spookily trim, unwrinkled, and brown-haired as he had back in the late fifties, when my sister and I, budding cultural élitists that we were, used to snicker at the moronic advice to teens contained in Boone's best-selling book of the time, *Twixt Twelve and Twenty*. The real business of the convention, Boone said by way of warming up the crowd, was "to reelect by acclamation the living God as our guide and source of light." That should not be a problem, given the big Guy's low negatives in the polls.

Three of Quayle's probable rivals four years hence—Pat Buchanan, Jack Kemp, and Phil Gramm—gave speeches during the first two nights, in that order. If one were to draw a graph with these three names, again in that order, on the horizontal axis and human decency on the vertical, the result would look like Mt. Fuji. Kemp is a species of miracle I don't pretend to understand. How did a person of such obviously sincere concern and, more amazingly, respect for the poor and downtrodden manage to find his way into Bush's cabinet and the hearts of Bush's delegates? It's a mystery, like Gorbachev and Yeltsin coming out of the Soviet Communist Party. Kemp's speech had not a trace of meanness or ugliness in it. He spoke of "those liberal democratic ideals which gave birth to our nation"—a daring turn of phrase in this crowd. And he finished by saying that "the message of Los Angeles" is that "we must be the party that gives everyone a stake in the system." His solutions are simplistic and wrongheaded, I think, but I can't help feeling affection for him, and I would sooner entrust power to him than to many a Democrat.

Buchanan and Gramm, on the other hand . . . now there's a scary pair.

Buchanan was the de facto keynoter of this convention, since his speech was the featured event of opening night's prime time, pushing Ronald Reagan into the Arsenio time slot. Buchanan, as sour as Kemp was sweet, lingered lovingly on his hates, which included Bill and (especially) Hillary Clinton, feminists, environmentalists, and of course gays and lesbians. Like Kemp, Buchanan built his peroration around the L.A. riots, but Buchanan drew a different lesson from that unhappy episode. With relish, he described how an Army unit faced down a mob that was about to torch an old folks' home, the only unburned, unlooted building on "a dark street." The mob retreated when "it met the one thing that could stop it: force, rooted in justice, backed by courage." Buchanan concluded with this sentence: "As those boys took back the streets of Los Angeles, block by block, so we must take back our cities, and take back our culture, and take back our country." There you have it: the vision thing. For Buchanan, the perfect metaphor for the political task facing his party and his country is militarized race war.

Senator Gramm, the nominal keynoter, gave a performance of unremitting negativity that was politically inept to boot. Keynote speeches traditionally incorporate a call-and-response gimmick. Gramm's was to describe, in his grating, contempt-laden voice, some proposed Clinton atrocity ("a new domestic spending spree," say), to ask theatrically, "Is that the change we want?," and thus to elicit a hearty "NO-O-O!" from the delegates. This was supremely dumb, because the one thing opinion polls have irrefutably established is that the public wants, precisely, change. All Gramm accomplished was to have the Republican Party, in convention assembled, repeatedly shout "No!" at the very mention of, precisely, change. Gramm also said that his test of any government program is to ask if it can pass muster with a Joe Sixpack type of his acquaintance, a "real honest-to-God working person" named Dicky Flatt. Dicky Flatt is apparently a staple of Gramm's speeches. Unfortunately, the name Dicky Flatt sounded to many of us, sitting in the cultural elitist section, like a coy slang term for penile flaccidity. "Bill Clinton," Gramm concluded this section of his speech portentously, "does not know Dicky Flatt." No, that's one thing Clinton has never been accused of. But neither does Bill Clinton know fear of Republicans, which is why Phil Gramm, if he gets his party's nomination in 1996, is likely to have to face a Democratic incumbent.

MARXISM: THE SEQUEL

HARRY GOLDEN, the late humorist and editor of the *Carolina Israelite*, once wrote, at a time when it seemed plausible that Barry Goldwater might someday make it to the White House, "I always knew the first Jewish president would be an Episcopalian." Something analogous seems to be going on with respect to the first sixties-style radical to occupy a position of genuine power in Washington. This long-awaited phenom turns out to be a Republican, and a right-wing one at that: yes, Newt Gingrich, the Speaker of the House.

Washington's other big-shot baby boomer, Bill Clinton, is often described as a product of the sixties. This is true as far as it goes—the saxophone, the blue jeans, the hugs—but the President is not now, nor has he ever been, a radical, politically or temperamentally. As a student, he was relentlessly mainstream, a straight-arrow, student-council, go-to-class, hit-the-books type, and he still is. Mr. Gingrich, in contrast, seems to have been rather more at home in (to use a term that is still a favorite of his) the counterculture: in 1968, while young Clinton was at Oxford, agonizing about his draft status, young Gingrich, safely deferred, was leading his fellow Tulane students in a raucous protest against the university administration's censorship of supposedly dirty pictures in a campus literary magazine. It is only as a mature adult, though, that Mr. Gingrich has wholeheartedly embraced what he is proud to call a radical agenda.

Goodness. There hasn't been so much loose talk in Washington about "revolution" since Abbie Hoffman and Jerry Rubin hit town to testify before the House Un-American Activities Committee. A Nexis database search for articles containing the words "revolution" and "Gingrich" immediately yields a warning that there are more than a thousand. Only when you specify articles published during the last week of January, say, do you get a manageable number; that week, it was two hundred and twenty-six. "This is a real revolution," Mr. Gingrich said in a typical recent talk, this one before the Republican National Committee. And, a few minutes later, "I am a genuine revolutionary; they [the Democrats] are the genuine reactionaries." On this occasion, the word "conservative" did not pass the Speaker's lips. It seldom does.

The resemblance between Mr. Gingrich's outlook and that of the campus revolutionaries of the sixties goes beyond a shared relish for the vocabulary of extremism. The Speaker has long been an enthusiast of Alvin and Heidi Toffler, the futurists. Last year, he wrote the introduction to the Tofflers' latest book, *Creating a New Civilization: The Politics of the Third Wave*, which consists of chapters from the Tofflers' previous books plus some new material, and his think tank, the Progress and Freedom Foundation, underwrote and published the book. Mr. Gingrich has been talking up Tofflerian ideas nonstop for a decade. "I want to urge you to set up a series of study groups to look at the Toffler revolution of a third-wave information revolution," he burbled to the American Hospital Association just last week.

It has been too little remarked that there is an eerie similarity between Tofflerism and Marxism. Look at the correspondences. Marxism—at least in its vulgar form—sees civilization as proceeding in three stages, each of which corresponds to one of the Tofflers'. In the Marxist analysis, feudalism (the equivalent of the Tofflers' agrarian First Wave) gives way to capitalism (the equivalent of the Tofflers' industrial Second Wave), and capitalism, in turn, gives way to communism (the equivalent of the Tofflers' cybernetic Third Wave). Each stage, in its time, constitutes a tremendous advance in human progress; each eventually becomes obsolete (the "contradictions," as the Marxists say, begin to get out of hand); and the next emerges, with much pain and dislocation, from the collapsing ruin of its predecessor. The first sentence of *Creating a New Civilization*—

A new civilization is emerging in our lives, and blind men everywhere are trying to suppress it.

—echoes the drumroll that opens *The Communist Manifesto*:

A spectre is haunting Europe—the spectre of Communism. All the powers of old Europe have entered into a holy alliance to exorcise this spectre.

In both the Marxian and the Tofflerian view, history is relentless, progressive, and ultimately irresistible. Marxism's ultimate vision, like Tofflerism's, is a vaguely defined future paradise of decentralization. How do we know we've reached the third stage, the inevitable culmination of human history? Simple: we see the withering away of the state—the federal government, anyhow.

Tofflerism and Gingrichism, like Marxism and Leninism, aren't identical in every respect; for example, the Tofflers favor employer mandates for health insurance and child care, and official recognition of nontraditional families. But the tone of what can fairly be called Tofflerism-Gingrichism is uncannily like that of Marxism-Leninism. There's a similar arrogance, a similar exhilaration that comes from being among the select few to whom the mysteries and the meaning of history are vouchsafed. There's a similar patronizing contempt for those who don't "get it" and are therefore fated to be swept into the dustbin of history. There's a similar worship of technology. There's a similar cult of toughness. (There's even a similar scorn for "liberalism.") Tofflerism, as surely as Marxism, is a variation on historical materialism. The fervor, the know-it-all certainty, the scientism, the "revolutionary" rapture—much of the new faith is weirdly familiar to anyone who has studied the history of the far left.

This doesn't mean that everything about the new faith is wrong, of course. Marxism produced Soviet totalitarianism, but it also produced stolid, sensible West European social democracy, and the Marx-like doctrines of Gingrich's Tofflerism might likewise produce something useful for the American future. What's attractive about Mr. Gingrich is his insistence that everything is on the table, that Washington can shed its habitual sense of diminished possibility, its cynical hopelessness about changing anything beyond the usual margins. But there is already reason to be on guard against a darker alternative. The apocalyptic three-stage theory of history, the belief in inevitable progress toward ever higher forms of society, the conviction that we, the revolutionaries, know what is best for the masses because we know the laws of history—this is a set of ideas that is not exactly inhospitable to hubris. In the orthodox Marxist version, it led to Stalinism; in a hippie-student version, it led to the excesses that everyone remembers as the worst of the radicalism of the sixties. And there is no obvious reason that those same ideas about history and inevitability and the greater wisdom of those who "get it" should not lead to something unpleasant today—even if, today, the certitudes about three stages and historical inevitability and all the rest can be found on the right and not the left.

—*The New Yorker*, February 13, 1995

COOKIE MONSTER

TAKE A LOOK at this passage from *To Renew America,* the new volume of political philosophy from Newt Gingrich, Speaker of the House:

> Just list some of the changes we are living through: laptop computers, cellular telephones, molecular medicine, new discoveries about the dinosaurs, home security systems that talk, composite materials that make cars lighter, microengineering, manufacturing in space, high-definition television, the video store—the list goes on and on.

Does any particular item jump out at you? Well, there's the talking-home-security-system thing, which adds a sinister note to the passage's generally sunny tone of techno-celebration. ("IN-TRU-DER DE-TECT-ED," one imagines such a system saying in a synthesized monotone, and, seconds later, "IN-TRU-DER TER-MIN-A-TED.") But the real jumper on the list, the item that comes cartwheeling off the page, is, of course, "new discoveries about the dinosaurs." What in the world is *that* doing there, amid the laptops and cell phones?

To Renew America consists mostly of policy prescriptions, attacks on whiny liberal elites, and encomiums for the Contract with America, and in these respects it has nothing to say that is not by now numbingly familiar. But it does offer glimpses of a couple of curious—and, truth be told, rather winning—aspects of the personality of the country's second most powerful public official. The dinosaur obsession is one.

As every parent knows, little boys love dinosaurs, because dinosaurs are big—bigger than mom and dad, bigger than school, bigger than just about anything, come to think of it, except Big Government. Gingrich mentions more than once that before he discovered politics he was planning to be a vertebrate paleontologist ("specializing in dinosaurs") when he grew up. Charmingly, he has retained his enthusiasm for the extinct giants into middle age. In addition to including breakthroughs in dinosaur research on his list of futuristic wonders, he specifies "people interested in dinosaurs" as a prime example of who might benefit from his education proposals. And he boasts, "I have a Tyrannosaurus rex skull in the Speaker's office." Awesome.

To Renew America offers copious evidence that Gingrich has also held on to another of his youthful interests: science fiction. The two works that "had a profound influence in my life," he recounts in some detail, were Arnold Toynbee's *A Study of History* (no surprise there) and *Foundation*, Isaac Asimov's epic trilogy about the decline and fall of the Galactic Empire—a series that, as Gingrich rightly notes, "remains one of the classics of science fiction." Farther on in *To Renew America* Gingrich devotes almost all of a chapter on science policy to sci-fi lit-crit. He asserts that his generation "is still seeking its Jules Verne or H. G. Wells," attacks his fellow dinosaur maven Michael Crichton for writing stories that are "just standard alarmist environmentalism," praises Arthur C. Clarke for having a "positive vision," and reflects on the differences between the movies *The Right Stuff* and *Star Wars*.

Perhaps it is Gingrich's passion for fantasy that makes his other book of the summer, the novel *1945,* several orders of magnitude more interesting than *To Renew America*, which, after all, is mostly Beltway boilerplate. *1945* is an example of "alternate history" fiction, a sci-fi subgenre in which the author speculates on what the world might be like if some historical event had turned out differently. Like Philip K. Dick's *The Man in the High Castle,* which is the recognized classic of the subgenre, *1945* has as its premise that Germany won the Second World War. In *1945,* a triumphant Hitler squares off against a United States that has defeated Japan but has stayed away from Europe.

1945 is a mess, of course, but it could be a lot worse. Newt Gingrich the novelist is to Philip K. Dick as Bill Clinton the tenor-saxophone player is to Sonny Rollins—awful, but more entertaining than you might expect. The difference between Clinton and Gingrich is that when the president dons his shades and picks up his horn he has to play his riffs himself, whereas the Speaker has a co-author—a genre veteran named William R. Forstchen—and a "technical editor," Albert S. Hanser. The writing produced by this team is standard guy-stuff pulpese. "The high-pitched stutter of a *Schmeisser* cut short the deeper rattle of the heavy machine gun," you read, and "Like a demon raptor deprived of its prey"—dinosaurs again—"the gunship pulled up and disappeared into the night." That sort of thing.

The tabloids have done their best to wring something salacious out of the three or four sentences in *1945* devoted to sex. But even the gorgeous Swedish Nazi-spy mistress of the White House chief of staff doesn't come across with much more than a "lethal pout." "He stirred at the movement of her fingers, which were no longer on his chest" is as steamy as it gets. When it comes to violence, however, Gingrich makes Time Warner look like a magazine company. The climax of *1945* is a lovingly described, incredibly bloody German commando raid on America's secret A-bomb installation at Oak Ridge. In the battle, General of the Army George C. Marshall personally hoses away several Nazis with an M-1 carbine and a machine pistol, and the bad guys are finally routed by—Timothy McVeigh please note—a ragtag citizens' militia, led by none other than Sergeant York, the combat hero of the First World War, now a sheriff in rural Tennessee. First, though, Gingrich lingers over the sadistic pleasures enjoyed by a particularly brutal SS officer:

> Richer popped the magazine out of his Luger as he gazed tenderly down at the half-dozen girls he had just talked out of their hiding place and then killed. It had felt so wonderfully good, especially when the extremely pretty one started to cry as, after first forcing them to kneel, he systematically shot her five friends, one after the other. [And] after she learned what was going to happen to her, she begged to be shot like the rest.

Three pages of mayhem later, Richer, wounded and helpless, is taken prisoner by the militiamen. One of York's comrades, a fellow sheriff, toys with the German a bit and then calmly fires a load of buckshot into his testicles. "They left Richer lying there, his groin a red mass," Gingrich writes. "He was still alive, but he wasn't having any fun." Add rhymes and a thumping beat, and presto!—a brand-new musical genre for Senator Dole to deplore: Speaka Rap.

In political debate, Gingrich often displays the qualities of a clever, if slightly maladjusted, teenage boy. When he is in one of his combative moods, he is insolent, sarcastic, self-righteous, narcissistic, and allergic to understatement. He loves catching people out, and dismisses criticism as unfair and motivated by malice or envy. As he shows in *1945*, far more clearly than in *To Renew America*, he also has more than his share of the exuberance and imagination (to say nothing of the aesthetics) of adolescence. Or perhaps it goes back further than that. "At heart," he writes in the final chapter of *To Renew America*, "I am still a happy four-year-old who gets up every morning hoping to find a cookie that friends or relatives may have left for me somewhere." After devouring *1945*, however, the reader who encounters cookies may be inclined to toss them.

—*The New Yorker*, July 17, 1995

BAD NEWS FOR BIGOTS

IN AMERICAN POLITICS, weirdness is routine. Still, it was more than routinely weird that, as the presidential primary campaign approached its climax, the struggle for the most powerful political office on earth found itself zeroing in on the moral peculiarities of an improbable educational institution by the improbable name of Bob Jones University. George W. Bush certainly didn't plan it that way. When his advance people lit on the Bob Jones campus as a good site for a South Carolina rally, they intended little more than a nod to Christian conservatives, or at most a roguish wink. Republican pols from Ronald Reagan to Dan Quayle had given speeches there. John McCain's own state chairman was a graduate of the place. No big whoop, right? Big mistake: all hell (a very real place in the Bob Jones scheme of things) broke loose. And all that hell—volcanoes of negative ads and push-polls, bubbling cauldrons of racial and religious divisiveness, sulfuric hysteria in the Republican ranks—provoked plenty of heated commentary, largely of the isn't-it-deplorable variety. But the controversy also showed that, beneath the surface and over time, there has been a tectonic change in American attitudes toward race—a change that deserves to be noticed and celebrated.

As the world knows, Bob Jones University had, until last weekend, a "policy" against interracial dating. Bush's failure to denounce that policy on the spot was a moral mistake. Bush, however, wasn't the only dog that didn't bark. Throughout the entire controversy, not a peep was heard in *defense* of the ban. A few prominent Christian conservatives defended what might be called Bob Jones's right to choose, but none expressed sympathy with the ban itself. Conservative politicians, when asked, responded with something approaching unanimity. If they didn't always speak with McCainian passion ("This ban on interracial dating is stupid, it's idiotic, and it is incredibly cruel," the senator said), they spoke plainly enough. The comment of Asa Hutchinson—congressman from Arkansas, House impeachment manager, and Bob Jones graduate, class of '72—was fairly typical. "The fact is," Hutchinson said, "you have an indefensible policy at Bob Jones University."

In other words, interracial dating (and all that it implies) has become so respectable that the most conservative, not to say reactionary, elements in American society feel it incumbent upon them to accept and even embrace it. This may seem unremarkable until one reflects how far it was from being the case a generation or two ago, when miscegenation was racism's trump card and even the most enlightened Americans, black and white, took it for granted that sexual fear was its unkillable heart. Civil rights leaders thought it politic to assure the white public that their movement was not aimed at "social"—i.e., sexual—integration. The makers of *Guess Who's Coming to Dinner*, which came out in 1967, were so worried about the explosiveness of their story of interracial romance that they loaded the dice by making the Sidney Poitier character a brilliant research physician. Cross-racial coupling is now so common on the screen (even the small screen) that it sometimes happens between unsympathetic characters.

This is not to say that black-white dating and marriage are without their special discomforts; any interracial couple can attest to the contrary. But there has been a huge change for the better. Last year, the Alabama legislature voted unanimously to remove an antimiscegenation clause (the nation's last, and already a dead letter, thanks to a 1967 Supreme Court decision) from the state's post-Reconstruction constitution. It's up to the voters to make the removal final in a November referendum. The margin probably won't be close. A recent *Atlanta Journal-Constitution* poll found that nearly two-thirds of Southern whites and more than nine-tenths of Southern blacks approve of interracial marriage. A quarter of the whites and half the blacks told the pollsters that such a marriage had actually taken place in their own families.

Although Bob Jones has now abruptly got religion where rainbow romance is concerned, it remains steeped in another mortal sin: anti-Catholicism. And in the reaction to this, too, there is encouragement to be found. On its Web site—which, in accordance with what is apparently a campus tradition of risible nomenclature, is www.bju.edu—the university explained that its position is simply a matter of trying to save Catholics (and Jews, and Muslims, and liberal Protestants, and so on) from the fiery pit:

> Our shame would be in telling people a lie, and thereby letting them go to hell without Christ because we loved their goodwill more than we loved them and their souls.
>
> If there are those who wish to charge us with being anti-Catholicism, we plead guilty. . . . All religion, including Catholicism, which teaches that salvation is by religious works or church dogma is false. . . . We love the practicing Catholic and earnestly desire to see him accept the Christ of the Cross, leave the false system that has enslaved his soul, and enjoy the freedom of sins forgiven that is available for any of us in Christ alone.

Bob Jones is essentially alone in clinging publicly to this sort of thing. Evangelicals and fundamentalists have rushed to disassociate themselves from the school's anti-Catholicism, and among conservative politicians the stampede to condemn it has been deafening. In large part, no doubt, this reflects an anxiety to maintain the anti-abortion political alliance with the Catholic Church. But it also suggests a willingness to place a higher value on commonalities of belief than on the jagged edges of religious doctrine. In 1960, Protestant divines ranging from Billy Graham to Martin Luther King, Sr., called for John F. Kennedy's defeat on religious grounds. Forty years later, religious prejudice, which never carried quite the sting of racism, has never been weaker. Only non-believers are left out of the atmosphere of ecumenical warmth: it is inconceivable that a professed atheist or agnostic could be elected president today, and even an unchurched Deist like Jefferson wouldn't stand a chance.

The likely truth is that most people, including most people who regard themselves as observantly religious, simply don't believe in the sort of God who would subject a virtuous person to eternal torture just because he or she believes in salvation through works rather than through grace, or vice versa (or doesn't believe in salvation at all). Whether this counts as a gain or a loss for true Christianity is for Christians, not secular magazines, to say. But it is certainly a gain for mercy, "and mercy rejoiceth against judgment."

—*The New Yorker*, March 13, 2000

SHEER HELMS

WHEN A "COLORFUL" CELEBRITY has achieved some sort of sustained and nominally respectable worldly accomplishment (record sales, business success, public office), has been around long enough to acquire the appealing vulnerability of old age, and has not been convicted of a capital crime, there's a powerful tendency to go all warm and fuzzy on him. So it is at the moment for Jesse Helms, the senior senator from North Carolina. With his announcement, last Wednesday, that he will not seek a sixth term next year, Helms became a certified legend—the feisty (but always courteous) conservative icon, the plainspoken Tarheel who never feared to be politically incorrect, the paragon of traditional values who always let you know where he stood and is destined to be remembered, as President Bush put it, as "a tireless defender of our nation's freedom and a champion of democracy abroad."

The strangest tribute came from Walter Russell Mead, a senior fellow at the Council on Foreign Relations and normally a levelheaded (if chronically puckish) observer. Writing in the *Wall Street Journal*, Mead described Helms as "one of a handful of Southern statesmen who ensured the triumph of the civil rights revolution"—and not, as you might suppose, by provoking disgust and indignation among the fair-minded with the crude racism that was his stock-in-trade (along with an "anticommunism" that treated liberal reform and Soviet tyranny as indistinguishable). According to Mead, the decisive contribution of Jesse Helms was that "once the civil rights legislation of the 1960s was enacted"—over Helms's unremitting and demagogic opposition, by the way—"he accepted the laws and obeyed them." Also, in edifying contrast to his counterparts of a century earlier, he refrained from "being directly and openly involved in the murder of black political leaders."

Talk about lowering the bar! But Helms never bothered with the soft bigotry of low expectations. He has always preferred the hard stuff, undiluted by the branch water of euphemism. Many of the Helms retrospectives of recent days have dated his entry into serious politics to 1960, when, after having spent most of his thirties as a banking lobbyist, he began delivering nightly five-minute commentaries on a Raleigh television station and on something called the Tobacco Radio Network—the job that propelled him into the Senate, twelve years later. But as far back as 1950, Helms, then twenty-eight, helped run what the Duke University historian William H. Chafe has called "the bitterest, ugliest, most smear-ridden campaign of modern times," the race to unseat Frank P. Graham, the former president of the University of North Carolina and probably the most distinguished North Carolinian ever to sit in the United States Senate. "The Graham campaign is generally viewed as the most pivotal in modern southern history since it set the precedent for the race-baiting and red-baiting tactics that were later employed so widely by politicians like Orval Faubus, George Wallace, and Jesse Helms," Chafe has written. "Helms, of course, helped invent these tactics." Over the succeeding half century, Helms changed but little. His own campaigns have invariably been powered by appeals to prejudice, racial and otherwise. In recent years the focus of his bigotry has shifted increasingly toward gays and lesbians. But his disdain for people of color (exemplified by his "humorous" habit, in private, of referring to any black person as "Fred") continues to find ways of expressing itself. He is the Senate's most reliable opponent of any measure aimed at securing the rights or improving the conditions of African Americans. In 1994, when Nelson Mandela visited the Capitol, Helms ostentatiously turned his back on him.

To be fair, the snub of the South African president probably had less to do with race per se than with foreign policy, the field in which Helms, who since 1986 has been either the chairman of the Senate Foreign Relations Committee or its ranking Republican, has done his worst mischief. His vaunted anticommunism was never based upon a principled belief in democracy. His support of the apartheid regime was of a piece with his enthusiasm for any dictatorship, no matter how brutal, that could plausibly be described as right wing. (He even supported the Argentine junta in the Falklands War with Britain.) He has crippled America's diplomatic corps, systematically starving the State Department of funds and capriciously blocking the confirmation of highly qualified ambassadorial nominees. But it is in his unrelenting hostility to international institutions that he has done his greatest and probably most lasting damage.

The gauzy story line of the past week requires Helms to have "mellowed," the main piece of evidence being his agreement, in 1999, to allow payment of some $900 million of the $1.3 billion in back dues the United States then owed the United Nations. Never mind that it was he who had abused the rules of the Senate to hold up the payments in the first place, or that the United States was on the verge of being deeply embarrassed by losing its right to vote in the General Assembly. The real significance of the episode is that what was supposed to be legally binding has now been certified as volitional. A new "principle"—that the solemn obligations of the United States are subject to abrogation without notice by congressional ideologues—has become ever more entrenched. America's U.N. bill, by the way, remains unpaid; it now amounts to $2.3 billion, a record, thanks to the machinations of such mini-Helmses as Tom DeLay, the House majority whip. Helms's heirs now populate the other end of Pennsylvania Avenue, too: the national-security apparatus of the Bush administration is heavily salted with his former assistants. Little wonder that the administration adds almost weekly to the long list of useful international treaties it proposes to reject, abrogate, or simply scrap. The retirement of Jesse Helms has been hailed (and mourned) as "the end of an era." If only that were true.

—*The New Yorker*, September 3, 2001

CAN YOU FORGIVE HIM?

IF A TALE of political migration is to have any real punch, it needs a touch of passionate intensity—and, as Yeats pointed out, that's what the worst are full of. The journey from moderate liberalism to moderate conservatism or vice versa is the stuff of watery op-ed pieces and policy monographs, but it doesn't provide much in the way of narrative drive. A cracking good story requires something stronger at one end or the other, or both. Stalinism supplied that something stronger a half century ago. Its apostates moved by definition from left to right, though many of them stopped well short of the opposite pole of the spectrum. Of the six contributors to *The God That Failed*, for example, five (Richard Wright, Ignazio Silone, Stephen Spender, André Gide, and Louis Fischer) ended up on the moderate left, and one (Arthur Koestler) turned away from politics. For these writers, the break was with political extremism itself as much as with its Stalinist manifestation. Other ex-Communists—one thinks of Whittaker Chambers and a multitude of lesser lights—took refuge in belief systems almost as Manichaean and doctrinaire as the one they abandoned.

The tradition of the left-to-right confessional has continued with writers like Norman Podhoretz, who led the neoconservative parade from standard liberalism to showy, confrontational anti-liberalism, and David Horowitz, who traded sixties-style infantile leftist anger for eighties-style infantile rightist anger. The political space such people inhabit has become, now that Communism and its Third World offshoots are in apparently permanent eclipse, the principal site of all-encompassing ideological certainty.

Partly as a result, there has been a bit of a drift—not quite a trend—in the other direction. It began quietly, when Garry Wills, along with a few other Catholic intellectuals, made the long march from *National Review* to the *New York Review of Books*. A younger writer, Michael Lind, has chronicled his conversion from neoconservatism to a kind of neo–New Deal politics he calls liberal nationalism. Now comes David Brock.

The texture of Brock's flight from the right was not at all like that of Wills or Lind. Their defection was the product of intellectual reflection; Brock's was the result of harrowing experience. What drove Brock was the wrongness of what he did, not of what he thought. As a frontline machine gunner in the Washington scandal wars of the 1990s, Brock inflicted heavy political casualties. But his own wounds came mostly from friendly fire, and many of these, he eventually realized, were self-inflicted. *Blinded by the Right: The Conscience of an Ex-Conservative* is the story of a change of heart, not of mind. It is also an astounding account of fin-de-siècle Washington politics. And it is an entertaining backstage sketchbook of scores of eccentric and mostly obnoxious characters, many of whom will be familiar to regular viewers of the cable news chat channels.

FOR A MAN not yet forty, Brock has had quite a career. As a student at the Berkeley campus of the University of California in the early 1980s, he had two arrows in his quiver. He was a crackerjack reporter for the *Daily Californian,* the student paper, where his scoops included an investigation of financial chicanery which forced the resignation of a university vice president. And he was a budding controversialist, whose rebellion against what was not yet called political correctness began when he covered a lecture by Jeane Kirkpatrick, President Reagan's United Nations ambassador, and saw her shouted down and silenced by a howling mob. Young Brock had worshipped Bobby Kennedy, voted for Jimmy Carter, and spent the summer after his freshman year working for one of Ralph Nader's organizations; after the Kirkpatrick episode, he started reading back issues of *Commentary,* sought out the few conservative professors on campus, and wrote opinion columns for the *Daily Cal,* which gleefully defied the prevailing left-wing orthodoxy. (One of them, a defense of the invasion of Grenada, prompted a demonstration against him personally.) Still, his ambition was to be a journalist, not a polemicist, and in 1985 he landed a news internship at the *Wall Street Journal.*

Brock's sojourn in New York went well, and in the normal course of events the *Journal* would have offered him a permanent position. Perhaps he would still be a member of the staff of reporters and correspondents which makes that paper (excepting its editorial and op-ed pages) a paragon of American journalism. At the time, though, a temporary hiring freeze was in effect at the *Journal*. For want of that particular nail, a horseshoe was lost, and then a great thundering herd of steeds, and then, very nearly, a kingdom—or its American equivalent, a presidency.

Brock settled for his second choice, a writing job at *Insight*, a weekly "newsmagazine" published under the auspices of the *Washington Times*, the jewel in the crown of the media satrapy owned by the Reverend Sun Myung Moon, the Korean messiah, and his Unification Church. At *Insight*, then at the Heritage Foundation, and, finally, at the monthly *American Spectator*, Brock became part of Washington's smart set of young and extremely conservative publicists, political operatives, lawyers, congressional staffers, and commentators. He soon eclipsed them all.

In 1992, Brock wrote a long article for the *American Spectator* portraying Anita Hill, the demure law professor whose testimony before the Senate Judiciary Committee had nearly derailed the nomination of Clarence Thomas to the Supreme Court, as a deranged liar manipulated by scheming feminist harridans. The article became a sensation when Rush Limbaugh read portions of it aloud on his radio program; the *Spectator*'s circulation quickly shot from thirty thousand to well over a hundred thousand. In the book version of "The Real Anita Hill," Brock adopted a more judicious tone. (He dropped the article's most notorious line, in which he had described Hill as "a bit nutty, and a bit slutty.") The grandees of respectable conservatism— George F. Will, William F. Buckley, Jr., the *Journal*'s editorial page—embraced *The Real Anita Hill*. It got a favorable review from Christopher Lehmann-Haupt in the *New York Times*, and it climbed to No. 2 on the *Times*'s best-seller list. (Only a book by Limbaugh himself kept it from the top spot.) Brock, at thirty, was suddenly the most famous young conservative writer in the country, a glamorous, swashbuckling "investigative reporter," the Bob Woodward of the right.

There was more—much more—to come. For his next big story, Brock took aim at the conservative movement's most hated, and most successful, nemesis: the new president of the United States, Bill Clinton. The resulting article, "His Cheatin' Heart"—eleven thousand words of sexual gossip retailed to Brock by Arkansas state troopers who had served on Clinton's gubernatorial bodyguard detail—was mainlined, pre-publication, into the media bloodstream via a well-managed leak to CNN. The *Spectator*'s circulation again soared, to three hundred thousand. Eventually, almost everything in the story would end up discredited. But that didn't stop it from creating an indelible image of Clinton. A few of its allegations—such as a (bogus) tale that the president had offered jobs to troopers in exchange for silence—were serious. The rest were trivial, such as an anecdote about a woman who had purportedly been summoned to Clinton's hotel room and left an hour later, supposedly remarking to a trooper that she was available to be the governor's "regular girlfriend." (Brock thought so little of this morsel of sleaze that he didn't bother to ask his source the woman's surname. He referred to her only as Paula.)

Brock now cut a bigger swath than ever in Washington's right-wing social circles and among the Limbaugh-listening masses. For his next book project, a promised hatchet job on Hillary Clinton, he got a million-dollar advance. But when the book came out, shortly before the 1996 election, it wasn't quite what his friends or his publishers had anticipated. *The Seduction of Hillary Rodham* was harsh in its depiction of Hillary's husband, and it took for granted the conservative critique of her politics as big-government, Hillary-knows-best radicalism. Even so, it was a real biography, well researched and mostly accurate, and it concluded, shockingly, that in spite of all her machinations and lawyerly evasions Mrs. Clinton was basically a well-intentioned, possibly even a decent, person.

As a result, Brock found himself ostracized by most of his suddenly former friends and disinvited to the sort of parties at which he had formerly preened. His second thoughts, which had been quietly taking shape for some time, were accelerated by two other factors. Brock is gay, a circumstance that was making him increasingly unhappy in a political movement often allied with homophobic bigotry—a movement, moreover, that had made him a star precisely because of his prowess as a sexual prosecutor. And, as the orchestrated scandalmongering that dominated Clinton's second term approached its apogee, Brock began to feel guilty. The perjury trap that led to Clinton's impeachment, after all, was sprung during a deposition in a malicious lawsuit that stemmed directly from Brock's "troopergate" article. Publicly and privately, step by step, Brock repudiated his former comrades, his former views, and the substance of most of the work that had made him famous. And he sat down to write another book.

. . . .

BROCK AND THE CIRCLE of young conservatives he joined when he came to Washington in 1986 called themselves the Third Generation. ("Barry Goldwater made the G.O.P. a conservative party; Ronald Reagan made it a winning electoral majority; now it was our turn.") They talked incessantly about "the battle of ideas," but ideas per se didn't much interest them. The catechism—cutting taxes on the rich, getting rid of regulations, and spending on defense are good; programs that redistribute income and provide services to the underprivileged are bad—required no revision. All that was required was to vanquish the enemy.

Blinded by the Right shows how deeply the conservatism of the past fifteen years or so was and is—to use an old term of abuse not much heard nowadays—reactionary. For most of the 1980s, anti-Communism and laissez-faire economics held the conservative movement together, and Reagan's sunny personality gave it a more or less genial face. When the Cold War faded and Reagan was replaced by the first George Bush—who ran for president on hard-right themes but governed as what the conservatives called a "squish," thereby earning their scornful indifference—the movement, leaderless but disciplined and well organized, was left to its own devices.

The enemy was "the other team": liberals, Democrats, environmentalists, peaceniks, victim-group whiners (black, gay, female, poor), civil liberties bores, and anyone who stood for such sixties countercultural values as, in Brock's summary, "abortion rights, gay rights, feminism, liberal judges, pornography, multiculturalism, affirmative action, and sex education in schools." For Brock, some of this entailed a certain cognitive dissonance. Openly gay at Berkeley, he had retreated behind the closet door when he got to Washington; but he continued to hold, if not to express, tolerant views on the "social issues." The female pals with whom he dished the dirt—including Laura Ingraham and Ann Coulter, the future scourges of Clintonian libertinism—were ambitious workaholics who permitted themselves plenty of sexual freedom. Brock took comfort from the comprehensive sexual hypocrisy of his "team," which seemed to validate his own. But he saw the earnest Democrats and liberal lobbyists of Washington, none of whom he actually knew, as extensions of the smug left-wing bullies he had encountered at Berkeley. The enemy's perfidy was something everyone—

Christian rightists, secular neoconservatives, conservative populists, and young militants fresh from the anti-P.C. wars on campus—could agree on. "The lefties, the takers, the coercive utopians," as Grover Norquist, an excitable conservative impresario, would later put it on the eve of the second president Bush's inauguration, "are not stupid. They are evil. *Evil!*"

Brock had flair and talent. He knew how to do what looked like investigative journalism, and he valued the credibility that his Anita Hill book had earned him. His success with the troopergate story inspired something called the Arkansas Project, financed by $2.5 million provided by the Pittsburgh-based billionaire Richard Mellon Scaife. Its goal was to produce evidence that Bill and Hillary Clinton were violence-prone sexual and financial criminals. The Arkansas Project's money was funnelled through the *American Spectator* to a variety of unsavory characters, racist Clinton-haters, and self-described private detectives in Arkansas. One of its investigations, a particular obsession of Scaife's, was of the Vincent Foster case. Foster, a Clinton family friend and a former Little Rock law partner of Hillary Clinton's, was a deputy White House counsel. In July of 1993, after being attacked in a series of *Wall Street Journal* editorials, Foster shot himself to death in a park outside Washington. Some on the right believed, or professed to believe, that he had been murdered by or at the behest of the Clintons, who were orchestrating a monstrous cover-up. R. Emmett Tyrrell, Jr., the editor of the *American Spectator*, assigned the story to a gullible British journalist named Ambrose Evans-Pritchard. What Evans-Pritchard turned in was so shoddy, Brock writes, that he, Tyrrell's executive editor, Wladyslaw Pleszczynski, and Ronald Burr, the magazine's publisher, agreed that it had to be stopped despite Tyrrell's determination to publish it. For help, Brock turned to Ted Olson, an informal but influential adviser to the *Spectator*. Olson had been Reagan's private lawyer; he was a sachem of the Federalist Society, an association of conservative lawyers and jurists whose membership included future justices of the Supreme Court; and he was a close friend and former law partner of Kenneth Starr's. Olson, Brock thought, was "the model of a sober, careful lawyer with impeccable judgment." Brock faxed him the piece. Olson's response was evidently not what he was expecting. Olson, Brock writes, "told me bluntly, in a tone of voice that I had never heard him use before, that while he believed, as Starr apparently did, that Foster had committed suicide, raising questions about the death was a way of turning up the heat on the administration until another scandal was shaken loose, which was the *Spectator*'s mission. The statement stunned me. Though I was all for harassing the administration, I was not ready to accept the reality that the *Spectator* was a propaganda organ." (The piece ran; the *Spectator*'s reputation, such as it was, was unaffected.)

The anecdote, like many that Brock tells, has elements of farce. But it also has a sinister side, and not only because Olson is now solicitor general of the United States. Brock's faith in Olson recalls the faith of Winston Smith, the hero of *1984*, in O'Brien, the Inner Party bigwig who Smith thinks shares his doubts about Big Brother, the Anti-Sex League, Hate Week, and the rest. When Smith (who, aptly, is an Outer Party member and low-level functionary in the Ministry of Truth) is arrested and O'Brien reappears as his interrogator, Smith, too, is stunned.

Indeed, the milieu that Brock describes is reminiscent of that of American Communism in the 1930s and 1940s. Obviously, organized American conservatism offers no moral equivalents of what the Communist Party U.S.A. and its front groups made it their business to defend or deny: totalitarianism, the Gulag, the tens of millions of murders committed by the Stalin regime. But the social and structural affinities are striking, and Brock himself touches here and there on some of their more obvious manifestations. (He notes a portrait of Lenin that Grover Norquist displayed on his wall as a symbol of ruthless commitment, and he remarks on the fact that some of his erstwhile comrades, such as Horowitz, made the transition from far left to far right without the slightest alteration in political style or temperament.) Like the American and other Western Communist parties in their heyday, the American conservative movement has created a kind of alternative intellectual and political universe—a set of institutions parallel to and modelled on the institutions of mainstream society (many of which the movement sees, or imagines, as the organs of a disciplined Liberal Establishment) and dedicated to the single purpose of advancing a predetermined political agenda. There is a kind of Inner Movement, consisting of a few hundred funders, senior organization leaders, lawyers, and prominent media personalities (but only a handful of practicing politicians), and an Outer Movement, consisting of a few thousand staff people, grunt workers, and lower-level operatives of one kind or another. The movement has its own newspapers (the *Washington Times*, the *New York Post*, the *Journal*'s editorial page), its own magazines (the *Weekly Standard*, *National Review*, *Policy Review*, *Commentary*, and many more), its own broadcasting operations

(Fox News and an array of national and local talk radio programs and right-wing Christian broadcast outlets), its own publishing houses (Regnery most prominent among them), its own quasi-academic research institutions (the Heritage Foundation, the American Enterprise Institute), and even its own Popular Front—the Republican Party, important elements of which (the party's congressional and judicial leadership, for example) it has successfully commandeered. These closely linked organizations (the vanguard of the conservative revolution, you might say) compose an entire social world with its own rituals, celebrations, and anniversaries, within which it is possible to live one's entire life. It is a world with its own elaborate system of incentives and sanctions, through which—as Brock discovered—energetic conformity is rewarded with honors and promotions while deviations from the movement line, depending on their seriousness, are punished with anything from mild social disapproval to outright excommunication.

Another echo was the conviction that the mainstream media—the conservative movement called it the "liberal," not the "capitalist," press, but the air of beleaguerment and conspiracy was the same—was little more than an engine of propaganda. Brock saw himself as an engagé journalist, presenting the "other side," willing to shape and select facts in support of an argument but not to make them up. As long as he had a "source," he had no compunctions about reporting things he did not know to be true, but he thought of himself as drawing the line at reporting things he knew to be false. He therefore experienced an epiphany in 1994, when he set out to demolish a competing account of the same events, *Strange Justice: The Selling of Clarence Thomas,* by two *Wall Street Journal* reporters, Jane Mayer and Jill Abramson, who, as it happens, had unfavorably reviewed *The Real Anita Hill* the year before. (Their review appeared in *The New Yorker,* where Mayer is now a staff writer; Abramson is now the Washington bureau chief of the *New York Times.*) Brock and Clarence Thomas's other supporters had portrayed him as having a prudish distaste for pornography; Mayer and Abramson reported that, on the contrary, he was a habitual renter of hard-core videotapes. While looking for a way to refute this, Brock discovered that it was true. Nevertheless, in his review he wrote that there was no evidence—none—"that Thomas had ever rented even one pornographic video, let alone that he was a 'habitual' consumer of pornography."

"When I wrote those words, I knew they were false," Brock confesses in *Blinded by the Right.* He adds, "Perhaps the errors of *The Real Anita Hill* could be attributed to journalistic carelessness, ideological bias, and my misdirected quest for acceptance from a political movement. In the review of *Strange Justice,* however, to protect myself and my tribe from the truth and consequences of our own hypocrisy, smears, falsehoods, and cover-ups, I consciously and actively chose an unethical path. I continued to malign Anita Hill and her liberal supporters as liars. I trashed the professional reputations of two journalists for reporting something I knew was correct."

The video-store lie was where Brock now understands that he touched bottom. It took him several more years to feel his way up through the dark, noxious mass he had done so much to create. His work on the Hillary Clinton book helped him find his moral bearings. In 1996, he debunked a concoction of Clinton-hating fantasies, *Unlimited Access,* whose author, a former F.B.I. agent named Gary Aldrich, had cited Brock as the source for one of his more outlandish claims. In 1997, in an article for *Esquire,* "Confessions of a Right-Wing Hit Man," he broke publicly with the movement, and, though he was still reflexively defending the accuracy of his Anita Hill and troopergate reporting, got fired by the *Spectator.* (The magazine has since faded into oblivion.) Later that year and throughout 1998, he told Sidney Blumenthal, a former Washington correspondent for *The New Yorker* who had become a Clinton aide, everything he knew about the Arkansas Project, and he did the same, on the record, for any reporter who called him. (Joe Conason, of the *New York Observer,* was one of the few who did.) In 2000, he voted for Al Gore.

This book completes Brock's project of purgation. Though he sometimes describes himself in the language of therapy (he writes of "filling my tortured need for friendship and affection and acceptance," etc.), the words he more often uses—words like "greed," "cowardice," "opportunism," "careerism," and "narcissism"—are not exactly drawn from the lexicon of moral relativism. *Blinded by the Right* is a valuable book. It is not an apologia. It is something rarer, and it is something that is owed not only from its author but also from the political cadre he has so spectacularly served and forsaken: an apology.

—*The New Yorker,* March 11, 2002

RUSH IN REHAB

"WE DO NOT NEED General Clark or any of the rest of you liberals. We don't need to change the definition of patriotism in order to conform to the antiwar, hate-America-first radicalism of the Democrat leadership. And that's what this is all about."

In case you don't happen to be a regular listener to *The Rush Limbaugh Show*, the above is a fair sample of the sort of thing the star of the show has been saying lately, or at any rate was saying until a week ago, when he checked in to a drug rehabilitation center. It's not very different from what he's been saying throughout the twenty years he's been talking about politics on the radio. We know the sample is fair, because it was the featured quote last Thursday on the home page of Limbaugh's own Web site, emblazoned in big blue letters right next to the smiling photograph of the patient himself. Limbaugh's target this time was Wesley Clark, because Clark is a leading candidate for the Democratic presidential nomination. As a four-star general, Clark led NATO's first and so far only major military action, which put a stop to ethnic cleansing in Kosovo; as a combat officer in Vietnam, he was severely wounded and awarded the Silver Star, the Bronze Star, and a Purple Heart. The person impugning his patriotism, Limbaugh, sat out the war in Vietnam—though not very comfortably, one must assume, since, as Joe Conason noted in *Salon*, the future scourge of cowards and slackers avoided the draft on account of "a persistent boil on his backside."

Limbaugh is a prime example of what is known as a chicken hawk—a noisy, preening master of the martial art of talking who, back when it was a question of getting anywhere near harm's way for the sake of his country, discovered that he had (as Vice President Cheney once put it, explaining his own absence from the fray) "other priorities." He has now joined another élite corps—the Vice Versa Virtuecrats, they might be called—whose members crusade against "moral relativism" and in favor of absolute standards of right and wrong backed up by draconian punishments while indulging themselves in devilment on the side. Like Newt Gingrich, who vowed to attack Bill Clinton in every speech for hiding his sad little dalliance with Monica Lewinsky while he himself was carrying on a years-long affair with a congressional staffer young enough to be his daughter, and William J. Bennett, who made millions promoting flinty self-discipline while gambling away comparable amounts in Las Vegas fleshpots, Limbaugh took a stern line on demon dope ("If people are violating the law by doing drugs, they ought to be accused and they ought to be convicted and they ought to be sent up") while himself possessing and consuming controlled substances in prodigious quantities. In Limbaugh's case, the difficulty goes beyond an embarrassing inconsistency between professed beliefs and private behavior, because the "problem" he has acknowledged having—being "addicted to prescription pain medication"—correlates strongly with committing acts that the law defines as crimes.

Limbaugh's colleagues in the right-wing jabber industry have come up with a consistent set of talking points in making the case that, in Ann Coulter's words, "Rush's behavior was not all that dissolute." One point is that it was "highly courageous" of Limbaugh to admit his addiction, as Brent Bozell wrote. This would be more persuasive if Limbaugh's admission had come before rather than after his addiction was described in detail in a *National Enquirer* story—a story whose essential outlines have since been confirmed by the non-supermarket press and whose particulars have been disputed by no one. (Limbaugh himself—presumably on the advice of his lawyer, Roy Black, whose other celebrity clients have included William Kennedy Smith and Marv Albert—has said only that the "stories you've heard contain inaccuracies and distortions.") Another point is that Limbaugh's ability to do his job while addicted is a testament to his greatness. "If this is what he's like on painkillers, imagine when he's off them!" Coulter exclaimed, adding, "Whoa! Set him loose once he's gone through detox!"

A third talking point is that Limbaugh is not like other junkies—the bad kind, who use drugs like heroin and cocaine. Sean Hannity, the Fox TV host, discerned a "difference between somebody who, as part of a medical treatment, had these things prescribed and it got out of hand over time, and somebody who is using drugs recreationally." Neal Boortz, an Atlanta-based radio shouter, said on MSNBC, "The addiction happened while he was under a legal regimen of these drugs. That is not at all the way people get addicted to heroin." And G. Gordon Liddy, the Watergate burglar turned pundit, said, "I would distinguish Rush's situation from someone who was a recreational drug user and was caught playing with fire and got addicted— moved up from marijuana to cocaine or something of that sort."

Actually, under federal law there is no distinction between Oxycontin, Limbaugh's reported pill of choice, and drugs like cocaine, methadone, and opiates. All are Schedule II drugs, which have medical uses but a high potential for abuse, and simple possession of any of them is punishable by up to a year's imprisonment. Though Limbaugh may well have been introduced to painkillers via a doctor's prescription, the suggestion that he became addicted to them under a doctor's care is almost certainly false. So is the suggestion that he wasn't taking them "recreationally"—i.e., to get high. The prescribed dose of Oxycontin, one tablet every twelve hours, is usually sufficient to relieve severe pain. The *Enquirer* has Limbaugh purchasing nearly twelve thousand during a four-month period in 2001—enough to soothe his back troubles for sixteen years.

Limbaugh deserves compassion no less (and no more) than any other drug addict. It would be a travesty of justice to lock him up for ingesting chemicals, an activity whose only victim, if any, has been himself. But the four hundred and fifty thousand Americans already in jail for breaking the drug laws also represent a failure of justice, and an even bigger failure of policy. (The United States imprisons more people for drug violations than the European Union imprisons for all causes combined, and the E.U.'s population exceeds the U.S.'s by a hundred million.) By the same token, it would be a travesty if Oxycontin—which has eased the sufferings of millions— were to be demonized as other psychoactive drugs have been demonized. Even if Limbaugh was using his drugs less to relieve pain than to procure pleasure, or if the pain he sought to relieve was less physical than existential, that may have been a problem, but it shouldn't be a crime.

Limbaugh's current sojourn in drug treatment is his third. If he fails again, he should have a fourth chance, and a fifth. Perhaps he will reflect upon the fact that if he weren't quite so lucky—if he were poorer and darker of skin, and if he had been obliged from the start to seek his treatment under the tender auspices of the criminal-justice system—he would already have had his third strike. Such a change of heart seems unlikely; drug rehabilitation comes easier than the political kind. Limbaugh may be a chicken hawk in the war on drugs, but that doesn't mean he deserves to be cannon fodder.

—*The New Yorker,* October 27, 2003

8. THE WAYWARD MEDIA

By the time I was seventeen I knew the names of every newspaper in every big and medium-sized city in the United States, plus the most important ones in Britain, France, Canada, and certain more exotic countries, such as Russia and India. This didn't impress my high school friends, but it proved to be an O.K. ice-breaker once I got to college and started meeting people from all over. Oh, you're from Fresno? What do you think of the *Bee*? From Kingston, Jamaica? You must be a *Daily Gleaner* reader. From Denver? Which do you prefer, the *Post* or the *Rocky Mountain News*?

I loved newspapers almost from the moment I learned to read, the bad ones as much as the good ones, mainly on account of how they looked. I especially liked the look of the Hearst papers—every big city had at least one—because of their eagle logos, chesty slogans ("An American Paper For the American People"), and urgent headlines. I collected newspapers instead of stamps. Their names were evocative as the names of railroads: the *Commercial Appeal* and the *Press-Scimitar* (Memphis), the *Item* and the *Picayune* (New Orleans), the *Evening Bulletin* and the *Public Ledger* (Philadelphia), the *Daily Defender* and the *Inter-Ocean* (Chicago). I read every newspaper history I could get my hands on, especially if it had pictures of old front pages. I devoured the Ballantine paperback edition of *The Press*, A. J. Liebling's collection of his "Wayward Press" columns from *The New Yorker*.

By and by, I became interested in what was actually in newspapers, i.e., news. Anyway, newspapers per se were getting less romantic. They kept dying off like old strip malls until only a handful of cities had more than one, and the ones that were left grew more and more stodgily alike. They became a subset of the media, which in turn seems to be becoming a subset of content. By the time that happened, though, I had already gotten detoured into magazines. I never did become a newspaperman. But a bit of the old love lingers. Television and magazines are all very well, or all very ill, but newspapers are still the fundament. They're like the agricultural surplus. What they do is primary; the rest is secondary. Without them we'd starve to death.

HEADLINE

IF THERE WERE a Pulitzer Prize for headline writing, this year's winner, hands down, would be William Brink, the managing editor of the New York *Daily News*. A little after five on the afternoon of Wednesday, October 29th, Mr. Brink was sitting at the news desk with a pencil in his hand and a chaotic heap of copy paper in front of him. As usual, he was trying to come up with something snappy for the next morning's front page, and he was batting around ideas with the editors and reporters who happened to be within earshot. At the *News*, the main headline is called the 120, because it's usually in large, 120-point block letters. When there's an unusually big story, as there was that day—President Ford had ruled out any federal help for the city until after a default—the headline is sometimes set in 144-point type. With two lines of eleven "units" each to play with, Mr. Brink would have to keep it terse. He wrote:

FORD REFUSES
AID TO CITY

A bit dull, and, anyway, FORD REFUSES was a half unit too long. He tried

FORD SAYS NO
TO CITY AID

That fitted, but it was still mundane. "What I wanted to do," Mr. Brink told us a couple of days later, "was to get across the idea that Ford hadn't just declined to help us; he had, in effect, consigned us to the scrap heap. He was cutting us adrift, sending us down the drain."

Then Mr. Brink wrote two words on his sheet of copy paper:

DROP DEAD

That was short, and sweet besides. Above, he wrote:

FORD TO CITY:

With the spaces, the colon, and the "I" counted as a half unit each, it came out to exactly eleven units. There was general approbation around the news desk. A grizzled deskman said, "Sounds like the old *Daily News.*" Michael O'Neill, the editor of the *News,* came out of his office, looked at the headline, laughed, and said, "Terrific." By the time people were getting to work on Thursday, Mr. Brink's headline had been reproduced on two million copies of the *News* and had been seen by every ambulatory literate or semiliterate in town. By Friday morning, it had been held up before the cameras by commentators on all three television networks. The wire services sent photographs of it, which appeared in hundreds of papers around the world. Last week, both *Time* and *Newsweek* displayed it prominently in their stories on New York's woes. It was, without question, the most successful headline the *News* has ever run.

Of course, headlines sell no bonds. As the saying goes (allowing for inflation), that headline and fifty cents will get you a ride on the subway. But morale hasn't been all that high in this city of late, and Mr. Brink's contribution cheered people up all over town. It was pugnacious, intemperate, outraged, biased, and pithy—a superb distillation of the New York–cabdriver idiom. The headline in that day's *Times* (FORD, CASTIGATING CITY, ASSERTS HE'D VETO FUND GUARANTEE; OFFERS BANKRUPTCY BILL) was, by comparison, a genteel, leisurely essay on urban finance.

All this started us thinking about *News* headlines in general. We've noticed a number of patterns over the years. For example, the *News* believes there's no such thing as a public figure with a name that can't be shortened. This is a world in which Brez, Henry K, Hubie, and Rocky are movers and shakers, as Khrush, DeG, and McGov used to be. Politicians with "funny" names, especially foreigners, run other risks. When a French premier of pre-DeG days started to lose political support, the headline in the *News* was

PFLIMLIN'S CHANCES
GROWING PFLIMSIER

When the topic is murder, as it so often is in *News* headlines, the preferred verb is "to slay." A psychiatrist's nefarious plans engendered this headline:

SHRINK HELD IN
PLOT TO SLAY 3

Crimes involving theft would be almost unheadlineable without the use of the letter "G," which stands for "grand," meaning a thousand dollars. Thus:

SOPHIA ROBBED
OF 600G GEMS

If the predicate is interesting or exciting enough, the subject can be dispensed with entirely in a *News* headline. Nevertheless, the verb has to agree with its absent noun, whether that noun is singular, as in

AXES WIFE, SONS
AND HANGS SELF

or plural, as in

BARE 21G DEAL
BY SCHOOL EXEC

Of course, this sometimes gives rise to confusing mock imperatives, as in

HURL ROCKS AT
NIXON IN CALIF.

Unlike the *Times*, which is constrained by the self-discipline of impartiality, the *News* feels free to indulge a sense of identification with its readers in its headlines. When Prohibition was repealed, the *News'* headline was YOU CAN DRINK! When the subway fare jumped a dime to thirty cents, the headline was an enormous OUCH! with a photograph of a token in place of the letter "O." This was the tradition in which Mr. Brink was working when he fashioned his masterpiece. We shook him warmly by the hand when we dropped in at the News Building the other day to congratulate him. He is a tall, big-boned man with a deeply lined, slightly flushed face. He has been with the *News* since 1970, before which he was a senior editor at *Newsweek,* and he has been managing editor for about a year. We asked him if he'd written any other one-twenties he considered noteworthy. He thought for a moment, and said, "We did one in Chinese when Nixon was over there. Let's see." He rummaged in a cabinet and pulled out a *News.* The headline (in English) was NIXON IN CHINA, and there were Chinese characters running down one side of the page. "We got a calligrapher to do this," Mr. Brink said. "It says, 'Welcome, Nixon,' or so we were led to believe. I got worried at the last minute, though. I started thinking maybe the calligrapher was pulling a joke on us. So I took it around to some of the Chinese restaurants on Second Avenue. I'd just go up to a guy and flash it. We didn't run it until I got three Chinese waiters to say 'Welcome, Nixon.'"

—*The New Yorker,* November 17, 1975

THE BIG TUNE-OUT

ON MONDAY, AUGUST 20TH, 1984, the Republican National Convention will be called to order in Dallas. On that first day, the delegates will hear from, among others, Frank J. Fahrenkopf, Jr., the shadowy, efficient chairman of the Republican National Committee; LeGree (can that really be his name?) Daniels, chairman of something called the National Black Republican Council; Representative Phil Gramm, the Texas apostate; Jeane J. Kirkpatrick, the former Democrat who serves as President Reagan's ambassador to the United Nations; Senator Howard Baker, a probable candidate for president in 1988; Margaret Heckler, the secretary of health and human services; Representative Guy Vander Jagt, 1980's grandiloquent keynoter; and this year's keynoter, Katherine D. Ortega, signer of dollar bills and treasurer of the United States.

Americans are entitled to feel some curiosity about each of these people. But those citizens who tune in to the network television coverage of the convention are likely to see and hear only two of them: Ms. Kirkpatrick, who undoubtedly will give those she regards as the softies in her erstwhile party pure unshirted hell; and Ms. Ortega, whose keynote address someone is sure to dub the Treasurer's Report. The rest of the television audience's time is likely to be taken up by a succession of already overexposed network correspondents and anchormen commenting on the predictability of it all and reporting to us and to each other that, in essence, "there's no story here."

"There's no story here." These happen to be the exact words used by a

network news executive—specifically, David Burke, a vice president of ABC
News and a very intelligent man—to describe the Democratic Convention
in San Francisco. Mr. Burke's contention is the first half of the case the networks have against the conventions—the other half being the ratings, which
some network spokesmen have tried to bathe in an aura of plebiscitary
democratic legitimacy. The network executives speak of low ratings for the
conventions (though in fact the ratings have remained fairly steady ever
since 1948, and have even gone up slightly since 1972). They do not yet dare
to apply this standard to the president's State of the Union Address, but that
day may come.

The bottom line, to use a phrase that is all too apt, is that there has been
less network coverage of this year's conventions than of any year's since 1948.
In 1980 the three networks devoted a total of about a hundred hours altogether to the two conventions. This year the time will be less than half that.
In San Francisco, ABC brazenly cut away from the Democrats' second
night to broadcast part of a rerun of "Hart to Hart," a show that is not
about Gary and Lee. NBC wasn't crass enough to go that far this time, but
NBC has made it clear that it intends to curtail its effort substantially next
time. CBS, to its credit, is arguing against the trend toward ever more
truncated coverage; but in the crunch, it will probably not resist. The Public Broadcasting System, which is more and more coming to resemble an
electronic airline magazine, disgraced itself thoroughly. Although C-Span,
the admirable cable-satellite public affairs network, had offered the system
its uninterrupted gavel-to-gavel podium coverage free of charge, not a
single one of the major public TV stations in the top ten markets accepted,
according to a survey by Bob Brewin of the *Village Voice*. The only real
bright spots were C-Span itself and the Cable News Network, which did
the kind of job the big networks used to do. Come 1988, it's entirely possible that the three big networks will "cover" the conventions via late-night
specials and occasional brief interruptions in their regular entertainment
schedules.

The contention that there was "no story" in San Francisco—and that
there is no story in Dallas—makes sense only if one begins with the assumption that the only question worth asking is the identity of the presidential and vice-presidential nominees. That is a singularly unimaginative
idea of what an American political convention is about. Granted, the role
of the convention has changed over the years. The system of primaries,

combined with campaign expenses so crushing that candidates are quickly squeezed out of the race, almost guarantees a first-ballot nomination known well in advance. Thanks to modern communications, the work of maneuver and compromise that used to occupy the convention now begins immediately after the last primary. But no story? Ridiculous. There were hundreds—no, thousands—of stories in San Francisco. All you had to do was look.

Gathered in Moscone Center were a couple of hundred members of Congress, nearly half the U.S. senators, the majority of the governors, and just about all the big-city mayors in America. With them were ex-cabinet officers, high-powered lobbyists, power brokers, pollsters, and political consultants; also, dozens of nationally known political writers, columnists, even novelists like James A. Michener and Mary McCarthy; also, representatives of just about every organized group in the country, from American Indians to rural gays; also, just plain prominent citizens from every state in the Union; also, assorted celebrities like Margot Kidder, Warren Beatty, and young Ron Reagan, on assignment from *Playboy*. And—also not least—television's own star correspondents and commentators. This astonishing assemblage of people had gathered in one gigantic, noisy room, talking with each other, gossiping about each other, scheming against each other, joking with each other, and, when things got dull, looking up at the podium, where there was always somebody one had heard of but usually never seen trying to give the speech of his or her life.

No story? Even leaving aside the political "angle," this gaudy, excessive, profoundly American scene is a TV talent coordinator's dream. To put it in terms a network executive might be able to understand, an American political convention is a mammoth combination of the *The Tonight Show,* the evening news, *Dynasty, Queen for a Day, People's Court, This Is Your Life, Saturday Night Live,* and the biggest *Phil Donahue Show* imaginable.

In fact, the only thing more amazing than the convention scene itself was the networks' ability to turn it into dull television. The opening night of the Democrats' gathering is a case in point. CBS and ABC deigned to go to the podium only twice, for the speech by former president Jimmy Carter and for Governor Mario Cuomo's keynote address. NBC also broadcast part of Representative Mo Udall's introduction of Mr. Carter. Apart from floor interviews, which varied widely in interest and appositeness, the networks devoted the rest of their time to the talking heads of various network per-sonalities, many of whom affected a world-weary cynicism.

Only the floor interviews gave some hint of the roiling human bazaar on the convention floor. And although there was a succession of interesting, even fascinating, other speakers on the podium, the viewer got no clue of that. Is it not possible that the TV audience might have appreciated a sample of New York Mayor Ed Koch's twenty-minute rant against cocaine push-ers? Or a taste of the talks by two women politicians who were considered for the vice-presidential nomination, Mayor Dianne Feinstein of San Fran-cisco and Governor Martha Layne Collins of Kentucky? Or a glimpse of the platform styles of Tom Bradley, Charles Manatt, Alan Cranston, Richard Hatcher, Julian Bond, Patricia Schroeder, Bill Clinton, or Coretta Scott King? Might it not have been worth at least mentioning, in view of all the talk about regional splits in the Democratic Party, that Governor Cuomo was introduced by his Texas counterpart, Mark White?

What television does really well, and what only television can do, is to show what is happening, as it is happening. The coverage of the conven-tions demonstrates that the network executives do not understand that their medium is best when it mediates least. Why else would they devote so much time to rambling colloquies between correspondents and anchors? These colloquies are not really journalism. They are proto-journalism, the equivalent of conversations between a newspaper's editors and its reporters. They are not the story or even the raw material for the story, but simply the editor's way of finding out if a story exists.

Showing such stuff when there is something real going on is a symptom of TV's narcissism. Another symptom is the complaint, voiced by some TV executives, that the conventions are no longer worth covering because they have become "media events." This complaint recalls the classic definition of "chutzpah": the man who murders his parents and then demands mercy on the ground that he is an orphan. Of course the planners of conventions try to attract TV coverage, but that is not a convention's sole or even main rai-son d'être, at least as far as the participants are concerned. Tens of thousands of busy people do not travel halfway across the country just to serve as a stu-dio audience for a television program—as the networks, which are obliged to employ shills to press game show tickets on reluctant tourists, ought to understand.

Still, the "media event" theme was one the networks harped on in San

Francisco, constantly noting as news the party's effort to manipulate them. On the third night of the Democratic Convention, for example, NBC's Roger Mudd reported that the party had asked the networks to move up their coverage by a half hour, but that the networks had refused. Mr. Mudd reported why the request had been made—so that George McGovern's speech, Gary Hart's address, and Walter Mondale's nomination could all occur during "prime time"—but not why it had been turned down, which was the other half of the story. There were no badgering interviews with network executives to get the answer to that one.

An ABC producer named Jeff Gralnick, perhaps by way of justifying his network's disgraceful performance, has been going around saying that the conventions are "dinosaurs." Leave aside the fact that the dinosaur, due to its great size and extreme rarity, is a most interesting beast. Is it really the conventions that are stumbling toward extinction? Or is it the networks? The network executives' inability to understand that the conventions are interesting is a confession of massive stupidity and lack of imagination. A network that can interrupt a political convention to show a rerun of an old detective serial thereby announces that it is ready for the boneyard. The networks are begging to be replaced—by videocassette recorders for entertainment, and, for news, by smaller, more maneuverable, less cynical, less star-choked cable operations.

No story? With all due respect, and not much is due, that is not for network executives to decide. The convention of a major American political party is not just another news item to be covered or not as some executive sees fit. Like it or not, the televised political convention has become part of the unwritten constitution of the United States. Do "only" half the people watch conventions? Well, only half the people vote in elections. No doubt both institutions have their problems, but abolition is not the answer for either of them.

No story? But that is a journalistic judgment. Somehow we suspect that the decision to miniaturize convention coverage is being made on other grounds. Cutting back will allow the networks to make a good deal more money; but that has always been the case. Why do the networks suddenly feel free to indulge themselves? Might it not have something to do with the *zeitgeist*—with the I've-got-mine moral atmosphere that has coincided with the rule of the Reagan administration? We have a government that has glorified the market, sanctified greed, devalued social goods, and legitimized contempt for public life. Is it any wonder the networks are insolent? There is a rumor that ABC has decided to reduce its coverage of the Republicans to an hour a night. Perhaps the other networks will follow suit. If it happens, a wee chicken will have come home to roost.

—Editorial, *The New Republic*, September 3, 1984

ENTERTAINMENT FOR MEN

I'D APPRECIATE IT if the following recommendation is greeted with a minimum of whistles, elbow digs, and Groucho Marx eyebrow flaps. Thank you. Now: check out *Penthouse* this month. It's interesting and, in a reversal of the usual alibi for buying magazines of this genre, more for the pictures than for the articles. Guccione's boys have had the astute if obvious idea of engaging the services of Debra Murphree, the New Orleans prostitute whose trysts with Jimmy Swaggart got that aptly named evangelist in a world of trouble. In exchange for, presumably, some multiple of her usual twenty-dollar fee, Murphree has told all to *Penthouse*'s team of crack reporters, who have spread the results over seven full pages of dense print. Their revelations leave unchanged the broad outlines of what has already been reported in thousands of family newspapers. But the highly specific details do flesh out a tale of degradation, hypocrisy, greed, furtive lust, revenge, and pathos so stern in its relentless trajectory to destruction that no novelist would dare invent it (except that Sinclair Lewis already did). More to the point, Debra Murphree has also posed for a series of photographs in which she reproduces the pornographic (*Penthouse*'s word, and it is exact) poses it was Swaggart's custom to ask her to assume. These are published in a sixteen-page section that is sealed shut by a perforated strip, thus forcing the casual drugstore peruser to lay out $4.50 if he (or she) wishes to gratify his (or her) curiosity—a clever innovation in magazine marketing, one that no doubt will be widely imitated.

The pictures show what Swaggart paid, first cheaply and then dearly, to see. Their chief interest, however, is not in what they have to say about Swaggart but in what they have to say about *Penthouse*. They are a devastating critique of the magazine in which they appear. The critique is clearest in the contrast between the pictures of Debra Murphree and the pictures of other naked women elsewhere in the magazine. The positions assumed by Murphree and by (for example) the "Pet of the Month" are identical. But while the Pet appears in lush color and is bathed in soft, warm light, Murphree has been photographed in harsh black and white in a brutal style reminiscent of the work of Diane Arbus. The Pet luxuriates on pastel satin sheets amid backgrounds of flowers and gilded antiques. Murphree lies on the coarse linen of a crummy motel bed in the light of an unshaded bulb hanging from a pasteboard ceiling. The Pet's skin is perfect and her makeup glistens. The pictures of Murphree deliberately emphasize her body hair, the pimples on her backside, the crude "Debbie" tattoo on her arm. The relation between the two sets of pictures is made explicit in a quote, supposedly a remark made by Swaggart to Murphree, that introduces the sealed section: "Pull your panties up your crack like a magazine I've seen. . . ." The basic business purpose of magazines like *Penthouse*—which was also Murphree's business purpose, at least with her most famous client—is the provision of an aid to male masturbation in exchange for cash. What is unusual is that this should be so forthrightly acknowledged by one of the two leading "respectable" skin magazines, and that the acknowledgment should be in a context that so strongly stresses the sordid, degrading, and exploitative aspect of the transaction.

Playboy, the other of the Big Two stroke books, also publishes a series of black-and-white photographs this month. These pictures too are of a naked woman. But the aim of the *Playboy* pictures—of Cindy Crawford, a beautiful *Vogue* model, taken by Herb Ritts, a well-known fashion photographer—is the opposite of that of the *Penthouse* ones. Where *Penthouse* uses black-and-white because it makes the pictures raw, ugly, and "realistic," *Playboy* uses black-and-white because it makes the pictures refined, pretty, and "artistic." *Playboy* has been trying for some years now to distance itself from the masturbatory nexus that called it and its competitors (notably *Penthouse*) into being. Hugh Hefner, the founder, is in semiretirement in California, and the now diminished empire is run out of the Playboy Building in Chicago by his daughter Christie, an intelligent woman of proclaimed feminist sympathies. Presumably as a result, *Playboy* has dropped the gassy blather about "philosophy," the ratings of porn videos, and the photos of Hef with pipe and bathrobe surrounded by off-duty Bunnies. *Playboy*'s pictures draw the line a bit closer than *Penthouse*'s, and the copy accompanying them is chock-a-block with girl-next-door banalities. (This month's Playmate likes rainy days, hates cruelty to animals.) *Playboy* tries to show its new attitude by publishing admiring articles about serious, accomplished women. All this is commendable enough in its tiny way. The problem is that because the magazine is no longer so stupid as to believe in itself and its mission, it has no spirit. Its smile is fixed, its eyes glassy, its cheeriness forced.

THE BIG SWAGGART-MURPHREE takeout was *Penthouse*'s revenge against *Playboy* for cornering the market, some months ago, on Jessica Hahn, the "church secretary" who defenestrated Jim Bakker. The synergistic parallels between the Bakker-Swaggart and *Playboy-Penthouse* rivalries are of course delicious, but the two magazines displayed their trophies in very different ways. *Playboy* chose to show Hahn in the Playmate style: wholesome outdoor backgrounds, frilly half-open dresses, flattering poses, airbrushed Kodachrome skin. Hahn is now installed in the Playboy Mansion West, reportedly recuperating from cosmetic surgery in preparation for another photo session. *Playboy*'s pictures of Hahn implicitly played to Bakker's fantasies, while *Penthouse*'s pictures of Murphree implicitly condemned Swaggart's (even as the rest of the magazine exemplified them). *Playboy* turned Hahn into a Stepford wife, a replicant who by now surely does love rainy days and hate cruelty to animals. *Penthouse* gave Murphree a check but left her in the gutter. *Playboy*'s hypocrisy was timorous and subtle; *Penthouse*'s is heedless and blatant. It's hard to know which approach is "preferable." As Gary Hart once said, let the people decide.

—Washington Diarist, *The New Republic*, July 4, 1988

CROSS TALK

ONE OF THE THINGS that has made local television news less and less tolerable in recent years is the spread of "crosstalk" or "backchat." This is the practice of having stilted exchanges between the main newsreader, called the anchorperson, and a reporter who has just finished reciting a story. The idea, I am told by friends who work in television, is (a) to please viewers by humanizing the little figures on the screen and (b) to add to the "credibility" of the anchorperson by demonstrating that he or she is "involved with the news" and "in charge." We see the reporter in his trench coat, standing in front of a building, holding his Eyewitness News Team microphone. "And so the mood here remains grim," the reporter is saying. "At city hall, I'm News Seven's Bob Bobson. Dave?" "Good report, Bob," says the anchorperson, swiveling his chair to address a monitor on which Bob's face may be seen, "but what would you say is the bottom line moodwise down there?" "Well, Dave, one highly placed source I talked to described it this way: nothing short of grim blah blah blah," natters Bob, as Dave nods sagely and such non-braindead viewers as may be watching think, "Please. Just give us the goddamn news."

The crosstalk virus has now infected the networks, the "CBS Evening News" being the chief carrier. I have thought long and hard about why this wretched practice is so peculiarly offensive. It's not just because the sight of Dan Rather being "spontaneous" is so excruciating. It's because the editorial work is supposed to be done *before* the program goes on the air. If whatever Dan is asking Leslie about is so important, if it's worthy of thirty or forty precious seconds of the twenty minutes CBS allots to summarizing everything that happened in the world that day, then why didn't Dan (who takes a screen credit as "managing editor" of his program) tell Leslie to put it in her story ahead of time? And if it isn't important, why is he asking her about it in the first place? I'm not sure which possibility is worse: that these embarrassing exchanges are staged, or that they're actually spontaneous. If they're staged, they insult our intelligence and compromise the integrity of the broadcast, such as it is. If they're spontaneous, they waste our time and that of CBS News, which even after recent cutbacks probably has enough competent people to fill a twenty-minute show with prepared material designed to communicate a maximum of information in a minimum of time. I mean, really. If newspapers treated their readers with the contempt television crosstalkers lavish on their viewers, then the *New York Times* would stop putting itself to the bother of writing stories. They'd just Xerox E. J. Dionne's notebook and give us that, along with a transcript of the afternoon story conference.

"WE ARE NOT gray grains of oatmeal in a porridge of privilege," said Lloyd Bentsen in his acceptance speech at the Democratic Convention. Just so. Also, we are not cowflops of complacency in a meadow of mediocrity. We are not quasars of querulousness in a galaxy of greed. We are not pousse-cafés of presumption in a cocktail lounge of cronyism. We are not BMWs of braggadocio on a parkway of plutocracy. We are not courtesans of callousness in a massage parlor of mendacity. We are not sun-dried tomatoes of sanctimony in a warm salad of wealth.

IT'S TOO BAD there isn't some way the Democratic Party could take obviously talented people and give them safe seats in the national legislature, the way they do in England. Because if there were, then Garrison Keillor would be senator from Minnesota and eventually, perhaps, president of the United States. I was never a *Prairie Home Companion* moonie, though I did like the bits where Keillor talked about Lake Wobegon, which reminded me of Jean Shepard's old radio monologues. I saw Keillor on *Nightline* a few years ago. I forget why he was being interviewed, but he handled Ted with a calm sagacity that was at once regal and democratic. I remember thinking, "This guy's Lincolnesque. Stick him in the White House." Anyway, what I'm building up to here is to note that the planners of the Democratic Convention did a good thing when they put Keillor in charge of the national anthem at the opening session. As we all know, the usual practice is for some overmiked diva or pop star to belt out the song with full orchestral accompaniment while everybody else stands there hoping not to go deaf. What Keillor did was to have a little group of elementary school kids sing it in wavering voices to the accompaniment of just a piano. The result was that everybody in the hall sang along in full voice, which for a moment turned the convention into a secular congregation. I normally hate group singing, but this time I'm convinced it established at the outset the feeling of unity and fellowship that ultimately became the dominant mood. I move a vote of thanks to Mr. Keillor.

I NOTICE A sudden outbreak of newspaper interest in the question of whether it is advisable to give money to panhandlers. The *New York Times* had a front-page story about this the other day, followed by an op-ed piece in which an expert argued that these people would be better off in soup kitchens or city-run flophouses, that giving money only encourages them, and that anyway they'll probably just spend it on booze or drugs. I don't find these arguments persuasive. I've had a "policy" on panhandlers for many years, one I'd like to "share" with perplexed readers. My policy is this: I always give a quarter and wish the person good luck. Always. No exceptions. That way I don't have to think about it. And the fact that my response is automatic and impersonal preserves both my dignity and the panhandler's. I view the transaction as an entitlement program. As a method of income redistribution, it is more efficient than any other form of public or private beneficence, because there are no administrative costs, no paperwork, and no delays. New York's Mayor Ed Koch, asked to comment on the panhandling crisis, advised people who feel guilty to go to a psychiatrist. But if you have a policy, guilt doesn't enter into it. Also, an hour with a psychiatrist costs the same as giving quarters to four hundred panhandlers. When I first evolved my policy, I only gave to people older than I was. If they were younger, I'd tell them, "Get a job." Now they're almost all younger than I am, and anyhow I've come to realize that panhandling *is* a job. It may not be a "productive" job, but then neither is asking redundant questions on TV.

—Washington Diarist, *The New Republic*, August 22, 1988

PRESS PASS

Manchester, New Hampshire

WELL, THE RESULTS ARE IN, and Pat Buchanan is the man of the hour. Good news for Democrats, Falangists, and ambitious ex-speechwriters-*cum*-media motormouths. Bad news for democrats, the White House, and ethnic groups ending in "ooze," such as Jews and Zulus. On the other side, we have a fwunt wunnah. The Tsongas victory shows that moderate Republicanism is alive and well, but only in the Democratic Party, and probably only in New England. Tsongas is not likely to travel well. After his free fall in the polls the week before the voting, Clinton has landed on his feet. If scandals are spirits, Clinton knows how to hold his liquor. He's still standing, but can he walk the line?

AS ALWAYS, the weekend before the vote attracted two types of media pyromaniacs. First, visiting firemen—anchorpersons, big-time columnists, talk-show heavies from Washington and New York, TV guys from Japan and other hard currency countries. Second, visiting firedogs: notebook-bearing Dalmatians, with or without visible means of support, who can't help jumping and barking when the bell sounds for the quadrennial conflagration. Persons in these two categories (I'm in the second) are well advised to avoid talking to voters, whose views, randomly solicited, are as misleading as those of taxi drivers. The electorate's wisdom is collective, not individual. As a last-minute visitor, one is better off confining one's canvassing to one's fellow hacks, especially those whose judgment one respects and who have been in the state for a while. One can do this on the fringes of campaign "events," such as rallies and shopping mall walkthroughs, and at the atriumlike bar of the Wayfarer, a hotel located unpicturesquely in the middle of a big parking lot south of Manchester. This is what I did, and I was astonished.

What astonished me was this. The group of people I'll call The Press—by which I mean several dozen political journalists of my acquaintance, many of whom the Buchanan administration may someday round up on suspicion of having Democratic or even liberal sympathies—was of one mind as the season's first primary campaign shuddered toward its finish. I asked each of them, one after another, this question: If you were a New Hampshire Democrat, whom would you vote for? The answer was always the same; and the answer was always Clinton. In this group, in my experience, such unanimity is unprecedented. It wasn't this way in 1968, when The Press was bitterly divided between Eugene McCarthy and Robert Kennedy; or in '72, when most liked McGovern but some preferred Muskie; or in '76, when Carter, Udall, Harris, and Brown all had their Press partisans; or in '80, when nobody liked anybody, but more disfavored Ted Kennedy than disfavored Carter; or in '84, when the Mondale-Hart split was about even; or in '88, when Babbitt nosed out Gore, Gephardt, and Dukakis in the informal Press primary. Obviously, Clinton is not yet the people's choice. He may never be. But he is The Press's. Why?

Only a little of it, I think, is due to guilt at the way the press (with the unhappy cooperation of The Press) trashed Clinton in the Flowers and draft affairs. Somewhat more is due to the middling qualities of the other declared candidates (though Harkin is the only one who seems to be actively disliked) and to Mario Cuomo's absence from the race (though the disgust with Cuomo, especially among those who had longed for him to run, has mushroomed of late). Almost none is due to calculations about Clinton's being "electable"; even those who think the political damage to Clinton is already fatal admitted they would have voted for him had they been New Hampshire Democrats. And none at all is due to belief in Clinton's denials in the Flowers business, because no one believes these denials. No, the real reason members of The Press like Clinton is simple, and surprisingly uncynical: they think he would make a very good, perhaps a great, president. Several told me they were convinced that Clinton is the most talented presidential candidate they have ever encountered, J.F.K. included. Above all, they are awed by his fortitude (his wife's, too). In New Hampshire he has walked through the valley of political death with voice uncracked, composure unruffled, energy undiminished, humor intact. He has shown no sign of self-pity or bitterness, which means either that he feels none, which would be impressive, or that he is capable of an utterly convincing bluff, which would be more so (and is a highly useful quality in a leader). The integrity of Clinton's private character, judges The Press, may be doubted; the strength of his public character, after this past month, may not be.

It works this way. Your typical member of The Press, call him Joe, respects what he himself cannot do. More precisely, Joe respects what he cannot imagine himself doing. Now Joe can just barely imagine, in his heart of hearts, that if he really, really tried, he could do the job of being a candidate as well as (for example) Bob Kerrey does it—could give as good a speech, could answer questions as knowledgeably, could campaign as vigorously. Joe cannot, however, imagine himself doing the job as well as Clinton, not in a million years; nor can Joe imagine himself standing up to Clinton's ordeal with Clinton's equanimity. Kerrey, unlike Joe, is a glamorous war hero, but Kerrey is also a normal guy—which is to say, he is ruled by irony and self-consciousness. Kerrey, like Joe, is aware of the ever-present danger of seeming ridiculous by seeming too serious. Clinton is different. Clinton can speak the language of irony when he chooses to, but he has no fear of earnestness. There are no visible gaps in his knowledge of public policy or his ability to expound his views lucidly. His gregariousness is as protean as Hubert Humphrey's used to be, with the difference that Clinton always seems interested in what the other person has to say, too. To all appearances, Clinton likes everybody he meets—a quality that may have something to do with his troubles—and he is capable, given the chance, of getting almost anyone to like him.

Few reporters think there was any real alternative to covering the Flowers imbroglio the way it was in fact covered. But this is not to say that journalists would not have professional reasons for welcoming a Clinton victory. No one likes the tangle of tabloid sleaze and invasion of privacy in which reporters have found themselves enmeshed during this campaign. But if the voters were to rise above the muck the respectable press, in the future, would have a powerful argument for doing likewise.

—New Hampshire Diarist, *The New Republic*, March 9, 1992

TOPLESS TABLOIDS OF GOTHAM

NORA (Myrna Loy): I read where you were shot
five times in the tabloids.

NICK (William Powell): It's not true.
He didn't come anywhere near my tabloids.
—*The Thin Man (1934)*

ASIDE FROM CERTAIN subatomic particles and unrefrigerated egg-salad sandwiches, few physical objects are more ephemeral than a tabloid newspaper. A tabloid is not a newspaper of record: the past is too far behind to worry about, the future too far ahead. Yesterday matters only insofar as it supplies copy. The day before yesterday is history—i.e., bunk. Tomorrow never comes, because by the time it does it's today. Today is the day that counts, because today's paper, and only today's paper, is on the newsstands. And today's paper, for our purposes, means today's tabloids—the New York *Daily News* and the *New York Post*. They're fighting it out, today and every day, for the hearts and minds of readers—the kind of readers who like to read fast or have to read slow. Their war may be fought in an eternal present, but it has been going on for a long time, on a battlefield soaked with the ink of newspapers living and dead. The casualties have been heavy. The combatants carry old scars and new wounds.

Let's define our term. The word "tabloid" originated in 1884, when a

British pharmaceutical firm registered it as a trademark for a medicinal powder that had been compressed into tablet form. It's a word that has seen a lot of service lately, having become a catchall for a whole range of related developments, mostly in the "media"—the ubiquity of trashy "reality" television, the crumbling of barriers between news and entertainment, the obsession with celebrity—but also in society at large. According to *Vanity Fair*, the 1990s is "the Tabloid Decade"—that is, the decade during which we have been told more about Marv Albert, Pamela Anderson, John Wayne Bobbitt, Joey Buttafuoco, Hugh Grant, Tonya Harding, Pee-wee Herman, O. J. Simpson, and, of course, Bill Clinton and his big-haired supporting cast than, strictly speaking, we needed to know. So there is tabloidism in the sense of a general coarsening of public life. There is tabloid television, as exemplified by programs like *Hard Copy* and *The Jerry Springer Show*, which are "tabloids" only metaphorically, the way *20/20* and *60 Minutes* are "magazines." And there are supermarket weeklies, like the *National Enquirer*—printed equivalents of the salt-rich offerings in the snack-food aisle. These phenomena are all very well (or all very ill), and they are descended etymologically from tabloids. But a real tabloid is something else.

A real tabloid is a daily newspaper. Its pages are "tabloid size"—that is, half the size of the pages of a "broadsheet," like the *New York Times* or the *Wall Street Journal*. But not every tabloid-size newspaper is a tabloid newspaper, as a glance at the *Christian Science Monitor* will confirm. A real tabloid is a specific thing, with specific qualities. The front page (sometimes distressingly called the cover) looks like the top half of an eye chart. It's dominated by a single huge headline in block type, plus some smaller headlines ("reefers," because they refer to stories inside the paper) and a photograph or two (the more dramatic the better). The back page is a front page, too, but about sports. Inside is a version of what appears in other daily newspapers, but with bigger headlines, shorter paragraphs, tough-guy columnists, and heavy emphasis on sensation, sports, and entertainment. The writing, at its best, is as direct and riveting as a ransom note.

The tabloid newspaper is an artifact of early- and mid-twentieth-century urbanism. Sixty years ago, three dozen American cities had one or two or even three of them. Apart from the *Philadelphia Daily News* and the *Boston Herald*, the American tabloid of the classical type is dead—except in New York, the last city in the land where the newsstands are crowded with newsprint. More than thirty dailies are published here, including trade and foreign language papers. And only in New York have not one but two heavy-weight tabloids stayed on their feet, wobbly but still game, to duke it out for the entertainment of the crowd. The *Daily News* has gone a little soft around the middle, and its footwork may have grown sluggish and its speech slurred, but it has stolid, sullen strength, and it still has the weight advantage. The *Post* has dazzling moves and not an ounce of fat, and it knows how to taunt an opponent, but its mouth is bigger than its fists, and there is some question whether it can go the distance. Neither was born yesterday. They've both been in training for this bout for a long time.

I N 1918, an artillery officer in the United States Army, Captain Joseph Medill Patterson, of Chicago, had a long talk in London with Lord North-cliffe, a Fleet Street press baron who was already well on his way to becoming the model for Lord Zinc in Evelyn Waugh's *Scoop*. Northcliffe had started the world's first real tabloid, the London *Daily Mirror*, in 1903. (It's still going strong, though Rupert Murdoch's much younger addition to the British genre, the *Sun*, is going a lot stronger.) Patterson, then in his late thirties, was the co-boss—with his cousin, contemporary, and comrade in arms Robert R. McCormick—of their family's newspaper, the *Chicago Tribune*. Captain Patterson and Colonel McCormick (they would be known by their titles of military rank for the rest of their lives) got along well enough, but it had been apparent for some time that the *Tribune* wasn't big enough for both of them. For one thing, their politics were incompatible. McCormick was a conservative, to say the least, and Patterson had been a prominent radical. (He had written popular "proletarian" novels and plays, and in 1908 campaigned for Eugene V. Debs, the Socialist candidate for president.) Patterson's 1918 visit with Lord Northcliffe crystallized an idea he had already been mulling over—that once the war was concluded he would see if he couldn't start a tabloid of his own, in New York, and match Northcliffe's success.

With seed money borrowed from the *Tribune*, an editorial staff of about two dozen, and spare floor space and off-hours press time rented from the New York *Evening Mail*, the maiden issue of Captain Patterson's folly hit the streets on Thursday, June 26, 1919. It was pretty bad. Its name—the *Illustrated Daily News*—made it sound like a genteel rotogravure; its headline type was delicate; its photographs were framed by fancy filigrees. But the paper got better fast. Within a year, the "Illustrated" had been dropped from the title, lending it a virile, almost biblical simplicity: give us this day our *Daily News.* A line cut of a camera—a Speed Graphic—was put between the words *Daily* and *News,* and a slogan was added underneath: NEW YORK'S PICTURE NEWSPAPER. Around the pictures themselves, no more curlicues: instead, thin rules that made them look sharp and crisp. A new headline display type was black and postery. Inside, the stories were short and punchy, and there were plenty of homely, wholesome features for the working-class families who were the *News*'s target readers: "Bright Sayings of Children"; "The Most Embarrassing Moment of My Life"; "The Inquiring Photographer," who every day asked half a dozen men and women in the street for their opinions about something; "Today's Riddle"; a fiction serial; and comic strips, like "Gasoline Alley" and "Harold Teen," that were salted throughout the paper instead of being grouped together on one page.

By the end of 1923, the *News* was selling over seven hundred thousand copies a day—more than any other New York paper, including William Randolph Hearst's *Journal.* The following year, Hearst started his own New York tabloid, unoriginally called the *Daily Mirror,* and Bernarr Macfadden, an eccentric bodybuilder and natural-health cultist who had made a fortune with *True Story* and other popular magazines, launched the *Evening Graphic.* The *Graphic* was a real pioneer of tabloidism, as distinct from the tabloid newspaper as such. It contained scarcely any news at all, with the exception of stories elaborating, often quite imaginatively, on events in the fields of crime, sex, celebrities, and entertainment. It captured—and helped create—the spirit of what became known as the Roaring Twenties. Its "Lonely Hearts" page inspired Nathanael West; its Broadway-gossip pages were conducted by an ex-hoofer named Walter Winchell; its exuberant lack of scruple made it the journalistic equivalent of bathtub gin. The *Graphic*'s most successful story is generally reckoned to have been the saga of Daddy and Peaches Browning. Edward Browning, a publicity-hungry real-estate magnate and aging playboy, married a pretty, chubby-cheeked fifteen-year-old shopgirl named Frances (Peaches) Heenan. Their romance was fodder for all three tabloids, but the *Graphic* was able to trump, so to speak, its rivals: only the *Graphic* was able to publish pictures of Daddy and Peaches in bed together, because only the *Graphic* had "composographs"—photographs in which the faces of real people were superimposed on scenes using models.

The *News* fought back with dramatic human-interest stories ranging from Lindbergh's transatlantic flight and Ruth's sixty homers to Valentino's riotous funeral. When Ruth Snyder, who with her lover had bludgeoned her husband to death, became the first woman to go to the electric chair—at Sing Sing, in 1928—the *News* sneaked in a witness with a small camera strapped to his ankle. As the switch was thrown, the *News* man pulled up his trouser cuff and, using a cable release threaded through a hole in his pocket, opened the shutter and closed it an instant later. The resulting picture was a little blurry—it looked like a German Expressionist painting—but on the front page, under a black, one-word headline (DEAD!), it was, unlike a composograph, disturbingly real.

The tabloid wars of the twenties ended in victory for the *News*. The *Graphic*, anathema to advertisers and out of synch with the sombre public mood brought on by the Depression, folded in 1932. The *Mirror* managed to limp on until the devastating newspaper strike of 1962–63. But the *News* went from strength to strength, gaining a hundred thousand readers a year. In 1944, its circulation passed the two-million mark.

Captain Patterson paid close attention to every aspect of the *News*. He selected and often suggested story lines for its comic strips, which included such icons of popular culture as "Little Orphan Annie," "Dick Tracy," and "Brenda Starr, Reporter." He supervised the construction of the News Building—a fine Art Deco skyscraper, opened in 1930, on Forty-second Street between Second and Third Avenues. He hired and fired editors, reporters, and columnists, and made sure that they (and all his other employees) were decently paid. (He also made sure that they didn't get too famous: in Patterson's universe, the paper was the star. In the *Mirror*, by contrast, columnists—particularly Winchell, who joined up when the *Graphic* began to fade—were kings.) Above all, Patterson decided what opinions were expressed in the *News*'s plainspoken, conversational editorials.

In the 1930s, those editorials backed the New Deal with gusto. The *News* even led the fund drive to install the White House swimming pool that allowed Franklin D. Roosevelt to exercise despite his crippled legs. But, as the decade drew to a close, the president's foreign policy began to alarm Patterson, who was a passionate isolationist and Anglophobe. When Roosevelt announced his plan to send supplies to Britain, Patterson turned on him, and the *News* denounced lend-lease as "a bill to make the president dictator of the United States." It did not help matters that four days after Pearl

Harbor, when the captain visited the commander-in-chief to offer his services in the war, F.D.R. humiliated him by giving him a sarcastic assignment: to reread his editorials from the previous year.

By the time Patterson died, in May of 1946, the *News*'s political line had become as reactionary as that of its parent, the *Chicago Tribune,* to which control of the *News* now reverted. When the Republicans won control of Congress that fall, the *News*'s Washington columnist, John O'Donnell, proclaimed that "the Commies" had been defeated, and sneered, "Franklin Roosevelt died too soon. A kindly fate plucked him from the world stage before the angry audience of his fellow countrymen had a chance to boo and yell their derision with all the fury of suckers who have just discovered that they've been trimmed to a fare thee well by the city slicker." The day's editorial expressed similar sentiments, adding the paper's regret "that J. M. Patterson, founder of this newspaper and its publisher for almost twenty-seven years, did not live to see this anti–New Deal triumph."

The paper that the captain left behind was selling 2 1/3 million copies a day and 4.5 million on Sundays: MORE THAN TWICE THE CIRCULATION OF ANY OTHER PAPER IN AMERICA, a standing box boasted. Patterson's body was barely in the ground when those figures began drifting gently downward. It's tempting to blame the founder's absence for the drop, but there were plenty of other, grander factors. Television—slayer of movies, slayer of radio, slayer of popular magazines, slayer of every form of human activity and inactivity except itself—happened. Suburbanization happened, exiling customers to places without newsstands and subways. Mass higher education (the G.I. Bill) happened. Industrial jobs melted away. Costs went up, and so did the street prices of newspapers—in the case of the *News,* from two cents (1948) gradually up to fifty cents (1994). Papers were shutting down like so many vaudeville theatres. All this was tough on everybody except the *Times,* which skimmed the cream of a growing class of the educated and the aspiring. The wonder is that the *News*'s circulation fell as slowly as it did. Daily sales took almost thirty years to dip below two million. Not until the nineties did the numbers settle into six figures. By then, the *News*'s main enemy was no longer the *Graphic* or the *Mirror,* or even television. It was the *Post.*

THE *New York Post* has the noblest pedigree of any newspaper in America. By comparison—as far as bloodlines are concerned, at least—journalistic grandees like the *Times* are jumped-up Johnny-come-latelies. The *Post* is the only screaming tabloid (for that matter, the only surviving periodical of any kind) to have been founded by a Founding Father—and not just any Founding Father but the handsomest, dashingest, and arguably most brilliant of them all, Alexander Hamilton. In the spring of 1801, Hamilton brought together a roomful of New York's richest and most staunchly Federalist merchants at the country house of Archibald Gracie (now the official residence of New York's mayors) and persuaded them to pledge the necessary capital. "We openly profess our attachment to that system of politics denominated FEDERAL," an editorial note on page one of the first issue declared, adding:

> The design of this paper, is to diffuse among the people correct information on all interesting subjects; to inculcate just principles in religion, morals, and politics; and to cultivate a taste for sound literature.

The *Evening Post*, as it was called then, stuck to that basic credo for generations, even as its politics shifted amid the tumult of events. It could be a little sketchy in the correct-information department—it was a four-page paper until the mid-1980s, and there wasn't room for everything—but few would question the justness of its principles (it backed Lincoln, denounced slavery, and advocated black enfranchisement) or the soundness of its literature (its writers included James Russell Lowell, Henry Adams, and Charles Eliot Norton). The *Evening Post* was guided by a succession of brilliant and formidable editors: the poet and essayist William Cullen ("Thanatopsis") Bryant, who held the job for fifty years; the Irish-born polemicist E. L. Godkin, who had founded *The Nation*, and who merged that political weekly, for a time, with the *Post*; and Rollo Ogden, who became a legendary managing editor of the *Times*.

At the turn of the century, the *Evening Post*'s circulation was only a little over twenty thousand—a pebble compared to Gibraltars like Joseph Pulitzer's *World* and Hearst's *Journal*, both of which, at various times, were selling a million copies a day. But it was the right twenty thousand, and what would today be called its readership profile attracted advertisers. (Pulitzer himself once told an interviewer that the *Evening Post* was his favorite newspaper. Asked why he didn't make the *World* more like it, he replied, "Because I want to talk to a nation, not a select committee.") "You will see few copies of the *Evening Post* in Hell's Kitchen," sniffed a handsomely printed promotional booklet in 1925. "On the commuting trains," it went on, "you see few *Evening Post*s in the smokers, but many in the club cars." After the Depression hit, though, things got dicey in the club cars. In 1933, the *Evening Post*—whose politics had by then become as stuffily conservative as its typography had always been—was sold to a Philadelphian, J. David Stern, and he jazzed it up a bit, dumbed it down a bit, dropped the "Evening" from its name, and made it a supporter of gaseous liberalism in general and F.D.R. in particular. In 1939, Stern sold it to a purportedly wealthy liberal named George Backer, or so the *Times* reported. Actually, the ownership passed to Mrs. Backer; she paid Stern nothing, but she assumed responsibility for the *Post*'s debts and losses. A couple of years later, Mrs. Backer, a member of the "Our Crowd" aristocracy of German-Jewish financial dynasties, divorced George and moved into the publisher's office herself. She stayed there for thirty-five years, and created the immediate precursor of the *Post* of today.

Mrs. Backer tended to go through husbands briskly, so eventually she reverted to her maiden name, Dorothy (Dolly) Schiff. In 1942, she turned the *Post* into a tabloid. Her *Post* used big, black headlines, but it never fully embraced the slam-bang style of tabloid news coverage. Its role was different.

During the 1950s and early 1960s, the morning papers were about class and the afternoon papers were about tribe. In the morning, the *Times* and the *Herald Tribune* were for the patricians, the *News* and the *Mirror* for the plebeians. In the afternoon, the *Journal-American* was for the Irish and Italian Catholics, the *World-Telegram* for the white-collar, white-bread, white Anglo-Saxon Protestants, and the *Post* for the Jews, the blacks, and (a little redundantly) the liberals. The *Post*, indeed, was the only daily voice of full-throated liberalism, not only in New York but in any big city in the land. Its columnists included Murray Kempton, Max Lerner, Eleanor Roosevelt, and James A. Wechsler, who was also the editorial-page editor. Its liberalism was firmly of the anti-Stalinist stripe, but that only made its crusades against such heroes of the right as Joseph McCarthy, J. Edgar Hoover, and (in his later, bitter years) Walter Winchell more glorious. People joked that the ideal *Post* story began, "His only crime was being born a Negro."

In circulation, the *Post* tended to run dead last. But by 1950 it had gradually worked its way into the black, and it achieved a goal that eluded its rivals: it survived. During the 1962–63 newspaper strike, Mrs. Schiff broke ranks with the other publishers and made a separate peace with the unions, putting the *Post* on newsstands all by itself for a month. After the strike, the *Journal-American* and the *World-Telegram* staggered on for a few years and then merged with each other and the *Herald Tribune* to form the *World Journal Tribune*, known briefly and without much affection as the Widget. This ghastly amalgam—which contained, one way or another, the bones of a dozen once great newspapers—expired like an overfed cannibal on May 5, 1967. The *Post*, now alone in the afternoon, enjoyed a decade of peace and, by its standards, something akin to prosperity. The confrontation with the *News* was about to begin.

In December 1976, Mrs. Schiff, who by then was well into her seventies, sold the *Post* to Rupert Murdoch. Murdoch, at forty-five, was already a formidable figure in his native Australia and in Britain, where he would soon add the venerable London *Times* to a stable that included the spectacularly successful ("soaraway") *Sun*, the mass-circulation Sunday *News of the World*, and a number of television interests. Acquiring the *Post* put him on the American map. His arrival marked the beginning of a decade and a half of turmoil in New York's tabloids, including theatrics, near-death experiences, multiple bankruptcies, last-minute rescues, and outright lunacy. As Winchell used to say: Let's go to press.

The year: 1977. The *News*, coasting on its famous FORD TO CITY: DROP DEAD headline—which some credited with deciding the 1976 presidential election—is smug. Within days of taking over the *Post*, Murdoch launches Page Six, a gossipy, attitudinous daily compendium of ministories about celebrities, media, and politicians; it becomes the new *Post*'s signature feature. British and Australian commandos hit the beach to teach the natives the sensationalist techniques of Fleet Street tabloid journalism. The stress is on crime and race, often in inflammatory conflation. Circulation begins to climb—still only a third of the *News*'s, but the bigger paper's complacency is shaken.

1980–81. The *News* fights back, launching an afternoon edition of its own, an upscale tab dubbed *Tonight*. It is an expensive disaster: aiming for sales of three hundred thousand, it barely gets into six figures, hemorrhages money, and folds in a year. The *News*, now politically centrist, endorses Carter for reelection. The *Post*, its Schiff-era liberalism spiked, backs Reagan. A *Columbia Journalism Review* editorial slams the *Post*: "The front pages regularly play to two emotions: fear and rage. And all too often what follows is meant to turn white against black, the comfortable against the poor. . . . The *New York Post* is no longer merely a journalistic problem. It is a social problem—a force for evil." Whoa, easy there! The *Post*'s losses mount—the big department stores shun it—but so do street sales, spurred by a cash-prize promotion called Wingo. The *News*'s deft counterstroke: a cash-prize promotion called Zingo.

1982–83. Reeling from the *Tonight* debacle, the *News* wins cost concessions from the unions; in Chicago, the Tribune Company renews its commitment to keep it afloat. The *Post* is now a morning paper. Its typography gets ever wilder; its "wood"—the daily cover headline, so called because in the days of handset type the biggest fonts were carved from wood—ever more outrageous. When a gunman shoots the owner of an after-hours strip joint in Queens and forces a female patron—a mortician—to decapitate the victim, the *Post* produces a masterwork: HEADLESS BODY IN TOPLESS BAR. According to *It's Alive!*, Steven Cuozzo's entertaining book about the *Post*, the auteur is Vincent A. Musetto, an assistant managing editor.

A New York edition is launched by *Newsday*, the prosperous, dignified Long Island tabloid-size paper founded in 1940 by Captain Patterson's daughter Alicia. *Post* and *News* staffers dismiss it as a tabloid in a tutu.

1987. In October, the stock-market crash poleaxes the city's economy, and the tabs feel the pain. The *News* wins more union concessions. In Washington, Senator Ted Kennedy, seeking revenge for *Post* assaults, slips a midnight rider into an appropriations bill which prevents Murdoch from getting a permanent waiver to own newspapers and TV stations in the same markets. Murdoch is forced to sell the *Post*, whose circulation is down to half a million from its Wingo-powered height of over nine hundred thousand. The buyer: Peter S. Kalikow, a tough-talking real-estate developer with no publishing experience.

1988. Kalikow turns out to be a surprisingly resourceful owner. He appoints attention-getting editors: first, Jane Amsterdam, the glamorous young founding editor of a trendy magazine called *Manhattan, inc.;* then Gerald Nachman, a fat, colorfully profane ex-TV producer. But a hubristic attempt to launch an elaborate Sunday edition is a fiasco. Losses mount at both tabloids.

1990–92. After a long, bitter strike that cripples the *News* for four months, Chicago runs out of patience. The *News* is "sold" to Robert Maxwell, pompous, portly owner of the London *Daily Mirror*. (Actually, Tribune Company executives pay Maxwell sixty million dollars to take the *News* and its obligations off their hands.) Meanwhile, Kalikow's business interests go south; he declares personal bankruptcy. Eight months after buying the *News*, Maxwell, facing margin calls from his bankers, vanishes from his yacht into the sea, a probable suicide; his fraud-riddled business empire collapses. The *News*—cashless and ownerless, its circulation dropping below eight hundred thousand—files for bankruptcy. The *Post* is in free fall: its claimed half-million circulation is revealed to be fifty thousand readers short.

1993. The climactic year: *annus horribilis, annus mirabilis.* Mortimer Zuckerman, Montreal-born real-estate entrepreneur and owner of *The Atlantic Monthly* and *U.S. News & World Report,* buys the *News,* rescuing it from certain death. He raids the prostrate *Post* for talent. At the *Post,* Kalikow, hounded into court by creditors, turns to a faintly shady financial operator, Steven Hoffenberg, for rescue. In a brilliant stroke, Hoffenberg hires a new editor: Pete Hamill, novelist, reporter, longtime writer of big-hearted, emotion-laden columns for every tabloid in town, romancer of Jackie Onassis and Shirley MacLaine, Brooklyn-bred man of the people at ease among the Manhattan élite, mentor to young writers—a tabloid saint. Hamill rallies the troops and brings the paper instant credibility, but within a month the Hoffenberg deal unravels.

Another rescuer appears, via the bankruptcy court: Abe Hirschfeld, a publicity-seeking septuagenarian parking-lot mogul with a dialect-joke Yiddish accent and a penchant for pointless runs for public office. Hirschfeld immediately fires Hamill and a score of other editors and managers, announces plans to fire hundreds more at random, and appoints Wilbert Tatum—race-baiting publisher of the *Amsterdam News,* a once great black weekly increasingly allied with Louis Farrakhan—to be editor of the *Post.* Suddenly, the parking-lot king's eccentricities take on a sinister cast. Chaos reigns; the paper's closing is hours away.

The staff revolts. Staking everything on a grand gesture, editors and reporters take control of the newsroom and put together one of the most remarkable issues ever published by an American newspaper. Page one is a huge woodcut of Alexander Hamilton with a tear rolling down his cheek. Hamill's name is defiantly restored to the masthead as editor-in-chief. The entire "news hole"—eighteen pages, including gossip columns and editorials—is devoted to a joyful excoriation of Hirschfeld and Tatum:

WHO IS THIS NUT?
HONEST, ABE DOESN'T KNOW
SPIT ABOUT JOURNALISM

HATE 'EM TATUM READY FOR SLIME TIME

AN URGENT APPEAL TO
POST READERS: HELP!

The edition captures the city's imagination. " 'Rage, rage against the dying of the light,' Dylan Thomas advised," a *Times* editorial praising the rebels begins. Governor Mario Cuomo, a favorite target of *Post* editorials, takes over the search for a new, responsible owner. Norman Mailer speaks at a rally. Hamill returns in triumph, fist pumping, to a foot-stamping newsroom ovation. (HE'S BACK, the next day's wood thunders.) Hirschfeld throws him out, but the judge puts him back and he edits the paper from a diner down the street. It's a beautiful week—a nicotine-and-ink-stained velvet revolution. But it can't last. Within days, a real rescuer appears—one who actually has the resources and the determination to save the *Post* from the abyss. Everyone is grateful, but in some quarters the gratitude has a queasy edge. The rescuer is Rupert Murdoch.

Cut to the present.

WHERE ARE THEY NOW? Well, Abe Hirschfeld is back where he likes to be: in the news, first for offering Paula Jones a phantom million dollars to drop her lawsuit against President Clinton, then for being charged with hiring someone to murder a business partner of his. Peter Kalikow is doing real-estate deals. Steven Hoffenberg is in jail for defrauding investors. *New York Newsday* is dead. Mario Cuomo is back in private life, having been defeated in 1994 for a fourth term, after getting the endorsement of neither the *News,* ideology notwithstanding, nor the *Post,* gratitude notwithstanding. Jane Amsterdam is in Westchester County, participating in carriage-driving competitions. Gerald Nachman is more visible than ever, on the cable-news chat channels. Mort Zuckerman is running the *News* and running through editor after editor—five of them so far. One editor he ran through was Pete Hamill, who lasted for the first eight months of 1997.

Today, Hamill writes books in his new apartment—an airy loft near Park Row, in the part of lower Manhattan that is haunted by the ghosts of scores of newspapers. Rupert Murdoch is thinking about the succession at his News Corporation, which has grown into a worldwide communications empire that includes movie studios and national and international cable- and satellite-television networks. And the *News* and the *Post* are circling each other in the ring, probing for weaknesses.

On the surface, the continuity between past and present at the *News* is much stronger than it is at the *Post*. The old *News* was a mass-circulation tabloid for working people; so is the new *News*. The new *News* looks recognizably like the old *News*. The title logo is essentially the same, with a stylized Speed Graphic still between *Daily* and *News*. (The old slogan, though, has been modified to the feebler NEW YORK'S HOMETOWN NEWSPAPER—a shot at the *Times*'s cosmopolitanism.) Politically, the old *News* was liberal and then it was conservative, while the new *News* is a hair to the left of center, but the paper's reporting, as ever, plays it pretty straight. The *Post*, by contrast, looks about as much like its ancestor as a Tokyo skinhead looks like the Mikado. The nineteenth-century *Post* was a somber, highbrow broadsheet aimed at the cultivated rich; the Dorothy Schiff *Post* was an earnest, middlebrow tabloid aimed at liberals; the Murdoch *Post* is a mischievous, lowbrow tabloid aimed, apparently, at converting the teeming urban masses to pickup-truck conservatism.

Yet the *New*'s greater continuity is not really a source of strength. Its past greatness hangs over it like a shadow—more a rebuke than an inspiration. And the discontinuities at the *Post* are not as severe as they appear. Through the *Post*'s many incarnations, its raison d'être has been the propagation of political opinion. If it made money, so much the better, but its survival has never depended on its balance sheet. And its news pages have never played it straight.

To paraphrase that 1801 editorial, the *Post* of today openly professes its attachment to that system of politics denominated RIGHT-WING REPUBLICAN. During last fall's New York senatorial campaign, the *Post* pulled out the stops for the incumbent, Al D'Amato. Eleven editorials promoted his candidacy or bashed his Democratic challenger, Representative Charles Schumer. The actual endorsement editorial was trumpeted with gigantic page-one wood: WE SAY D'AMATO. Coverage was extravagantly slanted. A double-page spread ostensibly devoted to examining the candidates' stands on education consisted of two items: a column attacking

Schumer for being allied with the teachers' union and an article headlined
D'AMATO WANTS PARENTS TO HAVE CHOICE. In the closing days of the campaign, the cheerleading grew risible. AL STORMS AHEAD was the wood for
the final Sunday's front page; inside, a story puffed a *Post* poll purportedly
showing D'Amato with a lead of 1.3 percent, although that lead, as the story
admitted in passing, "is well within the survey's 3.8-point margin of error."
(Other polls were by then showing Schumer coasting to victory.) Tuesday's
Post had a little squib entitled "Schumer Leads in Stretch Run," but it was
dwarfed by MAMMA HELPS GET AL'S CAMPAIGN COOKIN', with a heart-
warming picture of the senator and his doting mother. After Schumer won,
the *Post* editorialized loftily that D'Amato and the Republicans had deserved to lose, because the G.O.P. "chose to run a campaign in which it expected President Clinton's troubles and the economy's successes to grant it
easy victories." A fair point, but a curious one coming from a paper that had
spent the previous ten months attacking Clinton (in its news pages) as a
criminal, a weasel, a pervert, a felon who belongs in jail, and a tyrant using
his K.G.B.-style secret police to trash American liberties.

The *Post* is a raffish, intermittently unreliable redoubt of what Sidney
Blumenthal has termed the counterestablishment—the network of conservative and neoconservative publications and think tanks which has been
built up over the past generation in imitation of the supposedly monolithic
liberal establishment. Besides the *Post,* which provides (ideologically, at
least) a counter to the *Times,* Murdoch's contribution to the cause includes
The Weekly Standard, which counters *The New Republic,* and Fox News,
which counters Ted Turner's liberal-leaning CNN. All three lose money.

THE *News* and the *Post* bring distinct strengths and weaknesses to the daily
battle. The *News* has size. Its editorial staff is bigger—some three hundred
and fifty people, eighty-odd more than the *Post*'s. Though the *News* can no
longer claim to be the biggest-selling daily in the country, or even in the city
(at seven hundred and twenty-three thousand, it comes in sixth nationally,
after the *Wall Street Journal, USA Today,* the *Los Angeles Times,* the *New York
Times,* and the *Washington Post),* it still outsells the *Post* (which ranks fourteenth nationally) by three hundred thousand on weekdays and more than
four hundred thousand on Sundays.

To a reader—to this reader, at least—the *News* comes across as a paper
suffering from clinical depression, while the *Post* is more like a hyperactive

monomaniac, alternately amusing and obnoxious. By most conventional measures, the *News* is the better paper. If, God forbid, you had to pick one of them as your sole source of information about the world we live in, you would certainly pick the *News*. There's simply more news in the *News,* and that news is presented in a more balanced, less distorted manner. The *News*'s cityside columnists, Jim Dwyer and Juan Gonzalez, are stronger. Its TV listings are better. It has "Doonesbury." Its Washington columnist, Lars-Erik Nelson, is so smart that he moonlights for the *New York Review of Books.*

But the *Post* plays a better game of high-low. For the arugula set, it has enterprising, lively business pages, focussed cannily on media and Internet firms, and its many gossip columns—ranging from the hipness of Page Six to the sweetness of Liz Smith—are more fun. For the hamburger eaters, it has a topflight sports section. And when it comes to tabloid elan the *Post* cleans the *News*'s clock with metronomic regularity.

As a scientific example—scientific because the two papers were working from exactly the same raw material—let's take a recent day's developments in the Perelman-Duff divorce case, a current tabloid staple. Ronald Perelman, the Revlon supremo, and Patricia Duff, his beautiful blond ex-wife, are embroiled in what is known as a custody battle. At a hearing, Perelman was grilled about his income, his houses, their furnishings, his vacations, his household servants, his cars, his private jets—a toy store's worth of goodies for the tabs to sift through. The *Post* found the right detail to go with. Under an overline reading "New York's Cheapest Billionaire," the front-page wood shouts, I FEED MY KID ON $3 A DAY. The accompanying paparazzi-style photograph is more than a year old, but it's skillfully chosen: it shows Perelman crossing the street and reaching for his daughter's arm, but the little girl cringes away from him, clutching the hand of someone (perhaps a nanny) outside the frame. The story, by Dareh Gregorian, is peppered with cheeky epithets for the villain of the piece—"the makeup magnate," "the powder-puff poobah"—and begins, "High-living billionaire Ron Perelman says he can feed his year-old daughter on just $3 a day." It continues:

> "When Caleigh eats with me, she eats $3 worth of food a day," Perelman said. "She eats chicken fingers, hot dogs, cereal for breakfast, hamburgers and some pasta."
>
> "Three dollars? So about a $1000 a year would be appropriate? [Duff lawyer William] Beslow asked.

"Yes." Perelman replied. . . .

U.S. Department of Agriculture figures show $3.07 a day was the national average last year for a "low-cost" home-cooked food plan for a 4-year-old.

Perelman has a full-time chef on his staff.

Great stuff. How does the *News* handle the story? On page one, nothing. The wood is POTHOLE CITY, with a subhead reading "5,000 Craters in Last Week Wreak Havoc on Drivers." The picture—showing a couple of potholes that have been filled in—undermines the headline's alarm. Potholes are a city-desk perennial: there's a rash of them every time the roads thaw out after freezing rain. The *News*'s Perelman-Duff story, on an inside page, runs under the headline TYCOON'S LAVISH LIFE! The picture shows Perelman in an overcoat, smiling. "Billionaire Ronald Perelman yesterday reluctantly provided a rare peek into his privileged lifestyle world overstuffed with mansions, money and yachts," the story begins. The three-dollar food budget isn't even mentioned until the third paragraph. No numbers from the Department of Agriculture; that's a *Post* exclusive.

It's not always this one-sided, of course. The *News* has its good days too, and its readers remain surprising loyal. "There's a potent link between a huge stratum of people in New York and the *Daily News*," Jim Dwyer, who moved to the *News* after *New York Newsday* folded, told me recently. "It's read by people who run diners, by doormen, by housewives in the Bronx and Queens and Brooklyn. It's on every court officer's desk and in every police precinct." The *News* dominates the outer boroughs, where most of its press run is sold. The *Post* is stronger in Manhattan, where, on newsstands, it outsells not only the *News* but the *Times* as well. The *Post* is a "second read": most of its buyers read one of the other papers, too. This is bad for advertising but good for influence. New York's media elites read the *Times* for information and the *Post* for gossip and a giggle. The people who play softball with Mort Zuckerman in the Hamptons read the *Post*. They don't generally read the *News*—a source of great frustration for the star pitcher.

People who have worked at both papers agree that staff morale is higher at the *Post* than at the *News*. At the *News*, years of fratricidal strikes, mass layoffs, editorial revolving-doorism, front-office second-guessing, and obscure lines of authority have left the staff feeling, as one of them puts it, like "abused children with no self-esteem." Every office shakeup deposits a layer of bitter sediment. At the *Post*, the editorial bureaucracy is smaller and stabler. Ken Chandler, an old and able Murdoch hand, has been its editor since shortly after the Hirschfeld uprising. And the *Post* has the whole global Murdoch empire to move people into and out of—"kind of like the way the British had India," in Pete Hamill's phrase.

At the *News* cynicism is a shelter; at the *Post*, it's an opportunity. *Post* people have lower expectations, fewer hopes, and no pretensions, so they can get more fully into the fun of putting out a wild and crazy tabloid. If the chance comes along to do some honorable work (and it does, especially when there's no election coming)—well, then, so much the better. At the *News*, people have learned to keep their heads down. Even the two papers' new offices make for a happier *Post:* the *Post*'s are in Murdoch's spiffy glass box in the heart of media midtown; the *News*'s, in the dreary, remote West Thirties, have high ceilings, but the effect is more warehouse than cathedral, with windows far above eye level.

Because the *News* is privately held and the *Post* is a drop in the Murdoch ocean, estimates of both papers' financial viability are hard to come by. A reasonable guess is that the *News* makes a small operating profit and the *Post* loses somewhere between ten and thirty million dollars a year. The *Post* is therefore something unusual in the annals of down-market journalism: a vanity tabloid, supported by a rich patron as if it were the opera. Thanks to Zuckerman, the *News* is a viable business, but from the point of view of return on capital its continued existence, too, is a function of something other than its bottom line. Tabloids have become one of those subsidized cultural treasures that we New Yorkers get to enjoy simply because we live in New York.

And they are treasures. When I was a little boy, we had the *Times* delivered, but my father sometimes brought home the tabloids as a slightly naughty treat. Their look and feel excited me. By the time I was eleven or twelve, I was coming in from the suburbs to haunt the Newspaper Division of the New York Public Library, which occupied a floor of an industrial loft building not far from where the office of the *News* is now. I spent long, hypnotic afternoons in that repository of esoteric knowledge, turning the pages of fat, yellowing bound volumes not only of the *News*, the *Mirror*, and the *Post* but also of obscurer tabloids, tantalizingly vanished—the *Evening Graphic*, of course, and *PM*, and the *Compass*. Now the Newspaper Division is gone, too: it was closed in 1961, and bound volumes were simply thrown away after their contents were transferred, minus body and soul, to microfilm. But the jolt they gave me—the electric connection to a grittier, more tumultuous, jazzier world than mine, a world where people stay up late, wear snap-brim hats, and hear the sound of sirens—hasn't altogether disappeared. I still feel a tingle of it every morning when I get my hands on the newspapers. Especially the tabloids, whose todays are eternal.

—*The New Yorker*, February 22 & March 1, 1999

GEORGE WITHOUT TEARS

PRESIDENT CLINTON, who over the past five years has been the most important politician in America, has appeared during that time on the covers of *BusinessWeek*, the *National Enquirer, People,* and *Rolling Stone,* but he never made the cover of *George,* the "political lifestyle magazine" edited by John F. Kennedy, Jr. Indeed, of the forty-two issues of *George,* only three had covers that featured pictures of political figures. (Pointedly, all three—Richard Nixon, Ronald Reagan, and Newt Gingrich—were Republicans.) Twenty-two *George* covers had movie stars on them, seven had supermodels, four had television entertainment stars, three had television news stars, and the remaining three had, respectively, a pro basketball player, a country singer, and a dog dressed up as George Washington.

Inside, the package was tilted a little more toward politics than the wrapping suggested, but not enough to obviate the question of whether *George* was part of the problem or part of the solution. From the point of view of its critics within the journalistic profession, who were numerous but seldom harsh, it was part of the problem, administering one more small push to the American political system in the direction of issuelessness, triviality, alienation, celebrification, and lack of conviction. Kennedy's answer to this, essentially, was that these things had already happened, and that he was simply using them, judolike, to bring people back into "the process." In an editor's letter introducing the first issue, Kennedy wrote, "We believe that if we can make politics accessible by covering it in an entertaining and compelling way, popular interest and involvement in the process will follow." The idea was to attract people who, if they weren't reading *George,* would be perusing *Glamour* or *Maxim*—not *The Nation* or *The Weekly Standard,* let alone *Dissent* or *The Public Interest.* The question *George* wanted its potential critics to ask was not "Is this political magazine better than other political magazines?" It was "Isn't this political magazine better than nothing?"

The irony is that if *George* had been an unqualified business success the first question would have been irrelevant and the answer to the second would have been an ungrudging yes. But *George* was not a business success. It's only a little presumptuous to refer to *George* in the past tense, because its next two issues—September, which was already mostly done when John Kennedy's plane went down, and October, which is now planned as a memorial to him—will likely be its last. They will certainly be the last for the magazine as it is currently constituted. Even before Kennedy's death, there were obvious indications that Hachette Filipacchi—the French-owned publishing company that has underwritten *George* and puts out *Elle, Car & Driver, Premiere,* and a couple of dozen other American magazines—would withdraw its support at the end of the year, when its contractual obligations expire. Kennedy had been actively looking for new backers. *George,* according to the *New York Post's* well-informed "Media City" page, had been taking in revenues at a rate of eleven million dollars a year, four million short of breaking even. Its circulation had stalled at around four hundred thousand; its advertising pages were down 30 percent this year. None of this means that Kennedy could not have recruited a new angel to keep the magazine going for another five years. But he was the magazine's main business asset. He was also the shaper of its editorial vision—a vision so quirkily his that for a successor to keep putting the magazine out unchanged would be not just foolish but ghoulish.

"OUR COVERAGE of politics won't be colored by any partisan perspective—not even mine," Kennedy promised in that first editor's letter. Instead, *George* would treat politicians "not just as ideological symbols, but as lively and engaging men and women" and "as the personalities and pop icons they have become," and it would treat its readers as "skeptical consumers." Kennedy evidently thought that this model—of politics as nonpartisan ("post-partisan," in his preferred term), non-ideological, and upbeat, and of readers as consumers (to be distinguished, presumably, from citizens)—was a prerequisite to attracting the kind of big-time advertisers he was going after. But the model made *George* a dispiritingly passionless magazine. Its columnists were carefully balanced among liberals (Paul Begala, the former Clinton strategist), conservatives (Ann Coulter, a Clinton-hating television shouter), and neutrals (Claire Shipman, a network White House correspondent). Friendly feature stories about Democrats were offset by friendly feature stories about Republicans. *George* tried to make up in niceness what it lacked in bite. It seldom hinted that politics might occasionally be a clash of naked interest, or even a conflict between right and wrong. And if any sharp edges were left over they were buried under a gentle snowfall of celebrity celebration.

George looked like a fashion magazine, and most of the time, alas, appearances were not deceiving. Yet it published many good pieces. Some of the sharpest—for example, Lisa DePaulo's raw profile of Ruth Shalit, the young *New Republic* writer who sabotaged herself through plagiarism, and Timothy Noah's survey of the *New York Times*'s editorial board and its chief, Howell Raines—were about journalists. Curtis Wilkie contributed a tough piece on Trent Lott's Mississippi background and an exposé of Dexter King's handling of the legacy of his father, Martin Luther King, Jr. Ann Louise Bardach's story on Representative Mary Bono, which appears in the current issue of *George,* is full of fresh details about her personal background, her late husband, Sonny, and their involvement with Scientology (although, like many *George* articles, this one shows little curiosity about its subject's political beliefs).

The Clinton-Lewinsky scandal should have been *George*'s great opportunity. Suddenly, politics was more exciting, more dramatic, more suspenseful—in a word, more entertaining—than entertainment. A sprawling human epic packed with vivid characters, betrayals, skulduggery, ribaldry, and sex: what could be better suited to *George*'s pop-cult, personality-driven vision of politics? Yet the magazine froze up. For its first cover after the scandal erupted, *George* chose Tom Hanks—a tie-in with Hanks's HBO series about the Apollo program. As the impeachment drama neared its climax, the cover subjects included Peter Jennings, Sean Penn, and Garth Brooks. Kennedy was unable to break the mold. The scandal had glitz, but it was bitterly polarizing in a way that ill comported with *George*'s relentless cheeriness, and it plainly made Kennedy uncomfortable. His sympathies seemed to lie with Clinton, and in three of his editor's letters—which otherwise were almost always along the anodyne lines of "In this issue, we pay homage to the twenty most fascinating men in politics today"—he ventured some genuine, if timid, opinions. In the first of these letters he reviewed the history of the trial of President Andrew Johnson and wrote, "Although the current allegations against President Clinton seem freighted with legal implication, don't be fooled: The impeachment process has always been, at heart, a political contest." In another he wrote that "America has squandered the last year navel-gazing and hand-wringing." In the third he argued that "the human frailties of our public officials" are irrelevant to their public duties, noted that "Jack Nicholson may never tire of chasing starlets, yet we still go to see his films," and concluded on this jarring note: "So let's be consistent when it comes to politicians. They're famous and fabulous. Bob Livingston and Barney Frank for president!" The magazine's coverage of the scandal was incoherent. Of the twelve issues published during the yearlong uproar, six contained not a single feature article about it, offering instead filler like "Bruce Willis Kicks Asteroid." The pieces that did run ranged from a sober survey of Kenneth Starr's team of prosecutors to a tasteless essay, "Eleanor Mondale for Mistress," full of salacious anecdotes about the sexual adventures of the former vice-president's daughter and suggestions that if she wasn't already Clinton's mistress, then she ought to be.

Naturally, one couldn't read that last piece without thinking of the personal indiscretions of John F. Kennedy, Sr. *George* was haunted by ghosts and phantoms from the family closet. Kennedy's editor's letters frequently contained references to his lineage, some of them impersonal ("The Nixon-Kennedy debates ushered in the television age of politics"), others uncomfortably intimate ("My mother always said that the cocoon of the White House was a heavenly respite from the constant separations on the campaign trail"), still others coy ("An American president once said that a nation reveals itself through the men and women it honors"). Kennedy's most notorious editor's note—the one he chose to illustrate with an apparently nude photograph of himself, and in which he took two of his cousins to task—was painful to read:

> Two members of my family chased an idealized alternative to their life. One left behind an embittered wife, and another, in what looked to be a hedge against mortality, fell in love with youth and surrendered his judgment in the process. Both became poster boys for bad behavior. Perhaps they deserved it. Perhaps they should have known better. To whom much is given, much is expected, right?

When President Clinton turned fifty, *George*'s cover marked the occasion with Drew Barrymore made up as Marilyn Monroe, over the legend "Happy Birthday, Mr. President." But the most unsettling of Kennedy's editorial judgments of this kind was his decision to publish a long article by the mother of the assassin of Yitzhak Rabin, in which she claimed, on scant evidence, that her son had murdered Rabin because he had been goaded into it by an agent of the Israeli government. Kennedy wrote, "Several months ago, representatives of the family contacted the editors at *George* and asked whether we were interested in the piece. They were, no doubt, hoping that my own family history would bring added attention to their story, and they were probably right. . . . In no way is it intended to be an objective examination of the events surrounding the assassination. It is, however, a compelling look at one facet of an insular, conservative religious community within Israel. It may raise interesting questions. It may not." It may not?

IN MANY WAYS, *George* was most interesting as a reflection of the personal, family, and career pressures and conflicts that buffeted its editor. His involvement in the magazine rechannelled those conflicts without quite resolving them. Reading through the pile left me with an unexpected feeling: a sad wish, on John Kennedy's behalf, for the road not taken. It seemed clearer than ever that Kennedy would have been freer, happier, and more fulfilled if he had defied his mother's wishes and become an actor. If he had done so, it is far from outlandish to speculate, he might well have been wildly successful. He was handsomer than any leading man; he was joyful and athletic in physical movement; and, by all accounts, he had both a love of acting and a talent for it. The modesty and decency to which those who knew him have universally attested would have shone through on the big screen. Action thrillers, romantic comedies, historical dramas, sci-fi adventures—it's hard to think of a genre of motion picture he could not have excelled in. He would have been rich and famous in his own right—and as John Kennedy, not as John F. Kennedy, Jr. His lineage would have been no longer a burden but simply part of a golden Hollywood legend. His life would have been free of its parasitic, Peter Pan quality. Instead of being the editor of a marginal political magazine obsessed with the movies, he would have been, among other things, the natural and unquestioned leader of Hollywood's formidable community of liberal Democratic activists. From there he might even have become president. It's been done before.

—*The New Yorker*, August 9, 1999

WHAT'S UP, DOC?

THE RECENT COUP in the big marble palace on Capitol Hill turns out to have been a two-parter. Part One everybody knows about: just before Christmas, Trent Lott, of Mississippi, was forced out as the Republican leader of the Senate and replaced by Bill Frist, of Tennessee. It was a nice, clean trade-in, which not only substituted an attractive-seeming fellow for an unctuous incompetent but also changed the question of the day from "How come these guys are always pining for Jim Crow and white supremacy?" to "Isn't it reassuring that they got rid of that terrible man?" Part Two kicked in a couple of weeks ago, when the *New York Times* stopped referring to Lott's successor as Mr. Frist and started calling him Dr. Frist.

Like the switch from Lott to Frist, the switch from Mr. Frist to Dr. Frist was a canny move. "Dr." means "good." It means taking care of people, curing their illnesses, relieving their pain, binding up their wounds, saving their lives. It means honored, learned, respected. Its humanitarian glamour sprinkles fairy dust even on doctors of business administration. Its positive associations earn "Dr. Evil" a laugh even from people who have never seen Mike Myers touch his pinkie to the corner of his mouth. So having a leader who's a Dr. is a handy political prescription-drug plan for a party that is sometimes diagnosed as suffering from an eighty-year case of chronic compassion-deficiency syndrome, especially on "health-care issues."

Honorifics are something of an obsession at the *Times,* whose editors, having reflected deeply upon the subject, have codified their thoughts in *The New York Times Manual of Style and Usage.* The entry on "courtesy titles" is one of the longest. The gist of it is that in the *Times* every living person gets his or her last name preceded by a title—usually Mr., Mrs., or Ms.—unless he or she is being written about in the sports section or is a little kid or is a high-art legend (Pavarotti, for example) or has a goofy stage name like Meat Loaf. (The style book thinks it would be "overliteral" to call him Mr. Loaf.) The *Times* used to take the "Mr." away from anyone convicted of a felony, but that policy had to be dropped during the Watergate era, when the criminal classes and the ruling classes began to merge.

"Physicians' or dentists' titles should be used in all references," the style book directs. That's the plain language of the statute, but the justices of the Supreme Desk evidently interpret "all references" to mean "all references to physicians and dentists acting in a medical or dental capacity." The late Graham Chapman, of Monty Python's Flying Circus, was a physician, but he was always Mr. Chapman in the *Times*. Michael Crichton, M.D. and author, and Charles Krauthammer, M.D. and columnist, are mostly Messrs. Jonathan Miller, M.D., director, author, and pioneering sketch comedian *(Beyond the Fringe)*, is sometimes Mr. Miller, as when he's staging an opera, and sometimes Dr. Miller, as when he's lecturing on neurology, his medical specialty.

Is there a doctor in the House? There are eight, actually, plus three dentists, but the *Times* seldom gives them their medical honorific. The Senate has just the one, unless you count veterinarians, too, in which case it has three. (Wayne Allard, Republican of Colorado, is a good man to see about a horse. So is John Ensign, Republican of Nevada.) As for the new majority leader, in the hundred or so stories about him that the *Times* published before January 5th of this year Mr. Frist was beating Dr. Frist by a two-to-one margin. Since then, it's been Dr. Frist all the way.

Certainly, there's no disputing his entitlement to the title. He was still performing heart transplants during the Clinton administration. In 2001, he attended to a colleague, Strom Thurmond, who had collapsed on the Senate floor. (Mr. Lott, therefore, has Dr. Frist to thank that he was able to keep a speaking engagement at Mr. Thurmond's hundredth-birthday celebration.) And on New Year's Day just past, while on vacation in Florida, Frist happened on the scene of a gruesome auto accident and, as a press release from his office put it, "assisted with the intubation and resuscitation of three individuals."

Daniel Patrick Moynihan, of New York, and Phil Gramm, of Texas, are doctors, too, as was the late Paul Wellstone, and their doctorates—in international relations, economics, and political science, respectively—were highly pertinent to their legislative duties. (Now that they are gone, there are no more senatorial Ph.D.s, just the three sawbones.) The *Times* kept them in mufti all the same. Martin Luther King's degree was in theology, a field directly relevant to the work of a spirit-filled leader of Christian nonviolence, so it made sense for the newspaper of record to style him Dr. King. Benjamin Spock, M.D., who ran for president in 1972 as a third-party peace candidate, was always Dr. Spock. He was a pediatrician, not a Vulcan.

The most famous political doctor of them all, Henry Kissinger, is a special case. Dr. or Mr.? On the one hand, he's not a "real" doctor. On the other hand, his degree is in government, which passes the relevancy test. On the one hand, in what sounds a little like a twitch of Ivy League reverse snobbery, he once told the *Times,* which tries to accommodate people's wishes in such matters, that he preferred to be called Mr. Kissinger, so that's what the *Times* always calls him. (Well, nine times out of ten.) On the other hand, just about all the other papers that use honorifics call him Dr., and the secretaries in all his offices have always answered the phone, "Dr. Kissinger's office." On the one hand—oh, never mind. Let the International Criminal Court sort it out.

In any event, with the promotion of Frist in both the Senate and the *Times,* the Republicans have now opened up a doctor gap. One probable result will be a shortening of the odds against Howard Dean, the former governor of Vermont, who is running for the Democratic presidential nomination. Though he is a family practitioner who still occasionally saw patients when he was governor, his Dr./Mr. ratio in the *Times* is an alarmingly low one to three. Paging Dr. Dean. Call the copy desk.

—*The New Yorker,* January 27, 2003

L'AFFAIRE BLAIR

IN *The Fabulist: A Novel*, published last week by Simon & Schuster, Stephen Glass, once a young star writer for *The New Republic*, who, in 1998, was fired for fabricating a spectacular series of stories, tells the story of "Stephen Glass," a young star writer for *The Washington Weekly*, who gets fired for fabricating a spectacular series of stories. Like Stephen Glass, "Stephen Glass" fakes not only the stories but also the notes and documentation to back them up, the better to fool his magazine's editors and its fact checker, Victoria. Victoria maintains a "rulebook," which begins like this:

> acceptable forms of verification, in order of priority
> 1. *The New York Times*—the gold standard.

Whether as journalist, novelist, or character, Stephen Glass gets almost everything wrong—sometimes on purpose, sometimes because he just can't help it. But he got that one right. The *Times* remains the most important and, on balance, the best newspaper in the world. Its authority—slowly earned in the course of the century and a half since its founding, and especially the hundred and seven years since its purchase by Adolph S. Ochs, the great-grandfather of the present publisher, Arthur Ochs Sulzberger, Jr.—isn't just journalistic; it's downright ontological. It is scarcely an exaggeration to say that the *Times* defines public reality. Although newspaper readership in general is in decline, the *Times*'s circulation has been growing; it now stands at well over a million, half of which is accounted for by its national edition. The paper's overseas subsidiary, the *International Herald Tribune,* and its excellent Web site give it global reach. So when the *Times* makes a mistake—a big mistake, a ghastly mistake, a mistake that seems to compromise the soul of its mission—that's not just news. It's meta-news.

It's also, apparently, mega-news. A week ago Sunday, the *Times* unloaded a tale of journalistic malfeasance that began on the front page and jumped inside to four full broadsheet pages—some fourteen thousand words in all. In its gray bulk and solemn presentation ("an investigation by *Times* journalists has found . . ."), it resembled one of those multibylined "special reports" that Dave Barry once remarked ought to come affixed with the label "Caution! Journalism Prize Entry! Do Not Read!" Half of this behemoth consisted of a chronicle of the misbehavior of a young reporter, Jayson Blair, and of his editors' actions and (more often) inaction in response. The other half was a catalogue of specifics, examining thirty-nine articles by Blair that had been published during the previous three years and sorting his transgressions into categories like "Plagiarism," "Factual Errors," "Whereabouts" (Blair often faked his datelines, using e-mail and his cell phone to conceal the fact that he was still in New York, concocting descriptions of people and places with the help of the Internet and the *Times*'s own photo archive), "Denied Reports," and (in one instance) "Fabrications." Much of this stuff, from a reader's point of view, was trivial. When a reporter misidentifies the Historic Greater Friendship Baptist Church as the Historical Greater Friendship Baptist Church (especially when, as the catalogue goes on to note, the name is "rendered correctly later in the article"), the reader still gets the idea. When a reporter steals a quote from a rival's story, as Blair often did, the reader is misled about the enterprisingness and honesty of the reporter but not, or not necessarily, about the accuracy or significance of what the quotee has said. Perhaps the most consequential of Blair's fabulisms came in a story last October about the Washington-area sniper case, in which he asserted that a federal prosecutor had snatched a suspect out of an interrogation just as he was about to confess. That report, which the *Times* played as a page-one scoop, traduced the reputations of individuals and institutions.

The ultra-sophisticated view of the *Times*'s self-accounting is that it was overblown. Four full newspaper pages—isn't that a little too much information about the dismissal of a midlevel employee at corporation No. 486

in the Fortune 500? Wasn't this an act of self-aggrandizement dressed as contrition? Actually, that analysis applies better to Glass and his solipsistic novel, in which every character—including the sole sympathetic one, "Glass"—is cut from cardboard, and which seems to view apology as a for-profit industry with a launch interview on *60 Minutes*. (Glass's nonfictional fiction lacks the imaginative flair of his fictional nonfiction. Perhaps he should try fictional fiction, or just forget the whole thing and practice law.)

The *Times*'s report stirred memories of the last time a major paper had to deal with deliberate journalistic misconduct on such a scale. That was in 1981, at the *Washington Post*, when a young reporter named Janet Cooke—like Blair, a charming, charismatic, twenty-something-year-old—won a Pulitzer Prize for a story about an eight-year-old heroin addict who, it turned out, did not exist. The *Post*'s catharsis, like the *Times*'s twenty-two years later, reflected its particular journalistic style to the point of stereotype. The *Post*, known as a writer's paper, assigned the task to one person, Bill Green, a Duke University official who was serving as the paper's ombuds-man, or internal watchdog. Green's report, the same length as the entire *Times* package, was almost pure narrative. It was full of suspense, color, di-alogue, and melodrama, rendered in prose that approached the pulpy. ("Mil-ton Coleman"—city editor then, deputy managing editor now—"is a rangy, tall man. His quietness is deceptive. He pursues news as though it's his quarry, and admiring colleagues regard him as highly competitive. When he sits, he sprawls. He likes to work in a vest.") The *Times*'s approach was to "flood the zone," in a favorite phrase of Howell Raines, the executive edi-tor, who is an admirer of Bear Bryant, the late Alabama football coach. Five reporters and two researchers put the story together, and the writing is as bureaucratic as the method. ("The paper, concerned about maintain-ing its integrity among readers, tells its journalists to follow many guidelines as described in a memo on the newsroom's internal Web site.")

In both cases, what was more startling than the reporters' pathology was the degree to which so many warnings of disaster were ignored by so many editors of experience, including the papers' top leadership. Both papers ac-knowledged this; but the *Post*'s Green, it must be said, did so with greater candor and in greater depth than the *Times*'s team. In both cases, the peo-ple at the top said the right things about accepting responsibility. At the *Post*, at least one head eventually rolled—but it rolled sideways, and it quickly re-joined its body and resumed its upward trajectory. (The head was that of

Bob Woodward, who lost his job as metropolitan editor. He was immediately made assistant managing editor for investigations, the job he still holds.) Whether there will be even such non-Draconian consequences at the *Times* remains to be seen.

Last Wednesday, the *Times* held an emotional, sometimes bitter staff meeting in a movie theatre across the street. (It was closed to the press, including the *Times* reporter assigned to cover it, who was the only *Times* person barred from entry. He got his information the same way his colleagues from other news organizations did—at second hand. Such are the folkways of big-time journalism.) During the meeting, there were complaints that Raines, in his twenty months on the job, had proved forbidding, autocratic, and inaccessible, had played favorites, had ruled by fear, and had lost the trust of much of the newsroom. The executive editor apparently absorbed these painful charges and promised to do all he could to set things right. These are issues for Raines, Sulzberger, Gerald Boyd (the managing editor), and the staff of the paper to resolve. The health of the *Times* depends on their doing so.

Like Janet Cooke (and Gerald Boyd), Jayson Blair is African American. And, like the *Post,* the *Times* is a socially liberal institution, owned by a public-spirited family sensitive to the imperative of racial justice. The role of race in the present fiasco is anything but clear. But the first instinct of the *Times*'s executives was to deny absolutely that it had played any role whatsoever. That was absurd. At the meeting, according to the *Times,* Raines said, "I believe in aggressively providing hiring and career opportunities for minorities." A moment later, he added, "Does that mean I personally favored Jayson? Not consciously. But you have a right to ask if I, as a white man from Alabama, with those convictions, gave him one chance too many by not stopping his appointment to the sniper team. When I look into my heart for the truth of that, the answer is yes."

To the extent that Raines finds himself guilty of big-heartedness, of course, he can find himself innocent of bone-headedness. Still, it is a fact that the *Times*'s commitment to diversity has been exemplary. It compares favorably with that of almost every other media organization, present company included. This is not the place to rehearse the arguments in favor of affirmative action, or to review the two hundred and fifty years of slavery, followed by a hundred years of racial oppression, that lie behind those arguments. But affirmative action is strong medicine, and, as with any strong medicine, no great distance separates the therapeutic dose from the toxic one. It demands close monitoring of its institutional side effects. At the *Times*—in this instance, to a degree not yet fully understood—that monitoring seems to have failed.

The *Times* lamented, in its special report, that Blair's (and the *Times*'s) "widespread fabrication and plagiarism represent a profound betrayal of trust and a low point in the 152-year history of the newspaper." Still, the harm to the commonweal inflicted by Blair's banal lies amounted to rather less than, say, the harm done by the Pulitzer Prize–winning whitewash of Stalin's terror perpetrated by Walter Duranty, the paper's longtime Moscow correspondent, or, for that matter, the more recent harm done by its obtuse, petty, and wrongheaded obsession with the Clinton non-scandal known as Whitewater. The gravest damage of l'affaire Blair has been to the newspaper itself—and less to its public reputation than to its internal soundness, which is ultimately of greater importance. The health of the *New York Times*, as much as that of any single private institution in the land, is crucial to the health of the state, and to the state of public and political life in America. An outsider may be permitted to hope that the meeting at the movie house will be the beginning of a recovery. "When you make a mistake," Bear Bryant liked to say, "there are only three things you should ever do about it: admit it, learn from it, and don't repeat it."

—*The New Yorker*, May 26, 2003

RADIO DAZE

NEW YORK CITY is the home base of Fox News, *National Review,* and *The Rush Limbaugh Show.* We're in our tenth straight year under Republican mayors. And we're the world headquarters of heartless, rapacious, crush-the-workers Finance Capitalism. But none of that makes our town Nirvana for conservatives. Politically, we're blue through and through. Al Gore's margin over George W. Bush here was four to one, and the city's congressional delegation consists of twelve Democrats and one Republican. New York has its share of paleocons and more than its share of neocons (neoconservatism having been invented on the Upper West Side, circa 1968), but what we mostly have is noncons—that is, nonconservatives. We even have liberals.

You'd be hard put to notice that, though, from listening to the radio. As in the rest of the country, political talk radio here is dominated by the hard right. On the AM band, whose low-fidelity signal is perfect for shrill jabber, no fewer than four powerful stations feature "conservative talk." Two of them, WMCA and WWDJ, are "Christian" and heavily salted with attacks on homosexuality, abortion rights, and stem-cell research and support for school prayer, President Bush's judicial nominees, and Israeli maximalism. The other two pump out a steadier flow of viscous, untreated political sewage. WOR carries four hours daily of Bob Grant and Bill O'Reilly, reliable voices of irritable reaction. The biggie is WABC, which claims the largest talk-radio audience in the country. The station features fifteen hours a week of Limbaugh, fifteen of Sean Hannity, and ten of Mark Levin ("one of America's preeminent conservative commentators"). It recently dropped the malignant ranter Michael Savage, not because he told a "sodomite" caller, "You should only get AIDS and die, you pig"—that happened a little later, on Savage's short-lived MSNBC cable-television show—but over a contract dispute. (Savage's photograph remains on the home page of the WABC Web site, like Banquo's ghost.) As its call letters indicate, WABC carries the respectable imprimatur of the American Broadcasting Company, which owns it and provides its hourly newscasts, and, by extension, of ABC's parent company, Disney.

A generation ago, when WABC was New York's No. 1 Top Forty rock station, talk radio, here and elsewhere, was both smaller and more varied. In 1980, only seventy-five stations in the United States used the all-talk format, and most of them were politically anodyne. Conservative hosts were novelty items. Now there are more than thirteen hundred talk stations, the vast majority of which are relentlessly right-wing. New York, like a few other big coastal cities, has a squeaky voice or two on the marginal left. WBAI broadcasts Chomskian harangues, and WLIB, which carries mostly Caribbean pop music, dips an occasional toe into protest politics. On the whole, though, the New York lineup mirrors the far right's near-monopoly on political broadcasting nationwide. There is no real liberal or even just noncon counterpart to the radiocons, as we might as well call them. On (mostly) the FM dial, National Public Radio is an alternative but not an equivalent. NPR's *Morning Edition* and *All Things Considered*, like *The Rush Limbaugh Show*, are carried on some six hundred stations, and their audience is roughly the size of El Rushbo's—somewhere around fifteen million people per week. But these NPR programs are news-feature broadcasts; they adhere to the practices of journalistic professionalism, including the aspirational ideal of objectivity. Their sensibility may fairly be said to be "liberal" in the sense that liberal education is liberal—that is, open-minded and urbane, with a preference for empirical inquiry over dogmatic conclusion-mongering—but what little overt political commentary they offer hovers around the moderate middle. NPR's local talk-show hosts tend to be more overtly liberal, but they are always polite about it.

In contrast, Limbaugh and his scores of national and local imitators aggressively propagandize on behalf of the conservative wing of the Republican Party and the domestic and foreign policies of the Bush administration, with a stream of faxes and e-mails from conservative think tanks and the

Republican National Committee keeping the troops firmly on message. Neither NPR nor anyone else ever performed any such services for the Clinton administration, and no one is doing so today on behalf of the beleaguered Democratic opposition.

Anita and Sheldon Drobny, a couple of Chicago venture capitalists, have set out to do something about this. They have formed a company, AnShell Media, have pledged ten million of their own dollars to it, and are spending the summer trying to raise more money and assemble a fourteen-hour-a-day package of liberal talk radio and a national network of stations to carry it. It won't be easy to get this act together, and it'll be even harder to give it legs once it's on the air. The main obstacle, probably, is neither financial nor ideological but temperamental. Remember the old joke about politics being show business for ugly people? Well, right-wing radio is niche entertainment for the spiritually unattractive. It succeeds because a substantial segment of the right-wing rank and file enjoys listening, hour after hour, as smug, angry, disdainful middle-aged men spew raw contempt at reified enemies, named and unnamed. The radiocons seldom offer analysis or argument. To the chronically resentful, they offer the sadistic consolation of an endless sneer—at weaklings, victim-group whiners, cultural snobs, Hollywood hypocrites whose hearts bleed for the downtrodden though they themselves are rich and privileged, feminists, environmentalists, and, of course, "liberals," defined as the Clintons, other members of the "Democrat Party," and persons suspected of thinking that the state ought to help correct for various kinds of unfairnesses or calamities (economic, racial, climatic, medical) or of attaching themselves to some identity other than or in addition to "American" (black, gay, foreign, all humanity).

By contrast, most noncons—most people, for that matter—do not regard politics as entertainment. They regard it as politics. They wouldn't think it was fun to listen to expressions of raw contempt for conservatives—oh, maybe for a little while now and then, just as some occasionally tune in Limbaugh to give themselves a masochistic thrill or to raise their blood pressure, but not long and often enough to sustain an industry. When they want to be entertained, they watch comedy or drama. For the radiocon audience, political hate talk *is* comedy and drama. To their ears, it's music.

The radiolibs at AnShell Media are aware that previous attempts at liberal radio have been undone by dull earnestness. At the same time, they know that anger and abuse will not win them the audience they seek.

Accordingly, they plan to rely heavily, they say, on "comedy and political satire." As their headliner, they are trying to recruit Al Franken, the *Saturday Night Live* star and the author of such works of political science as *Rush Limbaugh Is a Big Fat Idiot* and the forthcoming *Lies and the Lying Liars Who Tell Them: A Fair and Balanced Look at the Right*. Good luck to them. God knows they'll need it. They should only break a leg.

—*The New Yorker*, August 11, 2003

9. WEDGE ISSUES

Capital punishment, I've always thought, is a pretty easy call. Should the state tell a person that it is going to kill him at some future date (maybe in three or four months, maybe in ten years), then lock that person in a cage for twenty-three hours a day until it is good and ready to go through with the killing, and then either tie him down and inject him with lethal poison or else put a hood over his head and strap him to a high-voltage device that cooks him to death? The person to whom this is done may fully "deserve" such treatment. But for the state to inflict it is demeaning. It is an offense to its own general dignity and to the specific dignity and humanity of the civil servants whom it asks to perform the deed. In the development of civilization, there was a time when "an eye for an eye" represented a moral advance, because it implied some notion of proportionality. And, certainly, there are still times when killing is morally permissible. There is such a thing as justifiable homicide. But there is a difference between, on the one hand, killing in self-defense, or even vengeful killing in hot blood, and, on the other hand, the thoroughly premeditated, perfectly passionless ritual killing of a helpless wretch by representatives of the authority charged with safeguarding the moral order.

As I say, an easy call. The same with the "drug war," proposals for constitutional amendments banning "flag desecration," and laws authorizing the police to break down the doors of people's homes and arrest them for engaging in private, consensual sex with other adults not related to them by blood. Why isn't everyone simply against all three, end of story? Abortion, affirmative action, and pornography present somewhat more complex moral challenges, but it is baffling to me how a person of goodwill, after examining these issues with care, could conclude that it would be either wise or good to criminalize the first, abolish the second, and abridge civil liberties in order to extirpate the third. Yet people, some of them people of goodwill, will persist in having opinions on these and similar subjects (gay marriage, stem cell research, the right to die) that diverge from mine.

These differences of opinion are what makes op-ed pages. They also provide raw material for political attack ads. And when public opinion or public policy is on the "wrong" side of one these issues—drug policy is a good example—the consequences can include unnecessary human suffering. So the arguments must be made, whether the calls are easy or hard.

BIG BOOBS

GUESS WHAT, Miss Liberty? Ed Meese has a birthday present for you.

On July 3, 1986, a few hours before President Reagan flies north to officiate at the centennial celebration of the world's biggest female statue, his attorney general, if all goes as planned, will release the final text of the report of his pornography commission. The resulting fireworks may rival the big show in the sky over New York Harbor. If they don't, it won't be because Meese hasn't tried.

In the conservative dialectic that defines the Reagan counterrevolution, the report of the Meese commission—known officially as the Attorney General's Commission on Pornography—is designed to be the antithesis of its ancestor, the notorious 1970 report of the federal Commission on Obscenity and Pornography. The two reports and the two commissions are indeed antithetical, and not only in the ways Meese intended. If the old commission was the federal equivalent of *Playboy,* the new one is the equivalent of *Hustler*—low-budget, weak on fact-checking, unsubtle, and fascinated by the perverse.

The 1970 commission had a budget of $2 million, a staff of twenty-two, and two years to complete its mission. That mission, as defined by Congress, was to analyze the obscenity laws, to study the effects on the public of the traffic in obscenity and pornography, and, if necessary, to recommend ways "to regulate effectively the flow of such traffic." The 1970 commission sponsored a wide range of original research by reputable scholars, psychologists, and universities. Its chairman, William B. Lockhart, appointed by President Johnson, was the dean of the University of Minnesota Law School.

The 1986 commission, by contrast, had a budget of $400,000 (the equivalent in 1970 dollars of around $150,000), a staff of nine, and one year to complete its mission. That mission, as defined by Ed Meese, was to study the impact of pornography and to recommend "more effective ways in which the spread of pornography could be contained." The 1986 commission sponsored no original research, and its consultants were mostly policemen and antiporn activists. Its Meese-appointed chairman, Henry Hudson, is a Virginia county prosecutor who conducted an avid campaign against adult bookstores, and who once told the *Washington Post,* "I live to put people in jail." While serving as chairman, Hudson was angling for a job—which he has since landed—as a U.S. attorney.

By all accounts the 1970 commission approached its duties with an open mind. Two or three of its members had taken public positions on pornography, but the rest had not. When it produced its recommendations, they included calls for "a massive sex education effort" aimed at "providing accurate and reliable sex information through legitimate sources," for the prohibition of public displays and the sale to minors of "sexually explicit pictorial materials," and—most surprisingly—for the outright repeal of federal, state, and local laws against "the sale, exhibition, or distribution of sexual materials to consenting adults." The Nixon administration indignantly disavowed the commission, and few of its recommendations were enacted. Not a single state repealed its obscenity laws. But those laws, already spottily enforced, fell increasingly into disuse as police departments turned their attention to more pressing threats to public safety.

The 1986 commission has been stacked to prevent unwelcome surprises. Of its eleven members, six have well-established public records of supporting government action against sexy books and films. One of the commissioners, for example, is a Franciscan priest who has condemned Dr. Ruth Westheimer, the chirpy radio sex adviser, for advocating orgasms in premarital sex. Another is a religious broadcaster whose best-selling book, *Dare to Discipline*—a title that would not be out of place in the bondage section of an adult bookstore—advocates corporal punishment of children. A third is a University of Michigan law professor who has argued in law review articles that pornography is not constitutionally protected. The Meese commission lacked the financial and staff resources of its predecessor, but since its conclusions were preordained it didn't really need them.

The Meese report will recommend a long list of stern measures. They include changing obscenity laws to make any second offense a felony rather than a misdemeanor, with a mandatory one-year jail term; prosecuting the producers of porn films under the prostitution laws (because the actors are paid for their work); changing the forfeiture laws to permit the government to confiscate the assets of any business found in violation of the federal obscenity laws (allowing, for example, the seizure of a whole convenience store for the sale of a single dirty magazine); and a big enforcement push, including the appointment of a "high-level" Justice Department task force on obscenity cases. Where the pornography in question is too mild to bring the obscenity laws into play, the report somewhat cautiously recommends "private action"—picketing, boycotts, and the like.

Under the federal sunshine laws, the Meese commission has conducted virtually all of its business in public—not only the hearings it staged in Washington, Chicago, Houston, Los Angeles, Miami, and New York but also the working sessions it held in tandem with the hearings. Given the appeal of the subject, the show played to curiously empty houses. Not a single major newspaper assigned a reporter to cover the story on a regular basis. The only reporters who turned up for every meeting, and who assiduously collected the chaotic pastiche of hastily written drafts and documents that will make up the final report, were two representatives of what might be called the trade press. Philip Nobile and Eric Nadler of *Forum*, a kind of journal of sexual opinion put out by the *Penthouse* empire, will publish their researches next month in a book, *The United States of America vs. Sex: How the Meese Commission Lied about Pornography*, which combines solid reporting with lively and intelligent polemics. It is thanks to an advance reading of their manuscript and collection of documents that I have some idea of how the commission went about its work.

IT WAS QUITE A SHOW. The commissioners heard two hundred and eight witnesses, including sixty-eight policemen, thirty "victims," and fourteen representatives of antipornography organizations. They were subjected to slide shows that were—in the words of the two ultimately dissenting commissioners, Ellen Levine, editor of *Woman's Day*, and Judith Becker, a Columbia University psychiatrist—"skewed to the very violent and extremely degrading," including, in one case, a picture of a man having sex with a chicken. They made field trips to "adult bookstores." They listened as a retired F.B.I. agent assured them that the pornography industry was dominated by organized crime. They engaged in many a zany, aimless conversation, including one discussion of necrophilia during which a commissioner wondered aloud, "Is it legal to have sex with a corpse if you're married to it?"

The "victims" who testified before the commission included former prostitutes, former abused wives and children, former junkies, and people who complained that a relative had spent the family savings on dirty books. All blamed their troubles on pornography, though the causal connections were never clear. One of the most curious victims was a wispy, neatly dressed man of thirty-eight who appeared, Bible in hand, at the commission's Miami hearing.

"I am a victim of pornography," the witness began. "At age twelve, I was a typically normal, healthy boy. My life was filled with normal activities and hobbies. All that changed the following summer when I went to visit relatives, a married couple, who decided to teach me about sex. . . . I saw a *Playboy* magazine for the first time in my life.

"All the trouble began a few months later, back at my mother's home. The house we rented had a shed out back, and that's where I found a hidden deck of cards. All fifty-two cards depicted hard-core pornography—penetration, fellatio, and cunnilingus. These porno cards highly aroused me and gave me a desire I never had before."

The witness then detailed his subsequent record of wrongdoing, all of it, according to him, ascribable to the fatal deck of cards. From shoplifting, he descended to masturbation, anal intercourse with another teenage boy, peeping on his mother, "oral and finger stimulation on my parents' dogs," reading sex magazines ("I used to read Hugh Hefner's *Playboy* philosophy, and I am sure through his help I bought the program of the sixties, hook, line, and sinker"), taking drugs, and—the ultimate degradation—"watching R-rated movies on HBO and Showtime cable."

In conclusion, the witness solemnly told the by now stupefied commissioners, "If it weren't for my faith in God, and the forgiveness of Jesus Christ, I would now possibly be a pervert, an alcoholic, or dead. I am a victim of pornography."

EVEN THE MOST ardently antiporn commissioners were embarrassed by this sort of testimony—much of which, Chairman Hudson admitted during one of the working sessions, was written and structured by the commission staff. At the beginning of March, that staff, under the guidance of its executive director, a thirty-four-year-old federal prosecutor from Kentucky named Alan Sears, presented the commissioners with a proposed draft of the final report. It quickly became apparent that this elephantine document—whose twelve hundred pages included two hundred pages of lurid, unsubstantiated "victim" testimony—owed more than a little to the porno-card school of discourse. One of the commissioners, Frederick Shauer, the Michigan law school professor, protested.

In a letter to his colleagues, Shauer set forth his complaints. He pointed out that the ex-F.B.I. agent who had testified on the connection between pornography and organized crime was a convicted shoplifter with (in the words of the judge who tried him) "a great propensity to lie." He noted that one publication cited in the draft was included only "because it was astoundingly gross, bizarre, and disgusting," and added: "But that does not make it legally obscene, and it does not make us any less of a laughingstock for including it." He called the section on constitutional law "so one-sided and oversimplified that I cannot imagine signing anything that looks remotely like this." On the "victim" testimony, he wrote: "If this section is included as is, we will have confirmed all the worst fears about the information on which we relied, and all of the worst fears about our biases." Finally, he announced his intention to write an entirely new draft himself, taking into account the views of the other commissioners. Six weeks later, he had done just that.

Whether Edwin Meese realizes it or not, he owes Frederick Shauer a great deal, for Shauer has saved him from issuing a report that it would have been superfluous to ridicule. The Shauer draft, two hundred and eleven pages long, immediately became the basis for the text of the report the commission will issue on July 3. Though the draft has its share of howlers, on the whole it is reasonable and civilized in tone. It is written in a calm, even stately style. It contains little in the way of hysteria. To the limited extent that it takes note of the views of those who disagree, it treats those views with civility. Yet it preserves the basic conclusion Meese had programmed the commission to reach.

That conclusion, as best I can make it out through the fog of professorial qualifications and unacknowledged internal contradictions, is that pornography is "harmful," and that therefore the police powers of the state should be mobilized to suppress it. More precisely, according to the report, certain kinds of violent and "degrading" pornography seem to cause certain ill-defined varieties of "harm"—though not nearly as much harm, the report admits in two separate places, as either "weaponry magazines" that focus on "guns, martial arts, and related topics" or "slasher" movies of the *Friday the 13th* variety.

The process by which this conclusion is reached relies on a spectacularly tenuous chain of causation. For example, in certain laboratory studies, male college students were shown certain movies—exactly what movies the body of the report does not say, though it seems that in one case the flick of the day was Lina Wertmuller's highly acclaimed *Swept Away*—and then were taken to mock rape trials. Afterward, they were asked to fill out questionnaires. According to the results of the questionnaires, the students who saw the movies seemed to show less sympathy for the complainants in the rape cases than did students who had not been shown the movies. From this it is concluded that pornography causes—well, maybe not sex crimes, exactly, maybe not even a disposition to "unlawful" sexual aggressiveness, but *something*. (And never mind that Edward Donnerstein, the University of Wisconsin psychologist whose findings the commission relies on, has repudiated its interpretation of his work.)

This is as intellectually rigorous as the report gets where the question of "harm" is concerned. Mostly it turns with relief to more capacious definitions. "An environment, physical, cultural, moral, or aesthetic, can be harmed," it argues, "and so can a community, organization, or group be harmed independent of identifiable harms to members of that community." Broad enough? Apparently not, for in the very next sentence we are assured that "the idea of harm is broader than that."

Another bit of slippery reasoning in the report concerns the report's division of pornography into four "classes." In this scheme, Class I, violent pornography, and Class II, "degrading" pornography, are definitely "harmful," while Class III, nonviolent and nondegrading materials (such as depictions of ordinary vaginal intercourse), is probably harmless, and Class IV, simple nudity, is definitely harmless. This definition would seem to put the vast bulk of commercially available erotica, including magazines like *Playboy* and *Penthouse,* in Classes III and IV. But in drafting this section, Shauer broadened the definition of Class II. Taking a leaf from Andrea Dworkin, the renegade feminist antipornography crusader, Shauer incorporated into

the "degrading" category "material that, although not violent, depicts people, usually women, as existing solely for the sexual satisfaction of others,
usually men, or that depicts people, usually women, in decidedly subordinate roles in their sexual relations with others." By this sleight of hand,
Class III suddenly became "quite small in terms of currently available materials," while erotica of the *Playboy-Penthouse* variety just as suddenly became "degrading"— and therefore, in the commission's view, subject to
suppression.

IF EVERYTHING had worked out according to plan, the release of the report of the Attorney General's Commission on Pornography would be the
signal for a gigantic national crusade, fronted by right-thinking political
leaders, against demon porn. The report is not scheduled for release until
July 3, but it is already safe to predict that the crusade will fizzle. For this,
thanks are owed the people of Maine.

On Tuesday, June 10, the voters of that rocky, laconic state were asked to
approve or disapprove a new, four-and-a-half-page statute that for ballot
purposes had been boiled down to a one-liner: "Do you want to make it a
crime to make, sell, give for value or otherwise promote obscene material
in Maine?" The statute itself anticipated some of the Meese report's recommendations (such as heavy jail sentences for sellers of naughty magazines), and its endorsement at the polls—which would have provided the
ideal fanfare for the report—was a far from unreasonable expectation. Maine
is one of the more conservative states of the region, remote from the so-
phistications of fleshpots like Boston. The local Roman Catholic bishop
campaigned for the referendum, as did a noisy and powerful movement of
politically active evangelicals gathered under the banner of the Maine Christian Civic League, which has been a force in the state since it led the fight
for Prohibition. The "no" forces, for their part, had the Maine Civil Liberties Union, Democratic Governor Joseph Brennan, and Maine's most famous author, Stephen King.

The turnout was the highest ever for any comparable election in Maine,
and the outcome was decisive: 16,101 citizens voted yes and 48,976 voted no,
a margin of better than three to one against. Whatever the good people of
the Granite State may think of smut, they are unambiguous in their dislike
of censorship and the busybodies who promote it.

Politicians are sure to take note of this result. While true believers such as Jeremiah Denton and Pat Robertson will continue to pound the table about porn, their more opportunistic, less principled colleagues will probably ease off. As Maine goes, they will reason, so goes the nation. Posturing against porn may not yet be quite the political equivalent of herpes—it will still be required of Republicans in places where the religious right is strong—but the issue has now lost much of its punch. As for the president, he may be expected to make a Saturday morning speech in order to please his friend Meese and to placate the constituency Meese represents. But the old trouper—who has a history of tolerance for sexual unconventionality among his Hollywood chums, his staffers, and his wife's social circle, who has a son working for *Playboy* and a daughter whose recent novel includes the normal quota of steamy sex scenes, and who himself divorced one actress and then married another after remarking that he was tired of not knowing the names of the starlets he was waking up next to—will probably refrain from expending much of his popularity on an issue that was never especially congenial for him and is now a proven political loser as well.

Still, even if the report fails to touch off the hoped-for national crusade, it is bound to play an important part in a decentralized but wider effort to constrict personal liberty and freedom of expression. Most of the fuss over dirty books occurs at the local level, in small cities and towns. Typically, an ambitious or perfervid prosecutor decides that obscenity busts are the road to political advancement or social salubrity, or an ad hoc group of self-righteous citizens tries to make its own narrow preferences mandatory for a whole community, particularly for its schools, libraries, and convenience stores. When such people succeed, the result is censorship of a small but tangible kind. They will get plenty of encouragement from the Meese report.

Experience shows that these vigilante actions are almost never aimed at violent or even "hard core" pornography. The targets are usually books that treat sex realistically, or, in the case of convenience stores, popular men's magazines. And the commission has shown the way.

Last February Alan Sears wrote to a number of large companies informing each of them that the commission had "received testimony alleging that your company is involved in the sale or distribution of pornography." He invited them to explain themselves, adding ominously, "Failure to respond will necessarily be accepted as an indication of no objection." Attached to the letter addressed to the Southland Corporation, which operates the 7-Eleven chain of convenience stores, was a photocopy of a page that read in part, "The general public usually associates pornography with sleazy porno bookstores and theaters. However, many of the major players in the game of pornography are well-known household names. Few people realize that 7-Eleven convenience stores are the leading retailers of porn magazines in America." There was no indication of where the page came from. (In fact, it was from the testimony of Donald Wildmon, executive director of a religious right organization called the National Federation of Decency.) A few weeks later, Southland removed *Playboy* and *Penthouse* from its stores.

No doubt the Constitution will survive. Yet the fact remains that in some areas convenience stores are the only places magazines are sold. *Playboy* and *Penthouse* publish not only erotica but also what might be called politica. Nobody buys these magazines for the articles, despite what husbands caught with them tell their wives. Still, the articles are sometimes read. *Playboy* and *Penthouse* are sources of faintly heretical ideas as well as sexy pictures. Their removal from their largest sales outlet by what amounts to government intimidation does not improve the political health of the country.

Furthermore, there's no logical reason why the commission's slippery-slope syllogism should be limited to porn. The syllogism goes like this: (a) stores have the right not to carry any publication they don't want to carry; (b) private citizens have the right to boycott or protest in front of any store that carries a publication they don't like; (c) government approval or encouragement of such private efforts doesn't violate the First Amendment. The issue here is a technique of suppression. Some would argue that it is freedom of political speech that is protected by the Constitution. Yet once it is established that indirect government pressure on magazine distributors is O.K., there is no guarantee that such pressure won't be applied to publications that the reigning ideologues don't like for political reasons. "Private action" isn't so private when government commissions explicitly encourage it.

The Meese report also will encourage the kind of local crusaders for decency who are forever trying to ban supposedly dirty books from schools and libraries. One doesn't need to exaggerate the likely impact of this sort of thing to understand that it will be real enough for the schoolteachers and librarians forced to choose between their consciences and their jobs. Finally, the commission will probably succeed in its goal of encouraging local prosecutors to do their worst. Given the commission's loose definition of harmful pornography and the advent of the Rehnquist Supreme Court, their worst might ultimately turn out to be quite bad.

Despite its many assertions to the contrary, the Meese commission has simply failed to demonstrate that pornography constitutes a meaningful threat to the public interest. At a minimum, the commission is guilty of what Levine and Becker, in their dissent, call "unacceptable efforts" to "tease the current data into proof of a causal link." But even if some such showing could be made, it would not follow that freedom of speech and of the press ought therefore to be abridged. The First Amendment contains no requirement that the speech it protects be harmless. On the contrary, speech that somebody thinks is harmful is the only kind that needs protecting.

The commission's report will be widely read, because even a government book about sex is still a book about sex. And it's especially irresistible if it's as fat, as obsessed with kink, and as full of inadvertent humor as this one. A final apposite example of the last: after a long section on the problem of "underprosecution," the commissioners conclude, "We urge that many of the specific recommendations we suggest be taken seriously."

How wonderfully lame. The logically required corollary, of course, would be this: "We urge that some of the specific recommendations we suggest not be taken seriously."

Though insufficiently inclusive, this seems wise.

—The New Republic, July 14 & 21, 1986

EXECUTIONS I:
BURNING QUESTION

THE SCENE at Florida State Prison the morning they gave Ted Bundy the chair was straight out of a sleazy teen exploitation movie. Two thousand people, many of them boisterous college students, gathered outside the prison. They held up signs saying things like I LIKE MY TED WELL DONE. Sales of BURN BUNDY BURN T-shirts were brisk. When the hearse pulled out of the prison yard there were whoops and high-fives. All that was lacking was for Bundy to push open the lid of his coffin and come bounding out in a hockey mask.

Despite the frat-house atmosphere, there was nothing either uniquely American or particularly novel about the Florida festivities. Celebratory scenes at executions were old news when Voltaire and Dickens were describing them; old news, for that matter, when Roman soldiers threw dice and passed around the wineskin at Calvary.

The death penalty is uncontroversial in Western Europe, where execution is unknown, and in the Islamic countries, where it is routine. The debate is in South Africa, where the gallows helps prop up apartheid; in the Communist world, where glasnost has brought forth a few mild calls for abolition; and of course in the United States, where a few months ago our nice new president was demanding death for what he called "narcotic drug kingpins" in every campaign speech.

As with so many other goods and services, America offers a greater variety of execution than any other country. Besides the electric chair, the thirty-seven capital punishment states employ poison gas, hanging, shooting, and lethal injection. Electrocution (seventeen states), invented in 1888, was sold as "scientific" and humane, though in fact it is probably painful and undeniably disgusting: the body convulses, smoke pours from its orifices, the smell of cooked flesh pervades the execution chamber, and the corpse is so hot it cannot be touched for several minutes. In our cool era lethal injection (fourteen states) is the happening thing. This grotesque parody of medical procedure takes from five to ten minutes, during much of which the prisoner may be awake and in obvious pain. In one recent botched execution in Texas the I.V. tube slipped out of the condemned man's arm and sprayed poison all over the room; that one ended up taking forty-five minutes.

However iffy the technology, the United States is moving on the numbers front. After a ten-year hiatus we restarted slowly, with six executions between 1977 and 1982. The pace has picked up smartly: Bundy made it an even hundred since 1983. Some twenty-two hundred people wait on the nation's death rows, a proud Republican achievement.

The Bundy case makes a good test of one's views on capital punishment, just as a fourteen-year-old girl impregnated by rape or incest makes a good test of one's views on abortion. Bundy was such a sadistic, bloodthirsty, thoroughly evil mass murderer that one needn't be a proponent of the death penalty to be sickened by the thought of him living peacefully to a ripe old age, borrowing books from the prison library and granting the occasional interview. Why then was it wrong to execute him?

There are two main arguments for capital punishment, one specious and one worthy of respect. The specious argument is that it deters. Despite massive efforts, no one has ever been able to show that capital punishment lowers the murder rate. "The available evidence," writes James Q. Wilson, no softy, "does not establish that the death penalty has a deterrent effect." This flies in the face of common sense; but just as the commonsense laws of Newtonian physics go haywire near a black hole, so commonsense notions of behavioral incentive may invert in the dark and clotted mental universe of murder. Bundy, for example, moved to Florida only after ascertaining that it is where the death penalty is applied most assiduously.

The argument worthy of respect is that society has a right and a duty to manifest a terrible anger in the face of a terrible crime. "The criminal law must be made awful, by which I mean inspiring, or commanding, 'profound respect or reverential fear,'" Walter Berns, an eloquent defender of the death penalty, has written. "It must remind us of the moral order by which alone we can live as human beings, and . . . the only punishment that can do this is capital punishment." There is an appealing majesty to this view. But it is not at all clear that this is the lesson executions teach. If the Florida celebrants were thinking high-minded thoughts about the moral order, they did not show it. And soberer citizens, reading about the previous day's electrocution in the morning paper, may equally draw the lesson that killing is O.K. when some sufficiently powerful entity finds a sufficiently compelling reason to do it.

Bundy's example to the contrary notwithstanding, capital punishment falls most heavily upon the black and poor, especially if their victims are white and rich. But this argues as powerfully for increasing the reach of the death penalty as for abolishing it. Nor will it do to dismiss capital punishment as "lawful murder," unless we are also prepared to dismiss imprisonment as "lawful kidnapping."

The great practical flaw of capital punishment is that it opens up the possibility of executing the wrong person. This doesn't seem to have happened lately, but it could. Eroll Morris's superb documentary film *The Thin Blue Line* details the case of Randall Adams, an almost certainly innocent man sentenced to death and saved from execution only by the fluke of an unrelated Supreme Court decision. (Adams still awaits justice in a Texas jail.)

Because we rightly fear such travesties, because we rightly abhor the calculus of accepting the execution of one innocent person to facilitate the execution of many guilty ones, we have elaborate procedures to prevent this most irreversible of all miscarriages of justice. But these indispensable procedures, because they take time, amplify the cruelty of capital punishment, which consists more in the waiting than in the killing.

Albert Camus likened the death penalty to "a criminal who had warned his victim of the date at which he would inflict a horrible death on him and who, from that moment onward, had confined him at his mercy for months. Such a monster is not encountered in private life." Camus was wrong: Ted Bundy was a monster worse even than that. And Camus was right: the penalty is too cruel, even when, as in Bundy's case, the cruelty is deserved. Berns correctly locates the meaning of execution in society's duty to instruct itself. Bundy killed cruelly and coldly, thus meriting death. So we killed Bundy, less cruelly but more coldly, thus demeaning ourselves. In giving Bundy his deserts, we—the social order—deprived ourselves of ours. And we are more important than any murderer.

—*The New Republic*, February 20, 1989

EXECUTIONS II:
FEDERAL DEATH

ON MARCH 15, 1963, in a converted auto-repair shop on the grounds of the state penitentiary in Fort Madison, Iowa, a twenty-seven-year-old man named Victor Feguer was hanged by the neck until dead. Feguer was a banal and hapless criminal. For all but a few months of his wretched life from the age of thirteen until he died, he was confined to penal institutions. During one of two brief interludes of freedom, he robbed and murdered a stranger. Because he had taken his victim across a state boundary, he was tried in federal court. The only witnesses to his hanging were people who had to be there—prison employees, morticians, a priest, a few reporters.

Victor Feguer was the last person executed under the auspices of the federal government, a distinction that he will lose next week. The intervening thirty-eight years have been an era of progress. Hanging has been all but abandoned in this land of ours. (It is still an option in the State of Washington, but the inmate has to put in a special request.) It was always a nasty business. If the drop was too deep, the result could be decapitation; if too shallow, slow strangulation. Still, even when a hanging is done well it is an unpleasant thing to see and hear. One of the witnesses to Feguer's death, a retired newspaperman, is still troubled by the sound-memory of the surprisingly loud thunk-crack of the rope snapping and the neck breaking. The prisoner dangled limply, but his heart continued to beat for nine minutes and forty-five seconds.

The execution of Timothy McVeigh, on May 16th, in Terre Haute, Indiana, will be altogether tidier, thanks to the fashionable technique of lethal injection, which has many of the trappings of a medical "procedure." And McVeigh represents a better class of federal executee. He is a decorated Army veteran—a recipient of the Bronze Star for his service in the Gulf War. He is clinically sane. He is unrepentant. He killed 168 people. No one can say he was not responsible for his actions. Opponents of the death penalty find him a hard case.

Politically, though, capital punishment has been something of a non-issue since well before McVeigh came along. In 1988, Michael Dukakis's opposition to it helped cost him the presidency; in 1994, Mario Cuomo's helped dislodge him from the governorship of New York. Politicians of the sort who used to oppose the death penalty—Bill Clinton, Al Gore, Joseph Lieberman, Charles Schumer, and Hillary Rodham Clinton are among the many names that spring to mind—now support it. Perhaps they are truly convinced, in the inmost reaches of conscience, that state-administered death is a good thing. A more charitable (some would say harsher) view is that they have made a Faustian bargain: they say they're for capital punishment, and in return they get to survive politically. Like many political compromises, it's not necessarily a bad deal. (Would their constituents really be better off represented by people who not only favor the death penalty but also oppose progressive taxation, public health care, and environmental regulation?) The tactical retreat of the anti-execution forces echoes the tactical retreat of the anti-abortion forces. The latter no longer talk much about criminalizing abortion or forcing women impregnated by rape or incest to carry to term; they talk instead about "partial birth" and "parental notification." The former don't say they think it's wrong for the state to kill people (in fact, they say they think it's right); they say they're troubled by the disparate racial impact, or the possibility that an innocent person might be executed, or the shoddiness of legal representation. And, of course, these are wholly legitimate concerns.

It is often argued, especially in Europe, that the prevalence of official homicide in the United States bespeaks a peculiarly American coarseness: what else can you expect from a country full of fundamentalist zealots and gun nuts? But the truth is that you don't have to be American to like the death penalty. Support for it is as high in, for example, Britain (68 percent) and the Czech Republic (67 percent), both of which have abolished it, as it is in the United States (67 percent in the most recent Gallup poll, down from 80 percent in 1994). Even in gentle Canada, where there has not been an execution since 1962, support for capital punishment hovers at around 55 percent. The real difference between them and us is that we have fifty-one governments (the states plus the feds) that have the right to decide for themselves about capital punishment, and each of those governments consists of independently elected executive and legislative branches—an arrangement that leaves plenty of scope for single-issue, hot-button politics. In Europe and Canada, only one outfit per country has that kind of power: the ruling party or coalition in the national parliament. Once a parliament abolishes capital punishment, it's very hard to unabolish it. And the European Union has made abolition a de facto condition of membership. A country that decided to bring back the gallows, the garrote, or the guillotine would have to pay a pretty steep price for the satisfaction of offing a few miscreants. But if capital punishment is ever to be abolished here, it will have to be done by the people, state by state and step by step. Our politicians won't save us from ourselves. They can't.

Even so, more and more Americans agree with something President Bush said a few weeks ago: "We understand how unfair the death penalty is." Of course he meant the death *tax,* so-called, and he quickly corrected himself. (Capital punishment *sí,* capital gains punishment *no.*) He was right the first time. The prospects for small, incremental steps are actually quite good. Polls show growing, sometimes majority, support for moratoriums like the one decreed last year by George Ryan, the Republican governor of Illinois. There is movement here and there—even, in a modest way, in the Texas legislature—toward suspending the death penalty until it can be determined that it can be justly applied. Unfair in practice is not the same as wrong in principle, but it will have to do.

—*The New Yorker,* May 14, 2001

WOUNDS OF RACE

I HAVE YET TO MEET a well-informed, unbigoted black American who would not firmly endorse the following statement: If you're black, you have to be twice as good to travel the same socioeconomic distance as a white person in this country—twice as talented, twice as ambitious, twice as determined.

To this, the average well-informed, unbigoted white American will reply: nonsense. Sure, that was true years ago, but today if you're black and minimally qualified all you have to do is show up, and bang—you're in college, you're in law school, you've got the job.

The gap between these two honest perceptions is a measure of the passion and pain of race in America. Race is the wound that will not heal, and the Supreme Court has just rubbed fresh salt in that wound with a series of decisions truncating the equal employment provisions of the Civil Rights Act of 1964—which, as of July 2, will have been the law for exactly twenty-five years. What a dismal anniversary present.

To read these decisions is to become aware of the dizzying moral fall from the Warren Court, a product of Eisenhower Republicanism, to the Rehnquist Court, a product of Reagan Republicanism. When the Warren Court took up this most divisive of American perplexities, it was careful to seek unanimity among its own members: *Brown v. Board of Education* was a 9–0 decision. The Rehnquist Court hacks away at settled precedent by repeated votes of 5 to 4. The Warren Court looked to the grandeur of the Constitution for guidance. The Rehnquist Court draws its arguments from abstruse (and questionable) points of contract law. The Warren Court took history (not just "legislative history") into account, and considered the building of social justice to be part of its writ. The Rehnquist Court renders its decisions in highly technical, almost impenetrable language wholly free of any hint of the suffering, the bitterness, and all the other human realities that inform the cases it decides.

"The linchpin of the 'impermissible collateral attack' doctrine—the attribution of preclusive effect to a failure to intervene—is therefore quite inconsistent with Rule 19 and Rule 24," writes Chief Justice Rehnquist in a typical passage of *Marin v. Wilks*—and that's about as exalted as his language gets. In that particular case, the Court, by the usual 5–4 majority, opened the way for endless legal assaults on an affirmative action program, the product of seven years of painful negotiations and lawsuits, that since 1981 has peacefully and effectively brought a measure of racial integration to the previously all-white fire department of Birmingham, Alabama.

After reading the decisions, I ended up sharing the dismay of Justice Blackmun, who wrote in dissent, "One wonders whether the majority still believes that race discrimination—or, more accurately, race discrimination against nonwhites—is a problem in our society, or even remembers that it ever was." But the cases themselves are less important than the larger questions about race (and about affirmative action) they raise.

The affirmative action debate takes place in a context shaped by the success of civil rights and the failure of social policy. The triumphant destruction of institutionalized segregation broke apart the old black communities in which people of all classes and levels of accomplishment lived together in oppression. The most ambitious, lucky, and talented were—and are—boiled off into the larger society. As an unintended consequence, those left behind have been distilled into an increasingly isolated, increasingly pathological, increasingly self-destructive subculture, the urban black underclass. Social programs designed to alleviate its condition have either proved unworkable or been starved. Reaganism's upward redistribution of income has sharpened the pain. But the failure is general. "Conservatives have ignored the problem, left the solution to 'market forces' or, worse, to social Darwinism," writes Joe Klein in a brilliant essay in the May 29 *New York* magazine. "Liberals seem to have abandoned critical thought entirely, allowing militants to dictate their agenda, scorning most efforts to impose sanctions on anti-social behavior by underclass blacks."

Affirmative action is a kind of homeopathic medicine, an effort to correct an immense historic injustice with small doses of "injustice" in the present. It is an effort to lift some blacks by main force into the middle class. It should properly be seen not as a sacrifice by whites for the benefit of blacks, but rather as a sacrifice by the present generation for the benefit of the next. The cost is paid today—by the whites shunted aside, and, more subtly, by the blacks obliged to doubt that their advancement is personally deserved. ("Social victims may be collectively entitled, but they are all too often individually demoralized," writes the black essayist Shelby Steele, quoted by Klein.) The payoff will come tomorrow, when a new generation of black children is born into the middle class—there to share, presumably, the routine advantages and complexes of a bourgeois upbringing.

The psychic cost of affirmative action to its purported "real-time" beneficiaries is very high. In the post-slavery century of segregated oppression, few members of what W.E.B. DuBois called "the talented tenth" were troubled by lack of self-esteem. They *knew* that whatever they had they had more than earned, because there was no other way to get it. Their affirmative action counterparts of today cannot be so sure. Yes, the jobs are easier to get—and in this sense the white perception is correct. But the respect that is supposed to come with the job—that comes with it more or less automatically for whites—does not come automatically for blacks. It cannot be "demanded," Jesse Jackson notwithstanding. It must be struggled for and earned. This applies to self-respect as well as to the respect of others. "You're not here because you're smart or because you worked hard, you're here because there's a program for hiring black people." That's a natural enough thought for whites to have, and they don't have to be "racist" in any classic way to have it. It's a thought, moreover, that on some level the black beneficiaries of affirmative action are obliged to share. That is a high hurdle to overcome—as high, psychologically, as segregation was. The fact that the hurdle is subjective and invisible, that it cannot be measured by outward signs, does not make it any the less real. That is why, when blacks insist they must be "twice as good," they are merely reporting the existential truth of their own experience.

In any event, affirmative action can work only at the margins. It can pull up only those who are ready to be pulled up. It can do little or nothing for the mind-numbingly dreadful problems of the underclass—the powerful, self-reinforcing nexus of crime, drugs, children bearing children, family atomization, despair, peer pressure to fail in school, and all the fearful rest.

Against those problems—the real problems—affirmative action is helpless; and, in isolation, it fosters a cycle of mutual racial resentment destructive to the political will that is needed. There is no sign of that political will. President Bush and the Republicans have absolutely nothing to say about it. The Democrats have scarcely more.

Political will is not going to be summoned until whites and blacks can agree that they are citizens of the same country. Black nationalism is a dead end, as many observers, black and white, have noted. So is what might be called white nationalism. And in this connection the tragic elements of American history hang heavy—not because they are acknowledged but because they are ignored. Many of our reigning national myths, important parts of America's civil religion, simply exclude black people. I have been trying to imagine what it's like for a black person to listen to a speech about how America is a "nation of immigrants" and the "land of opportunity." The truth is that this is *not* a nation of immigrants. It is a nation of immigrants and slaves. Our ancestors did *not* come here full of hope, seeking freedom and a better life. They came seeking freedom and they came in chains.

The speeches of politicians and other national leaders seldom take this into account. In their anxiety to draw happy, uncomplicated morals, they seldom tell the full American story. No wonder black people—whose roots in this country, on average, go back further than those of white people—are alienated.

Consider a couple of exceptions, drawn from the two greatest speeches ever delivered by Americans.

Fondly do we hope—fervently do we pray—that this mighty scourge of war may speedily pass away. Yet, if God wills that it continue, until all the wealth piled by the bondman's two hundred and fifty years of unrequited toil shall be sunk, and until every drop of blood drawn with the lash, shall be paid by another drawn with the sword, as was said three thousand years ago, so still it must be said, "the judgments of the Lord, are true and righteous altogether."

I still have a dream. It is a dream deeply rooted in the American dream. I have a dream that one day on the red hills of Georgia the sons of former slaves and the sons of former slaveowners will be able to sit down together at the table of brotherhood.

Abraham Lincoln and Martin Luther King, Jr., told the whole truth about America, and that is one reason they are deified in the American memory. Few of their contemporary successors emulate them. Yet what is needed, as the spiritual precondition to a material commitment, is a refurbished national mythology that takes account of the historical experience of all Americans. That is something politicians can begin to provide without spending a dime. The dilemma is not a black dilemma (or a white one) but an American dilemma. The answer is not "black history" but American history, not "black pride," (or white guilt) but American determination.

—The New Republic, July 10, 1989

FLAGELLATION

> Many a bum show has been saved by the flag.
>
> —*George M. Cohan*

AMID THE CURRENT HYSTERIA an important ontological point has been overlooked: you can't burn the flag. It can't be done. *A* flag, yes. *The* flag, no. *The* flag, the American flag, is an abstraction—a certain arrangement of stars, stripes, and colors—that exists (a) in the realm of Platonic ideals and (b) in the minds and hearts of people. To say this is not to denigrate the flag; on the contrary, it is to place the flag where it belongs, in a higher realm of existence than the material. *A* flag, any particular flag, is merely a copy. You can no more destroy *the* flag by burning *a* flag than you can destroy the Constitution by burning a copy of the Constitution.

The flag, as long as it exists in human hearts, is fireproof. The Constitution, however, is more vulnerable. It can be desecrated quite effectively—by amending it in ways foreign to its spirit and hostile to its purposes. Members of Congress rushed to do just that in the wake of *Texas v. Johnson*. George Bush, in the first truly sickening act of demagoguery of his young presidency, has now put the impetus of his support behind them.

Have you read the actual Texas statute the Supreme Court ruled on? It makes it "a Class A misdemeanor" for anyone to "deface, damage, or otherwise physically mistreat [a state or national flag] in a way that the actor knows will seriously offend one or more persons likely to observe or discover his action." What's surprising is not that this bit of legislative flotsam was struck down, but that four of the nine justices deemed it consistent with the First Amendment.

All the opinions in this case are notable for their passion. The dissenters' passion is reserved mostly for the flag, the majority's mostly for the Constitution. The dissenters venerate the symbol; the majority venerates the thing symbolized. Both have emotion on their sides. But the majority has logic, too.

Chief Justice Rehnquist devotes many pages to explicating the special meaning of the flag. His dissent is studded with verse: four lines of Emerson's "Concord Hymn," the opening stanza of "The Star-Spangled Banner," two full pages of "Barbara Frietchie." He succeeds beautifully in making the point that the flag is a powerful symbol of a particular set of sentiments and ideas. Or, as Justice Stevens puts it, in a transcendently absurd passage I can't resist quoting:

> The message conveyed by some flags—the swastika, for example—may survive long after it has outlived its usefulness as a symbol of regimented unity in a particular nation.
>
> So it is with the American flag.

What the justice means is . . . well, never mind. But Rehnquist and Stevens want to have it both ways. The flag conveys a message that nothing else conveys, but burning a flag (in Rehnquist's words) "conveyed nothing that could not have been conveyed and was not conveyed just as forcefully in a dozen different ways." These assertions, Justice Brennan remarks in a footnote, "sit uneasily" next to each other. If flying the flag is symbolic speech, so is burning one; and speech, in this country, is supposed to be free.

Rehnquist argues that we outlaw "conduct that is regarded as evil and profoundly offensive to the majority of people—whether it be murder, embezzlement, pollution, or flag burning." We don't, however, outlaw murder, embezzlement, and pollution because they're offensive. We outlaw them because they inflict palpable harm on actual people. Flag burning merely offends, and it offends by what it says.

When the decision came down, I allowed myself to hope it would be the occasion for nothing worse than a harmless festival of hokum calculated to bring pleasure to the shades of Mencken and Sinclair Lewis. And that's how it was, the first day.

The inimitable Bob Dole rushed a wild, all-caps statement up to the Senate press gallery. It began this way:

MAYBE THOSE WHO SIT IN IVORY TOWERS AGREE WITH THE SUPREME COURT. MAYBE, AS THE MAN WHO BURNED THE FLAG, MILLIONS OF PEOPLE HATE AMERICA. HATE THE FLAG. IF THEY DO, THEY OUGHT TO LEAVE THE COUNTRY. IF THEY DO NOT LIKE AMERICA, THAT'S FINE, GO FIND SOMETHING YOU DO LIKE. IF THEY DON'T LIKE OUR FLAG, GO FIND ONE YOU DO LIKE.

That was a paragraph to savor, especially the way the antecedents chased each other like enraged bees. Meanwhile, over on the House side, one rascal after another was having his say. The fifteenth to rise was Douglas Applegate, Democrat of Ohio, who, after proclaiming that it would be all right with the Court for his colleagues to rip down "the flag right here in this Chamber" and "defecate on it," shouted, "Are there any limitations? Are they going to allow fornication in Times Square at high noon?" As if on cue, up got Donald E. "Buz" Lukens, Republican (and underage girl fancier) of Ohio. "Mr. Speaker, what does it say to the world that Americans can now legally burn the flag? . . ."

The show got ugly the next day, when the texts of proposed amendments started filling the hoppers—amendments like this one, offered by seventeen members of the House:

SECTION I. The misuse or desecration of the symbol, emblem, seal, or flag of the United States is not protected speech under the first amendment to the Constitution of the United States.

SECTION 2. The Congress shall have power to enforce this article by appropriate legislation.

And so on. An America capable of writing this sort of tripe into its Constitution would be a country at once less serious and less funny than the country we thought we were living in. And less free, too.

President Bush's role in all this is unusually contemptible. His first reaction was to say that while he regards flag burning as "dead wrong," he could understand why the Court decided as it did. That was the reasonable, moderate fellow one stupidly keeps hoping is the "real Bush." After a day's reflection—and lunch with Lee Atwater—Bush decided that "the importance of this issue compels me to call for a constitutional amendment."

If Bush has his way, the Bill of Rights will be amended for the first time in American history—and for what? Because of what danger? Flag burning is extremely rare, and, though offensive, essentially harmless. It has no "importance." It is not even an "issue," since no one, apart from a few isolated political cultists, is in favor of it. So what's going on?

The mystery vanishes when one recalls Bush's use last fall of the Pledge of Allegiance "issue." Now, if he has his way, the same cynical manipulation of patriotic symbols, as perfected by political consultants, is to be enshrined in the Constitution. Negative campaigning is to be raised to the level of a civic sacrament. The desecration of the flag, which is not a problem, is to be made the pretext for the desecration of what the flag represents. For George Bush, nice guy, the defilement of the Bill of Rights itself is just another tactic for narrow partisan gain. And it's hard to see, at this point, who's going to stop him.

—*The New Republic,* July 17 & 24, 1989

GORE'S GREATEST BONG HITS

A WEEK OR SO AGO the latest chapter in the continuing saga of Al Gore's flaming youth erupted, as so many such stories do nowadays, from the subterranean depths where book publishing, journalism, and the Internet flow together. A new biography, full of purportedly titillating revelations, is set for publication a few months hence (in this case by Houghton Mifflin); a big magazine (in this case *Newsweek*, where the book's author, Bill Turque, works) buys the first serial rights; the magazine's editors, worried about the credibility of a source, develop qualms; an Internet reporter (in this case Jake Tapper, of *Salon*) gets a tip; and the gist makes its way via the tabloids to the mainstream papers (initially as a business section "media" story) and the TV political gab shows, where, at this moment, it contentedly bubbles and pops.

The story, in brief, is that John Warnecke, a former friend of Gore's, says that in the early seventies, when the two were neighbors and cub reporters at the Nashville *Tennessean*, they smoked marijuana together many, many times—more often, arguably, than the "rare and infrequent" pot use to which the vice president has long admitted. The tale is not especially scandalous, but it is irresistible, and not just on account of the comic picture it conjures up of the profoundly unwild and uncrazy Gore as an enthusiastic doper—a big stiff with a big spliff. What gives the tale piquancy, even an element of tragic dignity, is the apparent texture of the relationship between the two men, who, like Prince Hal and Falstaff, were once as close as brothers and then drifted far apart when their destinies diverged. Both had grown up in the bosom of the Washington elite: Albert Gore, Sr., was a prominent senator, while Warnecke's father, John Carl Warnecke, was a famous architect and was so close to Jacqueline Kennedy that she chose him to design her husband's gravesite. But young Gore's life took him on a path to Congress, the Senate, and the vice presidency, while young Warnecke's led to alcoholism, depression, and obscurity. The two have not spoken, Warnecke says, since 1988, when Gore called him to ask him not to talk to the press about their pot smoking.

At the level of national government, discussion of drug policy has been dormant since the 1980s ushered in the crack epidemic, just say no, three strikes and you're out, and the prison boom. The Clinton administration, the first to be run by people who grew up with soft drugs, chose to surrender to the reigning orthodoxy. Yet the failure of the twenty-year "drug war" has never been more apparent. The most damning evidence can be found in the most recent "Fact Sheet" handed out by the White House Office of National Drug Control Policy—the same office that is currently in hot water for offering television networks millions in financial incentives to insert antidrug "messages" into entertainment programs. The surest measure of the success of drug interdiction and enforcement is price: if drugs are made harder to come by, the price must increase. According to the "Fact Sheet," however, the average price of a gram of pure cocaine dropped from around $300 in 1981 to around $100 in 1997; for heroin, the price fell from $3,500 to $1,100. Only marijuana has gotten more expensive, but its potency has more than kept pace. Interdiction has functioned mainly as a protectionist and R & D program for the burgeoning domestic marijuana industry, whose product, once the equivalent of iceberg lettuce, is now more akin to arugula. The nickel bag is long gone, but not the nickel high.

Meanwhile, federal spending on drug control has gone from around $1.5 billion to around $16 billion, mostly for interdiction and criminal justice. State and local spending has likewise multiplied, bringing the combined annual bill to something in the neighborhood of $40 billion. The prison population, which fifteen years ago was under three-quarters of a million, will cross the two million mark sometime this month. Drug convictions account for the great bulk of that increase. The average drug offender in a federal prison serves more time than does the average convicted rapist, burglar, or mugger. This costly jihad has scared off some casual users, but it has done nothing to reduce the number of hard-core addicts.

These facts have not much intruded themselves upon the current political campaign. Below the presidential and would-be presidential level, though, there are modest signs of popular discontent with the drug-policy status quo. The voters of eight states, from California to Maine, have passed initiatives approving the medical use of marijuana. There is growing interest in practical alternatives to the regime of punitive prohibition, particularly the approach known as "harm reduction"—which, in the words of Ethan Nadelmann, of the George Soros–funded Lindesmith Center, "aims to reduce the negative consequences of both drug use and drug prohibition, acknowledging that both will likely persist for the foreseeable future." Even a few politicians have begun to call for fundamental reform, including Congressman Tom Campbell, the probable Republican nominee in this year's California Senate race, and Governor Gary Johnson, of New Mexico, also a Republican, who has undertaken a sustained rhetorical crusade against what he regards as the folly of the drug war.

With varying degrees of candor, three of the four plausible presidential candidates have admitted to (Gore and Bill Bradley) or alluded to (George W. Bush) past drug use. The fourth, John McCain, says he has never done drugs, but, as he said not long ago, he was already a prisoner of war when pot became popular in the military. ("Also, remember my age: sixty-three," he added apologetically.) Gore has taken the usual baby-boom politician's boilerplate—admitting one or two episodes of unenjoyable "experimentation"—a useful step further: for some years, he was an occasional (by his own account) or regular (by Warnecke's) marijuana user. During those years, he served in the Army in Vietnam, studied divinity and law, worked as a newspaper reporter, and prepared to run for Congress. Whatever the effect marijuana had on him (and he did, after all, once suggest putting a TV camera in orbit, aiming it straight down, and broadcasting a picture of the earth twenty-four hours a day on cable), his ability to function as a productive citizen does not appear to have been impaired.

One day, perhaps, an actual or potential president will acknowledge that there are meaningful distinctions to be drawn among different drugs and different ways of using and abusing them; and that there is something morally askew in a criminal-justice system that treats adults who sell drugs to other adults (let alone adults who merely grow marijuana plants) as harshly as it does violent, predatory criminals. That day can hardly come too soon, though when it does a great change may have already begun. "I wouldn't be doing this if I didn't think this was a Berlin Wall–type situation," Governor Johnson told an interviewer recently, explaining why he is willing to brave the indignation of the drug warriors. "You're going to get a critical mass here, and all of a sudden it's just going to topple."

—*The New Yorker*, February 7, 2000

LABOR'S CHINA SYNDROME

FOR ORGANIZED LABOR, last week's vote in the House of Representatives to establish "permanent normal trade relations" with China (that's the new, easy-to-swallow name for most-favored-nation trade status) was a disaster, and a self-inflicted one at that. Labor is surely right that the United States could do more to use its trade clout on behalf of human rights. But the defeat of the trade bill would have strengthened the most reactionary and belligerent forces inside China. At least, that was the dominant opinion among China's pro-democracy dissidents, who, by all accounts, welcomed the bill's passage as eagerly as their oppressor, the Communist Party, did.

American labor's problem, in any case, is not Chinese imports. And it's not that Chinese workers can't form unions. American labor's problem (and this is only a slight exaggeration) is that *American* workers can't form unions. The National Labor Relations Act of 1935—the Wagner Act—is still on the books. But it has been hollowed out by thirty years of court decisions and administrative rulings, and by the increasing willingness of employers to be ruthless. The legal deck is prohibitively stacked against the supposedly sacred right of workers to organize and bargain collectively. The law provides just enough protection to allow unions to maintain themselves in the steadily shrinking redoubts they conquered two and three generations ago but nowhere near enough to give them a fair chance to sign up new members.

Yes, it's against the law for an employer to fire an employee simply for joining, or wanting to join, a union. But this is not the kind of law anybody gets arrested for breaking. If a worker fired for talking union seeks legal re-dress (with or without the services of a lawyer, whose fees cannot be recov-ered), then the offending company might, at worst, have to reinstate the worker and fork over his or her back pay—after subtracting whatever sum he or she has managed to pick up doing odd jobs in the interim. By then, two or three years will have passed, and the organizing drive will have long ago been crushed. This is what has happened over and over, year after year. And this, not trade with China, is why the unions' share of the private-sector labor force has dropped from 35 percent in the mid-1950s to under 10 per-cent today. It is also, by the way, why the only unions that have consistently grown in recent decades are unions of public employees. It's not that toll-booth attendants, clerks in government bureaucracies, and schoolteachers are by nature tough, hardened militants or have bulging, ropy forearms. It's that their employer, the government, is in a poor position to routinely and brazenly flout the plain language of the law. Private companies have fewer disincentives to lawlessness. Under these circumstances, a company that does not break the law is practically guilty of fiduciary irresponsibility to its stockholders.

What labor needs is not to torpedo trade abroad but to persuade, or to force, Congress to do some dental work on the laws that purportedly pro-tect the right to organize. Suppose labor had used the threat of all-out op-position to China trade as a lever to get the Clinton administration and the Democratic Party to commit themselves to putting teeth in the labor laws. Would the laws have been revamped this year? Hardly. If labor-law reform ever happens, it will happen only when there is a Democratic Congress to pass it and a Democratic president to sign it—and, even then, only if both have been elected with a mandate to make the law fairer. Meanwhile, though, the unions could be devoting their still formidable resources to ed-ucating the public about the grotesque unfairness of the current labor-law regime—rather than to lobbying an unsympathetic Congress in a cause as dubious as it was doomed—and they could now jump into the political campaign with enthusiasm. (Of course, the China trade bill would have passed. But that happened anyway, didn't it?)

As it is, many sensible people inside the labor movement worry about a repeat of 1994, when the unions, having dashed themselves on the rocks of another failed trade battle (the one over the North American Free Trade Agreement), went into a political pout that contributed to the takeover of the House by Newt Gingrich and his band of non-union contractors. Not long afterward, the A.F.L.-C.I.O. pushed out its somnolent boss, Lane Kirkland, and installed an insurgent team of leaders under John Sweeney. Despite the legal obstacles, the new leaders poured money and energy into trying to organize the unorganized. They got college students involved. They brought back some of the movement's old idealism. They cemented labor's relations with former allies, like blacks, and new ones, like environmentalists. They helped the Democrats gain House seats in the 1998 election—an unprecedented event for a party in the second term of a presidency. It looked as if labor might be getting somewhere.

And now this. What a mess. What a sad mess. And it's sad not just for the unions. When the labor movement isn't drawing a bead on its own foot, after all, it tends to busy itself supporting things that are good for people who aren't even dues-paying members—things like health care and education. Labor's public-spiritedness is a rarity among "interest groups," and its concern for the suffering Chinese was no doubt genuine. But in this case labor wasn't selfish enough.

—*The New Yorker*, June 5, 2000

COPS AND WALLETS

NOT EVERY COP has heeded the call of the Patrolmen's Benevolent Association to boycott Bruce Springsteen. At last Tuesday night's concert at Madison Square Garden, a trio of police officers happened to be seated up in Section 110, to the left of the stage. Their identity wasn't apparent to the naked eye; in a Springsteen crowd, lots of people look like off-duty cops. But when the singer launched into the dirge that opens his newest unreleased song—"*41 shots . . . 41 shots . . . 41 shots . . .*"—the young men reached for the heavy leather wallets that hold their badges, flipped them open, and held them up like candles. Then they booed—a dicey move, because "Boooo!" sounds like "Bruuuce!," the affectionate lowing with which Springsteen's fans serenade him. But there was no mistaking the officers' meaning.

These are dispiriting times for New York's cops. Their prestige, which had risen in synch with an extraordinary drop in the crime rate, has been dented by a handful of incidents that drew attention to the dark side of their aggressive methods. The most serious of the incidents—the one that prompted Springsteen's song—was the case of Amadou Diallo, a Guinean immigrant who last year was shot dead on his doorstep; the gun that four plainclothesmen thought he was going for was only a wallet. Then, last week, after dozens of women were terrorized by mobs of men in Central Park after a Puerto Rican Day parade, the police were faulted for not being forceful enough.

The booing cops in the Garden echoed the sentiments of their spokesmen, whose attacks on Springsteen have ranged from the truculent (Springsteen is "trying to fatten his wallet by reopening the wounds of this tragic case," the president of the P.B.A. said) to the ugly (Springsteen is a "dirtbag," the local head of the Fraternal Order of Police said). Still, the fact that the cops were in the Garden at all—and scores more must have been there, too—suggests that something is wrong with the picture of Springsteen as just another rich, liberal star urging the offing of the pig. Here are the lyrics in dispute—first the three verses, then the refrain that follows each:

41 shots and we'll take that ride
'Cross this bloody river to the other side
41 shots . . . cut through the night.
You're kneeling over his body in the vestibule
Praying for his life.

Lena gets her son ready for school
She says "On these streets, Charles
You've got to understand the rules
If an officer stops you
Promise you'll always be polite,
That you'll never ever run away
Promise Mama you'll keep your hands in sight."

41 shots and we'll take that ride
'Cross this bloody river to the other side
41 shots . . . got my boots caked in this mud
We're baptized in these waters and in each other's blood.

Is it a gun?
Is it a knife?
Is it a wallet?
This is your life
It ain't no secret
It ain't no secret
No secret my friend
You can get killed just for living
In your American skin.

This is the song that has lately been denounced for "depicting Amadou Diallo as a victim of racist cops gone trigger-happy" (Stanley Crouch, in the *News*), for creating "the impression that New York's police officers are a bunch of trigger-happy cowboys" (John Tierney, in the *Times*), and for condemning the cops as "cold-blooded killers" and "murderers" (Eric Fettmann, in the *Post*). What's striking about the song (especially in contrast to the obtuseness of the attacks on it) is its imaginative sympathy. The first verse takes the point of view of one of the officers, whose action is not exactly that of a murderer. (Something like what Springsteen describes actually happened in the Diallo case.) The second verse is in a mother's worried voice. (Springsteen's later songs are full of parents trying warily to prepare their children for the realities of life.) The third verse brings the two voices together in suffering, with a subtle hint of redemptive hope. The refrain combines the voices, too, without quite blending them, in a way that makes clear that the American dilemma enmeshes us all. Unless any song suggested by the Diallo tragedy is deemed ipso facto antipolice—unless actual content does not matter—then this song is not antipolice. To see it that way is like seeing "Born in the U.S.A."—until now, Springsteen's most misunderstood composition—as antiveteran: after all, it fails to mention the many Vietnam vets who have gone on to positions of civic leadership.

Springsteen is said to dislike being called the Boss, but he is acutely aware of the responsibility entailed by the moral authority he has happened to earn. No other American artist has forged such a tender, reciprocally respectful relationship with such an enormous audience. (Springsteen's body of work may be the largest irony-free zone in American popular culture.) Springsteen was never likely, in Tierney's accusing words, "to play to the mob." His audience is not a mob. It is a public. As Tuesday's concert continued, the off-duty cops in Section 110 forgot their booing and gave way to the thick swell of emotion that slowly gathers whenever Springsteen performs. The cops pumped their fists joyfully, wiped away tears, and sang along with song after song. They knew all the words. When the new song is recorded and released, perhaps they will learn its words, too.

—*The New Yorker*, July 3, 2000

UNNATURAL LAW

LIKE "WHIST," "WHILST," and "self-abuse," the word "sodomy" has an old-fashioned ring to it. You don't even see it alluded to much anymore, except in punning tabloid headlines about the situation in Iraq. But it—or its kissin' cousin, the nearly as archaic-sounding "deviate sexual intercourse"—can be found in the criminal codes of thirteen states of the Union, where it is punishable by penalties ranging from a parking-ticket-size fine to (theoretically) ten years in prison.

Even at this late date, many people are vague about just exactly what sodomy is. Montesquieu defined it as "the crime against nature," which is not especially helpful. Blackstone called it "the infamous crime against nature, committed either with man or beast," which gets us a little further, but not much. Back in the U.S.A., the statute books tend to be franker. Some states bring animals into the picture, some don't. The Texas legislature's definition is nonzoological. According to Section 21.01 of the Texas Penal Code (readers of delicate sensibilities may at this point wish to skip down a few lines), " 'Deviate sexual intercourse' means: (a) any contact between any part of the genitals of one person and the mouth or anus of another person; or (b) the penetration of the genitals or the anus of another person with an object."

What the Lone Star State does and does not view as some kinda deviated preversion became of national interest last week, when the United States Supreme Court agreed to consider *Lawrence v. Texas*. The Lawrence of the case is John G. Lawrence, fifty-nine years old, of Houston, who, on the evening of September 17, 1998, was in his apartment with a guest, Tyron Garner, who is thirty-five. Texas got involved when police, having been tipped off by a neighbor that a "weapons disturbance" was in progress, busted down the door. (The tip was a deliberate lie on the part of the neighbor, who was later convicted of filing a false report.) What the officers found Lawrence and Garner doing is really none of our business, any more than it was any of Texas's; suffice it to say that it was consensual, non-violent, and noise-free. The two men were arrested, jailed overnight, and eventually fined two hundred dollars each. They appealed, a three-judge panel of a district appeals court reversed their conviction, the full nine-judge appeals court reversed the reversal, and the Texas Court of Criminal Appeals declined to do any more reversing. And so to Washington.

The statute under which Lawrence and Garner were convicted, Section 21.06 of the Texas Penal Code, is officially known as the Homosexual Conduct Law. Ironically, this statute was a product of the progressive mood of the early 1970s. In most of the states that still criminalize sodomy, it doesn't matter, legally, whether a couple engaging in behavior (a), above, consists of two men, two women, or one of each. That's how it was in Texas, too, until 1974. In that bell-bottomed year, the Texas legislature made hetero-sexual sodomy legal, but it couldn't quite bring itself to do the same for gays. The result is that Texas is now one of only four states (the others being Kansas, Missouri, and Oklahoma) where it is a crime for gays to please each other in ways that are perfectly legal for straights. The panel that over-turned the conviction saw this as discrimination on the basis of sexual ori-entation. The full state court disagreed. Rather, confirming what Anatole France called "the majestic egalitarianism of the law, which forbids the rich as well as the poor to sleep under bridges," the court pointed out that in Texas homosexuality is illegal for heterosexuals and homosexuals alike. No discrimination there.

According to the *Times*'s Linda Greenhouse, the Supreme Court prob-ably wouldn't have taken the case unless a majority had already decided to "revisit" *Bowers v. Hardwick* (1986), which upheld the constitutionality of Georgia's sodomy law. The decision in that case—by a vote of 5–4, as with so many of the Court's clunkers—was an embarrassment. Both its language and its reasoning were shockingly coarse. Writing for the majority, Jus-tice Byron White defined "the issue"—leeringly, sarcastically, obtusely, and repeatedly—as "whether the Federal Constitution confers a fundamental right upon homosexuals to engage in sodomy," or protects "a fundamental right to engage in homosexual sodomy," or extends "a fundamental right to homosexuals to engage in acts of consensual sodomy." Any such claim, he added, "is, at best, facetious."

Caricaturing the well-established constitutional right to privacy in this nyah-nyah way is like dismissing the First Amendment as being all about the right to make doo-doo jokes. It was left to the author of the dissenting opinion, Justice Harry Blackmun, to point out, quoting Justice Brandeis, that the case was really "about 'the most comprehensive of rights and the right most valued by civilized men,' namely 'the right to be let alone.' "

Justice Lewis Powell, who tipped the balance in *Bowers v. Hardwick,* expressed regret years later that he had voted the way he did. He's gone now. John Paul Stevens, who dissented, William Rehnquist, now chief justice, and Sandra Day O'Connor are the only holdovers from the Court that upheld Georgia's sodomy law (which, by the way, was thrown out, a few months after Lawrence and Garner were arrested in Houston, by Georgia's supreme court, for violating *Georgia's* constitution).

Half the states that had sodomy laws when *Bowers* was decided have got rid of them, and those that still have them seldom enforce them. But when they are enforced the consequences can be more onerous than it may appear. Lawrence and Garner aren't just out four hundred bucks; they may also be banned from certain professions, from nursing to school-bus driving, and are deprived of other privileges denied to persons who have been convicted of "crimes of moral turpitude." Anyway, sodomy laws are a standing insult to, among others, millions of respectable citizens who happen to be gay. They are an absurd anachronism and an obvious violation of the right to privacy. Whatever they may have represented in Montesquieu's day, or even Byron White's, in 2002 they are nothing but an expression of bigotry. If the Supreme Court takes a truly honest look at Section 21.06 of the Texas Penal Code, it will surely agree with the view of Dickens's Mr. Bumble: this is one case where, at bottom, "the law is a ass."

—*The New Yorker,* December 16, 2002

NORTHERN LIGHT

THE FOURTH OF JULY is one of the best holidays around: fireworks that get better every year, no gift-giving hassles, not too much commercial exploitation, nice weather (usually), no religious test for participation. And, no doubt, throwing off the yoke of perfidious Albion is something to celebrate. Still, every now and then a small regret intrudes that we weren't able to work out a peaceful resolution of our differences with the mother country. God knows we tried ("We have Petitioned for Redress in the most humble Terms," the Declaration of Independence notes sadly), but George III wouldn't listen to reason. A little less taxation, a little more representation, and, presto—227 years later, we might all be Canadians. Would that be so terrible?

Our big, easygoing neighbor to the north has its problems—too cold, a weak dollar, a reputation for paralyzing dullness—but its people are reasonably free, and they seem, on the whole, quite nice. Their contributions to popular music (Joni Mitchell, Neil Young, The Band, the McGarrigle sisters, Leonard Cohen, Alanis Morissette—the list goes on) are legion. Their anomalous gift for comedy (Martin Short, Dan Aykroyd, Mike Myers, and Jim Carrey are among the names that spring to mind) has made Ontario the Catskills of our time. By sending their soldiers to serve side by side with ours in Afghanistan, they supported us in our hour of need—the act of a true friend. By declining to participate in our Iraq adventure, they let us know that they sincerely thought we were making a mistake—also the act of a true friend. In matters of public policy they are often more enlightened than we are, without being snooty about it. Their health-care system is a mess, but it's a fairer, more humane mess than ours is. They have mastered the knack of having guns without using them to slaughter one another. They have a comparatively sensible approach to the drug problem: while our federal government tries strenuously to put marijuana smokers in jail, even (or especially) when the marijuana has been smoked for medical purposes in states whose people have voted to sanction such use, their federal government is about to decriminalize the possession of small amounts. And now—with a minimum of fuss, hardly any hysteria, and no rending of garments—they have made it legal for persons of the same gender to marry each other.

Meanwhile, south of the border down U.S.A. way, the Supreme Court issued its long-awaited decision in the case of *Lawrence v. Texas*. With surprising firmness, the Court struck down the remaining laws against "sodomy," thus bringing the United States to where Canada was a generation ago. Those laws, in Texas and twelve other states, had rendered it a crime, until last Thursday, to make love in the ways that, for anatomical reasons, are gay folks' sole option. It was a strong, solid decision, six to three, with only the hard-core hard right—Antonin Scalia, joined by William Rehnquist and Clarence Thomas—dissenting. In his dissent, Justice Scalia accused his colleagues of having "signed on to the so-called homosexual agenda." And what is that so-called agenda? Daisy chains on the church steps? Compulsory drag shows at school assemblies? "Eliminating the moral opprobrium that has traditionally attached to homosexual conduct," as in Scalia's own definition? No, it's worse than that. Just like in Canada, some of these people actually want to get married. *Pace* Joni Mitchell, they *want* a piece of paper from the city hall, keeping them tied and true.

For the moment, the only city halls in the Western Hemisphere that are issuing such pieces of paper are in Ontario, where, on June 10th, the provincial court of appeals declared that the old common-law definition of marriage, "the voluntary union for life of one man and one woman," did not comport with the Charter of Rights and Freedoms, Canada's version of the Bill of Rights, and that, effective immediately, marriage, at least in Ontario, is "the voluntary union for life of two persons." A week later, Prime Minister Jean Chrétien announced that, instead of trying to get the decision overturned, his cabinet would seek to codify it. Legislation is to be drafted over the next few weeks, vetted by Canada's supreme court, and submitted to the federal parliament. It's pretty much a lock that, perhaps as early as next fall, gay marriage will be the undisputed law of the land from St. John's to the Klondike.

This ghastly prospect was evidently on Scalia's mind as he composed his dissent in *Lawrence v. Texas.* If sodomy laws are unsustainable, he warned, then so are "laws against bigamy, same-sex marriage, adult incest, prostitution, masturbation"—masturbation? is that one still on the books?—"adultery, fornication, bestiality, and obscenity." Doom looms, it would appear. According to Scalia, "The Court has taken sides in the culture war," and the next step, logically, must be "judicial imposition of homosexual marriage, as has recently occurred in Canada." Leaving aside the question of who, exactly, gay marriage would be an imposition upon, this seems prohibitively unlikely. According to the polls, most people up there think gay marriage is O.K. Most people down here don't. And the Court's majority opinion, written by Anthony Kennedy, insists that it says nothing about "whether the government must give formal recognition to any relationship that homosexual persons seek to enter."

Still, a lot has changed since 1986, when, in *Bowers v. Hardwick,* the Supreme Court upheld a sodomy law like the one it threw out last week. The majority's language then was dismissive: the notion of "a fundamental right to engage in homosexual sodomy," sneered the late Justice Byron White, was "at best, facetious." Last week, the majority was respectful. "The liberty protected by the Constitution allows homosexual persons the right to choose to enter upon relationships in the confines of their homes and their own private lives and still retain their dignity as free persons," Kennedy wrote. He left the sarcasm to Scalia, whose tone seems to have embarrassed even Justice Thomas. The latter filed his own odd little note, seven sentences long, explaining that he thinks the Texas law is "silly," that if he were a member of the Texas legislature he "would vote to repeal it," and that "punishing someone for expressing his sexual preference through noncommercial consensual conduct with another adult" is deplorable. It's just that he can't do anything about it, because there's no such thing as a constitutional right to privacy.

A lot of people, including some conservatives, already think that if gays want to get married—if, in other words, they want to settle down, become pillars of the community, and bring up children in loving, stable homes—then perhaps a little encouragement is in order. But "Christian" conservatives disagree. So it'll be a while before we get gay wedlock here. Gay applicants for marriage licenses will have to join the queue at the city clerk's office in Toronto, which stayed open last Saturday and Sunday, in honor of Gay Pride Week. Good old Canada. It's the kind of country that makes you proud to be a North American.

—*The New Yorker*, July 7, 2003

10. HIGH CRIMES

Was the hounding of the President, 1998, as much fun for young conservatives as the 1973 edition was for young liberals? Certainly the two hatefests had a lot in common. In both cases, impeachment enthusiasts fairly leapt out of bed in the morning, full of hope that the day would bring another shameful or sordid revelation. Both cases offered suspense, the thrill of the chase, and a riveting cast of colorful, offbeat characters. Both were powered by right-wing conspiracies, directed by the White House in one case and against it in the other. Both had lies, and both had tape. Only one had sex, though.

Call it generational chauvinism if you like, call it political prejudice, but I would argue that the one without the sex was the more satisfying. Watergate was Shakespearean—the tragedies, the comedies, the histories, everything but the sonnets. Notwithstanding a Starr turn as Malvolio, the Clinton scandals (which should more properly be called the anti-Clinton scandals, since that was what was scandalous about them) were more like Kafka as told to Jacqueline Susann.

Woodward and Bernstein I most certainly was not, but during the summer and fall of 1973 William Shawn sent me down to Washington three times to kibitz at hearings of the Senate Watergate Committee, beginning with the opening-day testimony of John Dean, the former White House counsel. (The resulting "Talk" story leads off this section.) The second time, I sat next to Hunter S. Thompson, the *Rolling Stone* correspondent, who was a hero to young reporters aspiring to hipness. The witness was Patrick J. Buchanan, Nixon's rightmost speechwriter—and, as a total nonparticipant in burglaries, cover-ups, and other White House horrors, a pugnacious and indignant defender of his boss. While Buchanan talked into the microphones, Thompson mumbled under his breath. He delivered a stream-of-consciousness, improvised narrative that involved attaching a very long chain to the bumper of a pickup truck parked outside on Constitution Avenue, running the chain into the building, up the marble staircase, down the hall, into the hearing room, and around Buchanan's chest under his arms, and then signaling the guy in the the pickup to floor it and watching Buchanan shoot backward out of the witness chair, down the aisle, and bump bump bump down the stairs. . . . At my third hearing, Alexander Butterfield revealed the existence of the White House taping system. Most of the people at the press table weren't quite sure what to make of it, but at the lunch break the wisest among us, the white-haired, very tall, very distinguished-looking Richard Strout, of the *Christian Science Monitor,* stood up and said quietly, "Well, that's it. He's going to be impeached."

Most of the big post-Nixon 'gates have involved sex, which means that they also involved explanations, usually tortured, of why they weren't really "about" sex. (The exception was Iran-contra, which had no sex and therefore did not have to be sold as being about something other than what it was about.) The Gary Hart defenestration, treated elsewhere in this book, set the pattern. I defended Hart, whose politics I liked. But I also defended John Tower, the former Republican senator from Texas nominated in 1989 to be secretary of defense, whose politics I liked less.

I would have defended Clarence Thomas, too, whose politics I abominate. I didn't think that the offensive sexual banter which had discomfited his former subordinate Anita Hill was sufficient reason, in and of itself, to deny confirmation to someone who, I thought (probably wrongly), was no worse than whomever George H. W. Bush would nominate next for that particular Supreme Court opening and who, I thought (definitely wrongly), might grow in surprising ways. By the time my deadline rolled around, though, Thomas and his allies had succeeded quite thoroughly in changing the subject. They did this by alleging a monstrous conspiracy to destroy Thomas by means of fabricated calumnies delivered under oath by Hill. If there had been any truth in the story put out by Thomas himself, the White House, and (especially) the senior Republican member of the Senate Judiciary Committee, Orrin Hatch, then Hill would necessarily have been guilty of (at a minimum) perjury, and certain readily identifiable lawyers and lobbyists would have been guilty of (at a minimum) suborning her perjury. If Hill's accusers had believed what they were saying, then, Thomas's confirmation would have been followed by the prosecution of Hill and her coconspirators for felonies committed in furtherance of a criminal conspiracy. This did not happen. As soon as Thomas was confirmed, the anti-Hill propaganda apparatus in Congress and the White House fell as silent as an unplugged TV set. No investigations, no prosecutions, no lawsuits, no complaints—just a few homilies about the healing process and the need to be sensitive. This proves that those who made the allegations of falsification and conspiracy were lying and knew they were lying. Hatch and company, not Hill and her allies, were the ones who had deployed deliberate falsehoods in order to debauch a solemn process prescribed by the Constitution itself. And they've never been brought to account for it.

There's your scandal.

DEAN'S FIRST DAY

THE CAUCUS ROOM of the Old Senate Office Building is at once more intimate and more impressive than it appears on television. The cameras' wide-angle lenses exaggerate its length and breadth but give little sense of its height. One could pace off its length in twenty-five steps and its breadth in eighteen. The ceiling, which is decorated with rosettes and gilt fretwork, is thirty-four feet and six inches above the floor. Twelve marble Corinthian columns emphasize the surprising verticality of the room. Three high arched windows normally overlook a courtyard, but during the televised hearings of the Senate Select Committee on Presidential Campaign Activities their heavy red velvet curtains are kept drawn, and the only light is artificial. Four chandeliers, large but not massive, hang from the ceiling; their dozens of small glass globes are etched with eagles, Indian heads, and liberty caps. Just below the chandeliers hangs a steel bar nearly the width of the room, with eleven powerful theatrical-light fixtures attached to it.

The Caucus Room holds about four hundred spectators. The density of their crowding together increases roughly in proportion to their distance from the elongated, six-sided table behind which sit the members of the committee and of the committee staff. Flanking the witness table are four long press tables, each with seats for eighteen reporters, and behind it are several chairs for the witness's counsel (and, in most cases, wife). To the rear of them is another long press table, with seats for thirty-four reporters. Behind that is a row of wooden and red leather armchairs for the families of senators, and behind that are five rows of folding chairs, of which the first four are reserved for reporters and for Senate staff members. The twenty chairs in the last row are the only seats in the house for ordinary citizens. There is standing room in the back for some two hundred more. Along with congestion, informality of dress increases with distance from the action. And the nearer one is to the back of the room the more one is apt to be young or female or black.

Taped to the press tables are pieces of yellow copy paper with the names of the news organizations for which the seats are reserved; nearly every prominent newspaper, magazine, wire service, and broadcasting company in the United States, Great Britain, and Canada is represented, as are such European journals as *Der Spiegel* and the Stockholm *Dagens Nyheter*. (Places are reserved for at least seven papers from London alone; the *Observer*'s correspondent is the writer Mary McCarthy, who takes notes continuously in a small, dense hand.) The seats nearest the front, from which it is possible to see the face of the witness, are reserved for the wire services, the *New York Times*, the *Washington Star-News*, and the *Washington Post*, which is represented by (among others) Carl Bernstein, the young reporter who, with his partner, Bob Woodward, is as responsible as anyone for the existence of the Ervin Committee. The network men—Daniel Schorr of CBS, Douglas Kiker and Carl Stern of NBC, Sam Donaldson of ABC—are clustered near the door. Wires hang out from under their jackets like frugal bits of string.

By 9:45 Monday morning, the secretarial staff of the committee having worked through the night, the first ninety-eight pages of John Dean's opening statement were ready for distribution. Uniformed guards wheeled a cart laden with hundreds of pounds of legal-size paper onto the landing just outside the Caucus Room. From inside, Richard Strout, the venerable correspondent for the *Christian Science Monitor* (and, as TRB, for *The New Republic*), spotted the prey before anyone else. "Watch out!" he cried, and made for the door, nearly upending Tim Crouse, the somewhat younger correspondent for *Rolling Stone*.

A few minutes before ten, the seven senators and the two counsellors who are conducting the inquiry took their seats. They are by now among the most familiar men in the country, but in the flesh, without electronic metamorphosis, some of them seem subtly different. Senator Sam J. Ervin, Jr.—whose wonderfully active face suggests that of a Roman elder or an English country squire—looks a trifle bigger and younger than his televised facsimile, while Senator Howard H. Baker, Jr., looks a trifle smaller and older. Samuel Dash, the chief counsel to the committee, looks less severe and more humorous. Senator Lowell P. Weicker, Jr., of Connecticut, and Senator Edward J. Gurney, of Florida, are the tallest men on the committee; indeed, Senator Weicker is the tallest man in Congress, and when he walks through the crowd he is like a blimp floating gently over the heads of the spectators. Senator Gurney's walk is nimble and fastidious, as if he were stepping on water lilies to cross a pond.

At ten minutes past ten, Senator Ervin rapped his gavel and said, "This committee will come to order and the counsel will call the first witness." Mr. Dean was sworn in, and Mr. Dash said dryly, "I understand you have a statement to read."

Mr. Dean read his statement. He read until twelve-thirty, and he read from two o'clock until five minutes past six. Together with the portion that was handed out after lunch, it was two hundred and forty-five pages long— fifty-five thousand words, typed triple-space and all in capital letters on at least four different typewriters. He read at a steady rate of two hundred and twenty words per minute, in a clear, calm, regionless voice. As a performance, Mr. Dean's delivery more closely resembled the indifferent first reading of a one-character play than the lurid tale of fear, revenge, betrayal, arrogance, and lawlessness it was. But Mr. Dean's narrative, with its accumulation of detail, put his story of presidential involvement firmly in context and imbued it with a kind of remorseless, dramatic inevitability. The heads of the senators and the reporters were bowed as they followed Mr. Dean's narrative in their texts, which lay flopped on the tables in front of them like beached fish. Spectators entered and left the standing-room area as quietly as if the Caucus Room were a church. The high wooden door of the room was kept nearly closed; a leather strap from doorknob to doorknob kept the latch from snapping shut, as tape had kept open the doors of the Watergate office building on the day of the burglary. Most of the time, the loudest sound in the room, apart from Mr. Dean's voice, was the *whirr-click* of film advancing and shutters closing in the cameras of the dozen or so photographers who crouched between the witness's table and the Senators'. From the rear, Mr. Dean appeared almost perfectly still, and, indeed, throughout the day he displayed an extreme economy of motion, as if the slightest superfluous physical movement might upset some frail balance and open him to terrible danger. Upon his arrival, accompanied by his wife, his two lawyers, and a phalanx of plainclothes guards, he had gone straight to the witness chair and had sat down. As he read his statement, his lips hardly moved. When he was finished and the hearing adjourned, he left quickly, greeting no one, eyes ahead and slightly lowered, face small and drained, followed by his wife, with whom he exchanged not a word.

—The New Yorker, July 9, 1973

TOWER PLAY

ON THE DAY before the full Senate took up the matter of John Tower's fitness to be secretary of defense, the nominee got up in front of a ballroom full of lunching reporters at the National Press Club to give a speech.

Owing to a clerical error, I happened to be seated directly in front of the podium. From this vantage point, about six feet from the nominee, I was able to study him at leisure—especially the top half of his head, the only part that was continuously visible behind an imposing lectern. (Despite the name, Tower doesn't.) Occasionally, when he would lean to one side or go up on tiptoe to stress a phrase, I would catch a glimpse of the rest of his head, along with a flash of pin-striped English worsted, fine custom-made shirting, and silk tie.

John Tower has unnaturally black hair that lies against his boxy head in oiled strands that alternate with narrow strips of scalp. His ears are large and pointed, his mouth pinched, his eyes tiny and reddish under invisible brows. The flesh of his face is splotchy and suety. One could call his eyes "cruel" and his mouth "ungenerous," but that would be to fall into the pathetic fallacy. Oh, what the hell, let's fall the whole way: he looks like a mean, crafty imp. All that's lacking are the cloven hooves.

I dwell upon the physical details because the debate on Tower has been so very . . . *carnal.* It has become impossible to look at this ex-senator without picturing him in congress. The man can't take a sip of water without one's imagination transforming the glass into a square, amber bottle with three *x*'s on the label.

As the phrases of the prepared speech—"comprehensive review . . . strategic design . . . force posture"—floated over the fidgeting audience in Tower's rich announcer's voice, cards with questions scribbled on them were passed to the front. These, when read out, reflected the real concerns at the forefront of every mind. How can we believe your pledge to quit drinking? You say you've never broken a pledge—how about wedding vows? How come your old colleagues don't seem to like you?

The debate on the floor of the Senate began the next day. It is reaching its climax as I write, with Warren Rudman thunderingly deconstructing the Armed Services Committee's anti-Tower majority report, the Southern Democrats holding firm behind Sam Nunn, and Fritz ("You want 'em drunk and criminal—just drunk's enough for me") Hollings locked in bitter combat with Bob ("alcoholic abuse—isn't that a vicious personal attack?") Dole. Passion has boiled off the Senate's usual oleaginous coating of courtesy. What a show! For the moment, George Bush's Washington is no longer dull.

The show will probably have closed by the time this is read, almost certainly with Tower having been defeated. For what it's worth, I ended up rootin' for him, in a mild way. It's not that I have any doubt that he is a lush, a lecher, and a sleaze. Plainly he is all three. But what, when all is said and done, of it?

Senator Nunn made his strongest case on the booze front, arguing from the record that military crises have a way of breaking out during prime drinking time, often on a Saturday night. But Nunn, an observant Methodist, may be unaware that experienced drinkers know how to sober up fast when they need to.

As a senator, Tower was not reckoned to be among that august body's notorious drunks, and it surely counts for something that no one was able to point to a single instance when his tippling interfered with the performance of his official duties. Far from being useless after happy hour, he was known for his ability to outlast everybody else in late-night negotiating sessions.

During one of the many mock operatic moments of the debate, Senator Phil Gramm recounted Winston Churchill's bibacious exploits, paused dramatically, and intoned, "Was *he* unfit? *Ask—Hitler's—ghost!*" This isn't as absurd as it sounds. Brandy didn't make Churchill a great leader any more than heroin made Charlie Parker a great musician, but neither of them was impeded from greatness by his chosen vice; and Tower probably wouldn't be impeded from mediocrity.

Tower's real problem seemed to be sufficient contrition. Nunn complained that Tower had not "acknowledged and dealt with this [drinking] problem" in the approved Betty Ford Clinic manner. Tower's amazing pledge to swear off what, in a phrase worthy of W. C. Fields, he called "beverage alcohol" (a category that may or may not include hair tonic and fuel additives) had the content of penance but not the form. Its tone recalled an earlier, equally Fieldsian, remark of the nominee's: "I am a man of some discipline."

The lechery is by all accounts crude—Tower is apparently a one-man Shriners' convention, for whom chasing skirt is not a mere metaphor—but, again, its relevance to the job has not been demonstrated. And the sleaze, alas, was within the rules as well as the law. For Tower to make a quick million peddling real or ersatz inside dope to defense contractors was deplorable (even if it wasn't much compared with James Baker's running up the value of his bank stocks by making pro-bank decisions as secretary of the treasury). The remedy, however, is to change the old rules, not to punish Tower for breaking not-yet-written ones.

Like the rest of the audience at the Press Club, I didn't pay much attention to Tower's prepared speech, but a few days later, out of curiosity, I got hold of a copy. It turned out to have been a speech that might as easily have been given by a defense secretary in a Dukakis administration. The emphasis was on cuts ("significant and painful cuts," "cuts that will create a storm of debate both inside and outside the Pentagon"), on saying no ("a word that must slip easily off the secretary's tongue"), and on procurement reform. "Major and expensive systems will not survive"—that sort of thing.

Only words, perhaps, but the right words; and if President Bush is serious about shaking up the Pentagon, Tower might have been just the man to do it. He knew the field and the players better than any previous nominee to the post. He had lined up a loyal, cohesive, experienced team of prospective service secretaries to help him. And the fact that he had spent the preceding quarter century shoveling cash into the maw of the military-industrial complex had left him ideally positioned, politically and substantively, to tame it.

Still, the Tower nomination was a close call on the merits, and I might have felt differently if, like the senators who lined up against the nominee, I had read the fabled F.B.I. report. It's hard to feel all that sorry about seeing Tower go, and there is ample comfort in contemplating some of the side effects of his probable defeat. The coalition of Republicans and Southerners that has stymied every kind of reform since the end of the New Deal, except during Lyndon Johnson's first two years, has been fractured. Sam Nunn has got his halo dented, he has learned that he is a Democrat, and he has had the illuminating experience of coming under sustained attack from the right. And the ayatollahs of the Senate's "family values" caucus, having spent a week or more defending libertinism, substance abuse, and privacy, have been taught a hard lesson in tolerance. I'll drink to that, and John Tower is welcome to join me.

—Washington Diarist, *The New Republic*, March 27, 1989

WHAT A WHOPPER

CLARENCE THOMAS has won his seat on the Court, but he has forfeited his honor and besmirched his country. He did so beginning on Friday, October 11th, when the Senate Judiciary Committee and the global television audience returned from the dinner break to hear what he would have to say in response to the long, sad, calm story told by Anita F. Hill. Until that moment I had favored his confirmation—not because I thought him well qualified or liked his ideas, but out of a pragmatic calculation that whoever President Bush might nominate next would be less likely to grow in directions displeasing to his sponsors. Even after Professor Hill's testimony, I still hoped, rather wanly, that Judge Thomas would be able to explain. I hoped he would say that the whole thing was a ghastly misunderstanding—that Hill had bizarrely misinterpreted a thirty-three-year-old divorced man's clumsy attempts at courtship and ribald humor. Or, failing that, if he felt total denial was his only recourse, that she was evidently suffering from a severe delusion, that she needed help and deserved compassion, and that, by the way, the content of her delusion provided heartbreaking evidence of the internalization by some blacks of oppressive stereotypes. He did not say these things. Instead, he played the card of racial paranoia. In Thomas's telling, Hill's contentions were not delusions; they were lies. The proceedings were not a painful and (given the unauthorized leak of Hill's F.B.I. report) unavoidable airing of one woman's nightmarish fantasy; they were "a high-tech lynching for uppity blacks who in any way deign to think for themselves, to do for themselves, to have different ideas, or to refuse to kowtow to an old order." He was being "lynched, destroyed, caricatured"—

not for his alleged actions but for his ideas, and not by Hill's story but "by a committee of the U.S. Senate."

The next morning Thomas listened approvingly as Senator Orrin Hatch wove a lurid tale of a monstrous conspiracy by "interest groups" and "slick lawyers" to program Hill, *Manchurian Candidate*-style, with a viciously racist story pieced together from bits of old law cases and pulp novels. As Andrew Rosenthal has reported in the *New York Times*, this line of attack was a calculated strategy devised—hatched, so to speak—in the White House, with Bush's approval. It was a deliberate lie, as Hatch, Bush, and of course Thomas must have known—and as was indisputably proved on Sunday, when four associates of Hill's gave unchallenged testimony that she had confided in them about Thomas's behavior as long as a decade ago. Joseph Biden, the chairman of the committee, who handled the hearings with skill and patience, tried to let Thomas back away from it. In a colloquy that has been little noted, Biden gave Thomas every opportunity:

> *Do you believe that interest groups went out and got Professor Hill to make up a story? Or do you believe Professor Hill had a story, untrue from your perspective, that, as referred to here, groups went out and found? Which do you believe?*

> Senator, I believe that someone, some interest group, I don't care who it is, in combination, came up with this story and used this process to destroy me.

> *Got Professor Hill to say, to make up a story.*

> I believe that in combination this story was developed, or concocted, to destroy me.

> *With Professor Hill? That's a critical question. Are you saying, with Professor Hill? That a group—?*

> That's just my view, senator. There's no details to it or anything else. The story developed. I do not believe—the story is not true. The allegations are false. And my view is that others put it together and developed this.

> *And put it in Professor Hill's mouth?*

> I don't know. I don't know how it got there. All I know is that the story is here and I think it was concocted.

By embracing this poisonous accusation—that Hill's story was concocted, as opposed to merely unearthed, by "interest groups" working "in combination"—Thomas showed himself to be unfit for the powerful office he may well occupy into the 2030s. The accusation is worse than unproven: there is not a hint of a shadow of a fact to support it. In making it, Thomas displayed both a coarse contempt for the very concept of evidence and a stunning readiness to slash at the fabric of democratic trust. This should have been reason enough for the Senate to reject his nomination even if it is stipulated that he was entirely innocent of Hill's charges. But, of course, that cannot be stipulated. It is close to a certainty that she was telling something like the truth and he was not. She had no motive to lie; he did. There is no evidence that she is a vengeful woman, a fantasist, or even a Democrat; there is considerable evidence that he "discussed pornography" with, and forced his unwanted attentions on, other women too. For Thomas's version of their encounters to be true, Hill would have to have invented an elaborate delusional structure; for her version to be true, he would have only to have repressed (or rationalized away) a few troublesome memories. She would have to have been a psychotic; he would merely have to have been a man in a tight spot—which, manifestly, he was.

One thinks, in this connection, of Tawana Brawley, and of Al Sharpton. Brawley began with a relatively small lie, designed to save her some grief at home: some white men abducted her, and that's why she was out all night. The lie grew, to distract attention from its own inconsistencies. Enter Sharpton, and the small lie became a big lie, until an entire community was riven by racial bitterness and demagogy. To question Brawley's tale was to become a party not only to her victimization but to the victimization of black women by white men since the beginning of time. Thomas's lie—that nothing remotely resembling what Anita Hill said happened, happened—started out smaller than Brawley's. But it grew much bigger, big enough to engulf a nation, and by the end Thomas was telling an audience of tens of millions that he was being lynched, assassinated, and destroyed; that "our institutions are being controlled by people who will stop at nothing"; that the Senate was "ruining the country"; and that he, Thomas, was the victim of a malevolent, racist conspiracy so immense that it encompassed much of the political universe. Today Tawana Brawley is a minor celebrity on her college campus, and Al Sharpton remains a prominent "activist" in New York. They haven't done badly. But Thomas has done better. He is a justice of the United States Supreme Court.

—Washington Diarist, *The New Republic*, November 4, 1991

TALES OF THE TAPES

LAST THURSDAY MORNING, at the opening of the George Bush Library, in College Station, Texas, the weather was splendid and the mood was mellow. Mr. Bush was at his awkwardly modest best, and an amiable camaraderie prevailed as he posed with his White House fraternity brothers Gerald Ford, Jimmy Carter, and Bill Clinton. This being the nineties, the Bush Library is the first institution of its kind to open simultaneously with its own Web site (http://csdl.tamu.edu/bushlib/). There the browser learns, among other things, that the library's archive will contain "over thirty-eight million pages of personal papers and official documents," all of them "housed in acid-free storage (Hollinger) boxes in a balanced humidity and temperature atmosphere."

A rich trove for historians, this. But not quite as rich as it ought to be. For what the George Bush Library will emphatically not contain—and what the Gerald Ford, Jimmy Carter, and Ronald Reagan libraries do not contain and the eventual Bill Clinton library will not contain—is a faithful record of what was actually said in the Oval Office and the Cabinet Room and on the telephone by the president and his advisers as they deliberated on matters petty and great. For this state of affairs, as for soft money and cheap Chinese sneakers, we have Richard Nixon to thank.

The Nixon tapes were Nixon's undoing, of course. They are turning out, however, to be a historical resource of incalculable value. The same is true of the less extensive but still voluminous voice recordings of meetings and telephone conversations which were made by Nixon's two immediate predecessors, John F. Kennedy and Lyndon Johnson. Just how extraordinary these materials are has become clear in recent weeks with the publication of three new books: *The Kennedy Tapes: Inside the White House During the Cuban Missile Crisis*, edited by Ernest R. May and Philip D. Zelikow; *Taking Charge: The Johnson White House Tapes, 1963–1964*, edited by Michael R. Beschloss; and *Abuse of Power: The New Nixon Tapes*, edited by Stanley I. Kutler. All three are riveting, and, taken together, they show the power and variety of what amounts to a new kind of history. *The Kennedy Tapes*, drawn from transcripts of working meetings between October 16 and October 29, 1962, has the advantage of being a suspenseful, self-contained narrative of a single intense episode—the Cuban missile crisis, which in retrospect stands out as the most dangerous moment of the Cold War. In the cauldron of the crisis, the forty-five-year-old president emerges as everything his hagiographers have proclaimed him to be: calm, lucid, commanding, far-seeing. *Taking Charge* shapes itself into a character study. It consists almost entirely of telephone transcripts, and they give it a wonderfully intimate focus. As Johnson talks one on one with a staggering range of people—his wife, his closest assistants, his tailor, congressmen, relatives, civil rights leaders, cabinet members, columnists, J. Edgar Hoover, Robert Kennedy, and on and on—he is variously wheedling, ribald, resentful, scheming, gloomy, gleeful, gossipy, comforting, and stern. Vietnam is barely an annoyance at the beginning, but as the story progresses Johnson more and more often expresses vexation and bafflement over the still embryonic war, foreshadowing the nightmare that we know will eventually destroy him.

It was a long wait, but *Abuse of Power* finally, and satisfyingly, slakes the thirst for detail that was awakened on July 16, 1973, when a White House aide named Alexander Butterfield told the Senate Watergate Committee of the existence of Nixon's elaborate, voice-activated taping system. No wonder Nixon fought so desperately against the release of the Watergate tapes: just one of them was sufficient to force his resignation, and the rest—two hundred hours' worth, pried loose a year ago as the result of a lawsuit brought against the National Archives by Public Citizen and Professor Kuder—turn out to confirm everything you ever suspected, and more.

The criminality on display is voluptuous, and it begins in the first line of the book's first conversation, which was taped a full year before the Watergate break-in. The curtain rises on Nixon, H. R. Haldeman, John

Ehrlichman, and Henry Kissinger in the Oval Office. They are talking about the Pentagon Papers, which were published a few days earlier:

HALDEMAN: You maybe can blackmail Johnson on this stuff.

PRESIDENT NIXON: What?

HALDEMAN: You can blackmail Johnson on this stuff and it might be worth doing.

Nixon needs no urging. He quickly demands that a plan to knock over the Brookings Institution—a private think tank he suspects may have possession of documents embarrassing to his predecessor—be revived:

PRESIDENT NIXON: . . . I want it implemented. . . . Goddammit, get in and get those files. Blow the safe and get it.

Blow the safe, indeed. Throughout the six-hundred-plus pages that follow, the conversation seldom gets more elevated than this. Nixon and his assistants sound like regulars at the Ravenite Social Club. They are obsessed with breaking and entering: among the places they propose to burglarize are the National Archives (to steal more Johnson documents), the apartment of Arthur Bremer, the would-be assassin of George Wallace (to plant left-wing literature); and Nixon's own campaign headquarters (to make it look as if the Cubans did it, or the Democrats, or somebody). And as the coverup gives way to the coverup of the coverup, with Nixon and his men orchestrating all of it down to the smallest detail, *Abuse of Power* spells out subornation of perjury and obstruction of justice on a heroic scale.

The tapes from which these books have been fashioned are primary source material of a kind that is simply unprecedented, and it is almost impossible to overstate their value. They are about as close as we can come to the historian's dream of travelling in time and directly witnessing what actually happens, which is nearly always stranger, more complicated, and more disorderly than we assume—even, or perhaps especially, when the events in question have been written about ad nauseam.

The Kennedy, Johnson, and Nixon tapes opened a window on the past. Watergate slammed it shut. These books make one wish that the window could be thrown open again, on different terms. By all means, tape everything, and do it openly, not secretly. Wire the White House from top to bottom, and put the results under lock and key, rigidly protected by law from congressional subpoena or citizen lawsuit, for some suitable period of time. Forty years would be about right: long enough to insure the confidentiality of decision-making but short enough to let the events of one's youth be illuminated in one's old age. As it is, those thirty-eight million pages in College Station notwithstanding, there is a coming crisis in presidential historiography: the culture of scandal is dulling many of the basic tools of the historian. These days, a high government official can't even entrust private thoughts to private diary without risk.

It might be argued that if a system like the one proposed here had been in place during the early seventies, Nixon wouldn't have been forced from office. (In 2013, though, by way of consolation, we'd get to enjoy one hell of an eye-popping story.) But, by the same token, if the arrangements that obtain *now* had obtained then, Nixon would surely have beaten the Watergate rap—and the truth, in all likelihood, would have remained forever shrouded.

It wouldn't hurt for presidents and their lieutenants to know that posterity was in the room with them, listening. Given the overwhelming pressures on them to think in the short term, a little pressure to consider the long term would not be out of place. History has its claims. Why not marshal them in service to the future?

—*The New Yorker*, October 12, 1992

WHAT IT'S ABOUT

LAST WEEK, the government of our city began enforcing a zoning ordinance designed to curb porn shops, topless bars, strip clubs, and other pillars of the "adult-entertainment" industry. Under the ordinance, if a business establishment (a) is situated within five hundred feet of a church, school, home, or day-care center and (b) offers merchandise or activity more than 40 percent of which consists of smutty videos, dirty books, battery-operated dildos, naked women dancing suggestively, and the like, then (c) Mayor Giuliani's vice squad can move in and padlock the place. As a result, the window displays at Show World Center, which for some twenty years has been Times Square's biggest and busiest business establishment of its kind, are now filled with T-shirts, plastic Statues of Liberty, and piles of suitcases. Inside, gloomy corridors are still lined with lockable booths in which hardcore videos can still be viewed for a quarter per minute. But the merchandise shelves now hold perfume, sunglasses, and Walkmans, and the pornography salesroom now includes a sizable "Non-Adult Section," which stocks such mainstream titles as *Pillow Talk, F.I.S.T.,* and *The Nutcracker.* Whether all this has sufficed to push Show World Center's inventory below the 40 percent threshold remains to be adjudicated. But the position of the establishment's attorneys is clear: Show World Center is not about sex. It's about luggage.

So much for the week's doings in the cultural capital. What of the political capital?

"It's not about sex," Barbara Olson, who is identified as a former federal prosecutor, said recently on one of many editions of CNN's *Larry King Live* devoted to the investigation by the Whitewater independent counsel of the relationship between the president and the former White House intern. "It's about the Constitution." The Constitution? How high-minded, and how preposterous. The whole ghastly business—Kenneth Starr's four-year investigation, the massive public distractions and ugly private humiliations, the eons of airtime and acres of newsprint, the forced testimony of Secret Service agents and legal advisers, the crowning grotesquerie of the stained dress—has come down to a bizarre quest for the answer to a single question: Did two consenting adults, Bill Clinton and Monica Lewinsky, have sex with each other? This is not a good question. A good question would be: why is it surpassingly important to the public business of the United States and the world for that question to be asked, and, once asked, answered?

"It's not about sex, it's about lying," Alfred Regnery, the conservative book publisher, said on another Larry King program. No, it's about sex, and the kind of sex it's about—consensual but adulterous, furtive, and illicit—is by its nature incompatible with candor. To have sex of this kind is ipso facto to deceive, whether or not the deception is overt. Unless one is prepared to advocate open marriage—or, at least, to argue that adultery accompanied by press conference is somehow less reprehensible than adultery accompanied by discretion—the distinction is close to meaningless.

"This case and the investigation of Monica Lewinsky is not about sex. It's about perjury." That would be a former independent counsel named Joseph diGenova talking, also on CNN. If the president in his Paula Jones deposition did falsely deny an affair with Ms. Lewinsky, and if he makes the same denial in his August 17th testimony before Starr's grand jury, then he will indeed have lied under oath, twice. But he will have done so inside a kind of hermetically sealed experimental laboratory—a closed system consciously designed for no purpose except to maneuver him into committing a crime (and a singularly victimless crime at that). In terms of scale, the machinery that has been constructed to induce perjury stands in relation to the perjury it may or may not have induced as one of those enormous and expensive particle accelerators out West stands in relation to the trail of a neutrino.

"But the case is not about sex," said Tom Squitieri, a reporter for *USA Today*, on CNBC's *Equal Time*. "It's about obstruction of justice." Then what, exactly, is the justice that has been obstructed? And what, exactly, is the injustice that has been done, and to whom, as a consequence of this hypothetical obstruction? Obstacles may well have been placed in the path of an unaccountable prosecutorial bureaucracy that for obscure reasons has developed a single-minded obsession with discovering at any cost, and publicizing in sniggering detail, precisely what private sexual acts were engaged in by the president and the former intern. One can only hope so. But in what sense does the promulgation of details of this kind constitute justice? Doesn't this particular exercise in salacious nosiness *deserve* to be obstructed?

"It's not about the sex," Alvin Cooper, a clinical psychologist at Stanford University, said in a newspaper interview. "It's about the meaning that people put on sex." Here, at last, we may be getting somewhere. If few Americans believe that adultery should automatically be grounds for removal from office, still fewer would deny that adultery is almost always a selfish and hurtful thing. If the president had sex with the intern, then he behaved very badly, both toward "that woman," as he ungallantly called Ms. Lewinsky, and toward his own family. (His behavior would have been worse, however, if he had not tried energetically to keep it from becoming a public spectacle). But if public officials are to be judged by the moral texture of their private lives, why limit the inquiry to binary determinations of presidential adultery? Why not extend it to all high officials, and why not widen its scope to include the broader context of familial and affectional life? A good place to begin, perhaps, would be with the scores of senators and members of the House of Representatives who have been divorced. There is more than one way, after all, to be unkind.

"Apparently, it needs to be said repeatedly: The Monica Lewinsky–Bill Clinton investigation is not about sex," an important metropolitan newspaper, the *Chicago Sun-Times*, editorialized a few days ago. Well, it has been said repeatedly. Indeed, it has been said not only repeatedly but also ceaselessly, unremittingly, over and over again, and often—redundantly, in a word. And, if repetition could make a thing true, then it would be most emphatically and wonderfully true that the investigation of the relationship between the president and the former intern is not about sex. It would also be true that purchasers of *Playboy* and *Penthouse* are interested mainly in the articles. And that Show World Center is in business to sell souvenir key chains.

11. GHOSTS IN THE MACHINE

Where's Waldo? is the punch line of a standing *New Yorker* office joke, of which I am the punchee. It refers to my ferrety, unkillable persistence in trying to sneak favorable references to proportional representation and similar schemes for political betterment into the magazine. Sometimes the reference will be oblique—a mere allusion, intelligible only to experienced Waldo-spotters. Sometimes it's more overt but isn't brought up until the reader has been enticed by something more flavorful, as when I used a syrupy discussion of Oscar Week to suppress the reader's gag reflex before suddenly switching to an earnest endorsement of instant runoff voting. Sometimes it's unadulterated—two-hundred-proof wonkishness, straight up.

Beginning more than twenty-five years ago or so, when I first got a close look at the workings of Washington, I have believed with steadily increasing conviction that the peculiar failings of politics and public policy in the United States are caused mainly by the bizarre hydraulics of our electoral and governmental arrangements. Our problem is our constitution, broadly understood as the way our system is constituted. That means, first, the levers and pistons that are built into the eighteenth-century text of the written Constitution of the United States—the separation of powers, the bicameral Congress, the rule of two senators per state, federalism, the electoral college, and the near impossibility of getting an amendment ratified that might change any of these power relationships in any important way. But it includes as well a host of non-canonical rules and practices, ranging from the New Hampshire primary to the Senate filibuster to the geographic, single-seat, plurality-winner-take-all basis of legislative representation and executive election.

Once you begin to look at things from this angle, Waldo is everywhere. Why, for example, is the United States the only advanced industrial country that doesn't have some sort of universal health insurance? The usual debate over this anomaly pits those who think that it's because we Americans are self-reliant cowboys, who, unlike those docile Europeans, are suspicious of big government, against those who think that it's because Hillary screwed up. Some people think both. But how much do such explanations explain? The truth is that in the decades since the Second World War there have frequently been popular majorities for national health insurance in the United States. These majorities have been as large as the corresponding ones in Europe. In the matter of socially provisioned health care, the wishes of rambunctious, individualistic Americans are indistinguishable from the wishes of communitarian, regimented Europeans. It follows that the will of the people cannot possibly be the decisive variable. Nor can the cultural factors that might determine that will.

As for Hillary (and Bill), maybe she (and he) did screw up. But for that class of explanation to be conclusive, Harry Truman, John F. Kennedy, Lyndon Johnson, and Jimmy Carter would have to have screwed up, too. All ran on platforms advocating universal health insurance. The electoral victories of Truman, Kennedy, and Carter were narrow, but in 1964 Johnson won a huge mandate, sweeping large numbers of Democrats into Congress behind him. Johnson's political and legislative skills were at least as impressive as those of Clement Atlee, the mousy British prime minister under whom the National Health Service was established. Yet L.B.J. succeeded in getting coverage only for the old and the destitute—a magnificent accomplishment in American terms, but piddling compared to what Atlee and other Europeans had done a generation earlier. Americans, no less than the citizens of other democracies, want health care—want socialized medicine, if you like. And Americans, not once but five different times in fifty years, have gone to the trouble of electing presidents committed to it. The problem is that our clanking, creaking political-governmental mechanisms have proved incapable of delivering it.

The machine designed from scratch by the Framers and not much tinkered with since was a wonder of eighteenth-century political technology. It was a quantum leap upward from the Articles of Confederation. Its authors, from George Washington on down, took it for granted that their descendants would revise it and overhaul it in the light of experience. That never happened. And the Framers' instrument turned out to offer so much scope for obstruction and sclerosis that it has proved, on balance, a fitter instrument for conservative than for liberal purposes. But the system can be frustrating for conservatives, too. Ronald Reagan was sincere in his desire to shrink government, but he was unable to abolish even the tiny Legal Services Corporation, let alone the Department of Education. If it's hard for liberals to do things, it's almost as hard for conservatives to undo them. There are plenty of differences between Republican and Democratic administrations, but one way they are alike is that both are sluggish and neither is truly accountable. Might not the nation be better served by an alternation of energetic governments that could enact programs and be judged by them than it is by the tiny-brained herd of Apatosauruses that rules over us now?

If Americans don't bother to vote, maybe it's because voting is usually pointless. If Americans don't like government, maybe it's because we have so many of them that the buck never stops anywhere. I count three separately elected "governments" at the federal level—the presidency, the House, the Senate—overlapping with forty-nine state troikas and one unicameral, i.e., two-part, state government, Nebraska's. That makes a total of a hundred and fifty-two governments so far. (Then we have thousands of county, township, village, and city governments, most of which themselves have separately elected executives and legislative councils.) If Americans hate politicians, maybe it's because our chaotic pile of political systems offers so many perverse incentives for politicians to behave badly. If Americans don't feel represented by their representatives, maybe it's because they're not.

Allow me to elaborate.

LET'S GET REPRESENTATIVE

NOWHERE AMID the happy noise of the big two hundredth birthday party for the Constitution can one detect a popular clamor for changing that document. On the contrary, the emphasis is on thanksgiving and veneration; and despite the ghastly up-with-people tone of it all, the celebratory sentiments are worthier than the boosterism they engender. The Constitution, after all, is no ordinary scrap of parchment. It is more than the rules of a governmental game, more than an owner's manual for a political mechanism. Though other constitutions are like it (its Bill of Rights has been widely copied), it is not like other constitutions. Though firmly rooted in Enlightenment rationalism, it long ago acquired a mystical, almost occult significance.

In a sense, the Constitution of the United States *is* the United States. Our Constitution is central to who we are as Americans in ways that the basic laws of the French Republic or the Federal Republic of Germany, for example, are not at all central to the identities of Frenchmen or Germans. We may sing about purple mountain majesties and fruited plains, but we have no mystique of land or blood. We have no *patrie,* no *volk.* We come from all over the place, we're all different colors, and we don't all look alike. What unites us, finally, is a political compact, a constitution: *the* Constitution. It is the fount of America's very nationhood. No wonder we don't want to mess with it.

Because amending the Constitution is both difficult and dangerous, it has only been done three times on a large scale: before the mold had set (the

Bill of Rights); after it had been smashed by civil war (the Reconstruction amendments); and at Progressivism's high tide (direct election of senators, the income tax, women's suffrage). There is little reason to expect, alas, that the bicentennial can be turned into an occasion for change. But it is already the next best thing, an occasion for discussion. For the time being, it is possible to broach the subject of constitutional reform without being hooted down as a crank.

The more thoughtful critics of the system of government chartered by the Constitution point to two great flaws in it (which some regard as its greatest virtues): it is weak, and it is unrepresentative. The question is whether these two flaws could be remedied without seriously undermining the continuity that confers legitimacy. The answer, I would guess, is no and yes.

The weakness is endemic and probably ineradicable. Weakness is a function of the separation of powers between the legislative and executive branches. The separation of powers has been so central to the American system of government that abolishing it would probably make the system unrecognizable and thus threaten its historical legitimacy. The only effective way to get rid of the separation of powers would be to introduce a parliamentary system, in which the executive would be the creature of the legislature and the two branches would stand, govern, and fall together. Such a system would be strong, effective, and accountable. It would not, alas, be American.

Unrepresentativeness is another story. That problem, which is rooted in the geographic basis of representation, could be solved quite neatly.

The Congress of the United States does one thing, and one thing only, very well: it represents localities. When you go to the polls to vote for a candidate for the Senate or the House, you can be absolutely sure that you will have the opportunity to vote for someone to represent your state or your district. (You can even be sure that someone will in fact be elected to do just that.) What you cannot be sure of is that you will have the opportunity to vote for (let alone elect) someone to represent your point of view—or anything else about yourself you may consider important.

Two hundred years ago it was natural to make geography the sole basis for designing political constituencies. It is highly unnatural now. Back then most people lived out their lives within a few miles of where they were born. Now a third of the population uproots itself every two years. Then travel was slow and arduous. Now it is fast and easy. Then we had letters carried by stagecoach and sailing ship. Now we have telephones, modems, and Federal Express. Then we had torchlight parades and committees of correspondence; now we have tracking polls, *Nightline,* and national newspapers printed simultaneously in a dozen cities. The ties that bind are no longer just the ties of propinquity. The communities that count are communities of interest and belief—communities that are at least as likely to be national as local. Ideology, profession, class, even racial and sexual identity—these are the soil our roots grow in now, as much as or more than where we live.

John Stuart Mill would have understood this point. "I cannot see why the feelings and interests which arrange mankind according to localities," he once wrote, "should be the only ones thought worthy of being represented; or why people who have other feelings and interests, which they value more than they do their geographical ones, should be restricted to these as the sole principle of their political classification."

We would be better off, in other words, if our representative institutions represented what *we ourselves* regard as important about us, rather than representing only the states and districts in which we happen to live and everything else about us only capriciously or not at all. That is why we would do well to adopt the following:

AMENDMENT 27

Section 1. The Senate of the United States shall be composed of one Senator from each State, elected by the people thereof for six years, and an equal number of Senators elected at large by the whole people of the United States for six years.

Section 2. The one-third of the Senate elected every second year shall be divided as equally as possible between Senators elected by the several States and those elected at large.

Section 3. The Senators elected at large shall be elected by the Hare, or single transferable vote, method of proportional representation.

Section 4. The House of Representatives shall consist of the Members apportioned among the several states, and of one hundred members elected at large by the whole people of the United States.

Section 5. The Members of the House of Representatives elected at large shall be elected by the slate or party-list method of proportional representation.

Section 6. The Congress shall have the power to regulate, by appropriate legislation, the carrying out of the provisions of this Article.

This scheme would make the government of the United States dramatically more representative—more democratic—and it would do so without undue violence to time-sanctioned forms. Specifically, Amendment 27, with its use of national proportional representation to choose fifty senators and one hundred members of the House, would improve the quality of representative democracy in three ways:

First, it would allow important minorities to express themselves through the political system. Minorities are represented under the present dispensation—but only if they all happen to live in the same place. It takes about a hundred thousand people to elect a representative in an average district, scarcely more than that to elect a senator in some Western states. But much larger, much more salient minorities are shut out if they have the bad luck to be spread around. Under Amendment 27 a party or candidate would need the support of perhaps three quarters of a million Americans to win an at-large seat in the House, maybe four million to win one in the Senate—about the number of votes a Senate victory takes in the most populous states. These are not trivial numbers. (The actual thresholds would probably be higher, because turnout would almost certainly rise if you could vote for a person or party you actually agreed with and/or respected.) And the senators and representatives chosen in this way would represent what people want represented about themselves.

Second, Amendment 27 would make individual votes count. Voting in the United States is almost always purely a civic sacrament—a ritual of faith, not an exercise of political power. The only time your vote really "counts" is in a photo-finish election. If you happen to live in a "safe" congressional district, as the vast majority of Americans do, you might as well be disfranchised. In such a district your side can turn out 10 percent more votes than last time and it makes no practical difference. But under proportional representation 10 percent more votes means 10 percent more victories. As I'll explain, under P.R. all races are close and every vote counts—another reason turnout would undoubtedly be higher.

Third, Amendment 27 would permit the election of talented candidates whose political bases are in "constituencies" that don't happen to be local. It is good to have members of Congress who are grounded in particular places, and under Amendment 27 most still would be. But our geographically based electoral arrangements deprive us of the services of those who have had the wit or energy to leave home. In every country the ambitious, clever, and interesting people tend to abandon the provinces for the metropolis. They go to the big city because that is the way to accomplish something in business or the arts or scholarship. In Britain and France—even in Canada!—the political parties can tap such people and designate them to stand for provincial parliamentary seats; in Israel and Italy, they can run for seats at large. Not so here. Most of our best people are cut off from electoral politics because they lack a local base, and they lack a local base because they are some of our best people. The citizens of any self-respecting medium-sized city would be delighted to get Kareem Abdul-Jabbar to play for their basketball team, André Previn to direct their symphony orchestra, or Pauline Kael to review movies for their local newspaper. But few of these same good burghers would extend a political welcome to an "outsider," even one whose intelligence, eloquence, and knowledge of public affairs might make him or her better fitted for service in the House or Senate than some local lawyer or realtor. Arthur Schlesinger, Jr., for visiting professor at River City College? Of course. Arthur Schlesinger, Jr., for Congress? Never. Professor Schlesinger would be a catch, candidate Schlesinger merely a carpetbagger. Is it any wonder our legislative assemblies are filled with unimaginative people whose ambition and interests are narrow?

The framers saw the Senate as the protector of small states and as a chamber of notables. It would retain the first role because each state, regardless of population, would have its own senator. (This, by the way, would satisfy Article V's little-known requirement that the Constitution cannot be amended in such a way that any state is "deprived of its equal Suffrage in the Senate.") But with half its members elected by the Hare system, the Senate's character as a chamber of notables would be much enhanced.

The Hare system, named for its inventor, a mid-nineteenth-century British parliamentarian named Thomas Hare, is probably the most perfectly "representative" electoral system ever devised. Mill, its most passionate advocate, called it "among the very greatest improvements in the theory and practice of government." As it happens, the Hare system would be especially well suited for filling at-large seats in the Senate, only sixteen or seventeen of which would be up every two years.

The Hare system is simple for the voter, who has only to list his or her choices in rank order—first choice, second choice, third, and so on. The counting is what's complicated. The counting is also the key to the Hare system's advantage, which is that it makes every vote count. In simplified form, here's how it works (and pay attention, because I'm only going to explain this once):

Consider an at-large Senate election to fill sixteen seats, with 72 million people voting. (Come to think of it, you may need a pencil and some scratch paper to follow this.) The first-choice votes are counted first, and anybody who gets more than one-sixteenth of the 72 million first-choice votes, i.e., 4.5 million, is declared elected. Then, the second-choice votes of those whose first choice has won are added to the remaining candidates' totals—but only to the extent they represent a "surplus" for the winning candidate. This is done by multiplying the second-choice totals by a fraction representing the proportion of each winner's votes over 4.5 million. Any candidate who exceeds 4.5 million votes after this second round is declared elected. Meanwhile, at the other end of the field, the candidate with the lowest number of first-choice votes is declared eliminated, and his or her second-choice votes are distributed, at full value, among the remaining candidates. This cycle is repeated until all sixteen seats are filled. In the end, every vote has been fully used for winning candidates. No one needs to worry about "wasting" a vote on a candidate too popular to need it or too unpopular to use it. All clear?

No? All right, look at it this way. Let's say George Will gets 6 million first-place votes and Jeane Kirkpatrick gets 4 million. George is declared elected. His second-choice votes are then counted, and it turns out that 3 million of his people listed Jeane second. Those 3 million votes are multiplied by (6-4.5)/6—that is, one fourth—and the resulting figure, 750,000, is added to Jeane's total, giving her 4.75 million and putting her over the top. On the next round of counting, of course, her second-choice ballots would be distributed in similar fashion. And so on. This is sufficiently complicated that in the few places where the Hare system is used, such as in elections for the Irish Dail and the city council of Cambridge, Massachusetts, the counting can take days, because paper ballots are used. With computerization, though, it could be done in minutes.

If the above example displeases you, substitute the names "Jesse Jackson" and "Mary McGrory." Or "Michael Harrington" and "Irving Howe." The point is that Amendment 27 would open the Senate to the sort of people who might make floor debates worth listening to. With one or two exceptions it does not now contain such people. John Stuart Mill again:

> In the false democracy which, instead of giving representation to all, gives it only to the local majorities, the voice of the instructed minority may have no organs at all in the representative body. It is an admitted fact that in the American democracy, which is conducted on this faulty model, the highly cultivated members of the community, except such of them as are willing to sacrifice their own opinions and modes of judgment, and become the servile mouthpieces of their inferiors in knowledge, seldom even offer themselves for Congress or the State Legislatures, so little likelihood have they of being returned. Had a plan like Mr. Hare's by good fortune suggested itself to the enlightened and patriotic founders of the American Republic, the Federal and State Assemblies would have contained many of these distinguished men, and democracy would have been spared its greatest reproach and one of its most formidable evils. (*Considerations on Representative Government,* Chapter VII)

With sixteen Senate seats to fill, a voter could theoretically list sixteen candidates in order of preference. But there seldom would be much advantage in listing more than about a half dozen—and no advantage at all in "bullet voting," or listing only one candidate. It is perfectly reasonable to expect voters to be informed enough to be able to choose six candidates even from a large field in what would be a highly visible national election.

On the House side, however, with a hundred at-large seats to be filled at every election, the Hare system would offer too many choices. The solution is for each voter to cast a single ballot for a slate of candidates. The allocation of seats is in proportion to the vote. If the Democrats get 30 percent of the vote, the Republicans 22 percent, and the Right-to-Lifers 2 percent, then the Democrats get 30 seats, the Republicans 22, and the Right-to-Lifers 2. Each party draws up its own list, with the names of its most able and/or attractive candidates at the top, where they might make the cut.

I CAN IMAGINE many objections to Amendment 27, all of them rooted in legitimate concerns. It would weaken the existing parties. It would open the door to a host of little parties and single-issue and special interest groups to have their own members of Congress. It would risk giving some little extremist group the balance of power and thus inordinate influence over public policy.

Would it really weaken the parties? That would be quite a trick—a bit like wetting the ocean. Without question, Amendment 27 would result in the election of independent and minor-party senators and representatives. But on balance the major parties would be greatly strengthened. First, half the Senate and 80 percent of the House would still be elected by winner-take-all, first-past-the-post constituencies, the dynamics of which inexorably dictate a system of two broad coalition parties. (The expanded House of Representatives, by the way, would still have 115 fewer members than the British House of Commons.) Second, because Congress would be charged with making the rules governing access to the ballot, we can expect that those rules would be biased in favor of the big parties. Third, and most important, the national parties, which up to now have had at their disposal only the two quadrennial executive-branch nominations, would have the power to bestow 116 or 117 biennial legislative nominations as well. This would give the party organizations more clout than they have ever dreamed of.

What about Balkanization? In fact it would be less of a threat than one might expect. The experience of most countries that have proportional representation is that a stable two-party or two-coalition system emerges, with a few representatives of minor parties to add spice. In cases where no party wins an outright majority, the process of coalition-building more often acts as a moderating than a radicalizing influence.

The great counterexample, routinely cited by opponents of proportional representation, is Israel, where, because of the almost equal strength of Labor and the Likud, the balance of power has sometimes been held by a tiny, single-minded religious party, which has been able to force many of its orthodox strictures upon the secular-minded majority. Could that happen to us under Amendment 27? Thanks to the separation of powers, no. Even in the unlikely event some loony little political sect ended up holding the balance of power between the Democrats and their allies and the Republicans and theirs, the stakes would be far lower than under a parliamentary regime. The steepest price the loonies could exact would be a few extra committee seats and a chairmanship or two.

Anyway, what would be so terrible about a bit of political pluralism? Would it really be so bad if the anti-abortionists or environmentalists managed to elect a senator and three or four representatives? Or if black and sympathetic white voters succeeded in raising the number of black senators from zero to four or five and of black representatives from twenty-three to thirty-three? That would still be less than their rightful share—their "quota," if you like. The majority must rule, but shouldn't minorities (and every one of us is a member of some minority or other) have a voice?

A few years ago there was much worried clucking about the rise of the Greens in West Germany. They were said to have a disturbing penchant for "extraparliamentary" politics. Yet now they sit in the Bundestag, which has had the twin effects of strengthening the more responsible elements among them and of binding their followers more firmly to the democratic system. In fact it is the United States that has been the foremost stronghold of "extraparliamentary" politics. The most important American politician of the postwar era was not an officeholder but a protester, Martin Luther King, Jr., "Advanced" ideas of whatever stripe rarely find expression in our official political institutions, because the only way to get elected is to put together a majority or plurality coalition in a particular place.

Coalitions are built by blurring distinctions, not sharpening them. The best political discussions in the United States occur in universities, kitchens, little magazines, saloons—anywhere but in the halls of Congress. Amendment 27 would go some distance toward changing that. The discontented would no longer have to choose between fitful protest and frozen apathy; the citizenry would no longer have to choose between two banal local lawyers. All could go to the polls and vote, knowing that in doing so they were performing a consequential political act—and joining that now too often mythical symposium, the "national debate."

—*The New Republic,* June 29, 1987

TWELVE IS ENOUGH

BEFORE YOU automatically reject the proposal now making the rounds for a twelve-year limit for members of Congress as a dreadful idea—an antidemocratic, antipolitical, mechanistic "reform" that like so many other "reforms" would most likely end up making things worse, a bit of mischievous tinkering with the precious Constitution that has served us so well for two hundred years, a misguided gimmick that ignores the real problem (PACs, polls, gerrymandering, special interests, negative ads, cowardly politicians, ignorant citizens, whatever) and is probably nothing but a Republican plot anyway—before you agree with all these dismissals and turn your attention to more pressing matters, please consider three numbers.

Number number one: 37.1. Yes, it's a voter turnout figure, the op-ed writer's best friend. This particular figure represents the percentage of American over-eighteens who bestirred themselves to go to the polls in 1986, the last time the citizenry was invited to vote for members of Congress without the added glitz of a presidential contest. Compared with the turnout in any other arguably democratic country—France, Nicaragua, Norway, Hungary, El Salvador, Israel, Turkey, Italy, Lithuania, you name it—this is pathetic. It was the lowest since 1926, not counting 1944, when World War II made voting inconvenient for large numbers of people. And the public's true interest in House elections is even lower. According to *Congressional Quarterly*'s Rhodes Cook, if you factor out districts where there was a contest for governor or U.S. senator to lure people out, the turnout was a scandalous 27.6 percent. Only the most perverse élitists argue that this state of affairs is anything but a symptom of extreme political ill health.

Number number two: 98.3. This is the percentage of incumbent members of the House of Representatives who won their "races" for reelection in 1988, up from 98 percent flat in 1966. According to a recent study by David C. Huckabee of the Congressional Research Service of the Library of Congress, this number has remained in the 90s since 1974, and it is currently the highest it has ever been since the middle of President Washington's first term. And because more incumbents now choose to run than ever before, the reelection rate for the House as a whole is now in the 90s, too—92.4 percent last time out, to be exact. In the nineteenth century this figure tended to hover somewhere between 40 percent and 70 percent, once dropping to as low as 24 percent (in 1842); it hit the 70s after World War I and has been climbing more or less steadily ever since.

The 98.3 figure actually understates the political stasis of the House. Of the 409 incumbents who ran for reelection, six were defeated in November. But five of these had been tainted by one sort of scandal or another. So the grand total of representatives who lost their seats as a consequence of what we normally think of as politics—that is, a process in which the electorate chooses between competing sets of programs and policies—was exactly one.

Number number three: 36. This is how many years a single party, the Democrats, has controlled the lower house of the national legislature of the United States. By contrast, the British House of Commons has changed hands four times since 1954, the French Chamber of Deputies three times, the West German Bundestag five times, the Canadian House of Commons five times, and the Indian Lok Sabha three times. When it comes to one-party legislative dominance in serious countries, only Japan, Mexico, South Africa, and the Soviet Union are even in our league. And in the last two, unlike in the United States, the ruling party is a pretty good bet to lose the next election. No moral equivalence intended, of course. Or deserved.

In the light of numbers number two and three, the wonder is that number number one is so high. In the overwhelming majority of congressional districts, voting is increasingly an irrational act. Why bother, when 85 percent of the incumbents are getting more than 60 percent of the vote in their districts, when the *average* incumbent is getting 73.5 percent, when sixty-three members are returned with Brezhnevian majorities exceeding 94 percent? Except in the handful of districts where there are open seats or close races, voting may still make sense as a civic sacrament—as a way of refreshing one's soul with a sense of belonging to a democratic community—but it makes no sense as a form of political action. Better to spend the hour or so it takes to vote writing checks and sending them off to candidates in contested districts.

Against this background, the idea of a twelve-year limit begins to acquire a certain logic. Such proposals are neither new nor flakily marginal. A limit on congressional service was considered at the founding constitutional convention (which laid it aside as "entering too much into detail"), and the idea has won the support, over the decades, of a bipartisan list of luminaries including Abraham Lincoln, Harry Truman, Dwight D. Eisenhower, and John F. Kennedy. The current campaign for a constitutional amendment that would limit service to six two-year terms for House members and two six-year terms for senators (with an exemption for the present crew of incumbents, of course) is led by Senators Gordon Humphrey, Republican of New Hampshire, and Dennis DeConcini, Democrat of Arizona. Their ten co-sponsors span the Senate's ideological spectrum, from Jake Garn on the right to Nancy Kassebaum in the center to Tom Daschle on the left.

Even so, truth in packaging compels the admission that the current push is basically a Republican scam. All but three of the Senate co-sponsors are Republicans. The twelve-year limit was endorsed in the 1988 Republican platform. The letterhead pressure group promoting the idea, something called Americans to Limit Congressional Terms, is run out of a Republican political consultant's office and consists mostly of Republican ex-congressmen and state legislators (though it does include a few Democrats, of whom the most distinguished is former eight-term Representative Donald M. Fraser, now mayor of Minneapolis). Republicans are understandably eager to support any lunatic notion that holds out the promise of helping them break the Democratic stranglehold on Capitol Hill. But this just might be one of those rare cases where the narrow self-interest of the Republican Party is congruent with the public good.

The arguments for the term limit are surprisingly persuasive, especially where the House is concerned. Almost all of them are variations on a single theme: breaking the Gordian knot of entrenched incumbency which distorts our democracy from the polling place clear up to the Senate and (especially) House chambers. Out in that fabled land beyond the Beltway, the term limit would mean that at least once every twelve years (and probably more frequently), every citizen would get a fighting chance to vote in a genuinely *political* congressional election, which is to say one that would turn not on the goodies that good old Congressman Thing has procured for the district or the Social Security checks he has expedited or the campaign funds he has raised or the newsletters he has franked, but rather on the competing political visions and programs of parties and candidates. But the most interesting, and salutary, effects of the limit would be the ways in which it would change the political ecology of Congress itself.

A twelve-year limit would necessarily bring an end to the much-reformed but still pervasive and undemocratic rule of seniority. The House Speaker, the chairmen of important committees, and the other potentates of Congress have long been elevated by a decades-long, quasi-feudal process of favor-trading, personal alliance-building, ladder-climbing, and "getting along by going along." The term limit would leave Congress little choice but to elect its chiefs democratically, on the basis of the policy preferences and leadership qualities of the candidates. Like the Speakers of many of our state legislatures, these leaders would tend to be vigorous men and women in their forties and fifties—people in the mold of Bill Gray, Stephen Solarz, and Henry Hyde. The Dingells and Rostenkowskis would remain where they belong, on the back benches or in private life. This would be an important gain. And the frequent turnover of leaders—one who served more than six years would be a rarity—would be a spur both to brisk accomplishment and to attentiveness to the concerns and needs of the country.

The seniority system occasionally produces good leaders as well as bad ones, but there is no denying that it is grossly biased in favor of the most politically sluggish and unchanging parts of the nation. A swing district—one marked by close elections, and the robust debate and clamorous participation that those elections bring—has a hard time keeping somebody in office long enough to survive the glacial process by which congressional power is accumulated. It is precisely such districts that are most likely to elect representatives alive to the cutting-edge problems that most urgently require action. Systematically disempowering these districts and the people representing them, as the current arrangement so efficiently does, is insane.

A Congress invigorated by frequent infusions of new blood would be a more responsive, more democratic, more varied place. So would a Congress whose majority regularly changed from one party to the other, which a term limit would unquestionably promote. However bad this might be for the short-term partisan interests of Democrats like me, it would be good for the long-term interests of the country—and the party, too. Critics of the term limit idea argue that it would "weaken" Congress; and so it would, but in ways that would strengthen both its most useful functions and democratic governance in general. The one-party Congress has become a world unto itself, and the long period of Republican control of the presidency and Democratic control of Congress has produced an insidious mentality on Capitol Hill. The leaders of the Democratic congressional majority, veterans of decades of supremacy in their own little universe, no longer constitute an opposition. They conceive of themselves as ins, not outs—as leaders of one-half of a permanent coalition government. They may imagine that their own fiefdoms are secure, but their party is reaping almost all of the penalties of incumbency and almost none of the benefits. The foundations of Democratic congressional dominance are being relentlessly undermined, and once the structure topples, as eventually it must, rebuilding it will seem as hopeless a task as destroying it does now. A Congress shaped by a term limit would have a different and healthier mentality. During periods when it was controlled by the party that also controls the White House, it would be energetic in pursuit of that party's program; when in opposition, it would—for a change, and just as energetically—oppose.

The many Americans who deplore the decline of political parties in this country ought especially to welcome the term limit idea. By routinely undermining the totally independent, totally personal power bases that long-serving senators and representatives are able to build and maintain under the current system, and by dramatically increasing the number of elections fought on the basis of national issues, the term limit would enhance the strength and coherence of both national parties.

The term limit would mean that at any given moment something like sixty or seventy representatives, and perhaps half that number of senators, would be ineligible to run again. To critics of the proposal, this is one of its worst features. The lame ducks, say the critics, would be "unaccountable" and unresponsive to their constituents' wishes. But Congress's problem is hardly that its members are insufficiently obsessed with reelection, insufficiently attentive to polling data, and insufficiently ardent in pursuit of district pork barrel. The broader public good could only benefit from having a cohort of comparatively disinterested legislators, relieved from reelection pressures and free to consult their consciences as well as their pollsters and contributors. The critics add that the lame ducks might fall prey to corruption, legal or illegal. This phenomenon is not exactly unknown under present arrangements. But it would not be more likely to happen if most of the departing members are still relatively young and still ambitious. Why should they feather their nests at the cost of their reputations?

It's true, as the critics also say, that the term limits would deprive Congress of the services of legislators whom experience has made wise. This would be a real cost. But it would be a cost worth paying to be rid of the much larger number of timeservers who have learned nothing from longevity in office except cynicism, complacency, and a sense of diminished possibility. And it's not as if the job of being a congressman is so difficult that it takes decades to master. It's easier than being a first-rate school-teacher, for example, and no harder than such jobs as president, governor, or mayor—all of which are regularly performed very well indeed by people who have had no on-the-job experience at all.

In any case, the senators and representatives obliged to seek other employment after twelve years will not vanish from the face of the earth. They will be available for service in the executive branch, in industry, in advocacy groups, and in the academy. Few will become lobbyists, because the turnover on the Hill will quickly make their contacts obsolete and their influence unpeddlable. Many will run for other public offices. Representatives will run for senator, senators will run for representative, and both will run for president, governor, mayor, and state legislator. The result will be more and better competition for these jobs, too. This would not be such a bad thing. Membership in Congress would no longer be a life calling or a lifetime sinecure, but this would not be such a bad thing either. A shot at Congress would be an attractive option for the young and ambitious, for the old but still energetic, and for men and women in midlife who want something more meaningful than whatever success they have earned elsewhere. There would be no shortage of candidates. Though harder to keep, the job would be easier to get.

A Gallup poll taken in December found that 70 percent of the American public favors the idea of a term limit. This is uncannily close to the percentages of the public that (a) think Congress is doing a lousy job and (b) keep on voting to reelect the same old incumbents. Opponents of the term limit say that if voters are so fed up with Congress, there is a simple way for them to do something about it without tinkering with the Constitution: "Throw the rascals out," as the *Chicago Tribune* suggests. So why don't they? "The explanation," my friend Michael Kinsley wrote recently, "is that the voters are lazy hypocrites." Maybe they are, but that's not the explanation.

A given voter can vote to throw out a maximum of one rascal—three if you count senators. That's one-half of 1 percent of the total rascal contingent. The problem is not individual incumbents; it's chronic incumbency, and trying to solve it by removing one's own incumbent is like dealing with a community-wide epidemic of tooth decay by having your own molars extracted, whether or not they've got cavities in them. To tell a voter he can solve the problem of chronic incumbency by voting against his own representative is to recommend a particularly fruitless form of single-issue politics. The public's disgust is with Congress as an institution, and defeating one member out of 535 won't revamp Congress any more than firing the deputy assistant to the president for scheduling would revamp the White House.

Thanks to seniority, voting to remove a long-serving congressman necessarily means voting to replace him with someone who will have less power. It therefore means voting to deprive one's district (and oneself) of clout. That's fine if you truly think your representative is a rascal. But what if you simply think he's a mediocrity?

There has to be a better way, and the twelve-year limit just might be it. The movement for it deserves the support of all who think Congress is broke and needs fixing—even those who, unlike me, don't think the limit itself is a particularly good idea. Let's be realistic: the chances a term limit amendment will actually get enacted are pretty remote. Congress, for obvious reasons, is not likely to pass it, and the other route—a constitutional convention called by two-thirds of the state legislatures—has never been successfully traveled. But the movement to impose a limit, if it catches fire, could throw enough of a scare into the Congress we've got to induce it to make changes—in campaign financing, PAC spending, access to television, mandatory campaign debates, and so on—that would accomplish some of the same salutary results. The term limit movement is potentially like the nuclear freeze movement of the early 1980s. As a policy blueprint the freeze proposal left a lot to be desired. But the movement did a world of good by forcing the Reagan administration to offer serious arms control proposals of its own, most of which the Russians eventually accepted. The freeze movement was a cri de coeur. So is the term limit movement. Listen, Congress.

—*The New Republic*, May 14, 1990

BOOM VOX

THE VOICE OF THE PEOPLE is heard in the land, and it sounds like a bad rock concert. Heavy-metal listeners are familiar with a phenomenon that occurs when the speakers get too close to the microphone pickups on the guitars. The sound comes out and goes in, comes out and goes in, around and around, over and over, all in a fraction of a second, getting reamplified with each cycle—and the result is an earsplitting screech that not only obliterates the music (which was none too soothing to begin with) but also deafens performers and audience alike. This is known as feedback.

In politics, feedback, as in feedback from the voters, has a calmer, metaphorical meaning, referring to that part of the process of political accountability whereby an elected official's constituents let him or her know what they are thinking. The framers of the First Amendment to the Constitution had this kind of feedback in mind when they guaranteed "the right of the people peaceably to assemble, and to petition the Government for a redress of grievances." What they most certainly did not have in mind was the apparatus of modern electronic plebiscitarianism—the explosion of telecommunications and data-processing technology which, by wiring together a nexus of overwrought call-in shows, overnight polls, skittish politicians, and pandering parajournalists, has created a political noise machine that takes a skewed sample of the instantaneous opinions of the moment, amplifies and reamplifies it, and packages it as the authentic voice of mainstream America.

Instantaneous opinions are by definition unthinking, or nearly so, because thinking takes time, and time is what's annihilated inside the new political-feedback loop. The machine, which crackled with loud but intermittent static during last year's election campaign, has been emitting a continuous, piercing shriek throughout the first three weeks of Bill Clinton's presidency, as one overhyped issue or pseudoissue after another—Zoë Baird and her nanny problem, gays in the military, a possible cap on Social Security cost-of-living raises, Kimba Wood and *her* nanny problem—gets fed through its overloaded circuits. All this has been widely, if a little dutifully, deplored. But for every commentator who laments the rise of electronic mob rule there is another who praises it as a valuable innovation in participatory democracy, a salutary corrective to the supposed out-of-touchness of those whom the voters have elected to public office. If the people—or, rather, the simulacrum thereof comprising callers-in to radio talk shows and respondents to hastily conducted opinion polls—make the snap judgment that Zoë Baird is unfit to be attorney general, and if senators who initially (and correctly) saw her nanny infraction as substantively trivial suddenly reverse themselves and condemn her, it is considered bad form to suggest that "the people" might simply be wrong, the senators simply craven. Instead, what will typically be said is what at least one commentator has already said: that "the people were way out in front of the politicians on this one"—as if the speed of a judgment and its astuteness were one and the same. At the time of the Clarence Thomas hearings, the people, according to a poll, thought that Thomas was telling the truth and Anita Hill was lying. Now the people, according to a poll, think the reverse. Whom were the people way out in front of on *that* one? They were ahead of the politicians, to be sure (if only in the sense that the politicians hastened to follow), but weren't they also getting a little ahead of themselves?

The temptation to flatter the digitalized phantom that has been sanctified as "the people" seems to be irresistible. The chat shows and op-ed pages are filled with altogether too much condescending awe of the alleged sagacity of "the people"—too much prattle about how when you come right down to it the folks out there have so much more wisdom and, darn it, so much more plain old common sense than all us élitists. But the unconsidered opinions of the many are no better, if not necessarily worse, than the unconsidered opinions of the few. Considered opinions, regardless of the size of the group espousing them, tend to be sounder opinions, and it is because the many have lives to lead and livelihoods to earn, and are therefore unable to take part in the daily deliberations of government, that our democracy is representative rather than direct. It is weakened, not strengthened, when those who are chosen to conduct its daily deliberations—whether they are presidents, legislators, or private citizens on jury duty—cede judgment to distorted images of the popular passions of the moment.

The conceit behind the bogus democracy of the call-in shows is that because they are unfiltered they are superior. The mediating institutions of representative democracy—political parties, advocacy groups, professional associations, and the elected bodies themselves—are seen, in this model, as inherently evil and corrupt. But the call-in shows, for the most part, are marketing devices, not civic forums. They're in business to get boffo ratings—a goal that ought not to be confused with public enlightenment or political participation. "I'll admit to you I'm flattered, but I don't go into this studio every day saying, 'How can I influence Congress?,' " Rush Limbaugh told Ted Koppel on *Nightline* last Tuesday. "I'm here to attract an audience—I want to attract the largest number of people I can and hold them for as long as I can. That's my job." Shows like Limbaugh's deal in hysteria, resentment, and outrage—and what can be more fun, especially if you're stuck in traffic? The act of calling in to such a show can even be a constructive one. But it stands in relation to real political involvement as 900-number phone sex does to emotional involvement. If the people, opposed to "the people," are truly to be heard over the screech of the feedback loop, it would help to move the mike back an inch or two, and be skeptical of the inflated claims of electronic populism.

—*The New Yorker*, February 22, 1993

IDEA WOMAN

THERE WAS NEVER any doubt about Lani Guinier's qualifications to be assistant attorney general for civil rights. Radcliffe and Yale Law School; a clerkship with the chief judge of the United States District Court in Michigan; four years' apprenticeship as special assistant to Drew Days, who held the Justice Department's top civil rights job during the Carter administration; seven years as a highly successful litigator with the N.A.A.C.P. Legal Defense and Educational Fund; and, most recently, five years as a respected, energetic, and popular professor of law at the University of Pennsylvania Law School: no nominee for the post has ever been better prepared than Lani Guinier. That wasn't her problem. Her problem was her ideas.

Or, rather, a caricature of her ideas. She was one of "Clinton's Quota Queens," according to the careless headline on the *Wall Street Journal* op-ed piece that opened the assault, on April 30th. The headline, with its echo of "welfare queens," had a touch of raw racism not reflected in the article, which was by Clint Bolick, the litigation director of a conservative think tank called the Institute for Justice. Mr. Bolick merely used artfully chosen quotations from Ms. Guinier's articles in law reviews to portray her as demanding what he called "equal legislative outcomes, requiring abandonment not only of the 'one person, one vote' principle, but majority rule itself." Other critics, mostly but not exclusively from the political right, quickly piled on. Ms. Guinier "does not share the goal of a colorblind society. She is not an integrationist" (John Leo, in *U.S. News & World Report*). She "intends to abolish one of the cornerstones of American democracy—

majority rule" (Lally Weymouth, in the *Washington Post*). She stands for "racial polarization" and for "setting black and white politically and legally apart" (A. M. Rosenthal, in the *New York Times*). She is a "hard-left extremist" (editorial, *New York Post*), who favors "vote-rigging schemes" (Senator Bob Dole). She "is a firm believer in the racial analysis of an irreducible, racial 'us' and 'them' in American society" (editorial, *The New Republic*). It all sounded pretty awful. How could such a person be nominated for such an important position?

"At the time of the nomination, I had not read her writings," President Clinton said on Thursday evening, explaining why he had abruptly decided that she wasn't his choice after all. "In retrospect, I wish I had." One can heartily share that wish, and add the wish that when at last he did get around to reading her writings he had done so less hurriedly and more carefully. For the truth is that Ms. Guinier's writings—a three-inch-high stack of monographs, law-review articles, and speeches she submitted to the Senate Judiciary Committee—reward the effort of slogging through what she herself described as her "ponderous and dense" style. They do not show her to be an enemy of racial integration, a proponent of racial polarization, or an opponent of democratic norms. They do show her to be a provocative, interesting thinker whose speculations could nourish what is a nascent debate in this country about alternative electoral systems. Perhaps they still can.

In her most important writings—four long law-review articles published between 1989 and this April—Ms. Guinier returns again and again to the theme of the shortcomings of the system of legislative representation that is almost universal in the United States. That system is based upon single-member, winner-take-all, geographically based electoral districts. Because she writes from the perspective of a civil rights lawyer, her main concern is how blacks fare; and, because her specialty is the Voting Rights Act, her focus is on local government, the level of government most often affected by the act. Given the racial polarization that exists in our society—a condition that Ms. Guinier forthrightly recognizes but certainly does not advocate—black legislative candidates are seldom elected except in "majority minority" single-member districts. Voting-rights lawyers have therefore concentrated on forcing local jurisdictions to create "safe" black-majority districts, and also on eliminating at-large systems that have demonstrably allowed white majorities to shut even sizable black minorities out of representation altogether. Ms. Guinier takes a different tack. In common with many conservative, and some liberal, critics, she recognizes the moral and political costs of racial gerrymandering: while it does allow black legislators to be elected, it creates monolithically white districts as well as monolithically black ones; it depresses political competition, voter turnout, and interracial political alliances; it depends for its effectiveness on segregated housing patterns (and, in fact, gives black politicians an incentive to perpetuate such patterns). Ms. Guinier proposes as an alternative a variation on proportional representation which she calls, with typical infelicity, "proportionate interest representation." It's really a modified at-large system. In a citywide election for five council seats, say, each voter would have five votes, which she (to borrow Ms. Guinier's feminist usage) could distribute among the five candidates any way she liked. If a fifth of the voters opted to "cumulate," or plump, all their votes for one candidate, they would be able to elect one of the five. Blacks could do this if they chose to, but so could any cohesive group of sufficient size. This system is emphatically not racially based: it allows voters to organize themselves on whatever basis they wish. It has actually been tried in a few jurisdictions—including the proverbially American city of Peoria, Illinois—and has had notable success in all of them.

Pressed to justify his abandonment of Ms. Guinier, Mr. Clinton said that she had seemed to advocate proportional representation, a position he called "antidemocratic and very difficult to defend." Antidemocratic? That will come as news to the people of Germany, Spain, the Netherlands, the Scandinavian countries, and Austria, among other countries. Indeed, most of the electorates of Continental Europe, including those of the liberated East, elect their legislatures under some form of proportional representation; so do the Irish, the Italians, and the Israelis; and so will the New Zealanders, if, as is expected, they pass a referendum on the subject this fall. P.R., as its advocates call it, is the very opposite of undemocratic. It not only facilitates minority representation but also virtually guarantees majority rule (the majority most often being a legislative coalition). By contrast, single-member-district, winner-take-all systems, like ours and Britain's, often produce minority governments. The last peacetime British government that represented a majority of the British voters was Stanley Baldwin's, elected in 1935; and Bill Clinton himself, it should be remembered, owes his job to 43 percent of the voters. While there may be reasons to doubt the suitability of P.R. for the United States at the national level, lack of democratic purity is not among them. Mr. Clinton was right in calling P.R. "difficult to defend," but that is because Americans, by and large, are ignorant of the existence, let alone the details, of electoral systems other than their own.

In one or two of her law-review articles, Ms. Guinier also speculates, briefly and sketchily, about various ideas for requiring "supermajorities" and allowing "minority vetoes" in certain local legislative bodies, on certain issues, under certain exceptional circumstances. These notions, which she advanced in the interest of provoking discussion, are far more questionable than her ideas about electoral systems, but they are also far more tentative. Their purpose is not to guarantee "equal legislative outcomes"; equal opportunity to influence legislative outcomes regardless of race is more like it. Nor is there any evidence that she would have tried to have these notions judicially imposed had she been confirmed in the position for which Mr. Clinton nominated her. In any case, supermajority arrangements are not exactly foreign to American government. Supermajorities are required for passing constitutional amendments and for ratifying treaties. And Senator Dole, not long before he attacked Ms. Guinier for supposedly scorning majority rule, engineered the defeat of President Clinton's economic-stimulus bill through the most notorious form of the minority veto, a Senate filibuster.

Thanks to a combination of presidential weakness, congressional hysteria, public ignorance, and Lani Guinier's own intellectual adventurousness, the civil rights division of the Justice Department has been deprived of the services of a formidable lawyer. Ms. Guinier's ideas are now, in a sadder sense than before, academic.

—*The New Yorker*, June 14, 1993

FILIBUSTER I: CATCH-XXII

EVEN BEFORE the Senate opened the historic—or futile, we don't know yet—debate on health-care reform that now occupies it, the opponents of reform flourished their ultimate weapon. "Anything I can do within the rules of the Senate to prevent the government from taking over or controlling the health-care market, I'm going to do," Phil Gramm, Republican of Texas, declared at a news conference the day before the debate began. At the same news conference, Richard C. Shelby, Democrat of Alabama, put it more bluntly. "Would I mind filibustering against something like this to kill it?" he asked himself rhetorically, referring to the compromise bill offered by George Mitchell, the majority leader, and answered, "Absolutely not."

Mr. Gramm's "rules of the Senate" are really only one rule—Senate Rule XXII, which requires a three-fifths vote of the full membership to end debate. In practice, Rule XXII means that the real threshold for action in the Senate is not the simple majority we learned about in civics class—that is, fifty-one senators if everybody is present and voting, or as few as twenty-six if there are absences or abstentions—but an irreducible supermajority of sixty. By voting against "cloture," or simply by not voting for it, forty-one senators can veto any piece of legislation supported by the fifty-nine others. And, unlike a presidential veto, this one cannot be overridden.

A filibuster used to be a handmade artifact, requiring many days and nights of labor. Strom Thurmond, the Senate's longest-serving member, was a master craftsman in his racist youth: in the summer of 1957, he set the record, still unbroken, by holding the floor for twenty-four hours and eighteen minutes straight, trying to kill a mild civil rights bill. Then, beginning in the 1970s, production was automated. It is no longer necessary actually to conduct a filibuster; it suffices merely to announce one, and the Senate moves on to other business until the required sixty votes can be assembled or the targeted bill dies. No muss, no fuss, no embarrassing Cleghorns in string ties reading excerpts from the telephone directory far into the night. Filibustering has become a no-show job. Today's filibusters are almost always invisible, and, perhaps for that reason, most people are unaware that they are now more common than ever before, despite their antique image. Their use has been expanding exponentially, and that's not hyperbole. Here's the scorecard, according to a June study by the Congressional Research Service of the Library of Congress: during the eighteenth century, no filibusters; during the nineteenth, sixteen; during the first half of this one, sixty-six; during the 1960s, twenty; during the seventies, fifty-two; and during the eighties, ninety. During the nineties, if the pace set so far is maintained, the Senate will rack up some two hundred. Senators use filibusters or the threat of them not only to kill bills but also to weaken them, or to hold a bill or a nomination hostage for some wholly unrelated concession. The filibuster shadows everything the Senate does. It is one reason that Senator Mitchell's health-care bill is already weaker than its House counterpart, to say nothing of President Clinton's original proposal (which, in turn, was weaker than the Canadian-style "single payer" plan that many of his advisers, and probably he himself, would prefer if wishing could make it so).

There's one other little problem with Rule XXII: it's unconstitutional. Lloyd Cutler, White House counsel in two administrations, has made a compelling case for this proposition. The argument goes roughly as follows. First, the Constitution specifies that "a Majority of each [House of Congress] shall constitute a Quorum to do Business." Since a Senate quorum is fifty-one, and a vote to shut off debate is business, a rule that requires sixty votes to do that business (or any other) is quite plainly unconstitutional. Second, the Constitution specifies that the Senate must assent by a two-thirds vote—two-thirds of a quorum, by the way, not two-thirds of the full membership—in just five cases: treaty ratification, expulsion of a member, an impeachment verdict, the overriding of a presidential veto, and the proposing of a constitutional amendment. Since the framers specifically rejected proposals requiring supermajorities for other categories of legislation, such as laws relating to foreign commerce, they would not have smiled on a rule that invites senators to impose such a requirement at will. Third, the Constitution's provision allowing the vice president to break ties in the Senate is made nonsense by a rule that subjects the Senate's every move to a supermajority vote, which, by definition, cannot result in a tie. Q.E.D.

It's true that the framers did not specify that the Senate would do its normal business by simple majority vote, but that's because it didn't occur to them that they had to specify it, any more than it occurred to them to specify that senators should not dunk each other's powdered wigs in the inkwells. For, as the Supreme Court noted in 1892, "the general rule of all parliamentary bodies" that "when a majority is present, the act of a majority of the quorum is the act of the body . . . has been the rule for all time, except so far as in any given case, the terms of the organic act under which the body is assembled have prescribed specific limitations." Unfortunately, the Court, which is extremely shy of challenging the internal workings of Congress, is not about to outlaw filibusters.

If Senators Gramm and Shelby carry out their threat, Senator Mitchell is likely to make them do it the old-fashioned way, in the hope of showing them up as obstructionists. But, even if a filibuster is averted, President Clinton and his congressional allies face immense obstacles in their effort to bring the United States into line with the rest of the developed world by guaranteeing health insurance to its citizens. Unlike his reforming predecessors Franklin Roosevelt and Lyndon Johnson, Mr. Clinton has no mandate from an election landslide, no ideological majority in Congress, no atmosphere of crisis to help him rally support, and no party machine to discipline his nominal followers. Elected by a mere plurality, he has been further weakened by a series of trivial but chronic scandals. Under the circumstances, it's something of a miracle that he still has a chance, however slender and diminishing, of getting something done.

—*The New Yorker*, August 22 & 29, 1994

FILIBUSTER II: FILIBUSTED

THE SURVIVING DEMOCRATS of the Senate and the House of Representatives, now straggling back to Washington for this week's opening of the 104th Congress, are short on ideas, short on enthusiasm, and short on votes. About the only thing they have in surplus is explanations for the electoral disaster that befell them in November, helpfully provided by the op-ed irregulars of the opinion industry. The consensus in the industry, even that part of it generally sympathetic to the Democrats, is that the Democrats' problem was Bill Clinton. The president was too much the craven, eager-to-please compromiser (except, of course, in those cases—identifiable only in retrospect—when he pigheadedly refused to meet the other side halfway). The president foolishly made gays in the military his opening priority. (Never mind that it was the Republicans who turned up the volume on that issue, while Clinton, following "centrist" advice, tried desperately to quiet it.) The president failed to keep his promise of a middle-class tax cut (the price of keeping his much more important promise to reduce the deficit). The president miscalculated by focussing on health-care reform instead of welfare reform. (If he had done the reverse, the same attackers would have attacked him, and not unfairly, for putting too much emphasis on the problems of the poor and ignoring middle-class anxiety about health insurance.)

No doubt many of the complaints about Clinton—and there are plenty more where these come from—are valid. What the indictment lacks is any sense that the alternative to Clinton was not, and will not be, some abstract embodiment of personal and political perfection but, rather, another mortal politician with his own set of weaknesses and strengths, his own blindnesses, his own scuffed baggage. It's far from clear that the country would have been better served by Jerry Brown's lone-wolf populism, or Paul Tsongas's pinched deficit-obsession, or Bob Kerrey's ironic detachment, or even Al Gore's Beltway environmentalism—let alone by another four years of George Bush's fecklessness. The real-world alternatives to Clinton might not have made Clinton's mistakes, but they would surely have made their own. Nor is it obvious that Bob Dole or Phil Gramm or Dick Cheney, should one of them defeat Clinton two years hence, can be counted on to lead us to the New Jerusalem.

At this point, halfway between the last presidential election and the next (and thus, blessedly, at the maximum distance from both), it might be worth the Democrats' while to consider some causes of their distress more amenable to change than the imperfectability of human beings in general and Bill Clinton in particular. One direction for them has been pointed, albeit negatively, by no less a seer than Newt Gingrich, the author of, among other things, the Republican congressional victory. As his very first act of business in the Speaker's chair this week, Gingrich plans to gavel through a change in the House rules which would require a three-fifths majority for passage of any increase in tax rates. Here, then, is something for the new Democratic opposition to oppose: not only this new rule but also the use and abuse of "supermajority" gimmicks to prevent action in both Houses of Congress.

It's safe to say that if the 103rd Congress had managed to enact a health-insurance program the composition of the 104th would be somewhat different. But our political system, designed from scratch in 1789 on the basis of necessarily limited practical experience with democratic governance, is overwhelmingly resistant to coherent, ambitious action. Uniquely among serious democracies, ours requires the unanimous concurrence of three separately elected, essentially independent "governments"—House, Senate, and presidency—for legislation to be passed. One of those governments, the Senate, is not even pretendedly democratic, apportioned as it is by states rather than by people; and, within the Senate, the use of an extraconstitutional (and probably unconstitutional) maneuver, the filibuster, means that a working majority is not fifty-one of the hundred senators but sixty—the number required to invoke "cloture."

Just how undemocratic these arrangements are was shown by Tom Geoghegan, a Chicago labor lawyer and a fellow at Harvard's Institute of Politics, in a little-noticed preelection essay in *The New Republic*. Geoghegan ran the numbers, and found that senators sufficient to block action can represent a population base of as little as 10 percent. Even a simple majority of senators can represent just 16 percent of the people. By the same calculation, to get a bill through the Senate can require, in effect, a popular majority of 90 percent. This grotesquerie has gotten worse since the framers' day. In 1789, when the first Senate convened and the filibuster had not yet been invented, it took senators representing a population base of at least 33 percent to prevail.

Geoghegan's preferred solution would reconstitute the Senate along the lines of something closer to one person, one vote—a dangerously radical idea, perhaps, but one that was passionately advocated by James Madison at the Constitutional Convention and has lately been tried with some success in democracies ranging from Lithuania to South Africa. That's unlikely to happen anytime soon. But the filibuster just might be vulnerable. Two Democratic senators, Connecticut's Joseph Lieberman and Iowa's Tom Harkin, representing respectively the moderate and liberal wings of their party, have been plumping for a rules change that would turn the filibuster from a blocking mechanism into one that could merely delay. This suggests a ploy for the Democrats: issue a standing invitation to their Republican colleagues to join them in adopting the Lieberman-Harkin rules change—and then filibuster *everything*. Capital gains, death penalties, orphanages—the works. The Republicans, now a majority but not yet a supermajority, just might decide they would rather keep their Contract with America than perpetuate a disgraceful form of minority rule—one, moreover, that can cut both ways.

And the filibuster *is* disgraceful—so much so that its only legitimate use ought to be its own abolition. The Democrats will be tempted to use it as a routine legislative weapon. They shouldn't. In the long run, the filibuster is a worse deal for those who see democratic self-government as an instrument of public action (and have principled qualms about using the filibuster to begin with) than it is for those who wish the "public sector" would just go away. Say what you will about the reasons for last year's health-care debacle, the truth is that the stake that was driven through health care's heart was a filibuster—and not even a filibuster against health care. (The nominal target was the crime bill, but the delay ran out the health-care clock.)

Getting rid of the filibuster would also be in the short-term interest of the Republicans, and in the long-term interest of those among them who are confident of their party's electoral future, and who would like to use government to do something more creative and interesting than cancel itself out—Newt Gingrich, for example. The public fascination with term limits and the line-item veto—whatever one may think of the merits of those proposals—shows that voters are willing to consider systemic explanations as well as moralistic ones for their government's manifest failures. Filibustering the filibuster would be a way for the Democrats, despite their minority status, to get into the act.

—*The New Yorker*, January 9, 1995

THE CASE FOR PROPORTIONAL
REPRESENTATION

LAST NOVEMBER 8TH, I did something stupid. Well, maybe it wasn't completely stupid, but it was irrational, sentimental, and politically pointless: I voted. Specifically, I voted in the election for representative in Congress, in which the incumbent Democrat in my district, Jerrold Nadler, was running against a Republican, Michael Benjamin, and a Conservative, George Galip.

As a civic sacrament, this was a pleasant and worthwhile thing to do. I enjoyed the ritual of standing in line with my fellow citizens of every age and size and color. I enjoyed signing my name in the big voters' book, which is like St. Peter's ledger at the gates of heaven. I enjoyed exchanging small talk and smiles with the nice ladies from the Board of Elections behind the card table. I enjoyed going into the booth, and pulling the big lever from right to left to close the curtain, and pulling down the levers next to my choices, and hearing that satisfying chunk sound they make, and then pulling the big lever from left to right to open the curtain again. I'm glad I live in a city that still uses old-fashioned voting machines. No flimsy punch cards for us New Yorkers. As usual, I smiled at my fellow citizens on the way out and thought to myself, "Isn't this nice?"

And it was nice. What it was not was a meaningful political act. Voting gives you a nice warm feeling of being part of something big and great and wonderful—a civic miracle, the beautiful pageant of democracy. It's like putting a pinch of incense on the altar of our civic religion. But it is a snare and a delusion to confuse that warm, fuzzy feeling with politics or self-government.

The truth is that it didn't make a damn bit of difference whether I voted or not. Nadler got reelected by 82 percent of the vote that day. In 1994 he also got 82 percent. 1992 was a squeaker, though—he only got 81 percent.

But it's not just that it didn't make any difference whether I voted. It's worse than that. We are often exhorted by good government types that it isn't enough just to vote—if you want to make a difference, you have to get out there and get involved in old-fashioned, participatory grassroots politics. Well, let's suppose I followed this advice. Let's say I spent the entire summer and fall going door to door among my neighbors, manning a table on Broadway every weekend, organizing kaffeeklatsches, going around to civic groups, making speeches, doing everything I could to reelect Nadler—or everything I could do to defeat him, it doesn't matter which. Let's say my efforts were spectacularly successful, and I managed to convince one out of three anti-Nadler voters in the district to change their minds. In that case, Nadler would have been reelected by 88 percent instead of 82 percent—that's if I was for him. If I was against him, and I succeeded in convincing a like number of voters, he'd have been reelected by 76 percent.

I'm not saying you can't do serious politics if you live in my district. Presidential primaries and campaigns for statewide office are occasionally competitive. But campaigns for other offices—member of Congress, assemblyman, state senator, city council member—offer scope for what we know as politics only on those happily rare occasions when one of our Officeholders-for-Life goes to his or her reward. Otherwise, when I want to do something political, I give money to a Democratic candidate in a borderline Republican district somewhere out west or down south. I'm not the Lippo Group or AIPAC or the Tobacco Institute, but even at my level, which is to say the level of a twenty-five- or fifty- or hundred-dollar giver, my money means more than my vote, because I can send my money where it might do some good, but my vote is stuck right where it is.

You may say, "Well, your situation is unusual. You live in Manhattan, where everybody's a knee-jerk liberal Democrat. Most places aren't like that."

Actually, most places *are* like that. Not that most places are full of knee-jerk liberals—alas, they're not. But most places are just like the good old 8th Congressional District in that the results of their elections are preordained. Consider 1994, which was the last time people went to the polls to elect a new Congress without the distraction of a presidential race. This was a much more competitive election than usual, remember—this was the great epoch-making upheaval, with the Republicans sweeping in and the Democrats being swept out after forty years. And yet in that election, one-third of the American people had absolutely no chance of making a difference, because they lived in districts where the incumbent was either running unopposed or where the expected (and actual) margin of victory was more than forty percentage points. Another one-third of us had almost no chance of making a difference, because we live in districts where there might be some slight attempt to mount some semblance of a contest, but one candidate or party is so dominant that the result is as predictable as the outcome of a basketball game between Stuyvesant High School and the Knicks—a lopsided victory by more than twenty points.

So that leaves just a third of us living in congressional districts in which something resembling politics has a chance of taking place—where the top two candidates at least finish within twenty points of each other. And in only a third of that third is there a real contest, a close election, where the winner's winning margin is five points or less.

That's how it was in 1994. With very minor variations, that's also how it was in 1996. And that's how it will be in 1998. That's how it always is and until something is done that's how it always will be.

We have 435 congressional districts in the United States. In any given election year, in at most around 50 of those districts there will be a pretty close election, and therefore in those districts it makes sense to vote and organize and pass out leaflets and be a good citizen. In around another 100 districts there's a chance that given an extraordinary confluence of events—let's say, some massive Vietnam- or Watergate-style upheaval in the country, plus the incumbent being about to go to jail, plus an unusually attractive and well-financed challenger—you might get a meaningful contest. But in around 275 districts at the very minimum—and sometimes it's a lot more (in 1988, for example, it was about 100 more)—one side or the other is certain to get blown away. Crushed. Obliterated. Neutron-bombed. Again, in these districts it doesn't matter which side you're on, because if you're on the losing side your vote is wasted and if you're on the winning side your vote is superfluous. So you may as well stay home. And, of course, that's exactly what a lot of voters do—stay home. Not because they're lazy or apathetic, not because they don't care who wins, and certainly not because they're happy with the status quo. They stay home because they have better things to do on a nice fall Tuesday than engage in a politically pointless act of civic piety.

Such is the situation that obtains in areas inhabited by a substantial majority of the people of the United States. This may sound like a technicality, a bit of wonkish hairsplitting. But the implications are enormous. For example, one implication is that the kinds of political reforms that many public-spirited people advocate do not hold out anything like as much hope as their sponsors wish they did. You can eliminate all barriers to voter registration. You can have public financing of campaigns and strict limits on money in politics. You can ban thirty-second spots and sound bites. You can have free TV time for candidates. You can have free transportation to the polls. You can let people vote by mail or over the internet. You can send a delegation from the League of Women Voters to ring every doorbell in America and give everybody in the house a totally objective briefing on the issues and the candidates. You can do all this, and these would all be good things to do, and in the 10 or 15 percent of the country where contested elections take place these things would help. But not one of these reforms would make any important difference in the great majority of congressional or legislative districts. Neither would all of them put together. As far as the majority of eligible voters are concerned, they wouldn't change a thing. It still wouldn't be worth their while to vote. It still would be a waste of time and energy for them to get involved in grassroots politics in their local communities. These citizens would still sense a gigantic disconnect between voting on the one hand and having a meaningful political impact on the other. And they would be right.

The problem is built into the very structure of representation in our political system. It's built into the structure of our electoral and constitutional arrangements—the hydraulics of the way our particular system works.

A lot of the political pathologies we worry about in this country—things like low voter turnout, popular alienation from politics, hatred of politicians and politics per se, the undue influence of special interests, and the prevalence of negative campaigning—are not caused by the usual suspects, or not primarily caused by them. They are not caused by the low moral character of our politicians, the selfishness of the electorate, the peculiarities of America's national character and political culture, the power of money, or the ghastliness of television. They are artifacts of a particular political technology. They are caused by our single-member-district, geographically based, plurality-winner-take-all system of representation.

I can't prove this with survey data, but I'd be willing to bet a lot of money that most Americans, including most educated Americans, simply do not know that there is more than one way to have an election. Most Americans are simply unaware that there exists, on the one hand, the single-member plurality winner-take-all approach, which is what we have, and, on the other hand, the many forms and varieties of proportional representation—all of which have in common, essentially, that if a party gets 20 percent of the votes it gets something along the lines of 20 percent of the representatives, and if it gets 60 percent of the votes it gets something along the lines of 60 percent of the representatives.

And I would also guess that even among well-informed Americans who do know about different voting systems, the assumption is that most democratic countries, or at least a good cross-section, have chosen the same model as ours. In fact, the only countries that have this system are Britain and a few former British colonies, such as India, Pakistan, Canada, Jamaica, and the United States, plus one or two former American colonies, such as the Philippines. France, as always, is a special case; it has single-member districts but it also has runoffs. Every other democratic country in the world—including all the new democracies of central Europe—has looked at the options and has decided to go with proportional representation.

I've already mentioned the first flaw in our system: that it essentially disfranchises voters who happen to live in so-called safe districts, a group that includes the great majority of potential voters.

The second flaw: our representatives represent the wrong thing. Our House of Representatives does one thing, and one thing only, well: it represents localities. When you go to the polls to vote for a candidate for the House, you can be absolutely sure that you will have the opportunity to vote for someone to represent your district. In fact, you can be sure that someone will be *elected* to represent your district—even if you *don't* vote. And even the very worst congressmen generally do a good job of representing the district. Your representative may be a budget-cutting conservative or a peacenik liberal, but when it comes to closing a military base inside the district he or she forgets all about ideology and fights to keep that wasteful, warmongering military base open. This isn't hypocrisy. It's just the representative representing what the representative is supposed to represent: the district.

What you cannot be sure of when you go to vote is that you will have a chance to vote for someone to represent your point of view—or anything else about yourself you may consider important.

Two hundred years ago it might have made sense for geography to be the sole basis for designing political constituencies. It doesn't make sense now. Ask yourself: how many of the human and social connections in your own life that you care about are contained within the boundaries of your congressional district—or within any geographical boundaries, for that matter? The communities that count are communities of interest and belief, and these communities are at least as likely to be national as local. Ideology, profession, class, aesthetic taste, racial and sexual identity, shared beliefs about society—these are the ties that bind. And our system, unlike proportional representation, denies us the possibility of choosing to be represented according to those ties.

I didn't think of this point, by the way. John Stuart Mill thought of it. He was a passionate advocate of proportional representation—in fact, he was the very first P.R. bore. Here's Mill, in *Considerations on Representative Government:* Critics of proportional representation, he writes,

> are unable to reconcile themselves to the loss of what they term the local character of the representation. A nation does not seem to them to consist of persons, but of artificial units, the creation of geography and statistics. [The legislature] must represent towns and counties, not human beings. But no one seeks to annihilate towns and counties. Towns and counties, it may be presumed, are represented, when the human beings who inhabit them are represented. Local feelings cannot exist without somebody who feels them; nor local interests without somebody interested in them. If the human beings whose feelings and interests these are, have their proper share of representation, these feelings and interests are represented, in common with all other feelings and interests of those persons. But I cannot see why the feelings and interests which arrange mankind according to localities, should be the only ones thought worthy of being represented; or why people who have other feelings and interests, which they value more than they do their geographical ones, should be restricted to these as the sole principle of their political classification.

Flaws number three and four: A democratic political system should do two things at a minimum: enable the majority to rule—within limits, of course—and enable important minorities to be represented. Our system reliably does neither. And almost by definition it cannot do both.

We do a lot of complaining about the two-party system, but in a winner-take-all environment, where a plurality of votes in any given constituency gets you 100 percent of the representation, a two-party system is the only way to make sure that the majority has a chance of ruling. The alternative is minority rule. The minute you get more than two important parties in a system like ours, minority rule becomes routine. The British have shoe-horned three parties into a habitat suited for two, and as a result minority rule has become a way of life. The Tories have run the show for eighteen years, and throughout that time there has been a passionately anti-Tory majority in the electorate. Even under Margaret Thatcher the Conservatives never managed to get as large a share of the popular vote as Michael Dukakis got in 1988.

Even if there are only two parties, it's theoretically possible for a minority, even a small minority, to win it all, if the district lines are drawn right. We have 435 congressional districts. Suppose that in 235 of those districts, the Democrats win by an average of 55 percent of the vote, and that in the other 200 districts the Republicans win by 80 percent of the vote. Dick Gephardt becomes Speaker of the House, with a fairly comfortable margin. But the popular vote would be 61 percent Republican—as big a margin as F.D.R.'s in 1936 or Nixon's in 1972. And even if the split were a little more realistic—if the Democrats won by 55–45 in their 235 districts and the Republicans won by 60–40 in their 200 districts—the Republicans would still have a popular majority, and they would lose the election.

That's theory. What happens in practice? The same thing, only in somewhat less exaggerated form. This past November, as you know, the Republicans retained control of the House of Representatives. What you may not know is that the Democrats, overall, got more votes. It wasn't much of a margin—only around fifty thousand—but it was real, even though there's probably not more than one person in ten thousand who knows about it.

So much for majority rule. What about the other thing we can reasonably ask from an allegedly democratic election—that it allow minorities to be represented in the deliberations of government?

In this, our system is even more inadequate. It does an outrageously bad job of representing minorities—and not just racial minorities, but just about every kind of minority. The sole exceptions are those minorities that happen to be geographically concentrated to the point where they constitute a local majority. But woe betide a minority that is truly national—that is spread evenly throughout the country. That minority—and I'm talking here about political minorities, but the point holds for minorities of every kind—has no chance of getting itself represented in Congress.

Which brings us to flaw number five—gerrymandering. If you have districts, the districts have to have boundaries, and the boundaries are going to have political consequences. If the boundaries are drawn by some sort of nonpartisan commission, as some reformers would like, the consequences will be unintentional. If they are drawn by politicians armed with powerful computer programs, as they are in this country, the consequences will be very intentional indeed.

The politics of gerrymandering—and there is no such thing as redistricting without gerrymandering—are more than routinely sickening. There is almost always a deal across party lines to protect the seats of incumbents—and if someone has to be thrown to the wolves, it's often the most independent-minded member. (Back in 1970, that's what happened to the late Allard K. Lowenstein, probably the finest one-term congressman since Abraham Lincoln.) The system creates a horrible dilemma for African Americans and their political leaders. If they don't push for racial gerrymandering, they practically guarantee that no black legislators will be elected. If they do push for it, the price they pay can be very high. By condensing black voters into one district, they bleach out neighboring districts, which undermines incentives to build political coalitions across racial lines and, in the end, can result in fewer representatives aligned with black aspirations. It creates a black political class that has a vested interest in the preservation of residential segregation—and a society that can have either integrated housing or an integrated Congress but probably not both.

And of course racial gerrymandering provides the Rehnquist Court with an occasion for truly stomach-turning sanctimoniousness, as it explains why it is immoral and unconstitutional for legislators to use redistricting to give black folks a shot at electing someone to Congress but perfectly permissible to use redistricting to reach a preordained *political* outcome—because we wouldn't want the court interfering in "politics," would we?

If someone speaks out against the whole sordid business (someone like Lani Guinier, for example) and points out that under proportional representation you wouldn't need race-specific solutions, in fact you wouldn't need redistricting at all and therefore you wouldn't be able to have gerrymandering—if someone points out that under P.R. the voters can elect the politicians they want, rather than letting the politicians elect the voters *they* want—well, that someone finds herself ganged up on by ideological thugs, such as the editorial page editors of the *Wall Street Journal,* and by ignorant politicians (ignorant about P.R., at least) such as President Clinton.

A few more flaws in our geographically based single-member plurality-winner-take-all system:

By making a fetish of geographic provincialism, the system practically guarantees that people of distinguished accomplishment will not hold public office. Even in the metropolis, the choice in the United States always seems to come down to a a couple of banal local lawyers. That's flaw number six. Here's number seven: In our system, the fight for political power takes place in a relative handful of marginal districts. I've already mentioned one of the perverse effects of this—that it makes political activity pointless in most places. But it also magnifies the power of money, because it acts as a lens that collects money from all over the country and focusses it on a few places, where it can have overwhelming impact.

Flaw number eight: Because our electoral mechanisms tend to foster a two-party system, they also tend to make politics a zero-sum game. And the zero-sum game is what makes negative campaigning work. As every political consultant knows, negative campaigning depresses turnout across the board. The reason everybody does it is that it depresses the vote for the candidate who's being attacked more than it depresses the vote for the candidate who does the attacking. But if there are a couple of other viable parties on the scene—and for that to happen you've got to have some sort of proportional representation—a scorched-earth policy can backfire on you. So it doesn't happen as much.

One more flaw, number nine, which happens to be my favorite, because it's so wonderfully perverse.

One of the great mysteries of American politics is this. How is it that even though poll after poll, year after year, shows the public's approval rating of Congress to be roughly on a par with its approval of drug kingpins, that same public keeps reelecting that same Congress? More than 80 percent of incumbents are always reelected. Even in 1994, Year One of the Revolution, more than 90 percent of incumbents were reelected. Why? Why don't the voters throw the rascals out? Because they can't, that's why. A voter can vote to throw a maximum of one rascal out of the House of Representatives—and there are 435 of them. Telling a voter who doesn't like Congress that she can solve the problem by voting against her member of Congress is like telling a voter who is upset about the state of family values in America that she can solve *that* problem by divorcing her husband.

The weirdest paradox of our system is that it doesn't make sense to vote against a long-serving incumbent congressman even if that congressman stands for everything you despise politically. Thanks to seniority, replacing a veteran with a freshman necessarily means electing someone who will have less power. It therefore means voting to deprive your district (and therefore your neighbors and maybe even yourself) of clout. It means depriving your district of the concrete goodies that clout can bring. So if you succeed in defeating your nasty old congressman, you will change the ideological complexion of 1/435th of the House of Representatives—that's a little less than 1/4 of 1 percent. But you will deprive a lot of your flesh-and-blood neighbors of their jobs helping build a new post office. It's a lousy trade, and it's a lousy system that forces us to make it.

When I talk to people about this sort of thing—and as my friends can testify, I talk about it way too much—the immediate reaction I often get is, "Oh, yeah—you want a parliamentary system, like England." Or, "Look, the United States is different. We're a big country with lots of different groups, not like those little homogeneous countries in Europe. Maybe their system is good for them but it wouldn't be good for us." Or, "Oh, yeah, P.R.—that's what they have in Israel, right? Is that really what you want?"

And when I say no, they say, "Well, what *do* you want, then?" And I say, "If you must know, I think we should adopt a system like the one they have in Germany." And they say, "Oh, great, Germany—there's an ideal model. Hello?"

So I say, O.K., if Germany doesn't suit you, how about New Zealand?

Four years ago, the people of New Zealand decided they had had enough of their British-style winner-take-all parliament. So they had a referendum and adopted the German system—which, by the way, was designed under American auspices. There are a lot of ways to do proportional representation, but this one, I think, is the best, and perhaps the one that would be best suited to this country. Each voter gets two votes for the national legislature. You cast one of them for a local candidate and the other for a national party. Once all the votes are counted, the legislature gets filled out with people from the national party lists until the party percentages match up. If your party gets 30 percent of the popular vote but only wins 10 percent of the local seats, your party gets enough of its national candidates added so that it ends up with 30 percent of the total seats in the legislature. To keep out the lunatic fringe and to prevent a wholesale proliferation of parties à la Israel, there's a 5 percent minimum.

It works. Every election is a close election, because every increment in the popular vote gets your party more seats. Everybody's vote counts equally, no matter where you live. Grassroots politics is worth the effort in every corner of the country. There's majority rule, because the party with the most votes gets the most seats. There's minority representation, because the price of admission to the legislature is only 5 percent of the vote, and it doesn't matter where the votes are cast. Money is less decisive because it has to be spread around so much. Instead of being represented by someone you didn't vote for, as is the case for most Americans, you get to be represented by someone you *did* vote for. And turnout is through the roof. It's routinely in the 80s or low 90s in P.R. countries. If it should happen to drop to, say, 75 percent, which is as high as it ever gets in the winner-take-all countries, that becomes an occasion for national soul-searching and the appointment of blue-ribbon commissions.

If proportional representation is so great, you may be wondering, why weren't the Founding Fathers for it? Well, for the same reason they weren't for railroad regulation: the technology hadn't been invented yet. James Madison was a great supporter of what he *called* proportional representation. What he meant by that was that the more populous states should have more representatives (he prevailed on that point) and more senators (he lost on that one).

Nobody got around to conceiving of the kind of proportional representation I've been discussing here until the second quarter of the nineteenth century. But there's no doubt in my mind that the framers would have been for it. They prided themselves on being on the cutting edge. Here's Hamilton in The Federalist No. 9:

> The science of politics . . . like most other sciences has received great improvement. The efficacy of various principles is now understood, which were either not known at all, or imperfectly known to the ancients. The regular distribution of power into distinct departments—the introduction of legislative balances—the institution of courts composed of judges, holding their offices during good behavior—the representation of the people in the legislature by deputies of their own election—these are either wholly new discoveries or have made their principal progress towards perfection in modern times.

Proportional representation would have appealed to the framers' enlightenment rationalism, their fascination with clockwork—the high tech of its day. If there was any nineteenth century figure who was temperamentally akin to the framers and their hero, Montesquieu, it was John Stuart Mill—and, as we have seen, he was a passionate supporter of P.R. Another honorary Founding Father, you might say, was Alexis de Tocqueville. That's right: another P.R. fanatic.

All right. By now you may be wondering, Why is he telling us all this? Doesn't he realize that this idea is going nowhere? Doesn't he know that American politicians, who don't even want to touch campaign finance reform, are not exactly clamoring to abolish the mechanisms that got them their jobs in the first place? Isn't he aware that this is all just a wee bit academic?

Well, yes, of course I'm aware of all that. But I think that proportional representation is worth talking about and agitating for and organizing around—for two reasons.

One reason is that I don't actually agree that there is no chance we are going to get big structural political change in this country. Ten years ago, the idea that Soviet communism might simply disappear was absolutely unthinkable, out of the question. Yet it happened. I am similarly convinced that sooner or later the other shoe is going to drop in this country as well. Our structure of government might have been fine when we had untold natural resources and a tremendous margin of error—though, to be honest, it has never worked all that well. Fourscore and five years after it was founded, it collapsed into the bloodiest civil war in history because it was unable to find a political solution to the problem of slavery. But leaving that aside, the day will surely come when the United States will need a government that is capable of coherent, decisive action. We haven't got anything remotely resembling that kind of government today. I don't know how the change will come or what will precipitate it, but change is coming. Brothers and sisters, the end is nigh.

In the interim, though, I'm convinced that Americans are going to become steadily more interested in proportional representation and other kinds of fundamental constitutional reform. Right now even the best-informed Americans don't know what the options are. Rob Richie, of the Center for Voting and Democracy, recently paid a visit to the *New York Times* editorial board, and while I won't name any names I will say that even in that temple of civic knowledge ignorance in these matters is rampant. But that is about to change. In two weeks the British will have a general election, and the Labor Party will form a government. Labour is committed to holding a referendum on the adoption of proportional representation for elections to parliament. Polls show that a solid majority of the British people already favor changing to a German-style—make that New Zealand-style—system. When that referendum takes place, it will get the attention of élites in this country. Then the discussion will really begin.*

As noted, there's a second reason I think this stuff is worth talking about. Even if we don't adopt proportional representation anytime soon, even if we never adopt it, it's worth knowing about it as an analytic tool. We are in the habit of jumping to moralistic conclusions about our political and public problems. We automatically blame everything on bad people—bad politicians, bad media moguls, bad voters. Because we take it for granted that our political institutions are perfect, we have no choice but to blame the people who administer them when things go wrong. This is dangerous. It gives rise to a destructive anger against politics per se, a dangerously mindless populism. If we can begin to understand that we are up against a systemic problem, that many of our woes are due to the perverse incentives that our particular political arrangements create, we may at least be better equipped to steer clear of false answers.

We should not be afraid of going back to first principles. We should stop worshipping the framers of our Constitution and start imitating them. They were unafraid of fundamental change. We should be similarly courageous.

—Irwin Mann Memorial Lecture,
New York University, April 15, 1997

---

* Once in power, Labour slowly backed away from this commitment. Prime Minister Tony Blair appointed Roy Jenkins, one of his political mentors, to head a commission on the subject. The Jenkins commission recommended an ingenious compromise that would have introduced an element of proportionality into the system while retaining single-member districts for most of the seats, but even this proved too much. After 9/11 nothing more was heard about it. The new regional legislatures—the Scottish parliament and the Welsh assembly—are proportional. The system is rapidly spreading to local governments as well. And there is talk of converting the House of Lords into a kind of proportional representation senate. But P.R. for the House of Commons will probably have to await a "hung parliament" in which no party has a majority and the Liberal Democrats demand it as the price of forming a coalition.

LETTER FROM NEW HAMPSHIRE:
THIS MUST BE THE PLACE

THE WAYFARER INN, in Bedford, just south of Manchester, is the unofficial headquarters of the New Hampshire primary. Every four years, as winter approaches, the Wayfarer begins to fill up with the camp followers of national politics: advance people, consultants, television technicians, political reporters and pundits, gofers, campaign staffers—even, sometimes, actual candidates and their entourages. The Wayfarer has a hundred and ninety-four rooms, all but a handful of which can be had for about a hundred dollars a night—a hefty sum by local standards, but peanuts if you're on the expense account of a network or a big-city newspaper. The location is great. New Hampshire is shaped like a wine bottle, and most of its million-plus people have settled like silt at the bottom—the bottom, of course, being where political campaigns feed. From the Wayfarer, it's a five-minute drive to the heart of Manchester. Twenty minutes north gets you to Concord, the state capital. Twenty minutes south and you're in Nashua, the second-largest city, and halfway to Boston.

The Wayfarer is a strangely magical place. It's like a space station. It's surrounded on all sides by a concrete wilderness, from which, once you're inside, it seems utterly cut off. Four or five multilane highways collide haphazardly around it. Shopping centers and strip malls are plunked on the asphalt like boulders on Mars. Guided by a couple of discreet, easy-to-miss signs, you enter the Wayfarer by driving through the desolate parking lot of a boxy Macy's. Yet the Wayfarer somehow feels as if it were in the country. Trees and hillocks screen out the sprawl. The cozy entrance suggests rough timbers. In the details of its décor and facilities, and the unpretentiousness of its staff, the Wayfarer is an ordinary midrange business motor hotel. Its various wings, though, have been built in a splattered-out way, in different directions, on different levels, and in different shapes. Wandering the Wayfarer's angled corridors, you can't tell how big it is, or where it begins and ends, or where you are in it. Even after many sojourns there, I still have to find my way to the lobby by trial and error—a happenstance that, unless I'm in a hurry, is amusing rather than distressing.

Somewhere at the heart of all this, like the bridge of Captain Kirk's Enterprise, is the bar. It's an airy structure, with a high, steeply raked ceiling—a sort of modified A-frame—with thick wooden beams, a big fireplace, and an enormous projection TV set. Political posters from campaigns past adorn an entrance wall. Through tall windows on three sides may be seen a covered bridge over a picturesque stream, a waterfall tumbling over a canal lock, a white frame farmhouse, lots of trees. A flock of Canada geese occasionally stops for a waddle on the slope at the water's edge. You'd never know where you are, except that you're in heaven—political heaven, at any rate. At night, after the last rally or press conference, the room hums with the sound of political gossip. Sitting at the bar, you may catch a glimpse of David S. Broder or (more likely) Jack Germond. Every now and then, someone flips open a notebook or flicks on a tape recorder. You're in the quadrennial crucible of the conventional wisdom, and you never want to leave.

The Wayfarer opened in 1962. The site had been occupied by an old water mill, built in 1744 by a veteran of the French and Indian Wars and operated for two hundred years by his descendants. The last of them, in the 1950s, made pinewood furniture for the nostalgia market, including (notes a brochure) "a milking stool which proved to be popular as a TV viewing seat." A milking stool for watching television—that's a nice metaphor for the Wayfarer Inn. And the Wayfarer, come to think of it, is a nice metaphor for the New Hampshire primary itself. Both of them look, superficially, pretty much as they did thirty-odd years ago, while everything around them has changed; both incorporate elements of much older forms; both have a rustic appeal, even as they make use of the latest technology; both are magnets for the migrant circus known as "the political community"; and both, while inexpensive compared with their metropolitan counterparts, cost a hell of a lot more than they used to. (In 1962, a room at the Wayfarer could be had for seven dollars.) Time has given both of them something of the artificial aspect of a theme park, though it is by no means certain which is fake—them, or the brave new worlds that have metastasized around them.

I've been visiting New Hampshire during primary season ever since 1968, and what struck me this time was how familiar the basic rituals seemed, given the convulsive changes in politics—the big money, the eclipse of volunteer activism, the media craziness, the direct-mail revolution, the polling explosion. It all still happens, event to event, on a human scale—in hotel function rooms, on sidewalks, at civic clubs. It's still amazingly easy to see candidates, even meet them and ask them questions. On one recent two-and-a-half-day foray, I had no trouble catching a Bill Bradley rally at a Lions Club in Hudson, a George W. Bush speech and press conference at Manchester West High School, and a couple of John McCain "town meetings," in a Holiday Inn in Dover and a middle-school gym in Candia, with enough time left over to attend two all-candidate debates and have a late drink at the Wayfarer. Only at the debates was it obvious that something fundamental has changed.

These were held, one night after the other, at the University of New Hampshire, in Durham. Members of the press, around a hundred of us, were directed to a spacious, well-lit room in the student union, outfitted for the occasion with long tables, phones and modem lines, and a couple of tarpaulin-size video monitors. The candidates and their live audience were in an auditorium elsewhere on campus, but they might as well have been in Iowa. When the debate started, the monitors showed only what was being broadcast, so that neither the audience's reactions nor the facial expressions of candidates who were not talking could be seen. A few still photographers were in the auditorium, I was told, but no "pencil pool." None had been requested. From our tables in the student union, we were able to gather that (for example) Al Gore was more relaxed than usual. But if he had spent his time off camera with his tongue stuck out and his eyes crossed we'd have had to be told about it afterward.

Representatives of the various campaigns, naturally, were on hand to explain why their candidate had wiped the floor with the other guys. The importance of spin, however, is often exaggerated. The daily reporters—the ones who write the stories you read the next morning—don't have time for it. They have to grind out copy, fast. At these debates, in fact, spinners were barred from the filing room itself and relegated to an adjoining space, because the daily reporters had demanded a little peace and quiet. Some of the spinners had to be content with spinning each other.

There's nothing especially pernicious about any of this, and a good time was had by all. But it does point up the extent to which New Hampshire has become a television studio producing programs for the national market. The debaters were talking to voters not just in New Hampshire but in Iowa and Florida as well. The results of the New Hampshire primary have always been important, but the day-to-day details of what happened there didn't much matter outside the state. Now those details are instantly available to all.

IF YOU HAD TO PICK one of the fifty states and confer upon its citizens vastly more influence in the choice of a president than those of any other, you probably wouldn't pick this one. New Hampshire is small, provincial, and atypical. As a microcosm suitable for exploring the great issues, it stacks up indifferently at best. Economic policy? If New Hampshire were a country, as George W. Bush likes to say about Texas, it would have the fifty-fourth-biggest economy in the world—bigger than Chad's and Kazakhstan's combined! Tax policy? New Hampshire is the only state without either a personal income tax or a sales tax. Urban policy? Manchester is the two-hundred-and-tenth-largest city in the nation. It houses barely a hundred thousand souls. Race, the American dilemma? Of the nearly fourteen thousand black and Hispanic elected officials in the United States, New Hampshire has two. The state's African American population wouldn't fill the visiting-team side of Madison Square Garden.

But, then, no one appointed New Hampshire to have the first-in-the-nation primary except New Hampshire itself. It did so without (until recently) malice aforethought. In 1916, purely for reasons of Yankee thrift, the first primary was set to coincide with Town Meeting Day, when locals were congregating already. That date—the second Tuesday in March—remained unchanged for half a century and more, until, after 1968, it became obvious that primaries would henceforth monopolize the nominating process. Accordingly, the legislators of other states—imagining, poor dears, that their citizens, too, should have a substantial role in choosing the nation's chief magistrate—started horning in on the early action. Florida tried to move its primary to the same day as New Hampshire's, the first in a series of acts of aggression to which New Hampshire has responded like the czar's army drawing Napoleon into the wintry wastes of Russia. Back and back the date of the New Hampshire primary has fallen, election by election, out of March altogether and into February. This year, it's the first Tuesday in February, which happens also to be the first day in February. The gates of Moscow won't be reached until the New Hampshire primary is held on the day after the previous election.

RICHARD UPTON is a name not heard much nowadays, or ever, in constitutional-history classes, but it deserves to be. As surely as James Madison, Benjamin Franklin, Gouverneur Morris, or any of the other bewigged, buckle-shoed gentlemen who met at the Constitutional Convention in Philadelphia in 1787, Richard Upton is a designer of the system by which we choose our government—a framer, you might say. A Founding Father. In 1949, Upton was the Speaker of the New Hampshire House of Representatives. Until then, the voting in the New Hampshire primary had been only for convention delegates, whose affiliations with particular presidential candidates might or might not be known, and who usually won on the basis of their local prominence. Turnout was low, national impact quite rightly nil. In 1949, Upton decided to make the primary more interesting by allowing a direct vote for presidential candidates. His bill passed, without much fanfare, and was signed by the governor, Sherman Adams.

The new arrangement revolutionized presidential politics, beginning with the first time it was tried, in 1952. On the Democratic side, a rawboned freshman senator from Tennessee, Estes Kefauver, went to New Hampshire and pioneered the sustained "retail" campaigning that would eventually become mandatory in the state. President Truman, at first disdaining the primary as "eyewash," stayed in Washington but did nothing to keep his own name off the ballot. Sophisticates thought Kefauver was a clown (he campaigned in a Davy Crockett–style coonskin cap) and a sure loser (shortly before the voting, the Associated Press predicted that Truman would beat him by two or three to one). On the Republican side, Senator Robert A. Taft, the Ohio isolationist, also campaigned in person, but less extensively and, thanks to his chilly personality, far less effectively than Kefauver had done. Taft's opponent was General Dwight D. Eisenhower, who spent the winter in Paris, attending to his duties as supreme commander of NATO, while his supporters, led by Governor Adams, organized on his behalf. On Primary Day, Kefauver trounced Truman by ten points, and Eisenhower swamped Taft by a like margin. A few days later, Truman announced that he would not run for a second full term. Kefauver went on to win two-thirds of the vote in the fourteen remaining primaries that existed in those days, but not the nomination. The Republicans, desperate for a victory after twenty years of defeat, nominated the smiling general, who, once ensconced in the White House, made Sherman Adams his chief of staff. Its first time out, the modern New Hampshire primary had brought down one president and raised up another.

Ike's triumph established a rule that has held true in ten of the eleven subsequent elections: no one gets elected president without first winning the New Hampshire primary. Still, New Hampshire would not consolidate the importance it had so suddenly attained for sixteen more years.

In 1968, with Richard Nixon the prohibitive favorite on the Republican side, the action was among the Democrats, riven by the Vietnam War. Many people of a certain age remember that Senator Eugene McCarthy, of Minnesota, and his legions of freshly shorn "Clean for Gene" student volunteers dealt President Lyndon Johnson a defeat in New Hampshire that chased him out of the race and lured Robert Kennedy into it. They remember wrong: Johnson won. And among those who haven't forgotten the actual result, many have forgotten that Johnson's name was not even on the ballot. His supporters had to write him in.

It has since become routine for a New Hampshire winner to be seen as having lost and a loser to be seen as having won. The year 1968 marked the emergence of what has been called (if only by me) the expectorate—the congeries of political reporters, consultants, pollsters, commentators, and loiterers who decide how a candidate is expected to do, and who declare afterward that this or that candidate has done better or worse than expected and has therefore gained or lost momentum, if not the race. The expectorate's role is not entirely unhealthy: a primary such as New Hampshire's is part of a fluid process, like the first turn in a horse race, and the testimony of handicappers may therefore be of value. At the track, though, the opinions of touts and tipsters can't influence the odds once the starting gate snaps open. Nor can those opinions have any effect on the horses, or even— assuming that the race has not been fixed—on the jockeys.

The 1992 primary was the high-water mark of New Hampshire weirdness. President George Bush won but lost; Governor Bill Clinton lost but won. The president's margin over Patrick Buchanan, the right-wing populist commentator, fell short of the expectorate's never quite specified benchmark, and Bush came out weakened by his victory. Senator Paul Tsongas, a Massachusetts goo-goo, defeated a field of mostly more liberal Democrats by a sizable plurality. But the second-place finisher, the energetic governor of Arkansas, famously proclaimed himself the Comeback Kid and got away with it. Clinton's New Hampshire abracadabra remains the apotheosis of spin—the furriest, plumpest rabbit any politician has ever pulled out of a battered New Hampshire hat. Clinton then became the first and, so far, only person to be elected president without winning the New Hampshire primary.

OF COURSE, the lessons of primaries past—that you can win without winning, that the expectorate can trump the electorate, that (with a little spin) a candidate can come back from the dead—became visible only in retrospect. In 2000, retrospect is still down the road. We have only prediction, an altogether less satisfactory instructor. Because the leading candidates are so closely bunched in the opinion polls, the winners cannot be predicted. By the same token, however, it can be predicted that winning, this time, will require an actual plurality of votes. And it can be predicted that, once the results are in, no great issue will have been propelled to the fore, as Vietnam was in 1968. No such issue exists—not, at any rate, in the narrow space defined by American political possibility.

It has been a sedate, civil, and serious—in the sense of giving attention to substance—campaign. But Gore and Bradley have had to struggle to find things to disagree about. So, to a lesser extent, have Bush and McCain. What piquancy the campaign offers derives mostly from the backgrounds and personalities of the two leading Republicans. McCain is certainly the most interesting candidate in the race. He says in his stump speech that he is a "proud conservative Republican," and his voting record in Congress confirms the conservatism if not the pride. But his campaign doesn't feel particularly Republican. The openness and good fellowship aboard his campaign bus, the Straight Talk Express, are all they're cracked up to be. There's none of the feeling of being inside an ideological bunker, whether beleaguered or triumphant, which was so marked in the Reagan campaigns and still is in those of such latter-day Reaganites as Gary Bauer, Steve Forbes, and Alan Keyes. Nor is there the feeling of being deep inside the culture of Republicanism, as there was with Bush *père* and is with Bush *fils*. McCain, in his town-meeting Q&As, speaks with passion about campaign-finance reform and inspiring young people to public service. When he's asked about the budget surplus, he stresses that he doesn't want to give it all away as a tax cut. Bush, for his part, has worked hard to perfect a vocabulary of social concern, but the airless orthodoxy of the conservative movement—in which government is to be disparaged at every turn, and tax cuts and military spending are always good—still hangs heavy over his operation.

These are not, however, the sort of thing that epochs are made from. At the Wayfarer bar the other night, where in years past the pre-primary talk had been about Vietnam or nuclear war, the main topic was whether Bill Bradley should grow a beard. My drinking partner said no—Middle America would never stand for it. I said yes. He'd look great, and, God knows, something has to be done about that inflatable object between lip and necktie, especially given Gore's newly workout-chiselled jaw. Also, Lincoln had one.

—*The New Yorker*, January 31, 2000

THE LESSON OF RED KEN

EARLIER THIS MONTH, for the first time ever, the citizens of London went to the polls and elected themselves a mayor. This unprecedented event was little noted in the United States. Americans who read the inside pages of the big papers will be aware that London's voters, by picking a maverick who had been thrown out of the ruling Labor Party for running as an independent, stuck a gleeful Cockney finger in the eye of Prime Minister Tony Blair. To summarize the tabloidish high points: Kenneth "Red Ken" Livingstone, cheeky hero of London's Loony Left, trounces hapless, bearded Labor draftee Frank Dobson and skirt-chasing Conservative Steve Norris in rebuke to Blairite control-freakery after Labor-hopeful-slash-movie-queen Glenda Jackson quits and original Tory-nominee-slash-potboiler-novelist Lord Jeffrey Archer flames out in gamy sex scandal. Great copy. But seeing this story solely from the personality angle is like handicapping the Grand National by judging the jockeys without mentioning horses or hurdles.

The real novelty of the election was the way it was conducted: by a kind of instant runoff. Under London's ingenious arrangement, each voter gets to name both a first choice and a second one. If somebody wins an outright majority, that's it. If not, then all but the top two candidates are eliminated; the second preferences of the eliminated candidates' voters are counted up; the second-choice votes for the two finalists are added to their first-choice votes; and the one with the highest total wins. This is what in fact happened. In the first-choice voting, Livingstone got 39 percent—a smaller share, by the way, than Ruth Messinger got when she had her head handed to her by Mayor Giuliani in the 1997 New York City election. Ten other candidates— three major, seven minor—split the remainder, with Norris, the Tory, com- ing in second, at 27 percent. In the second-preference vote, Red Ken got another 12 percent—just enough for a bare majority—while Norris picked up an additional 13, for a total of 40 percent.

This was a little too complicated for the American press. For example, the *Times*—New York, not London—simply reported that Livingstone had won "with an estimated 51 percent of the vote," making it sound as if the voters liked Red Ken better than all his opponents put together.

It may seem pedantic to harp on what looks like mere procedure, but this is one case where the process is the forest. Red Ken is only a tree. The elec- tion he happened to win is part of a profound constitutional upheaval that, far more than any Third Way policy tinkerings, will be Tony Blair's lasting legacy. The only aspect of this upheaval to have received much attention over here is the abolition of hereditary membership in the House of Lords. That change, for all its *Masterpiece Theatre* appeal, is less important than the cre- ation of new regional parliaments in Scotland and Wales that are chosen in semiproportional elections. Most of the members of these parliaments rep- resent individual districts, but, in addition, a few extra seats are distributed among the parties according to their proportion of the overall total vote. That way, geographically dispersed and/or smaller parties get a share of representation, too. A similar scheme was used last year in the balloting for Britain's delegates to the European parliament in Brussels, and a modest move toward proportionality has been proposed for the British Parliament itself. London had a city council election on the day it elected Red Ken, and there, too, an innovative system was employed. The two biggest parties swept the district-based seats. But, thanks to proportionally distributed extra seats, the council has a fair sprinkling of Liberal Democrats and Greens as well.

All this ought to be of interest to Americans, because our electoral sys- tem is based on an eighteenth-century British model—single-district, winner-take-all elections decided by simple pluralities—that Britain is hav- ing second thoughts about. For Americans, London's instant-runoff idea presents especially intriguing possibilities. It's a way of opening up politics to a wider variety of voices without sacrificing the clarity and energy of a single directly elected executive. As a third-party or independent candidate, you can campaign hard without the risk of being a spoiler and handing the election to the candidate most hostile to your views. As a citizen, you can vote your heart without giving up your shot at picking the lesser evil. London's voting system allows the electorate to speak far more subtly and precisely than ours does. Red Ken won fair and square, because he was at least barely acceptable to a majority. He was the people's choice, but not their first choice. The voters gave him the job, but they were able to specify that they were giving it to him grudgingly. And, if there's one thing American voters would dearly love to be able to express, it's grudgingness.

—*The New Yorker,* May 29, 2000

BEST PICTURE

IN 1989, the Academy of Motion Picture Arts and Sciences, wishing to minimize the wounded feelings that can accompany being tagged a loser, changed the formula by which the envelope-rippers announce the recipients of the Oscars. The federal bureaucracy, always a bit behind the Hollywood curve, took more than a decade to catch up: not until the 2000 election did Washington get around to ditching the old, hurtful custom of having the voters say "And the winner is . . ." and replacing it with a more sensitive practice, whereby a group of chosen judges, wearing gowns that a Price Waterhouse accountant would die for, consult themselves and then announce, "And the presidency goes to . . ."

For the movie industry, it's been a rough political season. Campaign spending is through the roof. According to one estimate, by the time the polls close on Tuesday the studios will have shelled out a record sixty million dollars for full-page newspaper ads, billboards, videotape and DVD mailings, and other promotional goodies. That may not sound like much— Michael Bloomberg paid more last fall for a four-year lease on city hall— but it's thirty times the reported production budget for *In the Bedroom*, one of the contenders for Best Picture. And the Oscar electorate is a lot smaller than the mayoral one: fewer than six thousand people have the franchise. At these per-vote prices, a presidential campaign would cost a trillion dollars.

And that's just the "hard money." Hollywood has "soft money," too. Academy rules ban filmmakers from giving parties for Academy members and forbid studios to hold screenings that "feature the live participation of the film's artists before or after the screening" or include "receptions, buffets or other refreshments"—even a lousy bag of popcorn. But if somebody else throws the party, or if non-Academy riffraff are also invited to the screening, then bring on the caviar and the stars. In other words, "independent expenditures" are O.K. So is negative campaigning. This year, *A Beautiful Mind,* a front-runner in the big categories, has been the main target. The critics long ago pointed out that the film pretties up the facts about the real-life mathematician on whom the Russell Crowe character is based. Lately, though, anonymous leaks to the Drudge Report and other outlets of dubious respectability have "revealed" some nasty things which the mathematician (who, at the time, was in the grip of schizophrenic delusions that had him convinced he was the emperor of Antarctica) did and said, and which are omitted from the film. Crowe himself has been slammed for loutish behavior at an earlier awards ceremony. The "character issue" is big this year, both for source material and for actors, if not for what's actually on the screen. Meanwhile, the celebrity endorsements are flowing in, with Julia Roberts and Mel Gibson throwing their support behind Denzel Washington against Crowe. And three of the movie colony's most prominent ethnic groups—Brits, African American superstars, and hobbits—have been jostling for position. Oscar politics ain't beanbag.

Hollywood, it may seem, has learned all there is to learn from the world of "real" politics. And, God knows, vice versa. But maybe not. Take the wonky, but actually quite important, question of voting systems. To pick Oscar winners, the Academy uses what we call plurality voting and the British call "first past the post." The Oscar "goes to" whichever nominee—there are usually five—gets more votes than any one of the others. This is why mediocre, bombastic movies that are obviously disliked by the majority of Academy members and other discerning filmgoers are so often rewarded with golden statuettes. The nominees, however, are chosen differently. Academy members still get one vote each, but they can list up to five favorites in order of preference. Any film or actor that gets a fifth of the first-place votes is nominated automatically, and the rest are chosen by considering alternative preferences. As a result, meritorious work frequently makes it to the finals.

Something analogous is beginning to happen, in a small way, outside the zone of glitz. On March 5th, voters in San Francisco decided to adopt "instant runoff voting" for mayor and other officials elected citywide. That same day, clear across the country in bucolic Vermont, fifty-one town meetings passed resolutions asking the state legislature to adopt the same system for gubernatorial and other statewide races. Under I.R.V., voters can list their choices in order of preference. If no candidate tops 50 percent, the losers are dropped from the count one by one and the votes are retallied, with each voter's vote going to his or her top choice still in the race, until someone has a majority. (Computers do the math in a flash.) The system is an exotic novelty here, but it is used routinely in Australia, Ireland, and England, and, of course, in the nominating process of the Academy.

San Francisco and Vermont are special cases. San Francisco previously staged separate runoff elections between the top two finishers, which costs money and rewards zero-sum negative campaigning. In Vermont, if no gubernatorial candidate gets an absolute majority the legislature picks whoever it wants. That's already happened twenty-one times, and it's likely to happen again this year, because four plausible candidates will be on the ballot. But there are similar movements afoot in places—Alaska and New Mexico, for example—that, like almost all of America, currently use plain old plurality voting.

If the instant-runoff system begins to take hold, the impact on America's political culture could be profound. It would encourage civility, discourage fratricidal negative campaigning, prevent the election of candidates strongly opposed by majorities, and broaden the range of candidates while eliminating the third-party spoiler phenomenon. The two big parties would retain their primacy, but no one can say which would benefit. The only sure winners would be the voters. Remember them? The people who, on the whole, would rather be watching the Oscars?

—*The New Yorker*, March 25, 2002

FRAMED UP

ROBERT A. DAHL—whose new book's title asks the question *How Democratic Is the American Constitution?*—is not a crank. He is the Sterling Professor Emeritus of Political Science at Yale, and he is about as covered with honors as a scholar can be. He is a member of the National Academy of Sciences, the American Philosophical Society, and the American Academy of Arts and Sciences; a corresponding fellow of the British Academy; a recipient of the Talcott Parsons Prize, the Woodrow Wilson Foundation Award, and the James Madison Award of the American Political Science Association, of which he is a past president. He is the author of twenty-three books and textbooks, several of which are considered definitive landmarks in the field. His peers revere him. He has been called "the premier democratic theorist of our time" by Fred I. Greenstein, of Princeton; "the premier analyst of democratic theory and democratic institutions writing today" by James S. Fishkin, of the University of Texas; and "the foremost political theorist of this generation" by Theodore J. Lowi, of Cornell. Robert Dahl is eighty-six years old. He knows what he is talking about. And he thinks that the Constitution has got something the matter with it.

Treating the Constitution as imperfect is not new. The angrier abolitionists saw it, in William Lloyd Garrison's words, as "a covenant with death and an agreement with hell." Walter Bagehot (and a prominent American admirer of his, Professor Woodrow Wilson) thought it deeply flawed. Charles A. Beard considered it mainly an instrument for the protection of property rights, an analysis that he did not intend as a compliment. Academic paintballs have splattered the parchment with some regularity. But in the public square the Constitution is beyond criticism. The American civic religion affords it biblical or koranic status, even to the point of seeing it as divinely inspired. It's the flag in prose. It's something to be venerated. It's something to be preserved, protected, and defended, as the President swears by God to do. In the proper place (a marble temple in Washington), at the proper times (the first Monday in October, *et seq.*), and by the proper people (nine men and women in priestly robes), it is something to be interpreted, like the entrails of a goat. But the Constitution of the United States is emphatically not something to be debunked, especially in the afterglow of sole-superpower triumphalism. The few critics to have spoken up in recent years—Daniel Lazare, the author of a pathbreaking 1996 book, *The Frozen Republic: How the Constitution Is Paralyzing Democracy,* is one—have tended to be isolated and uncredentialled. Against this background, Dahl's apostasy merits attention.

How Democratic Is the American Constitution? falls somewhere between a little book and a big pamphlet—a hundred and sixty airy pages of text, with large type and wide margins. It has been adapted from a lecture series that Dahl gave shortly before the most recent presidential election. Perhaps because it was written to be spoken, it is conversational, informal, and relaxed. Dahl's premise is that the Constitution ought to be judged by "democratic standards"—that is, by whether it is "the best that we can design for enabling politically equal citizens to govern themselves under laws and government policies that have been adopted and are maintained with their rational consent." And his purpose "is not so much to suggest changes in the existing constitution as to encourage us to change the way we *think* about it." That premise is more controversial, and that purpose less modest, than either of them may sound.

Dahl's main points form an argument that goes roughly like this. Wise and great though the framers were, their vision was circumscribed by what they knew, what they mistakenly thought they knew, and what they lived too soon to have had any way of knowing. Even within those limits, they were hobbled by the political necessities of a particular moment, which forced them to swallow provisions to which the most eminent among them were strongly (and rightly) opposed. Later, in the nineteenth and twentieth centuries, an explosion of democratic theory, experience, and practice yielded up an abundance of new democratic norms and mechanisms. A few of these (such as the direct popular election of senators) were incorporated into the formal Constitution, and a few more (such as the idea of competing political parties and the practice of allowing citizens to vote for presidential electors) were jury-rigged into the informal constitutional structure. But many others were not, and, despite American power, the American system has not been a model for other democracies. Although it's difficult to separate constitutional systems from other factors affecting national well-being, there is no reason to believe that the American system does a better job than the democratic alternatives, and quite a few reasons to believe that it does a worse one.

THE MOST BLATANTLY undemocratic feature of the document that the framers adopted in Philadelphia in 1787 was its acceptance—indeed, its enshrinement—of slavery, which in its American form was as vicious and repugnant as any institution ever devised by man. Article I, Section 9 forbade Congress to forbid the slave trade (or, as the framers shamefacedly put it, "the Migration or Importation of such Persons as any of the States now existing shall think proper to admit") until 1808—twenty long years! Article IV, Section 2 made the citizens of the "free" states complicit in the crime by obliging them to return any runaway "Person held to Service or Labour in one State" to "the Party to whom such Service or Labour may be due," even if slavery itself was unlawful within the state to which the brave wretch had managed to escape. Most notoriously, under Article I, Section 2, a state's allotment of seats in the House of Representatives (and, by extension, its presidential electors) was determined by counting not only "free Persons" but also "three fifths of all other Persons." This was simply diabolical, because to the insult of defining a person held in bondage as three-fifths of a human being it added the injury of using that definition to augment the political power of that person's oppressors.*

It took the deaths of seven hundred thousand soldiers to cleanse the Constitution of these obscenities. Though Dahl does not emphasize the point, the Civil War—the bloodiest war in recorded history up to that period—represented a catastrophic failure of the Constitution itself. The po-

---

*The injury would have been greater, of course, if the insult had been less—that is, if the slaveholders had been able to augment their overrepresentation in Congress by counting each slave fully.

litical institutions it created had proved incapable of solving the nation's greatest problem. In the war, North and South both claimed to be the true inheritors of the founding generation. The South probably had the better of the argument, but the North won the fight and, with it, the point. The victors saw no great need to overhaul the document in whose name they had triumphed. So the Reconstruction amendments were substantive, not structural. The Thirteenth Amendment abolishes slavery (and, for the first time in the Constitution's text, drops the "such Persons" circumlocutions and finally uses the brutal word). The Fourteenth extends to all "the equal protection of the laws." And the Fifteenth guarantees the right to vote regardless of "race, color, or previous condition of servitude." But nothing was done to alter the political institutions that in 1860 had held four million people—one American in eight—in bondage and that, for the next century and beyond, denied millions of their "free" descendants both equal protection and the franchise.

Even so grotesque and obvious an injustice as apartheid in the public schools was beyond the ability of the national government to correct. And when, after ninety years, formal, official school segregation was outlawed, the deed was not done by the elected representatives of the people. It was done through the exercise of unelected, unaccountable, unchecked, quasi-legislative judicial power—one of the numerous features of the American constitutional system that the framers had no idea they were creating. The framers wanted an independent judiciary, for sure. They seem to have wanted some sort of judicial review, especially of state laws or actions that might impinge on the authority of the national government. And the language of the Bill of Rights—"Congress shall make no law respecting an establishment of religion," and so on—suggests that, even though the framers did not explicitly authorize the Supreme Court to overturn acts of Congress or presidential edicts that infringed upon guaranteed civil liberties, they would not have been scandalized by the Court's doing just that. But no one anticipated that the Court would gather unto itself what Dahl calls "the power to make policy decisions that affect the lives and welfare of millions of Americans." The framers did not create that power; the Court itself seized it, gradually and over time. What the framers did create, by establishing a government profoundly at odds with itself and often helpless against the veto power of determined minorities, was the power vacuum into which the Court was drawn. Somebody had to do something about school segregation, after all; it was a patent injustice and an international embarrassment, most Americans opposed it, and sooner or later it would have led to serious civil disorder. But at least the substance of *Brown v. Board of Education* (as opposed to the power behind it) was democratic. Could one say the same of *Dred Scott v. Sandford, Buckley v. Valeo,* or *Bush v. Gore?*

Once slavery was removed, the most undemocratic remaining provision of the Constitution was, and is, the composition of the Senate—its so-called equality of representation, whereby each state gets two senators regardless of population. This is often referred to as a "concession" to the small states, but in truth it was more like surrender to blackmail. The small states saw it as a deal-breaker, and they would brook no compromise. Dahl notes that Gunning Bedford, Jr., of Delaware, told his fellow delegates to the Constitutional Convention that, unless the big states yielded, "the small ones will find some foreign ally of more honor and good faith, who will take them by the hand and do them justice." The Senate was formed less by rational argument than by threats of treason and war.

You've probably never heard of Gunning Bedford, Jr. (I hadn't, until Dahl introduced me to him.) When it came to the composition of the Senate, though, the Gunning Bedford types exerted far more influence than James Madison or Alexander Hamilton, who were then left holding the bag. It was Madison and Hamilton, along with John Jay, who got the assignment of defending every last detail of the various Philadelphia compromises in the series of long op-ed pieces later collected as *The Federalist Papers* and treasured to this day by columnists and speechwriters composing encomiums to the providential perfection of the framers' handiwork. Dahl points out, amiably but sharply, that *The Federalist Papers* were an exercise in spin. "If we employ a dictionary definition of propaganda as 'information or ideas methodically spread to promote or injure a cause, nation, etc.,' then *The Federalist Papers* were surely propaganda," he writes. Madison and Hamilton had a job to do. It was a perfectly honorable job, but it obliged them to defend things they did not believe in. Madison had been the Constitutional Convention's most passionate advocate of giving the big states more senators than the small ones. Hamilton had been almost as adamant. "As states are a collection of individual men," he harangued his fellow delegates, "which ought we to respect most, the rights of the people composing them, or of the artificial beings resulting from the composition? Nothing could be more preposterous or absurd than to sacrifice the former to the latter. It has been said that if the smaller states renounce their *equality*, they renounce at the same time their *liberty*. The truth is it is a contest for power, not for liberty. Will the men composing the small states be less free than those composing the larger?"

Even if it were true that the condition of being a citizen of a state with a small population entails such grievous disadvantages that, to correct for them, the very votes of such citizens must be assigned a greater weight than the votes of other Americans, how much is enough? Are the special needs of people who live in small states—people who can, after all, escape their condition by moving somewhere else—greater than the special needs of people who are short, or people who are disabled, or (more to the point of American history) people who are black? Here's a little thought experiment, inspired by Dahl's reflections. Imagine, if you can, that African Americans were represented "fairly" in the Senate. They would then have twelve senators instead of, at present, zero, since black folk make up 12 percent of the population. Now imagine that the descendants of slaves were afforded the compensatory treatment to which the Constitution entitles the residents of small states. Suppose, in other words, that the 12 percent of Americans who are of African descent had as many senators to represent them as the Constitution allots to the 12 percent of Americans who live in the least populous states. There would be *forty-four* black senators. How's *that* for affirmative action?

Dahl is content, in this little book, to point out the grotesqueness of the Senate in the light of elementary democratic principles. There have been large historical consequences, too. At the moment, admittedly, the Senate is not a particularly unpopular institution. In contrast to the House, the Senate has many members who are widely known, so it has a human face. Liberals like the way the Senate derailed President Bush's plan to turn the Alaska wilderness into an oil patch. Conservatives like the way it thwarted President Clinton's health-care proposal. But, as these examples suggest, the Senate is essentially a graveyard. Its record, especially over the past century and a half, makes disheartening reading. A partial list of the measures that—despite being favored by the sitting president, an apparent majority of the people, and, in most cases, the House of Representatives to boot—have been done to death in the Senate would include bills to authorize federal action against the disenfranchisement of blacks, to ban violence against strikers by private police forces, to punish lynching, to lower tariffs, to extend relief to the unemployed, to outlaw the poll tax, to provide aid to education, and (under Presidents Truman, Nixon, and Carter as well as Clinton) to provide something like the kind of health coverage that is standard in the rest of the developed world. The rejection of the Versailles treaty and the League of Nations after the First World War and then of preparedness on the eve of the Second are only the best known of the Senate's many acts of foreign policy sabotage, which have continued down to the present, with its refusal to ratify international instruments on genocide, nuclear testing, and human rights.

Some will take all this as proof that the system has worked exactly as the framers planned. But, to believe that, one must believe that the framers were heartless, brainless reactionaries. They were not. They were practical, public-spirited men who preferred the lessons of experience to the dictates of theory. Unfortunately, since no one had ever before tried making a republic like the American one, there was very little experimental information to guide the designers. A generation later, Dahl thinks, they might have come to different decisions.

Much has been made of Madison's fear of majorities and abhorrence of parties ("factions"), which he expressed in Federalist No. 10. Madison was thirty-six when he wrote his Federalist essays. Dahl points to some fascinating material that shows how Madison's thinking evolved as he and the republic matured. At forty, Madison writes (in "Parties," an essay for Philip Freneau's *National Gazette*) that "parties are unavoidable" and that their dangers can be overcome "by establishing a political equality among all," by pursuing policies that discourage extremes of wealth and poverty, and "by making one party a check on the other." At seventy, while preparing for publication his notes on the debates at the Constitutional Convention, he writes that observations he himself made at the convention "do not convey the speaker's more full & matured view." He goes on to affirm, ungrudgingly, the importance of political parties as "a natural offspring of Freedom"; and he defends "an equal & universal right of suffrage" without property qualifications. At seventy-four, he writes that while no form of government "can be a perfect guard against the abuse of power," the republican form—"where the people govern themselves, and where, of course, the majority govern"— is less subject to abuse than any other. Finally, in 1833, with Andrew Jackson in the White House, Madison, now in his eighties, tells a correspondent that "a republican Government in which the majority rule the minority" is the "least imperfect" of all governments and that (just to drive the point home) "the vital principle of republican government is the *lex majoris parties*, the will of the majority." This greatest of republicans had ended by becoming a democrat.

AN OBSCURE PROVISION of Article V of the Constitution, which outlines the amending process, provides that "no State, without its Consent, shall be deprived of its equal Suffrage in the Senate." On its face, this appears to mean that an amendment changing the composition of the Senate would have to be ratified by every single state. Dahl writes, "In effect, those fifteen words end all possibility of amending the Constitution in order to reduce the unequal representation of citizens in the Senate." I'm not so sure. In theory, one can imagine a Senate with, say, one senator from each state, plus fifty more elected at large. That would preserve the "equal Suffrage" of the states, while providing, for a change, a bit of equal suffrage for actual people. Anyway, what if those fifteen words were themselves amended out of the Constitution? The idea that a constitutional amendment might itself be unconstitutional is probably too audacious even for the Supreme Court.

It will never come to that, alas. The amending process alone is enough to insure that the two-senators-per-state rule is forever safe. That process (which was designed, at least in part, to protect slavery) requires the assent of three-fourths of the states. The politicians of the smaller states (and to a much lesser but discernible extent the citizens thereof) would have much to lose from a democratized Senate. So what if the thirty-seven largest states—representing 95 percent of the nation's population—ratify an amendment? To kill it, all the thirteen smallest have to do is nothing.

The presidency is another aspect of the constitutional system that has turned out to be quite unlike what the framers envisioned. Parliamentary democracy was not even considered, because it hadn't been invented yet. (The British system of an executive beholden to a legislative majority, rather than to a monarch, did not fully take shape until the early 1830s.) Still, as Dahl notes, the framers came close to devising something akin to it: not once but three times, the Constitutional Convention voted to have the chief magistrate chosen by Congress outright. In the end, the delegates, remembering their Montesquieu, drew back—but only partly. The electoral college, they thought, would be a kind of nominating convention. If no candidate had an outright majority—and the framers assumed that this would be normal once George Washington had passed from the scene—the House would choose among the top five, later reduced to the top three, with each state delegation casting one vote. So the president would owe his job to Congress, even if Congress, having installed him, could remove him only with the greatest difficulty.

The convention gave the job of picking electors to the state legislatures—or, more precisely, to "each State," which would do the appointing "in such Manner as the Legislature thereof may direct." This, Dahl writes, opened a huge democratic opportunity in the following century, as one state legislature after another, under public pressure, yielded the power to choose electors to the voters. But this power is on loan only, as we learned in 2000, when the Florida legislature made clear its intention to name its own slate of electors if the recount went forth and came out the wrong way.

Just as the Fourth of July orators say, America has been an inspiration to peoples struggling for democracy. But, when it comes to actually designing the machinery, the American model has had no takers—not among successful democracies, at any rate. (The Philippines, Liberia, and some Latin-American countries, which have copied us, are not good advertisements.) Dahl surveys the twenty-two countries that have governed themselves democratically without interruption since 1950. Only six, including the United States, are federal, and in every case "federalism was not so much a free choice as a self-evident necessity imposed by history." Only four, all of them federal, have strong bicameralism. Only the United States, the United Kingdom, Canada, and France do not use one of the many variants of proportional representation, a nineteenth-century invention. We get bad marks in "democratic fairness" and "encouraging consensus." In "accountability," we're flunking. "Where are we to place responsibility for the conduct of our government?" Dahl asks. He goes on:

> When we go to the polls, whom can we hold accountable for the successes and failures of national policies? The president? The House? The Senate? The unelected Supreme Court? Or, given our federal system, the states, where governments are, in their complexity, a microcosm of the national government? . . . I, for one, am inclined to think that compared with the political systems of the other advanced democratic countries, ours is among the most opaque, complex, confusing, and difficult to understand.

In short, if our system "fails to ensure the fairness promised by the proportional vision, it also fails to provide the clear accountability promised by the majoritarian vision." Nor is that all. In so-called consensual democracies, polls show, voters who are on the losing side of an election are almost as satisfied with the political system as the winners—and both are more satisfied than citizens of majoritarian regimes like ours. Also: "When the United States is ranked with other established democracies on such matters as the rate of incarceration, the ratio of poor to rich, economic growth, social expenditures, energy efficiency, foreign aid and the like, its performance is something less than impressive." On the other hand, we do as well as anyone in maintaining civil liberties—thanks mainly to the Bill of Rights, one part of the Constitution with which Dahl doesn't have a beef. And, although Dahl doesn't mention this, we seem to be getting straight A's in world domination.

AS A PRACTICAL MATTER, we probably won't be able to change our constitutional system in any truly significant way. But we can, as Dahl suggests, change the way we think about it. If we worshipped the framers a little less, we might respect ourselves a little more. If we kept in mind the ways in which our constitutional arrangements distort our democracy and hobble our politics, we might gain a deeper, more useful understanding of the sources of our various national discontents. If we didn't assume that the system was perfect, we wouldn't assume that everything we don't like is the fault of bad people. We'd judge our politicians more shrewdly, and more charitably, if we reminded ourselves regularly of the constraints that the system imposes on them. We'd be less tempted by lazy moralism.

Our constitutional system is loaded with perverse incentives. To take a current example of how this plays out, many liberals feel exasperation, or even contempt, for what they regard as the timidity of the Democratic opposition to President Bush. Why, they wonder, isn't the Democratic congressional leadership full-throatedly demanding stronger environmental regulation, meaningful gun control, and tax policies that don't simply bloat the rich? It's not as if these positions were politically unpopular—all of them, polls show, are supported by solid majorities of the American public. But solid majorities of the American public don't have much to do with who wins American congressional elections. This fall, control of the House and the Senate will be decided in a dozen districts and a half-dozen states, and in those districts and states the issues don't necessarily cut the way they do in the country at large. So Democrats stick to Social Security and Medicare, Republicans stick to terrorism and "compassionate conservatism," and the general public wonders why "the issues" aren't being "addressed."

"My reflections lead me to a measured pessimism about the prospects for greater democratization of the American Constitution," Dahl writes. He sees little or no chance for the kinds of changes to which his analysis logically points. He does see some unspecified hope in "a gradually expanding discussion that begins in scholarly circles, moves outward to the media and intellectuals more generally, and after some years begins to engage a wider public"—specifically, a discussion of how our system stacks up against the performance of constitutional systems in other advanced democracies and against democratic principles. Our understanding of those principles will evolve indefinitely. "So, too," he writes in his final sentence, "will the implications of those principles for our democratic political system, and its Constitution, under which we Americans freely choose to live."

Dahl can be forgiven this one little flourish of sentimentality. As he knows very well—and has written a book to prove—our system is a lot less democratic than it should be. And we didn't choose it; it was here when we arrived. We just have to live with it. Better we should do so with our eyes open.

—*The New Yorker*, July 29, 2002

12. YUPPIES AND OTHER
LEFTOVERS

The pieces that follow have in common a deplorable failure to fall neatly into any of the other groupings in this book. Rather than consign them to oblivion, I decided to give them a safety net. Liberalism strikes again.

(If you're a conservative, just think of this section as a jail.)

The first of these essays, "The Education of Mr. Smith," was made possible by my lifelong annoyance with a Frank Capra movie. The second, "All the Fine Young Kennedys," was an attempt, unfortunately futile, to persuade the children of J.F.K. to follow their father's profession. The one entitled "Moby-Rick" is a special case. It would be a stretch to think of it as having much to do with politics, unless you count a vague sympathy for whales as political, but at least it's short. Its opening joke is a very oblique tribute to Peter de Vries, the great comic novelist. He was one of the *New Yorker* legends with whom I nominally overlapped during my early days at that magazine. De Vries was a literary giant—he must have been six and a half feet tall. Burly, too. I once saw him heading for the reception area on the writers' floor, but by the time I had worked up the courage to go up to him and stammer out something about how great he was, he had disappeared into the elevator. Anyway, the first line of "Moby-Rick" was inspired by the way de Vries once subtly updated a Robert Frost couplet by changing the case of a single letter:

Whose woods these are I think I know.
His house is in the Village though . . .

THE EDUCATION OF MR. SMITH

CONSIDER A YOUNG POL.

He is a first-time candidate for Congress. This means he was in school sometime during the period from the assassination of John F. Kennedy to the resignation of Richard M. Nixon—the period called the sixties. As a student he may or may not have marched, may or may not have dropped acid, may or may not have felt the exhilaration of putting his body on the line against the war machine. But he is likely to have been affected, even if glancingly, by the passions and moral certainties of that time. He is likely to have picked up the notion that a wrong is simply something to be opposed. He may even have been persuaded that his own conscience is the highest authority he can consult.

Chances are, sometime in his youth he saw Frank Capra's splendidly simpleminded 1939 classic, *Mr. Smith Goes to Washington*. It meant a lot to him. This is important because Mr. Smith (James Stewart) was not only a wonderful idealist but also a damn fool. With luck and a modicum of tact, Jefferson Smith could have become a powerful force for good in Washington. Instead, he allowed himself to be driven berserk by the discovery that his mentor and fellow senator from Montana, Joseph Paine (Claude Rains), occasionally indulged in practical politics.

Admittedly, Senator Paine's Willet Creek Dam appropriation was not a moral high point in the Senate's history. On top of enriching the party bosses, this particular infrastructure improvement was going to flood Senator Smith's precious Boy Rangers' camp. But water projects are as American as tobacco subsidies. And politics ain't beanbag.

The indignant Smith managed to destroy old Paine's career. But what our candidate doesn't know is that in the years after the movie ended, things did not go well for Smith or his ideals. Paine's successor turned out to be a philosophical opponent of government-subsidized recreation areas, which he regarded as socialistic. The Boy Rangers' camp, deprived of its funding, closed. Smith himself had so alienated the party faithful that he didn't even get the nomination. He returned to Montana, where he eventually found a position in the public-relations department of Boise Cascade. Jean Arthur, bored silly, moved back to Washington and got a job on the old *Times Herald.*

Maybe the problem was that Smith got his Senate seat by appointment. As our candidate will find out, none of this could have happened to a politician who'd ever had to run for anything.

IT IS SOMETIMES SAID that our politicians are poor because the pool of young people who enter politics is thin: no one with conviction runs for office anymore. But Mr. (and Ms.) Smiths come to Washington all the time. The problem is just that the system educates or, if you wish, conspires against them. Even among the towel-snapping, backslapping, student-council-president types who provide the roughage in our political diet, the desire to do good persists. A politician is by definition an egotist, but he is an egotist who identifies his ego with something larger. He is an egotist who is willing to take a risk. He is an egotist whose self-esteem is somehow bound up, however weakly, with some notion of public service. The same cannot so readily be said of other professions that involve the pursuit of power. There is such a thing as the public interest, higher than any and all private interests, and it is something of which a politician must at least be dimly conscious.

"One thing that has always surprised me is how much conscience you do find around here," says Representative Charles Schumer, Democrat of New York. Schumer, who is thirty-five years old, was elected to Congress at twenty-nine. "Every day you see congressmen raising their hands—or putting those little electronic voting cards into the machine—in ways that hurt them," he continues. "It far exceeds the number of businesspeople who will say, 'This time our company will not maximize profits, because it wouldn't be good for the country.'"

The questions of conscience faced by young politicians are of two kinds, the interesting and the uninteresting. Unlike the uninteresting questions— whether or not to take bribes, for instance, or whether or not to force one's staff to pay kickbacks—the interesting questions presuppose a functioning conscience. And they all boil down to a single dilemma: Should I make the decision at hand purely on its merits, as if it were the only decision I'll ever have to make? Or should I make the decision at hand with an eye to my future effectiveness?

The sine qua non of effectiveness, of course, is getting elected and, once elected, reelected. For members of Congress—distilled politicians, Richard Reeves calls them—the campaign never ends. When the cherry trees blossom for the first time after the election, the next primary is only a year away. The new member, no matter how idealistic, will want badly to win it and keep the seat.

Anyway, the satisfactions of the job are not limited to the privilege of serving one's fellow creatures. The member of Congress is a minor celebrity, a certified success. The building in which he works is seductive. It has none of the musty, cabbagy feeling of most government installations. The marble floors and walls of the Capitol, its high, frescoed ceilings, give his very footfalls the sharp click of purpose. Observe him on his way to an important committee meeting. (If it weren't important, he wouldn't be on his way to it.) An aide whispers at his elbow, a step behind. Tourists in loud sport shirts gape awestruck at him as he strides into the MEMBERS ONLY elevator. He feels so consequential, so—important. The texture of life on the Hill is a nonsexual erotic fantasy for the modern American male. (Though of course women, too, want to get reelected.)

"It's a game of king of the mountain," says Christopher Matthews, Speaker Tip O'Neill's administrative assistant. "You have to win every time or you lose everything. It's like that Hitchcock movie where the guy has to get his cigarette lighter to light twenty times in a row or they'll cut his finger off. Only in politics they cut off something more serious." No one wants to be an ex-congressman, one of the walking dead who haunt the Hill. "When you're a member, they give you respect," says one who isn't anymore. "The minute you lose, you owe it all back. It turns out they only lent it to you. My God, the way they look at you when you've lost. The way they *don't* look at you."

Effectiveness means reelection above all, but it also means cultivating many "they's"—contributors, party leaders, the press, one's own "image." At any given moment, on any given issue, the young politician rides a rapids of crosscutting moral eddies. He can vote the money, or he can vote his friends, or he can vote the party, or he can vote the district. Or he can vote the country, the planet, his conscience—different words for the phenomenon known to politicians, who skip the flowery language when talking among themselves, as "doing the right thing."

Money, friends, party, district, the right thing—all are moral frames of reference one can honor, except the first; and even the first can be a byproduct of motives that are not wholly ignoble. Consider them one by one.

The money. "The first time a guy runs for Congress," Edward Markey, a congressman from Boston, observes, "he puts his own home on the line, his friends and family come up with whatever they can, and it's always the biggest political miracle in the district's history. Then he discovers he has to raise another two hundred thousand dollars for next time. He can do it night after night with ten-dollar, twenty-dollar, fifty-dollar fund-raisers. Or he can go meet ten PAC [political action committee] guys, pick up five grand each, and he's done for half a year." He has gained not only money but also time—time he might spend, for example, with his family.

Money, the curdled mother's milk of politics, is the most humiliating, corrupting part of a politician's life; and the most corrupting money is business PAC money. Ideological money, the kind that comes in because somebody likes the cut of your philosophical jib, is universally regarded as the least corrupting. After that comes single-issue money: anti-abortion, antinuke, and so on. But business PACs are not interested in "issues" as the term is generally understood. They are interested in favors. Unless business PAC money is intended as a form of genteel bribery, a lot of stockholders are getting rooked.

The only thing rarer than a congressman who will deny that vote buying occurs is one who will admit that he is among the sellers. But the corruption doesn't have to be as gross as that. "There are various degrees of being for a bill—cosponsoring it, or fighting for it in committee, in debate on the floor, or in a leadership role on the floor," Les Aspin, chairman of the House Armed Services Committee, once told the lawyer and author Mark Green. "PAC funds can determine a member's intensity as well as position."

The classic formula for avoiding the moral snares of fund-raising is contained in a maxim attributed to various legendary pols of old: If you can't drink their booze, take their money, and screw their women and vote against them in the morning, you don't belong in this town. How easy to say. How hard to do.

The friends. Doing something because a friend wants you to has a warmer moral glow than doing it because you're being paid to. Politicians are human beings, and it pains human beings to disappoint their friends. "You get to know people personally," says Representative Patricia Schroeder, Democrat of Colorado. "You go to their houses, you meet their children. And then something comes up, something you know is wrong, and one of those friends looks you in the eye and says, 'If you don't vote for this, I won't get reelected. My life will be ruined.' And you know if you don't you will thereby sever the relationship forever and ever. That's hard."

Friendship is a virtue; but it is a private virtue, not always compatible with either the ambitions or the ideals of public life. True friendship can play you false, and false friendship can truly ruin you. Politicians may have computerized "friend" lists, but they are often lonely. That, far more than money, is why so many of them spend so much time with lobbyists. The best lobbyists go for months of dinners and golf without asking for anything so crude as a favor. The best lobbyists are like the best hookers: they make you feel you didn't pay for it.

The party. Strong political parties, which have become fashionable in theory in lockstep with their decline in practice, require discipline, and discipline requires the ability to reward and punish. Reform has not yet deprived the bosses of all their tools. In Congress the leadership can offer or withhold committee assignments, office space, campaign contributions, media exposure, and, less concretely but more tantalizingly, reputation as a responsible, influential shaper of policy, not a marginal maverick. Plenty of Democrats take public positions that are more liberal than their convictions, and plenty of Republicans take public positions that are more conservative than theirs, to win that reputation—and in the hope of being elected by their colleagues to the leadership groups of their respective parties. Later, they tell themselves, they will use the power assembled by doing small wrong things to do large right things. But of course that is always when "effectiveness" will be used—later.

There is virtue in voting the party, but it is the sort of virtue illustrated by a story told by Congressman Barney Frank, the witty Massachusetts

Democrat. At a city council meeting, the reformers were holding forth, one after another, about having the courage to do what's right. Finally a grizzled regular rose and said, "Whaddya mean, what's right? *Real* courage is the courage to do what's *wrong*—day after day, when you know damn well in your heart it *is* wrong."

The district. "They were mad at me till I explained myself," says Barney Frank about a time he went against the leadership. "Then they were furious." He had used the wrong explanation. "If you say, 'I've studied this, and it's bad public policy,' they get mad at you. If you say, 'I'd love to help you on this, but it'd get me in trouble back home,' they say, 'Okay, yes, fine, of course.'"

"Back home" is a mystical place, the source of the political Ganges, a place to be treated with deference. And there is a respectable body of democratic theory that holds that a legislative representative should be nothing more or less than the faithful instrument of his constituents' views. "I have colleagues who always try to vote as the majority of the people in their district would vote," says Dick Cheney, Wyoming's Republican congressman. "They poll everything. That's a legitimate way to approach the job. But I've noticed that the members who do it that way are generally unable to influence their colleagues."

A more sophisticated kind of democratic theory holds that there is more to the act of representing than being a Xerox machine for poll results. People look for a representative who is in general agreement with their views, of course, but they also seek someone who can represent them characterologically—someone who seems to incarnate qualities they admire. Those qualities may even include independence of judgment. The safer the district, of course, the more room the congressman has to exercise independent judgment. And the easier it is for him to flout the maxim known all over Capitol Hill: If you have to explain it, don't do it.

The right thing. Prayer in schools is what politicians call a horseshit issue. The arguments for it have no real moral weight. But if you do the right thing and vote against it, and you have a less than safe district, you will have a lot of explaining to do. You will have to spend an extra month of weekends back in the district, going from talk show to meeting to editorial board. You may or may not undo the political damage—probably you won't—but you are guaranteed to do some damage to your family life. The price of doing the right thing for your principles can be doing the wrong thing to the actual people you love.

If politicians simply voted their consciences—if they did the right thing every time—a good many issues would come out differently. When you ask members of Congress what would happen if the House voted by secret ballot, you get a surprising unanimity of judgment. Military pensions would be cut. Social Security cost-of-living increases would be capped. Tax loopholes for oil companies, among others, would be slammed shut. "Domestic content" for cars, textile quotas, subsidies to the shipping industry—all gone. School prayer—goodbye. Anti-abortion bills, which currently tend to pass by forty votes, would fail by a like margin. A strong gun-control law would be enacted; so would a tough immigration law. Israel would have to get along with less aid. The MX missile would be junked. Heroin would be legalized for terminal patients suffering intractable pain. And members of Congress would get one hell of a pay raise.

But there is no secret ballot, and the miracle is that once in a while a politician hears the inner voice despite the cacophony outside. Pols are invariably proudest of the times they took someone on—an echo, for some of them, of their youthful defiance of "the system." They prefer it if their adversary is the special interests or the money guys or the elitists or the single-issue screamers, but even if it's the electorate the experience can be exhilarating. To say, "This is as far as I go, and I don't care if it gets me defeated," is to know what freedom is.

But there are few opportunities to step so boldly into the moral sunshine. Our young pol learns that the real choices he must contend with leave him in the gray zone. From the best of motives, he begins to make compromises. He wishes to build his effectiveness. He seeks to accumulate credits that will be used at some future date in some unspecified way on some issue he doesn't know about yet. And then he begins to put his soul in danger. He begins to imagine that his political advancement is so important to the cause of good and right that the cause of good and right is served by his advancement in and of itself. He enters a realm of moral paradox in which compromising his conscience becomes superior as an ethical act to obeying it. He begins to reason like this: If I vote my conscience half as often and thereby have ten times as much power—why, won't I then do five times as much good as I did before?

MR. SMITH GOES TO WASHINGTON had its gala world premiere in the city of its title. In an official proclamation, October 16, 1939, was declared

Mr. Smith Day. There was a black-tie banquet at the National Press Club. Outside Constitution Hall, where the film was to be shown, a Marine band played as limousines discharged dignitaries. Inside, Frank Capra shared his box with the real senator from Montana, Burton K. Wheeler, the great Progressive who had been Robert M. La Follette's running mate in 1924. But during the movie there was a steady din of irritated whispering. A third of the audience walked out before the end. When the lights went up, Senator Wheeler coldly said goodbye and left immediately. No one in town had a kind word to say for the picture.

Capra, in his autobiography, dismissed all this as simply hypocrisy—the huffing of a bunch of "Olympian cuff-shooters" discomfited by the truth. Capra was wrong. The real story of our politics, for our hopeful young politician and for his elders, is a story both more elevating and sadder. More elevating because in Washington there is real heroism, which is the practical attempt to build something decent out of materials that are exceedingly imperfect. And sadder because there is real pathos, which is the idealism that has learned the practical way of the world so well that it has forgotten what it set out to build in the first place. Welcome to Washington, Mr. Smith. Be careful.

—*Esquire*, February 1986

ALL THE FINE YOUNG KENNEDYS

ONE OF LIFE'S little methods of reminding you that time marches on is the way a set of people that has always been older than you suddenly pops over to being younger. I first noticed this phenomenon with respect to ballplayers. (That's when I stopped thinking of baseball as a career possibility and started thinking of it as a metaphor.) After that, totemic groups started flashing by like exit signs on a freeway: cops, then heads of Third World revolutionary governments, then Wall Street boy wonders, then Reagan administration officials at the subcabinet level. This year, it's Kennedys.

I suspect 1986 will be remembered as the year the center of gravity of the Kennedy family shifted down a generation. There were always hordes of kids in the photographs taken at Hickory Hill and at the celebrity tennis tournaments, but this year a lot of those kids have suddenly emerged as adults, and they are doing adult things. Four in particular have broken out of the pack: Maria Shriver, who has just gotten married and is pursuing a successful career; Caroline Kennedy, who is about to do both of the above; and Kathleen Kennedy Townsend and Joseph P. Kennedy III, who are running for Congress.

One thing that is immediately striking about this list of new-minted Kennedy achievers is that it is three-quarters female. Despite their many virtues, the Kennedys of the 1950s, 1960s, and 1970s were a noticeably sexist lot, even by the standards of their own time. The J.F.K.-R.F.K.-E.M.K. generation produced no equivalent of Eleanor Roosevelt, Margaret Chase Smith, or Maurine Neuberger, or even of Barbara Walters. This was certainly not for want of female talent. The Kennedy sisters, Eunice, Patricia, and Jean, were and are intelligent, forceful people. With a bit of the encouragement their brothers were given so lavishly, any or all of them could have had large public careers. This omission is now to be rectified. The new batch of Kennedys is manifestly free of the look-good-shut-up-stand-by-your-man philosophy that ruled their elders. Kathleen Kennedy Townsend, now running for Barbara Mikulski's seat in Maryland, made her reputation by writing an article for the *Washington Monthly* that sought to reconcile feminism with older moral concerns. Her political style, admirably, is that of an austere, no-nonsense bluestocking. Maria Shriver is by contrast a glamour girl, and in interviews she has expressed her determination to play the traditional wifely role. Even so, her marriage to Arnold Schwarzenegger can be taken as a slyly ironic comment on her family's history of exaggerated machismo. Schwarzenegger, as he showed in *Pumping Iron* and *The Terminator,* is a clever fellow with a sense of humor about himself. But it's awfully hard to believe that Maria married him for his brains.

Caroline is not yet a public figure in her own right, but no doubt she will be one day. She is about to marry Ed Schlossberg, which is to say she has had the discernment to choose a man who, like your Diarist, is in his early forties and has a name that ends in "berg." (A pity she preferred a castle to a heart, but perhaps that is her tribute to Camelot.) After working for some years in the art world, she has gone back to school to take a law degree at Columbia. So it is not too farfetched to postulate a political career for her sometime in the future. It is pleasant to imagine that she, rather than one of her male cousins, will become the second President Kennedy. And the first President Schlossberg.

The male cousin most likely to present an obstacle to any such plan is the one who, come next January, will occupy the seat in Congress that for the past thirty years has been held first by John F. Kennedy and then by Tip O'Neill. Joe Kennedy has many opponents for the Democratic nomination in the Eighth District of Massachusetts, but only one of them, State Representative Thomas Vallely, had a chance to beat him. Vallely has the face of a young Tip and the war record of a young J.F.K., and his campaign slogan— "The Other Guy"—was to the point. But Vallely dropped out of the race two months ago, and the remaining candidates, worthy though several of them are, have gone nowhere. Get ready, Washington. Here comes Mighty Young Joe.

Joe Kennedy entered politics at the age of fifteen, when he worked his way through his father's funeral train, gravely shaking the hand of every last passenger on board. In 1979, speaking at the dedication of the John F. Kennedy Library, he delivered a wild attack on President Carter, who was on the platform with him. I was there as a member of Carter's staff, and I thought Joe's speech was puerile demagoguery. Still, it had energy. In recent years he has been running a company that sells heating oil cheaply to poor people. The universal applicability of his model is questionable; not everyone can get crude oil at a discount by having his picture taken with the suppliers. But this is surely no crime. I saw him for the second time in my life last week, at a campaign cocktail party in Belmont. His talk—a living-room version of his basic stump speech—was workmanlike, nothing more. What I hadn't expected—perhaps because my expectations were so low—was that he would be better at answering questions, which he did coherently and confidently, even when his views were obviously at odds with those of his mostly Harvard-affiliated audience. (He said he approved of the Libyan air raid, for example.) He has answers, though this is not necessarily the same as having convictions; and he is jocular, though this is not necessarily the same as having a sense of humor. He is big, sharp-toothed, handsome in a rougher way than his uncles and father. He conveys a faint air of menace. His raw political talent is immense, but because it and he are so unformed there is always the chance that he will turn out to be dangerous. He will probably not be boring.

Just one more. I am told that John, Caroline's brother, is trying to decide between law school and becoming an actor. I hope he picks acting. He is by far the best-looking Kennedy ever, and he would quickly become very big. The second J.F.K. as a movie star: this is the kind of big mythic medicine the country is going to need once the Reagan bubble bursts. Come on, John. It's your duty.

—Boston Diarist, *The New Republic,* June 16, 1986

MOBY-RICK

CALL ME, ISHMAEL. Or leave a message on my machine and I'll get back to you. Because I want to tell you about where I went last Sunday. It was kind of like that trip you took, in that it involved (a) boarding a vessel out of a picturesque port village in Massachusetts and (b) sailing upon the face of the deep in quest of Leviathan, as you might put it. The main differences were that I embarked at Provincetown instead of Nantucket; that instead of Queequeg, Starbuck, and that monomaniac peg leg Ahab, my shipmates were a half-dozen naturalists from the Center for Coastal Studies and about fifty camera-festooned tourists in plaid Bermudas and Reeboks; that our ship was provisioned with chili dogs and Cokes instead of salt pork and rum; that the journey took ten hours instead of three years; and that instead of harpooning the whales with tempered steel we just looked at them. But from the awesomeness-of-nature angle, the voyage of the *Dolphin VII* was not that different from the *Pequod*'s. Really, you'd have been right at home.

Whale watching is a chancy business, because the whales are not on staff. They do as they like and go where they please. Two summers ago the humpbacks, which are the best whales to watch because they are the most frolicsome, chose to congregate just north of the Cape. Even on a four-hour trip like those that depart Provincetown every hour of every day, one could be fairly sure of seeing dozens of them. This year most of the humpbacks have moved farther off, to Georges Bank, thirty miles to the southeast. The short trips are still worthwhile—I took one early in the week and saw three finback whales, including a mother and calf, plus a lone humpback. But I wanted more.

The *Dolphin VII*, like all the Dolphin Fleet whale-watching boats that operate out of Provincetown, is a specially built ocean-going craft, a hundred feet long. It has blue plastic benches and a smelly, noisy diesel engine, but if you stand at the bow the breeze is fresh, the noise minimal, and the swell pleasantly bouncy. Less than two hours into the trip, with the dunes of Truro still plainly visible, we saw our first whale spout in the distance, the spray rounded like a tree made of dissolving blue mist. As we bore down on the whale, he spouted twice more, then flicked his handsome tail in the air and was gone. Five minutes later he resurfaced, perhaps eighty yards from the boat; and this time, drifting with the engines banked, we could hear his spout as well as see it, a deep rumbling whoosh.

The pattern continued throughout the day, as whale by whale we drew nearer to Georges Bank. The whales grew exponentially more numerous as we sailed on. Once I saw a pair of tuna, darting synchronically from the water like chorines in a water ballet; twice I saw gliding sharks, or rather their ominous, jet-black, triangular fins; and, sixty-five times (I wasn't counting, but the naturalists were), we saw whales. Three of them were minke whales, a dozen were finbacks, and fifty were humpbacks. The minkes were shy and frisky and small, and kept their distance. The finbacks were shy and dignified and huge (they are the second largest creature on earth, after the blue whale); only a little of their shiny black backs broke the surface, the flatness of the curve suggesting the prodigious bulk beneath. The humpbacks were big and sometimes boisterous.

At Georges Bank as many as eight humpbacks would surround the boat at once. The whales showed no fear. Sometimes they swam slowly at the surface; sometimes they merely floated, apparently dozing between sonorous blows. Then, perhaps emboldened by their numbers and our proximity, they began to cavort. One of them rolled slowly on his side, the better to fix us with his eye, an orb the size of a baseball a third of the way down the length of his body, just in front of his side flipper. The whale was forty-five feet long. His flipper was fifteen feet long, and now he raised it full out of water and brought it swiftly back with a smack. Astonishing sight, astonishing sound! A bit farther off, one of his companions raised his tail, and— but draw back a bit, and let Melville describe it: "[U]nbent from the vast corpulence of his dignity, and kitten-like, [the whale] plays on the ocean as if it were a hearth. But still you see the power in his play. The broad palms of his tail are flirted high into the air; then smiting the surface, the thunderous concussion rebounds for miles . . . Excepting the sublime *breach*—somewhere else to be described—this peaking of the whale's flukes is perhaps the grandest sight to be seen in all animated nature." Nor did we have to wait long for the sublime breach. Some fifty yards away, a whale shot into the air, exuberantly twisted his full exposed length sideways, and, as if in slow motion, settled back upon the water with a mighty crash.

I was standing in the very front of the bowsprit, a tongue of metal that juts out from the boat. From there I could peer straight down into the water, so clear and calm that I could see twenty or thirty feet below the surface. I was then treated to the most majestic sight of all: with great deliberation, a whale swam slowly across the bow of the ship, directly below my eyes. Through the transparent water I could see his whole body. Under his gray-black back, his belly shimmered a dappled, whitish gray-green. He was as big as a sixteen-wheel tractor-trailer and as graceful as Fred Astaire. Then, breaking the surface a few yards from the bow, he let loose with a great blow, drenching us all in whale-mist. This was beyond the experience even of Melville's Ishmael, who reports, at second hand, that the whale's exhalation is foul and acrid. But my whale's breath was mild and odorless. As the ship turned to make for port, I felt damp but happy, and much moved.

PORTENTOUSNESS is the pitfall of whale writing. Melville recognized this, joking in Chapter 104 of *Moby-Dick* that he quarried his grandiloquent cetological vocabulary from a huge folio edition of Johnson, because the bulk of both lexicon and lexicographer made that dictionary especially suitable to the purpose. In the late eighties, earnestness about such whole-grain causes as whale preservation is unfashionable to the point of embarrassment. Even in sixties-throwback P-town, SAVE THE WHALES bumper stickers are less common than NUKE A GAY WHALE FOR CHRIST ones, which make the same point (and a couple of others) with a layer of self-protective jokiness. Nevertheless: save the whales.

—Cape Cod Diarist, *The New Republic*, September 7, 1987

THE SHORT HAPPY LIFE OF THE
AMERICAN YUPPIE

IT IS A GRAY DAWN when they come for the last yuppie. He is in an emergency detention center for cultural offenders, a loft building in lower Manhattan that has been converted many times. Built as a prison in the mid-nineteenth century, it has been, successively, a warehouse, a sweatshop, an artists' studio, and a luxury loft condominium; now it has come full circle. The yuppie's cell is roomy but very dark, so dark the pressed-tin ceiling and exposed brick walls cannot be seen. His last meal—a simple poached salmon, an arugula and endive salad, a white chocolate mousse, a California Chardonnay, Saratoga water, decaf espresso—remains almost untouched on one end of the Alvar Aalto table. He has sat all night at the other end, writing final letters—to his wife, his mother, his broker—in the little pool of light given off by the Conran's lamp he was allowed to bring in with him. He looks tired, the skin of his youthful face drawn under the tan. His Perry Ellis shirt and his Giorgio Armani trousers are a little wrinkled but clean. He has lived well. He plans to die the same way. When the guards come, he rises and greets them with grave dignity, then walks between them to the elevator and out into the central courtyard. As he stands blindfolded against the wall, the pitiless sentence of the Zeitgeist Tribunal is read aloud. The Commissioner of Revolutionary Public Safety offers him a final cigarette.

"Certainly not," the last yuppie says in a firm, even voice. "And as long as I am here, thank you for not smoking."

The commissioner steps back. The members of the firing squad raise their rifles. "Ready . . . aim . . ."

WELL, ONE CAN DREAM, no? But even if the revolution is not at hand, even if, on the contrary, the flow of Cajun restaurants, bijou grocery stores, futon dealerships, and vertical racquet clubs is at this moment reaching a flood tide of unprecedented frenzy, there are ample signs that "the yuppie phenomenon" is doomed—that it is, as Nicholas von Hoffman said of Richard Nixon a few months before his fall, the dead mouse on America's kitchen floor, and the only question is when someone will pick it up by the tail and deposit it in the trash.

To all appearances, yuppiedom seems to be still thriving. But the yup-towns of our coastal cities, where one is seldom more than a few blocks from a designer ice-cream outlet or a branch of Banana Republic, have been over-built by speculators gripped by the delusion that trend lines never change direction. The gleaming, empty towers of yuppiedom betoken not prosper-ity but imminent collapse. The intimations—political, demographic, cul-tural, economic, journalistic, and culinary—are everywhere that yuppiedom is (to use a popular yuppie phrase, possibly connected with the well-known yuppie preference for grilled fish and crunchy vegetables) dead meat.

POLITICAL INTIMATIONS. Yuppiedom is essentially a phenomenon of the Ronald Reagan era, inextricably tied to the values, follies, and peculiar conditions thereof. The word *yuppie* shot from obscurity to ubiquity dur-ing the 1984 presidential campaign and became associated with the two politicians who squeezed Walter Mondale's head like the tongs in an Ex-cedrin commercial, Gary Hart and Reagan himself. In 1987 Hart toppled off his perch like a coal-mine canary. As for Reagan, whose upscale eco-nomic policies, the *Wall Street Journal* once opined, "entitle him to inscrip-tion as the most aged Yuppie"—well, as of Inauguration Day 1989 at the latest, he's history.

Demographic intimations. Reagan notwithstanding, a yuppie is by defi-nition young. Or at least youngish. And today's youngster is tomorrow's geezer. It would be cruel to dwell on what it is like to spend hours in the li-brary squinting at *The Statistical Abstract of the United States,* but the bot-tom line (another yup favorite) is that a huge yuppie-age bulge, the famous baby boom, is moving through the population like a puppy through a python. The older members of this bulge have reached an age at which youth is something one feels nostalgic for. Just as crime dropped during the early 1980s when the younger baby boomers finally made it out of their teens, so yuppieness will fade when the older ones start moving to Florida. The Age of Aquarius ended when "aging hippie" became a routine sneer. We will soon begin hearing about "aging yuppies."

Cultural intimations. (1) For the fall season, ABC introduced a program called (and, irritatingly, spelled) *thirtysomething*, which treats the banal dilemmas of everyday yuppie life with *Masterpiece Theatre*-like reverence. (2) Your mother wears running shoes. (3) The *Readers' Guide to Periodical Literature*, which indexes magazines, had no items under "Yuppies" for the years 1900 to 1983 inclusive. For 1984 it had nineteen. For 1985 it had twenty-six. For 1986 it had fourteen. For the first three quarters of 1987 it had twelve. Now the bottom has dropped out. In the most recent monthly update of the "Readers' Guide," the entry reads as follows, in its entirety:

Yuppies—*See also* Dinks

Economic intimations. Until the great stock market crash of October 19, 1987, it had never occurred to yuppiedom that there might ever again be such a thing as a downturn in the business cycle. The crash wiped the condescending smile off many a smooth yuppie mug. The jokes began to circulate within hours of the Dow's 508-point tumble. (What's the difference between a pigeon and a yuppie stockbroker? A pigeon can still make a deposit on a new Mercedes.) But even before Black Monday, it was becoming clear that throughout the whole of the period of what was officially described as prosperity, the foundations of the economy were being systematically undermined by wild borrowing, excessive consumption, decreased savings, lunatic speculation, and unbridled corporate cannibalism—the full range of yuppieish follies that go by the name of Reaganomics. All this guarantees that the next recession will be nasty. When it really takes hold, as it is already beginning to, yuppiedom will be swept away, taking all the sushi-to-go outlets and chichi local business magazines with it.

Journalistic intimations. DROP SEEN AS BLOW TO YUPPIES—*New York Times* headline, after the crash. WILL THE YUPPIES RISE AGAIN?—same paper, two weeks after that. SUNSET FOR YUPPIES—*USA Today*'s answer, two days after *that*.

The yuppie obits came in so thick and fast that in far-off England the editor of the *Daily Telegraph* sent a memo to his staff ordering a "complete ban" on the very word.

Culinary intimations. Burger King serves croissants.

The end, plainly, is near. It is time to quit wringing our hands and start pulling our chins. It is time to put the yuppie experience in—yes—perspective.

WHAT WE ARE dealing with here is something that began as a demographic category with cultural overtones and ended up as a moral category. *Yuppie* is now understood almost universally as a term of abuse. If you doubt this, try turning to the person next to you in exercise class and saying cheerily, *"You're* a yuppie. What's it like?"

At best, you'll get a slightly edgy, "I'm not a yuppie—I hate sun-dried tomatoes" or some such; at worst, the person may physically recoil. (You won't get punched, though; yuppies don't hit one another.) Why is everybody so defensive? The reason, of course, is that "you're a yuppie" is taken to mean not "you're a young urban professional" but rather "you have lousy values."

To understand how this came to be, it may help to draw back a bit and consider the history of the rise and picaresque adventures of the word and its many meanings.

The y-word itself seems to have been coined during the late 1970s, but hardly anybody used it until 1983. Bob Greene is generally credited with being the first to use it in print, in a syndicated *Chicago Tribune* column in March 1983. *Yuppie* became a national buzzword during the 1984 presidential campaign. It rose in lockstep with the political fortunes of Senator Gary Hart, but it did not fall with them. The media fad for yuppiedom continued to build, climaxing with a cover story, "The Year of the Yuppie," in the December 31, 1984, issue of *Newsweek*. The cover illustration, by Garry Trudeau, showed Mike Doonesbury, in business suit and backpack and mounted on a ten-speed bike, crossing a bridge in a city park alongside a briefcase-carrying Joanie Caucus, in skirt, blazer, pearls, Walkman, and New Balance running shoes.

Everybody agreed from the start that a yuppie had to be a baby boomer, one of the seventy million Americans born between 1946 and 1964. Beyond that, the category was, and is, played like an accordion. If yuppies are people who make forty thousand dollars a year or more, live in cities, and work in professional or managerial jobs (the high end of *Newsweek*'s several definitions), then there are only about a million and a half of them. If they are just baby boomers who went to college, live in metropolis areas, and work in offices (the low end), there are more than twenty million.

Everybody also agreed from the start that yuppiedom was at least as much a matter of "lifestyle" as of statistics. Yuppies were defined more by what they consumed than what they produced. What they produced (as lawyers, brokers, bankers, accountants, consultants, executives) was intangible. What they consumed was quite tangible, a lot of it was imported, and a lot of it cried out to be made fun of. Right from the start, any random list of yuppie consumables—raspberry vinegar, Akitas, chèvre, Beamers (BMWs)—was good for a laugh, especially from yuppies themselves.

But along with the good-natured jokes, moral demolition of this new category began almost at once. When Gary Hart started winning primaries in 1984, the press and the political community flailed about for an explanation. The forces of Walter Mondale were ready to provide one. "Mondale's aides cannily strove to diminish Hart's appeal by restating it as one of class," William A. Henry III wrote in *Visions of America*, his fine history of the campaign, "and helped persuade the press to adopt a shorthand term for a previously unrecognized group, the Yuppies."

Yuppie promptly went into a moral free fall that continued long after Reagan was reelected. In a Roper poll taken in 1985, which found that 60 percent of adult Americans knew roughly what yuppies were (an impressive total, considering, for example, that only 34 percent know who is secretary of state), six times as many people thought yuppies were "overly concerned with themselves" as thought they were "involved in working for the betterment of poor people." When a half-dozen young go-go Wall Street investment bankers—prototypical yuppie heroes—were indicted for insider trading in the wake of the Ivan Boesky scandal, yuppiedom's descent into moral squalor was complete in all eyes but its own. That was accomplished by the crash, which brought yuppies face to face with something worse (in their eyes) than dishonor: failure.

The word, once relatively neutral, is now in routine use as a weapon of contemptuous dismissal. Examples can be found in every day's newspaper. Here is one from the fresh copy of the *New York Times* on my desk. Frank Rich is reviewing a new play. It is, he writes, "a cuter, softened *Streetcar Named Desire* for the yuppie 1980s, down to its Windham Hill-style jazz-fusion score and its upbeat ending." Yuppie equals silly. Yuppie equals superficial. Yuppie equals mindlessly bland.

Because the moral opprobrium attached to yuppiedom is so severe, the yuppie is always someone else. Consider the Harvard Business School, which the rest of the world regards as the holy of holies of yuppiedom—the secular monastery where the orthodoxy of money and success will be cherished and the sacred texts (*In Search of Excellence*, et cetera) preserved long after the dark ages return. Here we find a Cross pen in every inside pocket, an HP12C calculator in every Gucci briefcase, a Hermes scarf round every throat. Here we find a studied disdain for the unsuccessful: "The guy's a complete loser" is the most feared putdown. Here "V.C." means venture capital, not Viet Cong. Yet even here, among the only group of people in the world consisting entirely of future Harvard MBAs, the reluctance to be tagged with the y-word is palpable. To normal B-School students, yuppies are the ones who want to become investment bankers. To the future "eye-bankers," yuppies are the ones who will settle for nothing short of a job with one of the "bulge bracket" firms, such as Salomon, Morgan Guaranty, or First Boston. And in the eyes of the aspirants to employment with these firms, yuppies are the ones who will under no circumstances consider a job in the public finance or sales and training departments, insisting on corporate finance or mergers and acquisitions. As a check, I arranged to have one of these exotic creatures pointed out to me. I approached him—he was a windswept-looking young man in a V-neck sweater and wide-wale corduroys—and asked him politely if he was a yuppie. "No, not really," he said. "I mean, hey, I drive an American car."

YUPPIE, OF COURSE, is a play on words—many words. In the first instance, it is a play on *yippie,* the name adopted by Jerry Rubin and Abbie Hoffman for the Youth International Party they founded in 1968. The yippies were young, but they were neither international nor a party. They were a little band of anarcho-nihilist, media-manipulating politicos, who specialized in reducing solemn left-wing meetings to shambles with shouted demands for the abolition of pay toilets and who, gathering in Chicago's Grant Park during the 1968 Democratic National Convention, "nominated" Pigasus the Pig for president amid the fumes of tear gas and the thwack of police truncheons on longhaired heads. The connection between yippie and yuppie is direct. By 1983 Rubin, having dropped radicalism, was urging his former colleagues to join the "business community" and was promoting "networking" parties for young Wall Street types. It was one of those parties that was Bob Greene's hook for his column "Yippie vs. Yuppie," the one that introduced the new word to the general public.

Yippie, in turn, was a play on *hippie,* and here again the sinister, protean figure of Rubin makes an appearance. At the beginning of 1966, a year and a half before the "Summer of Love," hippies were still an embryonic phenomenon confined mostly to the Haight-Ashbury district of San Francisco. Apolitical and dreamy, the hippies had little contact with the radicals of Berkeley across the Bay. To bring the two communities of rebels, political and cultural, together, Rubin and others organized something called The Gathering of the Tribes for a Human Be-In, a rock-concert-cum-rally where some ten thousand people smoked pot, dropped acid, and listened to Allen Ginsberg chant "Ommm," the Grateful Dead and Quicksilver Messenger Service play hypnotic electric music, and people like Jerry Rubin denounce the Vietnam War and the established order. This event (which I attended, as it happened, a week before I went on active duty in the Navy) is as good a marker as any for the arrival of the counterculture as a mass movement. "Be-In" was itself a clever bit of wordplay (especially with "Human" in front of it), combining the political sit-in and teach-in with the psychedelic-mystical be-here-now to symbolize the marriage of the strains that produced the distinctive mass youth culture of the baby boomers, and eventually—so sinuously and unpredictably does the dialectic work its mysterious will—yuppies.

Hippies thought property was theft; yuppies think it's an investment. Hippies were interested in karma; yuppies prefer cars. Hippies liked mantras; yuppies like manna. Still, yuppiedom carried over from hippiedom an appreciation for things deemed "natural," an emphasis on personal freedom, and the self-absorption of that part of the counterculture known as the human-potential movement.

The etymological connection between yuppie and hippie is a reminder that the special power and poignancy of the yuppie idea cannot be understood without reference to that earlier time. And the 1960s get it coming and going. Among those members of the baby boom old enough to have experienced the sixties firsthand, yuppiedom is an expression of disillusionment (sometimes masking nostalgia). Among those too young for such direct experience, it is an expression of Oedipal revolt (sometimes masking envy).

The cleavage is sharp between the two kinds of yuppies, older and younger. And the older ones—those aged about thirty-two and above—are much, much more defensive.

The other ancestor of *yuppie* is, of course, *preppy*. *The Yuppie Handbook*, by Marissa Piesman and Marilee Hartley, was a clever, best-selling knock-off of the even more popular *Official Preppy Handbook*, edited by Lisa Birnbach and published in 1980; the connection was strong enough that the authors of the former felt obliged to title their opening chapter "Beyond the Preppie." We thus arrive at the pseudo-social science (to be redundant) formula $y = h + p$, a handy way of summarizing the most important streams that fed the yuppie flood. Yuppies partook of the preppies' interest in law, banking, racquet sports, and expensive clothes as badges of status. But yuppiedom, like hippiedom, is a democratic realm. Anyone can be a yuppie, just as anyone could be a hippie, while preppydom is, or pretends to be, an aristocracy of birth, a bastion of hereditary privilege. Ethnic minorities stand outside the charmed circle. Jews, for example, can go to prep school, and they have even been admitted to the most exalted eating clubs at Princeton, the most exclusive secret societies at Yale, the snootiest final clubs at Harvard; but even if they are named Guggenheim or Lehman, their preppyness is always provisional. No one named Lisa Birnbach can ever be a preppy in the fullest sense. What *The Official Preppy Handbook* did was enable Lisa Birnbach to become a yuppie. If one of yuppiedom's least-attractive consequences was to make money the measure of all things, one of its not-very-numerous redeeming features was to reduce somewhat the prestige of inherited wealth.

In the preppy variant of snobbery, material objects—the clothes, the cars—were implicitly viewed as the outward signs of an innate superiority. In the yuppie dispensation, status was conferred by the objects themselves. One no longer had to be part of a class to acquire artifacts of that class. This was a logical result of the commercialization of bohemia and the reduction of "good taste" to a series of tidy, standardized formulas pioneered by *New York* magazine and eagerly picked up by the whole of the upscale press. Status became a commodity; sensibility became something that could be ordered out of a catalogue. In the final nightmare, the Beatles' "Revolution" was sold to be used as a jingle in an athletic shoe advertisement, and the Byrds' version of Pete Seeger's "Turn, Turn, Turn," was auctioned off for similar humiliation at the hands of a newsmagazine.

Part of the pathos of yuppiedom is that the products yuppies so assiduously consume are more upwardly mobile than the people who consume them. The nickel Popsicle went public and became the $2.00 Dove Bar. The workman's dungarees split two-for-one and became the $50.00 pair of Guess jeans. The neighborhood joint serving dollar burgers and working-class American beer (Budweiser) got its MBA and became O. Henry's Drinking Establishment, serving $6.95 potato skins and working-class Mexican beer (Corona). The YMCA issued junk bonds and became a Nautilus health club. The repositioning of humble items of food and clothing as pricey, status-drenched luxuries is the signal triumph of yuppie marketing.

In Boston, where I've lived for the past couple of years, the restaurant of the moment is the Blue Diner. It is a "real" diner, built in 1947. The new people cleaned out the grease and spiffed up the old woodwork, and they serve "real" diner food: meat loaf, macaroni and cheese, American chop suey. But because this is a yuppie diner, the dishes are perfectly cooked and made with good, fresh ingredients. It costs three times as much as a "real" diner; on the other hand, the food is better—not three times better, but better. Such restaurants are yuppie culture at its best. The food's fine, but the customers' real appetites are social, not physical.

THE QUESTION REMAINS: why is everybody so mad at yuppies, including people who by any reasonable definition are yuppies themselves? "What, after all, is so terrible about quiche?" Michael Kinsley asks in a typically contrary 1984 essay entitled "Arise, Ye Yuppies!" Kinsley is comparing the 1980s to that previous era of self-satisfied consumption, the 1950s. "Are jogging and spinach salad really more decadent than golf and sirloin?" he asks. "Is the journey from an obsession with the perfect martini to an obsession with California Chardonnay really another stage in the decline and fall of American civilization?" Martinis have made a comeback, but the basic point remains valid. Many aspects of yuppie culture are clearly superior to what they replaced: small, efficient cars against gas-guzzling behemoths; neighborhoods of restored brownstones against suburban subdivisions; Woody Allen movies against Doris Day movies; gay friends against "homosexual panic"; the woman in the Liz Claiborne skirt against the man in the gray-flannel suit.

The fact is that for the most part, today's yuppies have better taste than yesterday's well-off young adult Americans, are less ostentatious in their display of wealth, are more apt to choose natural ingredients and fabrics over the chemical kind, set a far better example of healthful living, and are more tolerant. The source of the anger against them is not to be found in their own obnoxiousness or selfishness or hypocrisy, none of which is particularly striking. The source of the anger against them is to be found in the falseness of what they have been made to represent.

The premise of most of what has been said, written, filmed, and broadcast about yuppies goes like this: the yuppie is emblematic of his time and generation. He is a synecdoche—the part that stands for the whole. In a time of prosperity, boundless opportunity, soaring hope, et cetera, he is the vanguard, the leading edge. He is like everybody else, only more so. We're all doing well; he's just doing a little bit better. He is simply a sharper, more dramatic instance of a trend that is general throughout the society. Therefore he is a fitting symbol of his age.

Implicit in the premise is a promise: that we all can be, will be, yuppies. Both premise and promise are false. The anger at the yuppie is really anger at a lie.

Consider a few facts, dry but damning. They come from a just-published monograph called *Dollars and Dreams: The Changing American Income Distribution,* published by the Russell Sage Foundation and written by the respected economist Frank Levy.

During the decade between 1973 and 1984—the decade that ended by spitting out the word *yuppie*—the median American family saw its income *drop* from $28,200 to $26,433 (measured in 1984 dollars, as are all these examples). At the same time, the proportion of Americans classified as poor grew by nearly a third.

But who cares? The poor and the average are species yuppies scorn. What about our heroes? Well, the very rich got very much richer, but even people in yuppie income brackets had their problems. In 1973, families in what economists call the highest "quintile"—that is, the top fifth—were earning a mean average income of $68,278. In 1984,they were making less— $66,607, to be exact. That's nothing to hold a telethon over, of course, especially when the income of the poorest quintile was dropping at the same time from $9,136 to $7,297. But it's not the bonanza suggested by all the fuss about yuppies either. It's stagnation.

The baby-boom generation was brought up in the 1950s and 1960s to assume that the little lines on the economic charts would keep going up and up forever. It hasn't worked out that way. Despite all the blather about "going forth" and "morning in America," despite all the gourmet mustard and CD players, reality has fallen sadly short of expectations.

Consider: In 1973, men who worked full time had a median income of $26,000. If things had continued to go the way they did when the yuppies were kiddies, this would have hit $31,000 in 1984. In fact, men who worked full time in 1984 had a median income of $23,218.

Consider: In the 1950s and 1960s, a man of twenty-five could expect that his real income would increase some 110 percent by the time he was thirty-five. But a twenty-five-year-old in 1973 saw his income over the next ten years increase by only 16 percent.

Consider: The proportion of young married couples whose income exceeded $35,000 (again, in constant 1984 dollars) was exactly the same in 1984 as in 1973—and in 1973 many more of them were doing it on one paycheck.

Consider: In the 1950s, a typical thirty-year-old man needed 14 percent of his before-tax earnings to make the mortgage payments on a typical house. By 1973 this had risen to 21 percent, still not that bad. But by 1984, writes Levy emphatically, "a thirty-year-old man—now a member of the baby-boom cohorts—would have had to spend *44 percent* of his gross earnings to carry a median-priced home."

One thing that did go up during the pre-yuppie decade was consumer spending per capita, which rose by 15 percent. But that was not because everybody cut their hair and went into investment banking. It was because more women were working and because of a greater willingness to go into debt.

Levy again:

"The other thing that kept going up was anxiety, reflected in the mounting emphasis young people put on making money. For twenty years the American Council on Education has been polling college freshmen about their values, including the importance to them of 'being very well off financially.' Before 1972 this was rated as 'essential' or 'very important,' the two highest possible ratings, by about half the freshmen polled. In 1973 it jumped to 63 percent, and now it's comfortably into the 70s."

One side of the yuppie myth tells college kids that a BMW, a condo, and a summer place in the Hamptons is the just and expectable reward for a bit of hard work and cleverness. What they actually see around them tells them nothing of the kind. The other side of the yuppie myth tells them that if they're worried about money it's because they're selfish little creeps who want to pig out on sushi. In reality, they're worried because there's plenty to worry about.

Connoisseurs of linguistic trivia will recall that for a brief time, *yuppie* had competition from *yumpie*. (HERE COME THE YUPPIES!—headline in *Time*, January 9, 1984. HERE COME THE YUMPIES!—ditto, March 26, 1984.) Lumpy, frumpy *yumpie* lost out because it had a discouragingly unglamorous sound, because it lacked *yuppie's* rich associational resonances, and because the "um" in it stood for "upwardly mobile," as against yuppie's more cautious "urban." If you define being upwardly mobile as having more status than your old man, then yes, those designated as yuppies are also yumpies. According to the Mayer Mobility Measure, a new social-science scam expressly created for this article (I won't go into the details, but the MMM entails impressive piles of computer printouts, the product of crunching University of Chicago numbers on a Harvard computer), fully 75 percent of yuppies work at more prestigious jobs than their fathers did, compared with just 48 percent of non-yuppie adults. But if upwardly mobile means you live better than your parents did and you're sure your children in turn will live better than you—the American Dream is another name for this—then no. The vast majority of those tagged yuppies by the media have been heading down, down, down for more than a decade, and the worst is yet to come. The very word *yuppie* is a taunt, a lie, a fraud: insult added to injury.

ONE PERSON who understood almost from the beginning that there was something wrong with the yuppie paradigm was Ralph Whitehead, a professor at the University of Massachusetts and a Democratic Party guerrilla demographer whom Senator John Kerry once described as a cross between David Reisman and David Letterman. Since 1985, in articles and speeches, Whitehead has been arguing that the baby-boom generation is far too variegated and interesting to be stuffed into a single rubric. To take account of that variety, Whitehead came up with some alternative bumper-sticker categories of his own.

He pointed out that there are as many as twenty-five million baby boomers struggling along on family incomes between twenty thousand dollars and forty thousand dollars, a postindustrial working class whose members do the kinds of jobs that fall somewhere between physical labor and middle-management pencil pushing. They listen to rock and roll and they know what marijuana smells like, but they have kids to support.

They are trying in their own ways to fuse traditional values such as family and community with newer imperatives such as self-expression and individuality. Their idea of a good guy is Captain Furillo of *Hill Street Blues,* the tough cop who's not afraid to cry. These people are not yuppies. They are the sons and daughters of the old blue-collar class. With intentional rhyming resonance, Whitehead calls them the New Collars.

As for the new class of knowledge workers, Whitehead calls them, in another bit of postindustrial rhyming slang, the Bright Collars. Because the Bright Collars have some yuppie markings, they are sometimes victims of mistaken identity. There are nineteen million of them. They are knowledge workers—middle managers, social workers, teachers, bureaucrats, most lawyers, software engineers—products of the economic and technological transformation that has affected the age scale from the bottom up. ("As for yuppies," Whitehead says, "I haven't made up my mind yet if there's a thin, snotty stratum of them across the top of the Bright Collars or if *yuppie* is just the latest term for the top 3 percent of the American upper class. Or both.")

Unlike yuppies, neither New Collars nor Bright Collars are defined by consumption. They are defined by their place in a postindustrial society and economy that places a premium on differentiation and rejects the social principles of uniformity and patriarchy that have governed most of this century.

"If there's one thing that has come through in all the interviews and focus groups I've done with baby boomers, it's that these people have big egos but weak identities," Whitehead told me. "The big egos come from Dr. Spock, from the loosening of all kinds of moorings, from the sheer *size* of the baby-boom generation, which has gotten them used to being the center of attention throughout their lives. They really want to be somebody, but their culture and life experience no longer offers them the kind of off-the-rack identities that were available to their parents: 'Mom,' 'Dad,' 'homemaker,' 'soldier,' 'man,' 'woman,' 'American'—the big-ticket identities of the nineteen-forties and fifties. American culture was an assembly line. A handful of identities rolled out of the factory and you fit yourself to one. If you weren't black or gay or an artist or an uppity woman it was a pretty good system.

"But now the typical baby boomer is like a balloon stretched very tight. The air is the big ego and the thin, tightly stretched rubber is the identity. One pinprick and you're gone. Having to go elbow deep into the raw materials of American culture and fashion your own identity is tough. That's why a ready-made identity—especially if it has a nice sheen, like yuppie—was so attractive."

Whether or not one accepts Whitehead's terms, he is surely right that the drama of a generation trying to understand itself requires new ways of talking. A new social order requires a new language to describe it. The yuppie idea is one early attempt. But the first tremors of a new zeitgeist can already be felt, and when Wall Street laid its big egg last fall the rumble became too loud to ignore. The eruption ought to be interesting. The shape of the post-yuppie world cannot be predicted. What can be predicted is that it will be as different from what went before as the 1930s were from the 1920s or the 1960s from the 1950s. And it can be predicted that sometime around the year 2018, people will begin to wonder if the world is due for another decade of upheaval—like the one back in the 1990s.

In the new, second edition of the *Random House Dictionary of the English Language, yuppie* takes its place alongside *flapper* and *zouave,* just another word among 315,000 others. Entombed in the fine print, it will have a kind of existence—just as the carved letters on a tombstone have a kind of existence.

Shout out: Who killed the Yuppie? The answer is, It was you and me. We turned him into an effigy, and then we hanged him. He became the collective projection of a moral anxiety. We loaded onto him everything we hated about the times we had been living through—everything we hated about what we suspected we ourselves might have become. We made the yuppie the effigy of selfishness and self-absorption, of the breakdown of social solidarity, of rampant careerism and obsessive ambition, of the unwholesome love of money, of the delusion that social problems have individual solutions, of callousness and contempt toward "losers," of the empty ideology of winnerism and the uncritical worship of "success." Then we strung the little bastard up.

He won't be missed. Still, the food was good. I hope we can keep the food.

—*Esquire,* February 1988

BOOK HIM

FORTY YEARS AGO, people used to wonder what John F. Kennedy was going to get up to once he wasn't president anymore. His circle gloated that he would be only fifty-one after his second term. His plans for the post-White House years were unfixed. He talked vaguely of going back to the Senate, or being president of Harvard or Yale, or getting his hands on a newspaper—the New York *Herald Tribune*, perhaps, or the *Boston Globe*, or one of the Washington dailies. (Maybe he would have been the one to give Woodward and Bernstein the green light to pursue the Watergate story, except that, with J.F.K. around, Richard Nixon would never have been president.) Health permitting, Kennedy would have remained a power through the 1990s and beyond. "Clear it with Jack" might have become the Democratic mantra. If he were alive today he would be eighty-four—just right for a pinochle game with Saul Bellow, Nelson Mandela, and the pope.

One thing that ex-President Kennedy would have had to cope with would have been a slow, steady, decades-long drizzle of embarrassing revelations about his extramarital sentimental entanglements. For ex-President Clinton, that problem has already been taken care of. The Monica Lewinsky mess is a big reason that the deal Clinton made last week with Alfred A. Knopf will bring him a record advance. But nobody expects a dirtier book than the one Kenneth Starr has already written. Clinton's mortifying secrets have already been revealed, in rather too vivid detail. He can decide to spin them, interpret them, ignore them, or illuminate them, but he can't decide to keep them. Clinton's editors at Knopf, Robert Gottlieb and Sonny Mehta, were said to have been impressed by their new author's familiarity with and analyses of the memoirs of his predecessors. As Clinton knows, the presidential memoir is a relatively new phenomenon; and the territory of the *good* presidential memoir is entirely uncharted. Grant's memoir remains the best book ever written by an ex, but it was about his brilliant generalship, not his somewhat less brilliant presidency. (His editor, one Samuel L. Clemens, was almost as distinguished as Bob Gottlieb.) John Quincy Adams, Theodore Roosevelt, and Calvin Coolidge wrote memoirs of a sort, but the genre began in earnest at midcentury, when Herbert Hoover plunked down three indigestible volumes he had been hoarding and revising for twenty years. Since then, nearly every president who lived to tell the tale has tried to do so. (The sole exception is Bush the elder, who, in lieu of memoirs, has published a collection of nice little notes, his favored literary form, and a gray foreign policy tome, co-authored with Brent Scowcroft.) The memoirs of Truman, Eisenhower, Johnson, Nixon, Ford, Carter, and Reagan have ranged from O.K. to awful, with each tending to be worse than the one before. All of them have flashes of interest, sometimes inadvertent, but even the best tend to be dull, humorless, and narcissistic. Carter's memoir, for example, was as big a stinker as any other presidential doorstopper with an embossed dust jacket and an overoptimistic press run. He has since become a prolific and unghosted author of "small" books. Their variety is highly eccentric (a book about fishing, a children's story illustrated by his daughter, a collection of poems), but among them are a couple of mini-memoirs of genuine value, one about his first race for state senator and the other about his rural childhood. It's as if he were going back and doing the memoir thing over again, bit by bit.

Clinton won't have that luxury—not with an eight-figure advance breathing down his neck. He's going to have to get it right the first time. His book is supposed to come out in 2003. Even if he spends every waking moment chained to a word processor (an unlikely prospect), that's way too early. Presumably, Knopf reasons that new news sells better than old news. But nuggets of news are not what people buy books for. People buy books for two reasons. One is to have them, as prestige items or decorator accents; and this has been enough to propel most of the other presidential memoirs onto the best-seller lists for a month or two. The other reason is to read them. And for people to want to read them, they have to be—by some standard or other (however debased), in some way or other—good.

Knopf may or may not be right that the commercial value of the book will diminish with time, but in every other way delay will be of the essence. The book will have a better shot at literary (and maybe even commercial) success if it is published in 2005 or later—and not just because it wouldn't have to share the spotlight with (or hog the spotlight from) Hillary's and could be written without worries about how it might affect the 2004 election. Bill Clinton, it must be said, don't know nothin' 'bout birthin' books. His only previous foray into the field was a banal, slapped-together 1996 policy pamphlet whose title *(Between Hope and History: Meeting America's Challenges for the Twenty-first Century)* was nearly as long as its text. No one doubts that Clinton has the intellect, the energy, and (no snickering, please) the imagination to write something worth reading; the question is whether he has the perseverance, the discipline, and the patience. Authors crave approval as much as politicians do, but book-writing is lonely, spartan work. Round-the-clock gregariousness is not part of the job description.

Taking it slow isn't the same as taking it easy, the latter being one way in which Clinton runs second to his successor. Last week, on the same front page that carried (above the fold) the story of Clinton's book deal, the *Washington Post* reported (below the fold) on the kickoff of George W. Bush's summer vacation—four full weeks, a holiday worthy of a retired bond dealer or a German factory worker. By Labor Day, the *Post* calculated, "Bush will have spent 42 percent of his presidency at vacation spots or en route." Whether you think this is a good thing or a bad thing depends on how you like the results when Bush exerts himself. But at least it'll make for a shorter memoir.

—*The New Yorker*, August 20 & 27, 2001

13. 2000 + 9/11 = 2004

It's early yet. But so far, the third millennium, A.D., has been a severe disappointment.

It started out promisingly enough. The final third of the twentieth century, from 1966 to 2000, saw so much improvement in so many parts of the world that the soiled old idea of Progress seemed to be making a comeback. In 1966 humanity was hostage to a seemingly permanent Cold War, a militarized standoff that could end only in nuclear holocaust and therefore could not end at all. The United States was trapped in a hot corner of that Cold War. By pouring bombs, blood, and treasure into Vietnam, we were sullying our reputation, corrupting our institutions, and sapping our belief in ourselves. In our domestic politics, there were early tremors of the reactionary convulsions that would bring Richard Nixon and eventually Ronald Reagan to power. In 1966 the walls of formal racial oppression in the American South had not yet fallen, while in South Africa Nelson Mandela, sentenced to life imprisonment for treason, was breaking rocks in a prison lime quarry.

By the turn of the century the Soviet Union had ceased to exist. Russia in 2000, if not quite a democracy, was as free a country as, say, Mexico in

1980. The Cold War had ended peacefully, snuffing out the guttering candle of the totalitarian idea. (The secular totalitarian idea, that is; religious totalitarianism is another matter. In retrospect the Cold War looks more like a civil war within the secular, industrial West than a global conflict between "East" and "West.") Even in China, Communism was moribund as an ideology; the economy had gone capitalist, and the Chinese Communist Party, while holding on to the levers of state power, had given up any pretense of controlling the inner lives of its subjects. In South Africa Nelson Mandela was a revered elder statesman, having just retired from the presidency of what was now a troubled but genuine multiracial democracy. The United States, under its first Democratic president since Franklin Roosevelt to be elected more than once, was enjoying unprecedented prosperity, declining rates of crime, poverty, and social pathology, and a budget surplus that held out the possibility of expanded public investments in education, health, and science. America, its power unchallenged, faced no mortal enemies. Or so it seemed.

Things began to go wrong on Tuesday, November 7, 2000, deteriorated further on Tuesday, December 12, 2000, and got unimaginably, frighteningly worse on Tuesday, September 11, 2001.

On the first of those three Tuesdays, a hundred and seven million Americans went to the polls and, by a small but clear margin, chose Al Gore over George W. Bush to be the next president of the United States. But because of the way the national vote was distributed, the electoral college outcome depended on Florida, where Bush's brother was governor and his state campaign co-chairman the official charged with supervising elections.

On the second Tuesday, the United States Supreme Court peremptorily awarded the presidency to Bush. The decision was so shoddily reasoned and transparently partisan that the five justices who endorsed it declined to put their names on it, while the four dissenters did not bother to conceal their disgust. If the Court had allowed the Florida recount to go forward, Bush most likely would have become president anyway. The Republicans in control of the Florida legislature had made it clear that they were prepared to appoint their own slate of electors if the voters' slate was not to their liking. The election might have been thrown into the House of Representatives, as the Constitution specifies in cases where no candidate has an electoral-college majority. In the House Bush would have won easily, because with each state delegation casting one vote, Wyoming, Montana, and Idaho outweigh California and New York, just as the Bahamas, Liechtenstein, and Belize outweigh China and the United States in the U.N. General Assembly. Settling the election by the rules would have been messy and drawn out, and it would have forcibly reminded everyone of the truth in the old John Birch Society slogan "America is a republic, not a democracy." But rules are rules, and by ignoring them—by cutting off the process and installing Bush by fiat—the Court made a mockery not only of popular democracy but also of constitutional republicanism. Pardon my French, but Bush's installation was a *coup d'état.* Or, if French is no longer pardonable, it was what the Latins call an *autogolpe,* the sort of coup, usually bloodless, that is carried out from within the existing civilian governmental structure.

September 11, of course, was the blackest Tuesday of all. Not since Antietam had there been a day when so many died violently on American soil. In fact, the attacks on the World Trade Center and the Pentagon were the bloodiest acts of non-state terrorism in the history of the world. Horrific in themselves, they were all the more frightening because of what they revealed about the vulnerability of open societies and what they portended for the future. The existential threat of global nuclear conflagration had disappeared a decade earlier, and we had grown used to breathing easier.

Now came a new danger, less comprehensive but more relentless, more intimate, more irrational.

This new kind of terrorism—amplified by technology, carried out by undeterrable fanatics, controlled by no authority, and having no fixed address—cannot destroy the world. But it is far more likely than the superpowers' nuclear arsenals ever were to destroy certain parts of certain cities—cities important to the terrorists' demonology, New York not least. And the prospect that terrorism will disrupt economies and provoke reactions damaging to free societies threatens everyone.

The Bush administration's response to 9/11 was energetic and ruthless, but its energy was often misdirected and its ruthlessness not always aimed at its ostensible targets. The administration quickly squandered the national and international solidarity that had been the only beneficial side effect of the attacks. It brushed aside as irrelevant NATO's instant and unprecedented invoking of the all-for-one clause of its founding treaty, thus forfeiting the opportunity to give Europe an ownership share in the "war on terror," which soon became America's war, not humanity's. The administration resisted the idea of a new government department to coordinate domestic security, an idea that had originated with a pre-9/11, Clinton-era bipartisan commission. When it reversed itself and embraced the idea, it carefully poisoned the authorizing legislation with a union-busting pill, and then used the resistance of some Democratic senators (notably Max Cleland of Georgia, a triple-amputee hero of the Vietnam War) to smear them as unpatriotic and defeat them at the polls. And it shifted the focus of its attentions, along with the nation's formidable but limited resources, from Al Qaeda and terrorism to Iraq and "weapons of mass destruction."

For some liberals the war in Iraq was an easy call: they were, and are, against it. But for others—many others—it was not so easy. The debate among the latter went on in millions of living rooms and kitchens and cafés and offices, including the offices of *The New Yorker* (its pages, too). The debate also went on inside millions of skulls, including mine. In the runup to that war I ended up opposing it, but with great misgivings. In its aftermath— or, rather, in its second phase, which two years after the fall of Baghdad shows no signs of ending—I remain opposed, and my misgivings about my opposition have diminished.

It is now clear that Iraq's biological, chemical, and, most importantly, nuclear weapons did not exist. Public and Congressional support for the war, as well as the limited international support it enjoyed, was therefore purchased falsely and, to a degree not yet known, dishonestly. It is clear that there was no connection between Iraq and 9/11. It is clear that apart from the military assault itself, every aspect of the war, from buildup to sequel, has been mismanaged or worse, always on account of arrogance and ideological blindness. And yet, it is almost certainly true that the people of Iraq, despite the avoidable post-Saddam chaos and the suffering inflicted by insurgency and counterinsurgency, are better off without the murderous dictatorship that the "coalition" overthrew. Saddam Hussein was not just a "bad guy," he was the head of a regime that was as lethal as Stalin's to those brushed by its power. How could one not welcome the fall of such a regime? Of course, as a humanitarian exercise, the war has not been exactly cost-effective. Assuming Iraq does not drift into civil war, and assuming it eventually acquires a government that gives its people a modicum of physical security, basic services, and civil liberty, then we will have spent several hundred billion dollars, sacrificed the lives and limbs of many thousands of American soldiers and Iraqi civilians, and alienated untold numbers of friends and potential friends around the world in order to alleviate the plight of a nation of twenty million. That is noble, in a way. But even if such a happy eventuality comes to pass, the war will not necessarily have been retroactively justified. And think how much more suffering even half that money—never mind the human and political costs—might have relieved if directed elsewhere.

The most far-reaching argument for the war, the argument that energized the war's most determined advocates within the administration, was that it would somehow cut a Gordian knot in the Arab world. The liberation of Iraq would set in motion a cascade of changes within and among Arab and Muslim countries, pushing them toward democracy and secularism, shaking them out of their economic and social torpor, and eventually drying up the sources of Islamist terrorism. We don't know whether the Iraq war will end up having this effect. The signs, so far, are mixed, tending toward encouraging. We may never know, however, because even if the Arab world moves in a positive direction, and even if the struggle against terrorism seems to go well during the next few years, we will be hard put to be certain of the causes. Different policies might have produced, or not prevented, a similar result. We made many mistakes during the Cold War (Vietnam, Chile, Guatemala), but larger forces steered us to a favorable outcome in spite of them. *Post hoc ergo propter hoc* may be a logical fallacy or it may be merely a description. *Hoc* happens, and we can't always say why.

ONE QUADRENNIAL CYCLE later, I remain bitter about the election of 2000. I have not "gotten over it," and I do not expect to get over it until the White House has a new occupant. The fact that the 9/11 terrorists gave Bush what he could not earn on his own, a political majority, deepens the bitterness. War-bloated support, compounded by fear of terrorism: that is what enabled the Republicans to consolidate their control of the federal government by taking the Senate in 2002. And that, far more than gay nuptials or Karl

Rove's machinations, is why Bush won the second time around. His victory in 2004 is thought by many responsible observers to have wiped away the stain of 2000 and established his legitimacy as at last unchallengeable. I do not agree. After the *autogolpe*, it is customary for the new regime to be approved by plebiscite. *¡El presidente, sí!* The only reason Bush was even on the ballot this time was because of what happened last time, and what happened last time was not legitimate. Nevertheless, in 2004, Bush was elected. That I admit. But he was not "reëlected."

One person I decline to blame for the rise of George W. Bush is Al Gore. It has become axiomatic that Gore was a bad candidate in 2000. Too stiff, too patronizing, too much populist rhetoric, too much distancing himself from Clinton. Whatever. I said and wrote such things myself. Yet the stubborn truth remains: Gore did his job, which was to get more votes than the other guy.

Gore's plurality over Bush was several times that of John F. Kennedy over Richard Nixon in 1960. If you're going to rag on Gore for blowing it in '00, then, logically, you have to rag on Kennedy for blowing it in '60. (How *did* Kennedy blow it, by the way? The sailboats and the ridiculous Hahvahd accent? The preppy haircut? The obvious disdain for Middle America? The guy was a total elitist, that's for sure. But I think it was the debate. Kennedy was too slick, too smooth by half. A human being sweats. A grown man has whiskers. Kennedy showed he was neither.)

When I make this argument to friends, they say, "Gore should never have let it get within stealing distance." To me, this is like saying Masaryk was standing too near the window. But let it pass. Bad candidate or good, Gore, I feel certain, would have been a fine president. He was extraordinarily well prepared for the job, yet at the same time he was—is—a man of probing intelligence and curiosity, with, for a politician, an unconventional turn of mind. His presidency would have been interesting, surprising, a little quirky, even exciting.

Gore would have been the object of immediate, comprehensive, and contempt-laden abuse from the right-wing propaganda apparatus, of course. If the popular-vote/electoral-vote shoes had been on the other feet, the talk-radio assault on Gore's legitimacy would have been unusually vile. And I'm sure the apparatus would have blamed the Clinton-Gore-Hillary axis of evil for 9/11. But I haven't the slightest doubt that Gore would have run a far more intelligent, far more effective antiterror campaign than Bush has done. Gore's response would almost certainly have included the overthrow of the Taliban regime in Afghanistan; unlike Bush, Cheney, and Rumsfeld, he might even have committed enough troops to have prevented bin Laden's escape. Gore's response might also have included a threat to invade Iraq, but the threat would have been followed through only if Saddam's "nuclear program" had turned out to be genuine. Iraq or no Iraq, though, Afghanistan alone would have been enough to prompt a segment of the American left to turn on Gore. "Nader was right," these folk would have told each other. "This guy's as bad as Bush would've been, maybe worse."

John Kerry, while getting eight million more votes than Gore, failed to do what Gore did: win a plurality. Even so, Democrats have been far less inclined to blame Kerry than they were to blame Gore after 2000. In large part, this is because they themselves were invested in the campaign in a way they hadn't been four years earlier. Many Democrats, especially those who voted for Ralph Nader, had persuaded themselves that it didn't much matter who won in 2000. Few retained such illusions four years later. The 2004 campaign wasn't just Kerry's; it was theirs, and they were a more important part of it than he was. By measures both objective (checks written, hours and days volunteered) and subjective (intensity of feeling), the 2004 campaign was something new. It was a mass movement, an awakening of civil society, an expression of moral and civic seriousness.

It was commonly said that Kerry's supporters were motivated more by anti-Bush sentiment than by regard for their own candidate, but this misses the point. They were not, for the most part, "anti-Bush" (just as European critics of the Iraq war were not, for the most part, anti-American). Personal antipathy to Bush had little to do with their passion; neither did personal devotion to Kerry. They—we—opposed Bush on account of his policies, foreign and domestic, and saw Kerry as the vehicle for a set of alternative policies: a far from perfect candidate, but a decent, dignified, and honorable spokesman.

This is not to say that Kerry did not make mistakes. The most consequential of them was a failure to recognize that 2004 was essentially a one-issue campaign. The issue was terrorism. If he had understood this, his campaign and his ticket would have been quite different. (For a start, his running mate would have been Wesley Clark, not John Edwards.)

Kerry's strategists had polling data that showed majorities preferring their man's economic and other domestic policies to Bush's. The key to victory, they therefore concluded, was to change the subject. The trouble was that the voters Kerry was trying to persuade already knew perfectly well that they agreed with him on the economy; they were planning to vote against him anyway, because they thought Bush would be better at protecting them from terrorists. Shouting "But you agree with us on the economy!" louder and oftener could do nothing to answer their question, which was, "What good is a job if you're dead?" (It was this group that decided the election, which is why Bush has no mandate to privatize Social Security or eliminate the remaining progressive features of the tax code.)

Similarly, polls suggested that while a majority of voters approved of the president's "handling" of "terrorism," a majority disapproved of the war in Iraq. For this reason, the Kerry campaign made somewhat incoherent efforts to separate the two, attacking Bush for the latter while remaining relatively tongue-tied about the former. There was an empirical basis for these efforts, in the form of evidence that the desire of the Administration's most influential policymakers to invade Iraq long pre-dated 9/11. "War on terror" was an unfortunate and incomplete metaphor for a struggle of which diplomacy, intelligence-gathering, clandestine operations, and international police work are components at least as important as warfare. Nevertheless, the war on terror is a real phenomenon, and the Iraq war *is* part of it, because the Iraq war could not have been undertaken in its absence. The point is not that the two are unrelated, or that the one is merely a distraction from the other; it is that Iraq has been a self-inflicted setback in the war on terror, a strategic blunder—if not yet an outright defeat then a Pyrrhic victory.

Kerry understood that fear of the terrorist enemy was a major obstacle in the path of any challenger. That is why he laid so much stress on his own military service, which, in terms of simple physical courage, equaled or surpassed that of any presidential nominee since Theodore Roosevelt. In his four months in Vietnam, Kerry saw more action and exposed himself to more danger than most combat soldiers did in the four years of American participation in the Second World War. He was near the centerpoint of the concentric circles of his generation's sons of privilege: unlike Clinton and Cheney, he served; unlike Dan Quayle and George W. Bush, he went to Vietnam; unlike most of his fellow Vietnam veterans, he repeatedly faced enemy fire. And unlike all but a very few combat soldiers in all the century's wars, he not only risked death but inflicted it, close in. As Patton (or maybe just George C. Scott) might have put it, he made the other poor bastard die for his country. So why was Bush widely considered the more alpha male?

Everyone knows that Bush flew planes in the National Guard, but I doubt that one voter in a hundred knew that Kerry was a pilot, too; unlike Bush, he still is. (He has flown planes since he was a teenager, and has logged hundreds more flying hours than Bush.) Bush was a cheerleader; Kerry was an athlete, and he still finds release in daredevil sports, such as motorcycling and, yes, windsurfing. An old *Saturday Night Live* sketch asked the question: *¿Quien es mas macho?* The generally accepted view is that Bush's acquired cultural signifiers—Texas, baseball, regular-guy anti-intellectualism—trumped the real-world exploits of Kerry, whose habits and manners remain true to the background he shares with Bush (prep school, Skull and Bones, the New England Wasp ascendancy) even if he, unlike Bush, is no longer a reliable servant of their shared class interests.

But there's more than "culture" to why Kerry's military service didn't "work," politically. As the documentary filmmaker Errol Morris pointed out in a brilliant *New York Times* op-ed essay on the eve of Bush's second inauguration, Kerry painted his Vietnam service in the bold primary colors of "greatest generation" World War II nostalgia. But Vietnam was a morally complicated war, and Kerry's picture of his relation to it fatally lacked— dread word—nuance. What was unique about Kerry was that he was both a war hero and an antiwar hero. The two roles he played in the late nineteen-sixties were two sides of the same coin of conscience. Each half of his story deepened the other and gave it richer meaning, and the two together formed a "narrative" of maturation and character. In 2004, with the nation regarding itself as at war, Kerry decided to leave out the antiwar half of his bildungsroman. It's easy to understand why. But by leaving it out he invited the suspicion that he had something to hide. This was a gift to the group calling itself "Swift Boat Veterans for Truth," whose vicious "independent" campaign—which took the form of lies about Kerry's military service but was motivated by resentment of his post-military service—was a crucial element of Bush's electoral strategy. Kerry exposed the crime but was unable to explain the motive. Bush, meanwhile, constructed an alchemical "narrative"—the story of an aimless, irresponsible young man cleansed and reborn in Jesus Christ—that turned the lead of his combat-dodging, hard-partying, business-ruining twenties, thirties, and early forties into political gold.

Since the election, Kerry, in contrast to Gore four years earlier, has given many indications that he understands his duty to serve as a leader of the opposition. Perhaps he will run again in 2008, and, assuming he has learned from his mistakes, perhaps he will win. Certainly the Democrats will at some point regain control of the Senate. On the other hand, I do not expect to see the House of Representatives restored to Democratic control in my lifetime, though I do expect that in future elections Democratic candidates for Congress will garner substantially larger vote totals than Republican ones. But Republican state legislators, armed with computers and a singleminded will to power, have so perfected the science of gerrymandering that the people's vote will not be reflected in the people's house. That's one reason, one of many, that I find myself returning again and again to the need for structural reform of our imperfectly democratic political institutions.

BOTH SIDES NOW

RIGHT FROM THE START of the political season, it's been Clinton versus Clinton. No, not Bill versus Hillary—and, no, not Horndog Bill versus Statesman Bill. What seeing Al Gore and George W. Bush duke it out has most persistently called to mind is a contest between the two biggest personal political strengths of the current president of the United States. Like Clinton, one candidate has high intelligence—a penetrating mind, a command of the sweep and detail of public policy, and a wide-ranging intellectual curiosity. The other, also like Clinton, has emotional acuity—a talent for projecting ease and empathy, an ability to size up a person or a group of people, sense the vectors of hope and sentiment or anxiety and resentment rocketing around the room, and windsurf the breezes and gales of feeling toward his goal. It's been the analyst versus the salesman, the Apollo from Tennessee (via Washington, St. Albans, and Harvard) versus the Dionysus from Texas (via Kennebunkport, Andover, and Yale), thought versus instinct—in short, Smart Bill versus Warm Bill.

With those two sides to his coin, Clinton has managed to overcome formidable obstacles (many of his own making) and to mint surprising quantities of political gold. Gore and Bush went into their first televised debate last week each hoping to grab a piece of the other's half of the Clinton formula, and most of the post-debate analysis was devoted to assessing whether they had succeeded in addressing the weaknesses that, in their cases, are the conspicuous obverses of their strengths. The vice president was animated (for him), the governor well spoken (for him). But ninety minutes is a long time, and not much of it had expired before both men began to slip into the political-cartoon versions of themselves. Gore's audible sighs had the unattractive sound of condescension, and some of his anecdotes turned out to be inaccurate. Bush demonstrated that he knew enough about his own proposals to sketch them in outline, but he was helpless to defend them in argument. When Gore said repeatedly that his opponent's plans are skewed to favor the well-to-do, Bush could only reply, just as repeatedly, that Gore was guilty of "fuzzy math." (He was alluding, whether he knew it or not, to the arcane concept of "fuzzy logic," though he made it sound more like the stuffed dice over the dashboard.) Just what was wrong with Gore's arithmetic Bush did not or could not say.

The campaign of which that debate was, so far, the sodden climax is taking place under new and hopeful conditions, largely of Clinton's creation. Through unheralded perseverance and political skill, the president has succeeded in freeing the country from the fiscal (and ideological) binds that constricted political possibility for a generation. The result is political space in which proposals for public action can be considered on their merits and not simply dismissed as incompatible with public solvency. Bush deserves credit for using that new space to nudge his party away from the exotica of its extreme wing and toward an acknowledgment of social responsibility. With that, he may have changed his party for good, just as Clinton did his; Bush may be the first New Republican. He has a lively interest in certain issues, most prominently education. But there is little evidence that he acquired those interests until it became expedient to have them. Even his letters to his father, when the senior Bush was president, the *Times* reported recently, are mostly notes about job-filling and requests for autographs. Gore may be a bit of a drone and he has been known to pander, but he is also a rare phenomenon—a politician who formulated a series of substantive ideas about a difficult subject and then put them down in a book without the aid of a ghostwriter. Within the administration, he has been a force for focus, discipline, and firmness.

Bush and Gore are contemporaries who came to maturity against a particular background of public events: the civil rights struggle, the Vietnam War, Watergate, the emergence of environmentalism, "malaise," the Cold War and the nuclear arms race, Reaganism, and more. Gore thought hard and earnestly about all these things. Bush ran for Congress in 1978, but it was a race essentially without issues; he is not known to have come to grips with any public question until 1993. He was then forty-five years old and, having been frustrated in his attempts to become commissioner of baseball, took a flyer on a run for governor. Gore, by contrast, has always been alive to the difficulty of making his life and work correspond to his moral perceptions. The way the two men responded to Vietnam is the best example. Both voluntarily entered armed service, and both did so in large measure because it would have been embarrassing to their fathers if they hadn't. But Gore thought about his duty in broader terms, too. He was against the war and, after considering every option, including draft resistance and exile, concluded that the most useful contribution he could make to his beliefs would be to go into the Army, and to Vietnam, as an enlisted man. Bush's views on the war are unknown; he disposed of the problem by taking refuge as an officer in a unit of the Texas Air National Guard.

Vietnam, of course, brought out another pair of Clinton halves. The young Clinton saw the war as an agonizing challenge to conscience; he was more active in the antiwar movement than all but a few thousand of his contemporaries, much more so than Gore. Yet, like the young Bush, he looked for an easy way out. A spot in the stateside Guard would have suited him fine; in the event, he dodged and weaved until a low draft number came along to moot his problem. This was a case of Smart, Warm Bill versus Slick Willie. Come January, few will be sorry to see the back of Slick Willie. Smart Bill and Warm Bill are another story. At least one of them will be sorely missed. We'll find out which in November.

—*The New Yorker*, October 16 & 23, 2000

THEY'VE GOT PERSONALITY

AFTER THE POLLS CLOSE next week, we will learn what presidential politics in the year 2000 has been "about." Specifically, we will learn whether it has been about "issues" or about "personality."

If the campaign turns out to have been about "issues," then the Democratic nominee, Al Gore, will be elected, because he is the superior candidate in point of both command and positions. Positions, of course, are a matter of opinion. And the opinion here is that Vice President Gore has shown himself to be, in comparison with the Republican candidate, George W. Bush, more fiscally responsible (because he proposes to spend somewhat less of the chimerical surplus than does Governor Bush), more socially responsible (because he proposes to spend more of that surplus on social needs such as education and health care and divert less of it to individual consumption), and more egalitarian (because his plans for changing the tax code, combined with his spending plans, would ameliorate inequalities of wealth and income while Bush's would exacerbate them). To judge from the little that has been said during the campaign about America's relations with the rest of the world, Gore's foreign policy would be more energetic in its promotion of democratic values than Bush's, and probably more so than President Clinton's. Bush has offered few clues to what his foreign policy might be, except to say that he would build a missile-defense system whether or not it was technically workable or strategically advantageous and that he opposes the American military presence in Haiti (where, at last count, we had twenty-nine soldiers) and in the Balkans, where a unilateral withdrawal would have the effect of weakening the Western alliance and America's role within it. As for the superiority of Gore's command of the issues, this is not a matter of opinion—or, if it is, everyone's opinion is the same, even (to judge from his defensive jokes) Bush's: Gore knows more, understands more, and has thought more, and more coherently, about virtually every aspect of public policy, domestic and foreign, than Bush has.

On experience, which occupies a space somewhere between issues and personality, Gore is also the superior candidate. Bush's experience for all but six years of his adult life has been as a failed businessman in the Texas oil patch, and then as an arguably successful businessman in professional base-ball (not exactly a cutting-edge industry), where his role was that of a front man and his business success due largely to family connections and the use of public funds and the state's power of eminent domain in building a sta-dium. His sole foray into public life is the six years he has spent as gover-nor of Texas—a weak office, which he has held during an unchallenging period cushioned by unprecedented national prosperity. Gore's experience, twenty-four years of it as an elected government official at the national level, has been intense and, it is fair to say, distinguished. His experience compares favorably with that of anyone newly elected to the presidency for at least the past century and is inferior only to that of incumbent presidents running for reelection, and not all of them. Gore showed initiative and cre-ativity as a senator on environmental and strategic issues, and has done so as vice president in the areas of foreign policy and improving governmen-tal efficiency. By all accounts he has been an active and successful vice pres-ident, perhaps the best in the country's history.

Bush's point of superiority, then, is in the matter of "personality," and it is striking how narrowly that word seems to have been defined for electoral purposes. Personality apparently excludes, if not intelligence itself, then such manifestations of it as intellectual curiosity, analytic ability, and a ca-pacity for original thought, all of which Gore has in abundance and Bush not only lacks but scorns. Personality apparently excludes courage, which Gore, at least in comparison with Bush, also possesses. Gore put himself in harm's way during the Vietnam War; Bush did not. And Gore showed po-litical courage, to a modest but discernible degree, when as a senator he voted to support the Gulf War and engaged the question of strategic arms in a heterodox way that went beyond the well-meaning simplicities of the nuclear freeze movement. When he did these things it was clear that he might be putting his national political future at risk. Bush, as has been noted before in this space, has helped move the Republican Party away from antigovernment extremism and toward an acknowledgment of a degree of social responsibility. But these were obvious, and politically cost-free, moves in light of the collapse of the Gingrich revolution and the political and policy triumphs of Clintonism. Bush's main rival for the Republican nomination, John McCain, would actually have moved the party further in the same direction.

"Personality" is the descendant of what used to be called, back in the old days two or three months ago, "character." And character has seemed to mean, first, a disinclination to embarrass the country through spectacularly foolish sexual indiscretions, and, second, credibility. Bush and his running mate, Dick Cheney, have tried to get some mileage out of the first—how else can one interpret their solemn promises to restore "dignity" to the White House? (Gore's displays of sexual enthusiasm, though arguably indiscreet, are inarguably marital; and, if anything, he would make the country heartily sick of dignity.) But less was heard about dignity as the campaign progressed, and the Republican ticket's big focus shifted to credibility. Gore's tendency to embellish anecdotes, especially about himself, is real and undeniable. Even so, some of his alleged lies have turned out to be strongly rooted in factuality. He did not "create" the Internet, obviously, but he was one of a tiny handful of politicians who grasped its significance when it was in its infancy, and he did take the lead in writing legislation to spur its development. He and Tipper weren't the models for Oliver Barrett IV and Jennifer Cavilleri, in *Love Story*, but the young Albert Gore, Jr., was, according to the novel's author, Erich Segal, one of two models for Ollie. (Tipper, who is feisty but not Italian-American, was not a model for Jenny.) Other errors of Gore's have been insignificant or superfluous, such as his anecdote about a girl who had no desk in her science class of thirty-six students. It turned out that the desk shortage was limited to the day on which the photograph Gore saw was taken. The fact remains that a class of thirty-six is too large for effective teaching.

What gives the theme of Gore as liar its power is the cautionary example of Clinton's impeachable (if not convictable) falsehoods about the Monica Lewinsky episode; if it weren't for that, Gore's exaggerations, such as they are, might not even have been noticed, and there would almost certainly have been no attempt to paint him as a liar. Because of the Clinton factor,

Gore's exaggerations are seen as a moral problem. In the debates, Bush uttered inaccuracies that, unlike Gore's, falsify the underlying essence of his point—as, for example, when he said that Gore was outspending him in the campaign (when the reverse is true, to the tune of fifty million dollars) and that he fought to get a patients' bill of rights passed in Texas (when he actually vetoed one such bill and allowed another to become law without his signature), and that his health-care proposal would "have prescription drugs as an integral part of Medicare" (when this is precisely what Gore's plan would do, while Bush's would dismantle Medicare as we know it in favor of a system of subsidized private insurance). But these untruths have generally been chalked up to ignorance, not mendacity. It's the same with Bush's boast that, guess what, Texas is going to put three of James Byrd's killers to death, when the actual number slated for execution in that case is two. It is generally agreed that Bush did not realize that he was exaggerating; he was just a little fuzzy on the math. So he was not "lying" (though some of his hearers felt a moral chill all the same).

Apart from the mostly specious matter of credibility, "personality" comes down to likability. And likability is not even a matter of opinion; it is a matter of taste. Hard as it may be to believe, there are people here and there on the planet Earth who actually like Al Gore, and there may even be one or two who wonder if George W. Bush might not be such a nice guy after all. Still, there's no denying that a large number of people find Gore irritating; to prove it, there are polls, to say nothing of the panels of "undecided voters"—that is, clueless, ill-informed citizens who even at this late date cannot summon the mental energy to make up their minds—assembled by the television networks into on-camera focus groups. Gore can be awkward and tone-deaf, and he sometimes has trouble modulating his presentation of himself, and he plainly lacks the instinctive political exuberance of a Bill Clinton or even the slightly twitchy easygoingness of a George W. Bush. Gore is aggressive, assertive, and intensely energetic, qualities once counted as desirable in a potential president but now evidently seen by many as disturbing. At a time of domestic prosperity and tranquillity, when the United States has few mortal enemies and none that are capable of presenting an existential threat, much of the public seems to have developed a thirst for passivity, a thirst that Bush is eager to slake. This may explain the paradox that while Gore was widely judged the substantive winner of all three of the candidates' televised debates, and certainly the first and third of them, he lost the battle in the post-debate media echo chambers and, perhaps partly as a result, in the opinion polls. In the final debate, Gore stretched the rules (within the bounds of civility, but still), while Bush complained and turned beseechingly to the moderator for help. To caricature them both, Gore was a smart bully, Bush a hapless tattletale. Neither attribute is attractive, but it may turn out that fear of the first will outweigh contempt for the second. In that case, "personality" will definitely have triumphed over "issues," and the transformation of the presidency of the United States into the presidency of the student council will be complete.

—*The New Yorker*, November 6, 2000

COLLEGE HIGH JINKS

SOON AFTER THIS ISSUE of *The New Yorker* goes to press, we'll learn whether we have bought ourselves the ultimate Electoral College wooden nickel: a president-elect fresh from getting beaten in the vote of the people. If that happens, it will at least have the virtue of provoking a general outcry on behalf of changing the weird, archaic system by which we pick our presidents.* The more likely (if less obvious) danger is that it won't happen, and we won't recognize the damage which that system has already wreaked.

Way back in 1787, when the delegates to the original Constitutional Convention met in Philadelphia, the question of how the "chief magistrate" should be chosen was low on their agenda. The big fights were over the composition of Congress. The Rube Goldberg contraption the framers finally devised to elect the president was a last-minute improvisation, and God knows it looks like one. The idea was that (1) each state's legislature would "appoint" a number of "electors" equal to the size of its congressional delegation, (2) the electors would vote, and (3) if one candidate won a majority of votes from the entire Electoral College he would be elected, but (4) if none had a majority the election would be thrown into the House of Representatives, only instead of each representative getting one vote, each state would get one vote. All clear?

We now regard (4) as a goofy anomaly, but the framers envisioned it as

---

This part of my prediction did not come true, for reasons touched upon in "Recounted Out," page 608.

S.O.P. They knew that George Washington would win the first presidential election—and he did, unanimously. But after that, what? Well, the way the framers figured it, various grandees would get votes from their regions' electors, but, barring exceptional circumstances, none would get a majority. The "ultimate election," as James Madison put it, would take place in the House. So the usual pieties about the wisdom of the framers don't apply to presidential elections, because the system the framers thought they were designing had little to do with the system they actually designed, let alone with any system that would be acceptable to the people of a modern democracy.

One of the many things the framers couldn't anticipate was that the state legislatures, intent on maximizing the relative clout of their states, would award all their electors to the plurality winner. (Forty-eight states—all but Maine and Nebraska—do it this way.) That's what created the possibility of a candidate who takes the overall popular vote but narrowly misses in just enough big electoral-vote states to lose the election—something that has happened three times, and almost happened as recently as 1976. It also created the situation whereby, as we have just witnessed, the vast majority of citizens are left out of the campaign. If you live anywhere except those famous half-dozen "swing" states, you might have read about the big last-minute advertising blitzes, but you probably didn't see any of the ads. Nor are you likely to have seen hide nor hair of the candidates. Your vote wasn't worth the trouble of soliciting. The concentration on voters in swing states, perfectly rational from the candidates' point of view, means that voters (or potential voters) in non-swing states—and that's most of us—don't get campaigned for. No wonder turnout is unfailingly lower in "safe" states: a lot of people, quite reasonably, find something more profitable to do on Election Day.

One obvious solution, promoted by several senators, including Orrin Hatch and Strom Thurmond, would be to require that each state's electors be divided according to the shares of the popular vote. Besides minimizing the threat of a perverse outcome, that would put every part of the country "in play." Every state would be a swing state, and every candidate would have as much to gain from increasing his margins in his own "safe" states, and cutting down his opponents' margins in theirs, as from tipping the balance in, say, Wisconsin. However, because third-party candidates would suddenly have a shot at getting electoral votes, the quaint danger of throwing the election into the House, which hasn't happened since 1824, would become scarily real. That's why such proposals—along with congressional proposals supported by, among others, Bob Dole and Edward Kennedy for the other obvious solution, electing the president by popular vote—often provide for a special runoff election if no candidate tops 40 percent of the vote. But why stop at 40 percent? Why not try for—daring thought—majority rule? The Australians and the Irish use something called "instant-runoff voting," which allows voters to designate not only their top choice but also their second, third, and fourth; if there's no outright majority winner, the losing candidates are eliminated one by one and their supporters' alternative choices redistributed until, bingo, somebody goes over 50 percent. I.R.V. would guarantee us a president elected with at least the grudging support of a majority. As a bonus, it would enable people to express themselves by voting for third parties—such as the Greens, this year—without running the awkward risk of helping elect their most unfavorite candidate. Granted, it's a little on the Rube Goldberg side. But, after two hundred years of the Electoral College, aren't we used to that?

—*The New Yorker*, November 13, 2000

ALL PERFECTLY LEGAL

BY THE END OF LAST WEEK, the outcome of the 2000 election, though still formally undetermined, was not really in doubt. Two realities loomed like beasts in the mist: that George W. Bush will be the next president of the United States; and that Al Gore will emerge as the clear winner of "the popular vote"—our name for what other democracies that elect presidents call, simply, "the vote." Bush will be president because possession is nine-tenths of the law, and he has all along possessed, in the shifting official tabulations of the Florida tally, a tiny numerical lead in that state; and because his brother is the state's governor and his campaign co-chair the state's secretary of state; and because his allies and lawyers have stifled the recounts that might have counted; and because justice takes time, and there is no time; and because the Florida legislature, which is controlled by his party, is ready, if necessary, to set aside the troublesome vote of Florida's people and appoint electors of its own choosing. That would be unprecedented, and it would be cynical, and it would be arrogant, and it would be (in the generally accepted, commonsense meaning of the word) undemocratic. But it would not be, on the face of it, either illegal or unconstitutional.

For these reasons and more, Bush is, if not quite president-elect, president-appoint. As for Gore's plurality in the national popular vote, during the first couple of weeks after Election Day some observers suggested that it might be reversed by absentee ballots, which often break in a Republican direction. This is now prohibitively unlikely. In contrast to 1960, when John F. Kennedy's lead over Richard Nixon eventually fell from around 300,000 the day after the election to less than 120,000, Gore's lead has actually grown as the supplementary returns have trickled in. The day after the election it was 97,773; a week after that it was 230,449; and as of the end of last week it was 357,576. The largest packets of still uncounted votes are in states that Gore carried. By the time all the states have certified their totals later this month, Gore's plurality will likely be somewhere between 250,000 and 400,000.*

Whatever the official vote count in Florida, it now seems beyond dispute that more citizens of that state went to the polls intending to vote for Gore than for Bush. In order to demonstrate this, the butterfly ballots of Palm Beach—the ones that produced the curious phenomenon of Jews for Buchanan—need not be invoked. In a careful report published on November 19th in the *Orlando Sentinel*, Sean Holton and Jeff Kunerth analyzed the voting systems used in Florida. The most dependable—pen-marked, precinct-tabulated ballots, a system that allows a bad ballot to be kicked back immediately to the voter so that it can be corrected—was used mostly in counties where Bush was strong. The least dependable system, punch-card ballots, was used in counties where Gore was strong. "If all 67 counties had been using the same type of system," Holton and Kunerth conclude, "Gore might have gone ahead of Bush in the totals for Nov. 7, by a margin of more than 1,700 votes. This scenario emerges whether voters used the most reliable system or the least reliable—as long as it was used uniformly statewide."

It is important to stress that Gore's popular-vote plurality (as he himself has repeatedly acknowledged) has no constitutional or legal significance. But that does not mean it has no significance at all. It is the moral basis for his challenge to the Florida count, and a firm basis it is. It is also the political basis for that challenge: if Bush had been the one whose national plurality now stood at a third of a million, any effort by Gore to reverse the Electoral College outcome by nibbling at a Bush lead of a few hundred votes in a single state would have been unsustainable. It would have been seen—rightly, and not just by excitable conservative ideologues—as an attempt to steal the election. The effort, therefore, would never have been made. But

---

* Gore's final plurality over Bush was 543,614. The totals: Gore 51,003,238 (48.38%); Bush 50,459,624 (47.87); Ralph Nader (Green) 2,882,985 (2.74); Patrick Buchanan (Reform) 449,120 (0.43); Harry Browne (Libertarian) 384,440 (0.36); Other 232,922 (0.22). Looked at another way, the left-of-center majority over the right-of-center candidates was 2,593,039—Gore-Nader 53,886,223 (51.12%) versus Bush-Buchanan-Browne 51,293,184 (48.66).

politically and morally, if not constitutionally, Gore's popular-vote plurality makes all the difference in the world.

If, as seems close to certain, Bush takes office next month, he will do so by virtue of a series of maneuvers that will have been—though by definition legal and constitutional—contemptible. The moral and political legitimacy of his victory will remain to be earned. Bush ran as an opponent of "partisan bickering," and the substance behind that rhetoric will be severely tested. (On that score, it must be said, his behavior since Election Day has not been reassuring.) Gore ran as a fighter. Now he is going down as a fighter, and the fight he has waged has been a service to his party and—because it has shone the unflattering light of truth on America's electoral systems—to his country, too. As that fight approaches its dismal and probably inevitable end, Gore's determination—in the face of scorn from pundits and, at the beginning, even from some of his own supporters—has begun to look less and less like petulance and more and more like grit.

—*The New Yorker*, December 11, 2000

EPPUR SI MUOVE

THAT WAS A TOUGH concession speech Al Gore had to give the other night, but people have had to give tougher ones over the years. In 1633, a prominent, well-connected member of the high-tech community of Florence found himself on the wrong end of a decision by the then equivalent of the Supreme Court. Put on trial by the Inquisition, he was found guilty of advocating a doctrine described in the Holy Office's indictment as "absurd and false philosophically, because it is expressly contrary to Holy Scripture." This was a characterization with which the defendant was known to privately disagree. But he was anxious to avoid being cast as a troublemaker and eager for the healing to begin, so he said the words the occasion required. "I, Galileo, son of the late Vincenzo Galilei, Florentine, aged seventy years," he recited, "abjure, curse, and detest the aforesaid errors and heresies, and I swear that I will never again say or assert that the Sun is the center of the universe and immovable and that the Earth is not the center and moves." Before Galileo was led away to spend the rest of his life under comfortable house arrest, however, he kicked the ground and, according to legend, muttered, *Eppur si muove*—"But still, it moves."

Vice President Gore, too, offered the required pieties last Wednesday evening—about putting rancor aside, about love of country, about how "that which unites us is greater than that which divides us." He did so with considerable grace and a few touches of rueful humor. He permitted himself only the faintest of heretical intimations: a declaration that he continues to "strongly disagree with the Court's decision" (coupled, to be sure, with an assurance that he accepts it); a mention of "those who feel their voices have not been heard," which might be taken as a reference to those whose votes remain uncounted; and an explanation that he was conceding because he was concerned about "our unity as a people and the strength of our democracy"—that is to say, not because he had lost the election.

And indeed he did not, as far as science can determine, lose the election. He lost the postelection, in which the franchise, it turned out, was limited to certain members of the Supreme Court. The embarrassment of this was evident even to them. At exactly this time of year four decades ago, John F. Kennedy made up his mind that he was going to appoint his kid brother Robert attorney general. Benjamin Bradlee asked him how he planned to make the announcement. "Well," the president-elect replied, "I think I'll open the front door of the Georgetown house some morning about two A.M., look up and down the street, and, if there's no one there, I'll whisper, 'It's Bobby.'" The Court last week actually did what J.F.K. joked about, except that what the Court whispered into the darkness was nothing so forthright as "It's Bush." While millions watched in bafflement, network and cable television news correspondents, many of them lawyers trained to skim judicial opinions for the gist, struggled to make sense of the majority opinion's verbiage. It's no wonder they were confused: the crabbed, ugly language had been crafted to obscure what had been decided, and even who had done the deciding. As the indispensable Linda Greenhouse noted a couple of days later in the *New York Times*, the opinion, which was unsigned, was styled "per curiam," meaning "by the court"—"a label used by courts almost exclusively for unanimous opinions so uncontroversial as to not be worth the trouble of a formal opinion-writing process." It took the experts the better part of an hour just to deduce that the ruling was by a 5–4 vote: to solve the mystery, they had to identify the authors of the overlapping dissents, add them up, and subtract from nine. In the text itself, the only clue to the breakdown was an innocent-sounding sentence—"Seven Justices of the Court agree that there are constitutional problems with the recount ordered by the Florida Supreme Court that demand a remedy"—which suggested that the opinion, or part of it, had been agreed to by all but two justices. This was false. But it was only a drop in the rancid bucket of the majority's bad faith.

The in-house reviews were not kind. The Court's decision "can only lend credence to the most cynical appraisal of the work of judges throughout the land" (Justice Stevens). "There is no justification for denying the State the opportunity to try to count all disputed ballots now" (Justice Souter). "I dissent" (Justice Ginsburg, omitting the customary softener, "respectfully"). The decision is "a self-inflicted wound—a wound that may harm not just the Court, but the Nation" (Justice Breyer). The clarity of the dissenters' prose and reasoning only makes their anger and sorrow more striking.

On the basis of the available evidence—not least the ruthless determination of the Republican Party to use all the powers at its command, from the executive and legislative branches of the Florida state government to the five-person Supreme Court bloc (now exposed not as jurisprudential conservatives but as ideological and nakedly partisan ones), for the single purpose of preventing a fair count of the ballots of Florida's citizens—it may now be inferred, pending the eventual recount by scholars and journalists under Florida's freedom-of-information laws, that the president-elect (a suddenly Orwellian honorific) lost not only the popular but also the true electoral vote. Nevertheless, the election of 2000 was not stolen. Stealing, after all, is illegal, and, by definition, nothing the justices of the Supreme Court do can be outside the law. They are the law. The election was not stolen. It was expropriated.

—*The New Yorker*, December 25, 2000

ADVICE AND CONSENT

DURING THE WEEKS since the Supreme Court Five put a stop to the Florida count, late returns from the upper forty-nine have kept trickling in. Al Gore's plurality of the national popular vote now stands at well over half a million—539,947, to cite the weirdly precise figure promulgated by the Associated Press. Yet as recently as last week some newspapers were still referring to the election of 2000 as the closest in American history. It wasn't. It wasn't even the closest since Gore and George W. Bush were in junior high school; it was the third closest. Gore's plurality is nearly five times the size of John F. Kennedy's over Richard Nixon, in 1960, and 30,000 votes bigger than Nixon's over Hubert Humphrey, in 1968. The margin in those two races is routinely described as razor-thin. This time, the margin is razor-thin, too, but it's a strange sort of razor: a negative razor, a Rogaine razor, a razor that would grow whiskers on Occam himself—a razor whose edge, like some post-Newtonian astronomical singularity, is so exotically thin that it pops through a wormhole into an alternate universe where the dull outcuts the keen.

Actually, the counting didn't stop in Florida, either. Despite a certain backwardness where electoral technology is concerned, the Sunshine State has an unusually comprehensive sunshine law—one that allows public scrutiny of ballots. Under that law, various consortia of leading national and Florida newspapers are examining scores of thousands of disputed and/or uncounted ballots. It will be many weeks before the results of these tabulations are known. And it is theoretically possible that they will validate

Bush's victory, just as it is theoretically possible that, on account of random Brownian motion, all the molecules of air in one of the counting rooms will rush to a corner and the counters will be asphyxiated. But it's not likely. What is likely is that the independent counts will demonstrate that, no matter what standard is used, Florida, and therefore the presidency, was unjustly awarded.

By that time, of course, Bush will long ago have been inaugurated. *L'état, c'est lui.* Anyway, neither his unquestioned popular defeat nor his unmerited Electoral College victory will (or even should) make any difference to his assumption of executive power. These things should have made (but did not) a difference in Bush's selection of his cabinet, which, notwithstanding all the talk of healing and bipartisanship, is essentially what it would have been if Bush had won in a landslide. And they certainly should (and, one hopes, will) make a difference in the behavior of the congressional opposition—above all in the field of judicial selection.

The Constitution gives the president the power to appoint, "by and with the advice and consent of the Senate," "ambassadors, other public ministers and consuls, judges of the Supreme Court, and all other officers of the United States." In the case of cabinet officers, diplomats, and "other public ministers," "advice and consent" has come to mean simply consent. It has long been recognized that the appointment of judges is different, because judges serve for life and constitute a third, co-equal, and (as the country was forcibly reminded by the case of *Bush v. Gore*) occasionally sovereign branch of government. In practice, this difference has meant merely that consent is somewhat more apt to be withheld. That should change.

Given the special circumstances surrounding Bush's accession to the presidency, the Democrats of the Senate have not only a right but also something like a duty to make it clear in advance that they plan to take the "advice" half of the Constitution's formula seriously when it comes to the appointment of Supreme Court justices and other inhabitants of the higher reaches of the federal bench. It is very much to the point that one of those special circumstances is the composition of the Senate itself. Because that body is evenly split, with fifty Democrats and fifty Republicans, the Republican Party's control of it will be a function of the new vice president's ability to break ties—and, therefore, a function of the same judicial fiat that handed the White House to Bush. For this among other reasons (such as the actuarial accident that the Supreme Court consists of seven Republican and only two Democratic appointees), Senate Democrats have a moral as well as a legal right to use the threat of systematic obstruction to force the new administration to accord them a role in making judicial appointments that goes beyond the passive giving or withholding of consent. Advice, after all, is meaningless unless it is considered before a decision is made. As it is, the advice Bush will be getting on naming judges will be coming mainly from his attorney general, the defeated Senator John Ashcroft, who is about as far to the right as an American politician can get without rendering himself unfit for polite society.

In the Senate, which is a deeply undemocratic institution, the filibuster rule effectively gives a veto to any forty senators, whose states can represent as little as 10 percent of the population. During the first two years of the Clinton administration, when Republican senators were in the minority, they used filibusters to block many of Clinton's nominees for both executive and judicial posts; for the next six years, they used delay and inaction to block many dozens more. Like the process that decided the presidential election, the filibuster is legal, constitutional, and an affront to democratic (if not to "republican") values. It should not be used promiscuously. But it, and the threat of it, should be used. Two wrongs can't make a right, but sometimes a small wrong can limit a big one's damage.

—*The New Yorker*, January 15, 2001

GENEROUS GEORGE

GEORGE W. BUSH'S BUDGET address to a joint session of Congress last
week was, as now seems routine for big Bush set pieces, remarkably deft—
coherently organized, competently written, and ingeniously crafted to
soothe delicate sensibilities. If its literary aesthetics were Gersonian (with
the convention speech, the inaugural, and now this, Michael Gerson, Bush's
chief speechwriter, is three for three), its political aesthetics were Clintonian. "Year after year in Washington," began its most elegant triangulating
passage, "budget debates seem to come down to an old, tired argument: on
one side, those who want more government, regardless of the cost; on the
other, those who want less government, regardless of the need." Bill Clinton couldn't have, and never did, put it better himself (his "the era of big
government is over" was crude by comparison).

Clinton used the Republican lexicon of toughness and personal responsibility to camouflage a program whose overall thrust was egalitarian and
redistributive. Bush uses the Democratic lexicon of social concern in a way
that is symmetrical but not morally equivalent. One can argue that for a Republican president to speak warmly of public spending for education, the
environment, and health care signals a moral advance of sorts, even if the
driving force is political calculation. One can argue that lip service is better
than no service. But these lips are thin and pursed. Trumpeting "a new
prescription-drug benefit for low-income seniors," Bush declared, "No senior in America should have to choose between buying food and buying prescriptions." That applause line brought even Edward Kennedy lumbering

to his feet. Understandably, the president omitted the details—for example, this one: under the benefit he has proposed, a widow living on as little as $15,000 a year would get no help until she had already spent $6,000 on prescription drugs. That is, she would have to have already left more than a third of her meagre income at the pharmacy. To put it still another way, her "deductible" would be $115—per week, not per year.

When you strip away the homilies that everybody agrees on (or has agreed to agree on)—education good, racial profiling bad, environment good—you are left with the tax plan. And when you strip away those aspects of the tax plan that everybody agrees on (or has agreed to agree on)—a bigger child credit, a lesser "marriage penalty," a modest break for "working families," some provision for keeping family farms intact—you are left with an incomprehensibly huge gift to the well-off. The administration has dismissed, but has not been able to refute, independent analyses showing that 40 percent of the benefits of the Bush tax cut will accrue to the richest 1 percent of taxpayers; that the bottom 80 percent will get less than a third of the benefits and the bottom 20 percent less than 1 percent; that all the benefits of the proposed abolition of the estate tax will go to the heirs of the richest 2 percent; and that the richest 6 percent of that 2 percent will rake in half the estate-tax pot. The shape of the Bush tax program represents a seismic shift in the overall tax burden toward the bottom of the economic scale. And its size represents a massive diversion of actual and potential resources away from public activities that benefit the whole of society—activities like education, public health, and environmental protection, the very ones Bush endorsed at the outset of his speech—and toward the single purpose of augmenting the net incomes of the comfortable. That goal, by the way, is superfluous. From 1992, the year before a supposedly onerous new marginal tax rate kicked in, through 1998, the most recent year for which Internal Revenue figures are available, the average after-tax income of the richest 1 percent rose from about four hundred thousand dollars to just under six hundred thousand, and from 12.2 percent of the national net income to 15.7 percent. (Disparities of wealth, as opposed to income, are, of course, much higher.) Really, now—how urgently do these good people require a new subsidy from the other 99 percent?

All this was thoroughly aired before the election and its aftermath, which hovered invisibly over the House chamber last week. The question is not one of Bush's legitimacy. The new president—so the highest authorities assure us—holds office by virtue of a process that was legal and constitutional. But not even the Supreme Court could decree that the electorate endorsed his policies, the most conspicuous of which was the tax program he presented the other night. More people voted for Vice President Gore than for Governor Bush, and they didn't do so because Gore had the more pleasing personality. If you factor in the millions who opted for outriders—Ralph Nader to Gore's left; Patrick Buchanan, Harry Browne, and Howard Phillips to Bush's right—then the electorate's expressed preference for a budgetary and tax regime more liberal than Bush's goes from a mere plurality of half a million to an outright majority of two and a half million. Our ramshackle eighteenth-century institutional and constitutional arrangements enabled Bush to become president despite being defeated in the vote of the people. Those arrangements, fortuitously, also give the Democratic half of the Senate the power to obstruct a tax proposal which, in its disputed parts, comes down to greed. The use of that power would be another symmetry, and not a fearful one.

—*The New Yorker*, March 12, 2001

TUESDAY, AND AFTER

THE CATASTROPHE that turned the foot of Manhattan into the mouth of Hell on the morning of September 11, 2001, unfolded in four paroxysms. At a little before nine, a smoldering scar on the face of the north tower of the World Trade Center (an awful accident, like the collision of a B-25 bomber with the Empire State Building on July 28, 1945?); eighteen minutes later, the orange and gray blossoming of the second explosion, in the south tower; finally, at a minute before ten and then at not quite ten-thirty, the sickening slide of the two towers, collapsing one after the other. For those in the immediate vicinity, the horror was of course immediate and unmistakable; it occurred in what we have learned to call real time, and in real space. For those farther away—whether a few dozen blocks or halfway around the world—who were made witnesses by the long lens of television, the events were seen as through a glass, brightly. Their reality was visible but not palpable. It took hours to begin to comprehend their magnitude; it is taking days for the defensive numbness they induced to wear off; it will take months—or years—to measure their impact and meaning.

New York is a city where, however much strangers meet and mix on the streets and in the subways, circles of friends are usually demarcated by work and family. The missing and presumed dead—their number is in the thousands—come primarily from the finance, international trade, and government service workers in the doomed buildings, and from the ranks of firefighters and police officers drawn there by duty and courage. The umbra of personal grief already encompasses scores or even hundreds of thousands of people; a week or two from now, when the word has spread from friend to colleague to relative to acquaintance, the penumbra will cover millions. The city has never suffered a more shocking calamity from any act of God or man.

The calamity, of course, goes well beyond the damage to our city and to its similarly bereaved rival and brother Washington. It is national; it is international; it is civilizational. In the decade since the end of the Cold War, the human race has become, with increasing rapidity, a single organism. Every kind of barrier to the free and rapid movement of goods, information, and people has been lowered. The organism relies increasingly on a kind of trust—the unsentimental expectation that people, individually and collectively, will behave more or less in their rational self-interest. (Even the anti-globalizers of the West mostly embrace the underlying premises of the new dispensation; their demand is for global democratic institutions to mitigate the cruelties of the global market.) The terrorists made use of that trust. They rode the flow of the world's aerial circulatory system like lethal viruses.

With growing ferocity, officials from the president on down have described the bloody deeds as acts of war. But, unless a foreign government turns out to have directed the operation (or, at least, to have known and approved its scope in detail and in advance), that is a category mistake. The metaphor of war—and it is more metaphor than description—ascribes to the perpetrators a dignity they do not merit, a status they cannot claim, and a strength they do not possess. Worse, it points toward a set of responses that could prove futile or counterproductive. Though the death and destruction these acts caused were on the scale of war, the acts themselves were acts of terrorism, albeit on a wholly unprecedented level. From 1983 until last week, ten terrorist outrages had each claimed the lives of more than 100 people. The worst— the destruction of an Air-India 747 in 1985—killed 329 people; the Oklahoma City bombing, which killed 168, was the seventh worst. Last week's carnage surpassed that of any of these by an order of magnitude. It was also the largest violent taking of life on American soil on any day since the Civil War, including December 7, 1941. And in New York and Washington, unlike at Pearl Harbor, the killed and maimed were overwhelmingly civilians.

The tactics of the terrorists were as brilliant as they were depraved. The nature of those tactics and their success—and there is no use denying that what they did was, on its own terms, successful—points up the weakness of the war metaphor. Authorities estimated last week that "as many as" fifty people may have been involved. The terrorists brought with them nothing but knives and the ability to fly a jumbo jet already in the air. How do you take "massive military action" against the infrastructure of a stateless, compartmentalized "army" of fifty, or ten times fifty, whose weapons are rental cars, credit cards, and airline tickets?

The scale of the damage notwithstanding, a more useful metaphor than war is crime. The terrorists of September 11 are outlaws within a global polity. They may enjoy the corrupt protection of a state (and corruption, like crime, can be ideological or spiritual as well as pecuniary in motive). But they do not constitute or control a state and do not appear even to aspire to control one. Their status and numbers are such that the task of dealing with them should be viewed as a police matter, of the most urgent kind. As with all criminal fugitives, the essential job is to find out who and where they are. The goal of foreign and military policy must be to induce recalcitrant governments to cooperate, a goal whose attainment may or may not entail the use of force but cannot usefully entail making general war on the peoples such governments rule and in some cases (that of Afghanistan, for example) oppress. Just four months ago, at a time when the whole world was aware both of the general intentions of the terrorist Osama bin Laden and of the fact that the Afghan government was harboring him, the United States gave the Taliban a forty-three-million-dollar grant for banning poppy cultivation. The United States understands that on September 11 the line between the permissible and the impermissible shifted. The Taliban must be made to understand that, too.

As for America's friends, they have rallied around us with alacrity. On Wednesday, the NATO allies, for the first time ever, invoked the mutual-defense clause of the alliance's founding treaty, formally declaring that "an armed attack" against one—and what happened on September 11, whether you call it terrorism or war, was certainly an armed attack—constitutes an attack against all. This gesture of solidarity puts to shame the contempt the Bush administration has consistently shown for international treaties and instruments, including those in areas relevant to the fight against terrorism, such as small-arms control, criminal justice, and nuclear proliferation. By now, it ought to be clear to even the most committed ideologues of the Bush administration that the unilateralist approach it was pursuing as of last Tuesday is in urgent need of reevaluation. The world will be policed collectively or it will not be policed at all.

—*The New Yorker*, September 24, 2001

DIFFERENCES

IF THERE IS ONE proposition on which everyone has come to agree in the two and a half months since September 11, it is that the campaign against international terrorism is unlike any conflict in our country's, or the world's, experience. This one is different because, among other reasons, the primary enemy is neither a state nor an insurrection against a state but a stateless conspiracy motivated by grandiose religious nihilism; because that enemy commandeers the materials and fluidity of modern civilization for use against modern civilization itself; because the enemy's nature precludes either negotiation or deterrence; because the essential aim of the conflict has the support (sometimes actual, sometimes only nominal) of almost every government in the world, free and unfree; because the means by which the campaign must be conducted include unprecedented kinds of police, financial, and public-health work as well as military action; and because defeat is unthinkable and victory difficult to define.

"This war will not be like the war against Iraq a decade ago, with the decisive liberation of territory and a swift conclusion," President Bush said in his address to Congress on September 20th. "It will not look like the air war above Kosovo two years ago, where no ground troops were used and not a single American was lost in combat." And yet the astonishment of the events of the past two weeks has been how closely they resemble conventional notions—and conventional hopes—of what war is supposed to look like. A decisive liberation of territory is precisely what has been happening in Afghanistan since November 9th. A swift conclusion—to this most visible military phase of the conflict, at least—now appears within reach. While American special forces on the ground have presumably suffered casualties, the official total of American combat deaths remains, at this writing, zero. And the most striking contrast between the Kosovo air war and the Afghan one has been that the former was actually larger.

One way in which this conflict is indeed different is that there is no antiwar movement to speak of. For nearly half a century—from 1953, when the guns fell silent in Korea, until this year—the United States never went to war, whether directly or by proxy, without significant domestic opposition. Vietnam is the most obvious example. But congressional Democrats voted overwhelmingly against the Gulf War under the first President Bush, and the Bosnia and Kosovo interventions under President Clinton faced similar objections from Republicans. Lebanon, Nicaragua, El Salvador, Grenada, Panama, Somalia—all engendered protest, often substantial and well organized. This time there has been nothing of the kind. Apart from traditional pacifists, who oppose any use of force on principle, and a tiny handful of reflexive Rip Van Winkles, almost no one objects, in broad outline, to the aims and methods of the antiterrorism campaign. Former (and unrepentant) anti–Vietnam War activists have been among the most passionate advocates of the duty of the United States to defend itself. Conservative commentators have had a frustrating time of it rounding up the usual blame-America-first suspects, because so few of those suspects are out there blaming America first. To be sure, there have been Americans who have suggested that American policies, arrogance, and heedlessness nourished the soil in which terrorism has grown. But even these critics, with very few exceptions, have been careful to affirm that none of this could possibly justify either the attacks themselves or a failure to respond vigorously to them. The United States has not taken up its campaign against terrorism as a matter of choice, or in pursuit of some tertiary policy goal that is subject to rational questioning. There has been no real antiwar movement since September 11, 2001, for the same reason that there was none after December 7, 1941.

The administration has, of course, made policy decisions that have come in for criticism and deserve to come in for more, especially the Justice Department's ukases truncating attorney-client confidentiality, detaining aliens without explanation or accountability, and establishing military courts to try (and, in theory, to order the execution of) suspected terrorists in secret and without judicial review. But, to the extent that the military campaign itself has been an occasion for something resembling dissent, that dissent has taken the form of tactical fretfulness, as noticeable on the right as on the left. Liberals worried that the bombing of Afghanistan, with its inevitable civilian casualties, would only strengthen the resolve of the Taliban, alienate the Europeans, and inflame the much cited "street" to the point of endangering the existence of moderate Muslim regimes. Conservatives worried that diplomatic oversolicitousness, an insufficient commitment of ground forces, and a reluctance to extend the war to Iraq would guarantee disaster. And some who are both liberal and conservative (or is it neither?) took both positions. ("Having found refuge in places that America will not, or cannot, bomb," *The New Republic* editorialized in its November 19th issue, "it appears the Taliban will rule Afghanistan through the winter, thereby handing the United States a humiliating and gratuitous defeat.")

The truth is that no one anticipated the extraordinary military gains of the past two weeks, and no one can know what the next two weeks—or two months, or two years—will bring. Success has its snares; triumphalism is as misleading as defeatism, and more seductive. The shape of success in Afghanistan is too conventional for comfort. The defeat of the Taliban is not the same as the defeat of Al Qaeda, with its global reach; and the defeat of Al Qaeda would not be the same as the defeat of international terrorism. The struggle has begun well, but it has only begun.

—*The New Yorker*, December 3, 2001

RECOUNTED OUT

IS IT O.K. to talk about the recount yet? It wasn't the right time on September 10th, because the University of Chicago's National Opinion Research Center had only just finished organizing the data gleaned from its meticulous examination of a hundred and seventy-five thousand uncounted Florida ballots. It wasn't on September 12th, because the news organizations that had commissioned the study were otherwise occupied. It was the right time on November 12th, apparently: that was the day the news organizations got around to publishing their analyses of the results. But, judging from the lack of discussion that has ensued, it abruptly became the wrong time again on November 13th. Maybe it'll never be the right time. But what the hell. Let's talk about it anyway.

The first thing to say about the media recount (its formal name was the Florida Ballots Project) is that it was a praiseworthy endeavor—well designed, unbiased, thorough, and public-spirited. The consortium of news organizations—its eight members were the *New York Times*, the *Washington Post*, the *Wall Street Journal*, the Tribune Company, the *Palm Beach Post*, the *St. Petersburg Times*, CNN, and the Associated Press—did something admirable.

The second thing to say is that the courage that spurred the consortium into existence, a year ago, flagged at the end. Given that the consortium's goal was to catalogue all, or as many as possible, of the votes that had been cast by Florida citizens but not recorded by Florida authorities, one might have expected its members to emphasize the finding that corresponded to its goal. That finding, it turned out, was that, no matter what standard or combination of standards is applied, Al Gore got a handful more votes than George W. Bush. Faced with this conclusion, the consortium changed the question to who would have won if the original statewide recount had not been aborted. The reassuring answer to that question, again by a handful, was Bush.

It soon developed, however, that the news organizations had missed a crucial detail: if the recount ordered by the Florida Supreme Court had in fact gone forward, the circuit judge supervising it, Terry Lewis, probably would have directed the counting not only of "undervotes" (on which machines could detect no vote) but also of "overvotes" (on which machines detected markings for more than one candidate). The overvotes, according to the consortium's own numbers, would have yielded a hair's-breadth victory for Gore. This news was uncovered by the *Orlando Sentinel* (which got its scoop the old-fashioned way: a reporter picked up the phone and called the fellow) and by Michael Isikoff, of *Newsweek,* who found a contemporaneous memo from Lewis confirming what he told the *Sentinel.*

In any case, there is no longer any doubt that more Florida voters intended to vote for Gore than for Bush: according to the *Times,* some eight thousand Gore overvotes, net, were lost because of bad design (the notorious "butterfly" of Palm Beach) or confusing instructions (the two-page Duval County "caterpillar" ballot, which directed voters to "vote all pages"). But those votes were irredeemably spoiled, and the consortium did not consider them. In terms of those votes that were arguably valid, Florida—still—is too close to call. In every scenario, the margins are smaller than the five hundred and thirty-seven votes by which Bush officially prevailed—and smaller, too, than the margin of error.

We do know, without question, that the losing candidate outpolled the winning one in the nation at large. In modern times this was unprecedented, but it had almost happened three times within living memory: in 1960, when J.F.K.'s plurality was barely a hundred thousand votes; in 1968, when Richard Nixon's margin was half a million (about the same as Gore's in 2000); and in 1976, when a geographic shift of twenty thousand votes would have given Gerald Ford an Electoral College victory despite Jimmy Carter's popular majority of 1.7 million. Each of these close calls, as it happens, precipitated a serious bipartisan effort to abolish the Electoral College. In 1969, the House of Representatives overwhelmingly passed a constitutional amendment calling for direct popular election; President Nixon himself endorsed it and a substantial majority of senators favored it, but it was filibustered to death after an epic debate in the Senate. In 1977, President Carter proposed the same idea, and it met the same fate. But at least there was an energetic national discussion, in which most of the participants took it for granted that the election of a president who had lost the popular vote would be in some way an affront to democracy.

The dodged bullets of the sixties and seventies found their target in 2000. Yet no real national discussion ensued. The unthinkable happened, and the almost universal response was to not think about it. The reasons for this are pretty obvious. There are three. First, the Florida imbroglio burned up all the oxygen in which a larger debate might have occurred. "Who won Florida?" became the only question, obliterating the question of who won America. Second, this time the political legitimacy of an actual, not a hypothetical, president was at stake. After 1960, 1968, and 1976, those seeking to abolish the Electoral College could pursue their aim without the burden of appearing to replay the past as well as reform the future. By the same token, the sitting president could float benignly above the conversation, secure in the knowledge that, however narrowly, he was the people's choice.

The third reason, of course, is September 11th, which extinguished the last traces of any appetite for a discussion that might call into question the legitimacy of a president who has his hands full and who needs, and has, the support of a nation united in the struggle against terror. But by then, it must be said, the damage to democracy had already been done. Someday, perhaps, our anachronistic system of picking presidents will be brought into line with the fundamental American idea of political equality among citizens. An unhappy legacy of the election of 2000 is that that day now seems more distant than ever.

—*The New Yorker*, December 24 & 31, 2001

MINE SHAFT

IN A SEASON OF DOLOR—when the news is mostly of economic ruin, climatic foreboding, the abduction of children, and, of course, terrorism, war, and rumors of war—the rescue of the Quecreek Nine was an interlude of gladness. Nine coal miners trapped deep beneath a cow pasture in southwestern Pennsylvania, the equivalent of twenty-four stories straight down; the miners scratching and crawling their way through pitch-black, four-foot-high tunnels fast filling with icy floodwater to find one another and a pocket of stale air; the rescue team aboveground, improvising a plan to pump in compressed air to push the water back, snapping a drill bit, almost losing hope; the miners, preparing for imminent death, sealing notes to their loved ones in a watertight bucket; time and air running out; and then, finally, as midnight approached on the fourth night, a breakthrough, joy and weeping, the miners lifted out one by one, all nine of them, haggard but whole.

It's a fine, uplifting story, full of terror and suspense, grit and determination—a story that shows, as did the story of September 11 and its aftermath, that a working-class hero is something to be. And this story has what that one did not: a happy ending. So Hollywood said: We're there. A week after the rescue, the nine miners, plus one of the lead rescuers, inked a Tinseltown pact, as *Variety* might put it. Or, as *Variety* actually did put it: "The Walt Disney Co. has locked up a nearly $1.5 million deal for the exclusive book and TV movie rights to the personal stories of the nine Pennsylvania miners. . . . Mouse web ABC will produce a two-hour telepic about the rescue operation, while Disney publishing unit Hyperion is expected to release a book about their ordeal." That's a hundred and fifty grand per miner, before taxes and lawyers' fees—which is either a lot or a little, depending on what you compare it with.

If you compare it with what the miners (who, among them, had more than two hundred man-years on the job) were making before, it's a lot. Their yearly wages, which are about 40 percent higher than the county average, come to around forty thousand dollars each, counting overtime. So the Disney deal will yield them upward of three years' pay. On the other hand, if you compare it with what their employers get, it's a little. As the *Wall Street Journal* reported last week, the Quecreek mine, "although portrayed during the rescue efforts as a tiny operation, is closely linked to a web of companies controlled by the venture-capital arm of Citigroup Inc."

In 2001, Sanford Weill, the chairman of Citigroup, collected $18 million in salary and bonuses, which means it took him around five hours to rack up what one of those miners made all year. What about the miners' new boss? According to the calculations of *Forbes* magazine, Michael Eisner, the C.E.O. of Disney, received $723 million in salary, bonuses, and stock options from 1996 to 2001, a yearly average of roughly $145 million. That could pay the yearly wages of more than three thousand coal miners (and, thanks to mechanization, there are only seventy thousand in the whole country). To be fair, on an hourly basis Disney paid Eisner only thirty-five times what it's paying the miners for each of the seventy-seven hours they were trapped (though once you throw in the hours they'll have to spend talking to the film producers and book writers, it'll be more like a hundred times). Such is the magic of the market.

The Quecreek Nine, like a majority of coal miners and unlike the firefighters, cops, and hardhats of September 11, are non-union. But this is not necessarily a mark of their devotion to rugged individualism. The complicated ownership and contracting arrangements under which mines like Quecreek operate are designed largely to keep union organizers at bay. For coal operators, and in the private sector generally, it's just sound business practice to fire people who might be thinking of joining a union and then maybe pay a small fine for it a year or two later. (Public-employee unions do better at organizing, despite the fact that strikes in the public sector are generally illegal, because it's politically awkward for the government to flout the law.) If the Quecreek Nine had been members of the United Mine

Workers of America, the legendary union that, in its glory days under John L. Lewis, had more than half a million members and made presidents quake, their pay and benefits would have been a little sweeter, and they would have had a tough workplace-safety committee to represent them. Still, it's due mainly to the union's efforts that even non-union wages are as high as they are. And the federal agency that helped supervise the rescue, the Mine Health and Safety Administration, was founded, in 1969, partly as a result of pressure from the U.M.W.A.

Non-union though they were, the Quecreek miners conspicuously displayed the noblest of all trade-union virtues: solidarity. They prayed together; they shared the single sandwich that was their only food; they lashed themselves together so that in death their bodies would not be separated. Once rescued, they shared with all and sundry the cases of beer that a local distributor had given them. And when it came time to negotiate with the folks from Hollywood they did so as a group, instead of trying to cut individual and possibly more lucrative deals at one another's expense.

A week after the rescue, President Bush dropped in for a photo op with the miners and told them that "it was their determination to stick together and to comfort each other that really defines kind of a new spirit that's prevalent in our country—that when one of us suffers, all of us suffer; that in order to succeed, we've got to be united; that by working together, we can achieve big objectives and big goals." A beautiful sentiment. But, although the Bush energy policy calls for the extraction and burning of more and more coal, the Bush budget calls for a 6 percent cut in funding for the Mine Safety and Health Administration. It's hard to say which of these moves is the more unwise. According to Senator Jay Rockefeller, of West Virginia, the budget cut will result in a 25 percent decline in the mine agency's inspection workforce, whose job it is to prevent accidents like the one at Quecreek from taking place at all. The Quecreek Nine were saved; but last year forty-two miners were killed digging coal, as against twenty-nine in 1998. Solidarity forever. Just not at this point in time.

—The New Yorker, August 19 & 26, 2002

MANIFESTO

THE WORLD IS NOT a place that George W. Bush was terribly familiar with until recently. Any college student who has done a semester abroad has logged a lot more time under foreign skies than he has; and, as he himself told Jim Lehrer, of PBS, during the campaign, "I'm not going to play like I've been a person who's spent hours involved with foreign policy. I am who I am." It's different now, of course. He's still who he is, but he is also, as he likes to say, the president; and he has come a long way since September 11th. Bush now has a worldview. He has to have one: it's the law—specifically, the Department of Defense Reorganization Act of 1986, which requires every president, on a regular basis, to formulate his and his administration's thoughts about America's global role. Hence the appearance the other day of a pamphlet entitled "The National Security Strategy of the United States of America."

It's a curious document. At nearly thirteen thousand words, it's roomy enough to accommodate some favorite ideological tchotchkes. For example, as a way of enhancing "national security," it promises to press "other countries" to adopt "lower marginal tax rates" and "pro-growth legal and regulatory policies"—your doctor's names for tax cuts for the rich and environmental laxity. And it exalts economic relationships as more fundamental than political and social ones (a mental habit that orthodox conservative ideologues share with their orthodox Marxist counterparts), as in this passage praising free trade as a "moral principle": "If you can make something that others value, you should be able to sell it to them. If others make something that you value, you should be able to buy it. This is real freedom, the freedom for a person—or a nation—to make a living." (As distinct, presumably, from the secondary, not quite real freedoms of thought, conscience, and expression.) The main thrust of the document, however, is twofold. First, it stresses preemption over deterrence as a strategy for dealing with threats. Second, it posits that American military power must be the operating framework for this new strategy—not just as a practical expedient, temporary and unavoidable, but as an inherently valuable and permanent ideal.

"Traditional concepts of deterrence," the Bush authors write, "will not work against a terrorist enemy whose avowed tactics are wanton destruction and the targeting of innocents; whose so-called soldiers seek martyrdom in death and whose most potent protection is statelessness." It's hard to argue with this. Deterrence is a problematical doctrine for the world that has emerged in the past decade and especially in the past year. Deterrence worked well (well, worked) in the Cartesian clockwork universe of the Cold War, with its two balanced superpowers, each armed to the teeth, each with something to lose, one "good" and one "evil" but both essentially rational, both philosophically rooted in the Enlightenment, and both professing dedication to a vision of a secular democratic commonwealth. (The Soviet claim to such a vision was as false as the vision itself was attractive. The falsity gave communism its singularly diabolical, Orwellian character; the attractiveness was a factor in the final internal crisis of the regime, when, in the most ironic manner possible, the Soviet state withered away.) Of course, Cold War–era deterrence looks a lot better in retrospect than it did at the time. The superpowers came to it by default, as the best of a bad lot of choices. It came close to failing more than once, and its failure might have meant something akin to the end of the world.

Global fault lines are different now, and not so tidy. Liberal democracy versus fanatic Islamist fundamentalism: that's not a dialectic, or even a geographic rivalry—it's two worlds conceptually (though not, alas, physically) sealed off from one another. In the new situation, the consequences of nuclear use, though more horrible than those of any of history's previous paroxysms, would still be much less so than would have been the consequences of all-out nuclear war between the United States and the Soviet Union. The ultimate worst-case scenario is now obsolete, and vanishingly improbable. But the bad-case scenario, involving deaths in the tens or hundreds of thousands, is much, much more likely. Bush is right that traditional deterrence is inadequate in the case of stateless outlaw bands like Al Qaeda. And the reliability of deterrence in such cases as Iraq is at best debatable. "America is now threatened less by conquering states than we are by failing ones," the Bush authors write. "We are menaced less by fleets and armies than by catastrophic technologies in the hands of the embittered few." They're right about that, too.

So: preemption, yes—when demonstrably necessary, and as a last resort. But unilateral preemption? Not so fast.

The key phrase in the Bush document, judging by the number of times it is repeated (five), is "a balance of power that favors freedom." The authors do not define it, except by implication. The usual definition of a balance of power ("a state of peace that results when rival nations are equally powerful and therefore have no good reason to wage war," according to E. D. Hirsch, Jr.,'s *New Dictionary of Cultural Literacy,* an impeccably conservative source) is certainly not what they have in mind, since they also write, "Our forces will be strong enough to dissuade potential adversaries from pursuing a military build-up in hopes of surpassing, or equaling, the power of the United States." An overwhelming preponderance of power, not a static balance, is more like it.

The vision laid out in the Bush document is a vision of what used to be called, when we believed it to be the Soviet ambition, world domination. It's a vision of a world in which it is American policy to prevent the emergence of any rival power, whatever it stands for—a world policed and controlled by American military might. This goes much further than the notion of America as the policeman of the world. It's the notion of America as both the policeman and the legislator of the world, and it's where the Bush vision goes seriously, even chillingly, wrong. A police force had better be embedded in and guided by a structure of law and consent. There's a name for the kind of regime in which the cops rule, answering only to themselves. It's called a police state.

The Bush doctrine's answer to this objection is essentially this: Hey, we're the good guys. People—especially people who share our values, like the citizens of democratic Europe, but everybody else, too—should embrace American hegemony, because surely they know that we would use our great power only for good things, like advancing democracy, keeping powerful weapons out of the hands of terrorists, and facilitating peaceful commerce. And so we have done, most of the time; and so no doubt we would do, most of the time. But what a naïve view of power and human nature! Whatever became of the conservative suspicion of untrammelled power, the conservative insight that good intentions are not, are never, enough? Where is the conservative belief in limited government, in checks and balances? Burke spins in his grave. Madison and Hamilton torque it up, too. Are we now to assume that Americans are exempt from fallen human nature? That we stand outside history? It's as if the Bush authors' brains had been softened by an overdose of anti-"moral equivalency" vaccine. Conservatives used to fault liberals (often unfairly, but never mind) for thinking that there was no such thing as evil, that the Soviets (and the criminals, and the terrorists) were just put upon and misunderstood. Conservatives spend a lot of time congratulating themselves on their "moral clarity." The Soviet Union was an evil empire; Osama is evil; the axis of evil is evil. Nothing more need be said, nothing more need be understood. And if the other side is absolutely evil then we must be absolutely good, so it's fine for us to be absolutely powerful. We should be neither surprised nor indignant if our friends in Europe and elsewhere don't see things in quite the same way.

There's a contradiction at the heart of the Bush strategy. It implicitly recognizes that national sovereignty is in many ways an outdated and dangerous doctrine, one that must increasingly give way to other exigencies. Is the sovereignty of the Iraqi state to be valued more than the right of Iraq's neighbors and the rest of the world to be reasonably free of the fear of being vaporized or sickened unto death by Iraqi weapons of mass destruction? Of course not. So the Bush doctrine, in spite of itself, recognizes the logic of something like (to use a term that is the ultimate red flag for conservatives) world government. But its idea of world government looks very much like a benevolent American dictatorship—a dictatorship of the entrepreneuriat, you might say. And if the Europeans are a little alarmed, it's not just because of their own military insignificance, or because they're a bunch of weak-wristed, spineless wimps who resent the sight of somebody strong, tough, and decisive. It's because, from Napoleon through Stalin and beyond, a century and a half of blood-soaked history taught them that untrammelled national power seldom ends by reaching a salutary balance.

A huge opportunity was lost at the end of the Cold War, especially during the Clinton administration, when a long interlude of relative calm, combined with the rapid spread of democracy and market economics, opened up a chance for deep, thoroughgoing reform of the international system, including the United Nations itself, to make international organizations more energetic and more responsible and to create an international military capability that could be strong, flexible, and quick enough to, yes, police the world. Were these—are these—impossible goals? Why should they be? The nearly bloodless disappearance of the Soviet Union and the ideology behind it, the mostly peaceful transformation of the apartheid state into a multiracial democracy, the emergence of India and (Communist!) China as twin engines of capitalism—weren't these things impossible, too?

We have, increasingly, a global economy and a global society. The global polity is underdeveloped by comparison. If borders cannot protect the innocent, they should not be allowed to protect the guilty. There may be times, when all else fails, that unilateral American military action will be necessary, and Iraq may turn out to be one of those times. But the animating vision of American foreign policy should not be a Pax Americana, a global American empire, but a world of law and consent. American hegemony is preferable to fundamentalist Islamist hegemony, just as it was preferable to Soviet hegemony. But it's hard to imagine feebler praise.

When the United States government recognizes "friendly" military dictators abroad, we generally stipulate that their rule is expected to be transitional, that they are meant to regard their power as temporary and extraordinary, and that they are supposed to use it to prepare the institutional conditions for the introduction or reintroduction of democracy. A kind of global American military dictatorship may be for the moment something close to an unavoidable reality. But the Bush document seems to embrace it as a final end. It finds room for a denunciation of the International Criminal Court, but not for the slightest suggestion, however theoretical or remote, that a workable, democratic structure of international law might someday be a better, more just guarantor of peace and security than the power and intentions of any single country.

The Bush vision is in the end a profoundly pessimistic one, and, as such, more than a little un-American. It is, among other things, a vision of perpetual war. "World peace" used to be such an uncontroversially good thing that Miss America contestants, even at the height of the Cold War, could safely say that they were in favor of it. Now they'll have to say, "As Miss America, I hope to help little children and work on behalf of United States world domination." It's a dismal dream, and an ignoble guide for American foreign policy.

2000 AND TWO

SEVEN WEEKS AGO, the first anniversary of the World Trade Center and Pentagon attacks was commemorated with appropriately solemn ceremony. November 7th marks another anniversary, the second, of another American injury.

In terms of national and international upheaval, geopolitical importance, and, above all, human suffering, there is, of course, no comparison between the events of September 11, 2001, and those accompanying the presidential election of 2000. No evil conspiracy planned the latter; no one died on account of it; no children's dreams are haunted by it. Yet there is no doubt that American democracy suffered a grievous wound. September 11th presented a challenge to America's leaders, and by and large, especially in the early months, they rose to it. The challenge posed by November 7th, however, has never been met.

The most obvious aspect of that challenge is that for the first time since the nineteenth century the United States is governed by a president who, as a candidate, was rejected at the polls. *The Longest Night: Polemics and Perspectives on Election 2000* (California), a just published collection of essays by some two dozen distinguished scholars of law and history, includes several contributions from foreign observers. One of them, Shlomo Avineri, of Jerusalem's Hebrew University, notes sharply, "Certainly there is no other democratic society in which an executive president can be elected if he receives fewer popular votes than his major contender." But, as he points out, this possibility persists for good historical reasons, notably the patchwork way in which modern democratic norms were gradually and informally grafted onto the Constitution's eighteenth-century contrivances. In Avineri's words, "the democratization of the American system happened incrementally, not through revolution or rupture; new wine was poured into old vessels." He adds, "This nonviolent incrementalism is clearly praiseworthy; yet in Florida in 2000 it exacted its price."

It sure did. The victory of a popular-vote loser in the Electoral College, the leakiest old vessel of all, would have created a ticklish dilemma even if it had happened cleanly. It did not happen cleanly. Florida was an unremitting travesty, right down to the awarding of the state and the presidency to George W. Bush by the five most conservative justices of the Supreme Court, in a decision so shoddily reasoned and so at odds with their normal jurisprudential inclinations that the only plausible explanation for it is that they were simply imposing their political preference. How one feels about this depends at least partly on one's own political preference. But not even the most complacent Bush supporters could deny that their man was taking office under unusual circumstances.

The new president's response to all this was to ignore it. He made no attempt to broaden his government or to mitigate its program of putting money in the pockets of the rich, rolling back environmental protections, favoring energy extraction over conservation, and the rest. Bush's intransigence demanded a response, and it must be said that Gore did not provide one.

What might Gore have done? By a plurality of half a million, the voters had expressed a preference for his ideas (though not, one guesses, his personality) over Bush's. If you include the net third-party vote, the plurality becomes a clear center-left majority. Early on—even before the inauguration, perhaps—Gore could have said, first, that he did not question the legitimacy of Bush's claim to the office and would support him when possible; second, that the national popular vote, while constitutionally irrelevant, was the opposite of a political mandate for wrenching the country to the right; and, third, that he, Gore, believed that the popular vote had imposed upon him an obligation to speak for those whose interests and values would now be shut out of the executive branch of government. Then, perhaps in a series of monthly speeches, he should have spoken out, politely but firmly, on the issues of the moment.

Instead, he fell silent. He did not accept—and apparently did not perceive—the responsibility that his popular-vote victory had laid upon him. The other day, a Fox News poll had twice as many people saying that they would have felt "less safe" with Gore in the White House than they do with Bush. Does this reflect a belief (almost certainly incorrect) that Gore would have been less than vigorous in going after the terrorists? Maybe. But perhaps it also reflects a recognition that at a crucial moment he essentially left voiceless those who had placed their trust in him.

As for Bush, he is now spending the last days before the midterm election campaigning almost continuously to retain his party's control over the House of Representatives, recapture the Senate, and, by extension, consolidate the conservative Supreme Court majority that made him president in the first place. Trent Lott, the Senate Republican leader, explained the other day what would follow. "We will come out of the gate next year fast," he said, and listed these legislative priorities: confirming some fifty conservative nominees to the federal judiciary; expanding tax cuts, which go overwhelmingly to the very rich; enacting a prescription-drug plan that, bypassing Medicare, would require the elderly to buy coverage from private insurers; banning certain late-term abortions; and squelching any strengthening of gun control. This was the Republican agenda before 9/11, and it was unpopular enough that President Bush's approval ratings were steadily sinking. For good reason, it's still not popular. But, thanks to 9/11 and its aftermath, Bush is. And Democrats can be forgiven for feeling a little bitter that the political legitimacy he failed to earn at the polls ended up being conferred on him by Osama bin Laden.

—*The New Yorker*, November 4, 2002

TOO MUCH INFORMATION

WHEN IT COMES TO concocting fevered visions of the future as a way of illuminating the present, Jules Verne got some things right in his time, Aldous Huxley got others, and George Orwell got still others. In our time—in this terror-haunted interlude (we hope) of background-hum dread and well-founded paranoia—no literary divinator gets it righter than the sci-fi pulp master Philip K. Dick, author of *Clans of the Alphane Moon* and dozens of other books, and inspirer of some of Hollywood's spookiest dystopias, including *Blade Runner, Total Recall,* and *Minority Report.* And this is odd, given that he has been dead for twenty years. Too bad he's not still around. It would be interesting to get his take on the Information Awareness Office of the Defense Advanced Research Projects Agency of the Department of Defense.

The Information Awareness Office plays it so weird that one can't help suspecting that somebody on its staff might be putting us on. The Information Awareness Office's official seal features an occult pyramid topped with mystic all-seeing eye, like the one on the dollar bill. Its official motto is "Scientia Est Potentia," which doesn't mean "science has a lot of potential." It means "knowledge is power." And its official mission is to "imagine, develop, apply, integrate, demonstrate and transition information technologies, components and prototype, closed-loop, information systems that will counter asymmetric threats by achieving total information awareness."

The phrase "total information awareness" is creepy enough to merit a place alongside "USA Patriot Act" and "Department of Homeland Security," but it is not the Information Awareness Office's only gift to the language. The "example technologies" which the office intends to develop include "entity extraction from natural language text," "biologically inspired algorithms for agent control," and "truth maintenance." One of the office's thirteen subdivisions, the Human Identification at a Distance (HumanID) program, is letting contracts not only for "Face Recognition" and "Iris Recognition" but also for "Gait Recognition." (Tony Blair has pledged the full cooperation of the Ministry of Silly Walks.) Another of the thirteen, FutureMap, "will concentrate on market-based techniques for avoiding surprise and predicting future events"—a sounder approach, ideologically, than regulation-based liberal soothsaying.

The Information Awareness Office is working on some really cool stuff that will eventually turn up at Brookstone and the Sharper Image, like a PalmPilot–size PDA that does instantaneous English-Arabic and English-Chinese translations. But the office's main assignment is, basically, to turn everything in cyberspace about everybody—tax records, driver's-license applications, travel records, bank records, raw F.B.I. files, telephone records, credit-card records, shopping-mall security-camera videotapes, medical records, every e-mail anybody ever sent—into a single, humongous, multi-googolplexibyte database that electronic robots will mine for patterns of information suggestive of terrorist activity. Dr. Strangelove's vision—"a chikentic gomplex of gumbyuders"—is at last coming into its own.

It's easy to ridicule this—fun, too, and fun is something the war on terrorism doesn't offer a lot of—but it's not so easy to dismiss the possibility that the project, nutty as it sounds, might actually be of significant help in uncovering terrorist networks. The problem is that it would also be of significant help in uncovering just about everything, including the last vestiges of individual and family privacy. This is why William Safire wrote the other day that the program should simply be shut down, as was Attorney General Ashcroft's Terrorism Information and Prevention System (TIPS), which was going to enlist postal workers and the like as amateur spies.

At a minimum, a temporary shutdown, pending some sort of congressional review and the creation of safeguards, would seem to be in order. It will take years for total information awareness to get beyond the prototype stage. But if a working system ever does get up and running, you won't have to be Philip K. Dick to imagine the possibilities for mischief, especially if carelessness, to say nothing of malevolence, enters the picture. But not to worry. "The privacy of individuals not affiliated with terrorism" will be protected via "technologies for controlling automated search and exploitation algorithms and for purging data structures appropriately."

And who is offering this highly reassuring assurance? Why, the Director of the Information Awareness Office, John M. Poindexter, that's who. The office's Web site offers biographical sketches of the new agency's principal bureaucrats—or did offer them until the night of November 26th, when they mysteriously disappeared. Poindexter's is, or was, in the form of a résumé, of exactly the kind one would submit to a prospective corporate employer. It is a model of the genre: two crisp pages, neatly typed, no oddball fonts. The career it describes—Caltech Ph.D., flag-rank naval officer, White House senior staffer, high-tech business executive—is impressive. On the other hand, the information provided falls somewhat short of total. The passage concerning Poindexter's stint as Ronald Reagan's national-security adviser concludes as follows:

> Major events in which he played a significant role included: Strategic Defense Initiative, Grenada Rescue Operation, Achille Lauro incident, Libyan Operation to respond to terrorist attacks, Reykjavik Summit with Soviets, peaceful transition of government in the Philippines, support for the democratic resistance in Nicaragua, and an attempt to begin rationalization of U.S. relationship with strategically important Iran.

Cryptologists will detect in the last two items a reference to what made Poindexter, for a time, famous: the scheme to sell arms secretly to the mullahs of Iran and use the proceeds to get around a congressional ban on funding the anti-Sandinista guerrillas of Nicaragua. Poindexter's role in what became the messiest political scandal of the 1980s got him convicted of five felonies (including two counts of lying to Congress) and sentenced to six months in the federal penitentiary. He was saved from jail by an appeals-court ruling that his trial had been tainted by his own testimony, given under a grant of immunity, before a congressional committee. The facts of the case, however, stand. So does the conclusion of the trial judge, Harold H. Greene, that Poindexter's actions traduced the principle "that those elected by and responsible to the people shall make the important policy decisions, and that their decisions may not be nullified by appointed

officials who happen to be in positions that give them the ability to operate programs prohibited by law."

But even when intentions are good, as conservatives should know, it's not
enough. (The F.B.I. was supposed to be a bunch of clean-cut guys chasing
bank robbers, but by the mid-sixties it was putting tape recorders under
Martin Luther King's bed and urging him to commit suicide.) We may not
always have a leader as punctilious about civil liberties as President Bush—
and even he has some people around him (Poindexter, for one; Ashcroft, for
another) whose devotion to the Bill of Rights sometimes seems shaky.
Maybe the administration needs to catch up on its sci-fi reading. Philip K.
meant his dark visions as warnings, not as bureaucratic charters for George
W. Unfortunately, Bush doesn't know Dick.

—*The New Yorker*, December 9, 2002

BLIXKRIEG

THE MOST TASTELESS PASSAGE in last week's State of the Union message came about half an hour into the speech, as President Bush was enumerating his administration's successes against Al Qaeda. Three thousand suspected terrorists have been arrested, he said. "And many others have met a different fate," he went on. "Let's put it this way: they are no longer a problem to the United States and our friends and allies." Talk about smoking guns. You could almost see the president blowing across the upturned barrel of his Colt .45.

This was not the first Clint Eastwood moment in the history of the modern presidency. "Go ahead—make my day," Ronald Reagan said, back in 1985. "Read my lips," added his vice president, George H. W. Bush, in accepting the Republican presidential nomination in 1988. But they were merely promising to veto tax bills. Their bravado came with a twinkle. Bush the younger was talking about extrajudicial killings.

Under certain conditions—when the targets are known terrorists, arrest is not a practical option, and the risk to innocent civilians is small—such killings can be preferable to permitting escape. But for the president to boast of them so flippantly was not exactly an example of the moral clarity that is supposed to be his specialty. "They are no longer a problem." This sounded less like Reagan or Bush the elder than like—Well, let's put it this way. In a chilling account of Saddam Hussein's cruelties in the *New York Times* a couple of days before the speech, John F. Burns identified one of the dictator's favorite maxims: "If there is a person, then there is a problem. If there is no person, then there is no problem."

The president's swagger is the sort of thing that Europeans, especially "old" Europeans, have in mind when they grumble that our president is a callow cowboy. But the difficulty goes beyond the personality of George W. Bush. One cannot spend time in any of the other developed democracies without being struck by the damage the administration's wise-guy unilateralism has done, not only on the issue of Iraq but also on strategically marginal topics like the Kyoto environmental agreement, family planning, and the International Criminal Court. Everyone expected this pattern to change after the attacks of September 11, 2001. It didn't. The opportunity presented by Europe's instinctive solidarity—epitomized by NATO's decision to invoke, for the first time ever, the provision of its charter declaring that an attack against one is an attack against all—has been wasted. It's only natural that Europe, absorbed in creating a continental order based on nonviolent shared sovereignty, and the United States, whose unmatched military power confers unmatched responsibility, should view the world differently. Some degree of American unilateralism is inescapable. But this administration seldom bothers to observe the minimal decencies. Europeans remain proud of their participation in Afghanistan (just last week, Norwegian F-16s saw action in a battle against a holdout pro-Taliban warlord), but they have been steadily pushed toward seeing the struggle against terrorism as America's war, not theirs.

In the days after Bush's speech there was much discussion of whether he had "made the case." But the real question, whatever Bush says, is whether there is a case. In that connection, last week's most important speech was not the State of the Union. It was the report the day before by Hans Blix, of the United Nations Monitoring, Verification, and Inspection Commission (UNMOVIC), and it was not the whitewash that conservative commentators had preemptively decided it would be. In its drip-drip-drip way, the Blix report is completely consistent with the view that the Iraqi regime is cooperating only to the minimal extent required to avoid immediate attack and that it has no intention of giving up its murderous ambitions. The closest Blix gets to a conclusion—and it may be close enough—comes in this sentence: "Unlike South Africa, which decided on its own to eliminate its nuclear weapons and welcomed inspection as a means of creating confidence in its disarmament, Iraq appears not to have come to a genuine acceptance—not even today—of the disarmament which was demanded of it and which it needs to carry out to win the confidence of the world and to live in peace." To put what Blix is saying another way, if the Iraqi regime continues to resist disarmament then it must expect war. Even if one distrusts the Bush administration, it's hard to disagree.

It's also hard to disagree with the case for leaving the inspection regime in place for a time. As Blix reports, in two months UNMOVIC has built its staff in Iraq from zero to 260. It has eight helicopters and will soon have the use of unmanned aerial surveillance vehicles and U-2 aircraft. The chances of a conclusive discovery, or of a conclusive Iraqi effort to thwart one, are growing. A little more time, especially if it comes with a Security Council resolution unambiguously authorizing force if Iraq does not unambiguously disarm, would mitigate the damage to allied unity, lessen the (largely self-created) isolation of the United States, and create a basis for international burden-sharing in the rebuilding of Iraq.

The debate over Iraq has focussed almost entirely on the before and the after. What has hardly been discussed is the war itself. The administration's hawks and the op-ed falconers say it will be short and relatively bloodless. But wars seldom unfold as planned. Twelve years ago, Saddam's forces were massed in an empty desert. Today, though weaker, they are scattered throughout a thickly populated country the size of Germany. A war plan leaked last week to David Martin, of CBS News, calls for up to eight hundred cruise-missile strikes during the first two days—twice as many as during the forty days of the Gulf War. Martin quotes a Pentagon official as saying, "There will not be a safe place in Baghdad." The plan is called "Shock and Awe," and its goal is "the psychological destruction of the enemy's will to fight." Or perhaps that is merely the goal of the leak. But any campaign is likely to begin with bombs over Baghdad. Many people will die. And if Iraq's response to the bombing of its capital city is more like London's in 1940 or Hanoi's in 1966 than like Belgrade's in 1999—if its Army's will is stiffened rather than broken—then no one can say how much suffering and death might follow.

The other day, Secretary of State Colin Powell was reminded that his boss is in bed by ten and sleeps like a baby. Powell reportedly replied, "I sleep like a baby, too—every two hours I wake up screaming." The president's serenity is more worrying than the general's anxiety is comforting. And the storm approaches.

—The New Yorker, February 10, 2003

ATTACK ANXIETY

WRITING ON THE op-ed page of the *New York Times* the other day, Christopher Buckley reminisced about a previous era when Europeans turned out by the million to demonstrate in the streets against what they took to be American bellicosity. Twenty years ago, Buckley, who is now a well-known satirical novelist, was an aide to the then vice president of the United States, George H. W. Bush. What Europeans were protesting in 1983 was the pending deployment on their territory of Pershing 2 missiles, which their governments had earlier demanded in order to offset similar Soviet missiles that were already in place. At a Q&A session in London's Guildhall, with demonstrators shouting outside, a clergyman got up to say indignantly that he didn't want to see his children incinerated in an American-initiated nuclear war. According to Buckley, Bush managed to defuse the moment. "Look, I have kids, too," the vice president said plaintively. "Don't you think I want to see them grow up?"

Although Buckley doesn't mention it (he is making a different point, about the value of diplomatic tact), and although his boss probably didn't mean to be taken literally, the five Bush kids, at that moment, were not exactly toddlers. They ranged in age from twenty-three to thirty-six. But the eldest, if no longer a child, had not fully made the transition to adulthood. He had fumbled a congressional campaign that seemed to voters little more than a rich boy's indulgence; he had blown the first of his subsidized forays into the oil business; he was partying hard. He was still three years away from giving up drink, taking up religion, and beginning his fitful ascent.

Now the thirty-six-year-old is a fifty-six-year-old, and he is, ex officio, all grown up. He is the president of the United States, and a great deal hangs on the maturity and wisdom of his judgment. That, to some, is not a comforting thought.

George W. Bush is not perplexed about what must be done about Saddam Hussein's Iraq. He believes that there must be war, and soon, and he has lost no sleep over it. "If anyone can be at peace," he said the other day, "I am at peace about this." The president is one of those lucky people who know exactly what they think about Iraq—know it to a moral certainty, as the saying goes. Such people flourish on both sides. On one side is a set of mostly neoconservative policy intellectuals and civilian Pentagon officials, some of whom have been maneuvering for a decade toward the war that is nearly upon us. Their most reliable supporters, besides the president, are the sort of evangelical Christian conservatives who contemplate Armageddon with something like rapture. On the other side, equally convinced of their moral rectitude, are traditional pacifists and the sort of angry leftists for whom any exercise of American military power, because it is American, is wrong. They (along with activists from the mainstream Christian denominations, Protestant, Catholic, and Orthodox) provided the organizing energy and most of the platform rhetoric—though not the massive numbers—for the street demonstrations of February 15th.

Not everyone is so sure. Both among those who, on balance, support the coming war and among those who, on balance, oppose it are a great many who hold their views in fear and trembling, haunted by the suspicion that the other side might be right after all. In the American "homeland," the anxiety that this crisis is provoking is physical (a dread that, for obvious reasons, is perhaps stronger in New York and Washington than elsewhere), but it is also intellectual. The divisions are profound, and the most agonizing are not between people but within them. The phenomenon is visible in the tabular abstractions of opinion surveys. According to one fairly typical recent poll, conducted for the University of Maryland's Program on International Policy Attitudes, only a bare majority of the public favors the United Nations' authorizing an invasion as opposed to a "strengthened inspection process." But much larger—and therefore substantially overlapping—majorities, usually in the 70 percent range, say that they are convinced by the mutually exclusive arguments of both sides. They agree that the United States should not invade Iraq without the approval of the United Nations, and also that the U.N.'s disapproval must not be allowed to stand in the way; that Iraqi intransigence is such that the United States now has no choice but to invade, and also that strengthened inspections are preferable to invasion; that an invasion should begin soon, because Iraq's weapons of mass destruction will otherwise only become stronger, and also that an invasion should not begin at all, because it would provoke Saddam to use those weapons. When people have no idea of the consequences of a given course of action or inaction, they don't know which way to turn—or they turn both ways.

Last week, while the administration was strenuously hinting that war might be only days away, the full, catastrophic dimensions of its diplomatic endgame ballooned into view. On Saturday, the Turkish parliament unexpectedly rebelled, voting down a government proposal to let the United States use Turkish bases as the staging ground for a northern front in Iraq. All through the week, American officials, from the president on down, tried futilely to get commitments from enough of the six wavering nonpermanent members of the Security Council to guarantee the nine out of fifteen votes necessary, assuming no vetoes, to pass a new resolution sponsored by the United States, Britain, and Spain. By midweek, none had said yes, and Chile had said no. Canada, our friendly neighbor to the north, was said to be seething because a compromise that it had quietly, tentatively floated—it would have set a new but not distant deadline for full Iraqi compliance (the end of March, say), authorizing "all necessary means" if specific goals were not met—was deemed by the administration to be unworthy of even cursory exploration. Then, on Wednesday, the foreign ministers of France, Russia, and Germany stood together in Paris and pronounced the new resolution all but dead. Washington had not expected this, either. Patrick Tyler, on the front page of the *Times*, called it a "thunderbolt" that "may go down as the loudest 'No!' shouted across the Atlantic in a half-century or more." "In these circumstances," the Franco-Russian-German statement said (without quite explaining what "these circumstances" were), "we will not let a proposed resolution pass that would authorize the use of force. Russia and France, as permanent members of the Security Council, will assume all their responsibilities on this point." The word "veto" was not mentioned; but then, when President Bush speaks of America assuming its responsibilities with respect to Iraq, the word "war" is not usually mentioned, either.

After September 11, 2001, enormous crowds in Berlin and London and Paris, and even in Tehran, bore candlelit witness to their solidarity with wounded America. NATO, for the first time ever, invoked the provision of its charter declaring an attack against one to be an attack against all. With the blessing of the U.N. Security Council, the soldiers of a dozen countries fought alongside ours in Afghanistan. (Germans and French, among others, are still there.) Just a year and a half later, in almost every sizable city of Europe, North America, and the rest of the democratic world, the United States government became the target of what was apparently the largest coordinated one-day popular protest in the history of the world. In the Security Council, America's adversaries suddenly include, for the time being, at least, its putative friends, old and new alike. And wherever pollsters ply their trade they find—incredibly—that the publics of the democratic world regard the United States as a greater menace to peace and safety than Iraq.

How did it come to this? Some of the strain, as Robert Kagan argues, is structural, the natural result of asymmetries—of military strength, of historical experience—between America and Europe. And some is the consequence of European obtuseness, shortsightedness, hypocrisy, and wishful thinking. Russia and France (and, to a lesser extent, Germany) are not without blame in this crackup. Each in its own way is playing for advantage, worrying over its portion of influence in the world, calculating its economic stakes in Iraq and the Middle East generally. But it is the policies, attitudes, and ideological blindnesses of the Bush administration that have turned a chronic but manageable alliance problem into an acute crisis.

"The scale of the failure of U.S. diplomacy to give Bush workable alternatives to the situation in which he finds himself—going to war over the concerted opposition of allies and world public opinion—is staggering," Jim Hoagland, the normally hawkish foreign policy columnist of the *Washington Post,* wrote last week. The roots of that failure have been growing for two years. The administration trashed the Kyoto environmental treaty, the A.B.M. treaty, and the treaty establishing the International Criminal Court, and did so contemptuously and arrogantly, without offering compromises or remedies for their flaws; it demanded the ouster of Yasir Arafat while offering no resistance to the expansion of Israeli settlements in the West Bank; it defined the war on terrorism exclusively in the theological language of good versus evil, viewing any attempt to analyze terrorism politically as morally inadmissible; it undermined the power of the persuasive reasons for confronting Saddam (such as his consistent failure to disclose and dispose of his weapons of mass destruction) by mixing them with unpersuasive ones (such as his alleged cooperation with Al Qaeda); it created the impression that the U.N. effort to disarm Iraq has been a charade masking a predetermined plan to oust Saddam by force no matter what. Even among those who believe that an invasion of Iraq, sooner or later, cannot be avoided, some are asking, Where is the administration's wisdom, its sense of diplomatic touch, its Great Power modesty?

"I can only just go by my instincts," President Bush told Bob Woodward in an interview for *Bush at War*. Woodward adds, "It's pretty clear that Bush's role as politician, president and commander in chief is driven by a secular faith in his instincts—his natural and spontaneous conclusions and judgments. His instincts are almost his second religion." And if the commandment of his first religion is peace, that of his second, it seems clearer than ever, is war.

—*The New Yorker*, March 17, 2003

COLLATERAL DAMAGE

ONE OF THE characteristic horrors of what Raymond Aron called the century of total war was the expansion of the battlefield to encompass whole societies. In many of the twentieth century's conflicts, from the Philippines to Algeria to Vietnam and beyond, the distinction between soldiers and civilians offered the latter scant protection. In the bloodiest of all, the Second World War, both sides adopted a strategy of deliberately killing civilians and destroying cities—usually by means of aerial bombing, and always with the aim of breaking an enemy nation's will, or, failing that, its physical ability, to continue. The "good war," in this respect, was bad in the extreme. The damage inflicted upon London and Dresden, Rotterdam and Tokyo, Leningrad and Hiroshima, was anything but collateral. It was the whole point.

Whatever else can be said about the war against the Iraqi dictatorship that began on March 19th, it cannot be said that the Anglo-American invaders have pursued anything remotely resembling a policy of killing civilians deliberately. And, so far, they have gone to great tactical and technological lengths to avoid doing it inadvertently, too. Collateral damage is one of those antiseptic-sounding euphemisms that are sometimes more chilling than plain language, so hard do they labor to conceal their human meaning. It would be indecent to belittle the agony that has already been inflicted; you have only to imagine yourself, for example, as the parent or child of one of the dozens of people who were blown apart or maimed last Wednesday, and again last Friday, when stray bombs plowed into Baghdad marketplaces.

But this kind of "damage" is indeed "collateral," not only in that there is a serious effort to avoid it but also in that the intended purpose of the bombing of Baghdad, which so far has apparently been aimed only at military and government installations, has been to break not the will of the Iraqi people but the connections between them and their tyrannical rulers. Indiscriminate bombing would actually strengthen those connections, as we know from the experience of the Second World War and Vietnam. What we do not yet know is whether a different intention, backed by technologies of precision, will produce a different political result. And we do not yet know whether even the intention can survive the transition—which suddenly seems more likely than not—from a quick war of shock and awe to a grinding, protracted struggle, hand to hand and house to house.

The war in Iraq is a new kind of total war. The immense anxiety it is provoking throughout the Western world, perhaps most keenly in the United States, is more than a matter of compassion for the sufferings of people far away. The dread is a kind that hits closer to home. It is bound up with a set of fears that, in the runup to the war, had been invoked in different ways by both supporters and opponents of the impending conflict. One such fear is that "weapons of mass destruction," especially portable ones, will find their way into the hands of undeterrable terrorists. Another is that what began as a measured campaign against terrorist bands and the handful of rogue states that may or may not try fitfully to use them for their own purposes will morph into a globe-spanning, escalating struggle between the Islamic world and the United States. The Bush administration maintains that in the end this war will lessen both of these dangers; so, more conditionally, does the government of Prime Minister Tony Blair. Many others—in good faith, here and abroad—fear that in the end this war will do just the opposite.

The clash of arms is sharply limited in space, in time, and in the number of actual participants; but it is unlimited in its psychic presence in the lives of virtually every sentient person in the developed and half-developed world. The satellites that orbit the earth and the hundreds of millions of television sets that dot it insure that this is so. The fighting may not be total, but the audience is total; and in this sense the war is total. It is a world war. The war as it is seen here is not quite the same as it is seen elsewhere—elsewhere the screen shows more corpses and fewer retired generals with maps and pointers—but everywhere the war fills the field of vision. And this, too, brings its own kind of collateral damage.

One small example: Within hours of the war's beginning, the Cuban government began systematically arresting its nonviolent opponents and confiscating their papers, typewriters, and other records. Although the handful of leaders whose names are best known abroad have (for that reason) been left alone, those who have been seized make up the bulk of the active civic opposition, which, on account of the option of exile, is as small as it is courageous. Seventy-seven men and one woman were behind bars as of the end of last week, including the poet Raúl Rivero, once the Moscow bureau chief of Prensa Latina, the Cuban news agency, now an independent journalist; Oscar Espinosa Chepe, an economist and ex-foreign-service officer; and Marcelo López Bañobre, a former tugboat captain, now spokesman for the Cuban Commission for Human Rights and National Reconciliation. The predicament of these people, who are guilty only of bearing witness to facts the regime wants to suppress, is enviable compared with that of those who are suffering and dying in Iraq today, and also of those who have suffered and died there through the decades of Saddam's rule. There's a war on, and Fidel Castro knows it. Absent Iraq, what the Commandante is doing would be front-page news throughout Europe and the Americas; most likely he would not be doing it at all. "Human rights in Cuba can therefore be viewed as one of the first cases of collateral damage in the second Gulf war," Robert Ménard, secretary general of Reporters Without Borders, said on March 21st. "Human rights in other countries could also soon suffer the same fate." Mr. Ménard is French; even so, he was soon proved right. In Zimbabwe last week, hundreds of opponents of the Robert Mugabe regime were arrested or beaten. There is similar news from Belarus, but it is little seen or heard. The fog of war is thick, and it covers the globe.

—*The New Yorker*, April 7, 2003

BUILDING NATIONS

THE OTHER DAY, the *Times* quoted one of that ever-helpful breed, a "senior administration official," as expressing surprise at the horrendous condition of Iraq's "infrastructure," even before the destruction brought about by the war and its aftermath. "From the outside it looked like Baghdad was a city that works," the senior official said. "It isn't."

The quintessential city that works (or, at least, has a cleverly cultivated reputation for being the city that works) is, of course, Chicago. The ward heelers and aldermen of that city understand (or, at least, are celebrated in song and story for understanding) that political power flows not from the barrel of a gun, and not even, necessarily, from the ballot box (whose contents can change in the counting), but from the ability to fix potholes. Garbage that gets collected, buses and trains that take people places, cops that whack bad guys upside the head, taps that yield water when you turn them, lights that go on when you flip the switch, all lubricated by taxes and a bit of honest graft—these are what keep streets calm, voters pacified, and righteous "reformers" out of city hall.

By Chicago standards, Baghdad, along with almost all the rest of Iraq, is a catastrophe. For that matter, conditions are disastrous even by the looser standards of places like Beirut and Bombay. Reports from the scene are in general agreement on the essentials. Iraq is well rid of the murderous regime of Saddam Hussein. But the blithe assumptions of the Iraq war's Pentagon architects—that a grateful Iraqi nation, with a little help from American know-how and Iraqi oil cash, would quickly pick itself up, dust itself off, and start all over again—are as shattered as the buildings that used to house Saddam's favorite restaurants. In Baghdad, and in many other Iraqi cities and towns, civic society has degenerated into a Hobbesian state of nature. Despite the heroic efforts of a scattered minority of midlevel Iraqi civil servants, the services that make urban life viable are functioning, at best, erratically. More often, they do not function at all. "In the most palpable of ways, the American promise of a new Iraq is floundering on the inability of the American occupiers to provide basic services," the *Times*'s Neela Banerjee reported a few days ago. (Perhaps with an eye to educating her White House readers, she added that Baghdad is "about the size of metropolitan Houston.") Telephones are dead. Electricity and running water work, if at all, for only a few hours a day. Because the water pumps are hobbled by power outages, raw sewage is pouring into the Tigris River and is leaking into the fresh-water system, spreading disease and making the city stink. Hospitals that are secure enough to remain open overflow with patients, but they are short of food, medical supplies, and personnel. (Only a fifth of prewar health staffs are showing up for work.) Worst of all is the pervasive, well-founded fear of crime. Armed thugs rule the streets, especially in the pitch-black nights. "Amid such privations," Banerjee writes, "one of the few things that thrives now in Baghdad, at least, is a deepening distrust and anger toward the United States."

It's tempting to suggest that the Bush administration is failing to provide Iraq with functioning, efficient, reliable public services because it doesn't *believe* in functioning, efficient, reliable public services—doesn't believe that they should exist, and doesn't really believe that they can exist. The reigning ideologues in Washington—not only in the White House but also in the Republican congressional leadership, in the faction that dominates the Supreme Court, and in the conservative press and think tanks—believe in free markets, individual initiative, and private schools and private charity as substitutes for public provision. They believe that the armed individual citizen is the ultimate guarantor of public safety. They do not, at bottom, believe that society, through the mechanisms of democratic government, has a moral obligation to provide care for the sick, food for the hungry, shelter for the homeless, and education for all; and to the extent that they tolerate such activities they do so grudgingly, out of political necessity. They believe that the private sector is sovereign, and that taxes are a species of theft. To paraphrase Proudhon, *les impôts, c'est le vol.*

In a way, Iraq has become a theme park of conservative policy nostrums. There are no burdensome government regulations. Health and safety inspectors and environmental busybodies are nowhere to be seen. The Ministry of Finance, Iraq's equivalent of the Internal Revenue Service, is a scorched ruin. Museums and other cultural institutions, having been largely emptied of their contents, no longer have much use for public subsidies. Gun control is being kept within reasonable limits. (Although the occupying authorities are trying to discourage possession of heavy munitions, AK-47s and other assault weapons—guns of the type whose manufacture Tom DeLay and most of the House Republicans plan to relegalize back home—have been given a pass.) And, in the absence of welfare programs and other free-lunch giveaways, faith-based initiatives are flourishing. The faith in question may be Iranian-style militant Shiism, but at least it's fundamentalist.

The Bush administration no longer flaunts its contempt for nation-building abroad, but it remains resolutely hostile to nation-building at home. Its domestic policy consists almost solely of a never-ending campaign to reduce the taxes of the very rich. Not all of this largesse will be paid for by loading debt onto future generations. Some of it is being paid for right now, by cuts in public services—cuts that outweigh the spare-change breaks for less affluent families which the administration, in selling its successive tax elixirs, has had to include in order to suppress the electorate's gag reflex. The pain is especially acute at the state level, where net federal help is in decline. States are cancelling school construction, truncating the academic year, increasing class sizes, and eliminating preschool and after-school programs. Health benefits are being slashed, and a million people will likely lose coverage altogether. In many states, even cops are getting laid off.

As it happens, these are the very kinds of public services that America's proconsuls are promising to bring to Iraq. Of course, being nice to Iraq does not necessarily require the United States to be nice to itself. Nor does denying medicine to kids in Texas require denying it to kids in Baghdad. The connection is more karmic than causal. But it's also political. Whatever one may think of the global democratic-imperial ambitions of the present administration, they cannot long coexist with the combination of narrow greed and public neglect it thinks sufficient for what it is pleased to call the homeland. At some point—the sooner the better—a critical mass of Americans will notice.

—*The New Yorker*, June 9, 2003

UNSTEADY STATE

GEORGE W. BUSH says he wants to go to Mars—a motion that many of his fellow citizens would heartily second—but he probably doesn't mean it. The speech in which he announced his "New Vision for Space Exploration" was exceedingly vague about how and when the trip was to be made. It did say that in 2015 or maybe in 2020 Americans would be going back to the moon, where they would build a base for "human missions to Mars and to worlds beyond." An official likened this speech to President Kennedy's address of May 25, 1961, in which he asked the nation to "commit itself to achieving the goal, before this decade is out, of landing a man on the moon and returning him safely to the earth."

A week later came Bush's State of the Union address, the text of which one scans in vain for any mention of Mars, the moon, or space exploration. The subject has already been dropped. (By contrast, Kennedy's 1962 State of the Union reiterated and discussed the lunar excursion he had proposed eight months before.) Nor is a short attention span the only sign of Bush's lack of seriousness about his interplanetary venture. There is also its Wal-Mart price tag. The president is asking Congress for an extra two hundred million dollars per year, about what it costs to make a movie like *Waterworld.* Another couple of billion is to be cannibalized out of the existing space budget. This kind of money will get no one to Mars, but that isn't to say that Bush's project will yield no results. It has already led to the cancellation of maintenance on the Hubble Space Telescope, NASA's most scientifically valuable project, which means that the Hubble will go blind in three or four years' time. Bush's "New Vision" is a sharp stick in the eye.

Polls published between the two Bush speeches revealed a distinct lack of public enthusiasm for the president's space proposal, and it will be surprising if he mentions it again anytime soon. But "Mars," "the moon," and "space" are not the only words missing in action from the State of the Union. So are "unemployment," "AIDS," and "the environment." "Deficit" makes but a single appearance, as part of an utterly unconvincing, detail-free assertion that the gigantic budget shortfalls with which Bush has replaced the surpluses he inherited can be halved in five years if Congress would just "focus on priorities."

The word "war," on the other hand, makes a dozen appearances in the speech, while "terror" and its derivatives appear twenty times. The surrounding contexts suggest that Bush and his political handlers plan to use 9/11 and its aftermath every bit as ruthlessly this year as they did in 2002, when Republicans captured control of the Senate by portraying Democrats as friends of terrorism. (The most prominent victim of this strategy was Senator Max Cleland, of Georgia, who lost three limbs fighting in Vietnam, and who was defeated by ads showing his face alongside those of Osama bin Laden and Saddam Hussein.) In 2004, according to Bush, "we face a choice: we can go forward with confidence and resolve, or we can turn back to the dangerous illusion that terrorists are not plotting and outlaw regimes are no threat to us." If the choice he is talking about is November's (and what else could it be?), then this is slander. The illusion that Bush describes is shared by none of the four remaining Democratic candidates with a chance at nomination. Nor, by the way, do any of them doubt that the Iraqi people are better off without the regime of Saddam Hussein. And, while all four are for other reasons critical of Bush's Iraq policies, all recognize that, like it or not, the rehabilitation of Iraq is now an American responsibility.

The truth is that at this point no one can be sure whether the Iraq war, in its overall effect, will turn out in the end to have helped or hindered the larger campaign against Islamist terrorism. What does seem fairly clear is that Iraq's biological, chemical, and, especially, nuclear weapons did not exist. Public and congressional support for the war, as well as the scattered international support it enjoyed, was therefore purchased falsely and, to a degree not yet known, dishonestly. There has been a serious breach of trust, which cannot fail to have damaging results. "For diplomacy to be effective, words must be credible, and no one can now doubt the word of America," the president said in his speech, and for a moment one couldn't be sure one had heard him right. Was he speaking ironically? America's word—the present administration's, anyway—has in fact been cast into the deepest doubt, and that is one of the reasons its diplomacy has not been effective. Bush was talking about Libya's promise, post-Iraq, to abandon its (not very scary) nuclear ambitions, and what he actually meant, of course, is that no one now doubts America's will to make war. But that is not true, either. Iraq has stretched the Pentagon's legions thin, and the misinformation that the Administration promulgated, from whatever admixture of intelligence failure and deliberate distortion, means that it will no longer be possible to rally domestic or international support for military adventures in the absence of a clear and independently verifiable *casus belli*. Washington's word won't do.

Bush's only serious (that is, expensive) domestic program, as always, is yet another mammoth tax entitlement for the rich and the superrich. The new plan would make permanent his earlier tax cuts, which, in a gimmick designed to make future deficits look less terrifying, were scheduled to expire in 2010. This new round of relief for the unneedy, like the previous three, is to be financed (though the president didn't mention this part) by confiscating the Social Security "trust fund," curtailing federal activities that benefit society at large, and borrowing more trillions—taking out a fourth mortgage on the future, payable to foreign creditors. The rest of Bush's proposals were either ruinously expensive, socially poisonous non-starters (such as privatizing Social Security), or cheap cuts of wormy red meat for the conservative and evangelical base. Of the latter the cheapest was an exhortation to professional athletes to quit taking steroids, the wormiest a threat to deface the Constitution with anti-gay graffiti.

In last year's State of the Union, Bush's buzz phrase was "weapons of mass destruction," the threat of which justified the impending conquest of Iraq. This year's speech subsumed that phrase into the longer, mealier "weapons of mass destruction-related program activities," a usefully adaptable locution. Were teams of inspectors to fan out across Bush's domestic policies in search of solutions to the nation's problems, they would be less likely to return empty-handed if they settle for environment-related program activities (such as logging in national forests), education-related program activities (such as requiring tests without providing the funds to help kids pass them), and health-care-related program activities (such as forbidding Medicare to negotiate for lower drug prices). Like the speech itself, all this comes under the heading of winning the election-related program activities. Here's hoping it will prove equally effective.

—*The New Yorker*, February 2, 2004

NEW-TIME RELIGION

IT ISN'T EVERY DAY that the presidential nominee of the Democratic Party is a junior senator from Massachusetts who was educated at an elite boarding school and an Ivy League college and whose political career was founded on his war heroism as a young naval officer in command of a small boat and who has family money and a thick shock of hair and a slightly stiff manner and beautifully tailored suits and an aristocratic mien and whose initials are J.F.K. So rare is this phenomenon that the last time it happened was forty-four years ago, way back in 1960. That was also the last time that the nominee of the Democratic Party—or of either major party, for that matter—was a Roman Catholic.

There are plenty of other similarities between now and then, each of which comes equipped with its own corresponding difference. Here's one: in 2004 as in 1960, a large number of evangelical Protestant ministers have been alerting their followers to the danger posed by the man from Massachusetts. The difference is that last time they were against him because they were afraid he might be subservient to the Vatican. This time they're against him because they're pretty sure he won't be.

Here's another: in 2004 as in 1960, there are prominent Catholics who find it worrying or alarming or otherwise upsetting that their co-religionist is on the ballot for the office of President of the United States. In 1960, though, these prominent Catholics were mostly politicians, some of them the hard-bitten but cautious bosses of big-city Democratic machines. They loved John F. Kennedy, but they loved winning even more, and they feared that the time was not yet ripe to defy the bigotry that had traumatized them thirty-two years earlier. The crushing 1928 defeat of Al Smith, the only other Catholic who had ever run at the top of a major-party ticket, was exactly as distant in time, and as fresh in memory, as the crushing 1972 defeat of George McGovern is today (and the pols who saw McGovern when they looked at Howard Dean are the direct descendants of the ones who saw Smith when they looked at Kennedy). In 2004, the most prominent Catholic worrywarts are conservative prelates. Their fear is not that the candidate who happens to be Catholic will be defeated but that he will be elected.

Theodore Sorensen, the Unitarian who was President Kennedy's closest aide, wrote that while his boss faithfully attended Mass on Sundays, "not once in eleven years—despite all our discussions of church-state affairs— did he ever disclose his personal views on man's relation to God." John Forbes Kerry, who also attends Sunday Mass, has been similarly reticent about the intimate details of his spiritual beliefs. Nevertheless, Kerry's biography contains hints that his Catholicism is somewhat more devout than was that of his political hero and role model. Kerry was an altar boy, and as a youth he considered the seminary and a career in the priesthood. There is no evidence that any such thoughts ever crossed the mind of the first J.F.K. Yet, because Kerry opposes the recriminalization of abortion and supports stem-cell research to find treatments for such diseases as Parkinson's and Alzheimer's, a bevy of bishops have all but called for his defeat. The archbishop of St. Louis has said he would refuse to let Kerry take Communion, the central sacrament of Catholic inclusion, and lesser bishops in Boston; New Orleans; and Portland, Oregon, have chimed in with similar sentiments. The bishop of Colorado Springs has gone further, declaring that anyone who votes for a candidate who favors abortion rights or stem-cell research (or gay marriage or assisted suicide) will be denied Communion in his diocese. Of course, there are still lots of bishops, probably a majority, who think that using the Eucharist as a political bludgeon is a bad idea. Cardinal Roger M. Mahony, of Los Angeles, to name one, has said that Kerry is welcome to take Communion in his diocese. There is plenty of disagreement within the Catholic Church and plenty of debate in the Catholic press.

The salient division in American political life where religion is concerned is no longer between Catholics and Protestants, if it ever was, or even between believers and nonbelievers. It is between traditional supporters of a secular state (many of whom are themselves religiously observant), on the one hand, and, on the other hand—well, theocrats might be too strong a term. Suffice it to say that there are those who believe in a sturdy wall between church and state and those who believe that the wall should be remodeled into a white picket fence dotted with open gates, some of them wide enough to drive a tractor-trailer full of federal cash through.

President Bush is the leader of the latter persuasion, and his remodeling project has been under way for more than three years. This project goes beyond the frequent use of evangelical code words in the president's speeches; beyond the shocking and impious suggestion, more than once voiced in the president's approving presence, that he was chosen for his position by God Himself; beyond the insistence on appointing judges of extreme Christian-right views to the federal bench; beyond the religiously motivated push to chip away wherever possible at the reproductive freedom of women. It also includes money, in the millions and billions. The money is both withheld and disbursed: withheld from international family-planning efforts, from domestic contraceptive education, and from scientic research deemed inconsistent with religious fundamentalism; disbursed to "abstinence-based" sex-education programs, to church-run "marriage initiatives," and, via vouchers, to drug-treatment and other social-service programs based on religion. Though Congress has declined to enact the bulk of the president's "faith-based initiatives," the Administration has found a way, via executive orders and through bureaucratic novelties like the White House Office of Faith-Based and Community Initiatives and the Department of Health and Human Services' Compassion Capital Fund. "The federal government now allows faith-based groups to compete for billions of dollars in social-service funding, without being forced to change their identity and their mission," the president boasted a couple of weeks ago, in a commencement address at a Lutheran college in Mequon, Wisconsin. He did not mention that "their identity and their mission"—their principal purpose, their raison d'être—is often religious proselytization.

On September 12, 1960, Senator Kennedy, under pressure to confront what was quaintly known as the "religious issue," appeared before the Greater Houston Ministerial Association. "It is apparently necessary for me to state once again—not what kind of church I believe in, for that should be important only to me, but what kind of America I believe in," he said that day.

I believe in an America where the separation of church and state is absolute—where no Catholic prelate would tell the president (should he be a Catholic) how to act and no Protestant minister would tell his parishioners for whom to vote—where no church or church school is granted any public funds or political preference . . . .

I believe in an America where religious intolerance will someday end—where all men and all churches are treated as equal—where every man has the same right to attend or not to attend the church of his choice—where there is no Catholic vote, no anti-Catholic vote, no bloc voting of any kind—and where Catholics, Protestants, and Jews, at both the lay and the pastoral levels, will refrain from those attitudes of disdain and division which have so often marred their works in the past, and promote instead the American ideal of brotherhood.

With a bit of spiffing up for gender-pronoun correctness, it is just barely possible to imagine such a speech being delivered today by Senator Kerry. Could the same be said of President Bush?

—The New Yorker, June 7, 2004

BLUES

HERE IN THE BLUEST borough of the bluest city of the bluest state in all our red-white-and-blue American Union, it has not been a happy week. A cocktail of emotions was being felt in these parts after last week's presidential election, and the most potent ingredient was sadness. We've got the blues, and we've got 'em bad.

The grief that so many felt at Senator Kerry's defeat was quite unexpected, and profound enough that, for the moment at least, it held off bitterness and recrimination. On both sides, this was a campaign that vast numbers of people threw their hearts into. There was a huge volunteer outpouring for Kerry, from Bruce Springsteen and George Soros on high to the hundreds of thousands, maybe millions, who manned phone banks and traveled to "swing states" and wrote the first political checks of their lives. To be sure, something along these lines had happened before, in the campaigns of Adlai Stevenson, Eugene McCarthy, Robert Kennedy, and George McGovern on the Democratic side, and of Barry Goldwater on the Republican. But this time the scale was larger and the yearning was greater, because in contrast to the campaigns of 1952 and 1964 and 1968 and 1972, all of which had the quixotic quality of gallant but doomed struggles, the chance of victory in 2004 seemed real, especially as Election Day approached. And this time the stakes felt higher—higher than in any election for at least three decades and maybe longer.

During the campaign it was routinely remarked that the Democrats' fervor was rooted much more in anti-Bush than in pro-Kerry sentiments.

That was certainly true at the beginning, when many primary voters calculated that a decorated war hero, even one from liberal Massachusetts, would be more "electable" than a volatile Vermont doctor. It was far less true at the end. Grave and formal, steady and decent, more emotionally accessible as Election Day approached, John Kerry wore well. He earned the respect of his supporters and had begun to earn their affection. (Perhaps that will protect him from the kind of scapegoating to which Al Gore was so relentlessly subjected.) All Kerry needed to become thoroughly presidential was the presidency. His supporters risked heartbreak, and they found it.

Along with the sadness, there is puzzlement. Incumbents, especially in time of war, have a built-in advantage. But this incumbent had led the country into a war, the war in Iraq, that half the public had come to see as a mistake, and had led the country down what more than half the public saw, in pollster's shorthand, as "the wrong track." The election's outcome defies logic, and perhaps that is the point. The early analyses credited Bush's victory to religious conservatives, particularly those in the evangelical movement. In voting for Bush, as eighty percent of them did, many of these formerly nonvoting white evangelicals are remaining true to their unworldliness. In voting for a party that wants to tax work rather than wealth, that scorns thrift, that sees the natural world not as a common inheritance but as an object of exploitation, and that equates economic inequality with economic vitality, they have voted against their own material (and, some might imagine, spiritual) well-being. The moral values that stirred them seem not to encompass botched wars or economic injustices or environmental depredations; rather, moral values are about sexual behavior and its various manifestations and outcomes, about family structures, and about a particularly demonstrative brand of religious piety. What was important to these voters, it appears, was not Bush's public record but what they conceived to be his private soul. He is a good Christian, so his policy failures are forgivable. He is a saved sinner, so the dissipations of his early and middle years are not tokens of a weak character but testaments to the transformative power of his faith. He relies on God for guidance, so his intellectual laziness is not a danger.

What people on what might be called the cultural blue side, which includes many who voted for Bush, find deeply unsettling about him is not his religious faith—he is hardly the first devout president—but the way he speaks of making decisions with his gut, which, he has often suggested, takes its direction from God. In his second term, given the validation he received on Election Day, he is likely to be more confident—in himself, in his "instincts," and in Almighty Gut. He will be less inclined than ever to listen to his earthly father, or to his earthly father's earthly surrogates, such as Colin Powell.

Along with the sadness and the puzzlement, there is apprehension. Here in the big coastal cities, we have reason to fear for the immediate safety of our lives and our families—more reason, it must be said, than have the residents of the "heartland," to which the per-capita bulk of "homeland security" resources, along with extra electoral votes, are distributed. It was deep-blue New York (which went three to one for Kerry) and deep-blue Washington, D.C. (nine to one Kerry), that were, and presumably remain, Al Qaeda's targets of choice. In the heartland, it is claimed, some view the coastal cities as faintly un-American. The terrorists do not agree. They see us as the very essence—the heart, if you like—of America. And, difficult as it may be for some rural gun owners to appreciate, many of us sincerely believe that President Bush's policies have put us in greater peril than we would be facing under a Kerry (or a Gore) Administration. There is apprehension that the well-documented failure to devote adequate resources to the protection of our cities, seaports, and airports will not be remedied. There is apprehension that the colossal incompetence and bad judgment—accompanied by ideological hubris, diplomatic arrogance, and an eagerness to ignore or suppress inconvenient evidence—that have tied up our military might in the knots of Iraq will, having been rewarded at the polls, continue. There is apprehension that the anti-Bush sentiments that are manifest throughout much of the world will now transmute into fully fledged anti-Americanism. The governments of our estranged European allies, led by reality-based statesmen, will do their best to accommodate the practical fact of a second Bush term. But these are, after all, democratic countries, and their publics may not be so patient or so sensible.

And there is apprehension about where this Administration will try to take our society. In his victory statement on Wednesday Bush spoke of "a new opportunity to reach out to the whole nation." By Thursday, at his post-election press conference, this had been modified to "I'll reach out to everyone who shares our goals." One of those goals is to revamp the tax system in ways that would shift the burden further downward, including the permanent abolition of the inheritance tax. Another is to privatize part of

Social Security, which by definition would mean a reduction in guaranteed benefits for future retirees. Achieving the first of these goals would impose the pitiless culture of winners and losers on the beginning of life; achieving the second would impose it on life's end. Together they would constitute a fundamental revocation of an American social contract that was hammered out seventy years ago during the New Deal.

In Thursday's *Times,* a front-page news analysis argued that "it is impossible to read President Bush's reëlection with larger Republican majorities in both houses of Congress as anything other than the clearest confirmation yet that this is a center-right country—divided yes, but with an undisputed majority united behind his leadership." That is certainly true in institutional terms. But it is not true in terms of people, of actual human beings. Though the Republicans won nineteen of the thirty-four Senate seats that were up for grabs last Tuesday, for a gain of four, the number of voters who cast their ballots for Republican Senate candidates was 37.9 million, while 41.3 million voted for Democrats—almost exactly Bush's popular-vote margin over Kerry. When the new Congress convenes in January, its fifty-five Republicans will be there on account of the votes of 57.6 million people, while the forty-four Democrats and one independent will be there on account of the votes of 59.6 million people. As for the House, it is much harder to aggregate vote totals meaningfully, because so many seats are uncontested. But the Republicans' gain of four seats was due entirely to Tom DeLay's precedent-breaking re-gerrymandering of the Texas district lines.

The red-blue split has not changed since 2000. This is not a center-right country. It is a center-right country and a center-left country, but the center has not held. The winner-take-all aspects of our system have converged into a perfect storm that has given virtually all the political power to the right; conservative Republicans will now control the presidency, the House of Representatives, and the Senate so firmly that the Supreme Court, which is also in conservative hands, has abruptly become the most moderate of the four centers of federal power. The system of checks and balances has broken down, but the country remains divided—right down the nonexistent, powerless middle.

—*The New Yorker,* November 15, 2004

ACKNOWLEDGMENTS

WHEN A BOOK IS WRITTEN the way this one was—bit by bit, over a lot of years, and by accumulation, not conscious design—you end up with a pretty long thank-you list, because what you're thankful about isn't just a book. It's a career, and a good part of a life.

My list begins with seven people who at crucial moments steered me to something new and gratifying. Lillian Ross persuaded William Shawn to give me a job at *The New Yorker*. James Fallows recruited me for the White House staff. Jimmy Carter, in one of the lesser of his many services to his fellow creatures, trusted me to participate in American government at a high level. Martin Peretz may have given me hell sometimes, but he twice gave me heaven: the editorship of *The New Republic*. Tina Brown, an impresaria of nerve and dash, revived *The New Yorker* and brought me back to it. David Remnick, long may he reign, freed me (or was it fired me?) from editorial chores, handed me a giant bullhorn, and told me to start shouting. He is an editor of rocklike integrity and a man—make that a *mensch*—of Victorian energy and non-Victorian humor. Andrew Wylie decided I should have a book, and now, it seems, I have one.

At the *Harvard Crimson*, the only newspaper I ever worked for, I was lucky enough to encounter, among others, Andrew Weil, Raymond Sokolov, Joseph M. Russin, Richard B. Ruge, Faye Levine, Michael A. Lerner, Donald E. Graham and Mary (Wissler) Graham, Fred Gardner, Richard Cotton, and Jacob Brackman. At the National Student Association, it was Sam Brown, Michael Enwall, Gil Kulick, Karen Paget, and Philip Sherburne; and at *Newsweek*, John Burks and Rod Gander.

During my opening stint at *The New Yorker*, from 1969 to 1977, I learned from Martin Baron, Gardner Botsford, Pat Crow, Eleanor Gould, Ian Frazier, Anthony Hiss, Lee Lorenz, Suzannah Lessard, Mary Painter, Jonathan Schell, George W. S. Trow, and William Whitworth. At the Carter White House, my fellow sufferers included Jack Watson, Thomas Teal, Gordon

Stewart, Griffin Smith, Jr., Walter Shapiro, Alice Rogoff and David M. Rubenstein, John Ritch, Gerald Rafshoon, Jody Powell, Robert Pastor, Chris Matthews, Hamilton Jordan, Robert Hunter, Jerome Doolittle, Paul Costello, and Patrick Caddell.

Those who made working at Marty Peretz's *New Republic* entertaining as well as educational included Jack Beatty, Abraham Brumberg, Margaret Carlson, Jon Carroll, James Gibney, Michael Kinsley, Robert Kuttner, Vint Lawrence, Jefferson Morley, Sara Mosle, Laura Obolensky, Joan Stapleton, Steve Wasserman, Leon Wieseltier, and Robert Wright. I give special thanks to Dorothy Wickenden, my stalwart coworker of twenty-three years' standing, whom I met on my first day at *The New Republic* and who is now executive editor of *The New Yorker*. It was also at *TNR* that I made the acquaintance of my longtime and, I hope, lifelong friend and political crony Sidney Blumenthal.

My interlude at the Institute of Politics and the Shorenstein Center on the Press, Politics, and Public Policy of the John F. Kennedy School of Government of Harvard University, where I hid out for most of Reagan's second term, was enriched by the society of Dorothy Zinberg, Robert Reich, Nelson Polsby, Nancy Palmer, Jonathan Moore, Steven Kelman, Marvin Kalb, Teresa Donovan, Kurt M. Campbell, and Gautam Adhikari.

The staff of *The New Yorker* is a large and varied group of enormously talented and knowledgeable people. It has been my privilege to be part of that group for the past twelve years. Among the editors with whom I have worked, the writers who have toiled alongside me in the politics corner of the magazine, and the colleagues who have done whatever it took, and stayed no matter how late it got, to ensure that my expertly revised copy made it to the presses are Roger Angell, John Bennet, Cara Campbell, Peter Canby, Leo Carey, Will Cohen, John Cassidy, Gita Daneshjoo, Shana Davis, Sharon Delano, Matt Dellinger, Kevin Denges, Bruce Diones, Perri Dorset, Henry Finder, Boris Fishman, Jeffrey Frank, Tara Gallagher, Henry Louis Gates, Jr., Ann Goldstein, Dana Goodyear, Adam Gopnik, Philip Gourevitch, Seymour M. Hersh, Jilan Kamal, Dan Kaufman, Austin Kelley, Patrick Keogh, Raffi Khatchadourian, Ed Klaris, Joe Klein, Elizabeth Kolbert, C.S. Ledbetter III, Nicholas Lemann, Jacob Lewis, Lauren MacIntyre, Bruce McCall, Pamela McCarthy, Ben McGrath, Bob Mankoff, Sarah Mangerson, Jane Mayer, Luke Menand, Susan Morrison, Elizabeth

Pearson-Griffiths, Brenda Phipps, Emily Richards, Nandi Rodrigo, Adam Schatz, Mark Singer, Anne Stringfield, Kate Taylor, Jeffrey Toobin, Lawrence Wright, Daniel Zalewski, and, especially, Hellyn Sher.

For reasons that may or may not be obscure to them but are perfectly clear to me, I owe thanks to John Zeisel, Michael Sean Winters, Geoffrey Wheatcroft, Steven R. Weisman and Elisabeth Bumiller, Nicholas von Hoffman, Craig Unger, Daniel Thomases, Jeff Steingarten and Caron Smith, Michele Slung, Allison Silver, Pierre Schori, Murray Sayle, Helen Rogan, Rob Richie, Peter Pringle and Eleanor Randolph, Michael Naumann, Adam Moss, Peter Mezan and Pam Ridder, Christopher Lydon, Anthony Lewis, Michael Janeway, Wolfgang Ischinger, Christopher Hitchens, Katrina Hertzberg, Ernestine Guglielmo, Leonard Groopman, Jerry Groopman, Jeff Greenfield, Nathan and Sulochana Glazer, Franz-Olivier Giesbert, Timothy Ferris, Donald Fagen and Libby Titus, Edward Jay Epstein, Karen Durbin, Bill Drayton, Richard Cohen, Marcelle Clements, Alexander Chancellor, Daniel and Pearl Bell, Elizabeth Beautyman, and Katrina McCormick Barnes. My thoughts, deep and shallow alike, have been nurtured by a political cohort that includes Lorenzo Albacete, Eric Alterman, Bernard Avishai, Paul Berman, Joe Conason, E.J. Dionne, Jr., John B. Judis, Harold Meyerson, Jo-Ann Mort, George Packer, Michael Tomasky, and Sean Wilentz.

I mourn the passing of Robert F. Wagner III, Howard Simons, William Shawn, David Pickford, Daniel U. Newman, Andy Logan, William Lauroesch, Larry Hopp, Philip and Anna Hamburger, Bill Flynn, Henry Fairlie, Herbert H. Denton, Jr., James Chace, Maris Cakars, Jervis Anderson, and, above all, of my parents, Sidney Hertzberg and Hazel Whitman Hertzberg.

THIS BOOK EXISTS on account of the synchronous interest of Andrew Wylie, the literary agent, for whose mysterious intervention I will always be grateful, and Scott Moyers, at The Penguin Press. At Penguin, I am also indebted to Sophie Fels, Beena Kamlani, Darren Haggar, Claire Vaccaro, Amanda Dewey, Janie Fleming, Rachel Rokicki, Tracy Locke, and Ann Godoff. Dianne Belfrey helped me cope with the task of getting rid of the chaff and grinding the wheat into electronically bakeable form.

It is customary at this point to assert that one's spouse is one's best editor. In the present case, this is no mere sweet nothing. Virginia Cannon is a senior editor at *The New Yorker*. In addition to being her husband, I'm one of her writers. She actually *is* my editor. Her ear is unerring, her judgment infallible, and her attention to detail indefatigable. She even made me redo these acknowledgements. Everything that is good and true in my life is of her making, not least our son, Wolf. This book is dedicated to her and intended for him.

INDEX

FOR THE BEST IN PAPERBACKS, LOOK FOR THE

In every corner of the world, on every subject under the sun, Penguin represents quality and variety—the very best in publishing today.

For complete information about books available from Penguin—including Penguin Classics, Penguin Compass, and Puffins—and how to order them, write to us at the appropriate address below. Please note that for copyright reasons the selection of books varies from country to country.

In the United States: Please write to *Penguin Group (USA), P.O. Box 12289 Dept. B, Newark, New Jersey 07101-5289* or call 1-800-788-6262.

In the United Kingdom: Please write to *Dept. EP, Penguin Books Ltd, Bath Road, Harmondsworth, West Drayton, Middlesex UB7 0DA.*

In Canada: Please write to *Penguin Books Canada Ltd, 10 Alcorn Avenue, Suite 300, Toronto, Ontario M4V 3B2.*

In Australia: Please write to *Penguin Books Australia Ltd, P.O. Box 257, Ringwood, Victoria 3134.*

In New Zealand: Please write to *Penguin Books (NZ) Ltd, Private Bag 102902, North Shore Mail Centre, Auckland 10.*

In India: Please write to *Penguin Books India Pvt Ltd, 11 Panchsheel Shopping Centre, Panchsheel Park, New Delhi 110 017.*

In the Netherlands: Please write to *Penguin Books Netherlands bv, Postbus 3507, NL-1001 AH Amsterdam.*

In Germany: Please write to *Penguin Books Deutschland GmbH, Metzlerstrasse 26, 60594 Frankfurt am Main.*

In Spain: Please write to *Penguin Books S. A., Bravo Murillo 19, 1° B, 28015 Madrid.*

In Italy: Please write to *Penguin Italia s.r.l., Via Benedetto Croce 2, 20094 Corsico, Milano.*

In France: Please write to *Penguin France, Le Carré Wilson, 62 rue Benjamin Baillaud, 31500 Toulouse.*

In Japan: Please write to *Penguin Books Japan Ltd, Kaneko Building, 2-3-25 Koraku, Bunkyo-Ku, Tokyo 112.*

In South Africa: Please write to *Penguin Books South Africa (Pty) Ltd, Private Bag X14, Parkview, 2122 Johannesburg.*